D0163172

THE PAPERS OF
THOMAS JEFFERSON

THE PAPERS OF
Thomas Jefferson

Volume 2 · 1777 to 18 June 1779

Including the Revisal of the Laws, 1776-1786

JULIAN P. BOYD, EDITOR

LYMAN H. BUTTERFIELD AND MINA R. BRYAN,

ASSOCIATE EDITORS

PRINCETON, NEW JERSEY

PRINCETON UNIVERSITY PRESS

1950

London: Geoffrey Cumberlege, Oxford University Press

Printed in the United States of America by
Princeton University Press, Princeton, New Jersey

DEDICATED TO THE MEMORY OF

ADOLPH S. OCHS

PUBLISHER OF THE NEW YORK TIMES

1896-1935

WHO BY THE EXAMPLE OF A RESPONSIBLE
PRESS ENLARGED AND FORTIFIED
THE JEFFERSONIAN CONCEPT
OF A FREE PRESS

FOREWORD

THIS volume, covering the years 1777 to June 1779, marks the end of Jefferson's legislative career in the Virginia House of Delegates and the beginning of his term as governor. A few comments are necessary by way of amplification of the editorial policies outlined in Volume 1, inasmuch as the present volume embraces the first summaries of documents, the first record entries, and, most important of all, the first notable exception to the chronological arrangement in this part of the work.

Summaries. Letters, memoranda, legislative bills, tabular documents, enclosures, and other forms of record appearing in these volumes will be summarized if the matter is of slight importance or if the text is readily available elsewhere in print. As indicated earlier, summaries of letters or documents written by Jefferson will be confined to those of a trivial or duplicative nature and will be far less numerous than those of letters or documents written by others. Also, more documents will be summarized during the periods of Jefferson's incumbency of office than for other periods of his life, since such periods naturally produced a greater volume of routine and even trivial documentation. Occasionally, as in the case of the Bill to Enforce Attendance of Members of Assembly and the Bill to Enable Judges of the General Court to Hold Two Additional Sessions (see p. 188-9, below), fairly important documents will be summarized when there is a probability but not a certainty of Jefferson's authorship. Even important letters or documents will be summarized if they were enclosures and if they were not written by Jefferson.

An effort is made in these summaries to present in more or less detailed form the substance of the documents and not merely to provide calendar entries. In the fullest degree of summarization, direct quotations from the text will be employed frequently; in the least degree of summarization, an effort will be made to present enough of the substance of a document to enable the reader to form an intelligent opinion of its contents. It is scarcely necessary to point out that any degree of summarization involves the risk of distorting the meaning or misleading the reader through omissions and misinterpretations of phraseology; the editors have endeavored to guard against this danger by employing, in many instances, the precise phraseology of the original author. The text of summarized documents is presented in a smaller type than that used for documents printed in full. Captions are given in the same form as those for documents printed in full, and the descriptive, explanatory, and textual annotation follows the usual pattern. The place and date line of a summarized document is standardized and placed in italics on the left at the beginning of the text instead of occupying a separate line at the upper right. If the original text has no place or date, these, when ascertainable, will be placed within square brackets. For the specialist who wishes to obtain the full text of a document summarized, the descriptive note will give the location of the original document, the number of pages or parts of pages on which handwriting appears, and the location of a printed text, if known.

Record Entries. Record entries have the usual caption form, but all other matter in the entry is placed within square brackets, including place and date and editorial annotation. A record entry is merely a record of a document known to have been written but not at present located. See, for example, the record entry of Jefferson's letter to Benjamin Harrison of 7 June 1779 (p. 286, below), the manuscript of which was described in an auction sale catalogue of 1904. In all such record entries, the conclusive documentary evidence that originals once existed is given. Occasionally this evidence may even refer to or partially include the substance of the letter or document, and this is always included when available. Record entries will not be supplied for missing letters acknowledged in the replies to such letters; for example, we know from Jefferson's letter to Theodorick Bland of 8 June 1779 (see p. 286, below) that Bland had sent a "letter to Governor Henry of the 1st. instant," but the fact that this letter from Bland to Henry has not been located is stated in the note to Jefferson's acknowledgment of 8 June instead of being noted in a separate record entry under date of 1 June.

The Revisal of the Laws. The major part of the present volume is occupied by the Revisal of the Laws, a landmark in the formative period of American law for which Jefferson was the chief architect. It would seem at first glance that this is a departure from the chronological arrangement that the present volumes follow. If this does in fact amount to a departure, it is one that the editors feel is eminently justified. It could be argued, technically at least, that the Revisal as presented in this volume could be construed as a mere "enclosure" to the letter that Jefferson and Wythe addressed to Benjamin Harrison, Speaker of the House of Delegates, on 18

June 1779. For the "two bundles" of bills that constituted the basis for the Revisal were in fact covered by that letter. But, so it seems to the editors, far more substantial and valid reasons justify the inclusion of the Revisal of the Laws here.

First of all, many of the bills drafted by Jefferson in the years of his legislative activity from the autumn of 1776 to the middle of 1779 are to be regarded as an integral part of the Revisal, even though many of these bills were drafted and enacted into law independent of the program of revision. Some of these individual bills drawn by Jefferson pertain to such important matters as the courts of justice, entails, the Established Church, importation of slaves, naturalization of foreigners, &c. But, as Jefferson later characterized it, these bills were "details of reformation only." And, though many of these important statutes were later incorporated in the Revisal that aimed at adapting the entire legal code to the republican form of government, some were not, and all remained for the most part separate instances of Jefferson's integrated purpose. To have excluded all of Jefferson's legislative bills from the chronological series on the ground that such documents properly belonged to the legal volume would have been to separate them from their context so violently as to run the grave risk of distorting the record of Jefferson's career in these dynamic years. Obviously such legislative documents as the Declaration of Independence and Jefferson's draft of a Constitution for Virginia, though they are legal documents of the highest importance, belong in the context of 1776. Similarly the Bills for Establishing a Land Office and for Adjusting and Settling Titles and the various bills in which Jefferson presented his far-reaching program of education naturally belong with his most active legislative years. All of these and many more are the subject of discussion in the letters to and from Jefferson printed in the present and preceding volumes.

In view of these facts, the editors concluded that it would be wise to present the Revisal of the Laws in the chronologically arranged series of letters and documents of which it seems to form a logical part. Even so, there still remained the troublesome question of the proper chronological point at which the Revisal should be inserted. Some of its bills, as already noted, had been passed prior to 1779; the Report of the Committee of Revisors was not put into print until 1784; and most of the 126 bills embraced in that Report were not adopted until the years 1785-1786. However, the problem presented by this range of possible dates appeared to be more serious than it actually was. Obviously the Revisal of the Laws could not properly be printed in this series prior to the date of 18 June 1779, for the Committee of Revisors were at work on the revision until that time. Subsequent to that date, no argument for any given chronological point—whether 1784, 1785, or 1786—appeared more valid than for another. While, therefore, the Revisal of the Laws as here presented is in fact far more extensive than the Report of the Committee of Revisors as submitted by Jefferson and Wythe on 18 June 1779, the editors have treated the Revisal as, in effect, an appendage to the communication of that date. In the extended editorial commentary preceding the Revisal of the Laws, and in the annotations provided for each of the bills, the editors have extended the history of this legislative reform far beyond the date of 18 June 1779 and, in some instances, even beyond the year 1786 which marked the terminal point for legislative action on most of the bills in the Revisal.

GUIDE TO EDITORIAL APPARATUS

1. *TEXTUAL DEVICES*

The following devices are employed throughout the work to clarify the presentation of the text.

[. . .], [. . . .]	One or two words missing and not conjecturable.
[. . .][1], [. . . .][1]	More than two words missing and not conjecturable; subjoined footnote estimates number of words missing.
[ ]	Number or part of a number missing or illegible.
[roman]	Conjectural reading for missing or illegible matter. A question mark follows when the reading is doubtful.
[*italic*]	Editorial comment inserted in the text.
⟨*italic*⟩	Matter deleted in the MS but restored in our text.

2. *DESCRIPTIVE SYMBOLS*

The following symbols are employed throughout the work to describe the various kinds of manuscript originals. When a series of versions is recorded, *the first to be recorded is the version used for the printed text.*

Dft	draft (usually a composition or rough draft; later drafts, when identifiable as such, are designated "2d Dft," &c.)
Dupl	duplicate
MS	manuscript (arbitrarily applied to most documents other than letters)
N	note, notes (memoranda, fragments, &c.)
PoC	polygraph copy
PrC	press copy
RC	recipient's copy
SC	stylograph copy
Tripl	triplicate

All manuscripts of the above types are assumed to be in the hand of the author of the document to which the descriptive symbol pertains. If not, that fact is stated. On the other hand, the following types of manuscripts are assumed *not* to be in the hand of the author, and exceptions will be noted:

FC file copy (applied to all forms of retained copies, such as letter-book copies, clerks' copies, &c.)
Tr transcript (applied to both contemporary and later copies; period of transcription, unless clear by implication, will be given when known)

3. LOCATION SYMBOLS

The locations of documents printed in this edition from originals in private hands, from originals held by institutions outside the United States, and from printed sources are recorded in self-explanatory form in the descriptive note following each document. The locations of documents printed from originals held by public institutions in the United States are recorded by means of the symbols used in the National Union Catalog in the Library of Congress; an explanation of how these symbols are formed is given above, Vol. 1: xl. The list of symbols appearing in each volume is limited to the institutions represented by documents printed or referred to in that volume.

CSmH Henry E. Huntington Library, San Marino, California
DLC Library of Congress
ICU University of Chicago Libraries
MB Boston Public Library
MHi Massachusetts Historical Society, Boston
MiU-C William L. Clements Library, University of Michigan, Ann Arbor
MoSHi Missouri Historical Society, St. Louis
NN New York Public Library
NNP Pierpont Morgan Library, New York City
NcD Duke University
NjS Free Public Library, Summit, New Jersey
PHi Historical Society of Pennsylvania, Philadelphia
PPAP American Philosophical Society, Philadelphia
Vi Virginia State Library, Richmond
ViHi Virginia Historical Society, Richmond
ViU University of Virginia
ViW College of William and Mary

ViWC Colonial Williamsburg, Inc., Williamsburg, Virginia

WHi State Historical Society of Wisconsin, Madison

4. OTHER ABBREVIATIONS

The following abbreviations are commonly employed in the annotation throughout the work.

TJ Thomas Jefferson

TJ Editorial Files Photoduplicates and other editorial materials in the office of *The Papers of Thomas Jefferson*, Princeton University Library

TJ Papers Jefferson Papers (Applied to a collection of manuscripts when the precise location of a given document must be furnished, and always preceded by the symbol for the institutional repository; thus "DLC: TJ Papers, 4:628-9" represents a document in the Library of Congress, Jefferson Papers, volume 4, pages 628 and 629.)

PCC Papers of the Continental Congress, in the Library of Congress

RG Record Group (Used in designating the location of documents in the National Archives.)

5. SHORT TITLES

The following list includes only those short titles of works cited with great frequency, and therefore in very abbreviated form, throughout this edition. Their expanded forms are given here only in the degree of fullness needed for unmistakable identification. Since it is impossible to anticipate all the works to be cited in such very abbreviated form, the list is appropriately revised from volume to volume.

Biog. Dir. Cong. *Biographical Directory of Congress, 1774-1927*

Bland Papers *The Bland Papers: Being a Selection from the Manuscripts of Colonel Theodorick Bland, Jr.*

B.M. Cat. British Museum, *General Catalogue of Printed Books*, London, 1931—. Also, *The British Museum Catalogue of Printed Books, 1881-1900*, Ann Arbor, 1946.

B.N. Cat. *Catalogue général des livres imprimés de la Bibliothèque Nationale. Auteurs.*

Burk-Girardin, *Hist. of Va.* John Burk, *The History of Virginia . . . Continued by Skelton Jones and Louis Hue Girardin*

Burnett, *Letters of Members* Edmund C. Burnett, ed., *Letters of Members of the Continental Congress*

C & D See *Va. Gaz.*

Cal. Franklin Papers *Calendar of the Papers of Benjamin Franklin in the Library of the American Philosophical Society*, ed. I. Minis Hays

Chancellors' Revisal *A Collection of all Such Public Acts of the General Assembly, and Ordinances of the Conventions of Virginia, Passed since the Year 1768, as Are Now in Force. . . . Published under Inspection of the Judges of the High Court of Chancery*, Richmond, 1785

Clark Papers See *George Rogers Clark Papers*

Clayton-Torrence William Clayton-Torrence, *A Trial Bibliography of Colonial Virginia (1754-1776)*; printed as part of Virginia State Library, *Sixth Report*, 1909

CVSP *Calendar of Virginia State Papers . . . Preserved in the Capitol at Richmond*

Conv. Jour. See *Va. Conv. Jour.*

D & H See *Va. Gaz.*

D & N See *Va. Gaz.*

DAB *Dictionary of American Biography*

DAE *Dictionary of American English*

DAH *Dictionary of American History*

DNB *Dictionary of National Biography*

Evans Charles Evans, *American Bibliography*

Ford Paul Leicester Ford, ed., *The Writings of Thomas Jefferson*, "Letterpress Edition," N.Y., 1892-1899

George Rogers Clark Papers, 1771-1781; also *1781-1784* *George Rogers Clark Papers*, ed. James A. James, Illinois State Historical Library, *Collections*, VIII, XIX

HAW Henry A. Washington, ed., *The Writings of Thomas Jefferson*, Washington, 1853-1854

Heitman Francis B. Heitman, *Historical Register of Officers of the Continental Army*, new edn., Washington, 1914; also the same compiler's *Historical Register and Dictionary of the United States Army* [1789-1903], Washington, 1903

Hening William W. Hening, *The Statutes at Large; Being a Collection of All the Laws of Virginia*

JCC *Journals of the Continental Congress, 1774-1789*, ed. W. C. Ford and others, Washington, 1904-1937

JHB *Journals of the House of Burgesses of Virginia, 1619-1776*, Richmond, 1905-1915

JHD *Journal of the House of Delegates of the Commonwealth of Virginia* (cited by session and date of publication)

Johnston, "Jefferson Bibliography" Richard H. Johnston, "A Contribution to a Bibliography of Thomas Jefferson," *Writings of Thomas Jefferson*, ed. Lipscomb and Bergh, xx, separately paged following the Index

L & B Andrew A. Lipscomb and Albert E. Bergh, eds., *The Writings of Thomas Jefferson*, "Memorial Edition," Washington, 1903-1904

L.C. Cat. *A Catalogue of Books Represented by Library of Congress Printed Cards*, Ann Arbor, 1942-1946; also *Supplement*, 1948

Library Catalogue, 1783 Jefferson's MS list of books owned and wanted in 1783 (original in Massachusetts Historical Society)

Library Catalogue, 1815 *Catalogue of the Library of the United States*, Washington, 1815

Library Catalogue, 1829 *Catalogue. President Jefferson's Library*, Washington, 1829

OED *A New English Dictionary on Historical Principles*, Oxford, 1888-1933

Official Letters *Official Letters of the Governors of the State of Virginia*, ed. H. R. McIlwaine

P & D See *Va. Gaz.*

PMHB *The Pennsylvania Magazine of History and Biography*

Randall, *Life* Henry S. Randall, *The Life of Thomas Jefferson*

Randolph, *Domestic Life* Sarah N. Randolph, *The Domestic Life of Thomas Jefferson*

Report *Report of the Committee of Revisors Appointed by the General Assembly of Virginia in MDCCLXXVI*, Richmond, 1784

Sabin Joseph Sabin and others, *Bibliotheca Americana. A Dictionary of Books Relating to America*

Shepherd Samuel Shepherd, *The Statutes at Large of Virginia, from October Session 1792, to December Session 1806, Inclusive . . . (New Series,) Being a Continuation of Hening*

Swem, "Va. Bibliog." Earl G. Swem, "A Bibliography of Virginia," Virginia State Library, *Bulletin*, VIII, X, XII (1915-1919)

TJR Thomas Jefferson Randolph, ed., *Memoir, Correspondence, and Miscellanies, from the Papers of Thomas Jefferson*, Charlottesville, 1829

Tucker, *Life* George Tucker, *The Life of Thomas Jefferson*, Philadelphia, 1837

Tyler, *Va. Biog.* Lyon G. Tyler, *Encyclopedia of Virginia Biography*

Va. Conv. Jour. *Proceedings of the Convention of Delegates . . . in the Colony of Virginia* (cited by session and date of publication)

Va. Council Jour. *Journals of the Council of the State of Virginia*, ed. H. R. McIlwaine

Va. Gaz. *Virginia Gazette* (Williamsburg, 1751-1780, and Richmond, 1780-1781). Abbreviations for publishers of the several newspapers of this name, frequently published concurrently, include the following: C & D (Clarkson & Davis), D & H (Dixon & Hunter), D & N (Dixon & Nicolson), P & D (Purdie & Dixon). In all other cases the publisher's name is not abbreviated.

VMHB *Virginia Magazine of History and Biography*

WMQ *William and Mary Quarterly*

CONTENTS

CONTENTS

1778

1779

CONTENTS

CONTENTS

ILLUSTRATIONS

VOLUME 2

1777 to 18 June 1779

JEFFERSON CHRONOLOGY

VOLUME 2

1777 January 13. Attended meeting of Committee of Revisors at Fredericksburg.

1777 February. Drew up and subscribed to a subscription to support a clergyman in Albemarle.

1777 April 10. Reelected to House of Delegates for Albemarle county.

1777 May 8-20. Attended House of Delegates.

1777 May 16. Began correspondence with John Adams.

1777 May 28. Son born; died 14 June.

1777 October 30 to 1778 January 24. Attended, with some intervals, House of Delegates.

1778 April 9. Reelected to House of Delegates.

1778 May 12 to June 1. Attended House of Delegates.

1778 June 24. Made observations on eclipse of the sun.

1778 August 1. Mary (Maria) Jefferson, third daughter, born.

1778 November 30. Attended House of Delegates in custody of sergeant-at-arms; in attendance until Assembly adjourned, December 19.

1779 January. Saratoga Convention army came to Albemarle Barracks.

1779 February 24-25. Capture of Fort Vincennes by George Rogers Clark.

1779 April. Reelected to House of Delegates.

1779 May 8. Attended House of Delegates.

1779 June 1. Elected Governor of Virginia; notified and sent message of acceptance, June 2.

1779 June 16. Ordered Henry Hamilton, British commander captured at Vincennes, placed in irons.

1779 June 18. Reported, with Wythe and Pendleton, proposed Revisal of the Laws of Virginia, including the Bills for Proportioning Crimes and Punishments, for the More General Diffusion of Knowledge, for Amending the Constitution of the College of William and Mary, and for Establishing Religious Freedom.

THE PAPERS OF
THOMAS JEFFERSON

From Thomas Nelson

DEAR JEFFERSON Baltimore Jany 2d 1777

Colo. Zane delivered your Letters to me in this Town, and as I had it not in my power to execute what you desir'd, I gave them to him and desir'd he would negotiate the Bill and transact the other business, which he promis'd to do.

Our affairs have had a black appearance for the two last months, but they say the Devil is not so black as he is painted. We have at last turn'd the Tables upon those Scoundrels by surprize, as you will see by the enclos'd paper. It was very unfortunate for us, that Ewing and Cadwalader could not get over the River, for it is almost certain, that they would have surprized a large Detachment of Hessians at Mount Holly, and most probably they would have taken the greatest part of them. The Number of prisoners exceeds what the General makes them by 500. He is always very moderate. Could we but get a good Regular Army we should soon clear the Continent of these damn'd Invaders. They play the very Devil with the Girls and even old Women to satisfy their libidinous appetites. There is Scarcely a Virgin to be found in the part of the Country that they have pass'd thro' and yet the Jersies will not turn out. Rapes, Rapine, and Murder are not sufficient to rouse the resentment of these People. If they be not sufficient provocations I dispair of any thing working them up to opposition. Your friends John, Andrew and William Allen are with General Howe; and Dickeson is they know not where, but it is imagined that he is on board the Roebuck. This Gentleman, after giving his Vote repeatedly in Congress, for the emission of Continental Money, wrote to his Brother not to receive any of it in payment for his Debts, and his Letter was intercepted by the Council of Safety. What does he deserve?

The Allens have hamm'd themselves finely, for when they went to Howe, there was very little doubt, but he would shortly have been in possession of Philada., as indeed he might, had he play'd his Cards well; but now I am in hopes that will not take place, and that they will be treated as they deserve. There are some of the vilest Rascals in the City and Neighbourhood of Philadelphia that ever existed.

The General was inform'd a few nights ago, that a conspiracy was form'd by some people in Bucks County near his Camp to kidnap him as poor Lee was, but he has more prudence than to be caught in that manner, however the disposition of the Inhabitants of that County appears to be inimical to our cause, which you knew before. Adieu, THOS NELSON JR.

You dont like long Letters more than myself.

Our little friend Hopkinson has suffer'd greatly by these Free booters; They have destroy'd all his furniture, Cabinet of Curiosities and his fine Harpsicord, which I am told was the best that ever came to America. You Have little chance for the Tellescope. Old Weatherspoon has not escap'd their fury. They have burnt his Library. It grieves him much that he has lost his controversial Tracts. He would lay aside the Cloth to take revenge of them. I believe he would send them to the Devil if he could, I am sure I would. Thus endeth the postscript.

RC (DLC).

TJ's LETTERS to Nelson not located. There is the following entry in TJ's Account Book for 1776 under 6 Dec.: "sold my crop of tobo. (except 7 hhds.) to Carter Braxton for Willing & Morris @ 20/ pr. C. & recd. for it a bill on Willing & Morris for £50 Pennsylva. curry. = £40 Virga. which I enclosed to T. Nelson by Isaac Zane." OLD WEATHERSPOON: John Witherspoon, president of the College of New Jersey. His LIBRARY was not wholly destroyed. Several hundred volumes, including many bound volumes of tracts and pamphlets, are in the Princeton University Library. See also G. O. Trevelyan, *The American Revolution*, London, 1903, pt. II, Vol. II, p. 31.

From John Goodrich

SIR Jany 20th 1777.

I have been confined to a small Room upwards of two months which has much Impaired my health. Your Inquiry the Reason of the Alteration of my confinement will much Oblige me. I have been very Ill Treated by Mr. Jouette Sundry times. Your favour in allowing me to Board at Some Other house in this Place will oblige your Obedient JOHN GOODRICH SENR

P.S. One George Bruce of the Guard have Sundry times threatned my life, and is extremely Abusefull. Your Notice hereof will Oblige

J G

RC (DLC). Addressed: "Thomas Jefferson Esqr Present." Endorsed: "Goodrich's lre."

John Goodrich and his sons were under frequent consideration by the Virginia Convention and House of Delegates from 1775 to 1778: first, for payment for powder supplied to the colony by the Goodriches, for which John Goodrich, Sr., was imprisoned by Governor Dunmore, and later for violations of the nonimportation agreement and actions unfriendly to the American cause (VMHB, XV [1907-1908], 160-5; Sabine, *Loyalists*, I, 480-2; *Conv. Jour.*, Dec. 1775, 1816 edn., p. 95-6). TJ first became concerned with the Goodrich affair in his capacity as county lieutenant, when John Goodrich, Andrew McCan, and other prisoners of war were transferred from the Williamsburg jail to Charlottesville, 22 July 1776 (*Va. Council Jour.*, I, 81-2). On 2 Nov. 1776 TJ reported for the Committee of Propositions and Grievances on the petition of John Goodrich, Jr., on behalf of himself and company (JHD, Oct. 1776, 1828 edn., p. 37; MS: Vi, in clerk's hand, corrected by TJ). Thereafter Goodrich was moved to the home of Nicholas Lewis, where he remained until he escaped, 18 Aug. 1777 (*Va. Gaz.* [Purdie], 22 Aug. 1777). Goodrich was apprehended shortly after his escape and in 1778 was again sent to Charlottesville for imprisonment. The following letters relating to Goodrich's confinement and escape are found in TJ's papers: Margaret Goodrich to Mary Lewis, 12 Aug. 1777 (DLC: TJ Papers, 3: 374); John Goodrich to Nicholas Lewis, 18 Aug. 1777 (same, 3: 382); John Goodrich to Mary Lewis, 19 Aug. 1777 and enclosure, namely, Goodrich's bill to the colony of Virginia, 10 Aug. 1777 (same, 3: 373, 384). See also Patrick Henry to TJ, 26 Feb., 31 Mch. 1777; List of British Prisoners and Their Quarters, 25 Sep. 1777; Patrick Henry to TJ, 21 Feb. 1778; Edmund Randolph to TJ, 22 Feb. 1778.

From Patrick Henry

SIR Wmsburgh feb 26th. 1777

Mr. Frazer is appointed first Leiutenant instead of Mr. Mossom. The other Appointments of your County remain unaltered.

The inclosed Resolution respecting the prisoners will explain the Ideas of the Council Board on that Subject.

Thirty pounds cash accompany this. Such of the prisoners as you may judge most in want of Clothes, will be furnished in such manner as you think best. If absolute Necessity calls for more money, you will please to write me.

If[1] Goodrich and McCan (if the latter is not a prisoner of War) may both be indulged to the extent of one Mile round Charlottesville upon Bond and Security not to exceed those Limits. But this only in Case you shall be of Opinion no Inconvenience can arise from it. But if no Security can be given, or if given, you shall have any ground to fear unfriendly Behaviour from them, they must be confind under a [Serge]ants Guard.

Blank Commissions are sent herewith. With great Regard I am Sir Yr. mo. obt. hble Svt., P. HENRY JR.

RC (DLC). Addressed in a hand other than Henry's: "Thomas Jefferson Esquire. Albermarle." Endorsed: "Governor's lre. Feb. 26. 77. about Goodrich & McCann." Enclosure missing. On verso, in TJ's hand, Account of the Guard for British Prisoners (q.v., under 5 Oct. 1777).

The INCLOSED RESOLUTION: The order of Council of 26 Feb. that all prisoners of war, except marines taken on merchant ships, be sent to Philadelphia under escort of the Continental recruits from the several counties. For this resolution and other directions covered in the letter, see *Va. Council Jour.*, I, 355; for Goodrich, see John Goodrich to TJ, 20 Jan. 1777.

[1] This word was probably intended to be deleted after the qualification enclosed in parentheses was added.

Subscription to Support a Clergyman in Charlottesville

[February 1777]

Whereas by a late act of General assembly freedom of Religious opinion and worship is restored to all, and it is left to the members of each religious society to employ such teachers as they think fit for their own spiritual comfort and instruction, and to maintain the same by their free and voluntary contributions: We the subscribers, professing the most Catholic affection for other religious sectaries who happen to differ from us in points of conscience, yet desirous of encouraging and supporting[1] the Calvinistical Reformed[2] church, and of deriving to our selves, through the ministry of it's teachers, the benefits of Gospel knolege and religious improvement; and at the same time of supporting those, who, having been at considerable expence in qualifying themselves by regular education for explaining the holy scriptures, have dedicated their time and labour to the service of the said church; and moreover approving highly the political conduct of the Revd. Charles Clay, who, early rejecting the tyrant and tyranny of Britain, proved his religion genuine by it's harmony with the liberties of mankind, and, conforming his public prayers to the spirit and the injured rights of his country, ever[3] addressed the God of battles for victory to our arms, while others impiously prayed that our enemies might vanquish and overcome us:[4] do hereby oblige ourselves our heirs executors and administrators to pay to the said Charles Clay of Albemarle his executors or administrators the several sums affixed to our respective names on the 25th day of December next, and also to make the like annual paiment on the 25th. day of December in every year following until we shall withdraw the same[5]

or until the legislature shall make other provision for the support of the said Clergy. In Consideration whereof we expect that the said Charles Clay shall perform divine service and preach a sermon in the town of Charlottesville on every 4th. Saturday till the end of the next session of general Assembly and after that on every 4th. Sunday or oftener if a regular rotation with the other churches which shall have put themselves under his cure will admit a more frequent attendance.

And we further mutually agree with each other that we will meet at Charlottesville on the 1st. day of March in the present year and on   in every year following so long as we continue our subscriptions and there make choice by ballot of three Wardens to collect our said subscriptions to take care of such books and vestments as shall be provided for the use of our church to call meetings of our Congregation when necessary and to transmit such other business relating to our said Congregation as we shall hereafter confide to them.

February. 1777.[6]
Th: Jefferson, six pounds.[7]
Philip Mazzei sixteen shillings & eight pence
Randolph Jefferson two pounds ten shillings
Nicholas Lewis three Pounds ten Shillings
Saml Taliaferro [Twenty?] Shillings
Hastings Marks Twenty Shillings
Peter Marks Twenty Five Shillings
Richard Gaines ten Shillings
Lewis Cradock ten Shillings
Edward Butler ten Shillings
Benjamin Calvert 10/.
Richard Moore 10/.
John [. . .] 10-
A S Bryan twenty shillings
Thos. Garth Fifteen Shillings
James Minor Twenty Shillings
William Tandy twenty shillings.[8]
Jno Joüet £1.10.
Thomas Key 2.0.0
Richd. Anderson 2.0.0

MS (MHi); in an unidentified hand, with autograph signatures. This MS was copied almost literatim, but with one important change (see further on in the present note) from another MS (DLC: TJ Papers, 3: 406); the latter MS is in TJ's hand and contains a shorter list of signatures, all but one of them crossed out (see note 7, below). Thus the TJ MS served as a draft for the present document, but the draft itself had been temporarily used and then rejected because *it* provided for "Protestant Episcopalian" services (to be held at the same times, conducted by the same clergyman, &c.) instead of the "Calvinistical Reformed" services called for in the present subscription paper.

Each of these documents by itself is puzzling; when considered together, part of the puzzle is solved, but questions still remain. They present, of course, TJ's own answer to the question left unsettled in the Act for Exempting Dissenters of 1776, i.e., "Whether a general assessment should not be established by law, on every one, to the support of the pastor of his choice; or whether all should be left to voluntary contributions" (TJ's Autobiography, Ford, I, 54; see Hening, IX, 165, and Notes and Proceedings on Discontinuing the Establishment, 11 Oct. to 9 Dec. 1776, in Vol. 1). TJ obviously preferred leaving "all to voluntary contributions" and in his own parish organized the subscription for the support of THE REVD. CHARLES CLAY, the friend and patriot who had preached the Albemarle fast-day sermon in July 1774 (see TJ and John Walker to the Inhabitants of the Parish of St. Anne, printed above under 23 July 1774; and Testimonial to Clay, 15 Aug. 1779, below). Furthermore, TJ not only pledged the largest sum among the subscribers but continued payments for others as well as himself over several years (Account Books, 9 Mch., 18 Aug. 1778; 28 Apr., 15 Aug. 1779). This, however, does not clear up the question why the subscription was first framed for the support of Protestant Episcopalian services and rejected in favor of one in support of "Calvinistical Reformed" services. Since both papers named the same clergyman, it can only be supposed that Clay in his patriotic ardor proposed to (or temporarily did) withdraw from the Anglican faith in order to enter the Presbyterian or German Reformed ministry. The voluminous record of the later friendship of Clay and TJ throws no light on the episode.

1 Deleted in the TJ MS at this point: "a church in our opinion so truly Apostolical as."

2 The TJ MS reads: "Protestant Episcopalian."

3 This word not in the TJ MS.

4 The tribute to Clay's patriotism, from "and moreover approving highly" to this point, was interlined in the TJ MS in a minuscule hand.

5 The order of the wording of this passage is different in the TJ MS, but the substance is the same except for an incomplete phrase ("until we shall withdraw our subscription in open ves") preceding the long blank in the text.

6 Date in TJ's hand.

7 The five signatures on the TJ MS are those of Th: Jefferson, Jno. Harvie, Randolph Jefferson, Thos. Garth, and Philip Mazzei. All but that of Harvie, who subscribed "Four pounds" for the support of a Protestant Episcopalian clergyman, are crossed out and reappear, pledged for identical amounts, in the subscription as revised. Harvie's name, it will be noted, does not reappear, suggesting that some hope was held out for obtaining the services of an Episcopalian as well as a "Calvinistical" clergyman.

8 This name and sum are in TJ's hand.

Subscription to Support a Clerk of the Congregation in Charlottesville

[February 1777]

We the Subscribers agree to pay on the 25th. day of December in the present year 1777. and so on the 25th. day of December annually in every year after till we shall notify the contrary in writing to the Wardens for our Congregation, the sums affixed to our respective names, to such person or persons as by a majority of our Congregation, to be called together by the wardens for that purpose, shall from time to time be appointed to the office of clerk for the said Congregation, to assist the reverend Charles Clay in performing divine service whenever he shall attend at Charlottesville for that purpose.

Th: Jefferson thirty shillings.
Jno. Harvie twenty Shillings
Randolph Jefferson ten shillings
Peter Marks Five Shillings

MS (DLC); in TJ's hand, with autograph signatures. This subscription was drawn up at the same time as the subscription to support a Protestant Episcopalian clergyman, described in the notes to the preceding document. It accompanies that subscription in the TJ Papers and is not separately catalogued in DLC.

From Patrick Henry

SIR Wmsburg March 31. 1777.

By the Bearer Lieut. Jas. Meriwether I send two hundred and thirty six pounds 16/. for the recruiting Soldiers in your County and the adjacent ones, to serve in the Battalions of this Commonwealth. You are to be assisted by Your Field officers in chusing 1 Captain 2 Lieutenants and one Ensign of the most proper persons who have the best chance to raise these Men quickly and deliver them the money I send taking Bond and Security from them to account for the same to me when required. This done they are to proceed to recruit, the Captain 28 the first Lieutenant 20. the 2d. Lieutenant 16 and the Ensign 10. for their Quotas. At the end of 3 Weeks after they get the money they must inform me what success they have had, and they will be continued if like to get their Quotas, if not they will be discontinued and others appointed upon your recommendation which please to send after the expiration of the above Time, if the Quotas are not f[illed]. If you cant conveniently get all the field officers to assist in the appointm[ents] proceed with any one of them to send out proper persons in the recruiting Business and be sure to let me know their Success at the end of 3 W[eeks] after they get the money. I send but half the Bounty and enlisting may be for a full Company but if more is wanted send by any s[afe?] hand or borrow it by some means and I will send it when called for.

I must entreat that [you] Sir and every Gentleman in your County ass[ist] by your Influance and interest in filling [up] this Company without loss of time; and let [me] know by the Bearer how soon you think [it] may be done. The men may be well cloth[ed] here. I am Sr. your hble Servt., P. HENRY JR.

RC (DLC); in a clerk's hand and signed by Henry. Addressed: "The County Leiutenant of Albemarle." Endorsed by TJ: "Papers relating to enlistment of company for Colonial service. April. 1777."

To George Washington

May it please your Excy. Albem Virga. [ca. 1 April 1777]

The bearer Horseley enlisted for 2 years in a company raised in this county for one of the Virga. battal's of 1775. In the winter now past, and before his time was out, he was unfortunate enough to desert from the service. Having had lesure to repent he some time ago made application to me through a third person to advise him what to do. I let him know that (his life being forfeited) there was no person in this world who could save it but yourself; and that if he would come in I would venture to state the fact to your excellency that he might have all the benefit which a voluntary return to duty and resignation of his life into your hands would give him, and could not help hoping he would obtain your pardon if it could any way square with the rules you may have laid down. He has therefore voluntarily come in and put himself under the care of Capt. Marks of Colo. Lewis's battalion, by whom he will be delivered to you. Having now discharged my promise and returned I hope a good soldier to the use of his country; the residue remains with your excellency to whose decision his fate and my wishes are submitted. I am &c.

Dft (DLC). Endorsed by TJ: "Washington, Genl."

HORSELEY: TJ left a blank for the insertion of the first name of the bearer, who was possibly John Horsley, son of William and Mary Cabell Horsley (Brown, *The Cabells*, p. 175-6). From the context, the letter must have been written in the spring of 1777, probably early in April, because TJ turned over the prisoners of war to Capt. Marks on 31 Mch. to be conducted to Philadelphia with the Continental recruits (List of British Prisoners and Their Quarters, 25 Sep. 1777).

Writ of Election for Delegates from Albemarle County

[10 April 1777]

Agreable to an Ordinance of Convention the Freeholders of Albemarle County met at the Court House of the said County on Thursday the Tenth day of April One thousand seven Hundred and Seventy Seven in Order to Elect Delegates to represent this County in General Assembly. Thomas Jefferson and Jno. Harvie Esq. were by the said freeholders chosen as representatives. Given under my Hand and Seal this 10th. day of April 1777.

Isaac Davis Shf.

MS (Vi). Endorsed: "Albemarle Thos. Jefferson & John Harvie." Another MS (Vi), dated 9 Apr. 1778, and also signed by Isaac Davis, appointed TJ and George Gilmer delegates for Albemarle for the sessions of 1778.

ORDINANCE OF CONVENTION: i.e., the Constitution for Virginia, 1776, sect. v and vii (Hening, IX, 114-15), which provided that two delegates be elected to represent each county in the House of Delegates in accordance with the rules for elections which were already in existence under the act concerning elections passed in 1769 (Hening, VIII, 308-9). TJ attended the Assembly 8 May 1777 (JHD, May 1777, 1827 edn., p. 3).

Receipt for Bounty Money

April 15. 1777.

Received of Thos. Jefferson fifty one pounds four shillings to be given in bounty to such persons as shall enlist with me and I promise to execute a bond with sufficient security for employing it in that way.

John Jouett Jur

MS (DLC); in TJ's hand, signed by John Jouett, Jr.

For instructions to TJ concerning the distribution of bounty money, see Patrick Henry to TJ, 31 Mch. 1777. TJ submitted an account of the distribution of the money on 17 May 1777 (*Va. Council Jour.*, I, 412).

From John Harvie

Dear Sir [Before 18 April 1777]

Mr. Strother Jones proposes setting out in a few days for the Continental Army, where he wishes to Contin[ue] if he can Obtain an Appointment near the person of either of the Generals. Gentel and Agreable, he is favour'd with several Letters to Gentlemen of Rank in the Army Yet thinks an Introduction from you to General Washington or to any other General to whom you think proper will have Considerable Influence in his favour. He is restrained by his duty from waiting on you in person with this requisition. I dont deceive you in calling him a very deserving Young Gentleman of the most punctilious Honour whose Resolution is Unquestionable. He has had the Offer of Aid de Camp to Genl. Stephen. His only reason for refuseing of it is that a Good understanding did not formerly Subsist between his father and that General and dislikes being under an Obligation to a man whom his father has not always treated with the greatest r[esp]ect. I hope you will not think me two Assumeing [and wil]l treat this application as you think [it] merits. I am Sir yr most Obt Servt, JNO HARVIE

RC (DLC). MS mutilated. Addressed: "To Colo. Thomas Jefferson By Ch[r]istie." On verso: Draft of TJ to George Washington, 18 Apr. 1777.

This letter has been dated from the contents of TJ's letter to an unknown correspondent, 18 Apr. 1777, q.v. STROTHER JONES was the only brother of Harvie's wife, Margaret Jones (J. A. Waddell, *Annals of Augusta Co., Va., Supplement*, Richmond, 1888, p. 394). HIS FATHER: Gabriel Jones, who was, by tradition, a person of "extremely irritable temper, which, when aroused, expressed itself in the strongest terms he could command, mingled with no little profanity" (same, p. 393; see also TJ to Gabriel Jones, 29 Apr. 1779).

To George Washington

May it please your excellency [18 April 1777]

The bearer Mr. Strother Jones, son of Mr. Gabriel Jones of Augusta is now about to set out for the Continental army, where he wishes to be so placed as to gain military knolege. An offer of being Aid de camp to Brigadr. Genl. Stephens he thought himself in delicacy obliged to decline, on account of some misunderstanding which had subsisted between that gentleman and his father, tho otherwise he would much have wished for such an appointment. Should his good fortune draw him within the sphere of your excellency's notice, you will find him active, fearless, and of punctilious honour. Perhaps some occasion may arise wherein your Excellency or some of your generals may make an essay of his properties. Assured they will stand any proof [I] shall in such case think myself happy to have had any share in recommending a good subject to good hands. In the mean time any civilities which you Sir shew him will be acknoleged as obligations to Your Excellency's Most obedt & Most humble servt.

Dft (DLC). Written on verso of John Harvie's undated letter to TJ printed under the present date.

The date of this letter has been established by its similarity to TJ's letter to an unidentified correspondent, 18 Apr. 1777, q.v. On 14 May 1777, Washington appointed STROTHER JONES captain of Grayson's Additional Continental Regiment (Washington, *Writings*, ed. Fitzpatrick, VIII, 61; Heitman).

To ——— ———

SIR Virginia April 18. 1777.

The bearer hereof, Mr. Strother Jones, son to a friend of mine, is now setting out for the American army, to share in the defence of his country. He is from nature well-principled for war; bold, honorable and modest: but he is young also, and will need the fatherly hand of some one to lead him thro' the mazes of military delicacy and duty on so large a scale. I feel myself therefore interested in recommending him to your good counsels and offices. I thought myself happy in the little degree of acquaintance I was able to acquire with you while in Philadelphia. It was not sufficient I own to justify my troubling you on any occasion. But the idea you then impressed on me was that from a disposition to do good you would lend your friendly aid to any one deserving it. I am therefore induced to recommend the bearer to your patronage in the school of honour, not doubting you will find him grateful of advice and profiting by it. I am Sir With much esteem Your most obedient most humble servt., TH: JEFFERSON

RC (MHi); Dft (DLC).

There is no indication of the addressee of this letter and, since the copy intended for the recipient is among TJ's papers, it may never have been sent.

From Richard Henry Lee

DEAR SIR Philadelphia April 29th. 1777

If I were to consider punctilio more than the suggestions of friendship, I should expect an answer to some of the letters I have written you, before I dispatched another. But I ever hated ceremonies, and shall not commence ceremony with you. I wish it were in my power to give you any very interesting news, but alas, the slow assembling of an Army prevents any attempt from us upon the enemy, and will furnish them an opportunity of collecting reenforcements from all quarters. The french Ministry assure our Commissioners that few succors can be drawn from Germany, but we find they are endeavoring to supply deficiencies from among the Tories in the States of Connecticut, New York, and New Jersey, where they have secret emissaries in abundance. For these purposes of corruption, it seems that Lord Howe is furnished with a Secretary, who is the greatest Adept in the art of bribing that now lives. I am afraid this Country furnishes too good materials for him to work upon. The plan of the British Court, if they can find Men and money and should not be disturbed by other wars, as it was settled in January last, was to reenforce Carleton and Howe, the latter to enter New England with his whole force for their *extermination*, whilst the former kept the middle Colonies in awe by invading N. York thro the Lakes. Burgoyne with 10,000 men chiefly Germans, to attack Virginia and Maryland. The Southern and Middle Colonies to be put under *Military Government*. This may be relied on as fact, and shews, if it wanted shewing, the just and merciful spi[rit] that animates the Leaders of our Enemies in Council. And I assure you, those that execute in the field are faithful representatives. It is on all hands agreed, that our own Tories are more formidable to us than the British force and that a few Leaders among these, are the Authors of all the mischeif. Quere then, if it becomes not every Legislature to secure against their machinations by the most vigorous and discouraging laws? I realy believe that numbers of our lazy, worthless young Men, will not be induced to come forth into the service of their Country unless the States adopt the mode recommended by Congress of ordering Drafts from the Militia. This may induce the young and lazy to take the Continental bounty, rather than serve for nothing of that sort. If the 88 Batallions were once complete, adieu to British Tyranny and every chance for its succeeding.

Howes Army still remains on the Heights near Brunswick and Gen. Washington to occupy the Country round him.

Farewell dear Sir. Regard me as your affectionate friend,

RICHARD HENRY LEE

RC (DLC).

The last letter from Lee to TJ that has been located is that of 3 Nov. 1776. The absence of other letters indicates that perhaps some of the letters which Lee wrote to him were intercepted and that they never reached him. The resolution of Congress recommending DRAFTS FROM THE MILITIA was agreed to on 14 Apr. 1777 (JCC, VII, 262-3). For the action of Virginia and Massachusetts regarding drafts, see TJ to John Adams, 16 May 1777, and Adams to TJ, 26 May 1777.

Petition from Some Inhabitants of Albemarle County

[Before 12 May 1777]

To the Honourable House of Burgesses and Senators of the common wealth of Virginia the Petition of sundry Inhabitants and Freholders Situate in the south part of Albemarle county Humbly Sheweth, that your petitioners suffer many and great Hardships and inconveniencys from the Vast extent of said County in Traveling to the Court-house, the greatest part by far of your petitioners have from twenty to Thirty five Miles to the same the Roads extremely Bad and cannot be made much better as the lands are

Craggy and Mountainous two Rivers and many Creeks that are Rapid which add to the inconveniency and the court-house of the said county set many Miles from the Center to the North part to make the Situation more agreable as the part supposed to be about the Center was Mountainous which your petitioners are Occasionally to get Through on any Emergency the Inconveniencies so great that many of your petitioners become sufferers not having it in their power to Attend to their business without Riding The day before and the day after to Return. For these and other Reasons we [pray to?] have the County divided into two distinct Countys by Running a direct line from the Southwest point of the Louisa line, the Waters of Machunck Creek, to the Fluvanna River at the lower side of Scotts ferry Landing by which Division your petitioners conceive the greatest conveniency to themselves and no Individuals to be prejudiced. The court-house and Town of Charlottsville will answer the same purpose as at present and be near Centrical to the North part of the said County and your petitioners shall ever pray &c.

MS (Vi), in unidentified hand, signed by 133 individuals, including Wilson Miles Cary, Thomas Napier, John Moore, and John and William Clark. MS endorsed: "Albemarle Petn. for Division of the County. 1777. May 12. Refd. to Propns. &c. (Reasonable) by a line to be run from the most Western point in the Louisa line directly to the lower edge of Scott's ferry. 2d. & 3d. Resolutions." The passage "by a line . . . Scott's ferry" is in TJ's hand. TJ also drew a map (also in Vi) to accompany the petition (see reproduction in this volume).

On 12 May the petition was presented to House and referred to the Committee of Propositions and Grievances; the committee reported favorably next day, and TJ was appointed to a committee to bring in a bill. Bill was reported 14 May by Nicholas; it was passed 20 May and agreed to by Senate 3 June (JHD, May 1777, 1827 edn., p. 7, 9, 10, 20, 21, 56). No MS of the Bill has been found, but it is quite probable that TJ drew it; the Act as adopted is in Hening, IX, 325-7. This Act created the new county of Fluvanna, set up courts therein, authorized the governor to appoint the first sheriff, and erected the parish of Fluvanna from those parts of the parishes of Saint Anne and Fredericksville that lay within the new county. Wilson Miles Cary and Thomas Napier were elected to represent the new county in the House of Delegates; see Election Writ, 30 June 1777, below.

Bill for Regulating the Appointment of Delegates to the Continental Congress

[12 May 1777]

Be it enacted by the General assembly of the Commonwealth of Virginia[1] that there shall be annually chosen five delegates[2] to act on the part of this Commonwealth in General Congress any three of whom shall have power to sit and vote. The delegates to be chosen in this present session of Assembly shall continue in office till the day of and those hereafter to be chosen at the said annual election shall enter on the exercise of their office on the day of next succeeding their election and shall continue in the same one year; unless sooner recalled or permitted to resign by General assembly; in which case another shall be chosen to serve till the end of the year in the stead of any one so recalled or permitted to resign.

No person who shall have served[3] two years in Congress shall be capable of serving therein again till he shall have been out of the same one whole year.[4]

Each of the *said* delegates for every day he shall attend in Congress shall receive eight dollars, and also fifteen pence per mile going and the same returning together with his ferriages,[5] to be paid wherever Congress shall be sitting by the Treasurer of this Commonwealth out of any public monies which shall be in his hands.

Dft (Vi). In TJ's hand and endorsed by him: "A Bill for regulating the appointment of delegates to General Congress." Docketed in hand of John Tazewell: "1777. May 12. Read the first Time." On recto of Dft in unknown hand is the following: "Ayes 42 Noes 40."

The close vote on this Bill has been explained heretofore by the long-standing and bitter feeling between the factions represented by Benjamin Harrison and Richard Henry Lee. At the election of delegates by the Convention on 20 June 1776, the number had been reduced from seven to five, Harrison and Braxton had been left out, and TJ himself had been near the bottom of the list (Ford, II, 128-9; Malone, *Jefferson*, I, 240-1); this Ford attributes to the influence of the "Lee party," though TJ was not an object of the maneuver (see Fleming to TJ, 27 July 1776; R. H. Lee to TJ, 3 Nov. 1776; and Burk-Girardin, *Hist. of Va.*, IV, 225-6). Ford adds: "In turn the Harrison faction began a counter attack on R. H. Lee, but apparently first attempted to veil it under a general act of the assembly. For this purpose, May 12, 1777, they ordered the preparation of a bill regulating the appointment of delegates, and named Jefferson alone to draft it—the only case I have discovered of a single individual being so selected. He was already pledged . . . to a limited term of two years for this office; and a bill prepared on these lines would legislate Lee out of office. . . . Lee . . . seemed to have felt no ill-will toward Jefferson for his part in the affair." The pledge to which Ford refers is the Resolution TJ drafted while in Congress to limit service of delegates to two years and to provide rotation and continuity in a state's delegation (see under date ca. 1 July 1776). This was probably drawn by TJ after he had prepared his proposed Constitution for Virginia, the Second Draft of which provided that delegates should be appointed when necessary, but after serving two years should not be reappointed during an interval of two years; his Third Draft altered this to "one year" in each case; neither provided for rotation or continuity. These were principles to which TJ was committed, and to imply, as Ford does, that he permitted his stand on such matters to be used by the Harrison faction requires particular comment. (1) There is no proof that the Harrison faction "ordered the preparation of a bill" to veil the attack on Lee. The Journal of the House merely states: "*Ordered*, that leave be given to bring in a bill 'for regulating the appointment of delegates to General Congress,' and that Mr. Jefferson do prepare and bring in the same" (JHD, May 1777, 1827 edn., p. 8). It is possible to interpret this as being the result of TJ's request for leave to bring in such a bill; it is almost certain that he had the Bill already prepared when on 12 May leave was granted, for after leave was granted only three routine and apparently undebated measures were recorded in the Journal before he presented it. (2) Ford cites, but does not analyze, Campbell, *Bland Papers*, I, 57. This is a remarkable letter from John Banister, which deserves special attention because it was written on or shortly after 20 June 1777 (dated June 10, but see below), because Banister was a member of the legislature, and because he was one of those voted upon as a delegate to Congress. His testimony may, therefore, be given some weight, particularly since, in that letter, he says of R. H. Lee that "I am not very fond of that gentleman." What Banister does explain is that Lee was left out of the delegation because of an accusation that he had, in writing, demanded rentals from his tenants in tobacco or in gold or silver specie, fearing paper emissions would depreciate (see R. H. Lee to TJ, 3 May 1779); that the inference drawn by the House was that Lee, "being in an eminent station, and one of the first guardians and trustees of the rights of America . . . ought not to be further entrusted with the high office he had been appointed to"; that Banister himself had opposed the measure and method of removing Lee "as a most flagrant act of injustice, and as a precedent dangerous in its nature." (3) Lee demanded a hearing before the House, was accorded it, the Senate attended, and, on 20 June, the House voted him its thanks for the "services he has rendered his country" (JHD, May 1777, 1827 edn., p. 84); shortly thereafter, Lee was elected to Congress to fill the place of George Mason, who had declined to serve (same, p. 94). (4) If the Bill was engineered by the Harrison faction, it is surprising that one of the amendments offered—that making delegates in Congress ineligible for membership in the General Assembly—should have passed; for that amendment was probably aimed at Harrison himself, who was serving out TJ's unexpired term until 11 Aug. 1777 and who had been in attendance as a member of the legislature since 8 May (Burnett. *Letters of Members*, II, lxix-lxx). (5) Finally, and conclusively, the Bill as drawn by TJ would have excluded *both* Lee and Harrison, for both had been elected to Congress in 1775 and again in 1776 (same). Under the Bill as amended by the Senate, and as accepted by the House with the alteration that service should be for three years *successively*, both Lee and Harrison were rendered eligible and both were, in fact, elected *after* the present Bill was passed and before the new term began on 11 Aug. 1777; both were also rendered ineligible to serve in the General Assembly while serving in Congress (Hening, IX, 299). There is little room for doubt that the Bill as drawn by TJ and as presented here was merely his effort to achieve by legislation what he had failed to achieve in his Drafts of a Constitution in 1776 and in his Resolution drawn up for presentation to Congress shortly thereafter to obtain limited tenure, continuity of experience, and rotation in office; his stand was grounded on a principle he had announced a year earlier. On 14-15 May 1777 TJ's Bill was debated and amended, passing the House on 16 May; TJ carried it to the Senate and that house offered four amendments, of which the House accepted the second and fourth, amended the first, and disagreed to the third. The Senate receded from the last (JHD, May 1777, 1827 edn., p. 8, 10, 13, 15, 22). TJ was undoubtedly disappointed in the emasculation of his Bill, for at the Oct. 1777 session another bill, amending the one adopted in May, was passed. This bill provided that the number of delegates should be limited to seven, of whom any three, when more than five did not attend, should be sufficient to represent the State; that no one should be eligible to serve in Congress for more than three years in any term of six; and that compensation should be increased to ten dollars per day (Hening, IX, 388). Ford (II, 129) asserts that R. H. Lee procured the introduction of this amending act and that TJ was "apparently . . . the drafter" of it also; Lee was not a member of the legislature and, during most of the session, was in attendance at Congress. TJ, of course, was a member of the legislature at the Oct. 1777 session and the bill is similar in its first provision to that part which was deleted in May (see textual note 1); this bill was ordered to be brought in on 6 Nov. 1777 (TJ was absent from the House from

5 to 10 Nov.), and Bullitt and Meriwether were appointed to draft it (JHD, Oct. 1777, 1827 edn., p. 12, 14, 24, 34-5, 62, 85, 89-90, 96, 98, 108). The probability is that TJ did not draft this bill, for on 12 Dec. 1777 the House passed the following resolution (before the Act had been adopted) and TJ, who carried it to the Senate, was probably its author: "Although it is the wish of the General Assembly, that the representation of this Commonwealth in Congress, should consist of three members at least; yet, as it may sometimes happen, from unforeseen accidents, that three may not be present, and the State thereby unrepresented, *Resolved, therefore*, that from this time until the end of two months after the expiration of this session of Assembly, any two of the delegates . . . be empowered to give the vote of this State on any question in Congress, whenever there shall happen to be none other of the said delegates attending" (same, p. 76). However, the other bill concerning representation which is definitely associated with TJ is Bill No. 10 in the Report of the Committee of Revisors (q.v., under date of 18 June 1779).

[1] The phrase "of the Commonwealth of Virginia" was deleted by amendment in the House. Also, everything from this enacting clause to the end of the first paragraph was deleted, thus reducing TJ's Bill merely to the limitation of periods of service and to compensation.

[2] Dft originally read "to represent," which was crossed out, and "to act on the part of" was interlined as a substitution.

[3] This was amended by the Senate to read: "No person who shall have served three years as a member of Congress, or shall hereafter serve three years, including the time he hath heretofore served." The House in turn amended this to read, as it does in the Act as adopted: "no person who shall have served, or shall hereafter serve, as a member of Congress for three years successively, including. . . ."

[4] The House amended the Bill by inserting a paragraph rendering delegates to Congress ineligible to serve as members of either of the houses of the General Assembly.

[5] The words "eight" and "fifteen pence" are in the hand of Tazewell, the spaces which they fill having been blank in Dft as presented by TJ. At this point the Act reads: "in lieu of allowances heretofore settled by law." This had been established in 1775 at 45 shillings for each day's attendance, plus one shilling per mile for transportation, plus ferriage costs; in 1776 the per diem was reduced to 30 shillings; and in the Oct. 1777 session, as noted above, the compensation was raised to ten dollars (Hening, IX, 73-74, 133-134, 388).

To John Adams

Dear Sir Williamsburgh May 16. 1777.

Matters in our part of the continent are too much in quiet to send you news from hence. Our battalions for the Continental service were some time ago so far filled as rendered the recommendation of a draught from the militia hardly requisite, and the more so as in this country it ever was the most unpopular and impracticable thing that could be attempted. Our people even under the monarchical government had learnt to consider it as the last of all oppressions. I learn from our delegates that the Confederation is again on the carpet. A great and a necessary work, but I fear almost desperate. The point of representation is what most alarms me, as I fear the great and small colonies are bitterly determined not to cede. Will you be so good as to recollect the proposition I formerly made you in private and try if you can work it into some good to save our union? It was that any proposition might be negatived by the representatives of a majority of the people of America, or of a majority of the colonies of America. The former secures the larger the latter the smaller colonies. I have mentioned it to many here. The good whigs I think will so far cede their opinions for the sake of the Union, and others we care little for. The journals of congress not being printed earlier gives more uneasiness than I would ever wish to see produced by any act of that body, from whom alone I know our salvation can proceed. In our assembly even the best affected think it an indignity to freemen to be voted away life and fortune in the dark. Our house have lately written for a M.S. copy of your journals, not meaning to desire a communication of any thing ordered to be kept secret. I wish the regulation of the post office adopted by Congress last September could be put in practice. It was for the riders to travel night and day, and to go their several stages three times a week. The speedy and frequent communication of intelligence is really of great consequence. So many falshoods have been propagated that nothing now is beleived unless coming from Congress or camp. Our people merely for want of intelligence which they may rely on are become lethargick and insensible of the state they are in. Had you ever a leisure moment I should ask a letter from you sometimes directed to the care of Mr. Dick, Fredericksburgh: but having nothing to give in return it would be a tax on your charity as well as your time. The esteem I have for you privately, as well as for your public importance will always render assurances of your health and happiness agreeable. I am Dear Sir Your friend & servt: TH: JEFFERSON

RC (Adams Manuscript Trust, Boston). Addressed: "To John Adams esq. of the Massachusets delegation in Philadelphia. Free." Endorsed: "Mr Jefferson. ans. May 26. 1777."

This earliest known letter exchanged between TJ and John Adams began a correspondence that continued, with some intervals, for forty-nine years and that remains unrivaled, in the United States at least, for its revelation of the writers' minds and characters, its literary distinction, and its historical importance. More than one of the questions of high public policy with which the present letter deals, and on which Adams in his prompt answer (of 26 May) comments thoughtfully and characteristically, was to engage the attention of the two men for many years thereafter. Congress had recommended DRAUGHTS FROM THE MILITIA on 14 Apr. 1777 (JCC, VII, 262-3; compare TJ's opinion on volunteers in his letter to R. H. Lee, 5 June 1778). THE CONFEDERATION: On 8 Apr. 1777 Congress resolved, "That the report of the committee of the whole house, on the articles of confederation, be taken into consideration on Monday next, and that two days in each week be employed on that subject, until it shall be wholly discussed in Congress" (JCC, VII, 240). The JOURNALS OF CONGRESS for 1776 were not ready for distribution until 3 June 1777 (JCC, VIII, 412). On 13 June 1777 the Board of War recommended the daily printing of the Journals but no action was taken by Congress (same, p. 474, note). Congress adopted the report of the committee for regulating the POST OFFICE on 30 Aug. 1776 (JCC, V, 419-20; see also John Adams to TJ, 26 May 1777).

From Richard Henry Lee

DEAR SIR Phila. May 20. 1777

We are this moment informed here, that some evil disposed people (no doubt hired for the purpose) have industriously propagated among the N. Carolina Troops, and among the recruits of Virginia in the upper parts, *that the plague rages in our Army.* In consequence of which, it is said, the recruiting business stops, and desertions are frequent. There never was a more infamous and groundless falsehood. The Army is extremely healthy, and the wise[st] methods are pursued to keep them so. I mention this dear Sir, that some adequate plan may be adopted to stop the progress of such wicked lies as are now, with industry circulated thro the Country. Force having failed our enemies, fraud is substituted, and corruption is swiftly and silently pushed thro every quarter.

One plan, now in frequent use, is, to assassinate the Characters of the friends of America in every place, and by every means.

At this moment, they are now reading in Congress, an audacious attempt of this kind against the brave General Arnold. Farewell dear Sir, I wish you happy, RICHARD HENRY LEE

Nothing new in Jersey.

RC (DLC).

GENERAL ARNOLD sent a letter to Congress on 20 May enclosing a handbill printed in Pittsfield, Mass., by John Brown, 12 Apr. 1777, making serious charges against Arnold. The letter, demanding an investigation, was referred by Congress to the Board of War, which reported on 23 May, clearing Arnold's "character and conduct, so cruelly and groundlessly aspersed in the publication," (JCC, VII, 371, 373; VIII, 382; see also Van Doren, *Secret History*, p. 159-60).

From John Adams

MY DEAR SIR Philadelphia May 26. 1777

I had this Morning, the Pleasure of your Favour of the Sixteenth inst, by the Post; and rejoice to learn that your Battallions, were so far fill'd, as to render a Draught from the Militia, unnecessary. It is a dangerous Measure, and only to be adopted in great extremities, even by popular Governments. Perhaps, in Such Governments Draughts will never be made, but in Cases, when the People themselves see the Necessity of them. Such Draughts are widely different from those made by Monarchs, to carry on Wars, in which the People can see, no Interest of their own nor any other object in View, than the Gratification of the Avarice, Ambition, Caprice, Envy, Revenge, or Vanity of a Single Tyrant. Draughts in the Massachusetts, as they have been there managed, have not been very unpopular, for the Persons draughted are commonly the wealthiest, who become obliged to give large Premiums, to their poorer Neighbours, to take their Places.

The great Work of Confederation, draggs heavily on, but I dont despair of it. The great and Small States must be brought as near together as possible: and I am not without Hopes, that this may be done, to the tolerable Satisfaction of both. Your Suggestion, Sir, that any Proposition may be negatived, by the Representatives of a Majority of the People, or of a Majority of States, shall be attended to, and I will endeavour to get it introduced, if We cannot Succeed in our Wishes for a Representation and a Rule of voting, perfectly equitable, which has no equal, in my Mind.

Nothing gives me, more constant Anxiety, than the Delays, in publishing the Journals. Yet I hope, Gentlemen will have a little Patience with Us. We have had a Committee constantly attending to this very Thing, for a long Time. But we have too many Irons in the Fire, you know for Twenty Hands, which is nearly the whole Number We have had upon an Average Since, last fall. The Committee are now busy, every day in correcting Proof Sheets, So that I hope We Shall Soon do better.

A Committee on the Post office, too, have found, a thousand difficulties. The Post is now very regular, from the North and South, altho it comes but once a Week. It is not easy to get faithfull Riders, to go oftener. The Expence is very high, and the Profits, (so dear is every Thing, and so little Correspondence is carried on, except in franked Letters), will not Support the office. Mr. Hazard is now gone Southward, in the Character of Surveyor of the Post office, and I hope will have as good Success, as he lately had eastward, where he has put the office into good order.

We have no News from Camp, but that the General and Army are in good Spirits, and begin to feel themselves powerfull. We are anxiously waiting for News from abroad, and for my own Part I am apprehensive of some insidious Maneuvre from Great Britain, to deceive Us into Disunion and then to destroy.

We want your Industry and Abilities here extreamly. Financiers, we want more than Soldiers. The worst Enemy, we have now is

Poverty, real Poverty in the Shape of exuberant Wealth. Pray come and help Us, to raise the Value of our Money, and lower the Prices of Things. Without this, We cannot carry on the War. With it, we can make it a Diversion.

No poor Mortals were ever more perplexed than we have been, with three Misfortunes at once, any one of which would have been, alone, sufficient to have distressed Us. A Redundancy of the Medium of Exchange. A Diminution of the Quantity, at Markett of the Luxuries, the Conveniences and even the Necessaries of Life, and an Increase of the Demand for all these, occasioned by two large Armies in the Country.

I shall, ever esteam it a Happiness to hear of your Welfare, my dear Sir, and a much greater Still to see you, once more in Congress. Your Country is not yet, quite Secure enough, to excuse your Retreat to the Delights of domestic Life. Yet, for the soul of me, when I attend to my own Feelings, I cannot blame you. I am, Sir your Friend and most obedient Servant, JOHN ADAMS

RC (DLC); FC in Adams' hand (Adams Manuscript Trust, Boston).

The final compromise on representation in the confederation agreed that the votes of nine states were required for the passage of certain measures. Nothing came of Adams' proposal to introduce TJ's suggestion (Merrill Jensen, *The Articles of Confederation*, Univ. of Wis. Press, 1940, p. 142-5). For the difficulties in establishing the post office, see Wesley E. Rich, *The History of the United States Post Office to the Year 1829*, Cambridge, 1924, p. 51-4.

Bill to Prevent the Importation of Slaves, &c.

[16 June 1777]

To prevent more effectually the practice of holding persons in Slavery and importing them into this State[1] Be it enacted by the General Assembly that all persons who shall be hereafter imported into this Commonwealth by Sea or by Land whether they were bond or free in their native Country upon their taking the Oath of Fidelity to this Commonwealth shall from thenceforth become free and absolutely exempted from all Slavery or Bondage to which they had been subjected in any other State or Country whatsoever.[2] That it shall and may be lawful for any person by Deed duly executed in the presence of two or more Witnesses and acknowledged or proved and recorded in the General Court or Court of the County where he or she resides within eight Months from the making thereof or by their last Will and Testament in writing fully and absolutely to manumit and set at Liberty any Slave or Slaves to which they are entitled,[3] But no Slave absconding from the owner who resides in any of the thirteen united States of America, or any other state in amity with them, and coming into this commonwealth, or coming with the owner to dwell here, or attending him as a Servant, or falling to any Inhabitant of this Commonwealth by Marriage Will or Inheritance and not brought to be sold, shall not become free,[4] And if any Slave manumitted shall, within years thereafter, become chargeable to a Parish, the former owner, or his Executors or Administrators shall be compelled to reimburse the expenses of his or her maintenance, And so much of the Act of general Assembly made in the year of our Lord one thousand seven hundred and fifty three intitled "an act for the better government of Servants and Slaves" as is contrary to this act, is hereby declared to be repealed.[5]

MS (Vi). The first half is in the hand of John Tazewell, the remainder in an unidentified hand. Docketed in the same hands: "A Bill to prevent the importation of Slaves into this Commonwealth & for other purposes. 1777. June 16. Read the first Time."

There is no conclusive proof of TJ's authorship of this Bill. In his Autobiography, written in 1821, TJ makes the following statement: "this subject was not acted on finally until the year 78. when I brought in a bill to prevent their further importation. This passed without opposition, and stopped the increase of the evil by importation, leaving to future efforts its final eradication" (Ford, I, 51-2). There is no doubt that TJ erred in thinking the Bill passed without opposition. But Ford goes much further. He states that the earliest step toward limiting importation was the introduction of a bill in Nov. 1777; that the matter was taken up *de novo* at the Oct. 1778 session, where the Act was adopted before TJ arrived at the General Assembly on 30 Nov.; and that TJ "thus clearly had nothing to do with the first bill, and, as he did not take his seat at the second session till Nov. 30th, it is equally certain he had nothing to do with the one which was adopted" (same, p. 52). There are, however, the following points to be noted: (1) the earliest bill was introduced in the session of May 1777 (though this was done on 11 June and TJ had been granted leave on 20 May for the remainder of the session) and, as the notes below indicate, the Act as adopted in 1778 must have been an amended version of the present document and not, as Ford suggests, an entirely new draft; (2) Ford's argument assumes that TJ's mere absence from the House at the time the 1778 bill was introduced or acted upon is conclusive proof of the error of his claim, an untenable assumption in view of the fact that TJ on occasion drafted and submitted a bill for a committee of which he was not a member or even for a legislative body in which he had no seat; e.g., his Bill concerning escheats (4 June 1779) and his Bill providing for a constitution for Virginia in 1776; (3) TJ was extraordinarily scrupulous in making claims to authorship and in respecting the valid claims of others; (4) the famous passage in the Declaration of Independence on the slave trade, though admittedly polemical, was certainly a reflection of TJ's feelings on the subject, as was his argument in Howell v. Netherland in 1770 in which he argued that "under the law of nature, all men are born free" (Ford, I, 376); (5) it is also pertinent to call attention to TJ's assertion in the Autobiography that in 1769 he had suggested to Richard Bland an extension of the protection of certain laws to Negroes (an assertion which Ford also inferentially doubts, basing his inference on the absence of a record in the Journal of the House of Burgesses, though the effort may have been made in the committee of the whole or in some other manner not requiring a record), and at another time gave a detailed account of this effort of 1769 (same, I, 5; see also TJ to Edward Coles, 25 Aug. 1814). In the absence of positive evidence tending to refute TJ's assertion, the Bill is presented here because no other Virginian of the day had so publicly declared his opposition to the slave trade as had TJ and because the Bill, as drafted, contains a far-reaching statement of purpose in its preamble that would seem consonant with a Jeffersonian origin.

The legislative history of this Bill from June 1777 to final enactment in 1778 is as follows. On 11 June 1777 Isaac Zane, James Henry, and Philip Alexander were given leave to bring in a bill "to prevent the importation of slaves into this Commonwealth, and for other purposes." Zane reported it on 16 June, when the motion to read it a second time was defeated (JHD, May 1777, 1827 edn., p. 73, 79; TJ was granted leave of absence on 20 May for the remainder of the session). At the next session, on 8 Nov. 1777, Henry and Starke were ordered to prepare a bill on this subject; the fact that Henry was on the committee and that the title of the bill was precisely the same as that of the May 1777 session indicates merely a revival of the same Bill. Henry reported the Bill on 22 Nov., when it was read the second time and then referred to the committee of the whole. Discussion of the Bill was thereafter postponed seven times until, on 5 Jan. 1778, it was resolved that the committee of the whole would discuss it on 1 Mch. 1778—a date which, as all members knew, would fall after the close of the session (same, Oct. 1777, p. 17, 40, 45, 54, 71, 80, 84, 88, 92, 97, 101; the session ended 24 Jan.). Nothing was done at the May 1778 session to revive the Bill, though TJ was present and took a major part in the legislation that was passed. There was one resolution, however, that concerned Negroes and that TJ may possibly have moved: "That all free negroes or mulattoes, who enlisted, or shall enlist, to serve in the army during the war, shall be entitled to all the rights and privileges enjoyed by any subject of this State" (same, May 1778, p. 10). In view of the legal disadvantage under which persons of color rested, this was a radical proposal. TJ was a member of the committee to which this and other resolutions were referred with directions to bring in a bill or bills. But no separate bill on this proposal was introduced and none of the Acts adopted during the May 1778 session includes such a proviso. The substance of the resolution, however, is quite similar to the effort that TJ later remembered as having suggested to Richard Bland in 1769. The Bill that was finally enacted to limit the importation of slaves was introduced at the next session by Richard Kello, was debated at some length, and was amended both by the House and by the Senate (JHD, Oct. 1778, 1827 edn., p. 11-13, 19-20, 21, 23, 27, 29). The notes below indicate that the Act as finally adopted was an amended version of the one originally introduced at the May 1777 session and not, as Ford suggests, an entirely new bill. The entire process of enacting the Bill took place between 14 Oct. and 27 Oct., in contrast to the abrupt rejection in June 1777 and the long series of postponements in the Oct. 1777 session. As noted above, TJ did not take his seat until 30 Nov. 1778. Ford concludes from this that TJ had nothing to do with the Bill as finally adopted; despite this, TJ could have persuaded another member to introduce the Bill for him, just as he had done in other instances.

1 The Act as adopted merely states its purpose as that of "preventing the farther importation of slaves into this commonwealth" (Hening, IX, 471); the intent to "prevent more effectually *the practice of holding persons in Slavery*" was, of course, a much more drastic step.

2 Instead of this far-reaching proviso, the Act as adopted merely prohibited the importation of slaves by sea or by land.

3 The Act as adopted carried no provision for the manumission of slaves.

4 The Act as adopted provides for similar exceptions to those enumerated.

5 This repealing clause is also in the Act as adopted.

Election Writ Issued to Sheriff of Fluvanna County

[*Williamsburg*] *30 June 1777.* George Wythe, Speaker of the House of Delegates, directs Martin Key, Sheriff of Fluvanna co., to summon freeholders on some convenient day to elect "two of the most able and discreet men" of the county and to notify the elected delegates to attend legislature at Williamsburg in October "to consult of such things as may be for the glory of God, and for the honour and prosperity of the commonwealth."

Tr (Vi). Endorsed in unknown hand: "Fluvanna Writ for electing Delegates. Thomas Napier Wilson M. Cary. Oct. 1777." Also endorsed in TJ's hand: "The execution of this writ appears in a certain schedule hereto annexed." The annexed certification is in the hand of TJ, as are also two certificates of election issued to Napier and Cary respectively; all three documents are in TJ's hand, though signed by Martin Key, and all are dated 6 Oct. 1777; see petition to divide Albemarle co., under 12 May 1777, above.

To Silas Deane

HONORABLE SIR Virga Aug. 13. 1777.

The bearer hereof Mr. Shore comes to Europe on behalf of a mercantile house of which he is a member for the purpose of establishing a proper correspondence. With himself I have but little personal acquaintance, but consider his character as sufficiently certified when appointed to transact business by those with whom he is connected, whom I know to be men of business, punctual, able and wealthy. What the situation of our countrymen may be at present on European ground we know not. Lest it should be otherwise than secure I take the liberty of recommending Mr. Shore to your protection and good offices. Your knolege too of the subject which carries him to Europe will enable you to assist him perhaps with useful advice and good correspondencies. Any thing of this kind will be very obliging. Were there less to do here, I should wish myself with you but we as well as you have our hands full. Help the credit of our paper and we are no where else vulnerable. That is supported as yet by the zeal of the people. But it is dangerous to stretch the cord too far as we know not the precise degree of tension at which it may break. Something must be done very soon. Either no trade at all, or trade on a broad bottom. I feel within myself the same kind of desire of an hour's conversation with yourself or Dr. Franklyn which I have often had for a confabulation with those who have passed the irremeable bourne. But this being impossible I can only wish you for the public that success which we need and merit, and to yourself personally all pleasures present and to come.

Dft (DLC). Endorsed: "Deane Silas."
MR. SHORE: Thomas Shore, a merchant shipper and a purchasing agent for the state (*Va. Council Jour.*, I, 268)

advertised in Purdie's *Virginia Gazette* in July and August that he proposed embarking for Europe, soliciting commissions for the purchase of goods, all persons interested to apply to William Anderson of Hanover, Thomas Pleasants of Henrico, or himself.

To Benjamin Franklin

HONORABLE SIR Virga. Aug. 13. 1777

The bearer hereof Mr. Thomas Shores is a native of Virginia, and having lately in conjunction with some others established a partnership for the purpose of carrying on a trade to Europe, he comes to France on behalf of his house to establish a proper mercantile correspondence. I am less acquainted with him than his partners whom I know to be able, punctual, and of great genius for trade; and their appointment of him to transact for the house I consider as a certificate of his character. During the unknown footing on which an American may stand in Europe at present I thought it proper at his desire, to make him known to you, hoping that you would be so kind as to extend your protection and good offices to him should he need them during his stay.

I forbear to write you news, as, the time of Mr. Shore's departure being uncertain, it might be old before you receive it, and he can in person possess you of all we have. With respect to the state of Virginia in particular, the people seem to have deposited the monarchical and taken up the republican government with as much ease as would have attended their throwing off an old and putting on a new suit of clothes. Not a single throe has attended this important transformation. A half dozen aristocratical gentlemen agonizing under the loss of preeminence have sometime ventured their sarcasms on our political metamorphosis. They have been thought fitter objects for pity than punishment. We are at present in the compleat and quiet exercise of well organised government save only that our courts of justice do not open till the fall. I think nothing can bring the security of our continent and it's cause into danger, if we can support the credit of our paper. To do that I apprehend one of two steps must be taken. Either to procure free trade by alliance with some naval power able to protect it: or, if we find there is no prospect of that, to shut our ports totally to all the world, and turn our labourers into manufacturers. The former would be most eligible, because more conformable to the habits and wishes of our people. Were the British court to return to their senses in time to seise the little advantage which still remains within their reach from this quarter, I judge that on acknoleging our absolute independance and sovereignty, a commercial treaty, beneficial to them, and perhaps even a league of mutual offence and defence might be approved by our people, not seeing the extent or consequences of such an engagement, if nothing in the mean time done on your part should prevent it. But they will continue to grasp at their desperate sovereignty, till every benefit short of that is for ever put out of their reach.

I wish my domestic si[tuation had rendered it possible for me to have joined] you in the very honorable [charge confided to you. Residence in a polite court,] society with literati of the [first order, a just cause, and approving god will] add length to a life for whi[ch all men pray and none more than Your most obedient & humble servt.]

RC (PPAP). Dft (DLC). RC addressed: "To Doctor Benjamin Franklin at Paris"; endorsed: "From Jefferson Thos. Augt. 13. 1777." RC mutilated and signature cut out; missing portions of text supplied from Dft.

On 22 Jan. 1778, Thomas Shore wrote to Franklin from Cape François, enclosing letters of introduction from his friends in Virginia (*Cal. Franklin Papers*, I, 354). Franklin also received letters of introduction for Shore from Philip Mazzei, 5 Sep. 1777, and George Wythe, 6 Sep. 1777 (same, p. 291-2).

To John Adams

DEAR SIR Albemarle in Virginia. Aug. 21. 1777.

Your favor of May 26. came safely to hand. I wish it were in my power to suggest any remedy for the evil you complain of. Tho' did any occur I should propose it to you with great diffidence after knowing you had thought on the subject yourself. There is indeed a *fact* which may not have come to your knolege, out of which perhaps some little good may be drawn. The borrowing money in Europe (or obtaining credit there for necessaries) has already probably been essayed, and it is supposed with some degree of success. But I expect your applications have as yet been only to France, Holland, or such other states as are of principal note. There is however a smaller power, well disposed to our cause, and, as I am informed, possessed of abilities to assist us in this way. I speak of the Grand Duke of Tuscany. The little states of Italy you know have had long peace and shew no disposition to interrupt that peace shortly. The Grand Duke being somewhat avaritious in his nature has availed himself of the opportunity of collecting and hoarding what money he has been able to gather. I am informed from good authority (an officer who was concerned in the business of his treasury) that about three years ago he had ten millions of crowns lying dead in his coffers. Of this it is thought possible as much might be borrowed as would amount to a million of pounds lawful money. At any rate the attempt might be worth making. Perhaps an application from Dr. Franklin who has some acquaintance in that court might be sufficient. Or, as it might be prudent to sound well before the application, in order to prevent the discredit of a rebuff, perhaps Congress would think it worth while to send a special agent there to negotiate the matter. I think we have a gentleman here who would do it with dexterity and fidelity. He is a native of that Dutchy, well connected there, conversant in courts, of great understanding, and equal zeal in our cause. He came over not long since to introduce the cultivation of vines, olives &c. among us. Should you think the matter worth a further thought, either of the Colo. Lees, to whom he is known, can acquaint you more fully of his character. If the money can be obtained in specie, it may be applied to reduce the quantity of circulating paper, and in such a way to help the credit of that which will remain in circulation. If credit alone can be obtained for the manufactures of the country, it will still help us to clothe our armies or to encrease at market the necessaries our people want.

What upon earth can Howe mean by the manoeuvre he is now practising? There seems to me no object in this country which can either be of utility or reputation to his cause. I hope it will prove of a peice with all the other follies they have committed. The forming a junction with the Northern army up the Hudson's river, or the taking possession of Philadelphia might have been a feather in his cap and given them a little reputation in Europe. The former as being the design with which they came. The latter as being a place of the first reputation abroad and the residence of Congress. Here he may destroy the little hamlet of Williamsburgh, steal a few slaves, and lose half his army among the fens and marshes of our lower country, or by the heats of our climate. I am Dear Sir with the greatest esteem Your friend & servt., TH: JEFFERSON

RC (Adams Manuscript Trust, Boston). Dft (DLC).

The OFFICER of the TREASURY of the Grand Duke of Tuscany from whom TJ received information concerning the Duke's finances was Charles Bellini, who had served as a clerk in the Treasurer's office in Florence before coming to America in 1773 (WMQ, 2d ser., V [1925], 1). Bellini came to America with Philip Mazzei, the NATIVE OF THAT DUTCHY whom TJ considered a satisfactory emissary to secure funds for Congress (see Plan of Philip Mazzei's Agricultural Company, printed at end of 1774). In a letter to John Hancock, 19 Oct. 1778, q.v., TJ made another effort to interest

Congress in sending Mazzei abroad. Failing to gain the interest of Congress, Mazzei was commissioned by Patrick Henry, Governor of Virginia, in Jan. 1779, to undertake the mission to secure funds for the Commonwealth of Virginia (Howard R. Marraro, *Philip Mazzei, Virginia's Agent in Europe*, N.Y., 1935). HOWE'S MANOEUVRE: The British fleet had sailed southward; its objective was Philadelphia, but when it was seen off the Virginia Capes, Virginians assumed that an attack was to be made on Williamsburg, York, and Portsmouth (*Va. Gaz.* [Purdie], 22 Aug. 1777).

From Richard Henry Lee

Dear Sir Phila. August 25. 1777

It will not perhaps be disagreeable to you in your retirement, sometimes to hear the events of war, and how in other respects we proceed in the arduous business we are engaged in. Since the loss of Ticonderoga (into the cause of which, and the conduct of the commanding Officers, Congress have ordered inquiry to be made) and Gen. Burgoynes speedy march to Fort Edward, our affairs in that quarter begin to wear a favorable appearance. In addition to Burgoynes force, another Body of Men came down the Mohock river, by way of Oswego, and laid seige to Fort Stanwix, or Schuyler, as it is now called. At this place a battle ensued with the Tryon County Militia, in which the enemy were driven from the ground with the loss of more than 200 Indians and several regulars. Colo. Willet making a Sally from the Fort did great injury to the enemy and took from them a great quantity of baggage with 2 or 3 field pieces. However, the Militia having lost many Men in this Action and their best officers having been killed or wounded, they retired and left the enemy to return and lay Seige to Fort Schuyler, which the Garrison was bravely defending, when Gen. Arnold was detatched with a body of men to relieve the place. We expect every day to hear of his success. To the northward of this, in the N. Hampshire grants, Gen. Stark with 2000 Militia attacked Colo. Baum and 1500 Regular Troops behind works, and with Cannon. The consequence you will find in the inclosed Hand bill. This was an important victory, well timed, and will probably occasion Mr. Burgoyne to retire very quickly. If he does not, I can venture to *Augur* his destruction. He is at Saratoga and Fort Edward, with our main Army a few miles in his Front at the mouth of Mohock river. I expect Generals Lincoln and Arnold will presently be in his rear, after which, his chance of returning will be very small. Gen. Gates has joined the Northern Army and now commands in that quarter. Putnam with 5000 men commands on the heights of Hudsons river above N. York, in which place Gen. Clinton is left with about 3000 men. After Gen. Howe had long raised the curiosity of this part of the world, to know what could be his view in embarking his Army and coasting it for 5 weeks in a most oppressively hot season; at length, he appears at the very head of Chesapeake Bay where he remains with more than 200 sail of Vessels. His Troops not yet landed that we know of, but imagine they were put on shore yesterday. We are left yet to guess his Object. It may be supposed either for this City, or to conduct a line from Chesapeake to Newcastle and thereby inclose a large tract of Country between that Bay, Delaware, and the Sea. Let his plan be what it may, Gen. Washington, with a gallant Army is gone to enter a Caveat. The General with his Army passed thro this City yesterday, and they made a fine appearance. To aid the Army, and make the business secure, Congress has called for Militia from this State, Delaware, Maryland, and the Northern Counties of Virginia. Should Gen. Howe venture to enter the Country against this force, I think his ruin will be sure, notwithstanding we are told his Master depends on the "desperate efforts that Generals Howe and Cornwallis must make to redeem their Bankrupt honor." So, we learn from France, the King of England hath said. We have no reason to suppose, from our foreign intelligence that a war in Europe will immediately take place, but that every preparation for it is making remains without doubt; and in the mean time we shall surely receive most substantial Aid from our friends there. The fleet of France grows stronger daily, and with it, the spirit of the Court rises, as appears by the answer made to Lord Stormont when he told the french Minister that "the peace cannot continue long if N. America continued to draw supplies from France." "*Nous ne desirons pas la guerre, et nous ne le craignons pas.*" In truth, every art of falsehood and fraud has been practised to prevent a war there, but it seems clear that this will not *long* prevail. Dr. Lee is returned from Spain and is gone to the Prussian Court. That Monarch is fond of commerce and is desirous of being acquainted with the whole nature of ours. He is offended with the Court of London, and has no reason to fear its resentment. We have good reason to expect considerable advantage from his friendship. If our funds fail us not, and our Union continues, no cause was ever safer than ours. To prevent the former, most extensive and vigorous taxes should immediately take place. The sum in circulation is immense and no corrective can be applied but Taxation, nor was there ever a time when the vast plenty of money rendered that business more easy.

The Loan Office, with that, will I believe answer, and upon the success of our funds will probably depend the Unity of our exertions. The Confederation goes on but slowly, occasioned by the immensity of business created by the war. But I find our right to our Charter bounds, as stated by our Act of Government will be strongly contested. The Charter of 1609 it is said has been vacated, and that no transfer of that Charter right can be shewn from the Company to the people of Virginia. That therefore the ungranted lands were the property of the Crown, and being taken from it by common exertions, must become common Stock. Will you be so kind as favor me with your reasons and authorities in support of our right? I am with great regard & esteem, dear Sir Your most affectionate and obedient [Servt.],

Richard Henry Lee

RC (DLC). Addressed: "Thomas Jefferson esquire in Albemarle County Virginia. Free R. H. Lee." Enclosure missing.

The INCLOSED HAND BILL was published by order of Congress, 22 Aug., reproducing a letter of General Schuyler of 18 Aug. with an account of General Stark's victory and General Burgoyne's instructions to Lt. Col. Baum (Evans 15686; JCC, IX, 1086).

List of British Prisoners and Their Quarters in Albemarle County

[25 September 1777]

Prisoners	Quarters	Date
John Dow William Nichols	Thomas West	Feb. 2. 1777
William Holderness John Mann. Jacob Seading George Harvie Joseph Coupland John Normon Malcolm Shilcott	N. Lewis.	Jan. 30. 1777.
Thomas Ruth.	(Richd. Woods).	
Alexander Colvin.	(Jamieson)	
Hugh Granville Wm. Jamieson	Wm. Barksdale.	Feb. 3. 1777
Wm. Stokes John Duncan	Wm. Woods.	Feb. 3. 1777

George Tilley James Allen	Ben. Calvert.	Feb. 3. 1777.
Robert Ash Edwd. Tow	Peter Marks	Feb. 3. 1777.
Robert Scaten William Dodds.	James Marks	Feb. 3. 1777.
Wm. Chambers.	Feilder.	

Mar. 31. 1777. delivd. the above to Capt. Marks, except Dow, Seedeng, Shilcot, Colvin, Dodds. also there remains Townshend, McCann & Goodrich.

Dow was sent to Staunton Sep. 25. 1777.

N (DLC). In TJ's hand.

On 8 Apr., 24 June, and 22 July 1776, prisoners of war had been ordered sent to Charlottesville from Williamsburg and Richmond (*Va. Council Jour.*, I, 39, 81-2; CVSP, VIII, 157). They were placed in the custody of citizens of Charlottesville under the supervision of TJ as county lieutenant (see John Goodrich to TJ, 20 Jan. 1777). Under order of Council, 26 Feb. 1777, the prisoners were to be turned over to the commanding officer of the Continental recruits for the county, to be conducted to Philadelphia (Patrick Henry to TJ, 26 Feb. 1777). CAPT. MARKS was the commanding officer for the Continental recruits in Albemarle co. (Woods, *Albemarle County*, p. 263; Heitman). Of the prisoners who were retained after 31 Mch., Goodrich, McCan, Shilcott, and Townsend escaped on 18 Aug. (*Va. Gaz.* [Purdie], 22 Aug. 1777). No record has been found of the discharge or transfer of Seading, Colvin, and Dodds, but the guard was disbanded shortly after the transfer of Dow to Staunton.

Account of Guard for British Prisoners

[5 October 1777]

	£		
Acct of the guard as presented by Bernis Brown was for himself from Nov. 15. 1776 to May. 15. 1777. 181 days @ 2/	18	2	0
to 10. privates from Nov. 15. 1776. to Apr. 10. 1777. 146 days @ 1/4	97	6	8
to 4. privates from Apr. 10. to May 15. 35. days @ 1/4	9	6	8
to 6¾ ℔ candle		6	9
	125	2	1

Certified the above.

2d. acct.

Bernice Brown 139 days (to wit from May 15. to Sep. 29.)	13	18	0
Wm. Statham 139 days	9	5	4
Stephen Hughes 133. days	8	17	2
Horseley Goodman 133 days	8	17	4
David Statham 99 days	6	12	
	48	0	
Berenice Brown to dieting himself & one of the guard to Staunton with Dow	1	0	
	£49		

Octob. 5. 1777.

certified the above and that at the close of those charges the guard was disbanded

N (DLC). In TJ's hand, written on verso of Patrick Henry to TJ, 26 Feb. 1777.

From Lucy Chiswell Nelson

DEAR SIR October the 13 1777

I take the liberty of troubling you upon a Subject of very great consequence to myself, and which I have very much at heart. Mr. Nelson very early shewed his inclination to defend his Country by entring into the service in the 7th. Regiment as a Major, in which capacity he acquitted himself to the satisfaction of every body. He is since advanced to be Lt. Colonel in that regiment, where he distinguished himself in the late battle with the enemy. As he has a Family who very much want his presence, he is desirous of the Command of the last Battalion of Artillery, which is to be disposed by the Assembly at their next meeting; not that his Ardour is in the least abated but he thinks he can serve his Country as effectually here, and attend to his own Affairs which suffer much by his absence. You know my situation, with three young Children, must make me anxious for his success on this occasion; and as you have a good deal of Influence in the House, you will oblige me exceedingly by giving him your Interest. I am Sir Your Hble Servant,

LUCY NELSON

RC (MHi). Addressed: "To Thomas Jefferson Esqr. in Williamsburg." Endorsed. On verso of p. 1: TJ's draft of his reply of 24 Oct. 1777, q.v.

LUCY NELSON was the daughter of John and Elizabeth Randolph Chiswell (Randolph, *The Randolphs*, p. 48), not Lucy Grymes Nelson, wife of Thomas

Nelson, Jr., signer of the Declaration, as identified in Mass. Hist. Soc., *Jefferson Papers*, p. 10-11, where this letter is printed. On 24 Nov. 1770, she married MR. William NELSON (1746-1813) of Hanover co., eldest son of Thomas Nelson, Sr., of Yorktown, Secretary of the Colony from 1743 to 1776 (R. C. M. Page, *Genealogy of the Page Family in Virginia*, N.Y., 1883, p. 170; Heitman).

From John Harvie

DEAR SIR York Septr. [i.e., October] 18th. 1777

This Morning the Inclosed Interesting Intelligence was received by Congress from General Gates. As I am sure you will receive pleasure in reviewing even the Minutia of this great and Glorious Victory I shall make no Apology for sending you a Copy of the several Letters in the Rough dress you see them haveing made it off in a Hurry at the Clerks Table. Gates's Rapid Successes to the Northward does him honour as a Great and deserving Oficer. The British General Clinton some short time since reduced Fort Montgomery on the North River and placed a Strong Garrison in it. However Sanguine Spirits here prophecy his Speedy Evacuation of that post. I wish the Event may Evince the truth of their prediction but as I know nothing of the place I have no Opinion about it. We yet Command the Delaware above Fort Island and the Enemy have been repuls'd with some Damage in every Attempt that they have made on our Batterys and little Navy. The Commodore is a Gallant Oficer of whose conduct Congress have expressed their high approbation. The president inform'd me to day that there are a Body of troops in Motion for Wilm[ing]ton. Probably a few days will bring us good News from that Hospital. General Washington is with[in] 17 Miles of Philadelphia. His design no doubt is on[ce] again to force the British Lines. His troops are Ard[ent] and Spirited therefore we may hope every thing from the[ir] Vigour and Activity. Our Agent from Martin[ique] writes that he has every reason to expect an Im[medi]ate War in Europe. Pennsylvania is at pres[ent] a dead weight on us. Their Councils and Executi[ve] are puerile weak and Inanimate. They deserve to be D———. I have not patience with them, and Yet the[y] think it Matter of Right to Engroce every Of[fice] of trust and profit. I verily think a Majority of them would willingly see us Involv'd in the deepest destr[uc]tion. However for their Comfort they have Martial [Law] Suspended over them for 70 Miles around the Cit[y]. This Resolution pass'd before I came to Con[gress] or I should have had my doubts about [the propriety o]f the Measure.

As we have no press from whence you might see those things in print I thought it might partly Ease your Solicitude to give you this detail of publick Matters.

You'l hear of the Dunmore Militia's behaviour when Order'd to Camp. Pray do not suffer them to Escape Reprehension, or their Example will be fatal to our Militia. They say they could not be provided on the Road. I enquir'd at Frederick town as I came down and their pretence is without any kind of foundation. A well Regulated Militia may be our Salvation and Officers who are not Attentive to their duty ought to be broke like Glass and certain I am the Dunmore Feild Officers were not, two of whom are Delegates for that County. As you wanted your Workmen from Philadelphia you are Sensible they cant now be Engaged from that City. This gives me Uneasiness as there is no man on Earth for whom I would Execute a trust with greater pleasure. I have not yet had a very clear distinct View of Congress but have seen and heard enough to Convince me that it is not that Wise Systematic decent Assembly that you knew it two years ago. If I was with you I could enlarge on this Subject but at a distance Sub Silentio (for fear of Accidents) is the best policy. I fervently hope the next Choice of Delegates for our State will be Confind to men of extensive political Knowledge, Steady and Spiritted in their Rights with Capacity Sufficient to penetrate the designs of every Corner of the Continent. Rely on it our Confederacy is not founded on Brotherly Love and Able Statesmen are Surely wanting here. To make room for one of this Character I will with pleasure Resign if you Advise me that it will not be Imputed to Unworthy Motives (but that would restrain me if the Service was as bitter as Gall) for to you who know me so well it is Needless to say I do not possess talents for State Affairs and yet truly I am one of the Board of War without having the Skill in Military affairs of an Orderly Sergeant. Our Worthy president withdraws from Congress in about 10 days. Will you be Surprized if F. L. Lee Esqr. Succeeds him. That he will is the General Opinion at present. I wish in a publick Assembly no Gentleman was fond of high Offices. I have not heard a tittle from my Family since I left it. My wife is certainly Reprehensible for not writeing. Yet perhaps she is Excusible as I never knew her so Negligent before. As she really Merrits every tenderness from me, I feel the Strongest Anxiety to hear that she is well. I kn[ow] she cant be happy in my Absence. I am Dr Sir With the Greatest Sincerity Yrs,

JNO. HARVIE

RC (DLC). Enclosures: Copies, in the hand of John Harvie, of Horatio Gates to John Hancock, 12 Oct. 1777, together with the letters enclosed therewith, namely, John Burgoyne to Horatio Gates, 8 Oct. 1777, John Burgoyne to Horatio Gates, 9 Oct. 1777, Horatio Gates to John Burgoyne, 12 Oct. 1777 (DLC: TJ Papers, 3: 394-5).

There can be no question about the date of the letter, although Harvie wrote "Septr.," because the letters which he copied and enclosed were read before Congress on 18 Oct. (JCC, IX, 820). Gates' letter to Hancock is a detailed report of his successful encounter with Burgoyne of 7-10 Oct. and Burgoyne's retreat to Saratoga. The enclosure in Gates' letter, Burgoyne to Gates of 8 Oct., is a request for protection of the sick and wounded officers abandoned in the British retreat. The letter of Burgoyne to Gates of 9 Oct. requests the safe conduct of Lady Harriet Ackland to her husband, who was wounded and a prisoner of Gates' army. Gates' reply to Burgoyne of 12 Oct. is a sharp protest at the devastation and cruelty of the retreating British army for whose prisoners Burgoyne asked clemency from the Americans. For a full summary of the events covered in these letters see Patterson, *Gates*, p. 166-70. The letter from William Bingham, AGENT FROM MARTINIQUE, was also read and acted upon in Congress on 18 Oct. (JCC, IX, 820-1).

To Lucy Chiswell Nelson

DR. MADAM Oct. 24. 1777. Wmsbgh.

Colo. Nelson's merit and his present command place him in my judgment without a competitor, for the post to which you wish him appointed. It is a great happiness to me therefore that while I pursue the dictates of my own judgment I am at the same time subservient to your wishes. One truth only it behoves me to warn you of, that you may not be deceived by over-rating any one's assistance. No man, my dear madam, who acts above board has influence in any appointments here, beyond the weight of his own vote. If this appointment should be obtained for Colo. Nelson, it will be by the mere force of his personal merit. In thus undeceiving you however I do violence to my own gratification, as this error alone has produced to me the happiness of a letter from you.

Fortune seems to have drawn a line of separation between us. Though often in the same neighborhood some unlucky star has still shuffled us asunder. When I count backwards the years since I had last the happiness of seeing you in this place, and recur to my own lively memory of our friendship, I am almost induced to discredit my arithmetic. The affection I still retain for a family with whom I once lived in so much intimacy and confidence, recalls to my mind often and often the most pleasing reflections. That heaven may shield the breast in which your happiness is embarked and administer to you every comfort of this life is the prayer of Your sincere & affectionate friend.

Dft (MHi). Written on verso of Mrs. Nelson's letter to TJ, 13 Oct. 1777.

William Nelson resigned his commission in the Continental army on 25 Oct. 1777 (Heitman). The appointment as commander of the regiment of artillery raised for the defense of Virginia, which Mrs. Nelson solicited for her husband in her letter of 13 Oct., was given to Thomas Marshall on 15 Nov. 1777. Nelson's name does not appear among those nominated for the position by the House of Delegates, in spite of TJ's expressed interest in his appointment to the post (JHD, Oct. 1777, 1827 edn., p. 27). For TJ's early association with William Nelson's family see the letter of his father, Thomas Nelson, Sr., to TJ, 6 Mch. 1770.

From John Hancock

DEAR SIR York Town in Pennsylva. Octor. 25th: 1777.

I Had the honour to Receive your obliging favor by Mr. Harvey, with Forty seven Dollars, being an additional Donation of the County of Albemarle for relieving the poor of Boston which shall be faithfully applied to their Benefit.

My constant application to Publick Business both in and out of Congress, has so impair'd my Health, that some Relaxation has become absolutely necessary, and to morrow morning I set out for Boston with the Leave of Congress to be absent two Months, and I shall be happy to have it in my power to Render you or your Friends any Services during my Stay at Boston.

My best wishes attend you for every Good, & believe me, with Sentiments of Real Esteem & Regard, Dear Sir Your most Obed Huml Servt., JOHN HANCOCK

RC (NNP). Endorsed: "Hancock John Oct. 25. 1777."

TJ's letter to Hancock has not been found. TJ evidently sent it by John Harvie when the latter departed for Philadelphia to attend Congress. There is an entry in TJ's Account Book under 7 Sep. 1777: "inclosed by John Harvie to J. Hancock Boston money £14.2. note this was for John Walker, & was settled before I paid him the above balance."

From John Harvie

DEAR SIR [25 October 1777]

I wrote you about ten days ago that General Gates had obtain'd a Signal Victory over General Burgoyne on the 7th. Inst. and now have the pleasure of informing you that a few days after this defeat Burgoyne with his whole Army Surrend'd themselves prisoners of War to the American General. It is said the prisoners Stores &c. taken are as followeth Viz 1 Lt. General, 2 Major Generals, 7 Brigadier Do. 5000 privates, 2 English noblemen, 1 Irish Do.

15000 Stand of Arms 40 Brass Cannon and a Considerable Quantity of Cloathing. This great and Important News I transmit to you on the Authority of the Committee of Albany, Governor Clinton and General Washington's Letters to Congress (except the Enumeration of Officers &c. which we have from another Quarter). No one doubts the truth of this happy Event Yet many feel the greatest Anxiety for a Confirmation of it under General Gates's own hand. Almost every day brings us News of some advantage or other over the Enemy. Yesterday we received an account that General Howe had Abandon'd German Town and collected his whole force in Philadelphia and its Subberbs and that General Washingtons head Quarters was between German Town and the City. To day Major Clark Aid de Camp to General Green writes General Roberdeau that on the 22nd. at 4 in the afternoon the Enemy made Several Attacks on Fort Mifflin, but were as often repuls'd. The Cannonade was very Severe and Continued till eight in the Evening. The next Morning it was renew'd with Redoubled Vigour. Two large Ships endeavour'd to pass the Chevaux de Freze while a Brisk fire was kept up from Province Island. At the same time a party of 3000 Attack'd Red Bank so that a Continual Fire was kept on all sides which lasted from 6 in the Morning till 4 in the afternoon without the least Intermission at which time the Enemy Quitted the Ships, haveing first set them on fire, and they soon after blew up. The explosion was dreadful. Thus ended the Day. Every thing seems quiet this Morning (the 24 being the Date of his Letter). He believes this will be their last effort and that they will certainly quit Philadelphia. He was inform'd one of the Ships was call'd the Augusta and that 300 Hessians were drowned. Could you have thought these Forts and Batteries were so formidable? As this is Saturday evening and of Course Holliday with Congress haveing heard you several times mention Mr. Dechsay [Duché] with Approbation I will give you the Conclusion of a Severe Libel against Congress and the Army Address'd by him to General Washington. After Attempting to refute the Idea of foreign Assistance or a European War, Magnifying the power and Clemency of Great Britain, Reprobateing his own Conduct for the part he took Early in the Dispute, he very Modestly Advises the General to demand of Congress an Immediate Negotiation with Lord and General Howe and if they refuse a ready Compliance to disavow their Authority, give up the Seditious Members as proper Sacrifices to Government and treat for America in his own person at the Head of his Army. What think you of this Invidious Hypocrite now? On viewing what I have wrote you may infer this was a publick Address. No such thing, it was Couched in a Letter to the General in which he makes the warmest professions of Esteem and friendship and sent by a secret Emissary. I should have been more Minute if I was not certain you would see a Copy of the whole Letter in Virginia as the names of one or two of our Countrymen are mentioned with high Encomiums B and H and you know they have friends here who would not wish to See Mr. Dechsay's panygerick on them Conceal'd from the Eyes of the publick. I hope we shall get through Confederation time enough for our Assembly to take it up this Session as the Attention of Congress is principally Confin'd to this Object. I fear the Length of my Letters will exhaust your patience but as you know my Motive is to give you the fullest and Earliest Intelligence of Matters highly Interesting you'l require no Apology for prolixity. What am I to do with your Money for Colo. Spotswood as I understand he has return'd to Virginia? Be kind enough to inform Mr. Wythe that Doctr. Redman is in Philadelphia and that it is a Rule with Congress for no Seal'd Letter to go into the City. I have his to that Gentleman still in my possession and should be glad of his directions about it. I am Dr. Sir Yr. most Obt. servt.,

JNO. HARVIE

RC (DLC). Addressed: "To Thomas Jefferson Esqr. in Williamsburg Virginia." Endorsed: "Harvie John. about Sep. 20. 1777."

The letter has been dated on the basis of internal evidence. The error in TJ's dating in the endorsement was doubtless occasioned by Harvie's error in writing "Septr." for October in his letter of 18 Oct. 1777, above. This indicates that TJ must have added the endorsement at a later date, because he could hardly have mistaken the date of the events reported in the letter when he received it. Purdie's *Virginia Gazette* reported Gates' victories in the issues of 24, 31 Oct., 7 Nov. (Suppl.). B AND H: i.e., Carter Braxton and Benjamin Harrison. Duché's letter says, in part: "You have no longer a Randolph, a Bland or a Braxton, men whose names will ever be revered. . . . Your Harrison alone remains, and he disgusted with his unworthy associates. . . ." (W. C. Ford, *The Washington-Duché Letters*, Brooklyn, N.Y., 1890, p. 14-15). MONEY FOR COLO. SPOTSWOOD: TJ's Account Book has the following entry under 7 Sep. 1777: "sent by John Harvie to Alexr. Spotswood £26-.14 in full for the horse I bought of him."

The Petition of Thomas Johnson

and the Resultant Controversy between the House of Delegates and the Senate concerning the Right of the Latter to Amend Money Bills

[11 November 1777 to 24 January 1778]

I. PETITION OF THOMAS JOHNSON

II. REPORT OF COMMITTEE OF HOUSE OF DELEGATES ON RIGHT OF SENATE TO ALTER MONEY BILLS

III. REPLY OF SENATE TO HOUSE OF DELEGATES CONCERNING MONEY BILLS

IV. NOTES ON MONEY BILLS

V. COMMUNICATION FROM HOUSE OF DELEGATES TO SENATE CONCERNING MONEY BILLS

VI. REPLY OF SENATE TO HOUSE OF DELEGATES CONCERNING MONEY BILLS

VII. DRAFT OF A RESOLUTION CONCERNING MONEY BILLS

VIII. RESOLUTION OF THE HOUSE OF DELEGATES RESPECTING THE CLAIMS OF THOMAS JOHNSON AND OTHERS

EDITORIAL NOTE

THE documents brought together in this grouping require special comment. The issue with which they deal resulted directly from the inclusion in the Virginia Constitution of 1776 of an article drawn from colonial experience. That Constitution (q.v. under date of 13 June 1776) contained the following provision: "All laws shall originate in the House of Delegates, to be approved or rejected by the Senate, or to be amended with the consent of the House of Delegates; except money bills, which in no instance shall be altered by the Senate, but wholly approved or rejected." Jefferson's proposed Constitution for Virginia also contained the provision that money bills "shall be originated and amended by the representatives only." This extension of colonial experience, which in turn was derived from British constitutional usage, could scarcely be justified in terms of republican principles and, when the issue was brought on by the case of Thomas Johnson in 1777, Jefferson found himself in the anomalous position of having to appeal to parliamentary precedent to justify Virginia procedure. It is obvious, however, that his main object was to adhere strictly to the letter of Virginia's substantive law, however critical he may have been then and later as to the method by which that law became operative. The issue that arose with the case of Thomas Johnson and the two steers of Charles Yancey reveals Jefferson in his earliest role as a strict constructionist. It also brought forth his first severe criticism of Blackstone.

The Senate's position cannot be understood without reference to two facts which are apparent from the legislative proceedings of the time: (1) the House of Delegates seems to have been inundated with petitions for claims and pensions by soldiers, widows of soldiers, and others and to have been tending toward a liberal recognition of these claims which the Senate must have regarded as at times extravagant; and (2) the House of Delegates could have taken advantage of the provision in the Constitution denying the Senate any power to alter money bills by inserting riders or extraneous matter into such bills, a device to which it did resort later if not at this time, as the compromise solution offered by Jefferson clearly indicates (see Document VII below).

The first of these factors is apparent from an examination of some of the many petitions and claims presented in Nov.-Dec. 1777, a few of which were acted upon by the House of Delegates and amended by the Senate as set forth in Document VIII below. As these documents show, the House of Delegates had not always scrupulously observed the constitutional requirement and had acquiesced in the Senate's amendments to some money bills (Document II below) and, indeed, while the controversy over the case of Thomas Johnson was being carried on the House agreed to amendments by the Senate to a resolution concerning claims (JHD, Oct. 1777, 1827 edn., p. 135). Yet the House must have decided to make an issue of the case of Thomas Johnson not because it was an isolated one but because it was typical of the Senate's apparent determination to diminish the growing appropriations made by the House for claims. The following cases in addition to that of Thomas Johnson received no action during the Oct. 1777 session because the Senate insisted upon amending the House bills and because the House would not agree to such amendments. On 6 Nov. William Bristow petitioned for a pension because, while in military service, he had "caught a severe cold, attended with violent pains, which settled in his thigh and leg, and deprived him of the use thereof." The Committee of Public Claims rejected the claim on the ground that Bristow was in the Continental service; the House recommitted the petition and the Committee then recommended that £20 be allowed but charged to the accounts of the United States, to which the House agreed; the Senate, however, on 29 Nov. amended this resolution (same, p. 13, 32, 33, 38, 39, 49). On 29 Nov. John Carmack, Ezekiel Smith, John Looney, and Jonathan Drake petitioned the House stating that the auditors of public accounts had refused to allow their claims for taking care of "all the lost stocks of cattle and horses" which they had been engaged to protect on the return from the Cherokee expedition; the Committee of Public Claims recommended that £182 19s. be allowed to Carmack, £66 to Smith, £105 16s. to Looney, and £147 5s. to Drake; the House amended the committee report by deleting the words "ought to be allowed" and inserting the words "be rejected for want of sufficient proof"; however, on the following day, 9 Dec., the House passed a resolution designating Isaac Shelby, Daniel Smith, and Isaac Bledsoe commissioners to examine and adjust the claims and instructing the treasurer to pay to Carmack and the others whatever sums two or more of the commissioners agreed upon as due. The Senate on 23 Dec. approved this resolution, but with several amendments (same, p. 49-50, 66, 73, 89). On 18 Nov. Catlett Jones and Richard Epperson were each allowed £10 for immediate relief and £5 per annum for life by the Committee of Public Claims because of their disability incurred in the Kentucky service; their petition was recommitted by the House and the committee then recommended the same sum for Epperson but £20 for immediate relief and £10 per annum for life in the case of Jones, to which the House agreed. The Senate on 29 Nov. agreed to the resolution but with amendments (same, p. 31, 38-39, 49). On 24 Nov. Anne Hays (Hayes) petitioned the House to the effect that her husband had served in the artillery and had "died some time ago, leaving the petitioner, with six small children . . . quite destitute." The Committee of Public Claims recommended £20 for immediate relief and £5 per annum for a period of three years, to which the House agreed. The Senate on 13 Dec. approved the resolution but with amendments (same, p. 40-41, 60-61, 77). On 4 Nov. James Duncan, Richard Reeves, and William Grills presented a petition stating that they had lost their rifles in a boating accident on 25 Dec. 1776; the Committee of Public Claims recommended that the petitioners be allowed £5, £6, and £8 16s. respectively. The House approved this recommendation and on 21 Nov. the Senate concurred, but with amendments (same, p. 11, 32-33, 37).

This, in part, was the context in which the petition of Thomas Johnson and the resultant controversy between the House and Senate over money bills must be considered. All of the House resolutions respecting the claims stated above, including that of Thomas Johnson, were amended by the Senate and all were left indeterminate at the close of the session on 24 Jan. 1778 (see Document VIII below). The legislative history of the petition of Thomas Johnson may be summarized briefly. The petition was reported upon favorably by the Committee of Claims on 11 Nov. (see Document I), and the House concurred in allowing Johnson £15 5s. 6d. to cover damages and cost of suit that Johnson had sustained. The Senate amended the House resolution on 18 Nov., eliminating the cost of suit and reducing the amount allowed Johnson to a total of £12 12s. On 1 Dec. the House debated the Senate amendment, declined to accede to it on the ground that the Senate had no power to alter money bills, and sent Jefferson to the Senate with a request for a free conference on the subject. At the same time the House appointed him to the chairmanship of a committee "to draw up what is proper to be offered to the Senate" at the forthcoming conference; other members of the committee were Cary, Pendleton, Bullitt, and Meriwether. Jefferson drew the report for the committee; it was accepted by the House on 4 Dec. without modification (see Document II). After this statement of the case was adopted, the free conference was held on 5 Dec. Managers of the conference for the House were Jefferson, Cuthbert Bullitt,

Hugh Nelson, Cyrus Griffin, Joseph Carrington, and George Meriwether; managers for the Senate were Thomas L. Lee, Paul Carrington, James Holt, William Ellzey, Theodoric Bland, Edmund Winston, George Brooke, William Cabell, and James Taylor. The statement of the House's objections to the Senate amendment was transmitted by the conference committee to the Senate and, on 9 Dec. the Senate replied (see Document III). A further conference was held the same day between the conference managers for the House and for the Senate; Jefferson was not a member of the committee for the House on this occasion, though the personnel of the committee was the same as that on 4 Dec. except for his omission and for the addition of Richard Lee. However, on 2 Jan. 1778 he was appointed chairman of a committee to answer the Senate's statement of 9 Dec. The extent of his interest in the constitutional issue is measured in part by his several outlines of the Senate's arguments and of proposed answers to points made therein; by his extensive notes taken from debates in Parliament on similar controversies (see Document IV and notes); and by the elaborate and warmly expressed report of his committee which he drew up and which the House accepted with slight modification and transmitted to the Senate on 9 Jan. with the request for another conference (see Document V). Jefferson was appointed one of the House managers for this conference, which was held on 13 Jan. His reply to the Senate statement of 9 Dec. was delivered to the Senate managers. The Senate replied on 15 Jan. (see Document VI); this second statement by the Senate, however, when reported by the committee, was ordered to lie on the table. Jefferson did not report the result of the conference of 13 Jan. until 23 Jan., when the House postponed further consideration of the report; the report was not printed in the Journal of the House of Delegates and no manuscript copy of it has been located. (Same, p. 20, 32, 52-53, 54-56, 70-71, 97, 108-11, 113, 134; *Journal of the Senate*, Williamsburg: Dixon & Hunter, 1777, p. 16, 17-18, 42-44, 45-46). The controversy was, therefore, left in an inconclusive state when the session ended on 24 Jan., and the House made some effort to relieve various claimants who were in danger of suffering thereby (see Document VIII). At the next session of the legislature, Thomas Johnson presented a second petition to the same effect as the first; again the House approved his claim and again the Senate amended the resolution. The House tabled this amendment and nothing further was done on the matter at that session (JHD, May 1778, 1827 edn., p. 6-7, 15, 29). Finally, at the session of Oct. 1778 Johnson presented a new petition, the House approved the claim, and, on 7 Dec. 1778, the Senate approved the resolution without amendment (same, Oct. 1778, p. 73, 94, 101).

This belated action, though it relieved Thomas Johnson, did not settle the constitutional issue; the Senate merely receded from its former position of insisting upon amending the House resolution. The same thing occurred in June 1778, when a resolution by the House was amended by the Senate and the House disagreed with the amendment on the ground that the Senate had no power to alter money bills; on this occasion, which involved payment of allowances to officers of the General Assembly, Jefferson was a member of the conference committee and, after the conference was held, the Senate receded from its amendment; no exchange of statements took place between the two houses at this time (same, May 1778, p. 34-5). The issue, however, continued to disturb the relations of the two houses despite the explicit terms of the Constitution of 1776; occasionally it arose over the definition of the term "money bill" and occasionally because the House inserted other clauses in bills generally acknowledged to be money bills. In 1780 the House sent a supply bill (for emitting paper money) to the Senate which the Senate regarded as having in it several clauses which were "improperly incorporated in such a bill"; nevertheless, the Senate passed it because of the "necessities of the State and want of time," at the same time informing the House in writing that such a practice infringed the rights of the Senate and expressing confidence that such would not be repeated. It was, however, repeated at the next session, when the House attached to the supply bill two clauses providing that the money to be emitted should be made legal tender and providing also that it should be a felony to counterfeit such notes. After several conferences between committees of the two houses, the House of Delegates finally amended the supply bill eliminating the two clauses and at the same time passed another bill for punishing counterfeiters and for making paper money legal tender (JHD, Mch. 1781, Va. State Libr., *Bull.*, 1928, p. 23, 24, 25, 26-28, 29, 33, 38; Hening, X, 429, 430-31). This was an example of what Jefferson had noted in parliamentary history—that of "a bill tacked to a money bill & again untacked" (see Document IV). Thus the issue was unresolved a second time. In 1805 the House of Delegates adopted resolutions to the following effect: (1) the Senate possesses no constitutional power of amending any bill originating in the House on the subject of imposing or collecting taxes; and (2) the incorporation of these subjects in the same bill does not tend in any degree to deprive the Senate of its constitutional power of amendment of bills other than money bills. This raising of the old issue in 1805 is of particular interest because the House, at that time, relied upon Jefferson's full statement of the case in Jan. 1778 (Document V); on 1 Feb. 1805 the House resolved that 250 copies of its resolutions, "together with the report of a committee presented to the House of Delegates, on the 9th January, 1778, on a similar subject, be immediately printed for the use of the members of the General Assembly" (JHD, Dec. 1804, p. 113-14).

The troublesome question was not finally settled until the adoption of the Virginia Constitution of 1830, when the archaic provision of the Constitution of 1776 respecting the Senate's power to amend money bills was eliminated. The pertinent article of the Constitution of 1776 was allowed to stand unchanged in the new constitution except for the deletion of the words that are italicized in the following: "All laws shall originate in the House of Delegates, to be approved or rejected by the Senate, or to be amended with the consent of the House of Delegates; *except money bills, which in no instance shall be altered by the Senate, but wholly approved or rejected*" (Hening, IX, 115; *Code of Virginia*, Richmond, 1849, p. 40).

I. Petition of Thomas Johnson

[Before 11 November 1777]

To the Honl. The Speaker and Delegates of the Common Wealth of Virginia.

The Petition of Thomas Johnson Jun. humbly shewith that your petitioner was appointed a Captain in the County of Louisa[1] and raised his quota of men and when he was about to march to Join his Ridgment, was obliged to hire a Cart and two Stears of Charles Yancey to carry his mens baggage &c. as far as Carrs bridge and after they were arrived there, your petitioner was under the necessaty of carrying them to Fredricksburg as he could not get another carriage to convey the baggage; and after your petitioner had discharged the Cart and Stears as they returned home they both died; and your petitioner was sued by the said Yancey and obtained a Judgment in Louisa Court against your Petitioner for the sum of Twelve pounds Twelve shillings and cost of suit amounting to two pounds thirteen shillings and six pence which your petitioner is obliged to pay,[2] and as he incurred this expence and damage for serving the Publick he hopes you will take his case under consideration and make him such satisfaction as you in your wisdom shall think requisite and your Petitioner as in duty bound shall always pray &c.

Tr (Vi); Tr (Vi). Original signed petition missing; though it was presented before 11 Nov. 1777, both transcripts are undated and unsigned, and both were employed in 1778 by the legislature. The first is endorsed: "Petn. Thos. Johnson. May 13. 1778. referred to Claims. reasonable. £12.12. Principal 1-11-3, 1-2-3 Laws. Fees & Tax. [total] £15-5-6. Allowed. reported May 21st." The second is endorsed: "Petn. Thos. Johnson. refd. to Claims. 20th Novr. 1778. Allowed £12-12 Principal 2-13-6 Costs. [total] 15-5-6. reported Decr. 1st." Second Tr differs from first slightly as indicated in textual notes below.

Accompanying second Tr is a transcript of the record in the case of Yancey v. Johnson. According to this record, certified by John Nelson, suit was entered before the Louisa County Court on 10 Mch. 1777. Charles Yancey was represented by William Du Val, and Thomas Johnson by John Lewis when the case came up for trial on 12 May. Plaintiff charged that by agreement with the defendant the latter had hired "his Cart, a Negroe Fellow, and two valuable Steers, to go and carry Baggage of the Third Virginia Battalion as far as Carr's Bridge"; that it was expressly agreed "not to carry the said Steers (they being Young) any further than the said Bridge"; that the steers were valued at £16; and that, by breach of the contract, he had sustained damages amounting to £30. Johnson pleaded not guilty as charged, and the jury awarded damages to Yancey of £12 12s. plus costs. Included in this record were two affidavits, also certified by John Nelson: (1) copy of an affidavit signed by Thomas Johnson as captain of a company of the 3d Battalion, dated 9 Apr. 1776, stating: "I employ'd a Cart of Mr. Charles Yancy to go as far as Carr's Bridge, and no farther, with my Company, but finding it necessary that they should go as far as Fredericksburg I ordered them there with the Baggage, in which Rout the Yoke of Oxen that drew the Cart died"; and (2) copy of an affidavit signed by

Waddy Thompson, dated 15 May 1776, to the effect that Richard Jones and Bartholomew Warren had sworn that the oxen "that died in the Country's Service" were worth "twelve Pounds Current Money of Virginia."

1 Second Tr adds at this point: "in the year 1776."

2 Second Tr adds at this point: "as will appear by a Record of the said Court of Louisa." This indicates that the record of the case, summarized above, must have been prepared after the second of Johnson's petitions was considered at the session of May 1778.

II. Report of Committee of House of Delegates on Right of Senate to Alter Money Bills

[4 December 1777]

The Committee appointed have according to order prepared what they think may be proper to be offered at the conference which is to be desired with the Senate on the subject matter of their amendments to a resolution of the house of delegates for paying to Thomas Johnson the sum of £15-5-6.

The house of delegates has desired this conference in order to preserve that harmony and friendly correspondence with the Senate which is so necessary for the discharge of their joint duties of legislation, and to[1] prevent both now and in future the delay of publick business and injury which may accrue to individuals should the two houses differ in opinion as to the distinct office of each.

Tho' during the course of the last two and also of the present sessions of assembly they have acquiesced under some amendments made by the Senate to votes for allowing public claims and demands,[2] yet they are of opinion that an adherence to fundamental principles is the most likely way to save both time and disagreement, that a departure from them may at some time or other be drawn into precedent for dangerous innovations, and that therefore it is better for both houses and for those by whom they are entrusted to correct the error while new and before it becomes inveterate by habit and custom.

The constitution having declared that 'money bills shall in no instance be altered by the Senate but wholly approved or rejected' the delegates[3] are of opinion the Senate has no authority to amend their late vote for allowing to Thomas Johnson the sum of £15-5-6.

Should the term 'money bills' in the Constitution not immediately convey the precise idea which the framers of that act intended to express, it is supposed that it's explanation should be sought for in the institutions of that people among whom alone a distinction between money bills and other acts of legislation is supposed to have been made and from whom we and others emigrating from them have indisputably copied it.

By the law and usages of their parliament then all those are understood to be money bills which raise money in any way or which dispose of it, and which regulate those circumstances of matter, method, and time which attend as of consequence on the right of giving and disposing.

Again, the law and customs of their parliament which include the usage as to money bills are a part of the law of their land: our ancestors adopted their system of law in the general, making from time to time such alterations as local diversities required; but that part of their law which relates to the matter now in question was never altered by our legislature in any period of it's history; but on the contrary the two houses of assembly both under our regal and republican governments have ever done business on the constant admission that the law of parliament was their law.

When the delegates therefore vote that £15-5-6 of money whether raised or to be raised on the people shall be disposed of in paiment to Thomas Johnson for losses sustained by him on the public behalf, this is a vote for the disposal of money which the Senate are at liberty to approve or reject in the whole but cannot amend by altering the sum.

The delegates therefore hope that the Senate will concur with them in a strict and mutual observance of those laws by which both houses are bound,[4] and they are well assured that this subject being properly stated to the senate, they will forbear in future to exercise a practice which seems not authorized: but if there should be found any difference of opinion on this point the delegates will be ready to join in any regular proposition for defining with precision[5] the subject of their difference so as to prevent all doubts and delays in future.

Dft (DLC). Verso carries the following in TJ's hand: (1) outline of Senate's reply entitled "Heads of answer from Senate" (see Document III in this series) and (2) endorsement reading: "Pend[leton] T. Nelson Bullitt Banister Meriwether."

TJ's draft of the Report was adopted, without modification, on 4 Dec. 1777; it is printed in JHD, Oct. 1777, 1827 edn., p. 54-5, and also in *Journal of the Senate*, Williamsburg, 1777, p. 16. Also in DLC: TJ Papers, 232: 42051, there is a MS in the hand of Edmund Pendleton which he evidently prepared for the Committee to consider, reading as follows: "Reasons to be offered at a Conference with the Senate on the Subject matter of their Amendment to a Resolution of the House of Delegates for Paying to Captain Thomas Johnson the sum of for . Without entering into the merits of the Question whether the Amendment proposed in this Instance be a reasonable and proper one, the House of Delegates found it necessary previously to determine whether this was not such a Case wherein the Senate is restrained by the Constitution of Government from proposing any Amendment as being a Money Bill; and as Instances of a Similar nature will frequently Occur much time may be spent, various and contradictory determinations prevail, and Altercations may sometimes arise between the two Houses on such Occasions to the great delay of Public Business: To prevent which, and to preserve Harmony as well as uniformity of determination, the House propose to the Senate that a joint Committee to consist of members to be appointed by each House shall endeavour to define what is meant by the general words 'Money Bills' in the Act for forming the Constitution of Government, with such precision that no future doubts may arise thereon, and that such definition may be confirmed by Act of Assembly and remain a fixed Rule for the future conduct of both houses: which being done, the House of Delegates, if such Rule shall permit them, will proceed to consider the Amendment proposed in the Case above, and determine thereupon as to them shall appear proper." This compromise proposal was evidently rejected by the Committee as appearing to concede too much to the Senate at the beginning of negotiations.

1 Deleted in draft: "[increase?] the length of that time in future which should be devoted to the service of the commonwealth and of the United States of America in general, and which is now most."

2 Deleted in draft: "sometimes from a desire to avoid any difference even tho small and sometimes when hurried by public business and want of time."

3 Deleted in draft: "think it their duty to disagree to an amendment of the Senate."

4 Deleted in draft: "and that they will therefore pass the resolution in question without any amendments and that they will forebear in future."

5 Deleted in draft: "the rights of the two houses on this matter."

III. Reply of Senate to House of Delegates concerning Money Bills

[9 December 1777]

The Senate wish to have their institution clearly understood, and the bounds of their authority marked, satisfied that a wide door must stand open to contest, were this not to be the case. They prize very highly the harmony so justly valued by the House of Delegates; whilst that reigns, the public happiness will probably be most effectually sustained.

This principle, so useful in the conduct of affairs, will be best preserved by a firm adherence to rules already adopted. It was not apprehended a difference of opinion could arise upon a point, which the concurring judgment of both Houses had seemed to fix beyond the possibility of a doubt. No point of the Constitution, it was conceived, could be fixed with more precision than what an uninterrupted chain of precedents had ascertained, and those begun by the very persons who formed the government, and who certainly knew, in what sense they employed the words in which it was declared. A departure from this high authority, can serve only to introduce uncertainty into every part of the system; nor will the matter be mended, by a reference to those multiplied disputes, which have for ages agitated the Parliament of England, and which no time will decide: we find the Commons, so low down as the year 1671, obliged to assert their rights in these words: "That in all aids given to the King by the Commons, the rate or tax ought not to be altered by the Lords." This would be to prove what is clear by what is very obscure, to unsettle what is fixed, and to set up the Parliament of England, not our own Assembly, as the expositor of our Constitution. Nor will it avail to have recourse to the proceedings of Assembly, during the regal government, since the subjoined precedents[1] will shew that the King's Council was allowed, by the House of Burgesses, to alter and amend those bills which concerned the application of public money. The great outlines of the British Constitution, are to be discerned in the frame of our government; yet, when the constituent parts of our Legislatures are compared, so faint is the resemblance, that no ground remains for those jealousies, which have continually prompted the attempts of the Commons against the other House.

In the political system of England, you find a king, lords, and the representatives of the people, called the Commons. The first, claiming and frequently exercising powers and prerogatives, which carried destruction to all the rights of a free people. The second, an order of men distinct from their fellow subjects, possessing titles and dignities which flowed to them from the crown, and which therefore inclined them to the side of royalty. The third, composed of the humble Commons, at first scarce pretending to any thing, and enjoying even the liberty of speech by permission, but in the course of time growing gradually into importance by a prudent management of the purse of their constituents. In our legislature can be perceived only the representatives of the people, separated into two bodies, and mutually endeavoring to exercise faithfully their delegated power. In the one case, the guardians of the people could oppose no other barrier to the encroachments of arbitrary power: it was the single method by which they could gently admonish and reclaim the offending monarch, by withholding supplies until grievances were redressed; they say themselves, the poor Commons could no otherwise recommend themselves to the king. The House of Delegates, the representatives of a brave, free, and sensible people, have no earthly being to render propitious: they happily have only to approve themselves to heaven and their constituents. The framers of our Constitution knew well that the application of public money would, of necessity, be branched and interwoven with a great variety of legal regulations, which it was never meant to deny the Senate a power to alter or amend. They, therefore, with great propriety, selected from the language of parliament the term "money bill," under which appellation are included, according to the celebrated Judge Blackstone, in his Commentaries of the laws of England, all bills by which money is directed to be raised upon the subject. These being considered, we hope the House of Delegates will approve of the amendment of the Senate to their resolution for allowing to Thomas Johnson the sum of 15*l.* 5*s.* 6*d.*

MS not located. Text from JHD, Oct. 1777, 1827 edn., p. 70-1; printed also in *Journal of the Senate*, Williamsburg, 1777, p. 17-18.

1 The "subjoined precedents," also printed in JHD, are: "Journal of the House of Burgesses, 1770, page 267, amendments to tobacco law. 1771, page 101, 114, amendments to fee bill. 1772, page 160, do. to tobacco law. 1773, page 64, 65, do. to light house bill. Debates in Parliament, in 1671, page 443, resolution of Commons about money bills. Blackstone's Commentaries, vol. 1, page 170, explanation of the term 'money bills.'" For TJ's comments on these precedents, see text of his reply to Senate 9 Jan. 1778.

IV. Notes on Money Bills

[Before 9 January 1778]

1671. Apr. 19. Resolved that there is a fundamental right in the house of Commons alone in bills of rates & impositions on merchandise as to the matter, the measure, & the time. Parl. deb. 1st. v. 147. note the bill in questn. was a bill for impositions on merchandise.

Apr. 22. they object that instead of a discourse from the lords on the amendments to the bill they met with nothing but a debate of the liberties of their house in the matter, measure, & time, of rates upon merchandise with a demand that these liberties should be delivered up &c. ib. 153.

1678. July 2. Resolved that all aids & supplies granted to his majesty in parl. are the sole gift of the commons; that all bills for the granting any such aids & supplies ought to begin with the commons and that it is the undoubted & sole right of the Commons to direct, limit, & appoint, in such bills the ends, purposes, considerations, conditions, limitns., & qualifications of such grants, which ought not to be changed by the house of lords. ib. 290.

1679. May. 8. on amendmts by the Lords to a bill for granting a supply for paying off & disbanding the forces &c., the commons agreed to some, but disagreed to others: & assign this among other reasons 'that the amendments relating to Guernsey & Jersey is such a *disposition* of money, as the commons have great reason to be tender of from past experience. it alters the bill in several parts, & would be of dangerous consequence if admitted. ib. 353.

1689. July. 25. among the reasons assigned by the Commons for disagreeing to some amendments offered by the Lords to a bill for laying an additional duty on coffee &c are these '1. the commons have always taken it for their undoubted privilege (of which they have ever been tender & jealous) that in all aids given to the king by the Commons the rate or tax ought not to be any way altered by the lords. 2. the amendmt. being in point of time, the commons hope your Ldships will not now renew a questn. concerng. the *method* of granting aids, which formerly occasioned great debates, & which may now beget many conferences, & end in great inconveniencies.' 2. P. D. 347.

1700. Apr. 9. a bill tacked to another & passed. 3. P. D. 126

1712. Apr. 21. an instance of a bill tacked to a money bill, & again untacked. 4. P. D. 299. 303.

1713. May. 15. another attempt but miscarried. 5. P. D. 12.

1700. Apr. 9. the Lds. after having amended a bill relating to forfeitures, receded from them. 3. P. D. 126.

1701. June. 24. the Lds. had made some amendmts. to a bill for stating the public accounts. the reason assigned by the commons for disagreeing to one of them is in these words 'The commons do disagree to the 3d. amendmt. because their Ldshps. have, in a clause, directed the commons to allow & certify a pretended debt to Col. Baldwin Layton; whereas the *disposition* as well as granting of money by act of parl. hath ever been in the h. of comm.; & this amendmt. relating to the *disposal* of money does intrench upon that right.' 3. P. D. 182.

1702. Dec. 2. in an act for preventing occasional conformity the Lds. made several amendmts. the 8th. reduced the penalty of £100. to £20. the commons disagree & assign this reason. 'to the 8th. amendmt., line 34. the commons have disagreed because (tho' many other reasons might be offered from which the commons can never depart, yet at this time they think it sufficient to say) that the penalties left out by your Ldps. in this amendmt. are reasonable, & no more than what is necessary to make this bill effectual.' see the Ld's answer. 3. P. D. 218. 219. 225.

1702. Feb. 5. on a bill to appoint Commrs. to examine & state the publick accts. the Lds. had amended by adding commrs. the commons disagreed. the Lords answering their reasons (which are not stated) say 'to the third & fourth reasons their Ldshps reply that they are unwilling to enter into a dispute with the commons what is the proper work of either house, in relation to the granting supplies to the crown or taking or examining the accts. thereof; because they would avoid any controversies of that kind with the house of Commons, especially at this time, having by experience found that such debates have frequently been attended with ill consequences to the public. but upon this occasion &c. Lastly the house of lords cannot allow the *disposition* as well as granting of money by act of parl. to have been solely in the h. of comm.: & much less' &c. the commons reply 'altho' the lords in the preamble of the third reason, seem to wave the dispute; yet having in their last reason disallow'd the right of the commons, in *granting*, *limiting*, & *disposing* public aids, the commons think it of highest concern that this affair, being the main hinge of the controversy, should be cleared & settled. That the antient manner of giving aids was by indenture, to which conditions were sometimes annexed; the lords only gave their consent, without making any alteration: & this was the continued practice until the latter end of H. V. & in some instances until H. VII. That in the famous record called the Indempnity of the Lords & commons, settled by the king, Lds. & Comm. on a most solemn debate in 9. H. IV. it is declared that all grants & aids are made by the Commons and only assented to by the Lords. That the modern practice is to omit the Lds. out of the granting, & name them parties only to the enacting clause of aids granted to the crown, to which their Ldps. have alwais concurred, & on conferences, departed from their attempts of petty alterations, in acts relating thereunto. That if then all aids be by the grant of the Commons,*[1] it follows that the *limitation*, *disposition* & *manner of acct.* must likewise belong only to them.' the Lds. in their reply say 'that they declined all arguments concerning the rights of the commons in *granting limiting* & *disposing* public aids, & therefore forebore to answer any arguments of that kind, for that the business now depending &c. 3. P. D. 251. 254. 255. 256.

1702. Mar. 10. the commons say 'the grant of all aids is in the commons only: or if there be any *surplusage*, the commons only can apply it to the charge of the ensuing year.' and again 'that no cognizance the Lds. can take of the public accounts, can enable them to supply any deficiency, or to apply any *surplusage* of the public money' 3. P. D. 271. 272.

1678. Dec. 23d. the Lords having amended a bill for granting a supply &c. the Commons assign this among other reasons for disagreeing 'that the Commons have directed the paimt. of the money into the chamber of London, for it's security; & that their Lps. never before changed any such *disposition* made on a supply granted by the commons.' the Lords in their answer say 'that their Lps. cannot charge their memories with not having altered any such *disposition* made in a supply. but that nevertheless their Lps. do herein but claim the exercise of their right to make alterations according to their judgments.' the Commons still disagreed. the session was prorogued before the bill passed. 1. P. D. 320. 322.

MS (DLC). On last page of MS there is an endorsement of several lines in TJ's hand, consisting of notes of parliamentary procedure respecting the opening, reporting, and concluding of a free conference.

The Senate's reply of 9 Dec. (q.v.) aroused TJ to one of his most serious efforts. Between that date and 9 Jan. he not only carried on extensive research in parliamentary and colonial history, but also analyzed and outlined answers to the Senate reply of 9 Dec. On the rough draft of his committee report of 4 Dec. he jotted down "Heads of answer from Senate"; TJ's papers also contain (DLC, 3: 399) a two-page fragment of notes on the same subject, arranged in his characteristic manner of stating in exceedingly brief form an "obj." and then similarly stating an "ans."; also, on the last page of the rough draft of the answer of the House of Delegates of 9 Jan. TJ jotted down a final outline of that answer, presumably arranging the headings on the basis of the notes just referred to. These are not printed here since they add nothing substantial to the formal documentation of the controversy over money bills and since, as notes and outlines, they are similar to the methods employed by TJ in the legislative debates over the question of religious freedom in 1776 (see Notes and Proceedings on Discontinuing the Establishment of the Church of England, 11 Oct. to 9 Dec. 1776). However, the first part of the final outline just referred to (written on the draft of the reply of 9 Jan.) departs somewhat from the extended draft and therefore may be quoted (all words are expanded):

"1st. Remove objections, viz.

"I. Precedents. Answer. Precedent is considered not as making law but evidence of the law. Accordingly is only relied on in cases of Customary law, or Law by Usage. e.g. in cases of Law of parliament which is a customary law. But never in cases of written or statutory law. No customary law in this country but what is brought from England. Because settlement of country is within memory. And particularly on this question which is but of yesterday. Precedents of that convention which formed constitution derive no authority from that circumstance.

"II. Explain the term Money bill by shewing whence the idea was taken. Where will you find the idea? in France? Spain? &c. or in the law Civil? Ecclesiastical? Nowhere but in law of parliament—from them therefore definition must be sought. From that therefore trace it's extent. 1. for raising money by way of *tax*. They admit. 2. by duties on merchandize. 1.P.D.147.153."

[1] Marginal note by TJ opposite the asterisk: "cujus est dare, ejus est *disponere*."

V. Communication from House of Delegates to Senate concerning Money Bills

[9 January 1778]

Reasons to be offered at the conference to be desired of the Senate in answer to their reasons delivered at the last conference.

The house of delegates not being satisfied with the reasons urged by the Senate in support of their amendments to the resolution for allowing to Thomas Johnson the sum of £15-5-6 have desired this second conference to shew the insufficiency of the said reasons and to propose that some expedient may be adopted by the two houses for reconciling their difference of opinion.

The resemblance between the constituent parts of our legislature and that of Great Britain is supposed by the Senate so faint that no ground remains for those jealousies which have prompted the commons of Gr. Br. against their house of lords. This might have been, and doubtless was, urged at the time our constitution was formed as a reason why the Senate and delegates should have equal powers over money bills: but the argument having been then overruled, the powers of the Senate as to this point being fixed by the constitution on the same restrictive footing with those of the Lords in the British legislature, it is conceived not to be the proper question of this day whether the resemblance between them in general be faint or strong, well or ill grounded; but whether the constitution has not made them to resemble in this point?

Had those who framed the constitution, as soon as they had completed that work, been asked, man by man, what a money bill was, it is supposed that man by man they would have referred for answer to the well-known laws and usage of parliament, or would have formed their answer on the parliamentary idea of that term. It's import at this day must be the same it was then. And it would be as unreasonable now to send us to seek it's definition in the subsequent proceedings of that body as it would have been for them at that day to have referred us to such proceedings before they had come into existence. The meaning of the term must be supposed compleat at the time they used it, and to be sought for in those sources only which existed at the time. Constructions which do not result from the words of the legislator, but lie hidden in his breast till called forth ex post facto by [subsequent][1] occasions are dangerous and not to be justified by ordinary emergencies.

Nor do we by this set up the parliament of England as the expositor of our constitution, but the law of parliament, as it existed and was evidenced by usage at the time the term in question was inserted in our instrument of government; a law coeval with the common law itself and no more liable as adopted by us to subsequent change from that body than their common or statute law which we have in like manner adopted: to suppose this branch of law not existing in our code, would shake the foundation of our whole legal system, since every legislative proposition which has been passed or rejected since the first establishment of a legislature in this country has been determined to be law, or not law by the forms of parliamentary proceedings.

With as little justice may it be said that this is referring for the definition of a term to multiplied disputes, which have for ages agitated the parliament of England, and which no time will decide; that it is proving what is clear by what is very obscure, and unsettling what is fixed; since we conceive that researches into parliamentary history will decisively shew that their practice in this matter has been clear, fixed, and antient; and that for ages past it has produced no agitation unless we call by that name some groundless assertions by the lords in the course of the last century. But these assertions they departed from in practice at the very time they advanced them and at all times after, they stand contradicted by the declarations of the commons, and the constant usage of both houses, which agreeing together are supposed to form the strongest evidence what the law of parliament is on this point. To prove this right as uniformly claimed and exercised by the commons and assented to in practice by the lords the delegates will subjoin some proceedings of parliament in addition to the passage cited by the senate.

That a bill for raising money by way of tax is a money bill, is admitted by the Senate and need not therefore be proved.

That bills for raising money by rates and impositions on merchandize are also considered as money bills will appear on recurring to the parliamentary proceedings of 1671, in which it is affirmed 'that there is a fundamental right in the house of commons alone in bills of rates and impositions on merchandize as to the matter, the measure, and the time,' and also by their declaration of 1689. 'that the commons have always taken it for their undoubted privilege

1 Parl. Deb. 147, 153.

(of which they have ever been tender and jealous) that in all aids given to the king by the Commons the rate or tax ought not to be any way altered by the lords,' which is supposed to be the passage cited by the Senate as of the year 1671.

3. P.D.126 That bills for applying forfeitures in aid of the public revenue are not amendable by the lords appears by the proceedings of 1700 on the bill for applying Irish forfeitures to the use of the public, to which the lords were not permitted to make any amendments.[2]

The right of levying money in whatever way being thus exercised by the Commons, as their exclusive office, it follows as a necessary consequence that they may also exclusively direct its application. 'Cujus est dare, ejus est *disponere*,' is an elementary principle both of law and reason: that he who gives may direct the *application* of the gift, or in other words may *dispose* of it: that if he may give absolutely he may also carve out the conditions, limitations, purposes and measure of the gift, seems as evidently true as that the greater power contains the lesser. Parliamentary usage
1 P.D.290 has accordingly approved this reasoning. In July 1678 the commons resolved 'that it is their undoubted and sole right to *direct*, *limit*, and *appoint* in all aids and supplies granted to the king the ends, purposes, *considerations*, *conditions*, *limitations* and *qualifications* of such grants, which *ought not to be changed* by the
[1] P.D. [320, 322] house of lords.' In December of the same year the commons having directed the payment of money and the lords proposed an amendment thereto, the former declared 'that their lordships never before changed any such *disposition* made on a supply granted by the
[3] P.D. [182] commons.' In 1701 the lords having amended a bill for stating and examining the public accounts by inserting a clause for allowing a particular debt, the commons disagreed to the amendment and declared for a reason 'that the *disposition* as well as *granting* of money by act of parliament hath ever been in the house of commons; and that the amendment relating to the *disposal* of money does
3 P.D. 251. 254. 255. 256. entrench upon that right.' And to a bill of the same nature the year following, the lords having proposed an amendment by adding the names of some commissioners, the commons disagreed to the amendment and declared 'that their right in *granting*, *limiting*, *and disposing* public aids being the main hinge of the controversy they thought it of the highest concern that it should be cleared and settled.'[3] They then go on to prove the usage by precedents and declarations and from these conclude that the limitation, *disposition*, and manner of 'account *belongs only to them*.' In reply the Lords said 'they declined all arguments concerning the rights of the

commons in *granting*, *limiting and disposing* public aids and therefore forebore to answer any arguments of that kind'; but proceeded to insist that the business then depending was of quite another nature. And at some subsequent conferences between the two houses during the same session it was repeatedly declared 'that the lords could not supply any deficiency or apply any *surplusage* of the public money in case any should be found'; and this declaration does not appear to have been contradicted by the Lords either then or at any time after. [3 P.]D.271 272. 273.

These precedents are supposed to prove not only that the *disposal* or *application* of public money is equally with the raising of it the exclusive office of the commons, but also that it makes no difference whether it be of money *then actually in the treasury*, *or yet to be raised on the people*, nor whether the raising and disposing be *in the same*, *or in separate bills*.

Tho the precedents referred to by the Senate in the proceedings of the Council and H. of Burgesses in the years 1771, 1772, and 1773 (the first of which however we suppose to be mistaken for 1772) might perhaps be well accounted for from the nature of the amendments, from the history of the times, or from other causes, and tho' the delegates might produce from the same records proofs much more decisive in their favor, yet they decline resting it on that bottom, because they do not think that the present determination should be influenced by the practice of those who have themselves only copied from the same original.[4] Both their opinions and yours must be decided by an application of the same common rule. When the delegates therefore in their former reasons mentioned the proceedings of the Council and H. of burgesses they did not think it proper to refer to them as evidence of what the law of parliament was, but only to prove in general that they admitted it to be their law.

How dangerous it is to appeal to any other authorities from the parliamentary records the true text of decision will appear also by examining the whole passage of which a part only was cited from the commentaries of Judge Blackstone, a writer celebrated indeed but whether most for his attachment to the prerogatives of the crown or to the rights of the people would be worthy of consideration where the question is on one of those rights which have been of the greatest value to the people, the right of giving and disposing of their own money. That writer after the definition cited from his book by the Senate goes on to quote a passage from Judge Hale's treatise on the jurisdiction of parliament, which is to be parlmt.4. found more at large in Bro[ke's] abridgement entitled parl. pt. 4. There it appears to be a saying of Kirbie a clerk of the parliament who lays down in express terms or by direct implication these positions as of the law of parliament. 1. That the Lords may amend a bill for granting aids. 2. That if the amendment be by shortening the duration of the grant they need not return the bill to the commons for their concurrence. 3. That the king may alter a bill. Brook indeed adds a quaere to the case; but that judge Blackstone disapproved of it cannot be inferred from his words. It is therefore submitted to the consideration of the Senate whether a writer who can cite or refer to such positions without condemning them in decisive and unequivocal terms may be appealed to as an adequate and impartial judge of the subject. He refers to no authority whatever for that part of his opinion which the Senate quote and rely on.[5] But to waive further examination of the grounds of his opinion, the judges of the common law can take no cognisance of the law of parliament; it can never come judicially in question before them. Their sayings or opinions on the subject must be ever extrajudicial. And they have accordingly always disclaimed a right to give judgment on them. Definitions therefore of parliamentary law by any other court, by a member of a court, or by a private individual, must be rejected as inauthoritative in a parliamentary disquisition.

For these reasons the Delegates still think that the Senate have no authority to amend the vote in question. But open to conviction if it can be shewn they are wrong, and actuated by a strong desire to promote the public service as well as to preserve the constitution entire, they propose to the senate, if they should still adhere to their former opinions, that a select committee may be appointed by each house to meet together in free conference and endeavor to define the office of the two houses in bills, clauses, and votes relating to money, and that such definition, if approved by both houses, may be confirmed by act of assembly.

Dft (DLC). Undated, but drawn up by TJ between 2 Jan. 1778, when he was appointed a member of committee to answer the Senate's reply of 9 Dec., and 9 Jan. when the committee reported its proposed communication, of which this is the rough draft. The committee report is printed in JHD, Oct. 1777, 1827 edn., p. 108-11, with slight modifications, most of which may have been made by TJ himself in taking off a fair copy; also printed in *Journal of the Senate*, Williamsburg, 1777, p. 42-44. The paper on which TJ composed this document contained the following deleted passage at the top of the first page: "To all princes, states, potentates, & persons the General assembly of the Commonwealth of Virginia sendeth greeting." This may have been the heading intended for credentials to be given to Philip Mazzei for use on his European mission.

1 The brackets appear in draft but not in the printed versions.

2 The following paragraph is deleted

in draft: "3.P.D.218.219.225. They may not alter pecuniary penalties in bills as appears in the proceedings on a bill for preventing occasional conformity."

[3] The following is deleted in draft: "That the antient manner of giving aids was by indenture to which conditions were sometimes annexed; the Lords only gave their consent without making any alteration and this was the continued practice until the latter end of Henry the fifth and in some instances until Henry the seventh. That in the famous record called the indempnity of the Lords and commons settled by the king, Lords and commons, on a most solemn debate in the ninth year of Henry the fourth, it is declared that all grants and aids are made by the commons and only assented to by the Lords. That the modern practice is to omit the Lords out of the granting and name them parties only to the enacting clause of aids granted to the crown; to which their Lordships have always concurred and on conferences departed from their attempts of petty alterations, in acts relating thereunto. That if then all aids be by the grant of the commons, it follows."

[4] The printed version reads for the remainder of the paragraph: "Their practice and our opinions must be proved by the same common rule, the law and practice of parliament; their acknowledgement of the rule proves their submission to it; and that their practice should be tried by the law, not the law by their practice."

[5] The following is in the report as adopted by the House and printed in both House and Senate journals, but not in draft: "Are we then to take it upon his affirmation when contradicted by the uniform current of parliamentary usage?" It is interesting to note that this critical comment upon Blackstone is the part of TJ's report that underwent more change than any other passage. The draft is heavily scored in this paragraph, and embraces many deletions and interlineations. The inclusion of the sentence just quoted also indicates that TJ continued to amend the phraseology of the passage after composing the draft and before submitting a fair copy to the House. His temerity in challenging the authoritative position of Blackstone was both severe in its method and far in advance of the times (see Jerome Frank, *Courts on Trial*, Princeton, 1949, p. 1).

VI. Reply of Senate to House of Delegates concerning Money Bills

[15 January 1778]

The Senate conceive that, in the present Question, it is of no consequence whether the constituent Parts of our Legislature resemble the Lords and Commons of *Great Britain*, or whether the Senate is made to resemble the House of Lords in this or that Particular. Clearly pointed out as they have supposed the Office of the two Houses to be in the matter on which a Difference of Opinion has lately arisen, they have wished to determine the Question by recurring to the Act which gives our Constitution its present Form. On this Subject they suppose the Instrument of Government will give complete Information, since in Terms not easily misunderstood the Powers of the Senate are there defined. The Senate think, from the Proceedings of the first Session of Assembly under the present Government, the Members of which modelled the Constitution, it may be fairly inferred that they would have declared a *Money Bill* to be a Bill which directs money to be levied on the People. Had the Framers of our Constitution, in general Terms, assimilated the Power of the Senate over *Money Bills* to that of the Lords, this Assembly might very properly carry their Researches so far into parliamentary Proceedings as would enable them to determine at what Point that Power ought to be fixed. But the Term *Money Bill* being clearly defined, so tedious an Enquiry becomes not only useless, but may endanger the Constitution whenever a future House of Delegates shall wish to enjoy all the Rights an *English* House of Commons may at any Time have assumed. The Votes of the Commons in 1671, containing a Description of the Power of that Assembly in *Money Bills*, we do not conceive the Propriety of referring to the Proceedings in 1700, nor do we suppose the Bill for Application of *Irish* Forfeitures to be a *Money Bill*, because the Lords did not amend it. In that Instance the Commons had passed a Bill for granting an Aid to his Majesty by Sale of the forfeited Estates in *Ireland*, and by a Land Tax in *England*. A Majority of the Lords inclined to oppose the passing of this complicated Bill, because they looked upon the tacking of one Bill to another as an Innovation in parliamentary Proceedings, and tending to take away the Share they ought to have in legislative Authority. But as they could not reject the Bill without leaving the Necessities of the State unprovided for, they contented themselves with making Amendments to that Part which related to Forfeitures. To these the Commons disagreed; in several Conferences the Lords insisted; and the King, fearing the Consequences, desired them to pass the Bill without Amendments; to which they then consented.

In 1678 the Commons had passed a Bill for granting a large Supply to the King. The Lords made Amendments, to all of which, except one, the Commons disagreed. Each House adhered to its Vote, and the Bill was lost. In the same Year the Commons resolve that the Lords had never before changed the Disposition made on a Supply granted by the Commons. In 1679 we find several Amendments made to a Supply Bill by the Lords, and disagreed to by the Commons; yet in 1701 the Lords having amended a Bill for Supply, and examining the public Accounts, the Commons declare that the Amendments relating to the Disposal of Money does intrench upon their Rights.

In several of the Precedents referred to we have found Amendments made by the Lords to Bills of Supply, and agreed to by the Commons. In another Instance, when irritated by an Opposition to their Prejudices and favourite Opinions, we find them disagreeing to Amendments made to that Part of a Bill which directed the Application of Forfeitures. In another Instance, they say their Rights are invaded by an Amendment, not to a Bill of Supply, but only relating to the Disposal of public Money. Do the Votes of the Commons on such Occasions constitute the Laws, Customs, and Usages of Parliament? And are the Resolves of the Lords, expressly asserting their Authority, only groundless Assertions? It may be observed, that in every Instance the Votes of the Commons exactly correspond to the particular Occasions on which they are entered. They have never come to any Compromise of Privileges which might set Bounds to their Claims, and their Privileges are at this Day undefined by any Law.

The foregoing Precedents are supposed to prove that the Customs and Usages, and Practice of Parliament, are variable, uncertain, and indecisive.

When the Delegates had asserted that the Laws and Customs of Parliament forbad the Lords amending those Bills which raise Money in any Way, or which dispose of it, and which regulate those Circumstances of Matter, Method, and Time, which attend, as of Consequence, on the Right of giving and disposing, and that the two Houses of Assembly, both under our regal and republican Government, have ever done Business on the Admission that the Law of Parliament was their Law, the Senate were led to refer to the unvaried Rule of the two Houses under the present Establishment, and to such Precedents from the Proceedings of the Council and House of Burgesses as occurred in the last Year of the regal Government. We are unable to account for them, from their particular Nature, or from the History of those Times, nor do we recollect Proofs from the same Records more decisive on the other Side of the Question.

The Senate, however, do not desire to rest the present Question on those Proofs; they wish to rest it on the Constitution. They cannot conceive the Offices of the two Houses will be more accurately expressed, or defined in Terms less liable to Misconstruction, than are adopted in the Act of Government; they are not yet conscious that the Rights of the House of Delegates are invaded by the Vote which occasioned the present Dispute; but, willing to give every possible Proof of their sincere Intentions to promote the public Welfare, they have most cordially agreed to a free Conference, and have commanded us to lay before you the following Propositions, which, as they conceive, contain a full Definition of the Power of the two Houses in *Money Bills*, and suppose will therefore be approved by the Delegates.

1st. The Delegates have the sole Right to direct the levying Money on the People for the Exigencies of Government, and to fix the Rate, the Time of Payment, and the Mode of Collection, and the Senate shall not alter or amend any Bill for those Purposes.

2d. When any Bill, Resolution, or Vote, shall be sent to the Senate for their Concurrence, by which, or by any Clause thereof, any other Matter or Thing is directed or purposed, the Senate may alter or amend the same.

Text from *Journal of the Senate*, Williamsburg, 1777, p. 45-6. There is a MS copy of the Senate's reply of 15 Jan. in DLC: TJ Papers, 236: 42301-3, in an unidentified hand; it must have been received by TJ at the time, though the Senate ordered the report to lie on the table. The Senate reply, of course, contained the same compromise proposal that TJ had drafted already (Document VII below); neither seems to have been officially expressed at the time and certainly neither received legislative approval of the two houses, thus leaving the door open for a continuation of the controversy.

VII. Draft of a Resolution concerning Money Bills

[Before 13 January 1778]

That bills relating solely to the raising or disposing of public money in any way whatever are not amendable by the Senate.

That in other bills if some clauses or sentences relate to the raising or disposing of public money, and others relate to other subjects, the said clauses or sentences so relating to the raising or disposing of public money are not amendable by the Senate; but such other clauses relating to other subjects are amendable by them.

That votes of the house of delegates relating wholly to the raising or disposing of public money, or partly thereto and partly to other subjects are amendable or not amendable by the Senate in the same degree in which bills are or are not amendable by them.

Dft (DLC); in TJ's hand. Undated, but TJ must have drawn up this compromise proposal at the time he drafted the House reply of 9 Jan. or at least in time for the free conference of 13 Jan., for in the House reply he proposed that each house appoint a committee to "define the office of the two houses in bills, clauses, and votes relating to money," which of course is precisely what the present draft does. The draft contains several deletions, but they are of verbal significance only.

VIII. Resolution of the House of Delegates respecting the Claims of Thomas Johnson and Others

[24 January 1778]

Resolved, That the Consideration of the different[1] propositions of the Senate and this House for defining the precise meaning of the term money Bill in the Act of Government, ought to be refer'd to the next Session of Assembly: and that in the mean time[2] the several persons interested in the claims suspended in consequence of amendments by the senate shall receive on account thereof the sums following, that is to say

Thomas Johnson the sum of £12	Anne Hayes £20
Catlett Jones £20	James Duncan £5
Richard Epperson £10	Richard Reeves £6
William Bristow £20	Wm. Grills £8-16

Whereas the claims of John Carmack, Ezekiel Smith, John Looney and Jonathan Drake of the county of Washington cannot now be ascertained and it will be inconvenient to the claimants to [want for?] their whole money until the next session of Assembly, Resolved therefore that the Treasurer advance and pay to Anthony Bledsoe the sum of three hundred pounds upon his giving bond and security to pay the same towards the discharge of the said claims in proportion to the amount of each, accounting for the application of the same to the next meeting of the Assembly.

MS (Vi). Partly in hand of Edmund Pendleton and partly in hand of TJ. Docketed at bottom of recto: "Agreed to by the House of Delegates. Jan: 24. 1774 [i.e., 1778] J. Tazewell, C H D." Endorsed in another hand: "Resolution Jany. 24th. 1774."

Despite Tazewell's categorical statement on the face of the Resolution, the Journal of the House of Delegates contains no mention of such a resolution; this lapse may have occurred because of the great pressure of business during the last day of the session, the hectic nature of which is possibly reflected also in Tazewell's lapse in dating the Resolution. Yet the fact that Thomas Johnson presented petitions at the two subsequent sessions of the legislature would seem to indicate that the Resolution above did not take effect.

[1] The word "two" is deleted in manuscript and "different" interlined. This indicates that the Senate proposal of 15 Jan. (Document VI, above) was known to Pendleton and TJ though not officially communicated. It also indicates, perhaps, that Pendleton may have had in mind his own proposal for an accommodation of the differences of the two houses (see notes to Document II, above).

[2] The following is deleted in the manuscript: "this House will proceed to Consider the Amendments proposed by the Senate to the Resolutions for giving money to Thomas Johnson jr. and others upon the footing proposed by the Senate." From this point on the MS is in the hand of TJ, and it was probably he who deleted the passage just quoted and substituted therefor the remainder of the Resolution.

Notes and Documents relating to the Transylvania and Other Claims for Lands under Purchases from the Indians

[19 November 1777]

I. NOTES OF THOMAS BURKE'S SPEECH BEFORE THE HOUSE OF DELEGATES

II. DEPOSITIONS CONCERNING CLAIMS TO LANDS UNDER PURCHASES FROM THE INDIANS

EDITORIAL NOTE

THE documents here presented, together with many others in Jefferson's papers concerning land claims and policies in the West, were gathered by Jefferson partly because of his aim to use the great tracts of land "on the western waters" for the benefit of small farmers, for encouragement of immigration and population, for stabilization of credit, and for strengthening the bonds of union (see Editorial Note to Bills for Establishing a Land Office and for Adjusting and Settling Titles, 8-14 Jan. 1778). But they were also gathered into his personal archives in part because of a specific resolution of the House of Delegates. On 24 Jan. 1778—the last day of the session and just after the two land Bills referred to had been defeated by postponement—the House of Delegates ordered "That the clerk of this House do transmit a copy of the several papers filed in the office relating to the claim of Richard Henderson and Company and of the Indiana company, to George Mason and Thomas Jefferson, Esquires" (JHD, Oct. 1777, 1827 edn., p. 136); the House had already, on 24 Nov. 1777, ordered the matter of the claim of Richard Henderson & Company to be "revived" and heard before the House at the May 1778 session (same, p. 41).

The committee of two was a distinguished one, but its members were far from disinterested. Jefferson, in addition to his own views toward western lands which certainly did not coincide with the views of any of the land companies, had already inflicted a heavy blow upon Richard Henderson & Company in the Bills for Dividing Fincastle County and, even before being designated to receive the papers pertaining to that claim, had drafted a bill to open a land office in Virginia, by the terms of which he hoped to befriend the individual settler and to block some of the schemes of the proprietary interests. George Mason, generally speaking, shared Jefferson's views, though he was an active member of the Ohio Company and therefore was, in another sense, scarcely disinterested. The committee of two were intended, so to speak, as a sort of investigating committee, and Jefferson's work on this task may be compared with his work as a member of the investigating committee in

Congress in 1776 on the causes of the failure of the Canadian campaign. Both produced documents of value to the historian. Those in the present sequence are now published partly because of the great importance of the subject and of Jefferson's interest in it, partly because of the wealth of detail about westward expansion presented in these documents which have heretofore been relatively inaccessible.

On 4 July 1776 the Virginia Convention appointed William Russell, Arthur Campbell, Thomas Madison, Edmund Winston, John Bowyer, John May, Samuel McDowel, John Harvie, Abraham Hite, Charles Simms, James Woods, Hugh Innes, Paul Carrington, Bennett Goode, and Joseph Speed as commissioners to collect evidence in behalf of the government "against the several persons pretending to Claim Lands within the Territory and limits of Virginia, under Deeds and purchases from the Indians." Any two or more of the commissioners were empowered to summon witnesses at such places as they might designate, to administer oaths, to cross-examine witnesses produced in support of such claims, and to see that this evidence was fairly recorded (*Conv. Jour.*, May 1776, 1816 edn., p. 83-4). Though this evidence was to be collected "in behalf of the government," some of these commissioners, either personally or through family relationships—Charles Simms and Arthur Campbell, for example—were interested in land companies (Abernethy, *Western Lands*, p. 177, 222). During the next year some evidence of the sort was gathered; probably not all of it was preserved or even recorded. On 13 Apr. 1777 Henderson wrote to Joseph Martin, one of those whose deposition is recorded in Document II of this series: ". . . God knows what I shall do; on Tuesday next the examination of my witnesses will begin at the Wolfhills and I suppose will continue three days—Will it not be in your power to attend[?]" (Lester, *Transylvania Company*, p. 226). On 19 Nov. of the same year the House of Delegates voted to "revive" the proceedings on the claim of Richard Henderson & Company and to direct the commissioners to continue to gather evidence; five days later the House decided to consider the matter of the Henderson claim the third Monday of June, 1778. However, there was another postponement at the session of May 1778. Finally, on the last days of Oct. 1778 the issue was joined. On 26 Oct. the House took up the memorial of Richard Henderson & Company and invited members of the Senate "to take seats in the House" while the memorial and papers were being read. Thomas Walker petitioned in behalf of "himself and the representatives of Peter Jefferson and Thomas Meriwether, deceased," who had purchased under the Loyal Company; the Ohio Company presented a petition; and on 29 Oct. Henderson came forward with an offer of a compromise settlement for his company's claim—to accept only a part of the tract originally claimed and not "to contend for a jurisdiction independent of Virginia" (JHD, Oct. 1778, 1827 edn., p. 28, 35; Lester, *Transylvania Company*, p. 226-36).

On the day that Henderson submitted this compromise, he was depressed: "You know," he wrote to John Williams, "this is two years and a half that I have waited on the Assembly of Virginia on the subject of our Transylvania purchase. . . . Many of the members [of the House of Delegates] . . . find that the House are not by Law or the Constitution Competent to decide the question. To avoid every kind of dispute of this kind, we today presented a Memorial in which we signified our willingness to be concluded by the Assembly" (same, p. 230). It was on the following day, 30 Oct. 1778, that Thomas Burke delivered the speech of which Jefferson preserved an outline (Document I in this series). On the same day Henderson again wrote to Williams: "Burke made a great speech. . . . We could not have been better served on, or off, the Continent. You must be informed that in order to prepare the minds of our Judges, we found ourselves under a necessity of offering a surrender of a greater part of our claim to the Commonwealth in return for protection, &c." (Lester, *Transylvania Company*, p. 230). Burke's speech and, what was more important, Henderson's effort "to prepare the minds of our Judges" were more effective for the Transylvania claim than were the efforts of the Ohio and the Indiana Companies. On 4 Nov. 1778 the House of Delegates resolved that all Indian purchases of lands made in the past or to be made in future by any private persons not authorized by public authority were void. This was a blow to all of the companies, but not such as to render their cause hopeless (Abernethy, *Western Lands*, p. 221). The Transylvania claim fell under this blanket voidance and was even specifically voided; but at the same time the House voted to allow the Associates "a compensation for their trouble and expense." The nature of this compensation was set forth in a series of resolutions of 23 Nov., the second of which made a grant of land on the Green River to Richard Henderson & Company not to exceed 800,000 acres. This was unacceptable to the House, and the resolution was recommitted. On 30 Nov., at the beginning of the day's business, Jefferson "attended in custody of the serjeant at arms," was "discharged out of custody," and paid his fees. Later in the day the committee reported a recommendation of 400,000 acres as compensation and the House ordered a bill to be brought in for this purpose. On 8 Dec. a bill was reported, and, as finally passed, the total acreage was reduced to 200,000. Whether Jefferson's presence had anything to do with this final reduction cannot be ascertained (JHD, Oct. 1778, 1827 edn., p. 42, 79, 90-1, 105; the Act granting compensation to Richard Henderson & Company is in Hening, IX, 571). The land was so remote that it was not surveyed until 1796; as immediate compensation, therefore, it was valueless (Abernethy, *Western Lands*, p. 220; Lester, *Transylvania Company*, p. 234).

I. Notes of Thomas Burke's Speech before the House of Delegates

[19 November 1777]

Jurisdiction of this state extends to lands in question.

Henderson & co. nevertheless a right to the soil. Altho' he must shew their right to the whole, they wish only to retain a very small part and give up the rest in consideration of protection.

To make a good deed 3 essentials.

1. That it be *bona fide* made.
2. feoffor's right to sell.
3. feoffee's right to purchase.

1. Price and other depositions prove deed *bona fide* executed for valuable consideration.

2. Indians have a right in the grounds they occupy.

the right which god and nature gave them.

British empire and colony of Virga. have hitherto treated with them on that ground and therefore conclusive.

Cherokees derive right to lands in question thus—

if 6. nations had a right they ceded that right to crown of Gr. Brit. by the treaty of *Fort Stanwix.*

they could only convey a feudal right to the crown and not a right to the soil.

but whichever the right be it has been conveyed to the Cherokees, who therefore might well convey to Hend. & co.

by treaty of Lochabar grounds westward of a line from Holston to G. Canaway ceded to Cherokees.

H. of burgesses in 1769 say "a country westward of this line to the Ohio *to be purchased of the Cherokees* would open an advantageous trade" and address Ld. Botett. on the subject.

the community under another government gave up the point.

the Cherokees have obtained all the right that could have derived from the treaty of F. Stanwix by cessions of the crown of Gr. Brit. and of the colony of Virga.

3. Parties who purchased had a right so to do.

every freeman has right to use his own as he pleases, provided it be not to the prejudice of others.

on what ground can the purchaser's right be disputed.

upon two grounds.

1. being against a decree of the crown of Gr. Brit.
2. the great extent of territory.
1. Hend. & co. knew of, and despised the prohibition of the crown as tyrannical.

property of the soil not in the feudal sovereign.

Indignation against the royal proclamation.

wherever a subject goes he carries all his rights.

Rom. tree.

2. Extent of territory.

act of assembly no operation in this case.

difference of principles that govern the legislature and judge.

is any law which forbids purchase beyond such a quantity?

altho' inconvenient, was not unlawful.

where there is no right, assembly will not exercise powers.

Hend. & co. intend to give up all and take back part as the gift of the state.

Company been at great expence in exploring &c. &c.

N (DLC); with TJ's title at top of page: "Notes of Burke's argum. before H. of Deleg. in the case of Henderson's claim to Kentucke." Docketed by TJ: "Henderson & Co. Notes of Burke's argum."

The opening section of Thomas Burke's speech proves that it was based upon Richard Henderson's memorial of 29 Oct. 1778 in which he offered to make a compromise settlement (Lester, *Transylvania Company*, p. 230; Abernethy, *Western Lands*, 220). TJ did not take his seat at this session until 30 Nov. and hence could not have been present at the time the speech was made. It is probable that he based these notes on those of some other member who was present and made an outline of Burke's argument.

II. Depositions concerning Claims to Lands under Purchases from the Indians

[April 1777 to October 1778]

In pursuance of a Resolution of the last General Convention of Virginia appointing us Paul Carrington, Bennet Goode and Joseph Speed Commissioners for taking depositions touching Claims to Lands within the Territory of Virginia under Deeds and purchases from the Indians, We have this day met at the Court House of Mecklenburg County after twenty days notice being given to Richard Henderson and others who claim certain Lands under a purchase from the Cherokee Indians and John Williams Gent one of the Claimants attended and at his instance William Farrar of lawful Age being sworn is examined and Deposeth as follows: That the Deponant in the month of March 1775 was present at a Fort at Watauga at a time when a Treaty was held between the said Richard Henderson and others on the one part and the Chiefs of the Cherokee Nation consisting of Occonostoto the little Carpenter and all the other Chiefs as this Deponant understood, at which Treaty about twelve hundred of the said Nation attended and in the course of the Treaty which continued several days that the said Treaty was conducted with the greatest regularity, order and sobriety, that the deponent was not actually present during the whole Consultation being engaged as a Drover of Beeves for support of the said Indians but at the Conclusion of the Treaty the Deponent understood that in consideration of a large quantity of Goods then delivered by the said Richard Henderson and others (the value whereof the Deponent knows not) they the said Indian Chiefs did agree to sell to the said Richard Henderson and others a quantity of land, but how much or by what particular bounds, the Deponent doth not remember only that the River Louisa was to be one part of the boundary but cannot be particular as to the description but understood it was several hundred Miles in Extent; That in consequence of such agreement the Deponent understood Deeds were Executed—that he saw the goods delivered to the said Indians who divided the same, gave Henderson and Company peaceable possession and the whole appeared to be well satisfied and departed in a peaceable Manner. The deponent further saith that at the said Treaty the said Richard Henderson and Co. was at great expence in accommodating the said Indians having furnished a great Quantity of Beeves, flour, Corn, Rum and other necessaries to a very great amount. Further the Deponant saith not.

William Farrar

The Deposition of Patrick Henry Esqr.; who being first duly sworn deposeth and saith: That early in the Year one thousand seven hundred and seventy four as well as he remembers the honorable Wm: Byrd Esqr. deceased having said that the Cherokee Indians had offered to give him a Tract of Land some years before, and falling into Conversation on that Subject with this Deponent, He the said Wm: Byrd together with the Honorable John Page Esqr. deceased and this Deponent agreed to send a certain Mr. Kennedy to the Cherokee Nation to see if they were willing to part with some of their Land on the Waters of their own River in Virginia to Convey the same to them and not for the State. Col. Christian was to be a partner if the Scheme succeeded. Upon Mr: Kennedys return he Informed this Deponent that he had been to Col. Byrds and had let him know the Answer of some of the Indian Chiefs and Communicated the same to this Deponent, which was, that they were willing to treat on the subject. Not long after this, and before any Treaty was Resolved on, the Troubles with great Britain, seemed to Threaten serious Consequences, and this Deponent became a member of the first Virginia Convention, and a member of the first Continental Congress, upon which he determined with himself to disclaim all Concern and Connexion with Indian Purchasers for the Reasons following, that is to say. He was informed shortly after his Arrival at Congress of many Purchases of Indian Lands, Shares in most or all of which were offered to this Deponant and Constantly refused by him because of the Enormity in the Extent to which the bounds of those purchases were carried. Another reason for this refusal was, that disputes had arisen on the Subject of those purchases and this Deponent being a Member of both Congress and Convention, conceived it improper for him to be Concerned as a party in any of these Partnerships, on which it was probable he might decide as a Judge. The Deponent says he was further fixed in his Determination not to be concerned in any Indian purchase whatever on the prospect of the present War, by which the Sovereignty and right of disposal in the Soil of America would probably be claimed by the American States. After Conversing with the said Wm: Byrd and communicating his Sentiments freely on the Subject, the Deponant saith that the Scheme dropt, nor did it proceed further than is above related. The Deponent further says that Mr. Henderson and his Partners very soon after their supposed Purchase joined in a Letter to this Deponent; in which was contained as this Deponent thinks, a distant though plain Hint, that he the Deponent might be a Partner with them. The Deponent also says he received a great number of Messages from Messrs: Henderson &c. inviting him to be a Partner: That Mr. Henderson in his own person and Mr. Allen Jones (a partner in the purchase) both applied to the Deponent to join them in their Scheme but the Deponent uniformly refused and plainly declared his strongest disapprobation of their whole proceedings, giving as his Reason that the People of Virginia had a right to the back Country, derived from their Charter and the blood and Treasure they expended on that Account. The Deponent says that he is not now nor ever has been concerned directly or Indirectly in any Indian purchase of Lands and that he knoweth nothing of Mr. Hendersons Contract. The Deponent being asked whether application to the Legislature or the Crown was made for leave to purchase Lands of the Cherokees by the said Wm. Byrd or any other Person in the matter aforesaid He answereth that no such application was made that he knows of, that the only proposal to the Indians was, to know if they would treat on the Subject and further saith not. PATRICK HENRY

Thomas Price of lawful Age being first sworn on the holy Evangelists of Almighty God deposeth and saith: That at the request of Richard Henderson and Nathaniel Hart of North Carolina in the Month of October in the Year 1774, this Deponent accompanied them on their Journey to the Cherokee Nation: that about six Miles from the said Nation, they met with Attacullacullah (otherwise called the little Carpenter) a Cherokee chief with whom they held some Conversation, relating to the purchase of the Lands now in dispute: that in Consequence of this Interview Attacullacullah returned with them to the said Nation and consulted such of the Chiefs as were then at Home upon the Subject of the said Henderson's and Harts proposals: that thereupon the said Chiefs deputed Attacullacullah to attend the said Henderson and Hart to North Carolina, and there examine the Goods and Merchandize which had been by them offered as the Consideration of the purchase: that if the Goods and Merchandize were found upon Examination to be of sufficient Value to induce the said Nation to treat upon them, Attacullacullah was injoined to make report thereof; if not, in this Case he was injoined to desire the said Henderson and Hart to keep their Goods and Merchandize as they (the Cherokees) would still keep their Lands: And this Deponent further saith that Attacullacullah having been satisfied upon Examination, that the Goods and Merchandize were of sufficient Value to induce the said Nation to treat upon them about the latter end of January 1775 returned to Wattaugh in North Carolina with the said Henderson and this Deponent who carried with them thither the said Goods and Merchandize; that Attacullacullah immediately dispatched from thence Runners to the great Warrior Oconistoto chief of the said Nation desiring him to summon his people to attend at Wattaugh to hold a talk with a Gentleman from North Carolina concerning the land lying on Kentucky, that in Obedience to such Summons, about twelve hundred Cherokees consisting of Men Women and Children among whom were Oconistoto, Attacullaculla, Savinouha and about twenty five other Chiefs, from the Overhill Towns, Assembled at Wattauga: that the Terms upon which the said Henderson proposed to purchase the lands, were fully explained and made known to them by one John Vann, the Kings Interpreter: that after several days talk Oconistoto, Attacullacullah and Savinouha in behalf of the Cherokee Nation, signed, sealed and delivered an Indenture bearing date the 17th day of March 1775, whereby they granted, bargained, sold, aliened, enfeoffed, released &c confirmed unto Richard Henderson, Thomas Hart, Nathaniel Hart, John Williams, John Luttrell, William Johnston, James Hogg, David Hart and Leonard Hendley Bullock their Heirs and Assigns forever, all that Tract, Territory or parcel of Land situated lying and being in North America on the Ohio River, one of the Eastern Branches of the Missisippi River beginning on the said Ohio River at the Mouth of Kentuckey, Chenosa, or what by the English is called Louisa River, from thence running up the said River, and the most Northwardly fork of the same to the head spring thereof thence a South East course to the top ridge of Powells Mountain, then Westwardly along the ridge of the said Mountain unto a point from which a North West Course will hit or strike the head spring of the most Southwardly branch of Cumberland River thence down the said River including all its Waters to the Ohio River thence up the said River as it Meanders to the beginning &c: as by reference to the Indenture itself which this Deponent subscribed as a Witness and on the back of which where the aforesaid Courses are set forth are written these Words: "Memorandum the within Deed is referred to by Thomas Price in his Deposition Edmund Randolph" will together with several other Things appear: And this Deponent further saith that the Majority of the above mentioned twelve hundred Cherokees were at Wattaugh for three Weeks or thereabouts and all the Chiefs were present at the Conclusion of the Treaty & signing of the Deed: that during this time he did not discover any of the Chiefs, Warriors or any other Indian drunk or intoxicated except one Corn Tassel, a person of no Consequence in the Nation: that the Treaty was held publickly so that every person who chose to attend might distinctly hear what passed that the Indians were particularly cautious in appointing an Interpreter and such other persons, as were necessary for carrying on the Treaty, seeing that they appointed John Vann the King's Linguist, their Linguist on this Occasion and chose Ellis Harlem, Isaac Thomas, Thomas Benn, a half bred and this Deponent to Watch and see, that a faithful Report was made of every Thing which was spoken: That this Deponent attended the Treaty from the first day of it to the Execution of the Deed: that he at that Time understood the Cherokee Language, so as to comprehend every thing which was said and to know that what was observed on either side was fairly and truly translated:

that the Cherokees perfectly understood, what Lands were the subject of the Treaty, and that the Lands, contained within the Boundaries or Courses, specified in the above mentioned Deed, were actually contracted for by the said Henderson with the Cherokees and disposed of by the Cherokees to him and his Copartners the said Boundaries or Courses having been read and explained at large before the Execution of the Deed: And this Deponent further saith that the said Henderson after Oconistoto, Attacullacullah and Savinouha had executed the Deed on their parts applied to the other Warriors to execute it on their parts also; but was answered that what the three subscribing Chiefs had done, was done on behalf of the Nation: that he saw the Goods and Merchandize which were the Consideration of the purchase delivered to the Cherokees and heard no Murmurs or discontent after the distribution of them; but knows not the amount of their value: that tho' he hath been acquainted with the Cherokees for about twelve years he hath never heard any of them, except those of the Overhill Towns, claim the sole Right to the Land now in dispute: that Chenesta (a Chief of one of the Cherokee Towns in the middle settlement) was present at the Treaty and claimed no seat in Council, as being entitled to a Voice in the Sale of the Lands; but remained at a distance from the place where the Council sat, and in the Evening after the Execution of the Deed and delivery of the Goods and Merchandize informed this Deponant in Conversation that he, on behalf of the middle Towns, claimed no right to the Land, for that it was an affair of the Overhills, in which they might do as they please: That this Deponent hath frequently heard the Overhills claim the Lands from the Mouth of the great Kanhawah to the Tenessee: That during the Treaty no mention was made by the said Henderson, or any person for him, that the said Henderson, or any of his Copartners were Authorized to treat for the Lands in dispute by or in behalf of the Crown of Great Britain or any Government whatever, but that the Cherokees always understood, that the said Henderson treated for them as an Individual, and that they had conveyed them to him as such: And this Deponent further saith that he read that part of the abovementioned Deed which expresses the Boundaries or Courses of the Lands, thereby conveyed and is certain, that they were inserted and read to the Indians, before the Execution of it: that Attacullocullah resides in the Overhill Towns, is one of their Chiefs and first Councellors, and has equal Authority with any Man in the Nation: that Attacullacullah is advanced in Years, and generally thought to be as well acquainted with the

Claims of the Cherokees to Lands as any person in the Nation: that the Dragon Canoe (one of the Overhill Chiefs) told the said Henderson at the Treaty, that there was a black Cloud hanging over that Country pointing to the North West, adding that it was in the Way of the Tawas, Kickapoos, Piankasees, and Kuskuskoes, when they came to War against the Cherokees, and that they would kill white, as well as red people: that the Dragon Canoe at first hesitated about the disposal of the Lands to the said Henderson, alledging, that the Cherokees had formerly held the Land to the Sea and the white people had encroached upon them almost to their Towns: that the Cherokees maintained themselves by hunting and if they parted with these Lands they should have a great many Goods for them: that he has heard that the Lands Northwest of the great Mountain, lying on the Waters of Cumberland and Kentuckey were once inhabited by the Shawanese who were driven from Augusta, and that the Cherokees brag of having driven them from Augusta and afterwards from those Lands. And this Deponent further saith that one other Indenture bearing date the day of March 1775 was on the aforesaid 17th day of March 1775. Signed, sealed and delivered by Oconistoto, Attacullacullah and Savinouha whereby all that Tract Territory or parcel of Land beginning on the Holson River where the Course of Powells Mountain strikes the same, thence up the said River as it Meanders to where the Virginia line crosses the same, thence Westward along the line run by Donaldson &c. to a point six English Miles Eastward of the long Island to the said Holson River thence a direct Course towards the Mouth of the great Kanhawa until it reaches the top ridge of Powell's Mountain, thence Westward along the said Ridge to the beginning was conveyed to the said Henderson and his said Copartners in the same manner, with the same Limitations and every Circumstance the same as what took place in the first Deed as by reference to the Indenture itself which this Deponent has subscribed as a Witness, and on the back of which, where the last mentioned Courses are set forth are Written these Words "Williamsburg December the 27th 1776 I do hereby certify, that this is the second Deed referred to by Thomas Price in his Deposition, Edmund Randolph." And this Deponent further saith that Mannaturiia a Cherokee mentioned at the Treaty, [said] that he had a plantation about the big bone Lick and as it was his place of Abode he did not choose that it should be sold, upon which the great Warrior observed that the old Women would begin to talk when the Boys did: that the Deponent was at the Treaty of Lochabar in 1770: that he understood, that two Commissioners from Virginia were at that time there who were treating on behalf of Virginia for all the Land which lay on the Western Waters to the Eastward of a Line then to be run reserving the Land lying to the Westward thereof to the Cherokees; that at this last mentioned Treaty the Cherokees hesitated to part with the said land, so lying to the Eastward but became reconciled thereto, when John Stuart Superintendant of Indian Affairs, representing to them the Inconsistency of selling Lands to several persons of South Carolina, and yet refusing so to do to their Father (meaning the King of Great Britain) who wanted to settle his people thereupon. And this Deponent further saith, that of h[is] knowledge he knows that about nine or ten years ago th[e] Cherokees determined to Negotiate for peace thro' the Mediat[ion] of Sir William Johnson with the Northward Indians: that in Consequence of this Determination, thirty Cherokees, or thereabout, among whom were Oconistoto, Attacullacullah, and Savinouha went to Charles Town in South Carolina, in order to take Shipping for the Northward, taking this Deponent with them as their Interpreter as far as South Carolina: that they actually did take shipping for this purpose that he has been informed that these Cherokees, upon the Accomplishing their business divided into two parties, one intending to return by Water the other by Land: that in the party which was to return by Land Attacullacullah was one: that as Attacullacullah returned homewards down the Ohio he held a treaty with the Shawanese upon the subject of peace at which Treaty the Cherokees, as this Deponent has been informed threw down some Skins, telling the Shawanese, that the Deer from which those Skins had been taken, were killed by them (the Cherokees) for their Food on their Journey, and that the Skins therefore belonged to them (the Shawanese) that this Deponent heard James Branham a half bred who went as Interpreter to the Cherokees, who were to return by Land, laugh at them for their Cowardice in giving up the Skins: that this Deponent knows, that Attacullacullah brought, on his return Home from the Northward, from some of the Indian Nations about Fort Pitt; some of his own Countrymen, who had been made Prisoners: that this Deponent is Confident and certain, that Attacullacullah returned by Land, and that he, and his party did not arrive at Home till three Months, or thereabouts after the Arrival of Oconistoto and his party: that the Cherokees can give no Account of their Original or removal from any Country, but believe that their Nation have held the Towns and Country, which they inhabit and claim from Time immemorial. And further this Deponent saith not.

THOMAS PRICE

Andrew Lewis of lawful Age being first sworn on the Holy Evangelists of Almighty God deposeth and saith that he was particularly acquainted with the Cherokee Nation for two Years or thereabouts and is also acquainted with the six Nations: that he has heard that a part of the Shawanese formerly lived on Cumberland River, but has never been at the River himself. That he has always understood, that the Shawanese and Delawares have been Tenants at Will of the six Nations, on the Lands claimed by them and has himself heard the six Nations threaten to chastise the Shawanes and Delawares in case of Misbehaviour: that being a Commissioner on the part of Virginia at the Treaty of Fort Stanwix 1768 and obliged before all the treating Indians had assembled to repair to Chiswells Mines to treat with the Cherokees there, he as well as Doctor Thomas Walker at the instance of Sir William Johnston committed to Writing their Opinions of the Boundary between the Northward and Southward Indians: that Johnson informed this Deponent, that he would enquire into the matter from the Sachems and Memorials, at the same Time keeping their Sentiments from the sight of the Indians: that Johnson further informed this Deponent who knew nothing of the Indians Language that upon Examination of the Sachems singly and collectively he had found that the Cherokees had no right to the Lands off the Waters of their Own that is the Cherokee River towards the Ohio, and this Deponent further saith that Col. George Croghan informed Johnson when he was enquiring into matters of Fact respecting said boundary in presence of the Deponent that many years before at a Treaty held at the Shawanese Town on the South East side of the Ohio nearly opposite the Mouth of Scioto between the six Nations and the Ohio Indians and Cherokees, the Cherokees when they came to treat threw down several Deer Skins between thirty and forty at the same time informing the six Nations that the Deer from which they had been taken had been killed by them for their subsistance since they crossed the great Mountain which divides the Waters of the Tenessee from these of Ohio on their land and promising not to kill more on their return than were immediately necessary for food: that this Deponent is convinced that the last mentioned Treaty was held before the year fifty six in as much as in that year the Shawanese removed from their said Towns nearly opposite the Sciota and have not resided there since: that the lands on Kentucky and Cumberland Rivers this Deponent has further understood belonged to the six Nations: that he hath understood that the Shawanese and Delawares have used to hunt on those Grounds and particularly remembers that in the Month of October of the Year 1773 he himself saw same Delaware familys at the mouth of the Great Kanhawa who said they were returning from those Lands from hunting and also said that there were near three hundred Shawanese Men, Women, and Children, up the Kentucky that summer ahunting: that he hath understood that none but the Tributary's of the six Nations have ever lived upon any of the Waters which fall into the Ohio on the South East side except on the Waters of the Tenessee or below the Mouth of Tenessee ever since the supposed Conquest of that Country by the six Nations: That he hath never heard that any of the six Nations or any of their Tributarys have settled lower down on the Ohio or on the South East side than opposite the Mouth of Sciota except a part of the Shawanese who were said to have settled on Cumberland River but that he does not know whether the Shawanese were at the time of such their settlement Tributarys to the six Nations: that he hath never understood that the Cherokees owned or claimed any Lands above the Tenessee or its Waters until Stuart [. . .] Donaldsons line run: that as far as he knows or believes the Capital Towns and settlements of the Mohawks, Onandago, Tuscarorah, Cayugas, Oneidas and Senecas lie to the North of Pittsburg but that the towns and settlements of part of the Mingos who call themselves a part of the six Nations lie to the Southward of Pittsburg: that Stewart informed this Deponent that after the reduction of Fort Loudoun the little Carpenter urged to him the said Stewart upon coming to the Banks of Holson River on the South side that he (Stewart) must cross the river before him: that the Country on the other side was the White peoples: that he must conduct him (the little Carpenter) by going before as he (the little Carpenter) had conducted him (the said Stewart) in his (the little Carpenters) own Country: That at the time of this Observation an Army was marching from Virginia against the Cherokees which had Advanced as far as the Dunkard bottom and that a detachment was within a few miles of the Crossing place: that the little Carpenter upon coming up with this detachment which this Deponent commanded informed him that he was much surprized to find any white people there whatever as he never had the least intimation of their approach: that fort Loudoun had been invested some Months and reduced one

Month or thereabouts before the detachment fell in with the little Carpenter and that while it was invested several persons escaped therefrom some of whom came to the Virginia Camp: that from the Overhill Cherokee Towns to the Ohio river at the Mouth of Kentuckey is more than three hundred Miles: that from the mouth of Kentucky down the Ohio to the falls is about seventy Miles: that upon this Deponants upbraiding Stewart in the Year One thousand seven hundred and sixty nine for having agreed in a Treaty with the Cherokees to a line to be run from Chiswells Mines to the Mouth of the great Kanhawa and reminding him of the Conversation with Attacullacullah at Holson replied that had Governor Fauquier sent Commissioners to run a line between Virginia and the Cherokees when he was first applied to, he might have obtained a Line to the mouth of any River or any remarkable place of the Ohio above the Tenessee as the Cherokees cared little or nothing about that Country, but that as Fauquier had treated him with disrespect on this Occasion he was determined to let the Cherokees claim to their Wishes: that Croghan informed this Deponant that Lord Hillsbro' told him when in England that if the fine Country on the Western Waters was opened he should neither retain his settlers on his Estate in Ireland nor get others to go over to his new lands in Nova Scotia: that he hath frequently heard that the said Henderson &c. have Attempted to erect a Government separate and independant of that of Virginia and believes that the Copy of the Commission hereto annexed is nearly a genuine one. ANDREW LEWIS

John Donelson, of lawful Age being first sworn on the Holy Evangelists of Almighty God, deposeth and saith: That in the Month of August 1770. he received an appointment from Lord Botetourt, to be present at a Congress to be held at Lochaber on the 5th day of October in the same year by John Stewart, Superintendant of Indian Affairs in the Southern Department, and the Cherokee Indians concerning the purchase of certain Lands to be annexed to Virginia and to take Minutes of all their Proceedings that the Cherokee Chiefs and a considerable number of Inferior Indians being assembled at Lochaber a treaty was opened respecting the said Purchase. That the great Warrior the prince and the little Carpenter did then openly declare, that the Lands lying on the South East side of the Ohio and below the great Kanhawa belonged to their Nations. That the said Stewart seemed to support this Claim by many Arguments, which this Deponent does not at present recollect. And this Deponent further saith; that after some Time spent in the Treaty aforesaid, it was agreed between the said Stewart and Cherokees, that a boundary shou'd be run between Virginia and the said Cherokees beginning at Holson River Six Miles above big Island thence running in a direct Line till it should strike the mouth of the great Kanhawa, That the said Stewart, having been informed by Lord Botetourt that this Deponent wou'd probably be appointed Surveyor for running the said Boundary, gave him Cause to vary the same from what had been fixed at the Treaty aforesaid, if any Contract cou'd be Entered into for that purpose, while this Deponent was engaged in running the said boundary, in the presence of Alexr: Cameron, the said Stewarts Deputy. That this Deponant being actually appointed by the President and Council of Virginia Surveyor to run the said Boundary, begun in presence of the Cherokee Chiefs and the said Cameron at the Holson River, six Miles above Big Island to run the same. That in the Progress of the Work they came to the Head of Louisa now Kentucky River when the Little Carpenter observed that his Nation delighted in having their Lands marked out by Natural Boundaries proposed that instead of the line, agreed upon at Lochabar as aforesaid, it shou'd break off at the Head of Louisa River and run thence to the mouth thereof and thence up the Ohio to the Mouth of the great Kanhawa: That this boundary was accordingly agreed to by the said Cameron and this Deponent. That leave having been granted to Virginia by the King of Great Britain to treat with the Cherokees for a more extensive boundary, than that which had been established at the treaty of hard Labour, provided the Virginians would be at the Expence of purchasing the same. The General Assembly Voted the sum of £2500 Sterling for that purpose which sum of £2500 Sterling was accordingly paid to the Cherokees in Goods as a Consideration for the Lands which were ceded by them to Virginia at the Treaty of Lochaber aforesaid. That the House of Burgesses in Consequence of the Vote aforesaid, proceeded to recommend to Lord Botetourt Commissioners to attend on behalf of Virginia at the Treaty of Lochaber, but that Lord Botetourt did not Nominate any of the Persons so recommended. That the said Stewart informed this Deponent that the great Kanhawa was the boundary between Sir William Johnsons Superintendancy and his own: which information was Corroborated by the Copy of the Appointment of the said Stewart to superintend Indian Affairs, which Stewart shewed to this Deponent. That the said Stewart Complained, that the said Johnson had incroached upon his Department, in the Cession; which he obtained from the six Nations at the Treaty of Fort Stanwix of the Lands, lying South Westward of the great Kanhawa.

JOHN DONELSON

Thomas Walker Esquire of lawful Age being first sworn on the Holy Evangelists of Almighty God deposeth and saith that in the Month of April 1750. he named a certain River which he has since understood was at that time called Shawanese Cumberland, That he has often heard that the Shawanese have lived on Cumberland River but at what time he knows not. That the Shawanese and Delawares have been Tenants at Will to the six Nations for near thirty two years past, That the six Nations permitted the Shawanese and Delawares to live under their patronage and protection upon their (that is) the six Nations Conquered Lands, but that he never heard that the Shawanese had lived on Cumberland River by the Consent of the six Nations tho' at the same time he believed that such part of the Shawanese as lived there had not at that time been taken under the Protection of the six Nations. This Deponent further saith that he hath never heard that those lands or any part thereof of which Attacullacullah and other Indian Chiefs when at his House in the Month of August 1751. observ'd that they never went into them but they ran with Blood have been since included within the Territory of Virginia in Consequence of any purchase made from the Cherokees. That he is acquainted with the Cherokees and six Nations and has often transacted Business with them, That he has always understood, that the lands on the Kentucky and Cumberland River, belonged to the six Nations, as well from Information as by the Deed of Cession made to the british Crown at Fort Stanwix in 1768. in which the six Nations reserved the Liberty of hunting on the said Lands for themselves and such others as they thought proper, that he has been informed, that the Shawanese Delawares and part of the six Nations have actually used the said Lands for hunting. That he never heard that the Cherokees claimed the said lands until sometime after the Proclamation of 1763. when they were Claimed by John Stuart Superintendant of Indian Affairs for and in behalf of the Cherokees. That when he was first acquainted with these Lands he discovered no Inhabitants but perceived Vestisges of Houses. That he has understood it to be the Custom of the six Nations either to Exterminate or expell those Nations whom they Conquer from the Conquered Lands tho' they some times adopt some of the Conquered into their own Nation and in the particular instance of the Delawares they took them under protection even after Conquest, that he hath never understood that any Tribe of Indians had inhabited Tenessee River except the Cherokees nor any other Indians the South East side of the Ohio except the Shawanese who live partly opposite to the Mouth of Scioto River partly near the Confluence of the great Kanhawa with the Ohio and partly about twenty Miles below Fort Pitt. That after the reduction of Fort Loudoun Stewart in this Deponents presence informed General Lewis and several others that Attacullacullah upon their Crossing the Holston River when he conducted the said Stewart out of the Cherokee Country told him that he the said Stewart must go before as they passed through the White peoples' Country as he had gone before during their passage through the Cherokee Country. And this Deponent farther saith that one Croghan an Agent for the British Crown informed him that at a Treaty held at a Shawanese Town near the mouth of Scioto between some of the Chiefs of the Cherokees and the six Nations the Cherokees on coming into the Council House threw down a parcel of Skins telling those of the six nations that they had killed the Deer for food after they had come into their Country and the Skins were theirs (the six nations) that the distance from the Mouth of the Cherokee River to the Mouth of Cumberland is Computed by some to be about Twelve by others about fourteen Miles, that the Charter of King James to the Treasurer and Company of Virginia in the Year 1609 includes all that Territory which Richard Henderson claims. That some Surveys were made of the Lands in dispute for Officers in Consequence of the proclamation in 1763 some time before the first day of October 1774. That this Deponent is induced to believe that the said Henderson hath attempted to erect a Government independent of Virginia from his having seen a Commission said to have been given by him in the style of sole Proprietor of Transylvania to a Justice of the peace and has been also informed that a House of Representatives had been chosen and a Chairman and Clerk appointed; That he hath understood from Authority which he Confides in that the said Henderson hath appointed a Surveyor for his aforesaid Territories. That it is his Opinion that Donaldson's Line was intended as a Temporary Expedient only, that all the Indians with whom this Deponent hath been acquainted have described the Boundaries, or Limits of Lands between themselves and any other Nation of Indians by natural Marks such as Water Courses [and?] Mountains. That he hath understood that the Cherokees have disavowed the sale of the Lands lying between Cumberland Mountain and the

Ohio, to Mr. Henderson by the Copy of a Letter sent by Andrew Boyd from the Cherokees in Answer to a Letter wrote them by Lord Dunmore: This Deponent also saith that the Indians in the Disposal of their Lands always depute some one or more of the Chiefs, of their Nation to enter into the Contract on behalf of the whole. THOS. WALKER

William Christian of lawful Age being first sworn on the Holy Evangelists of Almighty God, deposeth and saith, that as to his being interested in the Event of the dispute between the Commonwealth of Virginia and Richard Henderson & Company, he has only to say that he has three Warrants from Lord Dunmore for three thousand Acres of Land or thereabouts actually located, near the Falls of Ohio, and on Salt River in the County of Kentucky as appears by the Platts. That before Donaldsons line was run he does not remember to have formed any Opinion upon the property of the disputed Land, but upon the running of that Line, he thought that, it in effect ceded the Land lying below the said Line upon the Waters of Clinch and Hoylsons River and Powells Valley to the Cherokees. That as well, as he now remembers, early in the Year 1774. it was agreed between the Honorable William Byrd, and John Page Esqr. deceased and Patrick Henry Esqr. Inhabitants of this Commonwealth, and this Deponent to propose contracting for some of the Lands so lying on Holston and Clinch River, and Powells Valley with the Cherokees. That one William Kennedy was accordingly appointed to go to that Country and sound the temper of the Cherokees whether they were willing to bring about a meeting and Treaty for such Lands. That the said Kennedy was sent to the Cherokee Nation for that purpose but this Deponent does not recollect what answer he brought back. That this Deponent does not certainly know whether this Scheme of purchasing the said Lands, wou'd have been continued, but it so happened that he and the other partners never met again upon the subject.

WM: CHRISTIAN

The deposition of Richard Callaway, as taken in the presence of Mr. Henderson. Richard Callaway, of lawful age, being first sworn on the holy Evangelists of Almighty God, deposeth and Saith: That he is a holder of about 3,000 Acres of land in the county known by the name of Transylvania, 2,000 of which or thereabouts he claims under a deed from Mr. Richard Henderson & Co: that at the time of taking such deed, it was agreed, that the Money, which this Deponent paid in Consideration of the same, amounting in the whole to about £20. Sterling, should be refunded to him, in case the Title of the said Company thereto should not be established. That this Deponent has the greatest confidence, that upon the event just mentioned the said £20. will be accordingly refunded, and that he therefore conceives himself to be in no manner interested in the dispute between the Commonwealth of Virginia and the said Company. And this deponent farther saith, that he settled in Transylvania some time before, and continued there until the said Henderson went to take possession: that this deponent knows, that the said Henderson sent and carried out a considerable number of settlers into that Country: that the said Henderson hath been at great pains to accommodate such settlers on many occasions, but particularly by furnishing them with ammunition and salt, as their necessities required: that about May 1775 this deponent proposed that a convention of all the settlers should be holden, for the purpose of framing regulations for the better maintaining Society: that one was accordingly holden in May 1775, at which delegates from all the settlements were present, when regulations were made respecting the wanton destruction of Game and such other subjects, as were essentially necessary to be provided for in their infant state without meddling in any manner with a form of Government: that the said Henderson's assent was to be first obtained, before those regulations became obligatory upon the different settlements: that at the said convention, in Consequence of a power of Attorney for that purpose directed by the Cherokees to Joseph Martin and John Farrar or either of them, livery of seisin of Transylvania was made to the said Henderson & Company in presence of the delegates all of whom, as well as those who represented such people, as had settled there before the said Henderson took possession, as those, who were deputed by such, as settled there afterwards, acquiesced therein: that this deponent being one of the said delegates subscribed the memorandum as to the livery of seisin, and saw all the other delegates do so likewise: that in the fall 1775 a quantity of powder was despatched from Boonsborough, the place of the said Hendersons residence, and within Transylvania, by direction, as this deponent believes, of the said Henderson, to Harrodsburg, a settlement in the same Country; which powder, as this deponent has understood was actually received at Harrodsburg, and was also absolutely necessary for its support: that this deponent being present at the late treaty at long Island remembers to have heard Oconostoto declare by the mouth of his Interpreters, that after he had sold the land to the said Henderson, he, the said Henderson, would not suffer his, Oconostoto's people so much as to hunt thereupon, or catch the Cray fish in the branches. And farther this deponent saith not.

RICHD: CALLAWAY

The deposition of George Croghan Esquire taken before Abraham Hite and James Wood in pursuance of a Resolution of the Convention of the Commonwealth of Virginia, respecting the Title to the Lands on the Ohio and branches thereof claimed by Richard Henderson Gent. and Company. The Deponent being first sworn on the Holy Evangelists deposeth and saith that in the year 1750 or 1751 he then being trading among the Shawanese at the mouth of Scioto, he saw several Shawanese and Cherokees who had just come over the Alleghany Mountain from the Cherokee Country, on which a Council was called of all the Indians thereabouts, when the Shawanese informed the Chiefs of their Nation who resided at Scioto that they were returned from the Cherokee Nation and had left their Women and Children with several of their young Men at the blue Licks on Kentucky River where they intended to reside and Hunt that Season; then added pointing to the Cherokees; these Cherokees are about forty or fifty in number and have come over with us to solicit you to make up a difference subsisting between them and the Wiandots, there were at the Council several Wiandots Delawares and six Nations. The Cherokees then addressed themselves to the six Nations and requested they might have Liberty to hunt between the Alleghany Mountain and the Ohio for that Season, as they knew the Country belonged to them. At a Treaty held at Fort Stanwix in November 1768. the six Nations in General Council assembled did sell to Sir William Johnston then Superintendant for Indian Affairs all the Lands lying between the Mountains and the Ohio, as low down as the mouth of the Cherokee River for the King of Great Britain's use when they declared that Country belonged to them they having Conquered the Nations who formerly resided thereon. For further particulars of that Transaction this Deponent refers to the aforesaid Treaty of Fort Stanwix. The Deponent further saith that he never heard the Title of the six Nations to the aforesaid County disputed by any Nation of Indians until a few years ago when a deputation of the six Nations going to the Cherokees Country informed him that the Cherokees had set up a Claim to it, and said that they the six Nations had no right to sell it, and that they were then going to the Cherokee Country in Order to settle that matter; that some of the said deputation returned by Water to New York, others returned by Pitsburg the spring following and informed him that the Cherokees acknowledged in public Council the right of the six Nations to the aforesaid Country to have been good. And the Deponent further saith that about thirty or thirty one years ago a party of Shawanese headed by one Charlie a Shawanese who had received permission from Monagatootha and the half King, who were fully impowered by the Chiefs of the six Nations for that purpose, took possession of, and form'd a settlement on a large River which falls into the Ohio between the Mouths of Oubache on the West and the Tenessee or Cherokee River on the East side of the Ohio, which River was afterward called and known by the Name of the Shawanese River, and that the distance from Fort Pitt to the Mouth of the Shawanese River is computed to be upwards of one thousand Miles and further this Deponent saith not. GEO: CROGHAN

The Deposition of Mr. John Reid of full Age in behalf of the Commonwealth of Virginia sayeth. That he was present at the Treaty held by Col. Richd. Henderson & Co. with the Cherokee Indians at Wataugah in March 1775. and heard the Draging Canoe propose to sell the land above Kentucky to Col. Henderson & Co: which said Henderson refused to purchase alledging the State of Virginia had already bought it. And said it was not that Land he wanted, that the land he wished to purchase was on the South side of the Kentucky. upon which the Draging Canoe withdrew from the Conference which was stopped for that day. The Deponent does not recollect any thing of consequence that occured until the day the deeds were signed by the Indians which was two or three days after the Draging Canoe proposed to sell the land above Kentucky. When Col. Henderson produced the Deeds to be signed by the Indians, They appeared to be uneasy on Account of the number. Col. Henderson informed the Indians there were eight or nine partners in the purchase, And he chose that each should have a Deed least they should be destroyed by fire or Water, upon which the Indians appeared to be more satisfied. When said Henderson presented the first Deed to Oconastota to be signed the Deponant desired said Henderson to read the Boundarys of the land mentioned in it to him which said Henderson refused to do, until the Deeds were signed. The Deponent then observed that it was not generous to get a people to sign a Deed who did not know what was in it upon which said Henderson beg'd the Deponent not to be a means of breaking the Treaty, as he had been at a great deal of Expence And said after that Deed was signed it should be read, And declared the other Deeds were like that one. The Deponent did not see the Deeds signed, tho he thinks it was and then saw Jesse Banton read some Instrument of Writing to the Indians, which he believes to be the Deed signed by them but was at too great a distance to hear what it contained, nor does he know whether the Deed was interpreted to the Indians, and thinks the Interpreter was present while the Deed or writing was read. On the Night after the Deeds should have been signed the Deponent went with Richard Paris to where the Indians were encamped and was told by said Paris that he understood Col. Henderson had got a deed for the lands upon this River which the Indians knew nothing of and would inform them of it. When the Deponent and said Paris came to the Indians Camps they found the Chiefs almost all drunk and said Paris informed Oconastotas Wife that the Chiefs had given a deed for the Lands upon this River, upon which she appeared to be very uneasy, and went away (as said Paris told the Deponent) to acquaint some of the Chiefs with it. Next Morning the Deponent and said Paris met at Oconastotas Tent and found a number of the Chiefs at it, who, the Deponant saw (as he apprehended) marking out sundry Water Courses which he took to be the main branch of Holsteins River seeing the Great Island laid down and the north Fork with sundry others which the Deponant does not recollect, and thinks they were the branches of Holstein. Said Paris then asked the Indian Chiefs if they had sold Col. Henderson the lands upon them Waters: The Indians replied (as the said Paris inform'd the Deponent) They had not nor would not. The same day sundry of Chiefs met at the place where the Conference had been held, and there informed said Henderson (as the Deponent was told by some of the Traders) that they had not sold the Lands upon these Waters; and had only allowed him a path through them to pass to the Kentucky; that said Henderson then applied to the Indians to allow him a small distance on each side of the Path for hunting to support the People on their way to and from the Kentucky, but does not know whether the Indians agreed to it. The Deponent further saith that he did not see any of the Indian Chiefs intoxicated until said Henderson paid them the Goods for the lands and he understood the Deeds were executed. The Deponent also saith he did not constantly attend at all the Conferences during the Treaty, nor does he know that said Henderson & Co. had any private talks with the Indian Chiefs during the Treaty. The Deponent saith that he does not know the Draging Canoe withdrew or absented himself from any of the Conferences during the Treaty excepting the time aforementioned. The Deponant also saith that many of the young Indian Men appeared to be much dissatisfied upon the division of the Goods, and set off home the same Night the Deeds should have been signed, And that he was informed one of the Warriors received only one Shirt for his part who said he had sold the land, and he could have killed more Deer in one day upon it than would have bought such a Shirt. That Col. Thomas Hart one of the Company took the Deponent into a House where the Goods designed for the Indians lay and shewed them to him; The Deponent asked said Hart if the Indians had seen the Goods, who, he thinks told him they had, and were well enough pleased with them And further sayeth not. JOHN REID.

The Deposition of James Robinson[1] of full Age taken in behalf of Richard Henderson Esqr. & Co. saith That he was present at the public Conferences during the Treaty Richard Henderson & Co. held with the Cherokees in March 1775. That at the opening of the Treaty said Henderson proposed to the Indians to purchase from them the lands lying from the Mouth of the great Kanawa down the Ohio to the Mouth of Tenessee but does not recollect the other boundaries then proposed. Said Henderson then asked the Indians if the lands within the bounds he had mentioned were theirs; the Indians had then some private or low talk among themselves and afterwards told said Henderson that the lands were theirs. Said Henderson then told them if the land was theirs he had Goods there to give them for it: this concluded the first days conference. Upon the second day of the Treaty the Indians proposed to sell said Henderson the land upon the North side of Kentucky, to which said Henderson replied he would not have that land as it was already claimed by the Virginians and if he could not get the lands he asked for he would keep his Goods. Upon which the Draging Canoe got Angry and withdrew himself from the Conference, And the other Indians immediately followed him and broke up the Conference for that day. Some person in hearing of the Deponent told John Williams one of the Copartners not to pay any regard to the Draging Canoe's going off in a passion as the head men might still be got to sign a Deed privately. Col. Williams replied he wou'd not give any thing for every Indian there to sign a deed unless it was done in open Treaty. When the Indians met said Henderson upon the third day of the Treaty said Henderson told them the Lands he had mentioned before were the lands he had brought his

Goods for; The Indians then by their Talk seemed inclinable to let the said Henderson have some land, but complained the Goods were too few for the number of Persons who were there, and if they gave him up land they hop'd he would consider them at another time. Said Henderson answered they had seen the Goods, and if they gave him the Land he would give them the Keys of the House in which they lay, and he could promise them no more. The Indians then agreed to sell the land as far as Cumberland River and said Henderson insisted to have Cumberland River and the Waters of Cumberland River which the Indians agreed to, after telling said Henderson them were their Hunting Grounds, And their Children who were then growing up might have reason to complain if they sold that lands which Argument they frequently made use of from the time they offered to sell the land below Kentucky also observing it was a bloody Country, and if he went to it they would not hold him by the hand any longer, and must do it at his own risque, and must not blame them if any thing happened to him. On the fourth day of the Treaty, a Deed was produced and read and interpreted Sentence by Sentence to the Indians which was signed by them, also several others which the Indians were told were exactly the same with that which they first signed. The Deponent saith when Oconastota and the Raven Warrior were about to sign the first Deed that John Vann Alias Joseph Vann, took them by the hand and stop'd them from signing and (as the Deponent was informed) told them to take care of what they were about, and it was what they would to sign, but to clear him of it and not blame him afterwards for it which caution the Deponent thinks was given the Indians by said Vann, in order to exonerate himself as he was then Interpreter for the Crown, and not on Account of any fraud or Collusion on said Hendersons part in his bargain with the Indians. Said Deponent thinks the boundarys mentioned in the Deed first read to and signed by the Indians were from the mouth of Kentucky, up the same to Donaldsons line thence along said line to perhaps Cumberland Mountain, thence to the South Branch of Cumberland River including Cumberland and the Waters of Cumberland to the Ohio, thence up the Ohio to the beginning. Some time in the Winter after the Treaty the Deponent saw said Vann, who told the Deponent he understood Henderson & Company claimed more lands than the Indians had given a Deed for, as he understood said Company claimed the land up the Tenessee to within ten Miles of the Cherokee Towns. Richard Henderson asked the Deponent if when he heard John Vann complain about the Claim made by the Company to near the Cherokee Towns, if he understood the Indians also complained of a settlement being made in Powell's Valley. The Deponent answered he did not hear Vann or any other person say whether the Indians were satisfied or dissatisfied about the Settlement. The Deponent also saith that Isaac Thomas told him the Cherokees denied altogether their selling any lands to John Carter below the North fork of Holstein; And further saith he knew Oconastota to deny in conversation with Col. Christian the sale of land which the Indians had actually sold and for which he knew him to sign a Deed. The Deponent also saith the little Carpenter told Col. Henderson that they (the Indians) sold said Henderson the land from where they then stood to the Kentucky purchase for a path, but does not recollect what extent of Country said Henderson was to have on each side of the Path, for which the Indians signed some instrument of writing but does not recollect whether it was read or interpreted to them. The Deponent saith the Deeds from the Indians to Henderson & Company were signed by Oconastota, the Raven, and he thinks the little Carpenter, the other Chiefs being present. The Deponent also saith he understood the Cherokee Indians were considerably indebted to John Carter for Goods, which the said Carter had formerly sold them, and for which he had no prospect of being paid unless he could purchase a certain Tract of Country from them and that he had promised Goods to pay the Indians for it, over and above what they were indebted to him; that the Indians refused to sell said Carter the lands which he wanted. That Richard Henderson proposed to the Indians to have said Carters books spoiled and he would give them Goods to the value of two thousand weight of leather, on condition they would give him the land he asked for, for a path to the Kentucky purchase, which the Indians agreed to and received from said Henderson the goods provided by Carter for them; that the Indians made a Deed to said Henderson & Co. for the said path way to the Kentucky purchase the bounds of which is not known to the said Deponent, who has since been informed by said Carter, that he said Carter had a deed made to him by said Henderson out of the Indian Deed for the path way. The Deponent thinks for all the lands said Carter wanted he purchased from the Indians; and further saith not. JAS: ROBERTSON

Isaac Shelby, of lawful Age, being first sworn on the holy Evangelists of Almighty God, Deposeth and saith That this Deponent has made several Entries for Lands in Mr. Henderson's Office, but does not conceive himself to be in any manner interested in the event of the dispute between the Commonwealth of Virginia and the said Henderson. That in March 1775. this Deponent was present at a Treaty held at Wattaugha between the said Henderson and the Cherokee Indians; that the Deponent there heard the said Henderson call the Indians when the Deed by which the said Henderson now claims was going to be signed, and desired that they would attend to what was going to be done; that this Deponent believes the Courses in the said Deed contained to be the very Courses which the said Henderson read therefrom to the Indians and were interpreted to them. That the said Henderson took the said Deed from among several others lying on a Table, all of which appeared to this Deponent to be of the same Tenor with that which he read. That at the time of this Treaty one Read who was there and suspected that the said Henderson intended to purchase some Lands which He himself had his Eye on, desired the said Deed to be read before it was signed, which was accordingly done and the said Read objected not thereto. That being present at the late Treaty at Long Island this Deponent remembers to have heard Occunastoto or the Tassell, (but which he does not recollect) say that ever since he had signed the Paper to Mr. Henderson He was afraid to sign one, and that Mr. Henderson ever since He had signed the Paper deprived Him of the privilidge of catching even Crawfish on the Land; That this Deponant was present at the Time of signing the said Deed at Wattaugha when every thing was conducted fairly on the part of the said Henderson, who after signing desired the Indians to go and take the Goods which he designed for them. And further the Deponent saith not. ISAAC SHELBY

Nathaniel Gist of lawful Age, being first sworn on the holy Evangelists of Almighty God deposeth and saith That about ten Years ago being accustomed to hunt on green River, which lies between Kentucky and Cumberland Rivers, this Deponent has taken notice of Traces of the Country thereabouts, having been inhabited at some great distance of Time before, but that it was then deserted, That at the Treaty at Loggstown about twenty years ago this Deponent was informed by one David Hendricks, that he the said Hendricks had been captivated by a party of Taawas as he was going to or returning from (but which this Deponent does not recollect) the blue Licks, where some Shawanese Towns were settled. That this Deponent being present at the said Treaty remembers to have heard an application made by the Commissioners on the part of Virginia, to the six Nations for the sale of Lands on the South East side of the Ohio, but that the six Nations replied that they could not dispose of the same without the consent of the Shawanese King, for that they the six Nations had given those Lands to the Shawanese to hunt upon. That this Deponent never knew nor heard that the Country between the Ohio and Tenessee Rivers was ever occupied by any other Nation except the Shawanese who as He has understood resided at the blue Licks aforesaid, but used all the said Country for hunting Grounds, and that He has been informed that the Cherokees hunted thereon by the permission of the Shawanese, about the Time of the aforesaid David Hendricks being made Prisoner. That this Deponent remembers to have heard at the aforesaid Treaty the half King say (who subscribed the said Treaty on behalf of the six Nations and who was acknowledged by the Chiefs and others of the six Nations, who were then present to have been appointed by their Countrymen to preside over the Tribes, which were settled from the head of the Ohio down to the Shawanese Towns, and also to Act for the six Nations and the said Tribes at the said Treaty) that the Country between the great Mountain and the Ohio from Loggstown to the Mouth of the Tenessee belonged to the six Nations, that in the year 1754. the Deponent heard Tiftoe who was the head Man of the upper Cherokee Towns, and a chief of the Cherokee Nation tell one Stallnicker at the said Stallnickers House on Holstein River that He Tiftoe had no right to give him leave to hunt on the other side of the great Mountain, but that any where on this side, he might hunt, as he cou'd give him Liberty so to do, as the lands on this side belonged to the Cherokee nation. That at the Time of Donaldsons running this Line this Deponent being at Blooms's on Holstein heard the Couwee Warrior, who was the first in the deputation of the Cherokees to see the line between North Carolina, and the Cherokees as far as Holstein say That He the Couwee Warrior had nothing to say as to giving a right to hunt on the other side of the great Mountain, but that all he minded was his own side meaning the side on which the Warrior then was. That this Deponent understood from this Observation of the Couwee Warrior, that the Lands on the other side of the great Mountain did not belong to the Cherokee Nation; that in the Spring 1776 this Deponent being present at a Council of the Cherokees held at Chote the place where that Nation usually held their grand Councils, heard Occunostoto; the King and head Warrior of the Cherokee Nation tell Cameron and Stewart, who were Agents for Indian Affairs on behalf of the

King of Great Britain, that Mr. Henderson had sent for Him Occunostoto, to Wattaugha to treat for the purchase of the Lands on the other side of the great Mountain, that he Occunnostoto, replied to him the said Henderson, that the Lands on the other side of the great Mountain were a dark place, and advised the said Henderson not to go thither, as he wou'd probably be cutt off by the Enemy; that upon his Occunnostoto's disclaiming, that the Cherokee Nation had any right to those lands the said Henderson urged him to sell whatever right the Cherokee Nation might have to the same; that Occunnostoto at the same time added, that the said Henderson had applied to him frequently to purchase some of the Cherokee Lands for a road from the Great Island to Cumberland Gap, but that he Occunnostoto always told Him in Answer that He reserved those Lands for his hunting Grounds and never wou'd part from them. That the Raven and Tassell two Chiefs of the Cherokee Nation, at the same Council declared that they knew what Occunnostoto observed, as is above mentioned, to be true; that at the late Treaty held in July 1777 at Long Island, where, as this Deponent believes all the Commissioners were present, but particularly as he remembers two from Virginia to wit, Colonels Christian and Preston, and one from North Carolina, vizt: Mr. Lanier, Occunnostoto repeated what is above said to have been related by him at the great Council of Chote, respecting the said Hendersons urging him to sell the Cherokee Lands for a road as aforesaid, and also the same Answer, as is above declared to be what He replied to the said Henderson. That upon Occonostoto being about to relate at the Treaty in 1777, what He did as is just mentioned, concerning what passed between Him, and the said Henderson, called upon the Chiefs and Interpreters who were present to set him right if He should say any thing which was wrong. That the Chiefs and Interpreters after Occunestoto had finished, confirmed what He had related; that at the said Treaty in 1777 the abovemention'd Cherokee Chief called the Tassell when He was going to subscribe the Deed by which the Line which is now to be run between the Cherokees on the one part, and Virginia and Carolina on the other was ceded, declared that tho' He cou'd safely rely upon those with whom he was then treating that his hand always trembled whenever He put his to a paper ever since He had been imposed upon as he had been by Mr. Henderson. That this Deponent supposed that the Tassell alluded in this last observation to the Deeds under which the said Henderson now claims. That this Deponent did not himself at the treaty at Loggs Town, nor at any time since understand the public Talks of the six Nations, but that what he relates as having been said by the six Nations, this Deponent heard interpreted to the Commissioners by one Andrew Mentieur [Montour] who was one of their Chiefs and a public Interpreter and also by other public Interpreters. That what this Deponent has said respecting the Treaty at Chote, he heard interpreted to Cameron and Steward by one George Lowry a public Interpreter. That what he has said respecting the Treaty at Long Island he heard interpreted to the Commissioners by Joe, commonly called John Vann and Charles Murphy two public Interpreters, but that this Deponent did not at the said Treaties of Chote and the long Island understand enough of the Cherokee Language to comprehend the public Talks there. And further this Deponent saith not. N: Gist

The Deposition of William Cocke of full Age in behalf of Richard Henderson Esqr: & Co. saith That Col. Richard Henderson proposed to sell the Lands upon Kentucky purchased by him from the Cherokee Indians, to the first Adventurers at twenty shillings sterling per hundred clear of all Fees or Expences; The Deponent saith he was himself one of the first Adventurers with said Henderson and remained as such about five Months, in which time an entry Book was opened for those that chose to enter Lands; that said Henderson gave public Notice to the Adventurers to come in and enter their lands, at the same time acquainting them that those who enter'd lands first should have the preference: The Deponent believes the entry Book was kept fairly and impartially. The Deponent also, saith that he purchased and paid for five thousand Acres of land upon the terms proposed to the first Adventurers, and believes he was indulged to purchase so large a quantity when others were permitted to enter only five hundred Acres on Account of his Services in clearing a road to Powell's Valley and when a number of the Adventurers were returning from Kentucky some of them wounded by the Indians his Undertaking to carry an express from said Henderson to Capt. Daniel Boone upon Kentucky. Shortly after the Arrival of the Deponent at Kentucky about the 20th of April 1775 there was a Town or settlement made by the Adventurers called Saint Asaph; Harrodsburg and Boonsburgh being settled some time before. Sometime after it was recommended or ordered (he is not certain which) by said Henderson to the Inhabitants to elect Representatives; that about the last of May a Convention met but does not know whether it was by Col. Henderson's appointment or only agreed upon among the people and their Representatives, with the approbation of said Henderson. That the Convention insisted said Henderson should not raise the price of the Land above three pounds Sterling per hundred Acres which he alledged he had not power from the Company to agree to, but said it was his opinion it would not be so much; That in the time the Convention sat the Deponent in private conversation with said Henderson and Mr. Luttrell told them he thought the Company might make very ample fortunes by selling the Land at twenty shillings Sterling per hundred, And the people appeared very uneasy at the uncertainty of the price the said Henderson & Co: might in future have for the Lands, as there was a prospect of its raising. The Deponent saith that he and a number of the Adventurers was informed by said Henderson at their first setting out to Kentucky that he expected the price of the Lands would be raised after the first year and that it was generally expected by the Adventurers, and this Deponent often heard said Henderson say in a public manner that he expected the price of the lands would be raised but did not know how much it would be as the Company had not agreed among themselves to what price it would be raised. This Deponent further saith that their civil and Military Officers were appointed by said Henderson but knows of none before the Convention met and thinks that power was given the Company by the Convention, that by Agreement the said Henderson & Company were not to be elected as members of the Convention but had a right to open the Sessions by laying before them the business of the Country and to put a negative on all laws that might be made. The Convention reserved to itself the right of Adjournment and thinks if the Members did not meet according to appointment then the said Henderson & Company had power to call them together. The Deponent saith that said Henderson produced the Deed from the Indians for the Kentucky Country, to the Convention, upon which an endorsement was made and livery of Seisin given by John Farrar who was empowered by the Indians to give the same by the delivery of a Twig and Turf, and the endorsement of such livery was witnessed by all the members of the Convention present. The Deponent saith that he knew James Harrod who settled the Kentucky the year before said Henderson went out to enter lands with said Henderson and the said Harrod informed the Deponent that he paid the said Henderson a Dollar saying at the same time it was the first money paid him in the Country for Land. The Deponent also saith he did not hear any of the Adventurers Complain that

said Henderson had deceived them by promising them Lands at a lower price before they left home, than he would sell them for when they arrived at Kentucky but has since his coming home heard people complain that said Henderson had raised the price of the land from twenty shillings to fifty shillings (the price for the ensuing year) and has heard them say they expected it would be raised to five pounds and when the Country would be settled they did not doubt but it would be fifty pounds. And further this Deponent saith not.
WM: COCKE

The Deposition of James Gilmore of full Age in behalf of the Commonwealth of Virginia saith That he went to Kentucky in the year 1775 also in the spring 1776 and that he heard no Complaints against the manner Richard Henderson & Co. kept their Land Office the first year. The Deponent was there in year 1776. There was a general Complaint among the People in regard to the Validity of said Hendersons & Co. Titles to the lands. That the People also complains John Williams one of the Copartners who kept the land Office in 1776 knowingly suffered two or more Entries to be made on one and the same piece of land. And this Deponent further saith not.
JAMES GILMER

The Deposition of John Lowry of full age, taken in behalf of the Common Wealth of Virginia, saith That he was at the Treaty held by Richard Henderson & Company with the Cherokees in March 1775. and at the beginning of the Treaty heard the Indians propose to sell said Company Lands upon the North East side or above new River which said Henderson refused to purchase but does remember his reasons for doing so. The Indians then proposed selling some lands between Kentucky and new River which said Henderson also refused to purchase saying the Virginians had already bought it. Said Henderson then inform'd the Indians where the lands lay [which] he wanted to purchase, which was from the mouth of [Kent]ucky some distance down the Ohio, but said Deponent does not remember how far. The Deponent saith the Indians appeared unwilling to sell the lands which said Henderson told them he wanted to purchase and desired said Henderson to return home; and they would look to the Virginians for the price of the Land, which they sold them above Kentucky, also telling the said Henderson the Country which he wanted was of Great Service to them as hunting Ground and that they looked upon their Cattle or Game in it to be as beneficial to them as the tame Cattle were to the white People. The Deponent saith the Indians agreed to sell the land to said Henderson & Co. which they wanted to buy, but does not know the boundary thereof nor is he certain whether he heard them, tho he thinks its probable he did as he was present at the Treaty. The Deponent does not recollect any other thing of Consequence that occurr'd until the Deed came to be signed which was done publickly. When the Deeds were produced for signing, Vann the Interpreter said something to the Indians, which said Henderson objected to desiring the said Vann might not say any thing but what he said Henderson understood; to which said Vann replied he came there to oppose the said Henderson and he would do it; said Henderson then told said Vann he did not regard any opposition he could make him. Vann then told said Henderson he had spoke to the Indians to clear him to their Father Stewart that he might not be blamed for their selling the Land. After the Deeds were signed by the Indians for the Kentucky Country, said Henderson then told the Indians he had bought the Land on Kentucky from them, and he had yet no path to it. The Draging Canoe then told said Henderson he had all the Country from there to the Kentucky purchase for a path but does not recollect that a Deed was given by the Indians for it, nor any Valuable Consideration given to them in lieu thereof. The Deponent also thinks the Goods the said Henderson & Co. had at the Treaty were to be given the Indians for the Kentucky purchase. The Deponent saith he does not remember to hear any thing said during the Conferences of an Eastern boundary to the Kentucky Purchase And further saith not.

JOHN LOWRY

The Deposition of Samuel Wilson of full age taken before Arthur Campbell, and William Campbell Gent. Commissioners appointed by the General Convention and General Assembly of Virginia to take depositions relative to a purchase of Land made by Richard Henderson Esqr. & Co: within the limits of Virginia which deponent being first sworn on the Holy Evangelists deposeth and saith That he purchased a Tract of Land lying on the North side of Holstein River on the Big Creek in a place call'd Carter's Valley from Col. Richard Henderson for which the Deponent has paid twenty pounds ten shillings but in case the said Henderson & Co. should not be able to make a Title to said Land the deponent does not doubt but they will repay him the Money and would be satisfied therewith. The Deponent saith that he is not otherwise interested in the purchase of the Land made by the said Henderson & Co. from the Cherokees. The Deponent farther saith he was present at all the public Conferences during the Treaty with Henderson & Co: and the Cherokees at Wattauga in March 1775. concerning the purchase of certain Lands lying upon the South side of Kentucky but does not know the other boundary lines. The Deponent saith that at the Commencement of the Treaty the Cherokees proposed to sell the Lands upon the North side of Kentucky which said Henderson & Co. refused to purchase alledging that the Colony of Virginia had already bought them. The Deponent farther saith that after the Cherokees sold the said Henderson the land below Kentucky they sold the Land from where they then stood unto the former purchase. The Deponent also saith, that the Indian Chiefs appeared to be perfectly sober during the treaty and that he did not see any spiritous Liquors given to them during the Conferences; and that the Chiefs appeared to be satisfied upon the Receipt of the Goods given them for the Lands which they sold to the said Henderson & Co. The Deponent farther saith that he saw Occonastoto and the Raven Warrior sign a Deed to said Henderson & Co: for the Lands aforementioned and believes it was also signed by others of the Chiefs. The Deponent also saith that when said Henderson & Co. proposed purchasing the lands below the Kentucky the Draging Canoe told them it was the bloody Ground and would be dark and difficult to settle it. The Deponent also saith that he did not understand the Cherokee Indians alledged the said lands were claimed by other Nations, and that they sold them as the proprietors thereof. The Deponent farther saith that he can neither write nor read Writing, and any thing he knows of the Indians talks in the Conferences was by the Interpreter John Vann. The Deponent also saith that sundry Indian Traders Ellis Harlim, Isaac Thomas, Edward Rogers, Tom Ben, Richard Paris and Thomas Price who appeared to understand the Cherokee Tongue were present at the Conferences and that the Indians seemed to design them as a Check upon Vann in case he should not interpret their Talks justly. And this Deponent farther saith not.

his
SAMUEL + WILSON
Mark

The Depositions of the following Persons taken at the House of Mr. John Ormsby in Pittsburgh this tenth day of March 1777. agreeable to Notice given Col. George Morgan Agent for the Indiania Company, before James Wood and Charles Simms pursuant to a resolution of the honorable the Convention of Virginia appointing them Commissioners for collecting Evidence on behalf of the Commonwealth of Virginia, against the several Persons pretending to claim Lands within the Territory and Limits thereof under Deeds or purchases from Indians. The Deponents being of full age and first sworn on the holy Evangelists, in the presence of the said Morgan, Mr. John Gibson and Mr. Thomas Smallman Members of the Indiania Company. Previous to the taking of the Depositions Mr. George Morgan acknowledged himself to be a Member of the Indiania Company and that he was appointed Agent to that Company but that he did not think himself authorized as the representative of the Proprietors to appear in defence of their Title, and at the same time inform'd the Commissioners that he had put an Authenticated Copy of their Grant from the six Nations, into the Hands of John Harvie Esqr. one of the Commissioners appointed to take Depositions respecting the said Grant, sometime in the fall of the Year 1776 desiring that the same should be admitted to Record in the state of Virginia, which Mr. Harvie promised should be done, Thomas Walker Esqr. (one of the subscribing Witnesses to the Grant, and who was one of the Commissioners on behalf of Virginia at the Treaty of Fort Stanwix) then being in Pittsburgh.

Major Edward Ward deposeth and saith that in the beginning of the Year 1754. William Trent Esquire was appointed by Governor Dinwiddie of Virginia, Captain of a Company to be raised, of which this Deponent was appointed Ensign by the said Trent: who assembled the Chiefs and deputies of the six Nations and requested of them permission to erect a Trading House at the Junction of the Alleghany and Monongahela Rivers, to carry on a free and open Trade with the six Nations and their dependants; which was granted by the said Deputies with this restriction, that he was to form no settlements or improvements on the said Land, but on the Contrary to evacuate the same when required by the six Nations. After which the said Capt. Trent inlisted a number of Men not exceeding thirty three, and proceeded to erect a Fort at the place before mentioned. That on the 17th of April following and before the Fort was nearly compleated, this Deponent who commanded in the Absence of Capt. Trent, was put to the necessity of surrendering the possession to a superior number of Troops Commanded by a French officer, who demanded it in the name of the King of France, at which time the half King and a number of the six Nations in the English interest were present. This Deponent further saith that in the Year 1752 and before his surrender to the French there was a small Village Inhabited by the Delawares on the South East side of the Allegheny River, in the neighbourhood of that place, and that old Kittaning on the same side of the said River, was then Inhabited by the Delawares that about one third of the Shawanese Inhabited Loggs town, on the West side of the Ohio, and tended Corn on the East side of the River and the other part of the Nation lived on the Scioto River. That the deputies of the six Nations after the Surrender joined the Virginia Forces commanded by Col. George Washington, who was then on his March at the little meadows and continued with him in the service of Virginia till after the defeat of Monsieur La Force and a party of French Troops under his Command. And the Deponent farther saith that subsequent to the defeat of Colo: Washington at the great meadows, the Shawanese, Delawares many of the Western Tribes of Indians, and an inconsiderable number of the Seneca Tribe, one of the Six Nations joined the French and prosecuted a War against the Frontiers of the States of Virginia, Maryland and Pensylvania, till the conclusion of the peace with the Indians in the year 1759. but that he ever understood the Body of the six Nations continued the firm Friends of the English. That in the year 1756 an Expedition was prosecuted from Pensylvania against the Kittanning a Town inhabited by the Delawares on the South East side of the Alleghany River, which was destroyed, a small number of Indians killed and the remaining part drove from this side the River, where they never after took possession by renewing their settlements to his Knowledge but on the contrary he understood they removed further to the Westward. The Deponent further saith that after the Evacuation of Fort Duquesne by the French on the approach of the British Army in the Year 1758 General Forbes by one of the deputy Agents for Indian Affairs made a requisition to the Chiefs of the six Nations for permission to reestablish a Fort at the same place for the purpose aforesaid and to prevent the French from returning which was granted, a Fort erected and garrisoned which continued in the possession of the british Troops till the Year 1772, when it was evacuated by them and taken possession of by the Deponent, who occupied the same till taken possession of by Major Connelly in 1774, with the Virginia Militia. That in the Year 1759 General Stanwix called a Council of the six Nations, Shawanese, Delawares, and other Western Indians, when the General by the deputy Agent inform'd the Indians assembled that he was then going to erect a strong Fort, and asked the permission of the six Nations for that purpose, which was granted upon a promise of a fair and open Trade, and a reservation of the right of the Lands to the Six Nations, and that it should be abandoned at any time when required by them. After which and in the year 1762 several settlements were formed by Emigrants from the different parts of America by Permission of the Commanding Officer for the purpose of accommodating Travellers on the public Roads. That a settlement and improvement was formed about four Miles above the Fort on the South East side of the Alleghany River by Colo. Croghan in consequence of a Grant from the six Nations. The Deponent being asked by Mr. Morgan, whether the Representatives of the Crown have not upon all occasions acknowledged the six Nations to be the sole proprietors of the Lands on the Ohio previous to the Treaty at Fort Stanwix in 1768, Answers that as well the Representatives of the Crown as the Superintendants and Commissioners from the Colonies for Indian Affairs have always uniformly acknowledged it. And being further asked what Commission he bore at the reduction of Kittaning and whether it would have been in the power of the Detachment who destroyed it to have retained the possession at that time? Answers that he commanded a Company, and that he does not conceive it to have been practicable to keep the possession. That it was judged expedient by the Commanding Officer to retreat in a few Hours, which was precipitately complied with. And being further asked whether he ever knew of any Engagement between the six Nations, and the british or American Forces on or near the Lands in Question, or whether the six Nations were ever conquered by either of them? Answers not to his knowledge. And being further asked by the Commissioners if he was acquainted what Indians composed the Party which attacked and were defeated by Colo. Boquet in the year 1763? Answers that he has heard that a few of the six Nations of the Seneca Tribe joined the Delawares and Shawanese, but does not know it of his own knowledge. And being further asked by Mr. Morgan whether the six Nations ever surrendered or transferred their right to the Lands in question except at Fort Stanwix in 1768. Answers that he never understood that they had Except their Grants to Colo. Croghan and himself. And the Deponent being further asked whether he knows of any settlements being formed within the Bounds of the Indiania Grant before the Year 1768? Answers that he does not, he being an Inhabitant of Pensylvania at that time. The Deponent being farther asked by Mr. Morgan what Troops they were who took the Kittanning at the time beforementioned? Answers they were part of the first Pensylvania Regiment under the Command of Colo. Armstrong and no others.

EDWD: WARDE

II. DEPOSITIONS

Richard Antis deposeth and saith that in May 1767 he settled and improved a plantation on the Monongahala River two Miles below the Mouth of turtle Creek, by permission of the Commanding Officer [at] Fort Pitt, that he has continued and now is in possession of the same and that his settlement was distant from the Pensylvania road about two Miles and on Braddocks Road. Being asked by Mr. Morgan if he knew of any settlements made between Grave Creek and the little Kanhawa, answers that he does not, that he never was there in his life. Being farther asked if he knew of any Settlements made on the West side of Monongahala before that time. Answers he was not acquainted with that Country at that time and does not know of any. The Deponent farther says that Conrad Winemiller, Philip Whitzell and Peter Ralliter settled Lands near him at the same time he made his settlement. REINHARD ANDES

William Powell deposeth and saith that he settled and improved a plantation on Turtle Creek by permission of Col. Reed the Commanding Officer at Fort Pitt, before November 1768. That he has Continued and now is in Possession of the same. The Deponent being asked by Mr. Morgan whether he knew of any settlements being made between the River Monongahala and Little Kanhawa prior to November 1768? Answers that he does not know of any, being a Stranger to that part of the Country.

his
WILLIAM × POWELL
mark

William Elliot deposeth and saith that he settled and improved a plantation about seven Miles from Fort Pitt, on the public Road at a place called the Bullock pens, in the year 1766. by permission granted by Col. Reed the Officer commanding at Fort Pitt, which bears date the 29th day of August 1765. That he has continued and is now in possession of the same, that he knows of the following Persons being settled in his Neighbourhood before the year 1768. vizt. Thos. Small, Eneas Mckay, Alexander McGregor, James Royal, Devereux Smith and Jasper Tubbs, and that he understood they were permitted by the Commanding Officer in the same manner. That the several improvements above mentioned are said to be within the Bounds of a Grant from the Indians to Colo. Croghan and are claimed by him. WILLIAM ELLIOTT

Simon Girty deposeth and saith that while the French were in possession of Fort Duquesne, he was made Prisoner by a party of Delawares, Shawanese [and French], that he was carried to Kittanning which was then inhabited by Delawares or Muncys, after which he was delivered to the Senneca's one of the Six Nation Tribes where he continued a Considerable time. That he always understood that the party who defeated Colo: Grant consisted of French Wiandots, Senneca's, Delawares Shawanese and Ottowas and that he heard that Heashota was with them. The Deponent further saith that the Party which defeated Capt. Bullitt consisted of about fifty five Indians and French, a majority of which were of the Senneca Tribe and the Deponent further saith that he heard Hiashota acknowledge that he was in the Engagement and commanded, when the Attack was made on Colo. Bouquet. The Deponent further saith that he never understood the Indians returned to this side the Allighany River or formed any Settlements after the Kittaning being destroyed and that he has been informed it is not Customary for Indians to resettle a Town after being destroyed by an Enemy or deserted on any other Occasion. The Deponent further saith that he does not know of any settlements being made between the mouth of Monongahala and the little Kanhawa till after opening the Pensylvania Land office. SIMON GIRTEY

Thomas Girtey deposeth and saith that he was made a Prisoner by a party of Indians most of whom were Delawares. That he Continued at the Kittaning till it was destroyed by the English, that the Delawares removed to the other side of the River and never returned after the Kittaning was destroyed to his Knowledge. That he does not know of any settlements being made within the Indiana Grant before the Year 1768. THO. GIRTEY

Colo: William Crawford deposeth and saith that his first acquaintance with the Country on the Ohio was in the Year 1758, he then being an Officer in the Virginia service. That between that time and the Year 1765 a number of settlements were made on the public Roads in that Country by permission of the several Commanding Officers at Fort Pitt. That in the fall of the Year 1765. he made some improvements on the West side of the Alleghany Mountains, in the spring of the year following he settled and has continued to live out here ever since. That before that time and in that year a considerable number of settlements were made he thinks near three hundred without permission from any commanding Officer, some of which settlements were made within the Limits of the Indiania Company claim and some others within Colo: Croghans. [From that] Time to the present the people continued to imigrate to this Country very fast. The Deponent being asked by Mr. Morgan if he knows the names of those who settled in the Indiania Claim in the Year 1766 and on what Waters? Answers that Zachel Morgan,

James Chew and Jacob Prichett came out in that year and was informed by them that they settled up the Monongahela, that he has since seen Zachel Morgans plantation which is on the South side of the line run by Mason and Dixon, and that he believes that to be the first settlement he made in this Country, and always understood the beforementioned Persons lived in his Neighbourhood, but that he himself was never within the limits of the Indiania Claim until the year 1771. or about that time. The Deponent being asked by Mr. Morgan if he knew or ever heard of any settlements besides those beforementioned being made in the Indiania Claim prior to the Treaty at Fort Stanwix? Answers that he understood James Booth settled there before that time but does not know of any others. Being farther ask'd if those settlements were not made contrary to orders of Government? Answers that all the settlements made to the Westward of the Allegheny Mountains at that time were contrary to the orders of Government. The Deponent being farther asked by Colo: Morgan if he knows what Troops took the Kittaning in the Year 1756. Answers that he always understood they were Pensylvania Troops Commanded by Colo. Armstrong. The Deponent being asked by the Commissioners, if he is acquainted with the settlements made within the Indiania and Colo. Croghans grants, and if any Surveys have been made therein by virtue of Warrants or orders of Council and whether there has not been many Transferances made of Lands within said Grants? Answers that the lands within the Limits of Colo. Croghans grants are thickly settled but except on the Mongahela River and middle Island Creek there are but few settlements on the Indiania Claim that he knows of. That he knows but of three Surveys made by Warrant, or orders of Council of the Government of Virginia within Colo: Croghans Grants but a number were made by virtue of Warrants from the Government of Pensylvania. That two Warrants under the Proclamation of the year 1763 are laid within the limits of the Indiania Claim, but no Surveys that he knows of were ever made. And that many transferances have been made of Lands within said Grants. The Deponent being asked by Mr: Morgan if he was acquainted with the quality of the lands in the Indiania Claim? Answers that he is well acquainted with the Lands and he thinks Nineteen twentieths of it is very bad. The Deponent being ask'd if any entries were made with the Surveyor of Augusta for Lands Westward of the Allegheny Mountain Answers that upwards of two thousand were made with him and Colo: Dorsey Pentecost, a number of them for lands within the before mentioned Grants which Entries he transmitted to Mr.

Thos: Lewis Surveyor of Augusta County pursuant to his directions, none of which Entries were made before the year 1775 or in the month of December 1774. The Deponent being farther asked by the Commissioners if he knows that the Indiania Company or Colo. Croghan ever ascertained the Boundaries by surveys, Answers that he does not know that the Indiania Company ever made any Survey of their Lands. That Colo: Croghan made a Survey of his Lands on Raccoon Creek in the Year W: CRAWFORD

Joseph Nicholas deposeth and saith that in the Year after Braddocks defeat he was made Prisoner by a party of Indians consisting of Shawanese and Delawares by whom he was delivered to the Cayugas one of the six Nation tribes where he continued seven years and upwards, that within the said time he knew several of the said Tribes go with other parties against the Settlements, and that he saw several small parties of the Seneca Tribe on their way to War against the Inhabitants, that it was always denied by the Chiefs of the six Nations that [they] were at War with the White people, but that he knows the Contrary in the Instances above mentioned. The Deponent being asked whether he ever knew any number of real Cayugas go to war against the white people? Answers that the Cayugas were greatly mixed with other Nations, but that the parties above mentioned spoke the Cayugas Language and resided in that Nation. JOSEPH NICHOLAS

The deposition of Charles Robertson, relative to a certain Claim (by virtue of an Indian purchase) of Richard Henderson & Co: to a certain Tract of Country accounted to be within the Chartered boundary of the Commonwealth of Virginia. He the said Charles Robertson deposeth and saith That [he] was at the Treaty held at Watauga between the said Richard Henderson & Co. and the Cherokee Indians in March 1775. and believes he heard every public Talk that was delivered by the parties. That as to the Treaty or Conferences being held fairly and openly the Deponent frequently took notice that both Colo. Henderson and the Indians would always cause to be present the white Men and Indian half breeds who understood both Languages as a Check upon the Interpreter, lest he should mistranslate, or leave out through forgetfulness any part of what either party should speak; and saith that he believes the treaty was held fairly and openly but does not remember the whole of the boundary altho' he believes the Indians understood all that was said by the said Henderson. That he does not remember the bounds of the lands proposed to be bought, only that it joined the Ohio, and in them was mentioned something about the Head Springs of Kentucky and he believes of Cumberland, and that 'tis his Opinion it was to keep the dividing Ridge between Cumberland and Tenase. That there was eight or nine different pieces of writing signed by the Indians who were told that the reason of their being so many was that there was so many different Partners in the Company and that each must have one for fear one should be destroyed and that every one might know where his Land was. That none but one of them was read to the Indians. Colo. Henderson told the Indians these Writings were all alike word for Word (and no one was hindered from reading them but does not know that any person did read them) and that they might have them all read if they chose it, to which they said they did not want them read. He does not know how many Indians signed these Papers, but he understood it was done by Consent of the whole as he did not hear any particular one make an objection. The Deponent frequently tried to count the number of Indians which he could not do exactly but from his best observations there was about one thousand in all counting big and little and about the one half of them were Men. He did not understand there was any more than one principal Man behind called Judges Friend who he understood had sent Word that what the other Chiefs agreed to he would abide by. On the second day of the Treaty the Draging Canoe went out displeased on hearing the proposals of the said Henderson as to what Lands he wanted to purchase because (as the said Indian said) the white people wanted too much of their hunting Grounds. On the first day of the Treaty the Indians offered to give up some Lands which they said Col. Donelson had agreed to give them five hundred pounds for and had not paid them but Colo. Henderson said it would not be worth his while to talk about buying that only as he had a House full of Goods for them and should be at yet greater Expence for Beeves and rum to entertain them upon. That towards the close of the Treaty when the Indians seemed like complying with Col. Henderson's proposals the said Henderson told the Indians there was land between them and his Country. He did not love to walk upon their Land. That he had more Goods Guns and Ammunition which they had not yet seen. After this something was said concerning Carter's Books being destroyed. The Draging Canoe in some part of the Treaty said there was bad people both of his Nation and the Whites. That there was a dark Cloud over that Country. He could vouch that his own Countrymen would not hurt him but was afraid the Northern Indians would, that it was good to have the Path clear and clean, but on hearing what Col. Henderson said about the Land between them and his the said Hendersons Country he (the Draging Canoe) said Stamping his foot on the Ground we give you from this place pointing towards the Kentucky at which the Deponent was displeased because he was acting as a Trustee to purchase the Lands on Watauga (in Conjun[ction] with the said Henderson as to the Expence of the Treaty) of the said Indians [as] he thought the said Company were then getting the Watauga Lands which he then had a promise of from the Indians and had the Goods ready to pay for it. The Deponent saith he is no ways Interested in the said Henderson's purchase. His business at the Treaty was as a Trustee from the Watauga people to buy that Country of them Indians. When the Draging Canoe stampt his foot on the Ground and said he gave up all the Land from that place the Deponent understood that not only the Lands at Watauga which he was about purchasing but the Lands in Carters Valley which borders on Clinch Mountain quite to the Ohio was then given up, and that if he ever obtained them it must be of the said Henderson which was the Cause of his being displeased. He knows nothing of any Deed being signed for these last mentioned Lands tho' he has understood since that the said Henderson did take a Deed for the Land from Watauga quite to the Ohio. The Deponent heard no discourse about a Boundary for these Lands Northward of Holston and on this side Cumberland Mountain except only what the Draging Canoe said when he stampt on the Ground as he was then speaking in behalf of the Nation. The Deponent never heard Colo. Henderson promise them any more Goods, the Indians appeared to be satisfied with what he had given them, and that previously he told them if they did not choose to take them they would still be Friends. The Deponent saith he saw these last mentioned Goods as well as all the others delivered and divided and saw Papers destroyed said to be Carters Book of Accounts against the Indians which he was informed by Colo: Carter amounted to more than £600. The Deponent never heard there was any other bounds read to the Indians than what was in the Deed. The Deponent heard there had been some Claim to this Country by the Northward Indians but that these Indians said it was their Land and what they would to sell it. And farther saith not. CHARLES ROBERSON

The deposition of Joseph Martin relative to a certain claim by virtue of an Indian purchase of Richard Henderson & Co: to a certain tract of Country accounted within the chartered limits of the Commonwealth of Virginia. Deposeth and saith that in the year

1769 he was on the North West side Cumberland Mountain on Cumberland River when eight Indians came to his Camp who called themselves Cherokees and he since knows one of them to be a Cherokee, which said they had orders from Cameron to rob all white people they found hunting on their Lands, and that they must take the deponents Gun with seven others that was in Company with him. The Deponent answered that it was not their Lands, that it was Lands their brother King George had purchased of the Northward Indians at which they said eight Indians seemed very Angry, and said it was their Lands, and if the Deponent and his Company was cross they would tie them and take them to Cameron at the Cherokee Towns. They then took several Rifles from said deponents Company with other Articles. The Deponent further saith he has heard of other persons being robbed in that part of the Country. That this deponent in the Year 1769. made an agreement with Doctr. Thomas Walker for a large body of Land in Powells Valley in which agreement Doctr. Walker excepted a certain Mill seat Plantation near Cumberland Gap. That shortly after Colo. Henderson made his Indian purchase he the said deponent sent word to Doctr: Walker he had an opportunity to secure his Mill seat place. In Answer to which Message Doctr. Walker wrote a Letter in which was Words to this effect. "That he was much obliged to Mr. Martin for securing him his place and to inquire of the said Henderson & Co: on what terms they would sell their Lands, and that if he had proper encouragement he would erect a Mill by the time Corn was fit to Grind." That the said Deponent hath made several Entries of Land with said Henderson & Co: to the amount of ten thousand Acres or thereabouts which he made a Conditional agreement for, with the said Proprietors and that he is not further interested in the said purchase made by Richard Henderson & Co. from the Indians. And this deponent further saith not. JOS MARTIN

The Deposition of Thomas Houghton relative to a certain Claim by virtue of an Indian purchase of Richard Henderson & Co: to a certain tract of Country accounted to be within the Chartered limits of the Commonwealth of Virginia. He the said Thomas Houghton deposeth and saith that he was at the Treaty held by the said Richard Henderson & Company with the Cherokee Indians at Watauga in March 1775 though he did not constantly attend the Conferences. From the Interpretation of the Indian discourses the Deponent believed the said Company did purchase a Tract of Country of these Indians the bounds of which he does not well remember though he thinks it bordered on the Ohio and the Kentucky. That in the Course of the Treaty Col. Henderson told the Indians he did not want to walk upon their Land to his Country. That he had yet more Goods and Ammunition. That he wanted a path to his Country, and that from the manner of the Indians pointing he understood they gave up the path Col. Henderson asked for. That he heard one Deed read at the request of the Indians as far as the end of the boundary line of the Land, that then he stepped off and never knew that the latter part of the Deed or any other Deed was read. That he was a Subscribing Witness to the Deeds and saw Oconostoto, the Raven and Little Carpenter sign them, and that he understood they were to sign in behalf of their Nation. That whenever he was present he observed there were more Men by that understood the Indian Language then Vann the Interpreter, whom he understood were to take notice that what either party said was fairly translated. That he saw the Goods distributed and that the Indians appeared to be satisfied. That he is no ways interested in the said Companys purchase; and has no reason to judge it was held any otherwise than fairly and openly. That he remembers there were several subscribing Witnesses among whom were Tilman Dixon and Castleton Brooks, and further saith not. THO. HOUGHTON

The deposition of Richard Callaway, as taken in the absence of Mr. Henderson. The said Richard Callaway farther deposeth and saith by way of explication to his former deposition on the same subject, that by the Country called Transylvania he understands a Country distinct and separate from Virginia: that he doth not recollect the form of the Deed under which he holds his land in that Country, farther than that there was a Warranty contained therein from the agent of the Company and all claiming under them. That the object of the Transylvania convention was no other than by some regulations by them to be established to prevent the wanton destruction of Game, to oblige the people to cultivate the lands, and to preserve order amongst them, but that he considered Mr. Henderson making his assent necessary to render the regulations they made obligatory, was assuming some part of the legislative power. That the convention was convened at the instance of Mr. Henderson to whom such a step had been recommended by this Deponent: that this Deponent knows not, whether any Writs were issued for electing the Delegates to that convention; that the convention chose Mr. Thomas Slaughter for their Speaker: that this deponent knows of no second house of legislature being constituted, except as far as

Mr. Henderson may be considered as such from acting as abovementioned, that all regulations made in the convention were presented to Mr. Henderson for his assent; but this Deponent knows, that no vote passed for excluding dissenters from the Church of England from setling in the Country or taking up lands: that this Deponent hath never heard that Mr. Henderson and Company or the Convention appointed or proposed to send a Delegate or Delegates to the American congress, nor that any such were sent, or application made to Congress to receive one: that the Surveyor General was elected by the Convention and the deputy surveyors appointed by him: that this Deponent believes the Magistrates were appointed by Mr. Henderson, but does not recollect the stile of their Commissions: that the Magistrates took certain Oaths of Office, which were administered to them by the first in the Commission and afterwards by some of them to him: that this Deponent was a Justice of the peace for the town of Boonsborough: that there were no settlers on these Lands at the time of Hendersons purchase: that the Ammunition, mentioned to have been furnished by Mr. Henderson to the settlers, was, as this Deponent has reason to believe, not paid for by them, but that part of the Salt, as he believes, was paid for by them, tho' this deponent received some from the said Henderson, for which he paid nothing: that this Deponent has never heard Oconostoto or any of the Cherokee Chiefs declare, that they had been imposed upon by Mr. Henderson, in respect to the sale of these lands, or deny having sold him the land he claims, but that at the late treaty at long Island he heard among the white people that they had said so: that this Deponent has heard, that military Commissions have been issued by Mr. Henderson, but does not know the substance, or stile of them, as he bore never an one himself: That this Deponent understood from Oconostoto's Expression, that concerning Henderson not suffering his people to hunt or catch the cray fish in the branches, that Oconostoto thereby acknowledged that he had sold the land to Henderson. RICHD: CALLAWAY

NB. This supplementary deposition was taken (before us) in the absence of Mr. Henderson, who consented to any Additions, that Mr. Callaway might choose to make.

Transylvania Sct.

R H Richard Henderson, Thomas Hart Nathl. Hart John Williams, John Luttrell, William Johnston, James Hogg, David Hart and Leonard Hendley Bullock Esqrs. true and absolute Proprietors of the Colony of

Transylvania To John Lythe, James Douglas, Valentine Harmon, John Grayson, Joseph Bowman, and John Jackson Esqrs: Greeting. On recommendation of the Delegates for the Town of Harrodsburgh, and by virtue of the powers and Authority by which we are invested, We do ordain Constitute and appoint the said John Lythe, James Duglass, Valentine Harmon, James Grayson, Joseph Bowman, and John Jackson Esqrs. Consovators of Peace and Judges of the Inferior Court of Record within the Town of Harrodsburgh and the District thereunto belonging, and full Power Exercising the said Authority, according to the directions of an Act of the Colony Convention of Transylvania pass'd at Boonsburgh the 23d. day of May last, You the said John Lythe, James Duglass, Valentine Harmon, John Grayson, Joseph Bowman, and John Jackson Esqrs: first taking the Oaths for the Qualification of Justices or Consovators of the Peace and Judges of the Inferior Court of Record prescribed by the aforesaid Act, Given under our hands at Boonsburgh this 5th day of June 1775.

RICHD. HENDERSON
NATHL HART
JOHN LUTTRELL

Tr (DLC); 55 p., in clerk's hand, with a few notations in hand of TJ and two extracts from Journals of the House of Delegates in hand of John Tazewell, dated 19 and 24 Nov. 1777 (see below). Without date. Some of these depositions relating to Henderson's treaty with the Cherokees at Sycamore Shoals in Mch. 1775 (together with a few not in this transcript) are printed in CVSP, I, 282-311; the dates given there indicate that the depositions were taken at intervals from Apr. 1777 to Oct. 1778. Present in the transcript but omitted here are: (1) Memorial of Richard Henderson, Thomas Hart, Nathaniel Hart, John Williams, William Johnston, John Luttrell, James Hogg, David Hart, and Leonard Hendley Bullock, presented to the Virginia Convention 15 June 1776 (printed in *Conv. Jour.*, May 1776, 1816 edn., p. 51-3); (2) the Convention's order of 4 July 1776 appointing commissioners to take evidence on this and other claims made under purchases from the Indians (same, p. 83-4); (3) two orders of the House of Delegates, 19 and 24 Nov. 1777, reviving the Henderson claim and ordering it to be heard in June 1778 (JHD, Oct. 1777, 1827 edn., p. 34, 41).

For the background of the Transylvania or Henderson claim see not only the Editorial Note to this sequence of documents but also that for the Bills for Dividing Fincastle County, 15 and 26 Oct. 1776. At some undetermined time TJ began preparing a detailed abstract of the present document. In DLC: TJ Papers, 3: 343 is a closely written summary of the depositions of Farrar, Patrick Henry, Price, and Lewis, with one or two remarks on Henderson's memorial: "Art. 7. They say they have no vote or right of representation in this assembly—ergo they consider as different stat [. . . .] 10th. They deny intending separate governments." The summary breaks off on the verso of this page in the midst of Lewis' testimony. Quite possibly TJ discontinued his study of the evidence after the postponement of May 1778, when he became deeply engaged in the work of revising the laws; and presumably he did not report to the Assembly until after the Transylvania question had been virtually settled, making it unnecessary for him to continue his abstracting. Another fragment of notes by TJ on the subject of the Henderson claim survives. It is in DLC: TJ Papers, 2: 229, and reads as follows: "Our charte[r . . . b]oundary Northwd. N. Carolina fixes Southwd. boundary @ 36½°. All between this our assumed territory. Regular mode of obtaining & granting to wit: first buy of Indians. 2dly. appropriate by pat. from crown. They insist on treaty at Lochabar 1770. & Donaldson's line. Urge their applicns. to memb. of Congress. If the parties underst\d. their purchase to be in Virga. & to be part of the Comw. as they say, why did they not record their deed according to act of ass."

[1] I.e., Robertson.

[2] Brackets in MS.

Draft of a Bill to Give the Articles of Confederation the Force of Law

[After 15 December 1777]

Whereas certain articles of confederation and perpetual union were on the day of last proposed by Congress to be entered into between the states of New-Hampshire, Massachusetts-bay, Rhode island and Providence plantations, Connecticut, New York, New Jersey, Pennsylva, Delaware, Maryland, Virginia, N. Carolina, S. Carolina, and Georgia,[1] in these words following to wit 'Article I. the stile &c. here insert the whole instrument which said articles have been approved of by the assembly of this commonwealth who have authorized and instructed their delegates to attend in Congress on or before the 10th. day of March next to ratify the same, in the name and on the behalf of this Commonwealth and it may be found that sundry of our laws formed before the ratification of the said Articles of Confederation, may in some instances be contradictory to and inconsistent with the said articles or some of them, and tho' it will be proper on revising these laws for the committee heretofore appointed for that purpose to render the same conformable to the said articles, yet in the mean time judges and others may be at a loss how to determine between them. Be it therefore enacted by the General assembly that so soon as the said articles of confederation shall be ratified in Congress by each and every of the states of New Hampshire, Massachusett's bay &c. the same shall be construed to have the force of a law within this commonwealth, and to repeal so much of all laws passed before such ratification as shall be found to be contradictory to the said articles of confederation or any part of them.

Dft (DLC); in TJ's hand; mutilated, part of the endorsement being torn away. Endorsed: "giving [the force] of a law to the articles of Confederation & perpetual union proposed to be entered into between the several states of America." Undated, but after 15 Dec. 1777.

On 15 Dec. 1777 the House of Delegates passed resolutions authorizing and directing the Virginia delegates in Congress to ratify the Articles of Confederation (JHD, Oct. 1777, 1827 edn., p. 80). The Senate unanimously agreed to the resolution on 16 Dec. (same, p. 81; see also TJ to John Adams, 17 Dec. 1777). There is no evidence that TJ's proposed

Bill was ever introduced or acted upon.

[1] Deleted in draft: "and approved of by this assembly to which the house of delegates by their resolution of the fifteenth and the Senate by the   of this present month and." Though this conclusively proves that TJ's proposed Bill was drawn up after 15 Dec. 1777, probably immediately thereafter, it is curious that he should have left blank the date that Congress proposed the Articles to the various states, since the resolution of 15 Dec. specifically referred to that proposal as having been made "the 17th day of November last."

Bill for Dissolving the Vestries of the Parishes of Meherrin and St. Anne

[16 December 1777]

Whereas it hath been represented to this present general assembly, that by the death and resignation of sundry members of the *vestries* of Meherrin parish, in the county of Brunswick, *and of the parish of St. Anne, in the county of Albemarle*, there is not a sufficient number of members to hold a vestry *in either of the said parishes*, by which means the business of the *same* hath been for a considerable time unsettled: Be it therefore enacted by the General Assembly, That from and after the passing of this act the *said vestries shall be* dissolved; and the sheriff of the county of Brunswick is hereby required to summon the freeholders of the *said parish of Meherrin*, and others entitled to vote, to meet at Randall's ordinary, in the said parish, on the second day of March next, *and the sheriff of the county of Albemarle, in the like manner, to summon the freeholders, and others entitled to vote in the said parish of St. Anne, to meet at the new church upon Hardware river on the same day*, then and there to choose twelve of the most able and discreet persons *of their respective parishes to be a vestry for the said parishes respectively.*

The *vestries* so chosen, after taking an oath of fidelity to this commonwealth, shall proceed to regulate and settle the business of *their respective parishes*, and shall have full power and authority to levy all salaries or arrears of salaries due to the *incumbents* of the said parishes before the first day of January last, also to assess and levy *such sums of money as shall be* sufficient to enable them to comply with their parochial engagements before that date, and to demand and recover of any collector or collectors all arrears of money or tobacco due to the said parishes and put into their hands to collect, *and to do any other act which the said vestries hereby dissolved might by law have respectively done had they continued full and undissolved.*

Hening, IX, 442-3. MS (Vi) in an unidentified hand, accompanied by two pages of amendments in TJ's hand. MS endorsed: "A Bill for dissolving the Vestry of the Parish of Meherrin in the County of Brunswick." Docketed, partly in hand of John Tazewell: "Decr. 16. 1777. Read the first Time. Decr. 22. Read the second time & commd. to Mr. [Henry] Tazewell Mr. McLin [Macklin] Mr. Jefferson. Decr. 24th to be engrossed." (Printed text is employed in order to indicate more clearly TJ's revisions of the Bill, which are also italicized for the same purpose.)

This Bill, as introduced on 16 Dec. 1777 by Henry Tazewell of Brunswick (and perhaps drawn by him, since it concerned a vestry in the county he represented), provided only for the dissolution of the vestry of Meherrin parish. On the second reading, however, it was referred to a new committee which included TJ and the committee was instructed to include in the Bill a clause or clauses for dissolving the parish of St. Anne in Albemarle county. This fact, together with the list of amendments in TJ's hand, makes it certain that the enlargement of the Bill was due to his prompting (JHD, Oct. 1777, 1827 edn., p. 78, 81, 87, 91, 96). See TJ's Testimonial concerning Charles Clay, 15 Aug. 1779.

Bill for Dividing the Counties of Augusta and Botetourt

[16 December 1777 to 12 January 1778]

[Whereas][1] it is represented to this present Session of Assembly by the Inhabitants of Augusta and Botetourt Counties that they labour under great Inconveniencies by Reason of the great Extent of the said Counties and Parishes Be it therefore enacted by the General Assembly that from and after the first Day of February next the said County and Parish of Augusta shall be divided by a Line beginning at the North side of the North Mountain opposite to the upper End of Sweedland Hill and running a direct course so as to strike the Mouth of Senaca Creek on the North Fork of the south Branch of Potowmack River and the same course continued to the Allegany Mountain thence along the said Mountain to the Line of Hampshire County and all that part of the said County and Parish of Augusta which lies to the Northward of the said Line shall be added to and made part of the said County and Parish of Hampshire and that the Residue of the County and Parish of Augusta be divided by a Line to begin at the South Mountain and running thence by Benjamin Yardley's Plantation so as to strik the North River below James Bairds House, thence up the said River to the Mouth of Naked Creek, thence leaving the River and running a direct course so as to Cross the said River at the Mouth of Cunningham's Branch in the upper End of Silas Harts Land, to the Foot of the North Mountain thence North fifty five Degrees West to the Allegany Mountain and with the same to the Line of Hampshire and all that part which lies North Eastward of the said Line shall be one distinct County and Parish and called and known by the name of Rockingham. And be it further enacted that from and after the said first Day of February the said County and Parish of Botetourt shall be divided by a Line beginning on the Top of the Ridge which divides the Eastern from the Western Waters where the Line between Augusta and Botetourt Crosses the same and running thence the same course continued North fifty five Degrees West to the Ohio thence beginning at the said Ridge at the said Lines of Botetourt and Augusta and running along the Top of the said Ridge passing the Sweet Springs to the Top of Peter's Mountain thence along the said Mountain to the Line of Montgomrie County thence along the same Mountain to the Kanhawa or new River thence down the said River to the Ohio. And all that part of the said County and Parish between and to the Westward of the said Lines shall be one distinct County and Parish and be called and known by the name of Green Brier. And be it further enacted that the remaining parts of the said Counties and Parishes of Augusta and Botetourt be divided into three Counties and Parishes as follows to wit, by a Line beginning on the Top of the Blue Ridge near Steels Mill and running thence North fifty five Degrees West passing the said Mill and crossing the North Mountain to the Top of the Calf Pasture Mountain thence along the said Ridge to the Line of Botetourt County thence North fifty five Degrees West to the Ridge dividing the Eastern from the Western Waters; and that the remaining Part of the said County of Botetourt be divided by a Line to begin at said Audley Paul's and running thence south fifty five Degrees East to the Top of the Blue Ridge thence along the same to the Beginning of the aforesaid Line dividing Augusta County. Thence begining again at the said Audley Pauls and running North fifty five Degrees West to the Allegany Mountain and along the same to the aforesaid Line dividing Augusta County and all those parts of the said Counties and Parishes of Augusta and Botetourt included within the said Lines shall be one distinct County [and] Parish and shall be called and known by the name of Rock Bridge, and all the remaining Parts of the said Counties and Parishes of Augusta and Botetourt shall each of them respectively be a distinct County and Parish and retain their respective names and for the Administration of Justice in the said Counties of Rockingham Green Brier and Rock Bridge after the commencement thereof a Court for every of them shall be held therein, for the County of Rockingham on the fourth Monday in every Month for the County of Green Brier on the third Tuesday in every Month and for the County of Rock Bridge on the first Tuesday in every Month, the first Court for the said County of Rockingham to be held at the House of Daniel Smith, for the said County of Green Brier at John Stewarts for the said County of Rock Bridge at Samuel Wallace's. And the Justices of the said Courts respectively or a Major part of them being present and having taken the Oaths required by Law and Administered the Oaths of office to the Sherifs every of the said Courts shall fix on a place for holding Courts in their Counties at or as near the Centres as the situation and convenience thereof will admit of, and shall thence forth proceed to erect the necessary Publick Buildings at such places and shall also appoint such places for holding Courts in the mean time untill such Buildings shall be compleated as they shall think fit, and shall have power to adjourn themselves to such places as they shall appoint and after the Publick Buildings shall be compleated the Courts for the said Counties shall thenceforth be held at such places.

And be it further enacted that it shall be lawful for the Governor or in his absence for the President with the advice of the Council to appoint a person in every of the said Counties to be the first Sherif thereof, and the Sherifs of the said Counties of Augusta, Botetourt and Montgomery shall have power to Collect and distrain for any Publick dues or fees which may remain unpaid by the Inhabitants of the Counties of Rockingham Green Brier and Rock Bridge and that part of the County of Augusta which is added to Hampshire and that part of the County of Montgomery which is added to Green Brier at the Time of their taking place and shall be answerable for them in the same manner as if this Act had never been made. And in all future Elections of Senators the said Counties of Rockingham and Green Brier shall be of the same districts of which the County they are taken from now are and the County of Rock Bridge shall be of the same district that the County of Augusta now is. And be it further enacted that at the place which shall be appointed for holding Courts in the said County of Rock Bridge there shall be laid off a Town to be called Lexington thirteen hundred feet in length and nine hundred in Width, and in order to make satisfaction to the proprietors of the said Land the Clerk of the said County shall by order of the Justice Issue a Writ directed to the Sherif Commanding him to Summon twelve able and disinterested freeholders to meet on the said Land on a certain Day not under five nor over ten days from the date who shall upon Oath Value the said Land in so many Parcels as their shall be Seperate

Owners which Valuation the Sherif shall return under the hands and Seals of the said Jurors to the Clerks Office and the Justices at laying their first County Levy shall make Provision for paying the said proprietors their respective proportions thereof and the property of the said Land shall on the return of such Valuation become vested in the Justices and their Successors one acre thereof to be reserved for the use of the said County and the residue to be sold and conveyed by the said Justices to any Persons and the money arising from such Sale to be applied towards lessening the County Levy and the Publick Buildings for the said County shall be erected on the Lands reserved as aforesaid. And Whereas many suits and Petitions are now depending before the Courts of Augusta and Botetourt in which the Process have not been executed on the Defendants who after the said Divisions will reside in the Counties of Rockingham Green Brier and Rock Bridge and in many other cases in Augusta County the Process have been executed but no proceedings have yet been had in Court and in which the Parties after the said Division will both reside in the said County of Rockingham. Be it therefore enacted that the Clerks of the said County of Botetourt in the first, and the Clerk of the said County of Augusta in each of the cases before mentioned shall make out a Docket of all such Suits and Petitions in their respective Courts and deliver the same to the Clerks of the said Counties of Rockingham Green Brier and Rock Bridge respectively together with all Papers filed therein and a Copy of all Costs including the Costs of their removal and shall take such Clerks Receipts for the same and thereupon the Courts of the said Counties shall have Jurisdiction thereof in as full and ample a Manner as if they had been originally Commenced in such Counties and the Courts of the said Counties of Augusta and Botetourt shall have Jurisdiction of all other Actions and Suits now depending therein in the same Manner as if this Act had not been made. Provided that the Clerk of the Court of Augusta may have his Choice of the Clerkships of the said Counties of Augusta and Rockingham and also that the Clerk of the Court of the said County of Botetourt shall have his Choice of the Clerkships of the said Counties of Botetourt and Green Brier but such Election shall be made at the first Court to be held for such Counties as they shall make Choice of and an Entry made thereof on the Records of the said Courts. And where no such Elections shall be made at such first Courts the Justices of the said Counties of Rockingham and Green Brier shall every of them appoint a Clerk of the Peace. Provided also that no appointments of Clerks of the Peace or of

Places for holding Courts shall be made unless a Majority of the Justices be present, if such Majority shall have been prevented from attending by unavoidable Accidents but in such cases the Appointments shall be postponed till the next Court Day and so on from Court Day to Court Day as often as such Accidents shall happen. And Whereas several of the Vestry of the Parish of Augusta will by the Division be taken into new Parishes whereby it is necessary to dissolve the said Vestry and the Inhabitants of the Parish of Botetourt having failed to elect a Vestry agreeable to an Act of Assembly in that case made and Provided. Be it therefore enacted that the Vestry of the said Parish of Augusta be and the same is hereby dissolved. And be it further enacted that the Inhabitants of every of the said Parishes of Rockingham, Augusta, Rockbridge, Botetourt, and Green Brier respectively shall meet at some convenient Times and Places to be appointed and publickly advertised by the Sherifs of the said Counties before the first Day of May next and then and there elect twelve able and discreet persons who shall be a Vestry for the said Parishes respectively but the Collectors of the Parishes of Augusta Botetourt and Montgomery respectively shall have power to Collect and distrain for any dues which shall remain unpaid by the Inhabitants of the said Parishes of Rockingham, Rockbridge, Green Brier and that part of Augusta Parish added to Hampshire and that part of the Parish of Montgomery which is added to Green Brier at the time of the Division's taking Place and shall be answerable for the same in like Manner as if this Act has never been made. And for altering the Court Day of the County of Dunmore and changing the name of the said County. Be it enacted that from and after the first Day of February next, the said County shall be called and known by the name of Shannandoe and that the Courts for the said County of Shannandoe shall be constantly held on the last Thursday in every Month.

And be it further enacted that the Court of the said County of Shannandoe shall have Jurisdiction of all matters and Suits now depending before the Court of Dunmore County, and all Officers Civil and Military within the same shall have power to execute their respective Offices in the said County of Shannandoe in the same manner as if this Act had never been made.

MS (Vi); in clerk's hand, with notation by TJ as indicated below in note 1 and also with interlineations in hand of John Tazewell. Endorsed in clerk's hand: "A Bill For dividing the Counties of Augusta & Botetourt and for other Purposes." Docketed in the hand of Tazewell: "1777. Decr. 16. Read the first time. 17. Read the second Time & commd. to Mr. Bowyer. Mr. Lockhart.

Mr. Poag. Mr. Harrison of C. C. [Charles City] Mr. Carter. Mr. Jefferson. Mr. Neaville. Mr. Hite. Mr. Montgomery. to be engrossed." Another MS (Vi); in clerk's hand, with blank spaces left throughout for names of places and for dates.

The situation presented by this Bill is comparable in many respects to the involved legislative history of the Bills to Divide Fincastle County (q.v., under date of 15 and 16 Oct. 1776). This legislation no doubt arose from the "great Inconveniencies" presented to the western inhabitants in attending courts and general musters at distant county seats, but there is also no doubt that the matter of creating new counties, and thereby increasing representation of the western region in the General Assembly, brought on internal conflicts of a sectional nature comparable to those reflected on a larger scale upon the question of admission of new states to the Union. TJ led the western "party" in forcing the Fincastle County division in 1776 and there is evidence that he led the fight over the division of Botetourt and Augusta the succeeding year. The petitions from the western areas included the following: (1) one from inhabitants of parts of Augusta and Botetourt counties asking to be set off into a distinct county; (2) one from Botetourt asking for a division of the county; (3) one from Augusta asking for a division of the county; (4) several from Washington and Montgomery complaining about the boundaries established in the Bills for Dividing Fincastle County; (5) one from Montgomery county praying that a portion of that county be annexed to the northwest corner of Botetourt; (6) one from Augusta praying that a part of that county be annexed to Hampshire; (7) several from Bedford and Henry counties asking for the creation of a new county. To most of these there were counter-petitions. All were referred to the Committee on Propositions and Grievances, of which TJ was a member. It is impossible to reconstruct the history of all this recommended and protested legislation, but it is obvious that the conflict was intense and that the ultimate outcome was often in doubt. For example, on 8 Nov. the Committee succeeded in gaining the postponement of consideration of some of the troublesome petitions to the next session of Assembly; this was, of course, a victory for the eastern "party." On 9 Dec. (the whole subject was constantly agitated in the intervening month) the Committee came in with recommendations which far exceeded what the western representatives were able to achieve in the Bill here presented: it recommended that Montgomery be divided and that a new county be formed out of Bedford and Henry. On 10 Dec. the House directed the Committee to prepare bills in accord with these and other recommendations, but the final enactment, of course, did not include those parts of Montgomery, Bedford, and Henry referred to.

On 16 Dec. Nicholas presented a bill from the Committee for dividing the counties of Augusta and Botetourt. It was read the second time on 17 Dec. and committed to a new committee composed of those whose names are given above; this Bill, apparently, was the one authorized on 10 Dec. On 24 Dec. TJ reported for the committee (he was not its chairman) that the bill should be amended. The "amendment" in this case was precisely similar in method to that of the Fincastle County Bills: it was to the effect that everything after the initial word "Whereas" should be struck out and an entire new bill be substituted. The Bill with this "amendment" immediately passed its second reading and was ordered to be engrossed. On 27 Dec. it was passed by the House and its title changed to "An Act for forming several new counties, and reforming the boundaries of two others." TJ carried the Bill to the Senate the same day. The Senate amended the Bill in important particulars and disagreed to others. (For the legislative history of these petitions and committee reports, &c., see JHD, Oct. 1777, 1827 edn., p. 6, 13, 14, 15, 16, 17, 18, 29, 33, 37, 43, 44, 46, 47, 61, 62, 65, 76, 80, 81, 84, 91, 93, 107, 111-12 [the amendments offered by Senate are printed at p. 111-12], 113.) The text of the Act as adopted is in Hening, IX, 420-4.

1 The initial word "Whereas" has been erased, and above it TJ wrote: "leave out from the word 'Whereas' & add [the following]." This is the "amendment" referred to above.

Bill Indemnifying the Executive for Removing and Confining Suspected Persons

[16-26 December 1777]

Whereas on the late appearance of a hostile Fleet in the Bay of Chesapeake, a large Body of Militia were collected and arrayed, and to prevent the dangerous Consequences which might have been produced by a Communication of Intelligence, to the Enemy, it became necessary for the Governor and Council, for the public safety, to remove and restrain, during the Imminence of the Danger, at a Distance from the Ports and Encampments of the said Militia, and from other places near the Ports and Harbours of this Commonwealth, certain persons whose affections to the American Cause were suspected and more especially such as had refused to give assurance of Fidility and allegiance to the Commonwealth, according to the Act of Assembly for that purpose made and provided; And it may happen that some of the said persons, so removed and restrained, may be dispossed to vex with Actions at Law those who were concerned in advising issuing or Executing the Orders for that purpose. Be it therefore enacted by the General Assembly, that the Governor, Members of the Council, and all others concerned in advising, issuing or executing the said Orders for the removal or Restraint of such persons, stand indemnified, and clearly exonerated from all Actions, Suits, and Damages, on Account thereof: And that if any Action or Suit should be brought by, or on behalf of any person, so removed or restrained for the recovery of Damages for such removal or restraint, against any person or persons so indemnified, the Defendant or Defendants may plead the General Issue, and give this Act in Evidence.

MS (Vi), in clerk's hand. Endorsed: "A Bill for indemnifying the Governor & Council & others for removing & Confining suspected persons during the late Public Danger." Docketed, partly in hand of John Tazewell: "1777. Decr. 22d. Read the first Time. Decr. 24th. Read a second time & to be engrossed."

This Bill, suggestive of a similar control of private citizens exercised for military purposes during World War II, was drawn by a committee of which TJ was a member; what part he may have had in it is not known. It was introduced 22 Dec. 1777 by Carter, read the second time on 24 Dec., and passed on 26 Dec. Apparently there was no debate or amendment (JHD, Oct. 1777, 1827 edn., p. 81, 88, 90, 92). The Act as adopted is in Hening, IX, 373-4. (See notes to Bill to Attaint Josiah Philips, 28 May 1778.)

To John Adams

Dear Sir Wmsbgh. Dec. 17. 1777.

Congress will receive by this post our approbation of the Confederation. It passed the house of Delegates on Monday and the Senate on Tuesday last. Tho' our house of delegates is almost wholly of those who are truly zealous, yet there have ever been a few who have endeavored to throw obstructions in our way. Objections to this important instrument came therefore not unexpectedly. The most difficult articles however were surmounted by the spirit of the house, determined to secure if possible the union of the states. One objection only, stuck with them. It was urged that by the 9th. article reserving to congress a power 'of entering into treaties and alliances' with the proviso immediately following that they should not give to foreigners an exemption from such imposts as should be paiable by natives; the congress would have the whole regulation of our trade, and consequently might grant a monopoly of it: and it was intimated that such a measure had been in contemplation; and might be given away by those states, which have no staple, as the price of commercial privileges to them. Some warm members kindled at this idea, and all seemed to be struck with it. The advocates however for the confederation insisted that Congress would have no such power by the confederation: that a power to treat, did not include ex vi termini a power to pass away every thing by treaty which might be the subject of a treaty; and consequently no more gave such power over our commerce than over every thing else; that the inference from the proviso was merely an *implication* and that congress were by that instrument to derive no powers by implication or construction, but such only (art. 2) as were *expressly* delegated to them: that by the 2d proviso in the same 9th. clause allowing each legislature to prohibit the exportation of any article to all places, an inference arose in our favor that we might prohibit it to certain places, and consequently to the very place making title to the monopoly: that it appeared Congress themselves did not suppose these words gave them so very ample a power over trade, because in a subsequent part they reserve in express terms a right of regulating our trade with the Indians. This reasoning removed the difficulty and satisfied the house that the instrument would give to congress no such powers. Yet there remains a great anxiety that an article so important should not be laid down in more express terms, and so as to exclude all possible doubt; and a fear that at some future day such a power should be assumed. As I am myself of opinion the instrument gives no such powers, I naturally conclude congress had them not in contemplation, and consequently that they would have no objections to pass an explanatory vote declaring that the Confederation will give them no such powers. If the confirming in their affections an assembly which have ever witnessed the highest respect for congress, would be an object with them, I know nothing which would produce that effect more powerfully than such vote passed before the final ratification of the instrument. Knowing your candour I have taken the liberty of mentioning this subject to you, that if you should think it worthy your attention you may favor it with the assistance of your abilities.

I greatly fear your requisition of money by quarterly paiments will be impracticable here. Our counties are so large that an annual collection is as much as we ever attempted to complete. Our people too are quite unaccustomed to be called on oftener than once a year. We are proceeding to make good our numbers in the feild by a draught. I am Dr. Sir with every sentiment of esteem Your friend & servt., TH: JEFFERSON

RC (Adams Manuscript Trust, Boston). Addressed: "To The Honorable John Adams esq. of the Massachusetts delegation at York-town Pennsylvania"; corrected in another hand to read "at Boston," with James Lovell's frank added. Endorsed: ". . . forwarded with a Note by Lovell Jas. Decr 30th 1777."

Before this letter arrived at York Adams had proceeded northward to embark as American commissioner to France; he sailed 13 Feb. 1778 (DAB). Virginia was the first state to signify its APPROBATION OF THE CONFEDERATION; the Articles had been adopted by Congress on 15 Nov., and Virginia ratified by a simple resolution of each house of its Assembly on 15 and 16 Dec. (JCC, IX, 907; JHD, Oct. 1777, 1827 edn., p. 80-1); see also TJ's Draft of a Bill printed under 15 Dec. 1777. That TJ, despite this prompt ratification, should have set forth the views and fears of the opposition so fully is evidence that TJ himself was deeply concerned lest Congress incline toward the doctrine of implied powers (see also his "strict constructionist" comments on Franklin's Proposed Articles of Confederation, June-July 1775).

Act to Empower the Justices
of Cumberland and Fluvanna Counties to Appoint New Places for Holding Their Courts

[*Williamsburg, 24 Dec. 1777.*] Act repeals Act of preceding session directing justices of Cumberland to lay off a town called Effingham where the courthouse was to be located; petitions both from Cumberland and Fluvanna request that Assembly authorize justices to "re-consider their said appointments" of places for the respective courthouses. The Act also repeals that part of the Act of the previous session creating the town of Effingham, since petitions from Cumberland request that it "not be laid off." Justices of both Cumberland and Fluvanna directed to Assembly on fourth Monday in Mch. 1778 and fix places near the center of respective counties for courthouses, pillories, prisons, stocks, &c.

MS not located. Text from Hening, IX, 437-8.

As originally introduced, this Bill pertained only to Cumberland co. At its second reading, 24 Dec. 1777, it was committed to a committee composed of Randolph, Carrington, TJ, and Bullitt. At the same time, most probably at TJ's motion, the committee were instructed to incorporate a clause or clauses pursuant to a resolution of 4 Dec. made by the Committee on Propositions and Grievances. That resolution was to the effect that the petition of inhabitants of Fluvanna county asking for permission to fix the courthouse in a more convenient location was reasonable. The House had directed the Committee of Propositions and Grievances to prepare a bill for this purpose, but no such bill had been reported. The committee appointed on 24 Dec. then amended the Bill so as to apply both to Cumberland and Fluvanna, reporting the amending Bill on 1 Jan., when the amendments were read the second time and the Bill ordered to be engrossed. It was passed on 3 Jan. (JHD, Oct. 1777, 1827 edn., p. 56, 89, 95, 98). Since TJ had had a part in the establishment of Fluvanna county (see Petition from Some Inhabitants of Albemarle County, under date of 12 May 1777), it is probable that the amendments offered to the Cumberland Bill were his. The location of the courthouse was not the only issue that disturbed the people of the new county of Fluvanna: scarcely had the session of Assembly opened in Oct. 1777 when a petition was received from Fluvanna claiming that the office of clerk of court had been purchased by one John Cobb for £250 (same, p. 7).

Bill concerning Inoculation for Smallpox

[27 December 1777]

Whereas the Small-pox, at this time in many parts of the Commonwealth is likely to spread and become general, and it hath been proved by incontestible experience that the late discovery's and Improvements therein have produced great Benefits to Mankind, by rendering a Distemper, which taken in the common way is always dangerous and often fatal, comparatively mild and safe by Inoculation, and the Act for regulating the Inoculation of the small-pox having been found, in many Instances, inconvenient and Injurious makes it necessary that the same shou'd be amended: Be it therefore enacted by the General Assembly, that any person having first obtained in writing to be attested by two Witnesses, the Consent of a Majority of the housekeepers residing within two miles and not separated by a River or Creek half a mile wide[1] and conforming to the following Rules and regulations, may Inoculate or be Inoculated for the small-pox, either in his or her own house, or at any other place. No Patient in the small pox shall remove from the House where He or She shall have the Distemper, or shall go abroad into the Company of any person who hath not before had the small-pox or been Inoculated, or go into any Public Road where Travellers usually pass, without retiring out of the same, or giving notice, upon the Approach of any passenger, until such Patient hath recovered from the Distemper, and hath been so well cleansed in his or her person and Cloths as to be perfectly free from Infection, under the Penalty of forty shillings for every offence; to be recovered, if committed by a married Woman from her Husband, if by an Infant from the Parent or Guardian, and if by a Servant or Slave from the Master or Mistress.

Every Physician, Doctor or other person, undertaking Inoculation at any House, shall cause a Written Advertisement to be put up at the nearest public Road, or other most notorious adjacent place, giving information that the small pox is at such House, and shall continue to keep the same set up, so long as the Distemper or any Danger of Infection remains there under the Penalty of forty shillings for every day that the same shall be omitted or neglected; to be paid by the Physician or Doctor, if the offence shall be committed when He is present, or by the Master, Mistress, Manager or principal person of the Family respectively, if the offence is committed in the absence of the Physician or Doctor. Every Physician Doctor or other person, undertaking Inoculation at any Public place or Hospital for the Reception of Patients, shall before he discharges the Patients, or suffers them to be removed from thence, take due care that their persons and Cloths are sufficiently cleansed, and shall give such Patients respectively a Certificate under his hand, that in his Opinion they are free from all Danger of spreading the Infection; under the Penalty of three pounds for every offence; and every person wilfully giving a false Certificate shall be subject to the Penalty of Ten pounds. If any person who hath not had the small-pox, other than those who have been or intended to be inoculated, shall go into any House where the small-pox then is, or intermix with the Patients, and return from thence, any Justice of the Peace of the County, on due proof thereof, may by Warrant cause such person to be conveyed to the next Hospital where the small pox is, there to remain until He or She shall have gone thro' the Distemper, or until the Physician or Manager of the Hospital shall certify that in his Opinion such person can not take the same; And if such person shall not be able to pay the necessary expences, the same shall be paid by the County. Every person wilfully endeavouring to spread or propagate the small pox, without Inoculation, or by Inoculation in any other Manner than is allowed by this Act or by the said recited Act in special Cases shall be subject the Penalty of five hundred pounds, or suffer six Months Imprisonment without Bail or Mainprize. All the Penalties inflicted by this Act may be recovered with Costs by Action of Debt or Information in any Court of Record, where the Sum exceeds five pounds, or where it is under, or amounts to that Sum only by Petition in the Court of the County where the offence shall be committed, and shall be one half to the Informer, and the other half to the Commonwealth, or the whole to the Commonwealth, where prosecution shall be first instituted on the Public behalf alone.

So much of the act of General Assembly intituled "An Act to regulate the Inoculation of the small pox within this Colony" as contains any thing contrary to or within the Purview of this Act, is hereby repealed.

MS (Vi), in clerk's hand. Endorsed: "A Bill to amend an Act intituled an Act to regulate the Inoculation of the small-pox within this Colony." Docketed by John Tazewell: "1778. Jan: 12. Read the first Time. Jan: 14. Read the 2d. time & commd. to Com: of the whole."

To what extent TJ contributed to this Bill cannot be determined, yet it unmistakably bears the impress of his mind and influence. The matter was obviously one of much importance, and the personnel of the committee assigned to bring in a law on the subject indicated the House's awareness of the fact; George Mason was chairman and the other members were Adams, [Edmund?] Pendleton, Nicholas, [Thomas] Nelson [Jr.], Richard Lee, Harrison, Hugh Nelson, and Jefferson. Their duty was to amend the Act of 1769. That Act imposed severe penalties upon any person who imported "any variolous or infectious matter" of the smallpox for the purpose of inoculating (£1,000); created a system of permissive inoculation through licensing by civil authorities, who had full power to refuse a license or, where granted, to establish such restrictions and regulations as they should think necessary and proper; and imposed a penalty of £100 for each offense for anyone inoculating or procuring inoculation without a license (Hening, VIII, 371-4). The severity of the Act and its centralization of control of the disease entirely in the hands of the civil authority must have been repugnant to TJ, who, in 1766, had gone to Philadelphia for the purpose of being inoculated. The preamble of the 1778 Bill stands in strong contrast to the Act of 1769, and part of its opening sentence seems to have an indubitable Jeffersonian ring: "it hath been proved by incontestible experience that the late discovery's and improvements therein have produced great Benefits to Mankind. . . ." This is precisely the sort of argument that TJ employed in 1801 in respect to the then "late discovery" of Jenner concerning vaccination. No member of the committee in charge of drafting this Bill studied the problem of smallpox so earnestly or contributed so much to its solution as TJ did, and, whether he proposed this amending Bill or drafted it, it is fairly certain that he shaped and influenced it in a greater or lesser degree. The committee to which TJ was appointed on 27 Dec. 1777 reported, through George Mason, on 12 Jan. 1778. The Bill then introduced was read the first time; on 14 Jan. it was read the second time and committed to the committee of the whole; on 20 Jan. it was further considered by the committee of the whole and amended; on 22 Jan. it was read the third time and passed; Mason carried the Bill to the Senate (JHD, Oct. 1777, 1827 edn., p. 93, 113, 115, 123, 126). The Act as adopted (Hening, IX, 371-3) follows the text of the Bill precisely except as noted below.

1 The Act reads: "not separated by a river, creek or marsh, a quarter of a mile wide."

From John Harvie

DEAR SIR York Town December the 29th 1777

Your Letter of November the 26th. was handed to me by the post before the last. The great Objects of the Assemblys Deliberations are of the most Interesting Nature and I have no Doubt they will bring them to Maturity with their Usual Wisdom. If the late Generous Spirit of Virginia in their Act for Cloathing and Measures for preventing of Forestalling does not Inspire the other States with a Virtuous Emulation the Avarice of Individuals will be more Fatal to the Liberties of America than the Sword of the Enemy. I have a great while past Shudder'd at the Rapid Strides of this Monster in Society, but lately he has broke through every feeble Fort Oppos'd to him, and threatens us with Inevitable Destruction unless his Carrier is Immediately Check'd by the joint Efforts of the United States. In Short the Avarice and disaffection of the people here is so great that they refuse any price that we can give for the Necessary provisions for the Army, and the Generals last Letter Couch'd in terms Strong and pathetic holds out a probability of the Armys Desolveing unless they are more fully and Constantly Supplied. You would Execrate this State if you were in it. The Supporters of this Government are a set of Weak men without any Weight of Character. No kind of Respect is paid by the people either to their Laws or Advice, and instead of Checking they in many Instances Countenance the Exactions of their Constituents being otherwise fearful of looseing their present Shadow of power. Two thirds of the State of Delaware are Notoriously known in their Hearts to be with our Enemys. They have not at present the Shadow of Government amongst them and their Representation to Congress has been withdrawn a Considerable time before I had a Seat in it. From this you must foresee that these Execrable States Clogg the Operations of the Continent in an Alarming Degree. Then what is to be done? Are we with this Conviction upon our Minds to suffer them for the want of Virtue and Vigour in their Governments to Involve the whole in the Worst of Calamitys or will not Congress be Justifyable (from the Necessity of the Case as Guardians to the Sacred rights of the people at large) in persueing such Measures as will Eventually save this Continent from perdition? The feelings of my own Heart tells me they will. Yet I Revere the Sovereignity of the States and the Civil rights of the people as much as any man liveing who is not Capable of more refin'd and deeper reflections than myself. Such I acknowledge see things of this Dilicate Nature in a more Enlarged Comprehensive point of View and by such I Ardently wish to be Instructed. Indeed my Honored Friend for such I esteem you, the present State and Condition of this Continent, Oweing to the Alarming disaffection in this Quarter, an Almost Universal discontent in the Army, a Reformation therein Meditated by Congress to Commence and be Carry'd into Effect this Winter with Numberless other Matters that I am not at Liberty to disclose even to you, requires the Wisdom of the first Characters amongst us to give them weight and Efficacy. Then why cant some of those who so fully come under this Description be prevail'd upon to give their attendance in Congress if it was only for a few Months? I am sure you know me two well to Impute this Earnestness to Unworthy Motives. It arises from the purest Intentions for the Interests of my Country. It would be Stupid Vanity in me not to be Sensible of my own lack of Abilitys to Constitute a Member of this August Assembly with Reputation to myself and Service to the publick, and other States in part of their Delegation equally Experience this Misfortune.

Your Supply of Cloathing came very Opportunely to Cover the Shivering Limbs of our poor Naked Soldiers. Thousands of them are now in the Hospitals for the want of even Wrags to keep them from the Cold. We hear Two Hundred thousand pounds worth of Goods (at Exorbitant prices) has been purchased in the Masachusets. We hope they will be soon forwarded to the Army.

There is no late Interesting Intelligence from either of our Army's. General Washingtons is now in Forge Valley about twenty three Miles from Philadelphia where they will probably remain Inactive the greatest part of the Winter. The Waste of the Enemy wherever they move is a Scene of Cruelty and distress. This dreadful Calamity is only Alleviated to the Whig by seeing the Torys property made one Common Ruin with his own, for all their late Ravages is Indiscriminate.

It would take a much wiser man than me to Unravel the Misterious Conduct of the French Court. They have not yet given us any publick Avowal of their patronage. Our Commissioners are never Admitted to publick or private Audiencies with their Ministers. What little Business they transact with them is by the Aid of a third person and their Scanty Supplies to us seem to be Conducted with Timidity Caution and Secrecy. Some Weeks past we daily expected to hear that they had taken a dicisive part for us, but our last Letters Advise us Not to be two Sanguine in our Expectations of Foreign Assistance but to place our Security in our own Resources with this only exception that a Capital Advantage over our Enemys in the Feild may give a different Turn to the refin'd politics in Europe and Operate powerfully in our favour. This we have Obtain'd in the Surrender of Burgoyne of which the French Court are now or must Shortly be Acquainted. It is only to you that I Communicate any thing of this Nature that can have the least Tendency to Damp the Ardour or Expectations of our Countrymen.

I have wrote to a gentleman of my Acquaintance in Lancaster to endeavour to find out and procure the Workmen you desire if to be had in that Town, there being none such that will engage in this. I have not received his Answer but have but little expectations from his Enquirys, as a Tradesmans prospects here is not a Moderate Compensation for his Labour. Nothing less than a small Fortune made without Merrit or trouble will Content him. I am told there is amongst the British prisoners in Maryland or Virginia some expert Workmen of the Trades you want. I have written to the Commissary of prisoners to Acquaint me with their Names and the places of their confinement. My design after Obtaining proper Information is to Get a permission from the Board of War for you to Employ such of them as you think proper, which I shall in due time Inclose you. This I think will be the Cheapest and probably the most Convenient way for you to Carry on your Buildings but of this you are the only proper Judge. Drums for our Militia has been an Object of my Enquirys since I first came here. They are not to be had on any Terms whatever. Our State is at present unrepresented, Mr. Jones haveing left us a few days ago. Our Assembly was kind to him. I wish they would Confer the same favour on another of their Servants. Indeed my Situation is disagreable here besides you knowing my very Narrow Fortune may Immagine that sometimes the Cares of a Husband and parent tell me there is a duty oweing to them as well as to my Country. I beseech you not to Consider this Sentiment as ariseing from a littleness of Soul or a Sordid Spirit, but I could not be just to the Woman who from much higher Expectations devoted herself to me if I now altogether Neglected the Interests of her and the little pledges she has presented me with. The Complication of this Letter will Convince you of the respect I must have for the man to whom I open my whole Soul without Ceremony punctilio or Reserve.

JNO. HARVIE

RC (DLC). Endorsed: "Harvie, John 1777. Dec. 29."

TJ's letter of 26 Nov. has not been located. YOUR SUPPLY OF CLOATHING:

By a resolution passed by the General Assembly, 27 Nov. 1777, the county lieutenant of each county was ordered to collect from its inhabitants clothing for the Continental troops raised in the county, such supplies to be collected by the deputy quartermaster general and conveyed with the greatest expedition to General Washington (JHD, Oct. 1777, 1827 edn., p. 43, 46). The WORKMEN whom Harvie was commissioned to secure for TJ were intended for work on Monticello which TJ continued throughout the Revolution (Kimball, *Jefferson: Road to Glory*, p. 159; for Harvie's further efforts to secure workmen, see John Harvie to TJ, 15 Sep. 1778). MR. JONES: Joseph Jones resigned his position in Congress, and Thomas Adams was elected in his place, 9 Dec. 1777 (*Letters of Joseph Jones*, ed. W. C. Ford, Washington, 1889, p. 5-6; JHD, Oct. 1777, 1827 edn., p. 64).

Oath of Allegiance Signed by Citizens of Albemarle County

[1777]

We whos names are hereunto subscribed do swear that we renounce and refuse all Allegiance to George the third King of Great Britain, his heirs and successors and that I will be faithfull and bear True Allegiance to the commonwealth of Virginia as a free and independent state, and that I will not at any [time] do or cause to be done, any matter or thing that will be prejudicial or injurious to the freedom and independence thereof as declared by congress and also that we will discover and make known to some one justice of the peace for the said state all treasons or traiterous conspiracies which we now or hereafter shall know to be formed against this or any of the united states of America So help me God.

George Gilmer	Th: Jefferson	Saml. Bowcock
James Quarles	Jno Harvie	Dd. Morris
Wm: Lewis	John Coles	John Wallace
Richd: Anderson	James Marks	Matt: Maury
Peter Marks	John Harris	Mask Leak
James Bridget	John Jouett	Robert Cobbs
John Feilder	Nichs. Lewis	Thos. Gouch
George Norvill	Ben Harris	Jams. Woods
Nathl: Haggard	Saml. Dedman	Js. Reid
Henry Mullins	Jas. Hopkins	Ben: Lacy
Tucker Woodson	C. Sims	Wm. Tandy Senr
Isaac Davis	James Kerr	John Reid
Saml. Taliaferro	Michl. Wallace	Jos. Holt
John Day	Randolph Jefferson	Wm. Law: Benge
Mica: Chiles	Jos. Hail	Ben: Jordan
Richd. Harper	David Allen	J. Henderson Jr.
Wm. Barton	Charles Kerr	Wm. Barksdale
John Grier	Benj. Henderson	Thos. Thorpe

Js. Wm. Crosthwait
R Dixon
J Marshall
Dan. Coleman
Wm. Wingfeild
Chrs: Wingfeild
Wm. Leak
Mar: Haggard
Pet: Balieu
Thos. West
Wm. Anderson
Ths. Anderson
Joseph Neilson
Wm. Colvard
Wm. Fossetts
E. Moore
Wm. Haines
Ed: Butler
R: Davenport Junr
Wm. Irvin V. D. M.
Jason Bowcock
Henry Shelton
Js. Minor
Andr: Bryan
John Fitzpatrick
John Stockton
Josiah Wood
Wittle Flannagan
Peter Forgarson
Nathl. Mcalester
John Henderson Jr
John Lewis Senr
W. Langford
Petr. Burrus
John Tandy
Richd. Goodall
Spencer Norvil
Orlando Jones
Nat: Morris
Wm. Michie
Ths. Craig
John McColloch
Chs. Lil. Lewis
Wm. Johnson
Zacha. Mills
John Thomas
Wm Hopkins
Clough Shelton
Saml Woodson

Thos. Overton
Thos. Martin Junr
John Wilkinson
Ben. Dod Wheeler
Peter Jackson
Henry Herd
John Jouett Jr
Isaac Davis Junr
Philip Mazzei
George Sanders
Richd. Gaines
Wm. Briscoe
Wm. Carrill
Robt. Sharpe Senr
Robt. Sharpe Junr.
Chs. Lewis Junr
David Gallasby
Isham Lewis
Henry Ford
Wm. Sandage
Wm. Chinault
Thos. Musick
Saml. Huckstep
Jacob Oglesby
John Wood 128
Thos: Collins
Arthur Graham.
Thos. Morgan
Chs. Hudson
Wm. Jeffers
Richd. Scott.
Bernice Brown
Wm. Statham
Stephen Hughs Jr.
Horslee Goodman
Willm: Shelton
Lity. Sullevan
Castn. Harper Sr:
John Nukeham
Saml. Benge
Richd. Carter
Jo: Wingfeild
Hen: Harper
Nichs. Hamner
Jos. Terril
Danl. Goldsby
Richd. Davenport
Chs. Tucker
Wm Hickcock

Hen: Copeland
Richd Goldsby
Heron Gains
John Prince
Castle: Harper Jr.
Danl. Coleman
Wm. Wingfeild
Chs. Wingfeild
Wm. Leak
Martin Haggard
Pet. Balieu
Thos. Fantrees
Js. Mcmannus
Saml. Ray
Ab. Eads
John Fantrees
Wm Sorrow
Willm. Fry
Chs. Goodman
Jos. Lamb.
Jo. Bailey
Rowland Horselee
Richd. Harvie
Alexr. McKenzie
Robt Thompson Jr.
John Kearby 180
John Black
Wm. Pilson
Robt. Pilson
Js. Epperson
John Lott
Rhcd. Sharp
Robt. Burrus
Hen. Randolph
Wm. Mcgehie
Saml Karr
Saml Mccord
Wm. Karr
Wm. Ramsay
David Nemo
Wm. Reynolds
Richd Watson
Thad. Reynolds
Danl. Reynolds
Frs. Browning
Wm. Rannald
Ab. Gollan
Wm Cleavland
Jas. Bird

Wm. Ballard	Francis Hoges	his
Ths. Jameson	×	John × Kerbie Junr
Geo. Mann	his mark	mark
Danl. Millar 207	Fran: Taliaferro	21 Apl 1779

Tr in Diary of George Gilmer (ViHi).

On 28 June 1777 the General Assembly passed "An Act to oblige the free male inhabitants of this state above a certain age to give assurance of allegiance to the same and for other purposes," and the House of Delegates directed that the public printer print, without delay, one copy of the Act for each magistrate within the commonwealth, together with a sufficient number of certificates, and send the same to the several counties (Hening, IX, 281-3; JHD, May 1777, 1827 edn., p. 110). The Act provided that all free-born male inhabitants above the age of sixteen, except imported servants, were to subscribe to the oath on or before 10 Oct. 1777 before the justices of the peace in their counties, boroughs, or cities and that the justices of the peace were to keep fair registers of the names of such persons; and before the first of January in every year following, to submit to the clerk of the court for the county a list of the persons who had signed. Upon signing, each person was to receive a certificate which read: "I do hereby certify, that hath taken and subscribed the oath or affirmation of allegiance and fidelity. . . . Witness my hand and seal this day of ." The presence of a copy of the oath of allegiance and of the names of the signers in George Gilmer's Diary (the original MS has not been found) seems to indicate that George Gilmer was the justice of the peace charged with taking the oaths and keeping a record of the signers. From the last entries it appears that the record was cumulative through Apr. 1779. Gilmer was a justice of the peace in Albemarle county, 12 June 1771 ("Justices of the Peace of Colonial Virginia," Va. State Libr., *Bull.*, XIV [1921], 109). The certificate which TJ received on signing the oath has not been located. The printed certificate issued to James Madison, 11 August 1777, is located in DLC: Madison Papers, 1: 28.

List of Militia by Counties

[1777]

militia in 1776.	raisd 1776			Militia 1777
1208		Accomack		120[ ]
1270	74	Albemarle	*	95[ ]
1150	84	Amelia	+	
2000	148	Augusta	*	243[ ]
6000		Augusta (West)		
650	74	Amherst	*	800
1400	100	Bedford		1369
1600	102	Botetourt	*	1510
1200	90	Brunswick		1300
650	38	Buckingham		650
1200	84	Berkeley	*	
983	74	Caroline	+	1026
350	30	Charles city		29[ ]
812	54	Charlotte	*	715
960	74	Chesterfeild	*	750

militia in 1776.	raisd 1776			Militia 1777
1400	74	Culpepper	+	
1000	74	Cumberland	*	
700	44	Dinwiddie		700
800	74	Dunmore		100[ ]
160	10	Eliz. city	*	142
450	38	Essex		55
1000	74	Fairfax	*	831
1100	74	Fauquier	*	
1264	90	Frederick		1000
2000	74	Fincastle		
		Fluvanna		26[ ]
900	64	Gloucester	+	80[ ]
520	38	Goochland	*	58[ ]
1000	74	Halifx	*	98[ ]
700	74	Hampshire	*	
900	74	Hanover		98[ ]
500	36	Henrico	+	
		Henry		60[ ]
193	16	James city	*	22[ ]
725	48	I. of Wight	+	60[ ]
450	36	K. George	*	35[ ]
600	54	K. & Queen	*	50[ ]
500	36	K. Wm.		50[ ]
200	16	Lancaster	*	292
1600	122	Loudoun	+	1700
600	36	Louisa	*	500
593	48	Lunenburgh	*	550
300	20	Middlesex	*	210
		Montgomery		750
850	58	Mecklenburgh		850
	222	Monongalia		1000
800	54	Nansemond	+	644
448	28	New Kent	+	418
1000	74	Norfolk	*	880
700	54	Northumbld.	*	739
		Northampton	*	430
	148	Ohio		
550	38	Orange	+	580
1550	94	Pittsylvania	*	923
		Powhatan	*	364
550	36	Prince Edwd.	*	570
450	30	Prince George	*	500
450	30	Pr'ss Anne	*	594
1000	74	Prince Wm.	+	800
470	30	Richmond	*	573
750	54	Southampton	+	1000

militia in 1776.	raisd 1776			Militia 1777
500	36	Spotsylva.		450
500	38	Stafford	+	500
350	28	Surry		350
660	46	Sussex	*	700
100		Warwick		100
		Washington	+	829
700	48	Westmoreland	*	663
	370	Yohogania		1000
300	20	York	*	244
	16	Wmsbgh.	*	214
		Norfolk borough		
55,255	4070			
		the numbers marked * are from accurate lists of 1777. those marked + are from the lists given in to the Governor in 1776. Botetourt when divided will be		
		Botetourt		589
		Green briar		532
		Rock-bridge		395
				1516

Tabular MS (DLC).

This list may have been drawn up by TJ in connection with his work on the committee appointed to bring in bills pursuant to resolutions on the state of the army, passed by the House of Delegates 4 Dec. 1777 (JHD, Oct. 1777, 1827 edn., p. 55). It could not have been completed until after 24 Dec., when the "amendment" to divide Botetourt County into three counties instead of two was agreed to (same, p. 91), and possibly not until after 12 Jan. 1778, when this bill was agreed to by both Houses (same, p. 113); but it must have been written before 1 Mch. 1778, the date the division of counties was to take place (Hening, IX, 420-4).

To George Rogers Clark

SIR Williamsburg Janry. 3d. 1778.

As some Indian Tribes, to the westward of the Missisippi have lately, without any provocation, massacred many of the Inhabitants upon the Frontiers of this Commonwealth, in the most cruel and barbarous Manner, and it is intended to revenge the Injury and punish the Aggressors by carrying the War into their own Country.

We congratulate You upon your Appointment to conduct so important an Enterprize in which We most heartily wish You

Success; and we have no Doubt but some further Reward in Lands, in that Country, will be given to the Volunteers who shall engage in this Service, in addition to the usual Pay: if they are so fortunate to succeed, We think it just and reasonable that each Volunteer entering as a common [soldier] in this Expedition, shou'd be allowed three hundred Acres of Land, and the Officers in the usual Proportion, out of the Lands which may be conquered in the Country now in the Possession of the said Indians; so as not to interfere with the Claims of any friendly Indians, or of any People willing to become Subjects of this Commonwealth; and for this we think You may safely confide in the Justice and Generosity of the Virginia Assembly.

We are Sir Yr. most Hble Servts.,

G: WYTHE
G. MASON
TH: JEFFERSON

RC (ICU); in the hand of George Mason; signed by Wythe, Mason, and TJ. Addressed: "To George Rogers Clarke Esqr." Endorsed by Clark: "Mssrs. Withe Mason Jefferson 3 Jany 1778"; in another hand: "abt. Expedition."

For a full treatment of the origin of the Kaskaskia expedition and the connection of TJ, Mason, and Wythe with it, see J. A. James, *Life of George Rogers Clark*, Chicago, 1929, p. 109-15; see also A. Marc Lewis, "Jefferson and Virginia's Pioneers, 1774-1781," *Miss. Valley Hist. Rev.*, XXXIV (1948), 571. In May 1779 the General Assembly enacted the following: "Every soldier who enlisted into the corps of volunteers commanded by Colonel George Rogers Clarke, and continued therein till the taking of the several posts in the Illinois country, shall at the end of the war, be entitled to a grant of two hundred acres of any unappropriated lands within this commonwealth" (Hening, X, 26). The same Act granted bounties of 100 acres to all other Virginia volunteers who had enlisted or reenlisted to serve for the duration of the war.

Bills for Establishing a Land Office

and for Adjusting and Settling Titles

[8-14 January 1778]

I. BILL FOR ESTABLISHING A LAND OFFICE AND ASCERTAINING THE TERMS AND MANNER OF GRANTING WASTE AND UNAPPROPRIATED LANDS

II. BILL FOR SETTLING TITLES TO UNPATENTED LANDS

EDITORIAL NOTE

These two Bills, despite the attention they have received from careful historians, remain a neglected milestone in public land policy. Abernethy has asserted that "the land office act of 1779 was a colossal mistake. In 1776 Jefferson had advocated the granting of tracts of fifty acres to each family lacking that amount. This would have been an improvement on the colonial head-right system, and it would have been a great aid to the growth of democracy in America. . . . There is an element of historical irony in the fact that Jefferson, the father of democracy, should have helped to draft the act by which democracy was defeated in Virginia at the moment when it might have had its birth. The result was that within a few years Robert Morris came to own one and a half million acres, and Alexander Walcott a million acres of Virginia's Western lands, and most of that remaining fell into the hands of other absentee speculators who paid, in depreciated currency, a price equivalent in some cases to about fifty cents the hundred acres. Thus the growth of the country was retarded, the resident population forced to protect the property of those who took no part in its defense, and the great public domain was exploited by a few individuals for their private gain" (*Western Lands*, p. 228). Insofar as this applies to the two land Acts of 1779, it is a sound appraisal; insofar as it implies that Jefferson's part in the drafting of the Bills justifies the inference that he approved the final terms of the laws as enacted, it is misleading. The publication of the manuscript Bills, here presented for the first time, makes possible a comparison of what Jefferson and George Mason, his principal coadjutor in this matter, originally intended with what the legislature finally did to these intentions.

That comparison reveals that what Abernethy considered the fatal omission of the first of these laws—the making of provision for future settlers—was not omitted from the Bill as presented to the legislature. Among the more interesting provisions of the Bill that failed to become law are those "for the Encouragement of Foreigners. . . . And for the more equal Distribution of Lands, and to encourage Marriage and Population by making provision for the Natives of the Country." These provisions, which accord so well with the views that Jefferson expressed in his Constitution for Virginia in 1776 and in his letters to Pendleton during the summer of 1776, go far to remove whatever irony there is in the association of Jefferson's name with the Land Acts of 1779. Jefferson, who had advocated use of western lands for those who would settle there, for opposing monopoly and exploitation, for attracting immigration, for supporting the credit of the state, and for strengthening the bonds of union by securing the adoption of the Articles of Confederation, wrote some of these far-sighted policies into the terms of his Bill as well as in the preamble stating its purpose. He was its chief architect. George Mason assisted in its preparation, though Mason was more interested in the second of the two Bills (see Mason to TJ, 3 Apr. 1779). But the Land Acts of 1779 were not passed until after Jefferson had become governor.

Both of these Bills suffered strenuous opposition. No doubt much of this was due to the feeling of many that opening up the West would drain off population and involve the whole state in costly Indian wars. But much also was due to the fact that, so long as there was no land office, the advantage lay with the syndicates and the large operators as against the individual settlers: fishing in muddied waters promised some advantages. Both Bills were introduced at the busy session of Oct. 1777. Both were postponed, were not submitted at the May 1778 session, and came on again at the October session of that year. The opposition still succeeded in its delaying tactics, and it was not until the session of May 1779 that the Bills finally became law. They are introduced here, some seventeen months in advance of their final enactment, in order to place them approximately at the time at which they were first drawn and also in order to correlate them with Jefferson's other legislative activities at this time. For example, during the interval that elapsed between the appointment of a committee and the introduction of the Land Office Bill, Jefferson was much preoccupied with the time-consuming dispute with the Senate over the Case of Thomas Johnson, &c. (q.v., under date of 11 Nov. 1777) and with the Supply Bill (q.v., under date of 20 May 1778).

On 13 Dec. 1777 the committee of the whole of the House of Delegates, in considering ways and means "for the better supporting the credit of the paper money issued . . . and the contingencies of government, and for the more punctual payment of this State's proportion of the continental expenses," recommended, in addition to the levying of many taxes and duties, that part of the unappropriated lands be disposed of, "and the money arising therefrom, applied in aid of the funds to be provided for discharging the public debt, and that a land office be established for granting waste and unappropriated lands." The committee appointed to bring in a Bill for this purpose consisted of Thomas Nelson, Jr., George Mason, Pendleton, Nicholas, Jefferson, Zane, Bullitt, Braxton, and Lyne. The Bill was introduced by Mason on 8 Jan. 1778; it passed two readings the same day and was referred to the committee of the whole. It was then postponed three times until, on 17 Jan., the House resolved to consider it on "the last day of March next"—an effective means of killing the Bill at that session, since all knew that it would end in a few days (JHD, Oct. 1777, 1827 edn., p. 77-8, 106, 107, 111, 113, 116, 119). Nevertheless, on the last day of the session, 24 Jan. 1778, the advocates of the Bill succeeded in obtaining the passage by the House of the following important resolutions: "Whereas, it is of the greatest importance to this Commonwealth, that the waste and unappropriated lands to which no person having just claim should be disposed of, for the purpose of creating a sinking fund, in aid of the taxes for discharging the public debt, and to the end that the claims to unpatented lands, under the former or present government, may not in the mean time be increased or strengthened; *Resolved*, That every entry, with the survey hereafter made in the country upon the western waters under any pretence or title whatsoever, until the land office shall be established and the manner and terms of granting waste and unappropriated lands, shall be void and of no effect; and that no persons hereafter settling in the country upon the said western waters, shall be entitled to any land or pre-emptions of land for such settlement, without paying for the same such consideration as shall be hereafter ascertained by the General Assembly, so as no family be entitled to more than 400 acres. *Resolved*, That all persons claiming any unpatented lands on the said western waters by order of Council, shall lay the same before the General Assembly on or before the 20th day of their next session, and be at liberty in the mean time to take the depositions of any witnesses they may choose, to examine such claims, giving reasonable notice thereof to the person appointed by the Governor and Council to attend such examination in the county, on behalf of the Commonwealth, in case such person shall be appointed" (same, p. 136). The Senate immediately concurred in these resolutions. The opponents of the Bill were apparently willing, temporarily at least, to agree to a limitation on the number of acres permitted so long as the Bill itself could be blocked—a limitation that was removed once the Bill was enacted (Abernethy, *Western Lands*, p. 219). Neither of the two land Bills was brought up at the next session.

On 14 Oct. 1778 a new committee was given leave to bring in a Bill "for establishing a land office." This Bill was introduced by Tazewell on 17 Nov. Jefferson arrived only on 30 Nov. at this session and George Mason departed on 5 Dec., circumstances which raise some doubt as to whether the Bill brought in was the same as that introduced on 8 Jan. 1778 (but see Document I, note 24). At any rate, a motion to read the Bill the second time was defeated, whether because of the strength of the opposition or the fact that Jefferson was too much preoccupied at this time with the Report of the Committee of Revisors is uncertain (JHD, Oct. 1778, 1827 edn., p. 11, 67, 100).

However, as soon as the House was organized for business at the session of May 1779 a committee was appointed to bring in the Bill, consisting of John Taylor, Strother, John Harvie, Moore, Jefferson, Munford, Baker, Tyler, Burr Harrison, John Washington, Carrington, Smith, Peyton, and Pickett. On 17 May, Mason was added to the committee, and at the same time the committee was directed to bring in the related Bill for settling claims to unpatented lands, a Bill in which, as a member of the Ohio Company, Mason was particularly interested. Taylor reported the Land Office Bill on 5 June. It was read the second time on 7 June and was passed by the House on the 17th. On the 22nd the Senate offered amendments which were accepted by the House. In the absence of a MS listing the various amendments, it is impossible to tell which of the many variations between the Bill and the Act that are listed in the notes were made by the House and which by the Senate; many, we may be certain, were made by Jefferson and Mason themselves (see Mason to TJ, 3 Apr. 1779), but the emasculation of the broad and liberal terms of the Bill was undoubtedly the work of the opposition in the legislature. The fact that the session was in its last days and the calendar heavily crowded may partly account for the ready agreement by the House to the Senate's amendments. It is worth noting that this Bill, for which Jefferson had fought so long, was introduced at its final passage only after he had been elected governor; he was not a member of the House, therefore, during the amending process (JHD, May 1779, 1827 edn., p. 6, 12, 37, 38, 49, 51, 53, 61).

One important feature written into the Act by way of amendment to Jefferson's Bill indicates the manner in which it was deflected from its original purposes and altered to suit the desires of the land companies and large speculators. This was the proviso that permitted warrants to be issued by any county clerk. This was changed so that only the Register of the Land Office could issue such warrants, a change which manifestly gave advantage to the large operator who could afford to keep one or more representatives on hand at such an office. Another feature of a similar purport is to be found in sections IV and V of the Act as adopted, sections not to be found in Jefferson's Bill. The stated purpose of these sections was to quiet titles, prevent controversies, and do "equal justice to the commonwealth and its citizens" in respect to those persons whose titles to lands—because of the "ignorance, negligence, or fraud of the surveyors"—included more acreage than they were entitled to under the bounds described in the grant. In such cases, anyone might challenge the title of the grantee to the "surplus": (1) if he took action during the lifetime of the patentee; (2) if he did so before *any transference or alienation of the lands had been made by the grantee*; (3) if he gave notice of his intentions to the grantee one year in advance; (4) if the grantee did not within the year obtain rights and sue out a patent for his own extra-legal "surplus" lands; (5) if he (the prospective claimant) caused, at his own expense, the *whole* of the grantee's parcel to be resurveyed in order to determine the extent of the "surplus"; (6) if he was willing, if successful, to let the grantee assign such surplus land in any part of his tract in one entire piece; (7) if he was willing to obligate himself to pay for the resurvey whether or not a surplus was discovered; and (8) if, finally, "for his unjust vexation" of the grantee, he was willing to expose himself to "an action upon the case at the suit of the party grieved." Considering also the fact that this section allowed all surveyors a margin of error of 5% (five acres "surplus" in every 100 surveyed), and that there were no corresponding penalties against the grantee for holding surplus lands, except the mere possibility that he might have to yield them up to someone perceptive enough to discover such surplusage and hardy enough to try to gain possession of it—it is obvious that (1) these sections added to Jefferson's Bill encouraged making plus rather than minus "errors" in surveys; and (2) they favored the holders of large tracts, for the reasons that surplusage in large tracts was much more difficult to discover, the risk and cost of challenging possession correspondingly increased, and many of the surveyors were closely affiliated with the land companies and land speculators (Abernethy, *Western Lands*, 132-3; 224).

The Bill for Adjusting and Settling Titles was George Mason's work primarily. This is shown not merely by the fact that the MS bears no indication on its surface of Jefferson's collaboration—although he indubitably worked with Mason on the Bill—but also by the fact that the major part of it is in Mason's handwriting. This is confirmed also by Mason's letter to Jefferson of 3 Apr. 1779 and by Jefferson's "Notes on my title to 485. acres of land surveyed for me Mar. 27. 1788. . . ."

(CSmH: HM5593) in which he makes the following statement: "The Revolution now came on, and suspended the means of obtaining grants of land. Independence was declared in 1776. But it was not till 3. years after that the legislature re-opened the land office. Mr. Mason then came forward with his plan of a land law. His great object was to remove out of the way the great and numerous orders of council to the Ohio co. Loyal co. Misissipi co. Vandalia co. Indiana co. &c. and the thousands of entries for lands with surveyors of counties, which covered the whole Western country. . . ." The object of Mason's Bill, then, was to remedy a complicated situation that had grown up; that of Jefferson's Bill to lay down the foundations of a broad and permanent policy.

There is, however, less discrepancy between the second of these Bills and its terms at the final enactment than there was between the Bill for Establishing a Land Office and its corresponding status as an Act. Both the Bill and the Act for settling and adjusting claims provided extraordinary powers for the commissioners. This delegation of judicial power to an administrative body was criticized before the year was out by Thomas Scott of Pennsylvania, who bitingly remarked: "Tryal by Jury is held sacred in their bill of rights and is totally taken away by this law" (Thomas Scott to Joseph Reed, printed below, 29 Nov. 1779). There was provision for appeal in certain circumstances from the commission's decisions, but even on appeal trials were conducted in summary form. It is ironic that Mason, the chief author of the Virginia Declaration of Rights, should also have been the primary author of this Bill; it is also ironic that the author of the Declaration of Independence should have agreed to such features.

On 5 Jan. 1778 the House gave leave for a Bill to be brought in "for adjusting and settling the titles of claimants to unpatented lands, under the former government" and appointed a committee to bring in such a Bill, consisting of George Mason, Pendleton, Nicholas, Jefferson, Zane, Bullitt, and Braxton. Mason introduced the Bill on 14 Jan., and on the 21st it suffered the same fate as the Bill for Establishing a Land Office—that is, it was killed by being ordered to go through its second reading on 19 Mch. At the October session a new committee was ordered to bring in a Bill for this purpose; Mason was added to the committee on 20 Nov. Hite presented the Bill on 7 Dec. 1778, and it was ordered to be read the first time on 10 Mch. 1779, a date at which the Assembly would not be in session. On 17 May 1779 it was ordered to be brought in by the committee appointed to bring in the Bill for Establishing a Land Office, of which John Taylor was chairman and Jefferson a member; Mason was added to the committee on 17 May. Taylor presented the Bill on 4 June. It was amended both by the House and the Senate, being passed by the former on 16 June and agreed to by the latter on the 21st (JHD, Oct. 1777, 1827 edn., p. 101, 115, 125; Oct. 1778, p. 43, 75, 101; May 1779, p. 12, 34, 38, 41, 43, 44, 47-8, 49, 51, 60).

I. Bill for Establishing a Land Office
and Ascertaining the Terms and Manner of Granting Waste and Unappropriated Lands

[8 January 1778]

Whereas there are large Quantities of waste and unappropriated Lands within the territorial Limits of this Commonwealth, the granting of which will encourage the Migration of Foreigners hither, promote Population, increase the annual Revenue, and create a Fund for discharging the Public Debt, Be it enacted by the General Assembly that an Office shall be and is hereby constituted for the purpose of granting Lands within this Commonwealth into which all the Records now in the Secretary's Office of Patents or Grants for Lands heretofore Issued, with all papers relating thereto,[1] shall be removed for their safe keeping and all future Grants of Lands shall Issue from the said Office in manner and form herein after directed.[2] A Register of the said Land Office shall be appointed from Time to Time by joint Ballot of both houses of Assembly, who shall give Bond, with sufficient Security to the Governor or first Magistrate of this Commonwealth, in the Penalty of   Current Money,[3] shall take an Oath for the due and faithful Performance of his Trust,[4] shall hold his Office during good Behaviour, be entitled to receive such fees as shall hereafter be allowed by Law and shall have power to appoint a Deputy to assist in executing[5] the Business of the said Office.[6] If any vacancy shall happen by the Death resignation or removal of a Register during the Recess of the General Assembly, the Governor or first Magistrate of the Commonwealth by and with the advice of the Privy-Council,[7] may appoint some other person, giving Bond and Security and taking an Oath[8] in like manner, to Act in the said Office, until the end of the next Session of Assembly.[9] [And for the Encouragement of Foreigners to settle here, and an Inducement to import Inhabitants from foreign Countries, Be it enacted that the antient custom of importation-rights shall be continued, and[10] every person removing from any foreign Country or at his charge importing any Inhabitants not being Slaves[11] to settle in this Commonwealth, shall in Consideration thereof, be entitled to fifty Acres of Waste or unappropriated Land, for each person so removed or imported, upon Certificate from the General Court, or any County Court within the Commonwealth, of due Proof thereof, in Open Court, by the Oath of the party, or other satisfactory Evidence, of the name of every person so removed or imported, the County from which he came, the Year of the arrival or Importation, that the person obtaining such Certificate had never before Proved or claimed his right to Land for any of those named therein, and that they have all of them taken the Oath of Fidelity to the Commonwealth.][12] [And for the more equal Distribution of Lands, and to encourage Marriage and Population by making Provision for the Natives of the Country Be it enacted that every Child,[13] free-Born[14] within this Commonwealth, after the Establishment thereof, shall upon his or her Marriage and Residence for one Year next after such Marriage, within this Commonwealth, be entitled to seventy five Acres of waste or unappropriated Land, upon Certificate, from any Court of Record, of due Proof having been made of such Nativity, Marriage and Residence, and that the party had never before made Proof or obtained Certificate thereof, but the Portion of Land so due to the wife shall, upon such Certificate, be granted to the Husband and his heirs.][15]

And whereas a certain Bounty in Lands hath been allowed to the Troops, on Continental Establishment, raised[16] by the Laws of this Commonwealth, and to the Troops upon Virginia Establishment, Be it enacted that the Officers and Soldiers of the said Troops, as well as the Officers and Soldiers to whom a Bounty in Lands may or shall be hereafter granted[17] by any Law of this Commonwealth, shall be entitled to the Quantity and Portion of[18] waste or unappropriated Land allowed[19] to them respectively by such Laws; the Commissioned Officers, upon Certificate from the General or Commander in Cheif of the Continental Army, or the Commanding Officer of the Troops on the Virginia Establishment, as the Case is; and the noncommissioned Officers and Soldiers upon Certificate from the Colonel or Commanding Officer of the Regiment or Corps to which they respectively belong, that such Officers or Soldiers have served the time required by Law; distinguishing particularly in what Regiment or Corps such service hath been performed.[20] And for creating a sinking Fund, in Aid of the Annual Taxes, to discharge the Public Debt, Be it enacted that it shall be lawful for any Citizen of this[21] [or of any other of the United states, to obtain a warrant for surveying waste or unappropriated lands, on paying the consideration of[22] for every hundred acres and so in proportion for a greater or smaller quantity, in the following manner; that is to say; if the quantity required exceed four hundred acres, such Consideration money shall be paid into the hands of the Treasurer, who shall thereupon give to such person a certificate of the paiment and of the purpose for which it was made, which, being delivered to the Register of the land office, shall entitle him to a warrant from the said Register as herein after directed: but if the quantity required, does not exceed four hundred acres, such consideration money shall be paid to the clerk of the county court, with whom the Register shall constantly lodge a due number of printed warrants with blanks for the name, quantity and amount of the consideration, which warrants shall be filled up and countersigned by such clerk and issued to the persons paying such consideration money.][23]

And whereas some of the united American States may not have within their respective Territories waste and unappropriated Lands sufficient to pay the Troops raised within the same, upon Continental Establishment, the Bounty of Lands Promised them by the American Congress, for which the Public Faith is pledged, and it may hereafter become Necessary for this Commonwealth to furnish a Proportion of such Lands for that purpose, on the general Account and Charge of the said united States, Be it therefore enacted that for any waste or unappropriated Lands, so to be furnished by this Commonwealth, no greater Price or Consideration than the Sum of three pounds Current Money, or ten Dollars per hundred Acres, shall be charged taken or Demanded.[24]

And be it enacted that upon application of any person or persons[25] having Title to waste or unappropriated Lands either by Importation-Rights, Native-Rights, Military-rights or the larger Treasury rights,[26] and lodging in the Land Office a proper Certificate thereof, the Register of the said Office shall Grant to such person or persons a printed[27] Warrant specifying the Quantity of Land, and the Rights upon which it is due, authorizing any Surveyor[28] to lay off and Survey the same; and shall regularly enter and Record in the Books of his Office all such Certificates, and the Warrants Issued thereupon;[29] with the names of the persons mentioned in any Importation-Certificates. A Surveyor shall be appointed in every County, to be[30] examined and Certified able by the Professors of William and Mary College and if of good Character commissioned by the Governor with a reservation in such commission to the said Professors, for the use of the college, of one sixth part of the legal fees which shall be received by such surveyor.[31] He shall hold his Office during good Behaviour, shall reside within his County, and before he shall be capable of entering upon the execution of his Office shall, before the Court of the same County, take an Oath, and give Bond with two sufficient sureties, to the Governor and his Successors,[32] in the Sum of five hundred pounds for the faithful execution of his Office and shall also take the Oath of fidelity to the Commonwealth. Residence out of the County, or absence therefrom for a longer time than one Month, unless by unavoidable necessity, shall vacate his said Office.[33] So many deputy surveyors, as by the said chief surveyor shall be certified necessary to do the Business of the County, shall be in like manner examined, Commissioned and Qualified for their Office, who shall be entitled to the whole fees allowed by Law for whatsoever services they shall perform accounting nevertheless for one sixth part thereof to the professors of the college of William and Mary as before directed and one other sixth part to their principal;[34] and if any Deputy Surveyor, or any other on his behalf and with his privity,[35] shall pay, or Agree to pay, any greater part of the Profits of his Office, sum of Money in gross, or other valuable Consideration to his principal for his recommendation or interest in procuring the Deputation, such Deputy and Principal shall be thereby rendered for ever incapable of serving in such office. No principal Surveyor shall be answerable for any misfeasance in office, by his Deputy. It shall not be necessary for the present chief, or deputy Surveyors of the several Counties, duly examined, commissioned and Qualified according to the Laws heretofore in force, to be again examined,[36] Commissioned or Qualified under the directions of this Act.[37]

Every person having Importation Rights, Native Rights, military Rights or Treasury rights,[38] and being desireous of locating the same on any particular waste and unappropriated Land, shall lodge them with[39] the Chief Surveyor of the County wherein the said Lands, or the greater part of them lie[40] directing the location thereof so specially and precisely as that others may be enabled with certainty to locate other warrants on the adjacent residuum, which location shall[41] be entered by the surveyor in a book to be kept for that purpose.[42] And if on such application at his office, the surveyor shall refuse to enter such location under pretence of a prior Entry for the same lands made by some other person, he shall have a right to demand of the said Surveyor a view of the Original of such prior entry in his Book, and also an attested Copy of it, paying such Surveyor for the same two shillings and six pence.[43] But it shall not be lawful for any Surveyor to admit the location of any warrant on lands within the limits of the Cherokee Indians, nor on any islands in the Ohio river or lands on the North-west side of the said river; nor on any lands Westward of the meridian of the mouth of the Cumberland river.[44]

Any chief Surveyor having a warrant for lands[45] and desiring to locate the same on Lands within his own County, shall enter such location[46] before the Clerk of the County, who shall return the same to the next Court, there to be Recorded; and the said Surveyor shall proceed to have the Survey made within as short a Time as may be,[47] by some one of his Deputies, or if he hath no Deputy, then by any Surveyor or deputy surveyor of an adjacent County.[48]

Every chief surveyor, shall proceed with all practicable dispatch,[49] to Survey all Lands entered for in his Office, and shall[50] either give to the party concerned personal notice of the Time at which he will attend to make such Survey, or shall publish such notice by affixing an advertisement thereof on the door of the Court-house of the County, on two several Court days if the party reside within the said county: and if he reside out of the county, then such publication shall be twice made in the gazette, the expence of which shall be paid by the Treasurer to the printer, to be repaid as hereafter directed:[51] which time so appointed shall be at least four[52] months after personal notice given or after the second advertisement so published: and, if the Surveyor shall accordingly attend and the party, or some one for him, shall fail to appear at the time with proper Chain carriers and a person to mark[53] the lines if necessary, his Entry shall become void,[54] and where the chief Surveyor doth not mean to Survey himself he shall immediately after the Entry made direct a Deputy Surveyor to perform the Duty who shall proceed as is before directed in the case of the chief Surveyor.

The persons employed to carry the Chain on any Survey shall be sworn by the Surveyor, whether principal or Deputy, to measure justly and exactly to the best of their ability, and to deliver a true Account thereof to such Surveyor; and shall be paid for their trouble by the party for whom the Survey is made. The surveyor at the time of making the Survey shall see the same bounded plainly by marked Trees, except where a Water course or antient marked line shall be the Boundary; and shall make the breadth of such[55] Survey at least one third of it's length in every part, unless where such breadth shall be restrained on both sides by mountains unfit for cultivation,[56] by Watercourses, or the Bounds of Lands before appropriated. Within three days after making[57] the Survey, and before he proceeds to make another,[58] he shall deliver to the said party or person so attending a fair and true plat of such Survey, with a Certificate of the Quantity contained, the hundred[59] wherein it lies, the course of the several Boundaries natural and artificial, antient and new, expressing the proper name of such natural Boundaries where they have any, and the name of every person whose former line is made a Boundary and also the nature of the warrant on which such survey was made, and shall at the same time redeliver the said warrant to the party.[60] The said Plats and Certificates shall be examined and tried by the said principal surveyor whether truly made and legally proportioned as to length and breadth and shall be[61] entered within two[62] months after the survey is made, in a Book well bound, to be provided by the Court of his County, at the County charge; and he shall moreover, in the month of July in every Year, return to the professors of William and Mary college and also[63] to the[64] office of his County Court, a true list of all surveys made by him or his deputies[65] in the preceeding twelve months,[66] there to be Recorded. Any Surveyor, whether principal or Deputy, failing in any of the duties aforesaid, shall be liable to be Indicted before the Judges of the General Court, and punished by fine or[67] by deprivation of his office and incapacity to take it again,[68] and shall moreover be liable to any party injured for all Damages he may sustain by such failure. Every County Court shall[69] have authority at any time to appoint two or more capable persons to examine the Books of Entries and surveys in possession of their chief surveyor and to report in what condition and order the same are kept, and, on his Death or removal,[70] to take the same into their own possession and deliver them to the succeeding chief Surveyor.[71] Every person for whom any waste or unappropriated Lands shall be so located and laid off, shall, within twelve months after the survey made, repay to the treasurer the expence of publishing in the gazette notice of surveying the said lands, where such publication shall have been made either for his notification or that of any other who had before entered for the same lands, (which fact the surveyor shall duly note in his certificate for the information of the Register) and shall also return the plat and certificate of the said survey into the land office, together with the warrant on which the lands were surveyed, and may demand of the Register a receipt for the same. And, on failing to make such return or if the breadth of his plat be not one third of it's length as before directed, it shall be lawful for any other person to enter a Caveat in the said Land office against the Issuing of any Grant to him, expressing therein for what cause the Grant should not Issue; or if any person shall obtain a Survey of Lands to which another hath by Law a better right, the person having such better right may in like manner enter a Caveat to prevent his obtaining a Grant till the Title can be determined, such

Caveat also expressing the nature of the right on which the plaintif therein claims the said Land. The person entering any caveat shall take from the Register a certified Copy thereof, which[72] he shall deliver, on the same day on which he entered his Caveat in the said office, to the Clerk of the General Court; or such entry shall become void. The said Clerk, on receiving the same, shall enter it in a Book, and thereupon Issue a Summons reciting the causes for which such Caveat is entered, and requiring the Defendant to appear on the seventh day of the succeeding Court and defend his right; and on such Process being returned 'executed,' the Court shall Proceed to determine the right of the cause in a summary way, without pleadings in Writing, impannelling and swearing a Jury for the finding of such facts as are material to the cause, and are not agreed by the parties: and shall thereupon give Judgment on which no Appeal or Writ of Error shall be allowed. A Copy of such Judgment, if in favour of the Defendant, being delivered into the Land Office, shall vacate the said Caveat; and, if not delivered within one month,[73] a new Caveat may, for that cause be entered against the Grant: And, if the said Judgment be in favour of the Plaintif, upon delivering the same into the Land Office, together with a Plat and Certificate of the Survey,[74] and the rights on which it is claimed, he shall be entitled to a Grant thereof; but, on failing to make such return[75] within six Months after Judgment so rendered, it shall be lawful for any other person to enter a Caveat for that cause against issuing the Grant: upon which subsequent Caveats, such proceedings shall be had as are before directed in the case of an Original caveat, and in any[76] Caveat where Judgment is given for the Defendant, the Court, if they think it reasonable,[77] may also adjudge to him his Costs.

The clerk of every county court shall, before his said court, give bond, paiable to the Governor and his successors in such sum as the court in their discretion shall direct, with two sureties to be approved by them, for the faithful discharge of the office of issuing land-warrants and shall half-yearly, to wit, in the months of January and July pay into the hands of the Treasurer all monies by him received for such warrants, deducting for his trouble per centum therefrom, and shall take from the said Treasurer a certificate thereof which he shall deliver to the Register, together with a true account on oath of the monies so received, of all warrants issued by him, specifying the name of the party and quantity of land in each, and of all blank warrants still remaining on hand: producing moreover to the said Register such warrants as shall have been taken back from the purchasers in exchange for others and a certificate from the court of the said county, signed by the presiding magistrate by order of the court, that so many blank warrants as are stated in the said account were by the said clerk produced to the court, examined and counted.[78]

The Register shall, before the meeting of every session of assembly; return to the Speaker of the house of delegates all Treasury certificates delivered to him since his last account rendered, together with [all?] of the same, and the names of the persons from whom they were received, and also an account of all reimbursements to the public for printed notifications which shall have been certified to him, to be laid before the said house of delegates and by them referred to the Committee which shall be appointed for settling the Treasurers accounts.

Due returns of the several articles herein before required being made into the Land Office, the Register, within not less than one, nor more than three Months,[79] shall make out a Grant by way of Deed Poll to the party having right in the following form. 'A. B. Esqr. Governor of the Commonwealth of Virginia, To all to whom these presents shall come Greeting. Know ye that in Consideration of [white Inhabitants imported to settle in this Commonwealth by C. D. or in consideration that C. D. is a native of this Commonwealth, hath married and resided therein for one Year next after such marriage or in consideration that E. D. is a native of this Commonwealth, hath intermarried with C. D. and resided therein for one Year next after such intermarriage; or in Consideration that C. D. and E. his Wife are natives of this Commonwealth, have intermarried and resided therein for one Year next after such intermarriage or, in consideration of][80] military service performed by C. D. to this commonwealth, or in Consideration of military service performed by C. D. to the united States of America, or in consideration of the Sum of paid by C. D. into the Treasury of this Commonwealth, there is granted by the said Commonwealth unto the said C. D. a certain Tract or parcel of Land containing Acres lying in the County of and hundred of &c.[81] with it's appurtenances: To have and to hold the said Tract or parcel of Land, with it's appurtenances to the said C. D. and his heirs;[82] to be holden of the said Commonwealth by fealty in free and common soccage. In Witness whereof the said A. B. Governor of the Commonwealth of Virginia hath hereunto caused the seal of the said Commonwealth to be affixed at on the day of in the Year of our Lord and of the Commonwealth A B.'

Upon which Grant the said Register shall endorse that the party hath title to the same, whereupon it shall be signed by the Governor, Sealed with the Seal of the Commonwealth and then entered of Record at full length in[83] Books to be provided and kept for that purpose by the Register[84] at the Public expence and being so entered[85] shall be certified to have been registered and then be delivered[86] to the party or his Order. A copy of such Record duly attested by the said Register shall be legal evidence of such Grant in all cases.[87] So much of all former Acts of Assembly as[88] direct the mode of proceeding in any case provided for by this Act are hereby repealed.

MS (DLC); 14 pages in clerk's hand, but with numerous corrections and additions in TJ's hand, as indicated in notes below. The title of the Bill, in clerk's hand, is at top of first page, but crossed out; it is, however, endorsed on Bill in TJ's hand: "A Bill for establishing a land office, and ascertaining the terms & manner of granting waste & unappropriated lands." Text of the Act as finally adopted is in Hening, X, 50-65. There are many evidences in the MS that the clerk who transcribed it employed a MS written by TJ; for occasionally the initial word of a sentence is written with a lower-case letter and TJ's characteristic "it's" for the possessive pronoun occurs in several instances.

[1] Following added in Act (by George Mason?): "and all certificates of surveys of lands now in the said office, and not patented."

[2] Act reads: "herein after mentioned."

[3] Act reads: "fifty thousand pounds current money."

[4] Act omits requirement concerning oath, no doubt because TJ had already drawn a general Bill requiring oaths of office of all civil officers before any could qualify; this was passed at the May 1779 session (Hening, X, 22-3).

[5] MS originally read: "to appoint as many Deputies as shall be [warranted?] in"; TJ altered this to read: "a Deputy to assist in executing"; and, by amendment, the Act was changed to read: "a deputy and clerks to assist. . . ."

[6] Act reads: ". . . said office, but shall nevertheless reside there himself," "there" referring to the location of the office. This was a point on which TJ had strong convictions (see his letter to Patrick Henry, 27 Mch. 1779) and he may have altered the MS to read as it does in the Act.

[7] Act omits "Privy."

[8] Act omits reference to oath.

[9] Act contains the following sentence at this point: "All copies of the records and other papers of the said office, or of the records and papers hereby directed to be removed from the secretary's office and lodged therein, duly attested by such register, shall be as good evidence as the originals would be." This addition also bears the mark of George Mason's hand, since he was greatly interested in unsettled claims; see note 1, above.

[10] The words "the antient custom . . . continued, and" are interlined in TJ's hand.

[11] MS originally read: "import white inhabitants to settle." TJ first changed this to read: "importing free Inhabitants to settle"; and then altered this to read as in the text.

[12] Despite the fact that the legislature allowed the preamble to stand as TJ had written it, including as one of its purposes that of encouraging "the migration of foreigners hither," this entire proviso (i.e., the part enclosed in square brackets, which are supplied) was deleted by amendment. TJ's desire to continue the policy of head-rights is quite in accord with the principles set forth in his proposed Constitution for Virginia in 1776 and in his correspondence in 1776 with Edmund Pendleton concerning land policy.

[13] The words "not being in Slavery which shall become [. . .]" are deleted in MS.

[14] The word "free-" is in TJ's hand.

[15] This remarkably interesting proviso (here enclosed in square brackets,

supplied) for the encouragement of marriage and population was deleted by amendment.

16 Act reads: "by the ordinances of convention or the laws. . . ."

17 Act reads: "allowed."

18 The words "and Portion of" are not in Act.

19 Act reads "engaged."

20 At this point the Act has the following: ". . . hath been performed, or death happened; and upon making proof before any court of record within this commonwealth by the persons own oath, or other satisfactory evidence of the truth and authenticity of the said certificate, and that the party had never before proved or claimed his right to land for the service therein mentioned, which proof the clerk of the court before whom it shall be made, is hereby empowered and required to endorse and certify upon the original certificate, making an entry or minute thereof in his order book and recording the same; and every county court shall annually, in the month of October, send to the register's office, a list of all certificates granted by their respective county courts upon any of the before mentioned rights, there to be recorded."

21 The MS contains at this point a slip on which the passage in square brackets (supplied) is written in TJ's hand; this slip is pasted over the following that TJ had deleted from the MS (the words italicized *outside* angle brackets were interlined in TJ's hand): "Commonwealth *or of any of the United States* to sue for and obtain a Grant of any waste and unappropriated Lands upon paying to the ⟨*Receiver General*⟩ *Treasurer* the Sum of   for every hundred Acres, and so in proportion for a greater or less Quantity, the said Lands having been Previously entered for and surveyed in the manner hereafter directed, and the said ⟨*Receiver General*⟩ *Treasurer* shall, and he is hereby impowered and required, upon such Payment to give the Person making the same a Certificate under his hand and Seal of the Sum received, and the Quantity of Land thereupon due to such person and his heirs, making a regular Entry and Record thereof in the Books of his office. Provided nevertheless that no Lands in the Cherokee Country, or on the Northwest side of the Ohio River, nor any of the Islands in the said River *nor to the Westward of the meridian of the mouth of Cumberland river* shall be Surveyed Patented or granted without the further Order of the General Assembly.

"And be it further enacted that the said Receiver-General shall and he is hereby required half yearly to wit in the months of April and October in every Year, to pay into the Public Treasury all the Money which he hath received the preceeding half Year for Land Certificates by him Issued as aforesaid, after deducting Commissions, at the Rate of two percentum for his Trouble; for which Money the Treasurer for the Time being shall be accountable to the Commonwealth."

22 Act reads "forty pounds."

23 This concludes the insertion in TJ's hand written on the slip pasted on the MS. The Act contains no such limitation as TJ's Bill proposed; it provided that "any person may acquire title to so much waste and unappropriated land as he or she shall desire to purchase," certificate therefor being obtained from the public auditors on a receipt from the treasurer that the person applying had paid in a stated amount of money and was entitled to a proportionate amount of land at the rate stipulated. The decentralized system of obtaining warrants proposed by TJ would have been an advantage to the small purchaser; the limitation of acreage was intended to have the same effect.

24 This paragraph was eliminated by amendment. Here TJ seems to have had in view the use of the western lands to promote the solidarity of the union and to induce small states with limited boundaries, such as Maryland, Delaware, and New Jersey, to ratify the Articles of Confederation. A similar proposal is in the form of a resolution passed by the House of Delegates on 18 Dec. 1778, a resolution that Abernethy (*Western Lands*, p. 223) apparently attributes to the influence of R. H. Lee. But what Lee proposed was a general cession of land north of the Ohio; what the resolution proposed was essentially what was already in TJ's Bill—a Bill that had failed to reach its second reading only two weeks earlier. The resolution of 18 Dec. 1778 was passed at the same time as the resolutions authorizing the Virginia delegates in Congress to ratify the Articles of Confederation, and it seems plausible to suppose that TJ, seeing that his Bill could not pass at that session, lifted from it the section that related to the national problem. If so,

that section was altered, for the resolution reads as follows:

"The more effectually to enable Congress to comply with the promise of a bounty in lands to the officers and soldiers of the army, on continental establishment:

"*Resolved*, That this Commonwealth will, in conjunction with such other of the United States, as have unappropriated back lands, furnish out of its territory, between the rivers of Ohio and Mississippi, in such proportion as shall hereafter be adjusted and settled by Congress, its proper quota or proportion of such lands, without any purchase money, to the troops on continental establishment of such of the United States, as already have acceded, or shall within such time, given or indefinite, as to Congress shall seem best, accede to the confederation of the United States, and who have not within their own respective territory, unappropriated lands for that purpose; and that a copy of this resolve, be forthwith transmitted to the Virginia delegates, to be by them communicated to Congress" (JHD, Oct. 1778, 1827 edn., p. 124-5; copy of resolutions is in DLC: PCC, 71, I). Nothing came of this proposal.

[25] The words "their heirs or assigns" are added in Act.

[26] The words "by Importation-Rights, Native-Rights" were deleted by amendment in accordance with earlier deletions (see notes 12 and 15, above). The words "or the larger Treasury rights" are interlined in TJ's hand; Act reads: "or treasury rights."

[27] The word "printed" is interlined in TJ's hand; the Act reads: "printed warrant under his hand and the seal of his office."

[28] Act reads: "duly qualified according to law."

[29] The words "with the names of the persons mentioned in any Importation Certificate" were deleted by amendment. The Act has the additional clauses at this point: "which warrants shall be always good and valid until executed by actual survey, or exchanged in the manner herein after directed; provided that no warrant on treasury rights, other than preemption warrants, to be obtained by virtue of this act, shall be granted or issued before the fifteenth day of October next; nor shall the surveyor of any county admit the entry or location of any warrant on treasury rights, except preemption warrants, in his books, before the first day of May next. Any person holding a land warrant upon any of the before mentioned rights, may have the same executed in one or more surveys, and in such case, or where the lands on which any warrant is located shall be insufficient to satisfy such warrant, the party may have the said warrant exchanged by the register of the land office for others of the same amount in the whole, but divided as best may answer the purposes of the party, or entitle him to so much land elsewhere as will make good the deficiency."

[30] Act reads: "nominated, examined, and certified able by the president and professors."

[31] The words "with a reservation . . . by such surveyor" are interlined in the hand of TJ. The Act adds, after the word "surveyor," the following: "for the yearly payment of which, he shall give bond with sufficient security to the president and masters of the said college."

[32] Act reads: "in such sum as he, with advice of his council, shall have directed for the faithful execution of his office" and omits requirement respecting oath of fidelity.

[33] This sentence was deleted by amendment.

[34] The words "accounting nevertheless . . . sixth part to their principal" are interlined in TJ's hand. The provisions in the Act concerning deputy surveyors vary from the MS, as follows: "All deputy surveyors shall be nominated by their principals, who shall be answerable for them, examined and certified able by the president and masters of the said college, and if of good character, commissioned by the governour, and shall thereupon be entitled to one half of all fees received for services performed by them respectively, after deducting the proportion thereof due to the college. If any principal surveyor shall fail to nominate a sufficient number of deputies to perform the services of his office in due time, the court of the county shall direct what number he shall nominate, and in case of failure, shall nominate for him."

[35] The words "and with his privity" are interlined in TJ's hand, as is the word "greater" in the same sentence.

[36] The word "examined" is omitted in the Act.

[37] Act reads: ". . . this act, nor in cases now depending before any court within this commonwealth."

[38] Act reads: "Every person having a land warrant founded on any of the before mentioned rights, and being desirous. . . ." TJ deleted the following from the MS: "or meaning to procure Treasury Rights by Payment of the Consideration in money before mentioned" and then interlined "or Treasury rights."

[39] In MS TJ deleted the words "apply to" and interlined "lodge them with."

[40] In MS TJ interlined the words "directing the location . . . enter such location" after deleting the following: "who shall thereupon enter the same in a Book to be kept for that purpose in the name of the person applying by such particular description as that the same may be known thereby so specially and precisely that others may make Entries for [*interlined by TJ*: locate warrants on] the adjacent residuum. When any person shall apply [*interlined by TJ*: at the office of any surveyor with a warrant for] to have an Entry made with any Surveyor for the survey of waste or unappropriated lands [*interlined by TJ*: desiring to locate the same] and shall be refused [*interlined by TJ*: to have his location entered]." The Act reads at this point: ". . . of them lie, who shall give a receipt for the same if required. The party shall direct the location. . . ."

[41] Act at this point has the following additional words: "bear date the day on which it shall be made."

[42] Act at this point has the following additional words: "in which there shall be left no blank leaves or spaces" between the entries. The Act also provides that if several persons should apply with warrants at the same time, they should be ranked according to priority of dates of warrants; if all bore the same date, priority should be established by lot. For persons living outside the county, the surveyor should, at time of making entries, settle a date for the survey and give notice in writing.

[43] The words "paying such Surveyor . . . and six pence" were deleted by amendment.

[44] The following was deleted in MS at this point: "Any Surveyor, when so required, at his own office, refusing to produce such original Entry, or to give an attested Copy thereof, or to enter such Land, for the party applying when no other hath a preferable Claim, or refusing to Survey himself for any person upon reasonable notice any Lands before entered, or to direct a Deputy surveyor to make such survey, and any deputy surveyor, on receiving such direction, refusing within a reasonable time to make such Survey, shall forfeit to the party requiring the same the full value of such Lands." In place of this deleted passage TJ interlined in the MS the words "But it shall not be . . . Cumberland river." This in turn was altered by amendment to read, as the Act does: "But it shall not be lawful for any surveyor to admit an entry for any land without a warrant from the register of the land office, except in the particular case of certificates from the commissioners of the county for tracts of land, not exceeding four hundred acres allowed in consideration of settlements, according to an act of assembly, entitled 'An act for adjusting and settling the titles of claimants to unpatented lands, under the present and former government, previous to the establishment of the commonwealth's land office.' No entry or location of land shall be admitted within the county and limits of the Cherokee Indians, or on the north west side of the Ohio river, or on the lands reserved by act of assembly for any particular nation or tribe of Indians, or on the lands granted by law to Richard Henderson and company, or in that tract of country reserved by resolution of the general assembly for the benefit of the troops serving in the present war, and bounded by the Green river and a south east course from the head thereof to the Cumberland mountains, with the said mountains to the Carolina line, with the Carolina line to the Cherokee or Tenesee river, with the said river to the Ohio river, and with the Ohio to the said Green river, until the farther order of the general assembly." The grant to Richard Henderson and Company is described in Hening, IX, 571 (passed at the Oct. 1778 session), and the resolution respecting the reservation of lands for officers and soldiers was passed on the last day of the same session, 19 Dec. 1778 (JHD, Oct. 1778, p. 125-8; Hening, X, 55). Only the first of five resolutions offered was adopted, the remainder being tabled; the Senate agreed to it the same day.

[45] The words "having a warrant for lands and" and "locate the same on" are interlined in TJ's hand. The words "for himself" are crossed out in MS.

[46] The words "make such Entry" are crossed out in MS and "enter such location" interlined in TJ's hand.

[47] Act reads: "as soon as may be, and within six months at farthest."

[48] The following is added in Act: "or his entry shall be void, and the land liable to the entry of any other person."

[49] The following is crossed out in MS: "either by himself, or by such Deputy as he shall direct."

[50] The following is added in Act: "if the party live within his county."

[51] The words "if the party . . . repaid as hereafter directed" are interlined in TJ's hand. This interlined passage is not in Act.

[52] MS originally read "one" and was altered to "four"; Act reads "one."

[53] The words "mark" and "if necessary" are interlined in TJ's hand.

[54] The following is added at this point in the Act: "the land thereafter subject to the entry of any other person, and the surveyor shall return him the warrant, which may, notwithstanding, be located anew upon any other waste or unappropriated lands, or again upon the same lands where it hath not, in the mean time, been entered for by another person."

[55] Act reads "each," probably a misreading.

[56] The words "by mountains unfit for cultivation" are interlined in TJ's hand.

[57] The words "Immediately on the close of" are struck out and "within three days after making" interlined in TJ's hand.

[58] The words "and separates from the party or person attending him" are deleted in MS. The Act altered the time limit for supplying a plat to "as soon as it can conveniently be done, and within three months at farthest after making the survey" and, of course, eliminated the qualifying clause "before he proceeds to make another."

[59] Act adds: "where hundreds are established in the county wherein it lies."

[60] The words "also the nature . . . to the party" are interlined in TJ's hand as a substitution for the following, deleted in MS: "whether the said survey is made in pursuance of an Original Entry in his office, or by Virtue of a Warrant and Rights, in which case such Warrant and rights shall be recited." Act also adds the following at this point: "The said surveyor may, nevertheless, detain the said certificates and warrants until the payment of his fees."

[61] The words "be examined . . . and shall be" are interlined in TJ's hand.

[62] Act reads: "three."

[63] The words "to the professors . . . and also" are interlined in TJ's hand.

[64] Act adds: "clerk's."

[65] The words "or his deputies" are interlined in TJ's hand.

[66] The following was added to Act at this point: "with the names of the persons for whom they were respectively made, and the quantities contained in each, there to be recorded by such clerk; and no person after the first day of May next, shall hold the offices of clerk of a county court and surveyor of a county, nor shall a deputy in either office act as deputy or chief in the other."

[67] The words "by fine or" are interlined by TJ; Act reads "indicted in the general court, and punished by amercement or deprivation. . . ."

[68] The words "or by fine and imprisonment" are deleted in MS. Act reads at this point: ". . . take it again, at the discretion of a jury."

[69] Act adds: "once in every year, and oftener if they see cause, appoint two or more. . . ."

[70] Act adds: "shall have power."

[71] At this point TJ attached a slip on which was written in his own hand the following paragraph for insertion in the Bill: "Any person holding a land-warrant may have the same executed in one or more surveys; and in such case, or where the lands, on which any warrant is located, shall not be sufficient to satisfy such warrant, the party shall be entitled to have the said warrant exchanged at the office from which it issued for others, of the same amount in the whole, but divided as best may answer the purposes of the party, and entitle him to so much land elsewhere as will make good the deficiency."

[72] Act reads: "within three days thereafter, he shall. . . ." The words "on the same day on which he entered his caveat in the said office" are, of course, not in the Act.

[73] Act reads: "three months."

[74] Act adds the following: "and also producing a legal certificate of new rights on his own account."

[75] Act adds the following: "and produce such certificates."

[76] MS was altered by TJ from "all Caveats" to "any Caveat."

[77] Act has the following additional matter at this point: "award him his costs, and may compel the plaintiff in any caveat, if they think fit, to give security for costs, or on failure thereof, may dismiss his suit; and in case the

plaintiff in any such caveat shall recover, the court may, if they think it reasonable, award costs against the defendant; provided that where any lands surveyed upon a land warrant as aforesaid, shall, in consequence of any judgment upon a caveat, be granted to any other person than the party claiming under such warrant, such party shall be entitled to a new warrant from the register for the quantity of land so granted to another, reciting the original warrant and rights, and the particular cause of granting the new warrant. And to prevent confusion and mistakes in the application, exchange, or renewal of warrants, the register of the land office is hereby directed and required to leave a sufficient margin in the record books of his office, and whenever any warrant shall be exchanged, renewed, or finally carried into execution by a grant, to note the same in the margin opposite to such warrant, with folio references to the grant, or other mode of application; and also to note in the margin opposite to each grant, the warrant or warrants and survey on which such grant is founded, with proper folio references to the books in which the same are recorded. All persons, as well foreigners as others, shall have right to assign or transfer warrants or certificates of survey for lands, and any foreigner purchasing warrants for lands, may locate and have the same surveyed, and after returning a certificate of survey to the land office, shall be allowed the term of eighteen months, either to become a citizen, or to transfer his right in such certificate of survey to some citizen of this, or any other of the United States of America. When any grant shall have been finally completed, the register shall cause the plat and certificate of survey on which such grant is founded, to be exactly entered and recorded in well bound books, to be provided for that purpose at the publick charge."

78 The preceding paragraph and that following were written by TJ on a slip attached to the bottom of p. 12. They are not in the Act, since TJ's decentralized system of issuing warrants through county clerks was not adopted.

79 Act reads "not less than six, nor more than nine months."

80 The parts enclosed in square brackets (supplied) are not in Act, having been deleted because of the deletions noted above (notes 12 and 15).

81 Act adds: "(describing the particular bounds of the land and the date of the survey upon which the grant issues)."

82 Act reads: ". . . and his heirs for ever," omitting the passage "to be holden of the said Commonwealth by fealty in free and common soccage."

83 Act reads: "good well bound books."

84 Act omits the words "by the register" and adds, after the word "expence," the words "and kept by the register."

85 The word "entered" is interlined in TJ's hand.

86 Act adds at this point the words "together with the original certificate of survey."

87 This sentence is not included in the Act, but the following sections are in the Act but not in MS: "Where a grant shall be made to the heir or assignee of a person claiming under any of the before mentioned rights, the material circumstances of the title shall be recited in such grant: And for preventing hasty and surreptitious grants and avoiding controversies and expensive law suits, *Be it enacted*, That no surveyor shall at any time within twelve months after the survey made, issue or deliver any certificate, copy or plat of land by him surveyed, except only to the person or persons for whom the same was surveyed; or to his, her, or their order, unless a caveat shall have been entered against a grant to the person claiming under such survey, to be proved by an authentick certificate of such caveat from the clerk of the general court produced to the surveyor; and if any surveyor shall presume to issue any certificate, copy, or plat as aforesaid, to any other than the person or persons entitled thereto, every surveyor so offending shall forfeit and pay to the party injured, his or her legal representatives or assigns, fifty pounds current money for every hundred acres of land contained in the survey, whereof a certificate, copy, or plat shall be so issued, or shall be liable to the action of the party injured at the common law for his or her damages at the election of the party. Any person possessing high lands, to which any swamp, marshes, or sunken grounds are contiguous, shall have the preemption of such swamps, marshes, or sunken grounds for one year, from and after the passing of this act, and if such person shall not obtain a grant for such swamps, marshes, or sunken grounds within the said year, then any other person may enter on and obtain a grant for the same

in the like manner as is directed in the case of other unappropriated lands. But nothing herein contained shall be construed or extend to give liberty to any person to survey, take up, or obtain a grant for any swamps, marshes, or sunken grounds lying contiguous to the high lands of any feme covert, infant under the age of twenty one years, person not being compos mentis, or person out of the commonwealth, according to the regulations of an act entitled 'An act declaring who shall be deemed citizens of this commonwealth,' but all such persons shall be allowed one year after the removal of their several disabilities for the preemption of such lands.

"And whereas, through the ignorance, negligence, or fraud of surveyors, it may happen that divers persons now do or may hereafter hold within the bounds expressed in their patents or grants, greater quantities of land than are therein mentioned; for quieting such possessions, preventing controversies, and doing equal justice to the commonwealth and its citizens, *Be it enacted*, That it shall not be lawful for any person to enter for, survey, or take up, any parcel of land held as surplus in any patent or grant, except during the life time of the patentee or grantee, and before any transference, conveyance, or other alienation shall have been made of the lands contained in such patent or grant, and until the party intending to enter and take up the same, shall have given one full years notice to such patentee or grantee of such his intentions, and in case such patentee or grantee shall not within the year, obtain rights and sue forth a patent for the surplus land by him held, it shall be lawful for the person who gave notice as aforesaid, upon producing a certificate from the clerk of due proof of such notice before the court of the county wherein such patentee or grantee resides, to demand from the register of the land office, a warrant to the surveyor of the county wherein such lands lie, to resurvey at the proper charge of the person obtaining such warrant, the whole tract within the bounds of the patent or grant, and upon such persons returning into the land office a plat and certificate of such resurvey, together with the warrant on which it is founded, and obtaining and producing new rights for all the surplus land found within the said bounds, he may sue forth and obtain a new grant for such surplus, which shall be granted to him in the same manner as waste or unappropriated lands; but the former patentee or grantee may assign such surplus land in any part of his tract as he shall think fit in one entire piece, the breadth of which shall be at least one third of the length; and in such new grant there shall be a recital of the original patent or grant, the resurvey of which the surplus was ascertained and of other material circumstances.

"*Provided always*, That if upon notice given as aforesaid, the original patentee or grantee shall within the year resurvey his tract, and it be thereupon found that he hath no more than the quantity of land expressed in his patent or grant, with the allowance herein after mentioned, the party giving such notice shall be liable to pay all charges of such resurvey, for which he shall give sufficient security to the said patentee or grantee at the time of the notice, otherwise such notice shall be void and of no effect; and moreover for his unjust vexation, shall also be liable to an action upon the case at the suit of the party grieved, and that in all such new surveys, the patentee or grantee shall have an allowance at the rate of five acres in every hundred, for the variation of instruments.

"*And be it enacted*, That where any person shall find any mistake or uncertainty in the courses or description of the bounds of his land, and desires to rectify the same, or shall hold two or more tracts of land adjoining to each other, and is desirous to include them in one grant, he may in either case, having previously advertised his intentions and the time of application, at the door of the courthouse on two several court days, and also having given notice to the owners of the adjoining lands, present a petition to the court of the county wherein such lands lie, reciting the nature and truth of the case, and such court may, and is hereby empowered to order the surveyor of their county to resurvey such lands at the charge of the party, according to his directions and the original or authentick title papers, taking care not to intrude upon the possessions of any other person, and to return a fair plat and certificate of such resurvey into the said court, to be examined and compared with the title papers; and if such court shall certify that in their opinion such resurvey is just and reasonable, the party may return the same, together with his material title papers in the land office, and demand the register's receipt for them; and in case any caveat shall be entered against his obtaining a new grant upon such resurvey, the same proceedings shall be had therein as is directed in the case of other caveats, and the general court upon hearing the same, may either prohibit such new grant, or vacate the caveat as to them shall seem just; but if no caveat shall be entered within six months after such return, or if a caveat shall be entered and vacated as aforesaid, the party upon producing new rights for whatever surplus land appears to be within the bounds, more than the before mentioned allowance of five acres for every hundred, may sue out and obtain a new grant for such lands thereupon, in which shall be recited the dates and other material circumstances of the former title, and the title papers shall be delivered by the register to the new owner. The judges of the general court shall once in every year and oftener if they see cause, appoint two or more capable persons to examine the record books and papers in the land office, and report in what condition and order they are kept, who shall compare all warrants of survey returned to the said office executed, with the list of those issued therefrom, and cancel all such as shall appear to have been properly executed or exchanged, an account of which shall be kept by the register, charging therein those issued, and giving credit for those cancelled as aforesaid. The treasurer for the time being shall annually enter into bond with sufficient security to the governour in the sum of one hundred thousand pounds, for the just and faithful accounting for according to law, all money which shall come to his hands by virtue of this act. And that the proprietors of lands within this commonwealth may no longer be subject to any servile, feudal, or precarious tenure, and to prevent the danger to a free state from perpetual revenue; *Be it enacted*, That the reservation of royal mines of quitrents, and all other reservations and conditions in the patents or grants of land from the crown of England or of Great Britain, under the former government, shall be, and are hereby declared null and void; and that all lands thereby respectively granted, shall be held in absolute and unconditional property to all intents and purposes whatsoever, in the same manner with the lands hereafter to be granted by the commonwealth by virtue of this act; and no petition for lapsed land shall be admitted or received for or on account of any failure or forfeiture whatsoever, alledged to have been made or incurred after the twenty ninth day of September, in the year of our Lord one thousand seven hundred and seventy five. *And be it farther enacted*, That he or she be adjudged a felon and not have the benefit of clergy, who shall steal, or by other means take from the possession or custody of another, any warrant from the register of the land office of this commonwealth, to authorize a survey of waste and unappropriated lands; or who shall alter, erase, or aid or assist in the alteration or erasement of any such warrant; or forge or counterfeit, or aid, abet, or assist in forging or counterfeiting any written or printed paper, purporting to be such warrant; or who shall transfer to the use of another, or for his or her own use, present or cause to be presented to the register for the exchange thereof, or to a surveyor for the execution thereof, any such warrant or paper purporting to be such warrant, knowing the same so transferred or presented for the exchange or the execution thereof to be stolen, or by other means taken from the possession or custody of another, or altered or erased, or forged or counterfeited; and he or she shall be adjudged a felon and not have the benefit of clergy, who shall falsely make or counterfeit, or aid, abet, or assist, in safely keeping or counterfeiting any instrument stamping an impression in the figure and likeness of the seal officially used by the register of the land office, or who shall have in his or her possession or custody such instrument, and shall wilfully conceal the same, knowing it to be falsely made or counterfeited."

88 Act adds at this point: "concern or relate to the entering, taking up, or seating lands or."

II. Bill for Settling Titles to Unpatented Lands

[14 January 1778]

Whereas the various and vague claims to unpattented Lands under the former Government,[1] covering the greater part of the Country on the Western Waters, may produce tedious and infinite Litigation and disputes, and in the mean time Purchasers would be discouraged from taking up Lands upon the Terms lately prescribed by Law, whereby the Fund to be raised in Aid of the Taxes for discharging the Public Debt would be in a great measure, frustrated; And it is just and necessary, as well for the peace of Individuals, as for the Public Weal, that some certain Rules should be Established for setling and determining the Rights to such Lands, and fixing the Principles upon which such Claimers shall be entitled to Patents;[2] to the End that subsequent Purchasers and Adventurers may be enabled to Act[3] with greater Certainty and Safety. Be it enacted by the General Assembly that all Surveys heretofore made by any sworn surveyor, acting under Commission from the Masters of William and Mary College,[4] and founded either upon Charter Importation Rights duly proved and certified according to ancient Usuage,[5] upon Treasury Rights for Money paid the late Receiver General, upon Entry's made[6] with the Surveyor of any[7] County for Tracts of Land not exceeding four hundred Acres, according to Act of Assembly upon any Order of Council or regular Entry[8] in the Council Books, or upon any Warrant from the Governor for the time being, for Military Service in Virtue of any Proclamation either from the King of Great Britain[9] or any former Governor of Virginia, shall be good and valid; but that all Surveys for Waste and unpatented Lands made by any other person, or upon any other pretence whatsoever, shall be, and are hereby declared null and Void;[10] And that all and every person or persons, his her or their heirs or Assigns, claiming Lands upon any of the before recited Rights and under Surveys made as herein before mentioned,[11] shall upon the Plats and Certificates of such Surveys being returned into the Land Office, together with the Rights, Entry, Order or Warrant[12] upon which they were respectively founded, be entitled to a Patent or Patents[13] for the same; Provided that such Surveys and Rights[14] be returned to the said Office within Months[15] next after the end of this present Session of Assembly:[16] and where two or more persons shall claim the same

Land under different Surveys, the person claiming under that Survey which was first actually made shall have the Preference.[17] That all persons their heirs or Assigns claiming Lands under the Charter and ancient Custom of Virginia, upon Importation Rights[18] duly proved and Certified in any Court of Record before the Passing of this Act, as also those claiming under Treasury Rights for Money paid the Receiver General[19] or under Proclamation-Warrants for Military service, and not having located or fixed such Lands by actual Surveys as herein before mentioned, shall be admitted to new Warrants and Entries[20] for the same in the manner directed by the Act intitled an Act for Establishing a Land Office and ascertaining the Terms and manner of granting waste unappropriated Lands upon Producing to the Register of the said Office[21] the proper Certificates, proofs or Warrants, as the case is, for their respective Rights, within Months[22] after the End of this present Session of Assembly.[23]

And be it enacted that all Orders of Council or Entries for Land in the Council Books upon the Western Waters[24] except so far as such Orders or entries respectively have been carried into execution by Actual Surveys in manner herein before mentioned, shall be, and they are hereby declared void and of no Effect.[25] And that no claim to Land within this Commonwealth for Military service, founded upon the King of Great Britain's Proclamation in the Year One thousand seven hundred and sixty three,[26] shall hereafter be allowed; except a Warrant for the same shall have been obtained from the Governor of Virginia, during the former Government,[27] or where such service was performed[28] in one of the Virginia Regiments; in which case such Claimant making due Proof thereof in any Court of Record[29] shall be admitted to a Warrant and Entry[30] for the same in the manner herein before mentioned.[31]

And whereas great numbers of People have settled in the Country upon the said Western Waters, upon waste and unappropriated Lands, for which they have hitherto been prevented from sueing out Patents or obtaining legal Titles by the King of Great Britain's Proclamations or Instructions to his Governors, or by the late change of Government; and the present War having delayed, until now, the opening a Land Office, and the Establishment of any certain Terms for Granting Lands, and it is just that those settling under such Circumstances, and Guilty of no neglect or omission on their part,[32] should have some reasonable allowance for the charge and Risque they have incurred, and that the property, so acquired should be secured to them; Be it therefore enacted that all persons, who at any time before the passing of this Act[33] have really and bonafide settled themselves,[34] or at his her or their charge have settled others, upon any waste or unappropriated Lands,[35] to which no other person hath any legal Right or Claim, shall be allowed for[36] every such Family or Settlement the Quantity of four hundred Acres of Land to include such settlement, and to every such Family as for their greater safety have settled themselves in Villages or Townships these shall be allowed their respective Improvements in such Village or Township, together with as much adjacent Land as will make up the like Quantity of four hundred Acres, each Family to have the Preferrance in such Land as they have actually occupied, so far as the same can be done; for which Quantity's, to be adjusted ascertained and certified by the Commissioners to be appointed by this Act in manner herein after directed,[37] they shall be respectively entitled to Warrants, and Entries with the[38] Surveyor of the County,[39] and upon the due return[40] of the plat and Certificate of Survey,[41] grants may and shall Issue to them and their Heirs[42] according to the Rules and Regulations of the said office. And if any such Setlers shall desire to take up a greater Quantity of Land than is herein allowed them, they shall,[43] on payment of the consideration money required from other purchasers, be entitled to the Preemption, of any greater Quantity of Land, adjoining to such Settlements, not exceeding one thousand Acres, and to which no other person hath any legal right or Claim.[44]

All persons, who before the passing of this Act, have made regular Entries with the Surveyor of any County, for Lands on the said Western waters to which no other Person hath a legal Right or Claim, and have not surveyed the same in Manner herein before mentioned, shall be entitled to the Pre-emption, at the State Price, of the Land so entered for; and those who have[45] marked out[46] for themselves any Waste or unappropriated Lands,[47] and made any Improvements thereon, shall also be entitled to the pre-emption, upon the like Terms, of any Quantity of Land not exceeding two thousand[48] Acres, to include such Improvements, or so much thereof to which no other person hath any legal Right or Claim:[49] Provided they respectively demand and prove their Claim to[50] such pre-emption[51] and take out their Warrants of Survey within Months next after the end of this present session of Assembly, and thereafter duly comply with the Rules and Regulations of the Land Office.

And be it further enacted that all persons claiming Lands on the said Western waters[52] and sueing out Patents[53] upon Surveys heretofore made, either under Entries[54] with the Surveyor of any County, or under any Order of Council or Entry in the Council Books[55] and those claiming Tracts of Land not exceeding four hundred Acres hereinallowed[56] them in Consideration of their Settlements,[57] shall be subject to the payment of the usual Composition Money, under the former Government, at the rate of ten shillings Sterling for every hundred Acres, to be discharged in Current Money at thirty three and one third percentum Exchange,[58] and to no other Charge or Imposition whatsoever, save the common office fees.[59] And Whereas it is represented to this present General Assembly[60] that upon the Lands surveyed for sundry Company's by Virtue of Orders of Council, many people have settled,[61] under the faith of the Terms of Sale Publickly offered by the said Company's or their Agents at the Time of such Settlements, who have made Valuable Improvements thereon, and are now refused Titles to the Lands so Surveyed and Settled, or a much higher price demanded from them: For Remedy whereof,[62] Be it declared and enacted that all persons so settled upon any Lands,[63] except only such Lands as before the Settlement of the same were notoriously reserved by the[64] Company for whom they were respectively surveyed for their own use, shall have their Titles confirmed to them by the Members of such Company's or their Agents, upon Payment of the price at which such Lands were offered for Sale,[65] together with Interest thereon from the time of the respective Settlements.[66]

And[67] whereas the Claims of various Persons to the Lands herein allowed to the Inhabitants in Consideration of their Settlements, as well as of those who by this Act are entitled to Pre-emption at the State-Price,[68] may occasion many Disputes, the Determination of which, depending upon Evidence which can not without great Charge and Trouble be collected but in the Neighbourhood of such Lands, will be most speedily and properly made by Commissioners in the respective Counties, Be it enacted that the Governor with the Advice of the privy Council may and He is hereby empowered to appoint by Commission under his Hand and Seal four of the most able and discreet Men in each and every County upon the western Waters (any three of whom may act) to continue in office six months from the End of this present Session of Assembly for the Purpose of collecting adjusting and determining such Claims. Every such Commissioner, before He enters on the Dutys of his Office,[69] shall take the Oath of Fidelity to the Commonwealth, and the[70] following Oath of Office "You shall swear that You will well and truly serve this Commonwealth in the Office of a Commissioner for the County of   for collecting and adjusting and setling the Claims and determining the Titles of such Persons as claim Lands in the said County in Consideration of having setled thereon, or of such as claim Pre-emption to any Lands therein,[71] under an Act of General Assembly intitled an Act for adjusting and setling the Titles of Claimers to unpatented Lands under the former[72] Government; and that You will do equal Right to all Manner of People, without Respect of Persons; You shall not take by Yourself, nor by any other Person, any Gift Fee or Reward for any Matter done or to be done by Virtue of Your Office, except such Fees or Sallery as the Law shall allow You; and finally in all things belonging to Your said Office, You shall faithfully justly and truly, according to the best of Your Skill and Judgement, do equal and impartial Justice, without Fraud Favour Affection or Partiality" which Oath shall be administered by any of the said Commissioners to the first of them in nomination who shall be present, and then by him to the others.

The said Commissioners shall have Power to hear and determine all Titles to Lands claimed in Consideration of Settlements[73] made thereon, as also the Rights of all Persons claiming Pre-emption to any Lands within their respective Countys,[74] either for Entries made with the County Surveyor, or for the other Considerations mentioned in this Act, and shall imediatly upon Receipt of their Commissions, give at least twenty Days previous Notice by Advertisements at the[75] Churches and Meeting Houses[76] in their County, of the time and Place at which they intend to meet, for the Purpose of collecting hearing and determining the said Claims and Titles, requiring all Persons interested therein to attend, and put in their Claims; and may adjourn from place to place, and time to time, as their Business may require; but if they should fail to meet at any time to which they shall have adjourn'd, neither their Commission, nor any matter depending before them shall be thereby discontinued, but they shall proceed to Business when they do meet, as if no such Failure had happened: they shall appoint and administer an Oath of Office to their Clerk, be attended by the Sherif, or one of the Under Sherifs of the County, be empowered to administer all Oaths to witnesses or others necessary for the Discharge of their Office, to punish Contempts in the same Manner as the County Court, and enforce good Behaviour in their Presence;[77] they shall have free Access to the County Surveyor's Books, and may order the same to be laid before them at any time or place of their sitting.[78]

In all Cases of Dispute, upon Claims for Settlement, the person who made the first actual Settlement, his or her Heirs or Assigns, shall have the Preference; and in all Disputes for the Right of Preemption on Entries made with the County Surveyor, the Person, his or her Heirs or Assigns, who made the first Entry.[79]

The Clerk shall keep exact minutes of all the proceedings of the Commissioners, and enter the names of all the Persons to whom either Lands for Settlement, or the right of Pre-emption, as the Case is, shall be adjudged, with their respective Quantitys and Locations.[80] Upon application of any Person claiming a right to any such Lands, and complaining that another pretends a Right in Opposition thereto, the said Clerk shall issue a Summons, stating the nature of the Plaintiff's Claim, and calling on the Party opposing the same to appear at a time and place certain, therein to be named, and shew Cause why a Grant of the said Lands may not issue[81] to the said plaintiff: the said Summons shall be served on the Party by the Sherif of the County,[82] and such Service being return'd thereon, and the Party appearing, or failing to appear, the Commissioners may proceed to Trial, or for good Cause shewn, may refer such Trial to a further Day. The Clerk shall also have Power, at the Request of either Party, to issue Subpœnas for witnesses, to appear at the time and place of trial; which shall be had in a summary way, without pleadings in writing; and the Court in conducting the said Trial, in all matters of Evidence relative thereto, and in giving Judgement, shall govern themselves by such Rules and Principles of Law or Equity as are applicable to the Case, or wou'd be the Rule of Trial, of Evidence, or of Decision, were the same before the ordinary Courts of Law or Equity; save only so far as this Act shall otherwise have specially directed. Judgement, when rendered, shall be final,[83] and shall give to the Party, in whose favour it is, a Title against all others who were Partys to the Trial; and if after such Judgement rendered, the Party against whom it is, shall enter the said Lands forcibly, or forcibly detain the same, it shall be lawful for the said Commissioners, or any one of them, or any Justice of the Peace for the County, to remove such Force, in like manner as if it were committed on Lands holden by Grant actually issued.

The said Commissioners shall deliver to every Person to whom they shall adjudge Lands for Settlement, a Certificate thereof under their Hands, and attested by their Clerk, mentioning[84] the Quantity, and describing as near as may be, the particular Location; noting also therein the Quantity of adjacent Land to which such

Person shall have the Right of Pre-emption: and to every other Person to whom they shall adjudge the Right of Pre-emption to any Lands, they shall in like Manner deliver a Certificate specifying the Quantity and Location of such Land, with the Cause for Pre-emption;[85] for every[86] of which Certificates, the Party receiving the same shall pay down to the Commissioners the Sum of ten Shillings, besides a fee of two Shillings and six Pence[87] to the Clerk; And the said Certificates[88] shall entitle the Persons respectively receiving them to an Entry and Survey, or warrant for the said Lands in such way and on such Terms as herein before prescribed upon producing the same to the Surveyor of the County, or to the Register of the Land Office, or to the Treasurer, or County Court Clerk, as the Case may require. The said Commissioners[89] shall transmit to the Register of the Land Office, under their Hands and attested by their Clerk, an exact List or Schedule, in alphabetical order, of all such Certificates by them granted, and a Duplicate, so signd and attested, to the County Surveyor, for their Information;[90] and in order the more effectually to preserve to such Persons the priority and preferrence of Location, and the Benefit of Pre-emption, for and during the before mentioned Space of Months from and after the passing of this Act.

The said Commissioners for every Day they shall be actually employed in discharge of their Office shall be allowed the Sum of Shillings[91] each; they shall be accountable for all the money they shall have received upon issueing Certificates as aforesaid, except the Fee to the Clerk, and shall settle a fair Account[92] with the Treasurer; who is hereby empowered to pay them whatever Ballance may appear due to them thereon, and to receive from them any Ballance which shall be by them due to the Commonwealth.

The Clerk and Sherif shall receive, for their Services, the fees heretofore allowed by Law for the same Services in the County Court,[93] to be paid by the Party, and collected in like manner as is directed in the ordinary Cases of the same nature;[94] provided that the Clerk shall not be allowed any further or other fee for entering and issueing a Certificate than is herein before mentioned.[95]

When the Register of the Land-Office shall make out a Grant or Patent to any Person[96] or Persons for Lands due to him her or them in Virtue of this Act, He shall recite therein[97] the Rights or Cause for which the same became due "according to an Act of General Assembly passed in the Year of our Lord one thousand seven hundred and seventy seven[98] entitled an Act for adjusting and setling the Titles of Claimers to unpatented Lands under the former Government"[99] and if any Part thereof is due in Consideration of[100] purchase money paid to the Commonwealth the same shall be[101] distinguished. And whereas at the time of the late Change of Government many Caveats against Patents for Lands which had been entered in the Council Office were depending and undetermined, Be it enacted that all such Caveats, together with the Documents and Papers relating thereto,[102] shall be removed into the Clerk's Office of the General Court, there to be proceeded on, tryed and determined[103] in the manner directed by Law for future Caveats.[104]

MS (Vi); 13 pages; in hand of the same clerk who copied MS of Bill for Establishing a Land Office; with erasures, additions, interlineations, &c., by TJ and by George Mason as indicated in notes below. Endorsed on p. [12], in hand of John Tazewell: "A Bill for adjusting & settling the Titles of Claimers to unpatented Lands under the former Government. 1778. Jan: 14. Read the first Time." Endorsed, p. [13], in hand of George Mason, with same title as that on p. [12] and docketed by John Tazewell: "1778. Jan: 14 Read the first Time." Just beneath this was another line partially erased: "[Jany . . . & Committed]." Text of the Act as adopted at session of May 1779 is in Hening, x, 35-50, where the title is: "An Act for adjusting and settling the titles of claimers to unpatented lands under the present and former government, previous to the establishment of the commonwealth's land office."

1 Act reads: "the former and present government, previous to the establishment of the commonwealth's land office"; the words "covering the greater part of the Country on the Western Waters" are not in the Act.

2 Act reads: "upon which legal and just claimers shall be entitled to sue out grants."

3 Act reads: "proceed."

4 Act, following the enacting clause, reads: "That all surveys of waste and unappropriated land made upon any of the western waters before the first day of January, in the year 1778, and upon any of the eastern waters at any time before the end of this present session of assembly, by any county surveyor commissioned by the masters of William and Mary college, acting in conformity to the laws and rules of government then in force, and founded. . . ."

5 Act adds: "as far as relates to indented servants, and other persons not being convicts."

6 Act reads: ". . . paid the receiver general duly authenticated upon entries on the western waters, regularly made before the 26th day of October, in the year 1763, or on the eastern waters at any time before the end of this present session of assembly, with the surveyor. . . ."

7 Act reads "the" instead of "any."

8 Act reads: "or entry in the council books, and made during the time in which it shall appear either from the original or any subsequent order, entry, or proceedings in the council books, that such order or entry remained in force the terms of which have been complied with, or the time for performing the same unexpired, or upon any warrant. . . ."

9 The famous Proclamation of 1763 is in Hening, VII, 663.

10 Act includes at this point the proviso that all officers or soldiers, or their heirs or assigns, claiming under Governor Dinwiddie's proclamation of 1754 offering a bounty in lands to the officers and soldiers of the first Virginia regiment, if they had returned to the secretary's office surveys "made by virtue of a special commission of the president and masters of William and Mary college," could have their claims validated by taking out warrants on their proclamation rights, resurveying the lands, and then proceeding according to the Land Office regulations.

11 Act reads: ". . . mentioned, against which no caveat shall have been legally entered."

12 Act adds: "or authentick copy thereof."

13 Instead of "Patent or Patents" the Act reads: "grant or grants for the same in manner and form herein after directed."

14 The words "and Rights" are interlined in George Mason's hand.

15 Act reads: "twelve months."

16 Act adds at this point: "otherwise they shall be, and are hereby declared forfeited and void."

17 Act omits the clause: "and where two or more . . . shall have the preference."

18 Act adds: "as before limited."

19 Act adds: "duly authenticated"; one and one half lines erased in MS following this point.

20 Act reads: "admitted to warrants, entries, and grants for the same."

21 One and a half lines erased in MS following this point.

22 Act reads: "the like space of twelve months."

23 Four lines have been erased in MS at this point. In the Act the following additional provisions were inserted: "and not afterwards. All certificates of importation rights proved before any court of record according to the ancient custom, and before the end of this present session of assembly, are hereby declared good and valid: And all other claims for importation rights not so proved, shall be null and void; and where any person before the end of this present session of assembly, hath made a regular entry according to act of assembly, with the county surveyor for any tract of land not exceeding four hundred acres, upon any of the eastern waters, which hath not been surveyed or forfeited, according to the laws and rules of government in force at the time of making such entry, the surveyor of the county where such land lies, shall after advertising legal notice thereof, proceed to survey the same accordingly, and shall deliver to the proprietor a plat and certificate of survey thereof within three months; and if such person shall fail to attend at the time and place so appointed for making such survey, with chain carriers and a person to mark the lines, or shall fail to deliver such plat and certificate into the land office, according to the rules and regulations of the same, together with the auditors certificate of the treasurers receipt for the composition money herein after mentioned, and pay the office fees, he or she shall forfeit his or her right and title; but upon performance of these requisitions, shall be entitled to a grant for such tract of land as in other cases."

24 The words "upon the Western Waters" are not in the Act.

25 The Act has the following additional terms at this point: "and except also a certain order of council for a tract of sunken grounds, commonly called the Dismal Swamp, in the south eastern part of this commonwealth, contiguous to the North Carolina line, which said order of council with the proceedings thereon and the claim derived from it, shall hereafter be laid before the general assembly for their further order therein."

26 The date is omitted in the Act.

27 Act adds: "as before mentioned."

28 Act reads: "by an inhabitant of Virginia or in some regiment or corps actually raised in the same."

29 The Act adds: "and producing a certificate thereof to the register of the land office within the said time of twelve months, shall be. . . ."

30 Act reads: "warrant, entry, and grant."

31 Act adds the following at this point: "but nothing herein contained shall be construed or extend to give any person a title to land for service performed in any company or detachment of militia."

32 Act omits the words "and guilty . . . their part."

33 Act reads: "before the first day of January, in the year one thousand seven hundred and seventy eight."

34 Act adds: "or their families."

35 Act adds: "on the said western waters."

36 Act reads: "for every family so settled, four hundred acres of land, or such smaller quantity as the party chooses, to include such settlement." In addition, the Act provided that where any settler had had a survey made under any order of the colonial government, since 26 Oct. 1763, for less than 400 acres, he could take up as much additional unappropriated land as, with the amount surveyed, would amount to 400 acres.

37 The terms of the Act differ concerning these settlements "in Villages or Townships": "And whereas several families for their greater safety have settled themselves in villages or townships, under some agreement between the inhabitants of laying off the same into town lots, to be divided among them, and have, from present necessity, cultivated a piece of ground adjoining thereto in common: *Be it enacted*, That six hundred and forty acres of land whereon such villages and

towns are situate, and to which no other person hath a previous legal claim, shall not be entered for or surveyed, but shall be reserved for the use and benefit of the said inhabitants until a true representation of their case can be made to the general assembly, that right and justice may be done therein; and in the mean time there shall be allowed to every such family, in consideration of their settlement, the like quantity of land as is herein allowed to other settlers adjacent, or convenient to their respective village or town, and to which no other person hath, by this act, the right of preemption, for which said quantities to be adjusted, ascertained, and certified by the commissioners to be appointed by virtue of this act, in manner herein after directed."

[38] The words "Warrants, and Entries with the" are in the hand of George Mason; the Act reads "to entries with."

[39] Act adds: "wherein the land lies, upon producing to him certificates of their rights from the said commissioners of the county, duly attested, within twelve months next after the end of this present session of assembly, and not afterwards; which certificate the said surveyor shall record in his books, and then return them to the parties, and shall proceed to survey the lands so entered, according to law."

[40] Act adds: "to the land office."

[41] Act adds: "together with the certificates from the said commissioners of the rights, by settlement upon which the entries were founded."

[42] The words "or Assigns" are deleted in MS but the Act reads: "heirs or assigns, in manner before directed."

[43] TJ deleted the first and last seven words of the following in MS: "be entitled to the Preemption, at the State price to other purchasers," and interlined the words "on payment of the . . . other purchasers."

[44] At this point the Act includes the following: "And to prevent doubts concerning settlements, *It is hereby declared*, That no family shall be entitled to the allowance granted to settlers by this act, unless they have made a crop of corn in that country, or resided there at least one year since the time of their settlement."

[45] The words "have made regular entries . . . and those who" are written in the margin of MS in hand of George Mason and the words "on the said western waters" within this marginal clause are interlined in the hand of TJ. The Act reads: "All persons who, *since* the said first day of January, in the year one thousand seven hundred and seventy eight, have actually settled on any waste or unappropriated lands on the said western waters, to which no other person hath a just or legal right or claim, shall be entitled to the preemption of any quantity of land, not exceeding four hundred acres, to include such settlement at the state price to other purchasers. And all those who, *before* the said first day of January, in the year one thousand seven hundred and seventy eight have" (italics supplied by the editor).

[46] Act adds: "or chosen."

[47] Act reads: "and built any house or hut or made other improvements thereon."

[48] Act reads: "one thousand."

[49] Act adds: "but no person shall have the right of preemption for more than one such improvement."

[50] The words "and prove their Claim to" are interlined in the hand of George Mason; Act reads "and prove their right to."

[51] The corresponding passage in the Act differs from this: "before the commissioners for the county, to be appointed by virtue of this act within eight months, pay the consideration money, produce the auditor's certificate for the treasurer's receipt for the same, take out their warrants from the register of the land office within ten months, and enter the same with the surveyor of the county, within twelve months next. . . ." The Act also has the following section not in MS: "All locations made by officers and soldiers upon the lands of actual settlers, shall be void, but the said officers, soldiers, or their assignees, may obtain warrants on producing the commissioners certificate of their several rights, and locate their claims on other waste and unappropriated lands. To prevent the locations of those claiming under warrants for preemption, from interfering with such as claim under certificates for settlements, and to give due preference to the latter, so far as respects their rights to tracts of land not exceeding four hundred acres; the register of the land office shall particularly distinguish all preemption warrants by him issued, and no county surveyor shall admit any such warrant to be entered or located in his books, before the expiration of ten months as aforesaid. And where any such warrant shall not be entered and located with the county surveyor, within the before mentioned space

of twelve months, the right of preemption shall be forfeited, and the lands therein mentioned may be entered for by any other person holding another land warrant; but such preemption warrant may, nevertheless, be located upon any other waste or unappropriated lands, or upon the same lands where they have not in the mean time been entered for by some other."

[52] Preceding five words are interlined in TJ's hand; they are not in the Act.

[53] Act reads: "grants."

[54] Preceding seven words are in hand of George Mason, written over an erasure.

[55] Act reads: ". . . books, for which rights have not formerly been lodged in the secretary's office, and also those suing out grants for tracts of lands upon the western waters. . . ."

[56] Preceding twelve words are in Mason's hand.

[57] Act adds: "or under former entries with the county surveyor, for lands upon the eastern waters."

[58] Act adds: "before the grant issues."

[59] The following additional section is in the Act at this point: "And to all such persons, their heirs or assigns, who having title to land under the former government, had not only surveyed the same, but had lodged their certificates of survey, together with their rights, in the secretary's office; and although no caveat hath been entered, have not obtained patents, grants shall issue in consideration thereof, upon the payment of the office fees only."

[60] Act reads: "whereas it hath been represented to the general assembly."

[61] Act reads: "settled without specifick agreement, but yet under. . . ."

[62] The clause "and are now refused . . . For Remedy whereof" is not in the Act.

[63] Act reads: ". . . upon any unpatented lands, surveyed as before mentioned. . . ."

[64] Act reads: "respective companies for their own use. . . ."

[65] Act adds: "when they were settled."

[66] Act adds the following provisos at this point: "provided they compromise their claims with the said companies, or lay them before the commissioners for their respective counties, to be appointed by virtue of this act, and have the same tried and determined by them, in manner herein after directed: And provided also, that where any such survey contains more than four hundred acres, no one settler shall be entitled to a greater quantity than three hundred acres, unless he takes the whole survey, to include his settlement, and leave the remainder in one entire and convenient piece where the same is practicable."

[67] From this point (the concluding five pages) the MS is entirely in the hand of George Mason.

[68] Act adds: "as well as of the settlers on the lands surveyed for sundry companies by orders of council as aforesaid."

[69] Instead of commissioners in each county, the Act provides a district system, as follows: "That the counties on the western waters shall be allotted into districts, to wit: The counties of Monongalia; Yohogania, and Ohio, into one district; the counties of Augusta, Botetourt, and Greenbrier, into one district; the counties of Washington and Montgomery, into one other district; and the county of Kentucky, shall be another district; for each of which districts, the governour, with the advice of the council, shall appoint four commissioners under the seal of the commonwealth, not being inhabitants of such district (any three of whom may act) to continue in office eight months from the end of this present session of assembly, for the purpose of collecting, adjusting, and determining such claims, and four months thereafter for the purpose of adjusting the claims of settlers on lands surveyed for the aforesaid companies."

[70] The preceding eight words are not in the Act; the oath of office in the Act is in the first person, and the word "district" is substituted for "county."

[71] Act adds: "and also of such settlers as claim any lands surveyed by order of council, for sundry companies."

[72] Act reads: "and present government, previous to the establishment of the commonwealth's land office."

[73] Act reads: ". . . of Settlements to lands, to which no person hath any other legal title, and the rights. . . ."

[74] Act reads: ". . . respective districts, as also the rights of all persons claiming any unpatented lands, surveyed by order of council for sundry companies, by having settled thereon under the faith of the terms of sale publickly offered by such companies or their agents." The words "either for Entries . . . in this Act" are not in the Act.

[75] Act adds: "forts."

[76] Act adds: "and other publick places in their district."

77 Act adds: "and award costs."

78 The Act adds at this point a clause giving commissioners authority to pay, out of fees received for certificates, £3 to the county surveyor and £2 to the county sheriff for each day's attendance.

79 This paragraph is written over an erasure of six and a half lines; concerning the second category of disputes, the Act substitutes the following: "In all disputes for the right of preemptions for improvements made on the land, the persons, their heirs or assigns respectively, who made the first improvement, and the persons to whom any right of preemption on account of settlement or improvements shall be adjudged, shall fix the quantity at their own option at the time of the judgment, so as not to exceed the number of acres respectively allowed by this act, or to interfere with the just rights of others."

80 Act adds: "and also the names of all such persons to whom titles shall be adjudged for lands within the surveys made by order of council for any company with the quantity of acres adjudged, and in what survey; and if the same is only part of such survey, in what manner it shall be located therein, the name or style of the company, and the price to be paid them, with the time from which the same is to bear interest."

81 Act adds: "or a title be made."

82 Act adds: "where he resides, or wherein he may be found."

83 Act adds: "except as herein after excepted."

84 Act reads: ". . . the number of acres, and the time of settlement, and describing. . . ."

85 Act adds: "with a memorandum for the information of the party in each certificate of the last day on which the lands therein respectively mentioned can be entered with the county surveyor."

86 Act reads: "every hundred acres of land contained within the said certificates."

87 Act reads: "ten shillings to the clerk for each certificate so granted."

88 Act adds: "produced within the times herein before respectively limited to the surveyor of the county, or to the register of the land office, with the auditor's certificate of the treasurer's receipt for the payment due on the preemption, as the nature of the case may require."

89 Act reads: "And to prevent frauds or mistakes, the said commissioners immediately upon having completed the business in their district, shall transmit."

90 The remainder of this paragraph is not included in the Act. The Act, however, has the following not in MS: "They shall in like manner, and upon payment of the same fees, deliver to every person to whom they shall adjudge, a title to any unpatented land, surveyed for any company by order of council, a certificate mentioning the number of acres to which they have adjudged the title, what particular survey the same is in, and for what company made, the price to be paid such company, and the date from which the same is to bear interest, and where there is a greater quantity of land contained in the survey, describe as near as may be, the manner the land to which they have adjudged title, shall be laid off and bounded; and shall also immediately upon having completed the business in their district, transmit to the clerk of the general court, under their hands, and attested by their clerk, a list or schedule in alphabetical order, containing exact copies of all such certificates by them granted, to remain in the said clerk's office for the information of the said companies, and as evidence and proof of the respective titles.

"*Provided nevertheless*, That if the parties, their heirs or assigns, to whom such titles shall have been adjudged, shall not within six months at farthest, from the time of their respective judgments in their favour, pay or tender to the company to whom the same is due, or their agent, the price and interest so fixed by the said commissioners, the title of every person so failing, shall be forfeited, and shall be from thence forward, to all intents and purposes, null and void; any thing herein to the contrary thereof notwithstanding."

91 Act reads: "eight pounds each."

92 Act adds: "upon oath" and also states the substance of this clause differently.

93 Act adds: "and the witnesses the same allowance for their attendance."

94 Act adds: "and the clerk shall have the same power of issuing executions as the clerks of the county courts."

95 The following paragraphs, not in the MS, are in the Act: "But as by this summary mode of proceeding, some persons at a great distance may not have timely notice, and may be unable to appear in support of their claims, for remedy whereof, *Be it enacted*, That no grant shall issue upon any of the claims determined by the said commissioners, until the first day of December, 1780, and in

the mean time, any such person injured by their determination, his or her heirs or assigns, may enter a caveat against a grant thereupon, until the matter shall be heard before the general court, and may petition the said general court to have his or her claim considered; and upon its being proved to the court that he or she laboured under such a disability at the time of the meeting of the commissioners thereupon, the court shall grant him or her a hearing in a summary way, and if it shall appear upon trial, that the petitioners claim is just, such court may reverse the former determination, and order a grant to issue for such land or any part thereof, on the terms herein before mentioned, to the person to whom they shall adjudge the same.

"*And be it farther enacted*, That all claims for lands upon surveys under any order of council or entry in the council books, shall by the respective claimers be laid before the court of appeals; which shall meet for that purpose on the sixteenth day of December next, and shall adjourn from day to day until the business be finished; or if it be proved to the court that any such claimer is unable to attend and prosecute his claim, or for other just cause to them shewn, they may order such claim to be tried before them on some future day. All such claims shall be heard and determined in a summary way, without pleadings in writing, upon such evidence as in the opinion of the court, the nature of the case may require; and no such claim shall be valid, but such only as shall be so heard and established by the said court of appeals, and on their certificate that any such claim hath been by them established, the register is hereby required to issue a warrant or grant thereupon, according to the nature of the case, and the rules and regulations of the land office; and the attorney general is hereby required to attend the said court on behalf of the commonwealth.

"*Provided always*, That nothing herein contained shall extend to officers, soldiers, or their assignees, claiming lands for military service. The register of the land office shall regularly record all land warrants issued by virtue of this act; they may be executed in one or more surveys, and may be exchanged or divided so as best to suit the purposes of the party, and shall remain in force until lands shall have been actually obtained for them, in the same manner with the warrants to be issued by virtue of the before recited act for establishing a land office."

[96] Act reads: "a grant to any person."

[97] Act adds: "as the consideration."

[98] Act reads: "nine"; the 1777 date in MS proves that this MS, and therefore that of the Bill for Establishing a Land Office, were written at least as early as the Oct. 1777 session, perhaps being drawn before the session was convened.

[99] The title in the Act is the same as that given above in the descriptive note.

[100] Act adds: "the ancient composition money, or the new."

[101] Act reads: "shall be properly distinguished, and in every other respect the grant shall be drawn and pass in the form and manner prescribed by law for the future grants of lands from the commonwealth."

[102] Act reads: ". . . Caveats, with the papers relating thereto."

[103] Act reads: "proceeded on and tried in the manner directed. . . ."

[104] The following passage, not in MS, is included in the Act: "but the same shall be determined according to the laws in force at the time they were entered; and upon the determination of any such caveat, a grant shall issue in the name of the person to whom such land shall be adjudged, his or her heirs or assigns, upon producing to the register of the land office, within three months at farthest from the time of such judgment, an authentick copy thereof, together with the auditor's certificate of the treasurer's receipt for the antient composition money due thereon, at the rate of exchange herein before mentioned; but where the person recovering had before paid rights into the secretary's office, a grant shall issue in consideration thereof upon payment of the office fees only."

Bill for Sequestering British Property

[13 January 1778]

Whereas divers persons, subjects of Great Britain, had, during our connection with that Kingdom, acquired estates real and personal within this Commonwealth and had also become entitled to debts to a considerable amount, and some of them had commenced suits for the recovery of such debts before the present troubles had interrupted the administration of Justice, which suits were at that time depending and undetermined; and such estates being acquired and debts incurred under the Sanction of the laws and of the connection then subsisting, and, it not being known that their sovereign hath as yet set the example of confiscating debts and estates under the like circumstances, the public faith and the law and usages of Nations require that they should not be confiscated on our part, but the safety of the United States demands, and the same law and usages of Nations will justify, that we should not strengthen the hands of our enemies during the continuance of the present war, by remitting to them the profits or proceeds of such estates or the interest or principal of such debts: Be it therefore enacted by the General Assembly that the lands, slaves, stocks, and implements thereto belonging within this Commonwealth, together with the crops now on hand or hereafter to accrue and all other estate of whatever nature not herein otherwise provided for of the property of any British subject, shall be sequestered into the hands of Commissioners to be appointed from time to time by the Governor and Council for each particular estate, which Commissioners shall have power, by suits or actions to be brought in the names of the proprietors, to receive and recover all sums of money hereafter to become due to the said proprietors of such estates; to direct by agents, stewards or overseers the management of the said estates to the best advantage; to provide out of the monies so received and recovered, and the crops and profits, now on hand, or hereafter accruing, for the maintenance, charges, taxes and other current expences of such estates, in the first place, and the residue to carry into the continental loan-office within[1] this Commonwealth, and to take out certificates for the same from the said Office, in the name of the proprietor of such estate; which certificates shall be delivered in to the Governor and Council, before whom also a fair account on oath of the receipts and disbursements for the said estate shall be annually laid; and, if wrong, shall be subject, at their instance, to be revised and adjusted in the name of the proprietors, and all balances due thereon from the said Commissioners to be recovered in a Court of Justice according to the ordinary forms of the law, and such balances, so recovered, to be placed in like manner in the said continental[2] loan-office. And the Governor and Council shall once in every year lay before the General Assembly an account of the said certificates, put into their hands specifying the names of the owners; and shall see to the safe keeping of the same, subject to the future direction of the Legislature. And where any such estate is holden in jointenancy, tenancy in common, or of any other undivided interest with any citizen of this Commonwealth, it shall be lawful for such citizen to proceed to obtain partition by such action, suit or process to be instituted in the General Court or high Court of Chancery as is allowed to be had against a citizen in the like case and service of process in any such suit on the Commissioners appointed for such estate, and orders, judgments, and decrees thereon to be rendered shall be, to all intents and purposes, as valid and effectual, as if the party himself had appeared in defence. Saving nevertheless to such defendant, if the partition be unequal, such redress as shall be hereafter allowed him by the legislature against the party Plaintiff, his heirs, executors or administrators, and against the lands themselves allotted to the Plaintiff on such unequal partition and not sold to any person for valuable consideration actually and bona fide paid or agreed to be paid: but all lands so sold after partition shall be absolutely confirmed to the Purchaser and all claiming under him, according to the terms of his purchase in like manner as if the vendor had held an indefeasible estate therein. And the said Commissioners shall use their best skill and endeavors to obtain a fair and equal partition for their principal, for which purpose they may employ necessary agents and counsel at his expence. And for this and all other their trouble and expences such allowance shall be made them out of the profits of the estate as to the Governor and Council shall seem reasonable.

And be it further enacted that it shall and may be lawful for any Citizen of this Commonwealth owing money to a subject of Great Britain, to pay the same, or any part thereof, from time to time, as he shall think fit, into the said continental[2] loan-Office taking thereout a certificate for the same in the name of the Creditor, with an endorsement under the hand of the Commissioner of the said Office, expressing the name of the payer, and shall deliver such certificate to the Governor and Council, whose receipt shall discharge him from so much of the debt. And the Governor and Council shall in like manner lay before the General Assembly once in every year an account of these certificates, specifying the names of the persons by and for whom they were paid, and shall see to the safe-keeping of the same, subject to the future direction of the legislature.[3]

And be it further enacted that all suits which were depending in any court of Law or Equity, within this Commonwealth on the twelfth day of April in the year of our lord 1774[4] wherein British subjects alone are Plaintiffs, and any Citizen of this Commonwealth is a defendant, shall stand continued (unless abated by the death of either party) in the same state in which they were at that time, and where Citizens and British subjects are joint Plaintiffs against a citizen, the Court may proceed to trial and judgment, but execution as to so much of any debt sued for and recovered in such action, as will accrue to such British subject, shall be suspended till further direction of the Legislature. And in all such suits wherein any Citizen of this Commonwealth is a Plaintiff and any subject of Great Britain is a defendant, the Court may proceed to trial, judgment, and execution, saving to the defendant such benefit of rehearing or new trial as shall be hereafter allowed by the legislature.

MS (Vi); in clerk's hand, with interlineation by TJ (noted below). Endorsed by John Tazewell: "A Bill for sequestring British Property enabling those indebted to British Subjects to pay off such Debts & directing the Proceedings in Suits where such Subjects are Parties. 1778. Jan: 17th. Read the first Time." Also MS (Vi) in clerk's hand containing amendments to the foregoing Bill.

For the broad outlines of Virginia's policy toward loyalists and debts owed British subjects, see Isaac S. Harrell, *Loyalism in Virginia*, Durham, 1926; the above Bill and the consequences of its enactment are discussed at p. 80ff. For a variant of the Bill for Sequestering British Property, see Report of the Committee of Revisors, Bill No. 36, 18 June 1779. The justification of the present Bill, as stated in the preamble, stands in some contrast to that stated in the Bill Concerning Escheats which TJ also drew (q.v., under 4 June 1779); the former implied that confiscation was contrary to "the public faith and the law and usages of nations"; the latter, which was an Act of confiscation, referred to the earlier Act as a measure merely undertaken to prevent waste and destruction and justified confiscation in those terms. TJ's taking the lead in the matter of treatment of British property and debts owed British merchants was no doubt due in large part to his anxiety to stabilize the finances of the state and to halt inflation; during these years his utterances show that he thought the chief danger to the state came from the insecurity of its credit. Since Virginians were obliged by law to accept paper money as legal tender, it seemed logical that others should be required to do so also. In addition to logic and legality, members of the General Assembly were under some pressure to adopt such measures, as shown by a petition of 185 persons from Mecklenburg co. in May 1777, declaring that merchants and factors refused to receive paper money in settlement of debts. TJ and many other members of the Assembly were involved in indebtedness to British merchants. TJ estimated the debts owed by colonial planters at the opening of the Revolution to be between two and three million pounds sterling; to liquidate these debts in depreciated paper money would benefit debtors, and, by increasing the stability of the paper issued by the state, would turn private liabilities into public assets.

Unfortunately, this general sequestration Bill and its clause respecting debts did not achieve the ends hoped for by TJ and others: of the enormous debt in sterling owed to British merchants, only £273,554 of paper money was paid into the loan office, having a sterling value of £15,044, and these payments were made only by about five hundred persons. Among these were TJ, Wythe, Carrington, Pendleton, and other leaders. Yet both Wythe and Pendleton, as judges, later ruled that, because of the terms of the Treaty of Paris, payments into the loan office of Virginia did not discharge debts due British subjects.

On 13 Jan. TJ was appointed chairman of a committee to bring in a Bill on this subject; he reported it on 17 Jan. On 21 Jan. it was read the second time and amended by the House; it was passed on 22 Jan., and TJ carried it to the Senate, where it was agreed to without amendment the same day (JHD, Oct. 1777, 1827 edn., p. 113, 119, 125, 126). The Act as adopted is in Hening, IX, 377-80. For a fragment of a committee report that may possibly have been drawn up in connection with the proviso for liquidating British debts by payments of Virginia currency, see the next document succeeding this.

1 The words "continental loan-office within" were deleted by amendment and the words "loan office of" substituted therefor.

2 The word "continental" was deleted by amendment.

3 The following section was added by amendment: "Provided that the Governor and Council may make such allowance as they shall think reasonable out of the said Profits and Interest arising on Money so paid into the Loan office to the Wives and Children residing in this State of such Proprietors or Creditors."

4 The words "on the twelfth . . . our lord 1774" are interlined in the hand of TJ.

Draft of a Resolution concerning Money Due British Subjects

[ca. 13 January 1778]

And whereas his Britannic majesty did on the day of 1775 undertake by the strength of his fleets to shut up the several ports and havens of the American states and to intercept all commerce between the said states and other parts of the world, to which proceeding the British parliament had previously given their sanction by an act entitled an act[1]

whereby the monies belonging to the subjects of his Britannic majesty in the hands of the citizens of this Commonwealth being rendered useless to such citizens who could no longer employ them to any profit, it becomes just that[2] no compensation should be yeilded for the use thereof during the time that[3] their commerce shall be so interrupted and cut off.

Resolved therefore that it is the opinion of this Committee that nothing should be demandeable under colour of interest or by way of damages for the use or detention of any monies due from any Citizen of this Commonwealth to any British subject from the said day of 1775 till it shall appear to this assembly that by a restitution of trade the said monies shall become again profitable to the holders thereof and the said states[4] at the time of their rupture with Gr. Br. were unprovided with any naval power which might[5] such interruption of their commerce and still are unprovided with such a one as may open the same in defiance of the hostile navy.

Dft (DLC). On the same page and on its verso is a list of books, principally legal, omitted here. The draft is undated, and, as proved by the beginning phrase "And whereas," is only part of what must have been a longer preamble to a committee report.

In the absence of the complete text of this committee report, there can be no certainty as to its date or the particular legislation to which it applies. It may belong to the year 1776 (see TJ's Bill for Suspending Executions for Debts, 6 Dec. 1776) or it may even refer to the resolutions passed 19 Dec. 1776 calling upon the governor to put into effect the Statute Staple of 27 Edward III, c. 17 (*Va. Gaz.* [Purdie], Suppl., 20 Dec. 1776, where both resolutions and Statute Staple are printed). Or it may refer to the Bill Concerning Escheats and Forfeitures from British Subjects which TJ drew (q.v., under date 4 June 1779). Or it may possibly refer to some other part of the legislation respecting British subjects or even to a bill that was never enacted. It is placed here because (1) the general sequestration Act passed at the close of the session of Oct. 1777 was the first drastic legislation affecting property of enemy aliens, and (2) because that Act not only contained the first provision for payment of debts owed British subjects but also contained one clause (inserted by amendment) which by inference at least was at variance with the suspension of interest provided for in this draft (see Bill for the Sequestration of British Property, note 3, preceding).

1 The Act of Parliament referred to here must have been that of 22 Dec. 1775, "An Act to prohibit all Trade and Intercourse with the Colonies," Force, *Archives*, 4th ser., VI, 237.

2 The words "they should pay" are deleted in draft.

3 The words "the said ports and harbours shall continue" are deleted in draft.

4 The words "during their former connection with Gr. Br. being unprovided with" are deleted in draft.

5 There is no interruption at this point, but TJ must have omitted one or more words. Perhaps he intended the clause to read, for example, "which might have prevented such interruption. . . ."

Bill Appointing the Place for Holding the High Court of Chancery and the General Court

[20 January 1778]

Whereas by the acts constituting the High court of Chancery and General court, the said courts are to be holden at such place as the legislature shall direct, and no place hath as yet been appointed for that purpose:

Be it therefore enacted by the General assembly that for the term of one year after the end of this present session of assembly, and from thence to the end of the session then next ensuing, the said courts shall be holden in the Capitol in the city of Williamsburgh.

And be it further enacted that it shall be lawful for the said High court of Chancery to appoint from time to time their own Serjeant at arms who shall be attendant on the said court to perform the duties of his office; for which he shall receive such fees as shall be allowed by law.

MS (Vi); in TJ's hand. Endorsed by him: "A Bill appointing the place for holding the High-court of Chancery & General court, & empowering the sd High court of Chancery to appoint their own Serjeant at arms." Docketed in hand of John Tazewell: "1778. Jan: 20th. Read the first Time. Jan: 22d. Read 2d. time & to be ingrossed."

This Bill, as the above indicates, was rushed through at the close of the session. TJ and Edmund Pendleton were appointed on 20 Jan. to a committee to bring in the bill; TJ reported it the same day; it passed the third reading on 23 Jan., and the Senate approved it the same day, precisely as written (JHD, Oct. 1777, 1827 edn., p. 123, 126, 131-2). Text of the Act is in Hening, IX, 434.

From Patrick Henry

SIR — Williamsburg 21st. February 1778.

You are desired to receive into your Custody John Goodrich the Elder, who is ordered to be removed from Bedford County, the place of his present Confinement; and will be delivered by the order of the County Lieut: of Bedford. He is to be Safely kept and prosecuted agreeable to directions of Assembly by the Attorney General. I am Sir, Yr. hble Servt.,

P. HENRY

RC (DLC); in an unidentified hand and signed by Henry. Addressed: "The County Lieutenant of Albermarle." Enclosed in Edmund Randolph to TJ, 22 Feb., following.

The ATTORNEY GENERAL: Edmund Randolph (DAB).

From Edmund Randolph

DEAR SIR — Williamsburg Feby. 22. 1778.

The council board has been so much crouded with business of late, that I could not procure an order for the removal of Goodrich to Albemarle, 'till this morning. I should not have delayed to comply with the resolution of Assembly so long, had it not been necessary to examine him in the county, in which it is supposed he committed the crime. The order for his removal went by express to day to the county lieutenant of Bedford. Inclosed is an order to the county lieutenant of Albemarle, to receive him, and convey him to the proper place for his examination. Not knowing, whether you, or who else, may be in that post, I send the order to you. The letters too will accompany this, and I beg the favour of you to return them to me, if the examining court should think him deserving a farther trial.

What his offence, as grounded upon these letters, may be, I cannot at present tell. I could wish, that the court would settle distinctly in their own minds, before they put him into my hands, of what nature his crime is. You will oblige me by directing the court, if you should be present at his examination, how to proceed in this affair. I am Dr. Sir with great regard yr. mo. ob. Servt.,

EDM: RANDOLPH

RC (DLC). Addressed: "To Thos. Jefferson Esqr." Enclosure: Patrick Henry to TJ, 21 Feb; other enclosures missing.

After John Goodrich, Sr., escaped from custody in Albemarle co., 18 Aug. 1777 (see John Goodrich to TJ, 20 Jan. 1777), he was apprehended, ordered to be confined in Botetourt co., and later transferred to Bedford co. before being again sent to Albemarle for trial (*Va. Council Jour.*, I, 475; II, 20). No record of his trial has been found. However, he was apparently released (Sabine, *Loyalists*, I, 481). Purdie's *Virginia Gazette* of 19 June 1778 reported that "old Mr. Goodrich, and one of his sons, in two armed vessels, lately went into Ocracock inlet and burnt four vessels, and carried off five more, that were loaded and ready to proceed to sea." In Sep. 1778 he was still raiding the Virginia coast. Congress ordered two frigates to cruise off the Capes in quest of the "Notorious" Goodriches, and the Virginia Navy Board also sent out cruisers to apprehend them (*Va. Council Jour.*, II, 184, 186). Sometime thereafter Goodrich returned to England, where he died in 1785 (VMHB, XIV [1907], 443-4). It is interesting to compare the cases of John Goodrich, Sr. and Josiah Philips and particularly to compare Randolph's doubt about the charge to be preferred against Goodrich with his (or the court's) decision not to apply the Bill of Attainder to Philips (see notes to Bill to Attaint Josiah Philips, 28 May 1778).

To Isaac Zane

DEAR SIR Monticello Feb. 26. 1778.

Having been unable to get waggons to set off hitherto for our pans and the day on which we were to send for them, approaching, I thought myself bound to send express with the money to answer my engagement. The bearer I hope will be with you on the 1st. day of March which if I recollect was the ultimate day I required. He will deliver you one hundred and eighty pounds, the price of two pans according to what occurs to me of their weight and price. Should there be any difference it may be settled when I send the waggoners, if either of them should be trusty, or at any rate when I see you in assembly. I shall hope two pans more from you in the spring, as it has given our people here great satisfaction to see a probability of being supplied with salt at a low rate, and the two pans now sent for will yeild but a scanty supply. Write me by the bearer any interesting news. The draught went down very easy in this part of the country except in the neighboring worthless county of Fluvanna. Great opposition had nevertheless been talked of before. I asked you when I saw you last whether you would be willing to part with the spirit level you had of Ld. Dunmore's estate. What was your answer? For I have forgotten. I am engaged in a great work in the canal way. It would therefore be very convenient to me both as an undertaker and a philosopher settled in a country where god almighty has rendered the art of levelling as requisite as in any part of his creation. Against this, weigh your own necessities and determine. If in my favor, the bearer who is one of my trusties, will bring it safely tho' on horseback, only being apprised by you of the nature of that care which is requisite. Fix your own price. I wish I could have come instead of sending, but my day of leisure is not yet at hand. I wish you every felicity & am with more than religious form Your assured friend,

TH: JEFFERSON

P.S. I am using my best endeavors to get waggons to go for the pans; they shall be taken out of your way as soon as possible. Remember my stoves.

RC (André deCoppet, New York City, 1948).

PANS: Iron pans constructed for the purpose of obtaining salt from sea water; see TJ's Account Book, 27 Feb. 1778: "sent by Humphrey Gaines to Isaac Zane in part of my subscription for salt pans £25." An intimate and philosophical friend of TJ's, Isaac Zane conducted the Marlboro Iron Works in Frederick co. (Cartmell, *Shenandoah Valley Pioneers*, p. 436-7). There is no record that TJ obtained the spirit level here asked for.

From Richard Henry Lee

DEAR SIR York May 2. 1778.

We are this moment made acquainted by the War Office that an Express was immediately to depart for Virginia, and I take the opportunity of enclosing by him the last papers, which contain all our news, except it be a report that seems not illy founded, that Genl. Amhers[t] and Adml. Keppel are arrived at Philadelphia as commissioners from the King and Parliament of G. B. to carry into execution the very curious plan that one of the inclosed papers contains. Tis happy for America that her enemies have not sufficient ability to give even a specious appearance to their wicked designs. In this case the Peasantry here develope the cheat. We have no news, not a scrip from our Com[mission]ers. The Gold and the Sea power of our enemies have [preva]iled to deprive us of most important dispatch[es.] Adieu my dear Sir,

RICHARD HENRY LEE

Gen. Lee is fully exchanged and is sent for from [. . .] to attend the Army. For Gods sake, for the love of our Countr[y,] my dear friend, let more vigorous measures be quickly adop[ted] for re-enforcing the Army. The last draft will fall greatly short of the requisite number. Our enemies are sore pressed, wisdom and vigor now will presently compel G. B., proud as she is, to acknowledge our Independency.

RC (DLC). Addressed: "Thomas Jefferson esquire, or in his absence To the honorable George Wythe esqr. at Williamsburg in Virginia." Franked: "R. H. Lee By Express."

The EXPRESS by which this letter was transmitted was detained a day because of the arrival of news from France, and Lee's letter of 3 May, below, was sent by the same messenger. The false rumor that Lord Amherst and Admiral Augustus Keppel were among the COMMISSIONERS FROM THE KING AND PARLIAMENT was widely circulated (*Va. Gaz.* [D & H], 8 May 1778; Burnett, *Letters of Members*, III, No. 230). The British commissioners had set out for America on 16 Apr. but did not arrive in Philadelphia until 6 June; for a full treatment of the appointment of the commissioners, the plans of the King and Parliament, and the failure of the mission see Van Doren, *Secret History*, ch. III and IV.

From Richard Henry Lee

DEAR SIR York 3d. May 1778

Having detained the Express that he might carry you the news that we heard was on its way from France, I am furnished with an opportunity of congratulating you on the important event of a Treaty of Commerce, and one of Alliance and Amity, having been signed at Paris on the 6th of February last, between France and these United States. Having been as particular as we could on this subject in the Delegates letter to the Governor, I must beg leave to refer you to that for further information, being compelled to shortness here as the Express waits. Great Britain has now two Cards to play but which she will choose we cannot tell, altho we certainly ought in wisdom to be prepared for the worst. She may either acknowledge the Independency of America and make a Treaty of Commerce with her and thus be at peace with us and with all the World; or she may submit to the uninterrupted progress of French commerce to avoid a war with that Power and yet push her whole force against us this Campaign and thereby injure us extremely if we are not prepared with a strong force to prevent it. She has now at Philadelphia 12,000 Veteran Troops, and may possibly collect and send over 8000 more for a last effort. This consideration points out the necessity of having a strong Army immediately. I do sincerely hope that our Assembly will vigorously and early take up this consideration, because I am sure that their last plan will not procure our quota by a considerable number.

I am dear Sir most affection[ately,] RICHARD HENRY LEE

RC (DLC).

After Congress had adjourned on Saturday, 2 May, Simeon Deane, a brother of Silas Deane, arrived with dispatches from the American commissioners in France, including the treaties of commerce and alliance between France and the United States, concluded on 6 Feb. by Benjamin Franklin, Silas Deane, and Arthur Lee. Congress convened in special session to receive the messages and in regular session, 4 May, ratified the treaties (JCC, XI, 417-58). The DELEGATES LETTER TO THE GOVERNOR is printed in Burnett, *Letters of Members*, III, No. 250.

From Richard Henry Lee

DEAR SIR York the 11th of May 1778

We have once more ventured into the field of composition as the inclosed Address will shew you. And I have the pleasure to acquaint you that Congress have unanimously ratified the Treaties with France, and directed the ratifications to be presented for exchange in due season. The inclosed pamphlet I t[ake to] be a production of Dr. Franklin. It is well written, and was published first in Holland. When it began to make a noise, the B. Minister procured its suppression, but this, as usual, raised the public curiosity and procured it additional Readers. We have translated it here, and omitting one or two paragraphs that are not now true, it will be published next week in the Gazette of this place. The reasons are good and may be well used in these States to support public credit. Suppose you were to have a translation published by way of supplement to our Virginia Gazettes?

My heart is so bent upon the success of our Country that it grieves me extremely to hear a probability of measures being adopted that I am sure will injure us. I am told that application will be made to this Assembly to revoke Monsr. Loyeautes commission from the last. Is it possible that such an application can be attended to? Thus to treat a Gentleman of unquestioned ability, of reputation in France, and after we have applied to that Court to obtain leave for his longer residence among us than his furlough permitted! His character will not be hurt b[y] it, but how mutable shall we appear. And how totally wrong it will be thus to dismiss an able, zealous, and most industrious Artist, whilst we remain utterly ignorant of the necessary knowledge that he is both able and willing to instruct us in. I think the wise Men of our Assembly will suppress the spirit of vain ambition that prompts to this selfish application.

We are told that the enemies movements at Philadelphia denote their departure, but these perhaps may be designed to amuse us, and prevent the collection of a strong army.

I am dear Sir sincerely yours, RICHARD HENRY LEE

RC (DLC). Enclosures missing.

THE INCLOSED ADDRESS: "An Address to the Inhabitants of the United States . . . 9 May 1778" was printed at York by Hall & Sellers, at Lancaster by John Dunlap, and frequently reprinted throughout the states (JCC, XI, 474-81; XII, 1284-5; Evans 16097-16104). The PAMPHLET was probably "A Comparison of Great Britain and the United States in Regard to the Basis of Credit in the Two Countries" (Franklin, *Writings*, ed. Smyth, VII, 1-8) MONSR. LOYEAUTE: Anne-Philippe-Dieudonné de Loyauté was engaged as inspector general of artillery, fortifications, and military stores as the result of a report presented by R. H. Lee, for a committee of which TJ was also a member, in the House of Delegates 23 Jan. 1778 (JHD, Oct. 1777, 1827 edn., p. 132-3). On 18 May the House of Delegates resolved that Loyauté's appointment did not entitle him to military command. This resolution was carried to the Senate by TJ, and may, therefore, have been proposed by him (same, May 1778, p. 11). As a result Loyauté resigned his position on 20 May (*Va. Council Jour.*, II, 135-6), but was subsequently given a commission as lieutenant-colonel (Lasseray, *Les français sous les treize étoiles*, I, 288-90).

Bill Granting Free Pardon to Certain Offenders

[13 May 1778]

Whereas the American Congress by their resolution passed on the 23d. day of April last past, reciting that persuasion and influence, the example of the deluded or wicked, the fear of danger or the calamities of war may have induced some of the subjects of these states to join aid, or abet the British forces in America, and who, tho' now desirous of returning to their duty, and anxiously wishing to be received and reunited to their country, may be deterred by the fear of punishment: and that the people of these states are ever more ready to reclaim than to abandon, to mitigate than to increase the horrors of war, to pardon than to punish offenders: did recommend to the legislatures of the several states to pass laws, or to the executive authority of each state, if invested with sufficient power, to issue proclamations, offering pardon, with such exceptions, and under such limitations and restrictions, as they shall think expedient, to such of their inhabitants or subjects, as have levied war against any of these states, or adhered to, aided or abetted the enemy, and shall surrender themselves to any civil or military officer of any of these states, and shall return to the state to which they may belong before the 10th. day of June next: and did further recommend to the good and faithful citizens of these states to receive such returning penitents with compassion and mercy, and to forgive and bury in oblivion their past failings and transgressions.[1]

Be it therefore enacted by the General assembly that full and free pardon is hereby granted to all such persons without any exception who shall surrender themselves as aforesaid, and shall take the oath of fidelity to this Commonwealth within one month[2] after their return thereto.

MS (Vi); in TJ's hand. Endorsed by him: "A Bill granting free pardon to certain offenders." Docketed by Edmund Randolph: "Read first time May 13. 1778. Read second time May 14. 1778. committed to morrow to whole house." Accompanying this MS is a slip in Randolph's hand headed: "Amendments to the bill of pardon." There was, however, only one amendment offered (see note 2, below).

This Bill, which stands in marked contrast to that for attainting Josiah Philips drawn by TJ a few days later, failed of passage for some unknown reason, despite its having been recommended by Congress and its having passed the House in short order. On 13 May TJ, along with Page, Lawson, and Meriwether Smith, was appointed to bring in a Bill on the subject. He apparently had requested leave to do this, and must have had the Bill already prepared, for he reported it the same day. On 14 May it was read the second time and referred to the committee of the whole; two days later the Bill was debated in committee and one amendment was offered. On 18 May it was read the third time and passed; TJ carried the Bill to the Senate (JHD, May 1778, 1827 edn., p. 6, 7, 10, 11). Apparently the Senate considered it useless to pass such a Bill in the short time remaining before 10 June; it was never reported back to the House and did not become law.

[1] Thus far the Bill recites the resolution of Congress almost verbatim (JCC, X, 381-2). Congress ordered 500 copies of its resolution printed in English and 200 in German for "circulating . . . amongst the American levies in the enemy's army." Since the resolution of 23 Apr. limited its recommendation to 10 June 1778, it is obvious that little good would have been accomplished by enacting such a law late in May.

[2] Changed in committee from "month" to "week."

Bill for Raising a Battalion for Garrison Duty

[16 May 1778]

For garrisoning the fortifications and batteries erected for the defence of the several ports and harbours within this commonwealth be it enacted by the Gen. assembly that a battalion of infantry to consist of 8 companies and each company of 68 rank and file shall be raised within this commonwealth by such persons as shall be appointed by the gov. and council [for] that purpose; that each company shall have one drummer and fifer and be commanded by a captain, two Lieutenants an ensign and 4 serjeants and the whole by a Colonel, Lieutenant Colonel and Major; the commissioned officers shall be appointed by the governor and council, and the staff by the feild officers: that the said battalion shall have the same bounty, pay and rations as are allowed in the Continental service, to commence from the time of their rendezvous, shall continue in service 3. years from that time unless sooner discharged and shall be subject to the same rules and articles of discipline and government save only that the powers of confirming the sentences of courts martial in capital cases or of pardon in the same cases shall be in the governor and council.

Every person authorized by the Governor and council to enlist for the said battalion shall receive for every man he shall so enlist the sum of 10 dollars: but it shall not be lawful for him to enlist any artificer employed by contract in writing for hire in the public manufactories of fire arms or at any iron works,[1] nor any [indentured] apprentice in such manufactory or work nor any imported servant; without leave in writing from the manager of such manufactory or work or owner of such servant.

The Treasurer[2] shall from time to time pay all monies necessary for the enlistment, bounty, pay or subsistence of the said battalion, such monies for enlistment and bounty being drawn for by warrant from the Governor and council, and previous to their payment entered in account against the person receiving the same in the Auditor's office; and the monies for pay and subsistence by warrant from the Auditors to be entered in account in like manner: and the Auditors shall from time to time call for settlements of the said accounts, for vouchers for the due expenditure of the monies received, and for repayment of all unexpended sums to the treasurer and certificate thereof by him; and if any person fails when called on so to account such proceedings shall be used against him as are prescribed by an [act of] Gen. assembly passed in the year [1777] for recovery of monies due to the public.

If any person enlisted for the said battalion shall at any time be ordered to march out of the Commonwealth, such order shall amount to a discharge.[3]

And for further encouragement to those who shall [enlist] into the said service,[4] they[5] shall be free from [all draughts, except in] case of an invasion of the Commonwealth [, or insurrection therein, from the] time of their discharge for so long a time as they shall have actually been in the [said service.]

Dft (DLC); in TJ's hand, written on address leaf bearing, in an unidentified hand, the address: "Thomas Jefferson esquire in Wmsburg." Title in TJ's hand at top of recto: "A Bill for raising a battalion of infantry for garrison duty." The draft is much faded and text has been collated with Act as adopted, indecipherable words in the former being supplied from the latter and placed inside square brackets (Hening, IX, 452-3).

On 16 May 1778 the committee of the whole on the state of the commonwealth reported several resolutions. One of them was as follows: "*Resolved*, that for the purpose of garrisoning the fortifications and batteries, erected for the defence of the several harbors within this Commonwealth, a battalion of infantry be enlisted, to serve three years, unless sooner discharged, and to receive the same bounty, pay, rations, and other advantages, as are allowed to continental officers and soldiers; and that, for their greater encouragement to enlist, the public faith be pledged, that they shall not be sent out of the Commonwealth." TJ was one of a committee of thirteen to which this and other resolutions were referred with recommendations to bring in a bill or bills. Carter, chairman of this committee, introduced the present Bill on 18 May and it was read the first time; on 19 May it was read the second time, debated, and amended by the House; on 20 May it was read the third time and passed. It was further amended by the Senate and agreed to by the House 30 May (JHD, May 1778, 1827 edn., p. 10, 11, 12, 13, 29). Except as noted below, the Act as adopted coincides exactly with the text of the Bill as drawn by TJ.

[1] Deleted: "public or private."

[2] Deleted: "is hereby authorised and required."

[3] The Act as adopted has the following additional clauses at this point: "That all soldiers who shall enlist into the regiment of artillery now raising for the defence of this state shall be entitled to the same bounty and clothing as the troops now to be raised by this act are entitled to. That the said regiment of artillery shall be officered in the same manner, and that the officers thereof shall receive the same pay and rations as is customary in artillery regiments in the service of the United States of America."

[4] The Act has the additional words "or artillery" at this point.

[5] Deleted: "shall be furnished, while they continue therein, with such clothing and other neces[saries] from [the] public stores so far as [possible?] at the prices at which articles of the same kind and quality usually sold [in] the year 1774, and."

Bill Establishing a Clerkship of Foreign Correspondence

[18 May 1778]

Whereas it is necessary for the Governour and council to be provided with a person learned in the modern languages for assisting them in a communication with foreign states, and that a competent salary for such person should be provided by law; be it therefore enacted that a clerkship of foreign correspondence be henceforth established, under the direction and controul of the Governor and council, who shall from time to time at their will appoint such person to the said office as they shall find worthy of confidence and qualified to perform the duties thereof and remove him in like manner at their will. Such clerk having taken before them an oath of fidelity to the Commonwealth, and of secrecy in all cases where he shall be specially charged with secrecy, may enter on the exercise of his office, and shall receive for his trouble a yearly salary of two hundred pounds to be paid by the treasurer in quarterly paiments on warrant from the Auditors, who are hereby required to enter such warrants in account against such persons.

MS (Vi); in TJ's hand. Endorsed by him: "A Bill establishing a clerkship of foreign correspondence." Docketed in hand of Edmund Randolph: "May 19th. 1778 read 1st. time. May 20. read 2d. to be engrossed."

On 18 May 1778 TJ was appointed a member of a committee under directions to bring in such a Bill; the Bill was introduced the following day and apparently passed both houses without debate. It was enacted as TJ drew it, without amendment (JHD, May 1778, 1827 edn., p. 11-14, 21; Hening, IX, 467). See Report of Committee of Revisors, Bill No. 14, under date of 18 June 1779. TJ undoubtedly had his friend Charles Bellini in mind in proposing such a clerkship (see notes to TJ's letter to Giovanni Fabbroni, 8 June 1778).

Bill Providing Speedy Remedy against Defaulters to the United States

[18 May 1778]

Whereas divers persons receiving money of the United states of America for publick uses, apply it to different purposes, and when called on refuse or neglect to repay the same; others enter into contracts for supplying the army and navy of the United states with provisions and other necessaries, and fail or refuse to comply therewith; and whereas in like cases respecting this commonwealth in particular, speedy remedy was given by an act of general assembly past in the year 1777. intituled 'an act to establish a mode for the speedy and summary recovery of such sums of money as are or may become due to the publick, and for enforcing all contracts entered into with government' and it is expedient that the same speedy remedy be given in like cases respecting the United states: Be it therefore enacted by the general assembly that where in any case a remedy is by the said act given to this commonwealth, or any of it's agents or contractors, in a like case the same remedy shall be given to the United states, their agents and contractors; and where by the said act such proceedings are directed to be instituted by the Treasurer in the name of the Governor for the time being, in a like case respecting the United states the proceeding shall be instituted by their deputy pay-master general within this Commonwealth and in the name of the President of Congress for the time being.

MS (Vi); in TJ's hand. Endorsed by him: "A Bill providing speedy remedy against ⟨*those who deny or dela*⟩ defaulters to the United states." Docketed in the hand of Edmund Randolph: "May 19th. 1778 read the first time May 20th. read 2d. time & to be engrossed."

On 18 May 1778 TJ was appointed member of a committee to bring in such a Bill. It was introduced by Carter and read the first time on 19 May; on 20 May it was read the second time and amended; on 21 May it was read the third time, passed, and carried to the Senate; the Senate agreed to it on 28 May (JHD, May 1778, 1827 edn., p. 11, 12, 13, 14, 21). The Act as adopted is in Hening, IX, 462-3. The amendment noted in JHD must have failed, for the Act as adopted is precisely in the words of TJ's draft.

Bill Empowering the High Court of Chancery to Supply Vacant Offices

[19 May 1778]

Be it enacted by the general assembly that the judges of the high court of chancery or any two of them may before the next term appoint a clerk thereof in the room of him who lately died by writing under their hands and seals and at any time hereafter when that office or the office of serjeant at arms shall by any means become vacant may in like manner appoint a successor and such succeeding clerk or serjeant having in any court of record taken the oaths required by law shall exercise the same power perform the same duty and be intitled to the same fees and profits as he might have exercised performed and been intitled to if he had been appointed in term-time. The clerk of the high court of chancery shall be paid by the treasurer out of any public money that may be in his hands a salary of the rate of[1] by the year until the general assembly shall make such other provision for him as will encourage a man of sufficient ability to accept the office. Any party thinking himself aggrieved by a decree of the court of a county city or borough in chancery and not having entered an appeal from the decree at the time it was pronounced may appeal from such decree[2] at any time within three months after passing this act or within one month after the decree pronounced[3] lodging for that purpose with the clerk of the high court of chancery a copy of the proceedings in the suit and a petition suggesting error in the decree signed by some counsel attending the high court of chancery and also lodging with the petition a bond executed by the appellant or his agent and a surety or sureties with the like condition as is annexed to other appeal bonds and affidavits or solemn affirmations verifying the sufficiency of the sureties and the clerk shall there upon issue a summons against the appellee requiring him to appear and answer the said petition and appeal and shall also issue a supersedeas if necessary to enjoin from proceeding in execution of the decree and the court shall and may hear and determine the appeal in the same manner as if the appeal had been entered at the time the decree was pronounced.[4]

MS (Vi); in clerk's hand with interlineations by TJ. MS mutilated as indicated in note 4, below. Endorsed: "A bill empowering the judges of the high court of chancery to supply certain vacant offices, making a temporary provision for the clerk thereof, and establishing a method of appealing to that court in particular cases ⟨*and prescribing rules for reviewing decrees of the late general court in chancery*⟩." Docketed in hand of Edmund Randolph: "May 19th. 1778. read the first time. May 20. read 2d. time & to be engrossed."

On 19 May TJ and Cyrus Griffin were appointed to bring in such a Bill; TJ reported it the same day and must have been its author, since he drafted the earlier bills pertaining to the High Court of Chancery. The Bill passed the third reading 21 May and TJ carried it to the Senate, where it was agreed to on 28 May (JHD, May 1778, 1827 edn., p. 12, 13, 14, 21). Text of the Act, which was adopted without altering Bill save as noted below, is in Hening, IX, 458-9.

1 Act reads: "one hundred and fifty pounds by the year."

2 Preceding four words interlined by TJ.

3 The words "three months . . . decree pronounced" are inserted in TJ's hand.

4 MS mutilated. At this point the words "no bill of re-" are deleted and the MS is torn so that, in the next line, only the words "shall be admitted in the high c[ourt]" are discernible. The Act, however, ends with the text as given above; and the additional matter that the Bill contained originally must obviously have been that part "prescribing rules for receiving decrees of the late general court in chancery" (see descriptive note, above). It is to be regretted that the clerk's method of recording a deletion by amendment apparently took the drastic form of tearing off that part of the MS that was no longer needed for legislative purposes.

Bill Providing a Supply for the Public Exigencies

[20 May 1778]

Whereas in order to carry into effect the several acts passed at this present session of General assembly for raising a regiment of horse, for raising a battalion of infantry for garrison duty, for raising volunteers to join the grand army [for recruiting the continental army] and [other purposes therein mentioned, and the resolutions of the twenty ninth of May one thousand seven hundred and seventy eight, for making good the losses of certain sufferers in the town of Norfolk,][1] it will be necessary to make a further emission of ⟨*bills of credit*⟩ treasury notes and to provide for the redemption thereof; be it enacted by the General assembly that it shall be lawful for the Treasurer to issue treasury notes in dollars or parts of a dollar for any sum which may be requisite for the purposes aforesaid in addition to the sums issuable by former acts of assembly, so as the said sum to be issued by authority of this act do not exceed [six][2] hundred thousand dollars. And he shall cause the said notes to be engraved and printed in such manner and on such paper as he shall judge most likely to secure the same from being counterfeited, and shall appoint proper persons to overlook the press, and to number and sign the notes upon the best terms on which he can procure them.

And whereas there is reason to beleive that the taxes imposed by an act passed at the last session of General assembly for raising a supply of money for publick exigencies[3] will be more than sufficient to answer the purposes expressed in the said act; be it further enacted that after the taxes which shall be levied by authority of the said act shall have effected the purposes to which they are appropriated by the said act, so much of what shall remain as shall be sufficient for the redemption of the notes to be issued by authority of this present act, shall be applied to that purpose, and if so much as shall be sufficient shall not remain, further provision shall be made by law for making good the deficiency and redeeming the whole before the first day of December which shall be in the year of our lord 1785.

If any person shall counterfeit, ⟨*or aid or abet in counterfeiting*⟩ any of the said treasury-notes issued by authority of this act or shall be accessory thereto, or shall pass any such counterfeited note ⟨*in paiment*⟩ knowing the same to be counterfeit, he shall on conviction thereof suffer death without benefit of clergy.[4]

MS (Vi); in TJ's hand. Endorsed by him: "A Bill providing a supply for the publick exigencies." Docketed in the hand of Edmund Randolph: "May 20. 1778. read first time May 21. 1778. read 2d. time to be ⟨*engrossed*⟩ committed." Text of the Act as adopted (Hening, IX, 456-7) has been collated with MS. Accompanying this is a list of three amendments in Randolph's hand; see notes 1 and 2, below.

On 16 May TJ was appointed member of a committee to bring in a supply bill; it was introduced by Carter on 20 May, read the second time on the 21st, amended by the House on the 29th, and passed on the 30th (JHD, May 1778, 1827 edn., p. 10, 13, 15, 26, 28, 30). The Act was passed as TJ drew it, save as indicated in notes 1 and 2, below.

1 The passages in square brackets are supplied from the Act as adopted, spaces having been left blank in TJ's MS of the Bill. Both were supplied by amendment. The Acts referred to in the preamble of this Bill are in Hening, IX, 445-56.

2 The word in square brackets supplied from the Act; see note 4.

3 See Hening, IX, 349-68, for this Act of the preceding session levying various taxes and duties. TJ had been on the committee to draw up the bill for providing a supply that had been hotly debated during Jan. 1778 (JHD, Oct. 1777, 1827 edn., p. 77-8, 105, 108, 112-20, 123, 126, 133).

4 This paragraph is written in TJ's hand on a separate slip of paper. On it is written "600,000 D" in TJ's hand, perhaps as a note of the decision taken by the House on the amount to be inserted in the blank he had left in MS. It is worth noting that, in the Bill for Proportioning Crimes and Punishments (q.v., Bill No. 64, Report of the Committee of Revisors, 18 June 1779), counterfeiting

was not made a capital offense. This would seem to indicate that that famous Bill was drawn sometime between 20 May 1778 and 1 Nov. 1778 (TJ to George Wythe, 1 Nov. 1778; but see Malone, I, 269).

Bill to Amend an Act for Raising a Supply of Money

[21 May 1778]

Whereas [⟨*Whereas*⟩ by an act of the last session of General assembly intituled an act for raising a supply of money for public exigencies it was enacted that a tax or rate of ten shillings for every hundred pounds value should be paid, among other things, upon all slaves by the owner or proprietor; and that the value of such slaves should be estimated by assessors to be appointed in every hundred: and it hath been already seen that such valuations will be very unequal, slaves of the same value being estimated at three or four times more in some places than in others, insomuch that the said tax on this particular is like to be very heavy on some citizens of this commonwealth and light on others which is unequal and unjust; and it is beleived that if one certain rate by the head be fixed on all slaves, bearing the same proportion to their averaged value as the said pound rate bore to their respective values it will be more equal in the whole, it being supposed that in most parcels of slaves there will be nearly the same proportion of valuable and of indifferent be it therefore enacted by the General assembly that as well for the present as the remaining years of the term during which the said act is to continue in force a tax of ⟨*ten*⟩ fifteen shillings by the head shall be paid on all slaves of whatever age or sex, in lieu of the said rate of ten shillings in every hundred pounds value; and in like manner the double of the said tax by those who by the said act were to pay a double rate. And where the assessors shall before notice of this act have given in their assessment to the Commissioners, and shall have noted therein the number of slaves for which they shall have assessed a pound rate on the proprietor the commissioners shall extend against such proprietor the tax aforesaid in lieu of the pound rate on the said slaves extended by the assessors; and where they shall not have so noted the number of slaves they shall be required by the said Commissioners forthwith to do it. And if any person shall have paid such pound-rate before notice of this act if the same were greater than the tax hereby imposed he may require the sheriff to refund the difference or overplus and on failure may recover the same before any justice if the sum be under twenty five shillings and if it amount to that sum then on motion before any court giving such sheriff ten days notice thereof: and if the pound rate so paid were less than the tax hereby imposed, then the sheriff shall collect the difference or deficiency in like manner as by the said act he was authorized to collect the said pound rate. And doubts having arisen where slaves are hired whether the said pound-rate should be paid by the owner or hirer, and as a like doubt may arise, as to the tax hereby imposed it is declared that the said tax is paiable by the owner, unless otherwise settled by contract between the parties.][1]

[⟨*And whereas by the said act*⟩ by an act of the last session of general assembly intituled an act for raising a supply of money for public exigencies[2] the several county courts were required to take bonds with sufficient sureties of their respective sheriffs in the penalty of £3000 for the faithful collection and accounting for all the taxes thereby imposed, which sum in many counties will be less than the amount of the taxes to be collected in the same counties; be it therefore enacted that the bonds heretofore taken under direction of the said act shall be cancelled and in lieu thereof others shall be taken by according to the directions of the said act save only that the penalty of every such bond shall be equal at least to what may be the whole amount of the said taxes in the judgment of the court of the county using the best means in their power to inform themselves of such amount. And whereas][3] the Court of Hustings for the City of Williamsburg, were not authorised by the said Act to take bond with sufficient sureties from the Collector for the true and faithful Collection and accounting for the money arising from all duties and taxes thereby imposed on the inhabitants of the said City: Be it therefore enacted by the General Assembly that the Court of Hustings shall, at their Court to be held in the months of June or July in the present year and in the six following years in the months of April or May, take bond with sufficient sureties of the Serjeant of the City in the Penalty of three thousand Pounds payable to the Treasurer of the Commonwealth for the time being for the use of the Commonwealth, with Condition for the true and faithful collection and accounting for all the duties and taxes imposed by the above recited Act and paying the Money for which he shall be accountable according to the said Act. And if the Serjeant shall refuse or fail to give such surety, the Court shall appoint some other person to collect the said taxes and take the like bond and surety of him; which bond shall be recorded in the

Court and an attested Copy thereof transmitted by the Clerk without delay to the Public Treasurer, which shall be admitted as evidence in any suit or proceeding founded thereon.

MS (Vi); in clerk's hand, with two lengthy amendments in TJ's hand (these are inserted in the text as indicated in the notes below). The Bill is endorsed: "A Bill To amend an Act, intituled 'An Act for raising a supply of money for publick Exigencies.'" Docketed in Edmund Randolph's hand: "May 21. 1778. Read first Time. May 22. 1778. read 2d. time and to be committed to the whole to morrow." Also, accompanying MS, are notes of amendments in Randolph's hand indicating precisely the original form of the Bill, the defeat of one of TJ's amendments, and the acceptance of another. The text of the Act as adopted is in Hening, IX, 468-9.

On 21 May 1778 Nicholas and Page were ordered to bring in a bill on this subject. Nicholas presented it the same day. On 26 May TJ's amendments were reported; the amended Bill was passed on 27 May (JHD, May 1778, 1827 edn., p. 14, 16, 17, 18, 2 [misplaced], 20). As presented, the Bill consisted only of the paragraph indicated in note 2, below. TJ proposed two amendments to this Bill, to be inserted after the initial word "Whereas," with appropriate changes in the enacting clause. The first of these amendments failed, as indicated in note 1, below. The second of his amendments, which succeeded, then became the first section of the Bill, requiring further changes in the enacting clause; its text is in this form and position in the Act as adopted. Thus the original Bill became an appendage to TJ's amendments.

1 This entire paragraph is written in TJ's hand and may have been intended as a separate bill, since it began "Whereas by an act of the last session of General assembly intituled . . ."; but when Nicholas brought in his and Page's Bill, TJ struck out the word "Whereas" in this amendment and interlined above it: "after the word 'whereas' insert," obviously meaning the initial "whereas" of the Nicholas Bill and meaning to insert after it all of the passage here enclosed in square brackets (supplied). This amendment failed of adoption.

2 The words "by an act . . . public exigencies" were interlined in the hand of Randolph after the amendment indicated in Note 1 had been defeated and after the words in angle brackets had been struck out. Thus TJ's second amendment became the first section of the Act.

3 The preceding passage enclosed in square brackets (supplied) is in TJ's hand and was adopted without change. Bill as introduced consisted of the initial word "whereas" plus all that follows this point, except that "said Act" was substituted for title of Act amended.

Bill to Enforce Attendance of Members of Assembly

[*Williamsburg*, *26 May 1778*] Preamble of Bill asserts that public business has been delayed and heavy and unnecessary expenses incurred "thro' want of a sufficient number of members to proceed to business." Provides that any delegate or senator not attending on opening shall pay "the sum of   for every day that he shall continue absent" when the house of which he is a member is unable to do business for want of a quorum. Fines to be recovered by prosecution in the general court unless in the meantime the offending member can satisfy the house that he was detained on public business or that he, his wife, his child, or his parent had been ill; no other excuses admissible. If on trial defendant alleges that he did attend on any of days when house could not do business, burden of proof rests on him. Finally, if any member of either house should depart before the end of the session without permission, entered on the journals of the house of which he was a member, he forfeited all wages that he was otherwise entitled to.

MS (Vi); clerk's copy, endorsed: "A Bill to enforce the attendance of the Members of the General Assembly." Docketed in hand of Edmund Randolph: "May 27. 1778. read the first time. May 28. 1778. read a second time. rejected."

There is no evidence that TJ drew this Bill, but he was a member of a committee of three charged with the duty of drawing it (JHD, May 1778, 1827 edn., p. 3 [misplaced], 21, 22).

Bill to Enable Judges of the General Court to Hold Two Additional Sessions

[*27 May 1778*] Since there are only two sessions of the General Court (March and October), persons committed for criminal offenses "are obliged to undergo a long and painful confinement before they can be brought to trial, which is contrary to justice, and the principles of the constitution." Henceforth there shall be two other sessions (June and December) to hear *only* "treasons, felonies, misdemeanors, and other pleas of the commonwealth cognizable" before the court at other sessions. Act also provides that judges may qualify at any of the terms of the General Court.

MS not located; Act as adopted is in Hening, IX, 460-1.

On 25 May 1778 TJ was appointed to a committee of four, of which Henry Tazewell was chairman, to bring in a bill "establishing Courts of Oyer and Terminer." Tazewell introduced it on 27 May; the following day it was read the second time and recommitted to a new committee of five persons, of which Tazewell was also chairman and TJ a member. The Bill was reported again on 29 May, read the third time on 30 May, and approved by Senate the same day, with an amendment which the House in turn amended and which the Senate accepted (JHD, May 1778, 1827 edn., p. 2, 20, 22, 26, 28, 30). There is no conclusive evidence of TJ's authorship, but, as the chief architect of Virginia's judiciary system under the Constitution of 1776, he must have been concerned by the problem which this Bill was intended to solve. The preamble with its emphasis upon justice and constitutional principles also has a Jeffersonian sound. But perhaps the best evidence of TJ's authorship is to be found in an amendment that he wrote into a subsequent Bill to keep that Bill from interfering with the purpose of the Act of May 1778 (see Bill to Amend the Act Establishing a General Court, under date of 27 Oct. 1778).

Bill to Attaint Josiah Philips and Others

[28 May 1778]

Whereas a certain Josiah[1] Philips labourer of the parish of Lynhaven[2] and county of Princess Anne together with divers others[3] inhabitants of the counties of Princess Anne and Norfolk and citizens of this commonwealth contrary to their fidelity associating and confederating together have levied war against this

Commonwealth, within the same, committing murders, burning houses, wasting farms and doing other acts of hostility in the said counties of Princess Anne, and Norfolk, and still continue to exercise the same enormities on the good people of this commonwealth: and whereas the delays which would attend the proceeding to outlaw the said offenders according to the usual forms and procedures of the courts of law[4] would leave the said good people for a long time exposed to murder and devastation. Be it therefore enacted by the General assembly that if the said Josiah Philips his associates and confederates shall not on or before the[5] day of June in this present year render themselves to the Governor or to some member of the privy council, judge of the General court, justice of the peace or commissioned officer of the regular troops, navy, or militia of this commonwealth in order to[6] their trials for the treasons, murders and other felonies by them committed, that then such of them the said Josiah Philips his associates and confederates as shall not so render him or themselves, shall stand and be convicted and attainted of high treason, and shall suffer the pains of death, and incur all forfeitures, penalties and disabilities prescribed by the law against those convicted and attainted of High-treason: and that execution of this sentence of attainder shall be done by order of the General court to be entered as soon as may be conveniently after notice that any of the said offenders are in custody of the keeper of the public gaol. And if any person committed to the custody of the keeper of the public gaol as an associate or confederate of the said Josiah Philips shall alledge that he hath not been of his associates or confederates at any time after the day of in the year of our lord[7] at which time the said murders and devastations were begun, a petty jury shall be summoned and charged according to the forms of the law to try in presence of the said court the fact so alledged; and if it be found against the defendant, execution of this act shall be done as before directed.

And that the good people of this commonwealth may not in the mean time be subject to the unrestrained hostilities of the said insurgents, be it further enacted that from and after the passing of this act it shall be lawful for any person with or without orders, to pursue and slay the said Josiah Philips and any others who have been of his associates or confederates at any time after the said day of[8] aforesaid and shall not have previously rendered him or themselves to any of the officers civil or military before described, or otherwise to take and deliver them to justice to be[9] dealt with[10] according to law provided that the person so slain be in arms at the time or endeavoring to escape being taken.

Dft (Vi); in TJ's hand. Endorsed by him: "A Bill to attaint Philips & others unless they render themselves to justice within a certain time." Docketed by Edmund Randolph: "May 28. 1778. read the first time. May 29. 1778. read 2d. time & to be engd. Examined." The Act as adopted has the same title and precisely the same wording as the Bill except for the words supplied in the blank spaces left by TJ (Hening, IX, 463-4). The deleted parts, indicated in notes below, tend to prove that this draft of the Bill is TJ's original composition, not a fair copy such as he usually employed in reporting a bill.

The background of this extraordinary case is to be found in the following: Henry, *Henry*, I, 611-13; *Elliot's Debates*, III, 66, 140, 193, 223, 236, 274, 298, 450; W. P. Trent, "The Case of Josiah Philips," *Amer. Hist. Rev.*, I (1895-1896), p. 444-54. Ford (II, 149) states that this Bill "was a violation of article 8 of the Virginia Declaration of Rights and was afterwards cited by Edmund Randolph . . . as such, in the following words: 'There is one example of this violation in Virginia, of a most striking and shocking nature,—an example so horrid that, if I conceived my country would passively permit a repetition of it, dear as it is to me, I would seek means of expatriating myself from it. A man who was then a citizen, was deprived of his life thus: from a mere reliance on general reports, a gentleman in the House of Delegates informed the house that a certain man (Josiah Philips) had committed several crimes, and was running at large perpetrating other crimes. He therefore moved leave to attaint him; he obtained that leave instantly; no sooner did he obtain it, than he drew from his pocket a bill ready written for that effect; it was read three times in one day and carried to the Senate. I will not say that it passed the same day through the Senate; but he was attainted very speedily and precipitately, without any proof better than these vague reports. Without being confronted with his accusers and witnesses, without the privilege of calling evidence on his behalf, he was sentenced to death, and was afterwards actually executed.' " Also, St. George Tucker asserted that the judges of the General Court refused to apply the Act of attainder and that Philips was "put upon his trial, according to the ordinary course of law" (Tucker, ed., *Blackstone*, I [1803], Appendix, p. 293). TJ was in France when Randolph produced his amalgam of errors, and may not have seen the speech until 1815. On 27 July 1814 William Wirt wrote TJ asking what he knew about the case and merely referring to the fact that "Mr. Henry was much censured by Mr. Ed. Randolph, in the convention of 1788"; TJ replied that the censure of Henry was without foundation; that he remembered the case; and that "Philips was a mere robber, who availing himself of the troubles of the times, collected a banditti, retired to the Dismal swamp, and from thence sallied forth, plundering and maltreating the neighboring inhabitants, and covering himself, without authority, under the name of a British subject. Mr. Henry, then Governor, communicated the case to me. We both thought the best proceeding would be by bill of attainder, unless he delivered himself up for trial within a given time. Philips was afterwards taken; and Mr. Randolph being attorney General and apprehending he would plead that he was a British subject, taken in arms, in support of his lawful sovereign, and as a prisoner of war entitled to the protection of the law of nations, he thought the safest proceeding would be to indict him at Common law as a felon and robber. Against this I believe Philips urged the same plea; but was overruled and found guilty" (TJ to Wirt, 14 Aug. 1814).

The next year, however, TJ answered Randolph's charges much more fully, though he attributed his errors to the zeal of an orator who "in the ardor of conflict, [loses sight] of the rigorous accuracies of fact" (TJ to Girardin, 12 Mch. 1815). In this same letter TJ said that Randolph's decision to try Philips at common law was "a course which every one approved, because the first object of the act of attainder was to bring him to fair trial." TJ rewrote that part of Girardin's history so as to coincide with his memory of the proceedings on this Bill, and Girardin published TJ's revision (Burk-Girardin, *Hist. of Va.*, IV, 305-6). TJ did not, however, recall the ironic fact that Randolph himself, as clerk of the House, had docketed the Bill, though he repeated the account he had given Wirt of Randolph's decision not to make use of the Act.

While there is no clause in the Virginia Declaration of Rights or the Constitution of 1776 specifically prohibiting the legislature from passing bills of attainder, as, for example, there is in the Federal Constitution (Art. I, sect. 9), Coke and others had condemned such bills long before the American Revolution (C. H. McIlwain, *The High Court of Parliament*, 1910, p. 225). Yet to find such a bill proposed and drafted by TJ and enacted into law under his leadership is, to say the least, surprising. It is far more so to find him, so late as 1815, speaking of the "*proper* office of a bill of attainder." Yet, so far as such a Bill could be justified in terms of the principles of a republic, his distinction between proper and improper use accords with the nature of the Act of Attainder of 1778: "When a person, charged with a crime, withdraws from justice, or resists it by force, either in his own or a foreign country, no other means of bringing him to trial or punishment being practicable, a special act is passed by the legislature, adapted to the particular case. This prescribes to him a sufficient term to appear and submit to a trial by his peers; declares that his refusal to appear shall be taken as a confession of guilt, as in the ordinary case of an offender at the bar refusing to plead, and pronounces the sentence which would have been rendered on his confession or conviction in a court of law. No doubt that these acts of attainder have been abused in England as instruments of vengeance by a successful over a defeated party. But what institution is insusceptible of abuse in wicked hands?" (TJ to Girardin, 12 Mch. 1815). The Bill that TJ drew, though it was indeed an attainder limited by the condition that Philips surrender himself before a certain date to be tried according to regular judicial procedure, nevertheless was an assumption by the legislature that (1) Philips was a common criminal and was not acting under a British commission, and (2) that the legislature could of right make such a distinction affecting the life and liberty of an individual. Since this was assuming to the legislature a power over the rights of an individual usually regarded as belonging within the province of the judiciary and under protection of established legal procedures, the least that can be said about the Bill of Attainder of 1778 is that it was an extreme violation of TJ's belief in the principle of the separation of powers of government.

There is no doubt that Josiah Philips had been duly charged with crime, had withdrawn from justice, had resisted it by force, and had continued from 1775 to 1778 in his course of pillage and terrorism. On 20 June 1777 the council authorized the governor to issue a proclamation offering a reward for the capture of Philips and two other leaders of a group of "evil disposed persons, to the number of ten, or twelve, [who] have conspired together, to foment a Dangerous Insurrection"; Patrick Henry issued the proclamation the same day. On 3 Jan. 1778 the council authorized the governor to issue a warrant for £55 "for the purpose of rewarding sundry persons for apprehending Josiah Philips who was outlawed by the Governor the 20th June last as a Traitor to the State." Apparently Philips, after being captured, must have effected his escape, for on 1 May 1778 the council received word from Col. Muter that "the noted Traitor has again made an Insurrection in Princess Anne County at the head of fifty Men." The council authorized the governor to call out 100 of the militia from Nansemond, to offer a reward of $500 for apprehending Philips dead or alive, and to divide any booty among the captors of the traitor. By 27 May, however, Governor Henry laid before the council a letter he had received from Col. John Wilson saying that the militia was ineffective and recommending "the Removal of such Families as are in League with the Insurgents as a Step . . . absolutely necessary"; the council advised Henry to send this letter to the Assembly and to order out a company of regular troops (*Va. Council Jour.*, I, 435; II, 58, 127, 140). According to TJ's letter to Wirt of 14 Aug. 1814, Henry consulted TJ before laying Wilson's letter before the council and both agreed upon a bill of attainder; Trent (p. 446) asserts that TJ had probably instigated the letter which Henry transmitted to the House. The last may be so, but TJ was probably mistaken in recalling that he and Henry had agreed upon a bill of attainder. For what Henry asked the legislature to consider was Wilson's proposal about the removal of some families: "thinking that the Executive power is not competent to such a purpose, I must beg leave to submit the whole matter to the general Assembly, who are the only Judges how far the methods of proceeding directed by Law, are to be dispended with on this occasion" (*Official Letters*, I, 282-3). (During the preceding year, on a threatened invasion, the governor and council had authorized the militia "to remove and restrain, during the imminence of the danger . . . certain persons whose affections to the American cause were suspected," and the legislature had subsequently passed an Act of Indemnification for this use of executive power, indicating that Henry must have felt that on such a matter he did lack power; Hening, IX, 373-4). Henry's letter of 27 May was laid before the House on the same day, together with Wilson's letter; the House immediately resolved itself into the committee of the whole and debated the matter. On 28 May the committee of the whole again discussed the problem of the insurgents and agreed upon the following resolution: "Information being received that a certain   Philips, with divers others, his associates and confederates, have levied war against this Commonwealth within the counties of Norfolk and Princess Anne, committing murders, burning houses, wasting farms, and doing other acts of enormity, in defiance of the officers of justice, *Resolved, that it is the opinion of this committee*, that if the said   Philips, his associates and confederates, do not render themselves to some officer, civil or military, within this Commonwealth, on or before the   day of June in this present year, such of them as fail so to do ought to be attainted of high treason; and that in the meantime, and before such render, it shall be lawful for any person, with or without orders, to pursue and slay, or otherwise to take and deliver to justice the said   Philips, his associates and confederates." (Trent, p. 447, asserts that "the report of the committee of the whole has been found in Jefferson's own handwriting"; no such MS has been located, but in all probability TJ did draw the resolution just quoted, since its language in all respects is so similar to that used in the Bill.) TJ was appointed chairman of a committee of three to draft the Bill; he reported it the same day, when it was read the first time. On 29 May it was read the second time; on 30 May it passed the third reading; TJ carried it to the Senate and the Senate approved it the same day (JHD, May 1778, 1827 edn., p. 20, 22, 23, 24, 28, 33).

Philips and some of his confederates were apprehended before the time limit set by the Act of Attainder had expired. "Last Tuesday the noted Josiah Philips, and James Hodges, were safely lodged in the publick jail by the sheriff of Princess Anne. They were taken the 4th instant, at night, in Norfolk county, with three others of the gang, who are soon expected here likewise" (*Va. Gaz.* [Purdie], 19 June 1778). Their fate is recorded in the following newspaper account: "On Friday the 16th commenced, and continued to the 21st, the trial of sundry prisoners from the publick jail, when Josiah Philips, James Hodges, Robert Hodges, and Henry M'Clellan, from Princess Anne for robbing the publick waggons (and who were accused of murder, treason, and sundry other outrages) were capitally convicted" (*Va. Gaz.* [Purdie], 30 Oct. 1778). They were executed on the gallows near Williamsburg on 23 Nov. 1778 (*Va. Gaz.* [D & H], 4 Dec. 1778).

[1] Both in the report of the committee of the whole and in the Bill, here and elsewhere, TJ left blank spaces for Philips' given name. "Josiah" is filled in here and elsewhere in the Bill in Randolph's hand.

[2] Lynhaven is in Randolph's hand.

[3] TJ deleted the following at this point: "citizens of this commonwealth associating and confederating themselves together, have again."

[4] Philips had, of course, been outlawed by executive proclamation in 1777. See above.

[5] The Act reads: "last day of June." Since the Act was passed 30 May, this meant that Philips and his associates had only one month in which to deliver themselves up to justice or be attainted of treason.

[6] The Act agrees with the reading of the Bill at this point, though possibly TJ, in the haste of drafting, omitted the word "stand."

[7] The Act reads: "first day of July in the year . . . one thousand seven hundred and seventy seven."

[8] The Act reads: "first day of July."

[9] The word "executed" is deleted in MS.

[10] The words "as before directed by this act" are deleted and the phrase "according to law" interlined.

To Richard Henry Lee

Dear Sir Williamsburg, June 5, 1778.

I am now to acknowledge the receipt of two of your favours, during the session of Assembly, but there being little to communicate to you, and that, being a busy time with me, has prevented my doing it sooner. The Assembly rose on Monday last; their only act, which can shortly aid our army, was one for raising a regiment of horse, which, I think, will be raised as fast as it can be accoutred. Another act they passed, will, also, produce aid to our army, I hope, but it will be some time first; it was for giving great encouragement to soldiers, and appointing recruiting officers all over the country, to attend all public places. By a third act, they foolishly repeated the experiment of raising volunteers; the first attempt was pardonable, because its ill success could not be foreseen; the second is worse than ridiculous, because it may deceive our friends; I am satisfied there will not be a company raised. I wish Congress would commute a good part of the infantry required from us, for an equivalent force in horse. This service opens to us a new fund of young men, who have not yet stepped forth; I mean those whose indolence or education, has unfitted them for foot-service; this may be worth your thinking of. We passed the bill of pardon, recommended by Congress, but the Senate rejected it. Your letter, about enlarging your powers over the confederation, was not proceeded on, because the nature of the enlargement was not chalked out by you so intelligibly as enabled the house to do any thing, unless they had given a *carte blanche*. Indeed, I believe, that, had the alterations proposed been specified, unless they had been mere form indeed, it might have been difficult to obtain their consent. A Frenchman arrived here a week ago, with a vast cargo of woollens, made and unmade, stockings, shoes, &c. fit for the army, fifty-thousand weight of powder, and other articles; the master had once sold the whole cargo, to the governor and council, for 5*s*. 3*d*. the livre, first cost; but, on suggestions from some of our forestallers, and those from Maryland, he flew off. Our bay is clear of the enemy. Nothing new here. I set out for Albemarle, within a day or two. Mr. Harvie will be with you in about three weeks. My compliments to your brethren of the delegation, and am, dear sir, Your friend and servant, Thomas Jefferson

MS not located. Text from R. H. Lee, *Memoir and Corr. of R. H. Lee*, II, 187-8.

TJ was on the committee ordered to bring in the Bill for raising volunteers (Hening, IX, 445-9; MS: Vi), and the Bill for raising a regiment of horse (same, p. 449-51; MS: Vi), but there is no evidence that he had any part in their composition.

To Giovanni Fabbroni

Sir Williamsburgh in Virginia June. 8. 1778

Your letter of Sep. 15. 1776 from Paris came safe to hand. We have not however had the pleasure of seeing Mr. De Crenis, the bearer of it in this country, as he joined the army in Pennsylvania as soon as he arrived. I should have taken particular pleasure in serving him on your recommendation. From the kind anxiety expressed in your letters as well as from other sources of information we discover that our enemies have filled Europe with Thrasonic accounts of victories they had never won and conquests they were fated never to make. While these accounts alarmed our friends in Europe they afforded us diversion. We have long been out of all fear for the event of the war.[1] I inclose you a list of the killed, wounded, and captives of the enemy from the Commencement of hostilities at Lexington in April 1775. till November 1777. since which there has been no event of any consequence. This is the best history of the war which can be brought within the compass of a letter. I believe the account to be near the truth, tho' it is difficult to get at the numbers lost by an enemy with absolute precision. Many of the articles have been communicated to us from England as taken from the official returns made by their General. I wish it were in my power to send you as just an account of our [losses] but this cannot be done without an application to the war office which being in another country is at this time out of my reach. I think that upon the whole it has been about one half the number lost by them. In some instances more, but in others less. This difference is ascribed to our superiority in taking aim when we fire; every soldier in our army having been intimate with his gun from his infancy. If there could have been a doubt before as to the event of the war, it is now totally removed by the interposition of France; and the generous alliance she has entered into with us.

Tho' much of my time is employed in the councils of America I have yet a little leisure to indulge my fondness for philosophical studies. I could wish to correspond with you on subjects of that kind. It might not be unacceptable to you to be informed for instance of the true power of our climate as discoverable from the Thermometer, from the force and direction of the winds, the quantity of rain, the plants which grow without shelter in the winter &c. On the other hand we should be much pleased with cotemporary observations on the same particulars in your country, which will give us a comparative view of the two climates.[2] Farenheit's thermometer is the only one in use with us. I make my daily observations as early as possible in the morning and again about 4. o'clock in the afternoon, these generally showing the maxima of cold and heat in the course of 24 hours. I wish I could gratify your Botanical taste; but I am acquainted with nothing more than the first principles of that science, yet myself and my friends may furnish you with any Botanical subjects which this country affords, and are not to be had with you: and I shall take pleasure in procuring them when pointed out by you. The greatest difficulty will be the means of conveyance during the continuance of the war.

If there is a gratification which I envy any people in this world it is to your country its music. This is the favorite passion of my soul, and fortune has cast my lot in a country where it is in a state of deplorable barbarism. From the [line] of life in which we conjecture you to be, I have for some time lost the hope of seeing you here. Should the event prove so, I shall ask your assistance in procuring a substitute who may be a proficient in singing and on the harpsichord. I should be contented to receive such an one two or three years hence, when it is hoped he may come more safely, and find here a greater plenty of those useful things which commerce alone can furnish. The bounds of an American fortune will not admit the indulgence of a domestic band of musicians. Yet I have thought that a passion for music might be reconciled with that oeconomy which we are obliged to observe. I retain for instance among my domestic servants a gardener (Ortolano), weaver (Tessitore di lino e lan[o),] a cabinet maker (Stipettaio) and a stonecutter (scalpellino lavorante in piano) to which I would add a Vigneron. In a country where, like yours, music is cultivated and practised by every class of men I suppose there might be found persons of those trades who could perform on the French horn, clarinet or hautboy and bassoon, so that one might have a band of two French horns, two clarinets and hautboys and a bassoon, without enlarging their domest[ic] expences. A certainty of employment for a half dozen years, and at [the] end of that time to find them if they chose it a conveyance to their own country might induce [them] to come here on reasonable wages. Without meaning to give you trouble, perhaps it mig[ht] be practicable for you in your ordinary intercourse with your pe[ople] to find out such men disposed to come to America. Sobriety and good nature would be desireable parts of their characters. If you think such a plan practicable, and will be so kind[3] as to inform me what will be necessary to be done on my part, I will take care that it shall be done. The necessary expences, when informed of them, I can remit before they are wanting, to any port in France with which country alone we have safe correspondence.

I am Sir with much esteem your humble servt., T. J.[4]

ENCLOSURE

Number of the Killed, Wounded, and Captives of the British Army in the Course of the American War.

1775	KILLED	WOUNDED	PRISONERS
At Lexington & Concord	43	70	
Bunker's hill	746	1,150	
Ticonderoga, St. John, & Quebeck	81	110	340
1776			
on the Lakes by general Arnold	53	64	
at Fort Sulivan in South Carolina	197	260	
at the Cedars in Canada	40	70	
at Norfolk, & the great bridge in Virginia	129	175	40
in Long Island	840	1600	65
at Harlem & Hellgate near New York	136	157	49
at New York on Landing	57	100	
at Fort Washington near New York	900	1,500	
at Fort Lee	20	35	
at Trenton the 26 of Decber.	35	60	948
at Princeton in New Jersey	74	100	
1777			
in Boston road by Commodore Harding	52	90	750
in Sundry transports			390
at Danbury	260	350	
at Iron hill in Delaware State	59	80	20
at Brandwine in Pensylvania the 11th. Sepber.	800	1,176	
on Reading road by Genal. Maxwell	40	60	
at german Town near Philadelphia the 4th. Octber.	180	975	20
on Staten Island by Genal. Sulivan	94	150	278
at Bennington near the Lakes the 4th. Octber.	900	1,300	30
at Forts Montgomery & Clinton Hudsons River	580	700	
at Forts Mifflin & Red-Bank near Philada.	328	70	84
Genal. Burgoin's Army at Saratoga	2,100	1,126	5,752
Prisoners, & deserters before the Surrender			1,100
Total	8,844	11,528	9,866.

In all Wounded, Killed, and Prisoners, 30,238
Men already Lost to England 18,710

Dft (DLC); heavily corrected; the more important excisions are given in the textual notes. Tr (MiU-C) of the recipient's copy, which was evidently intercepted and is now missing; endorsed: "Copy of a private Letter from Williamsburgh in Virginia dated June 8-1778. Sent by the way of Spain, to a foreign gentleman abroad." Tr is incomplete, omitting more than half the text. It includes, however, the table of British losses which was enclosed by TJ and which is not found with the draft. That table is therefore printed here from the transcript.

YOUR LETTER OF SEP. 15 1776: TJ corrected the year, apparently from 1777 to 1776, for Tr reads 1776; see Fabbroni's letter of that date. On the cover of Fabbroni's letter TJ made memoranda for his reply. These read as follows:

"state of killed & [. . . .]
alliance
lies in Engld. diversion
musician harpsichd. singer. organ.
band. viz

2 horns &c ⟨*clarinet*⟩ &c bassoon.	Cab. makr. Gardener. Stone cutter weaver vigneron

wines. Vendée
Thermometer &c
a gardener. Ortolano
a stone-cutter. Scalpellino lavorante in piano.
a cabinet-maker. Stipettaio.
weaver. Tessitore di lino e lana."

Intercepted with TJ's letter was a letter from his friend Charles (Carlo) Bellini to Fabbroni; an undated translation of it is also in MiU-C. It provides an illuminating account of Bellini's life in Virginia: he describes himself as "Secretary to the State of Virginia for foreign affairs [he was actually a translator, see notes to Bill Establishing a Clerkship of Foreign Correspondence, 18 May 1778], and Professor of Modern Languages in this University [College of William and Mary]." The substance of his letter is repeated in one he afterward addressed to Mazzei, 12 Aug. 1778, printed in two Florentine journals later that year and reprinted in English by A. Pace, WMQ, 3d ser., IV (1947), 350-5.

1 Deleted in draft: "since the battle of Bunker's hill, which proved to us experimentally that the want of discipline might be supplied by native courage and a cordial tho' governable animation in the cause for which we are contending. Our enemies indeed obtained the feild on that day by superiority of numbers, but their loss was five times greater than ours."

2 Text of transcript of the intercepted letter (except for complimentary close and signature) ends at this point. The British high command was not interested in TJ's musical plans.

3 Deleted in draft: "as to write me a line, with advice what money may be necessary to remit, I will take care to do it for their transportation hither; I would remit it according to your advice to any port of France, with which country only we have safe correspondence. I shall always be glad to receive your letters and to do any friendly offices which you or your friends may require hence."

4 Supplied from transcript. Draft is unsigned.

To Samuel Henley

REVEREND SIR — Williamsburgh, June 9, 1778.

Mr. Madison I believe informed you by letter written some time ago that one of your boxes of books left in his care burst open in removing it from the college to the president's house for greater security. This accident discovered them to be in a state of ruin. They had contracted a dampness and stuck together in large blocks, insomuch that they could not sometimes be separated without tearing the cover. I happened to be in town and was of opinion with Mr. Madison that it was necessary to overhaul them and give them air. Indeed we both thought—I think it would be for your interest to have them sold, as books are now in considerable demand here, and, packed as they are in boxes, they must sustain injury. There are many of them which I would be glad to take myself at their stirling cost and would remit you the money by the way of France. That cost might be fixed either by note from yourself, informing me what they cost you, or by the estimate of anybody here in whom you trust. Upon a presumption that you could not but approve of the proposal to have them disposed of and the money remitted, for the reasons before given and others which you may apprehend but would be improper for me to explain, I have taken the liberty of laying apart many of them for myself, leaving with Mr. Madison a catalogue of them, and ready to return them to him if you shall direct it. I shall be glad of your answer as soon as possible, and will gladly serve you in the care of any interest you may have left here. The reasons are obvious which restrain this letter to matters of business. As soon as the obstacles to friendly correspondence are removed I shall be glad at all times to hear from you. I am Reverend Sir Your friend & servant.

MS not located. Text from Ford, II, 160-1, where it was printed, without signature, from a copy furnished by John Boyd Thacher of Albany. The letter was sold in the Thacher Sale, Anderson Auction Co., N.Y., 13 Mch. 1914, lot 160.

SAMUEL HENLEY, a professor at William and Mary College, left America about the beginning of the Revolution (WMQ, 1st ser., XXVI [1917-1918], p. 226-31). For a summary of events leading to this letter, which never reached its destination, see TJ to Samuel Henley, 3 Mch. 1785.

To James Mercer

DEAR SIR Albemarle June 14. 1778.

Mr. Dick presented me at the assembly in December Mr. Ogilvie's debt, at which time I was not able to answer it, and as he told me he should be in Williamsburgh again before the rising of the assembly, I omitted to take a memorandum of the amount. If you will be so good as to let me know what it is, I will by the first safe opportunity send it to you. If you have any news of the British army's departure, a French war declared, or other important event a communication of it by the bearer (who returns on receiving your answer to this) will oblige Dear Sir Your friend & humble servt.,

TH: JEFFERSON

RC (André deCoppet, New York City, 1949). Addressed: "To James Mercer esq. Fredericksburgh." Endorsed: "Jefferson Thos June 1778 [2?] times I was willing to receive a Specie Debt in paper. it was demanded but he coud not pay."

Information on this transaction is not available in TJ's Account Books, though see TJ to Thomas Adams, 11 July 1770 for TJ's earlier effort in Ogilvie's behalf.

From Richard Henry Lee

DEAR SIR York in Pennsylva. 16 June 1778

I thank you for your favor of the 5th which I received yesterday. It is the only satisfactory account I have received of the proceedings of our Assembly. The enemy have made many insidious attempts upon us lately, not in the military way, they seem tired of that, but in the way of negotiation. Their first, was by industriously circulating the bills of *pacification* as they call them, before they had passed into Acts, in order to prevent our closing with France. These bills received a comment from Congress on the 22d. of April, which no doubt you have seen. The inclosed paper will shew you the second attempt from Lord Howe and Gen. Clinton, with the answer of Congress. The third movement happened very lately, when Clinton desired a passport from Gen. Washington for Dr. Ferguson to come to Congress with a letter from the newly arrived Commissioners Lord Carlyle [Carlisle], Wm. Eden esqr. and Governor Johnston. The General refused the passport until Congress should give leave. The letter from Clinton was transmitted here, but the impatience of the Commissioners did not suffer them to wait for an answer. Thro the medium of the General, leaving their Secretary Dr. Ferguson behind, the packet arrived containing a letter from the Commissioners with a copy of their Commission. Their letter is a combination of fraud, falsehood, insidious offers, and abuse of France, Concluding with a denial of Independence. The sine qua non being withheld, you may judge what will be the fate of the rest. An answer has not yet been sent. In due time you will have both the letter and its answer. I dont know whether to call Governor Johnston an Apostate or not. He has been in opposition to the Ministry and has spoken some speeches in our favor, but I believe he has never been a friend to American Independence. However, there seems no doubt but that he has on this occasion touched Ministerial gold. The others are notorious Ministerialists. It is amazing how the Court of London does mix pride, meanness, cunning, and folly, with Gasconade, and timidity. In short the strangest composition is there formed that ever disgraced and injured Mankind. The King of Prussia has declared in terms explicit, that he would follow France in acknowledging our Independence and his hobby horse is, to become a maritime power. Yet he seems, by his movements disposed to quarrel with the Emperor about the divisions of the Bavarian dominions, the Elector being dead without Heir of his body, the next Heir who is the Elector

Palatine must loose his right between the two great Spoilers. We have been long amused with accounts of the enemy abandoning Philadelphia. I believe they will do so when they can stay no longer, but not until then. They have certainly removed all their heavy Cannon, Baggage &c. And fearing a french war every Moment, they keep in readiness to depart. We did late[ly] shatter extremely a 20 gun ship belonging to the enemy in [the] North river, and sent her away to York, in no condition for service. I observe by our last delegation, that my enem[ies] have been again at work, however, they shall not gain their point of withdrawing me from the public Councils.

I am dear Sir your affectionate friend and obedient Servant,

RICHARD HENRY LEE

RC (DLC). Enclosure missing.

The BILLS OF PACIFICATION and the reply of Congress were widely published in America (see *Va. Gaz.* [D & H], 8 May 1778). The letters of HOWE and CLINTON were transmitted to Congress in a letter of Gen. Washington, 4 June 1778, read and acted on in Congress on 6 June (JCC, XI, 572-5). The letter from the COMMISSIONERS was received in a letter of 11 June from Gen. Washington, read in Congress 13 June 1778 (JCC, XI, 605; see also R. H. Lee to TJ, 3 May 1778).

From Richard Henry Lee

MY DEAR SIR York the 23d. June 1778

The inclosed Gazette will shew you the progress, and perhaps the end for some time, of our negotiation with the British Commissioners. They, with their whole Army have abandoned Philadelphia, and our Troops are in possession of that City. The enemy are pushing thro Jersey for South Amboy, and in their front is Gen. Maxwell with a brigade of Continentals and the Jersey Militia. They have impeded the enemies progress by breaking up the roads and bridges; and we have just been told that Maxwell has attacked and gained an advantage over part of their army. Gen. Washington with 13,000 men is in hot pursuit of the enemy. He was about crossing Delaware the day before yesterday. If our Army can come up with them before they embark, we may have a second edition of Burgoyne. Governor Johnsone tries every art to gain admission among us. He abuses his Masters, flatters America, and is willing to yield us every thing if we will be perfidious to our Ally and again submit to the domination of his King and Parliament. This Man possesses in abundance Scottish cunning and Scottish impudence. But it is too late in the day. The Sunshine of liberty and independence prevails over the dark arts of Tyranny and its Tools.

We hope in 6 or 8 days to ratify the Confederation (all but two or 3 small States, at the head of which is Maryland and all of whom I have no doubt will soon fall in) with amendments—after which Congress will adjourn to Philadelphia. I am dear Sir affectionately yours, RICHARD HENRY LEE

RC (DLC); Tr (PPAP). Enclosure missing.

To David Rittenhouse

DEAR SIR Monticello in Albemarle. Virginia. July 19. 1778.

I sincerely congratulate you on the recovery of Philadelphia, and wish it may be found uninjured by the enemy. How far the interests of literature may have suffered by the injury or removal of the Orrery (as it is miscalled) the publick libraries, your papers and implements, are doubts which still excite anxiety. We were much disappointed in Virginia generally on the day of the great eclipse, which proved to be cloudy. In Williamsburgh, where it was total, I understand only the beginning was seen. At this place which is in Lat. 38° 8′ and Longitude West from Williamsburgh about 1° 45′ as is conjectured, eleven digits only were supposed to be covered. It was not seen at all till the moon had advanced nearly one third over the sun's disc. Afterwards it was seen at intervals through the whole. The egress particularly was visible. It proved however of little use to me for want of a time peice that could be depended on; which circumstance, together with the subsequent restoration of Philadelphia to you, has induced me to trouble you with this letter to remind you of your kind promise of making me an accurate clock, which being intended for astronomical purposes only, I would have divested of all apparatus for striking or for any other purpose, which by increasing it's complication might disturb it's accuracy. A companion to it, for keeping seconds, and which might be moved easily, would greatly add to it's value. The theodolite, for which I spoke to you also, I can now dispense with, having since purchased a most excellent one.

Writing to a philosopher, I may hope to be pardoned for intruding some thoughts of my own, tho' they relate to him personally. Your time for two years past has, I beleive, been principally employed in the civil government of your country. Tho' I have been aware of the authority our cause would acquire with the world from it's being known that yourself and Doctr. Franklin were zealous friends to it, and am myself duly impressed with a sense of the arduousness of government, and the obligation those are under who are able to conduct it, yet I am also satisfied there is an order of geniusses above that obligation, and therefore exempted from it. No body can conceive that nature ever intended to throw away a Newton upon the occupations of a crown. It would have been a prodigality for which even the conduct of providence might have been arraigned, had he been by birth annexed to what was so far below him. Cooperating with nature in her ordinary œconomy, we should dispose of and employ the geniusses of men according to their several orders and degrees. I doubt not there are in your country many persons equal to the task of conducting government: but you should consider that the world has but one Ryttenhouse, and that it never had one before. The amazing mechanical representation of the solar system which you conceived and executed, has never been surpassed by any but the work of which it is a copy. Are those powers then, which being intended for the erudition of the world, like air and light, the world's common property, to be taken from their proper pursuit to do the commonplace drudgery of governing a single state, a work which may be executed by men of an ordinary stature, such as are always and every where to be found? Without having ascended mount Sina for inspiration, I can pronounce that the precept, in the decalogue of the vulgar, that they shall not make to themselves 'the likeness of any thing that is in the heavens above' is reversed for you, and that you will fulfill the highest purposes of your creation by employing yourself in the perpetual breach of that inhibition. For my own country in particular you must remember something like a promise that it should be adorned with one of them. The taking of your city by the enemy has hitherto prevented the proposition from being made and approved by our legislature. The zeal of a true Whig in science must excuse the hazarding these free thoughts, which flow from a desire of promoting the diffusion of knowledge and of your fame, and from one who can assure you truly that he is with much sincerity & esteem Your most obedt. & most humble servt.,

TH: JEFFERSON

P.S. If you can spare as much time as to give me notice of the receipt of this, and what hope I may form of my clocks, it will oblige me. If sent to Fredericksburgh it will come safe to hand.

RC (PHi). Dft (DLC). Dft contains numerous excisions and substitutions not recorded here.

THE ORRERY (AS IT IS MISCALLED): I.e., Rittenhouse's planetarium, then at the College of Philadelphia and now in the Library of the University of Pennsylvania. (An earlier one constructed by

Rittenhouse had been bought in 1770 by John Witherspoon for the College of New Jersey.) TJ objected to the name because it derived from the fact that a rude planetarium had been built for Charles Boyle, Earl of Orrery, earlier in the century; the popular rather than the correct name was, however, used by Rittenhouse and most others (OED; William Smith, "A Description of a New Orrery," Amer. Philos. Soc., *Trans.*, old ser., I [1771], 1-3; M. J. Babb, "The Relation of David Rittenhouse and His Orrery to the University [of Pennsylvania]," *General Magazine and Historical Chronicle*, XXXIV [1931-1932], 221-32; H. E. Gillingham, "The First Orreries in America," *Jour. Franklin Institute*, CCXXIX [1940], 81-99; Edward Ford, *David Rittenhouse*, Phila., 1946, ch. V). THE GREAT ECLIPSE to which TJ refers occurred on 24 June 1778 (information from Prof. John Q. Stewart, Princeton University); see further, Rev. James Madison to TJ, 26 July, and John Page to TJ, 19 Aug. 1778.

From Richard Henry Lee

DEAR SIR Philadelphia July 20th 1778

The condition of our affairs is much changed since last I had the pleasure of writing to you, as by the favor of his Most Christian Majesty we now are become Masters of the Sea, on our own Coast at least. Ten days ago arrived in the Delaware a french Squadron commanded by Count D'Esteing consisting of 12 sail of the Line and 4 frigates, having of Seamen and land Troops 11,000 Men on board. There is one Ship of 90 guns, one of 80, 6 of 74, three of 64 and 4 frigates. Having missed the English here, they have proceeded to N. York in quest of them, and are now before that Harbour, the depth of water being unfortunately insufficient to admit such large Ships. The English, whose fleet is inferior, are well contented to remain within the Narrows, and suffer Monsr. the Count to intercept every Vessel coming to N. York. He has already taken 15. Sail. But the french Admiral being an Officer of great activity and spirit, he seems not content with this small work, and therefore I believe he will go immediately to R. Island where he can easily destroy the Ships, and with the assistance of our force there, make prisoners of 2000 British Troops on that Island. With this Squadron came Le Sieur Gerard Minister Plenepotentiary from his most Christian Majesty. He is a sensible well bred Man, and perfectly well acquainted with the politics of Europe. From him I learn that the Court of France consider the Message of the King of England to his Parliament and their answer, upon the Count Noailles notification of our Alliance, as a denunciation of War on the part of G. Britain, and that they mean to Act accordingly, without an express declaration, leaving this last to England. We are busied now in settling the Ceremonials for the reception of foreign Ministers of every denomination. And I assure you it is a work of no small difficulty. When this is finished, Monsr. Gerard will have his audience in Congress—I suppose this week. Gen. Washingt[on] has crossed the N. River, and will cooperate with the Admiral in Measures to be concerted against the Comm[on] enemy. The B. Commissioners have sent us a second letter, very silly, and equally insolent. The preleminaries insisted on by Congress (an acknowledgement of Independence or a withdrawing of their fleets and Armies) not having been either of them complied with, this letter is to receive no answer. We have detected and fully exposed Govr. Johnstone, who under the plausible guise of friendship and Virtue, has endeavored to bribe Members of Congress—The whole body indeed as well as individual Members. The Confederation i[s] ratified by 10 States, there remains only Jersey, Delaw[are] and Maryland; but I suppose their obstinacy will e'er long submit to their interest, and a perfect coalition take place. I am, much hurried, tho with great esteem, dear Sir your most obedient Servt,

RICHARD HENRY [LEE]

RC (DLC).

The committee on the public reception of Conrad Alexandre GERARD, of which R. H. Lee was a member, reported on 16 June. The report was debated on 17, 18, and 20 June. Gérard was publicly received by Congress on 6 Aug. 1778 (JCC, XI, 688, 696, 698-701, 707-8, 753-7). The ratification of the CONFEDERATION was taken up in Congress on 22 June (JCC, XI, 631), but the hope that the three remaining states would ratify the Confederation in the current session of Congress was not fulfilled (Merrill Jensen, *The Articles of Confederation*, Univ. of Wisc. Press, 1940, p. 191-6).

From Rev. James Madison

DEAR SIR

WMC.[1] July 26th 78

I was very glad to see your Observations, tho they differ considerably from those we made here. The same Misfortune of a cloudy Morning prevented us from seeing the Beginning, but we had a very good View of the End which Mr. Page made at 11h 3′ 25″ and myself at 11h 3′ 27″ tho' I think the Altitude of the Sun was such as must render the Observations uncertain to a few Seconds. The End of total Darkness was at 45′ 30″. This was pretty nearly determined, for the Return of Light was almost instantaneous. There was really something awful in the Appearance which all Nature assumed. You could not determine your most intimate Acquaintance at 20 yds. distance. Lightening Buggs were seen as at Night.

I began on the 17th. to make corresponding Observations and

had the Time very accurate. Rittenhouse got to Phila. Time eno' to make an observation, but he likewise saw only the End and informs that it was at 11 14′ 40″ M. Time. The Effect of Parallax will doubtless make a considerable Difference.

If you should be at Home in October you may have an Observation on an Imm. Jup. Sat. on the 5th at 8h 25′ 11″ and another on the 12th at 10h 20′ 56″—for this Pla[net] they are more to be depended upon than other observations because the Theory is better known.

We have Nothing new, but what the Papers will communicate, except the Landing of 4000 French Troops near Sandy Hook. The 90 and 82s it is said cannot get over the Bar. The Count D'Estaing is the Author of a Book called Des Egaremens de Julie and distinguish'd himself in the E. Indies last War as a brave Officer.

I hope to have the Pleasure of seeing you in October. If any Thing worth while should occur shall be happy to communicate and also to hear from you. Mr. B. returns best Compts & I beg Leave to pre[sent] mine to Mrs. Jefferson, and am with sincere Regard Yrs., JA: MADISON

RC (DLC).

TJ's OBSERVATIONS on the total eclipse occurring 24 June 1778 have not been found. IMM. JUP. SAT.: I.e., an immersion [of one of] Jupiter's satellites. DES EGAREMENS DE JULIE: More correctly *Les Egaremens de Julie*, an erotic novel published in 1756 and reprinted as recently as 1949, has been doubtfully attributed to Jacques-Antoine-René Perrin by various authorities; it was not by D'Estaing. MR. B.: Unidentified; he may have been Charles Bellini.

[1] I.e., College of William and Mary.

From Robert Carter

SIR Nominy Hall 27 July 1778

Your favor inclosing £36 11 0 is now before me, which Sum I consider as a full discharge of your Bond payable to me, conditioned to pay £27 10 0 which Bond is herein inclosed, striped of its Seal &c. You are pleased to Say that the practical part of musick afforded you much Entertainment and that you wanted an Organ. I have two daughters, who practice upon keyed Instruments; their music Master did enter into the continental Service, who lately resigned his commission. The Girls and Mrs. Carter are in Expectation of Mr. Victors returning to his former Calling. I had imbibed a very destructive notion touching the Religion of revelation that it was of human Institution only and that the Civil power had closed in with it for temporary advantages only. It does not appear fit to mention, here, the probable motives that lead to this deistical Opinion. I do now disclaim it and do testify that Jesus Christ is the Son of god; that through him mankind can be Saved only; that the old and new testament contain the word of god that they are written by inspired Men and for mans Instruction. In a Catalogue of the Westover Library, lately published, there are many Books on divinity part thereof I would have bought but was disapointed therein. I have lately Sent a list of Books to a house in france. Your Invitation I think on with pleasure, but I fear my Situation will not allow me to visit you at your house Shortly. I am Sir your most obedt & very hum. Servt., ROBERT CARTER

FC (NcD).

YOUR FAVOR: Probably TJ's letter (not located) was dated 26 May 1778, for his Account Book under that date records sending to Carter "by Richard Parker £36-11 being principal & int. of my bond." WESTOVER LIBRARY: The library of the Byrd family, the most important private collection of books in colonial Virginia; a catalogue was published late in 1777 (*Va. Gaz.* [D & H], 19 Dec. 1777), but no copy has been found; however, J. S. Bassett in his edition of William Byrd's *Writings*, N.Y., 1901, p. 413-43, prints a list of the titles at Westover from a MS catalogue now in the Library Company of Philadelphia.

From Alexander Purdie

SIR July 27th. 1778.

I got your Favour about 3 o'Clock yesterday Afternoon by your Servant. I have not above Half a Dozen Papers left, therefore it is out of my Power to furnish the Subscribers with last Week's Gazette. Indeed there was no News of any Consequence in it. I have sent one for you, and another for Dr. Gilmer. Since our last, we have a Confirmation of Capt. Jones's taking the Drake 20 Gun ship and carrying her into Brest, also of his Setting Fire to some Vessels at Whitehaven, where 50 of his Sailors landed privately, at Night, and spiked up several Cannon, to secure their Retreat, which they did, in the Bustle, about 4 in the Morning. The Vessel then stood over to the Scotch Coast, landed at Kircudbright, and went to Earl Selkirk's House, about a Mile from Town, from whence they carried off all the Silver Plate.

Philada. July 16th. Genl. Washington, with the Army under his Command, was at Paramus last Sunday, within 21 Miles of King's Ferry, where they were to cross the North River. Genl. Clinton's, with his Army, pitched their Tents the Same Day on Staten Island. French Fleet taken two Prizes one from London to N. York, the other from Antigua bound to Philada. Baltimore, July 21. Count

D'Estaing's Fleet, two of the largest excepted, safe arrived within Sandy Hook where they lie at Anchor. 4000 Troops landed from their Fleet at Black Point in Shrewsbury, New Jersey, to cooperate with the American Army. All the American Ships of War are ordered to join the French Admiral, who had himself invited them to come and help him to destroy and captivate the Enemy's Ships; those which the Americans take to be their sole Property.

The British Fleet consists of about 30 Vessels, great and small, at New York, with a large Number of Transports. Lord Howe and Adl. Gambier straining every Nerve to give Count D'Estaing a warm Reception. Several Ships lately arrived from New York from Rhode Island. One of 50 Guns came thro' the dangerous Passage of Hell Gate. 20 Ships, to be made Use of as Fireships, fell down towards the Narrows, at the Entrance into New York Bay, which it is said is strongly fortified.

Dr. Berkenhout, and ——— Temple, Esqr. it is said are on their Way from England to America, supposed to have been Sent on a private Embassy to Congress. The four Letters you enclosed will go by next Post. Mr. Clarkson told me he should keep a set of Papers for you, as you directed. Genl. Lee's Trial is not over, that we know of. He has written a very impertinent Letter to Genl. Washington. I did not hear the Contents only one Expression. He asks Genl. W. if he accused him of Timidity, or what? If of Timidity, he could convince him to the contrary. His Behaviour and Deportment at the Battle were unaccountable, and rendered him odious to the whole Army. I am, Sir, Your ob hum Servt,

A. PURDIE

RC (CSmH). Endorsed: "Purdie Alexr."

TJ letter to Purdie is missing, and there is no means of identifying the FOUR LETTERS he enclosed. MR. CLARKSON: John Clarkson, Purdie's nephew and successor as publisher of the *Virginia Gazette* at Williamsburg, 1779-1780 (Brigham, *American Newspapers, 1690-1820*, II, 1162).

From Richard Henry Lee

DEAR SIR Philadelphia 10th Augt. 1778

I agree entirely with you concerning the importance of the confederation, and have never failed to press it. Ten States have ratified —Jersey, Delaware, and Maryland have not, and one of them, Maryland, has adjourned until November, so that the new Congress under the Confederation cannot meet this year at the time proposed by the Confederacy. The inclosed paper contains all the

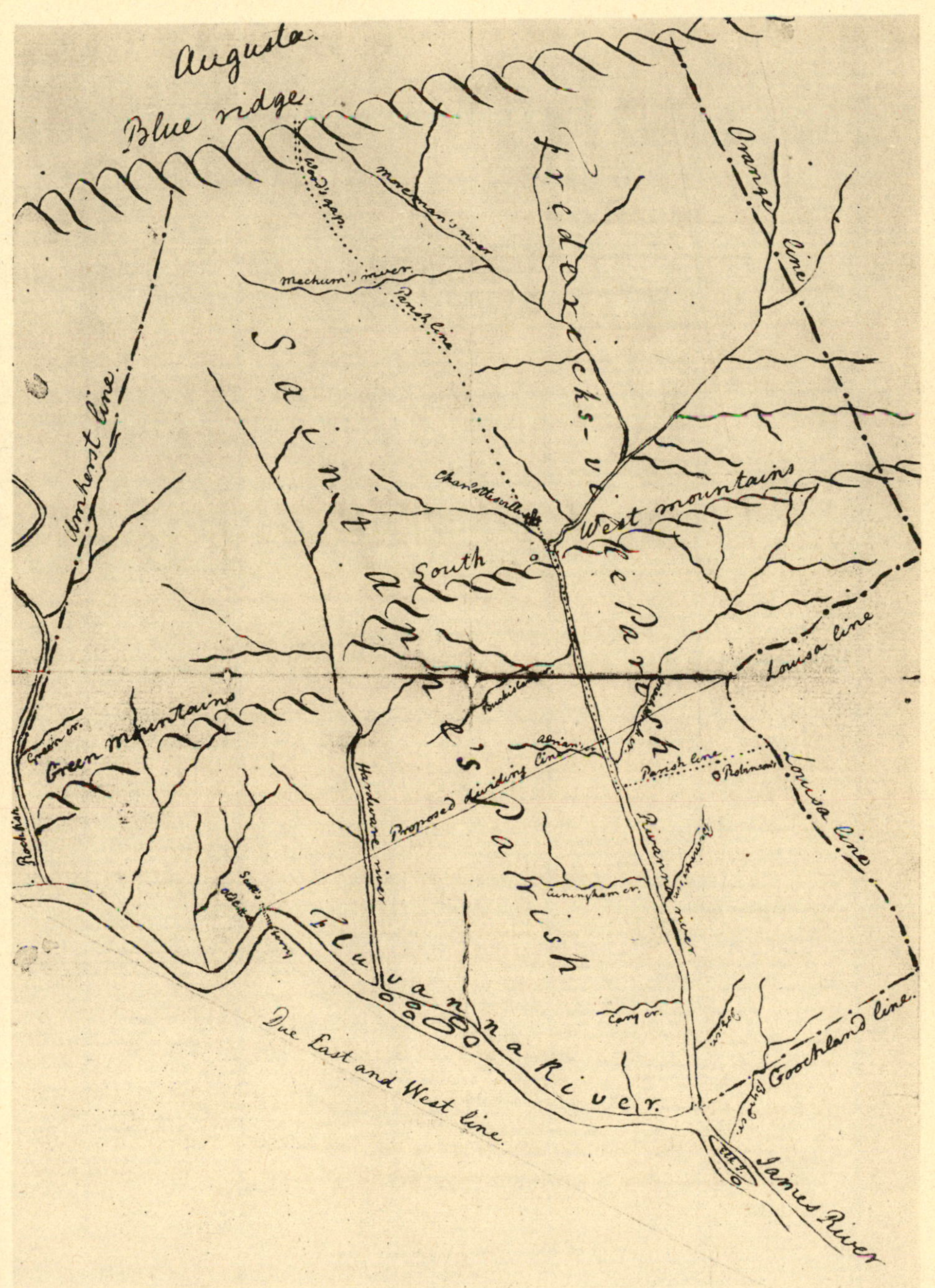

Jefferson's Sketch Map of Albemarle County

Dear Sir Monticello in Albemarle Virginia. July 19. 1778. (6) 132

I sincerely congratulate you on the recovery of Philadelphia, and wish it may be found uninjured by the enemy. how far the interests of literature may have suffered by the injury or removal of the Orrery (as it is mis-called) the publick libraries, your papers & implements are doubts which still excite anxiety. we were much disappointed in Virginia generally on the day of the great eclipse which proved to be cloudy. in Williamsburgh where it was total, I understand only the beginning was seen. at this place which is Lat. 38°. 8' and Longitude West from Williamsburgh about 1°. 45' as is conjectured, only eleven digits were eclipsed. it was not at all seen till the moon had advanced nearly one third over the sun's disc. afterwards it was seen at intervals through the whole. the egress particularly was visible. it proved however of little use to me for want of a time piece that could be depended on, which circumstance together with the subsequent restoration of Philadelphia to you has induced me to trouble you with this letter to remind you of your kind promise of making me an accurate clock, which being intended for astronomical purposes only I would have divested of all apparatus for striking or for any other purpose which by increasing it's complication might disturb its accuracy. a companion to it for keeping seconds, and which might be moved easily would greatly add to it's value. the theodolite for which I also spoke to you I can now dispense with having since purchased a most excellent one.

Writing to a philosopher I may hope to be pardoned for intruding some thoughts of my own tho' they relate to him personally. your time for two years past has I believe been principally employed in the civil government of your country. tho' I have been aware of the authority our cause would acquire with the world from it's being known that yourself & Dr. Franklin were zealous friends to it, and am myself duly impressed with a sense of the arduousness of government, and the obligation those are under who are able to conduct it, yet I am also satisfied there is an order of geniusses above that obligation & therefore exempted from it. no body can conceive that nature ever intended to throw away a Newton upon the occupation of a crown. it would have been a prodigality for which even the conduct of providence might have been arraigned had he been by birth annexed to what was so far below him. cooperating with nature in her ordinary oeconomy we should dispose of and employ the geniusses of men according to their several orders & degrees. I doubt not there are in your country many persons equal to the

Draft of a Letter to Rittenhouse in 1778

Dear Sir Monticello in Albemarle. Virginia. July 19. 1778.

I sincerely congratulate you on the recovery of Philadelphia, and wish it may be found uninjured by the enemy. how far the interests of literature may have suffered by the injury or removal of the Orrery (as it is miscalled) the publick libraries, your papers & implements, are doubts which still excite anxiety. we were much disappointed in Virginia generally on the day of the great eclipse, which proved to be cloudy. in Williamsburgh, where it was total, I understand only the beginning was seen. at this place which is in Lat. 38°-8' and Longitude West from Williamsburgh about 1°-45' as is conjectured, eleven digits only were supposed to be covered. it was not seen at all till the moon had advanced nearly one third over the sun's disc. afterwards it was seen at intervals through the whole. the egress particularly was visible. it proved however of little use to me for want of a time peice that could be depended on; which circumstance, together with the subsequent restoration of Philadelphia to you, has induced me to trouble you with this letter to remind you of your kind promise of making me an accurate clock; which being intended for astronomical purposes only, I would have divested of all apparatus for striking or for any other purpose, which by increasing it's complication might disturb it's accuracy. a companion to it, for keeping seconds, and which might be moved easily, would greatly add to it's value. the theodolite, for which I spoke to you also, I can now dispense with, having since purchased a most excellent one.

Writing to a philosopher, I may hope to be pardoned for intruding some thoughts of my own, tho' they relate to him personally. your time for two years past has, I believe, been principally employed in the civil government of your country. tho' I have been aware of the authority our cause would acquire with the world from it's being known that yourself & Doct^r. Franklin were zealous friends to it, and am myself duly impressed with a sense of the arduousness of government, and the obligation those are under who are able to conduct it, yet I am also satisfied there is an order of geniusses above that obligation, & therefore exempted from it. no body can conceive that nature ever intended to throw away a Newton upon the occupations of a crown. it would have been a prodigality for which even the conduct of providence might have been arraigned, had he been by birth annexed

Fair Copy of the Letter to Rittenhouse

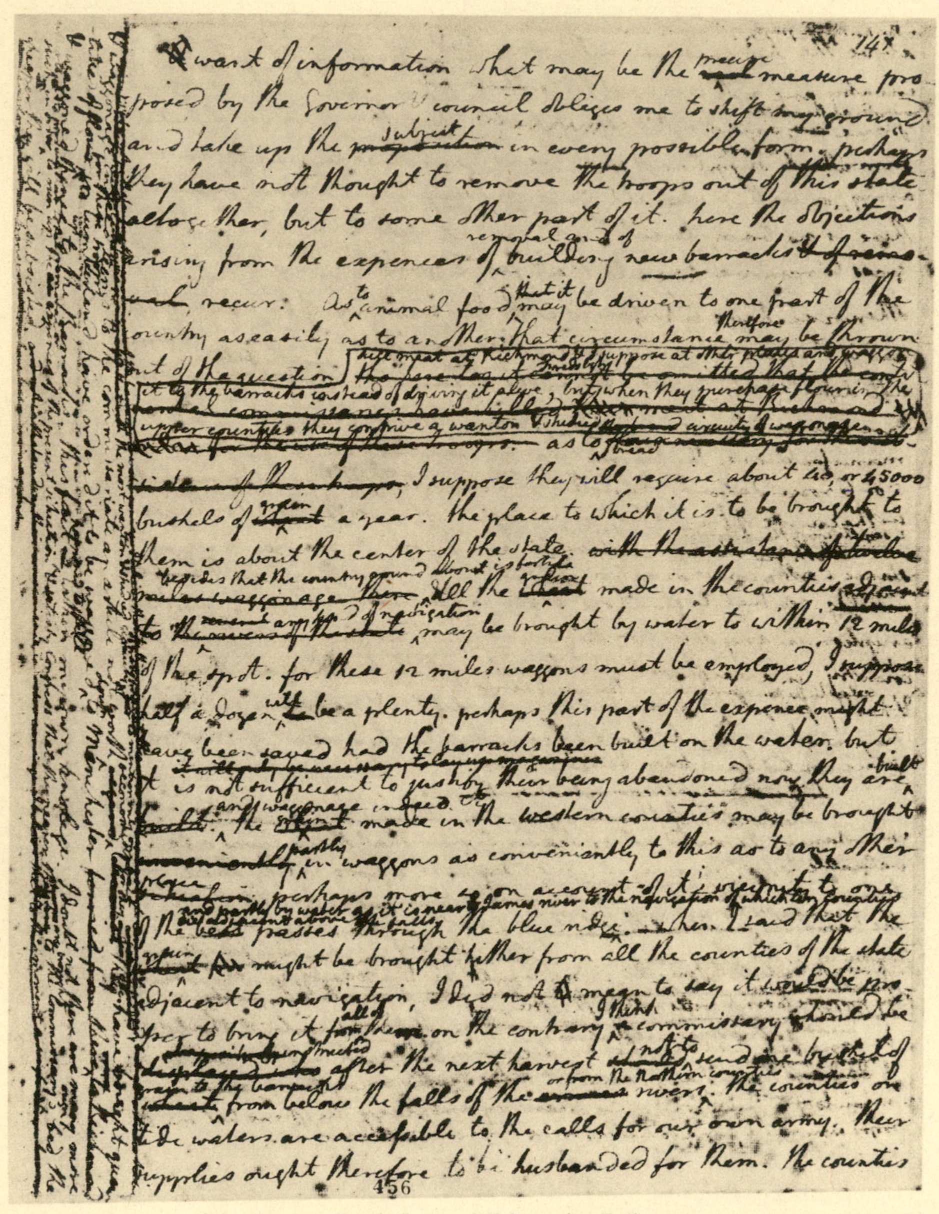

want of information what may be the measure proposed by the Governor & council obliges me to shift my ground and take up the subject in every possible form. perhaps they have not thought to remove the troops out of this state altogether, but to some other part of it. here the objections arising from the expences of removal and of building new barracks recur: as to animal food, that it may be driven to one part of the country as easily as to another: that circumstance may therefore be thrown out of the question. as to bread I suppose they will require about 40, or 45000 bushels of grain a year. the place to which it is to be brought to them is about the center of the state. besides that the country round about is fertile all the wheat made in the counties adjacent to any kind of navigation may be brought by water to within 12 miles of the spot. for these 12 miles waggons must be employed; I suppose half a dozen will be a plenty. perhaps this part of the expence might have been saved had the barracks been built on the water; but it is not sufficient to justify their being abandoned now they are built. the wheat made in the western counties may be brought partly in waggons as conveniently to this as to any other place, perhaps more so on account of it's vicinity to one of the best passes through the blue ridge. when I said that the grain might be brought hither from all the counties of the state adjacent to navigation, I did not mean to say it would be proper to bring it from them. on the contrary I think the commissary should be instructed after the next harvest not to send one bushel of grain to the barracks from below the falls of the rivers. the counties on tide waters are accessible to the calls for our own army. their supplies ought therefore to be husbanded for them. the counties

Page from a Draft Letter Written by Jefferson to Patrick Henry in 1779 news we have, except that it is well reported that Lord Howe being reenforced by 4 Ships of the Line sailed from N. York on thursday last with his whole force to Attack the french Squadron now at Rhode Island. Howe has a greater n[umber] of Ships, but Count D'Esteing has heavier Metal. The attack by Sea and Land was to be made this day on the enemy at R. Island, where they have 5500 men strongly posted and 3 or 4 frigates. Our force will be about 14000 men besides the Squadron. Success seems certain if Ld. Howe does not get up in time to prevent it. The Count D'Esteing is an Officer of approved merit, and his Ships very strong in every respect, so that I think he will check the British insolence on the Sea as we have already done on the land. No war in Europe on the 10th of June, nor do I believe G. Britain means to resent the proceedings of France. It seems to be a contest between the two Nations which shall be last in declaring War. Some advantages to accrue from Treaties is the cau[se] of this. To us it matters little, since we so pow[er]fully experience the aid of France. For it is certain this Squadron is to Act with and for us so long as the enemy by continuing here renders it necessary. There is great probability that the Emperor of Germany and the King of Prussia will fall out about the Bavarian dominions. Theirs will be a battle of Giants, each party having 300,000 men, the best disciplined Troops in the world. France, I fancy, has taken measures to avoid engaging in this quarrel, that her whole force may be employed against England.

The design against Detroit is abandoned for the present, and a force will be sent into the Indian Country to chastise their late insolences. I heartily wish that the wisdom of our Country may be early next Session employed to regulate our finance, restore public credit, determine about our back lands, and if possible get rid of our public Commerce. If it succeeds with us, I believe it will be the first instance that has ever happened of the kind. But many there are of injury derived from such Trade. Whilst necessity impelled, it was unavoidable, but now that private Commerce will furnish abundan[ce] of all things, I incline to think our interest will consist in withdrawing from governmental Trade. Remember me to Mr. Mazzie. I am yours dear Sir very sincerely,

RICHARD HENRY LEE

RC (DLC).

TJ's letter to Lee on the importance of the Confederation has not been located. On 11 June 1778, Congress resolved to send an expedition to DETROIT, but on 25 July resolved to defer the expedition because of inability to procure supplies for the venture (JCC, XI, 588-9, 720-1).

From John Page

Williamsburgh, 19 Aug. 1778. Critical discussion of TJ's "Observations on the late Eclipse" as sent to Rev. James Madison (see Madison to TJ, 26 July 1778). "I have annexed the Method used by the famous Short for finding the Effect of Parallax in a Transit of Venus, only applying it here to the Moon."

RC (DLC); 5 p. containing 4 rough astronomical diagrams. Text faded beyond legibility at many places.

To Richard Henry Lee

Dear Sir Monticello. Aug. 30. 1778

Your letters of June 16. and Aug. 10. came safely to hand. I am in great pain for the French fleet. Operations by land I have more confidence in. What are we to think of the handbill said to have been circulated by Mr. Mauduit and published in our papers as certified by your brother? Is it genuine? If they really are coming to their senses at last, and it should be proposed to treat of peace, will not the Newfoundland fisheries be worthy particular attention, to exclude them and all others from them except our tres grands et chers amies et alliees. Their great value to whatever nation possesses them is as a nursery for seamen. In the present very prosperous situation of our affairs I have thought it would be wise to endeavor to gain a regular and acknoleged access in every court in Europe, but most the Southern. The countries bordering on the Mediterranean I think will merit our earliest attention. They will be the important markets for our great commodities of fish (as Roman catholics) wheat, tobacco and rice. The two last commodities particularly may be vended in any quantities in Turkey. This power is moreover likely to be in our scale in the event of a general war. Emigrants too from the Mediterranean would be of much more value to our country in particular than from the more Northern countries. They bring with them a skill in agriculture and other arts better adapted to our climate. I beleive that had our country been peopled thence we should now have been farther advanced in rearing the several things which our country is capable of producing. To negotiate a general reception and on good terms for our capital commodities with these powers and to deduce from thence a number of settlers I think would be of great and immediate value. I have been led the more to think of this from frequent conversations with Mazzei, whom you know well, and who is well acquainted with all those countries. Do you not think he might be usefully emploied thither to act in conjunction with Mr. W. Lee wherever he should be? His connections in Tuscany are good, his acquaintance with capital men there, in Rome, and Naples great. He also resided some years in Constantinople where he contracted a knolege of the customs of the country, the mode of doing business there and of some respectable characters which might perhaps render him more able to be useful to us than many others. To some of these places perhaps your brother would not chuse to go. I beleive he would be particularly active in procuring emigrants which I own is with me almost as great an object as trade. Our own country wants nothing but skilful labourers to raise with success, wine, oil and silk. From the Levant and Archipelago we might hope to have introduced together with the people many useful plants, esculant, medicinal and for manufacture, and arts useful tho' as yet unknown to us. If his integrity did not of itself ensure his zeal; his real and pure principles of republicanism would do it. He is a good oeconomist, besides and would render the agency but little expensive, as I imagine he might make such a tour and return within the year. He must be very unsuccessful indeed should he procure us no benefit which would compensate to us the expence of a few hundred pounds. Perhaps it might be well to render the powers of such an agent subordinate to our principal commissioners, and to authorize them to direct the plan of his proceedings ex re natâ. Having no news to write you I scribble these thoughts for your consideration. Perhaps in your station you may mould them into something for the public good. I am Dear Sir Your friend & servt.,

TH: JEFFERSON

RC (ViHi). Addressed: "Richard Henry Lee esq. of the Virginia delegation Philadelphia." Endorsed: "Augst. 1778 Thos. Jeffers."

Israel MAUDUIT, agent in England for the colony of Massachusetts and an ardent defender of Great Britain's rights in America, in Mch. 1778 produced a printed paper declaring himself in favor of American independence. This paper was transmitted by Lord North to the King on 25 Mch. 1778 in a letter strongly advocating a cessation of the American war (DNB; Sir John Fortescue, *The Correspondence of King George the Third*, London, 1928, IV, 77-8). For TJ's interest in the proposed mission of MAZZEI to southern Europe, see also Plan of Philip Mazzei's Agricultural Company, printed above at the end of 1774; TJ to John Adams, 21 Aug. 1777; and TJ to John Hancock, 19 Oct. 1778.

From John Harvie

DEAR SIR Septr the 15th. 1778.

I should have done myself the pleasure of Answering your letter of July the 19th. several weeks ago, if I had not wished to have made a through enquiry after the workmen you want to

Employ previous to my writeing to you on that Subject. Ben Randolph professes an Inclination to Accomodate you with an House joiner and tells me that he has been Constant in his researches after one since I informed him that his recommendation to me of a proper Character in that way would be rendering me an Agreable Service to you, but from his and other Accounts of the Scarcity of Skillful hands now following this Branch of Business and the Exorbitant prices prevalent in this City and its Vicinity, I would by no means advise you to depend on one from this Quarter. I cant hear of a Stone Cutter of any kind, the prisoner that I hoped to have Engaged for you who was a Master of this Trade being in Common with a Number of others moved from where I formerly heard of him to some other place of Confinement that I am not able [to] discover. It is possible that a number of the Convention prisoners may be sent to Virginia this Fall or Winter. If so probably some Tradesmen of the Professions you want may be found amongst them and procur'd. Whilst I stay here I shall still Continue to look out for the person you want and shall never Consider a triffling Enquiry in this Way a trouble even for a Stranger and much less so for a man to whom I acknowledge myself in many Instances most Sensibly and highly Oblidged.

Haveing sent the papers Regularly to my wife since I have been here I expect their Contents have been Usually Desiminated through the Neighborhood wherefore I Conjecture a Circumstantial Account of the Action on the 28th Ultimo at Newport with the timely Regular and well Conducted Retreat of General Sullivan from Rode Island has either Struck your Eye or Ear. A Letter received last Evening from that General makes the Enemys loss in Kill'd and wounded in the Action (above) amount to upwards of One thousand men. The Hurry and Bustle of the Enemy in New York Indicates a Movement some where. General Washington Conjectures to the Eastward and therefore designs very soon to break up his Camp at White Plains, posting his Army on Ground more Advantageous for covering our Works on the North River and Counteracting their measures in the New England States. A Marauding Division of the Enemys Light Infantry and Dragoons have made a Descent from Newport on the Massachusetts Burnt many Valuable Houses in their Route and distroyed a Magazine of Considerable Consequence at Bedford in that State.

It is reported by pretty good Authority that ten 74 Gun Ships of Byrons Squadron has lately join'd Admiral Howe which Combined fleet now Hover about Boston Harbour. Upon the Appearance of this formadable force the Count D'Estaigne Stationd his Ships except those which are Damaged in Nantucket Road and Erected Batteries on George Island which Command the Entrance and Afford a Cross fire to the Ships which will render it extremely difficult, if possible, for a fleet greatly Superior in force to Enter. However I acknowledge I rather Consider the Count at present in a perilous Situation, but hope that the Brest fleets Arrival will again make him Out Number the Enemy.

I have Spoken at least a Dozen times to Dunlap relative to his account against the Albemarle Subscribers for his paper. He has not yet render'd it in. I will certainly Settle it before I leave this City. I intended to have been at the October General Court Early in the Session, but there is such a Strange Remissness in our Delegates if I leave Congress now, our State will be unrepresented at a time two when Business of the Utmost Consequence to us particularly is in Agitation. I must therefore Sacrifice My own private Interests to a publick Duty. The Moment F Lee or Mr. Smith arrive I quit this place I hope for ever. Adieu,

JNO. HARVIE

I have sent Mrs. Harvie the two last papers.

RC (DLC).

TJ's letter of 19 July has not been located. For Harvie's earlier efforts to secure workmen for TJ, see his letter to TJ of 29 Dec. 1777. Francis Lightfoot LEE took his seat in Congress on 9 Nov. and Meriwether SMITH on 28 Sep. Harvie left Congress about 19 Oct. (Burnett, *Letters of Members*, III, No. 522, where Harvie's account with the Commonwealth for attendance is printed in note 2).

Virginia Troops in Continental Service

[30 September 1778]

General Washington's return of Virga. troops Sep. 30. 7[8]

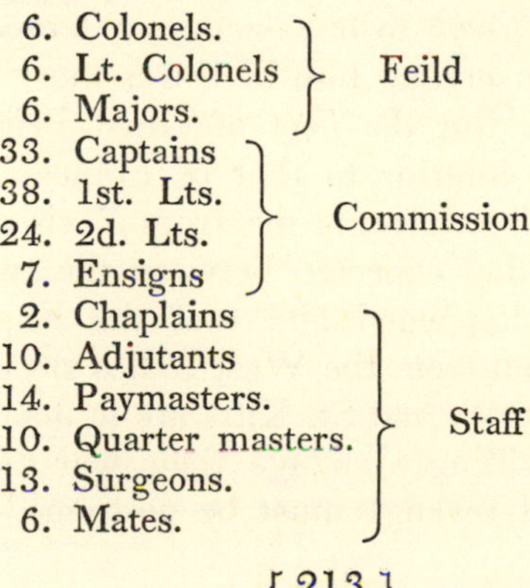

6. Colonels.
6. Lt. Colonels
6. Majors.
} Feild

33. Captains
38. 1st. Lts.
24. 2d. Lts.
7. Ensigns
} Commission.

2. Chaplains
10. Adjutants
14. Paymasters.
10. Quarter masters.
13. Surgeons.
6. Mates.
} Staff

13.	Serjt. Majrs.	Non commission
11.	Quartr. Mastr. Serjts.	
11	drum Majors.	
6.	Fife majors.	
215.	Serjeants	
105.	Dr. & fifers	
1753.	present, fit for duty	Rank & file
339.	sick present.	
805.	sick absent.	
875.	On command.	
36.	on furlough.	
[3]808	Total	

Reduced to 11. regiments.

MS (DLC). Entirely in TJ's hand.

In Sep. 1778 the fifteen Virginia regiments in Continental service were reduced by consolidation to eleven; see Gwathmey, *Hist. Reg. of Virginians in the Revolution*, p. 859.

From Richard Henry Lee

DEAR SIR Philadelphia October 5. 1778

A few days past, since the last post left us, Mr. Harvey presented me your favor of August the 30th, to which this is an answer; and which I shall direct to Williamsburg upon a supposition that the Assembly has called you there by the time the letter can reach that place. The hand bill you have seen was certainly written by Mauduit, and circulated under the auspices of administration. It was intended to feel the national pulse, and to prepare its mind for the reception of events, which are now become unavoidable. I agree with you Sir that the fishery is a most important point nor will the limits of Canada be with less difficulty settled in those negotiations which precede a peace. The arrival of Adm. Byrons Squadron has given to our enemies a temporary superiority in those Seas. The sending him here was more necessary than it can be called bold. But the fleet of Great Britain is, by this detachment, rendered inferior to that of France in the Channel of England. My brother informs me from Paris July 4 that an engagement is every day expected between the two fleets. Later accounts say it has happened and that the English fleet was beaten. Our information from the West Indies says that Dominica is fallen, and that Jamaica and St. Kitts are in Jeopardy. I believe our enemies would willingly change their war of conquest into a war of revenge, but revenge must be postponed to safety; and

I think they will rather endeavor to save what remains, than endeavor to get back what they have lost, or to gratify their malignity put Canada, Nova Scotia, the West Indies, and even G. Britain and Ireland in danger. But wisdom points to precaution, and they may attempt Boston as some think, in order to destroy the french Fleet. If they do and fail in the attempt, they will be defenceless in every part of the world by the destruction of the only army on which they can hang their hopes. I have a very high opinion of the republican principles and of the ability of Mr. Mazzei, and I think that if Mr. Maddi[son] were sent to Genoa with him for Secretary we might have a good chance to succeed in borrowing there one of the millions, five of which are absolutely necessary to sustain, and restore our falling currency. To cultivate a good understanding with the nations in the south of Europe is undoubtedly wise policy, and may produce the most profitable consequences. These affairs will come present[ly] under the consideration of Congress, when I shall not forget the usefu[l] possessions of Mr. Mazzei. Mr. Izard is the Commissioner for Tuscany, my brother William is appointed both for Vienna and Berlin. He has been sometime at the former Court, but the latt[er] refuses to receive a Minister from us or to acknowledge yet our Independance, altho he did by his Minister most unequivoca[lly] promise my brother he would do so, as soon as France should set the example. Since this, he has quarreled with the Emperor about the Bavarian succession, and wanting the aid of Hanover, Hesse, Brunswic &c. he chooses to be well with England. The Emperor is not a little puzzled in the same way and for the same reasons. Tis a matter, not of the greatest moment to us at present, since the war between the two Giants will swallow up [in] their respective vortices the lesser Tyrants and thus prevent h[im] of England from bringing German Auxiliaries to distress o[ur] Alliance. There is nothing that threatens so much injury to [our] cause at present as the evil operations of Engrossers. If something decisive is not quickly done by the Legislatures to stop the progress of Engrossing, and to make these Miscreants deliver up their ill gotten collections, the American Army must disband, and the fleet of our Allies remain in Boston Harbor. I know the root of this evil is in the redundance of money, but until the latter can be reduced some measures are indispensable, to be taken with the Engrossers. You will see the expedients devised by us. A more radical cure will follow shortly, in a proposition of Finance now under consideration. I am so greatly pressed with business that I

cannot now write to Mr. Mazzei and must beg the favor of you to make this apology for me. [Be so k]ind as remember me affectionately to Mr. Wythe & Colo. [. . . if] he is with you. I am affectionately yours,
RICHARD HENRY LEE

P.S. Colo. Baylor, with a Corps of 60 light Dragoons, was lately surprised in the Jerseys, between Hackensack and the North River—Himself made prisoner, and his party chiefly put to the Bayonet, it is said, in cold blood.

RC (DLC). Addressed: "Thomas Jefferson esquire at Williamsburg in Virginia." Endorsed.

Lee's supposition that the Assembly had called TJ to Williamsburg was valid, but TJ did not attend until 30 Nov.; on 7 Oct. the sergeant-at-arms of the House was ordered to enforce TJ's attendance and on 30 Nov. TJ came into the House in his custody (JHD, Oct. 1778, 1827 edn., p. 3, 90). The cause of TJ's delayed attendance is unknown, but was probably intentional on his part (see TJ to George Wythe, 1 Nov. 1778). He was engaged at this time in drafting the important Bill for Proportioning Crimes and Punishments, and his researches for the work of the Committee of Revisors must have occupied much of his time during Oct. and Nov. For the action of the Virginia legislature on ENGROSSERS, see Bill No. 89 in the Report of the Committee of Revisors, 18 June 1779.

From Cyrus Griffin

Philadelphia Octo. 6th 78

You will be good enough, my dear Sir, to excuse this Letter. There are but few Men indeed with whom I could wish to be thus candid. It appears to me that Congress will shortly be dissolved. If the large Emissions of Money, and visionary Expeditions do not bring forth our destruction, I greatly fear that *Party* will complete the matter. Congress exhibit not more than two or three Members actuated by Patriotism. Great questions are carried every day in favor of the East-ward, and to the prejudice of the Southern States. Great questions are now upon the Carpet and if determined in the affirmative will do excessive Damage to Virginia and Maryland particularly. At present we are under secrecy —perhaps in a little time I shall think myself obligated to quit Congress; I will not sit in a house whose proceedings I cannot assent to with honor, nor is it in my abilities to oppose them with success. I value most what our great Politicians value least. Congress are at present a Government of Men. It would astonish you to think how all affairs proceed upon the interested Principle: Members prostituting their votes in expectation of mutual assistance upon favorite Points. I am apprehensive that in geting free from oppression in one quarter, we are likely to establish it in another; by avoiding one set of Plunderers we are certain to fall into the clutches of a still more dangerous set. I am sorry our good Friend Harvey is about to leave Congress; he is a valuable man in times like the present, a man of great virtue and boldness of Spirit. If the Land office should be established, put him at the head of it; his abilities and honesty will be highly necessary in that Employment. The motions of the Enemy are very uncertain; there is an expedition going forward on the part of General Clinton, but to what object is merely conjecture, perhaps to Boston—New England and the French Fleet are powerful inducements. All Circumstances considered, I believe they are going to guard the remaining parts of their Dominion. In the mean time they will destroy everything they possibly can, and I should not wonder if Philadelphia itself was reduced to ashes before their departure. As yet Spain have taken no part to our advantage, indeed Arthur Lee still remains at Paris. The Court of Berlin have refused William Lee the Commissioner of Congress to that quarter: He is now gone to Vienna, the most accomplished Metropolis in the World. We are plagued to death with quarrels and recriminations relative to our Commissioners abroad; these men will involve the Continent in perdition. It is absolutely necessary that Dean should be sent over to Europe for the most valuable purpose in the world, but some Gentlemen are determined to ruin an innocent Character, notwithstanding he alone has the great merit of concluding that valuable Treaty with the Minister of France. Tell MacLurg and President Maddison they are both [re]miss in not answering my Letters. The next I write you will be in a different stile; this only by way of preface. I must beg to trouble you with my best respects to Mr. Wythe.

I am dear sir, your obdt humble servant, C. GRIFFIN

RC (DLC). Endorsed: "Griffin Cyrus." Closing portion of text faded.

PHILADELPHIA . . . REDUCED TO ASHES: Philadelphia had been evacuated by Sir Henry Clinton in June; this may be a slip by Griffin for New York.

Bill to Amend an Act for Raising a Supply of Money

[14 October 1778]

Whereas the Taxes Collected by virtue of the Act intituled "an Act for raising a supply of money for Public Exigencies" are not sufficient to answer the purposes of the said Act[1] and Whereas great inequality and injustice have arisen from the various opinions of Assessors in their valuation of Taxable property, and greater evils are still likely to arise if the same mode of Taxation is pursued.[2] For Remedy whereof Be it enacted by the General Assembly that in aid of the Taxes imposed by the above Recited act an additional Rate or Tax of Twenty Shillings for every hundred pounds value shall be paid for all Manors Messuages Lands and Tenements Slaves Mulatto Servants to thirty one Years of Age Horses Mules and Plate on the first Day of August One thousand seven hundred and Seventy Nine, and the like additional Tax or Rate shall be paid on the said first day of August in each of the five next Succeeding Years, by the Owner or Proprietor of such Estates respectively, that a Rate or Tax of [thirty shillings][3] including the former Tax upon Money for every hundred pounds shall be paid for all money exceeding five pounds which shall be in the possession of one Person on the [first][3] day of [May][3] That an additional Rate or Tax of [four shillings][3] for every pound of the amount of all Annuities, including the Quitrents payable to the Proprietor of the Northern Neck, except those in lieu of Dower and such as have been or shall be settled by the General Congress or the Assembly or Conventions of this Commonwealth as a provision for Wounded Soldiers or their families be paid by the annuitant Respectively on the said first Day of August in each of the said Six Years. That an additional Tax or duty of [twenty shillings][3] per Wheel upon all Riding Carriages [one shilling][3] per head on all neat Cattle and [ten shillings][3] per Poll upon all Tithables above the Age of twenty one Years (except Soldiers Sailors, Parish Poor and such as Receive an Annual Allowance in consideration of Wounds or injuries Received in the Public Service) except also Slaves and Mulatto Servants to thirty one Years of Age who being property are Rated ad valorem[4] as aforesaid shall be paid by the owner or Person enlisting such Carriages and Tithables respectively on the said first Day of August in each of the said Six Years that an additional Tax of [six pounds][3] for every Ordinary licence shall be paid down to the Clerk of the County or Corporation Court at the time of granting such Licence from the time of passing this Act until the first day of December one thousand Seven Hundred and eighty four. That an additional Tax or Rate of [twenty shillings][3] for every hundred pounds of the neat income of all offices of Profit be paid on the said first day of August one thousand Seven hundred and Seventy Nine and each of the five next succeeding Years. That an additional Tax or duty [one shilling][3] per Gallon be paid for all Spiritous Liquors hereafter to be distilled in this Commonwealth to be paid by the distiller or distilled in any other of the United American States and imported into this by Land or Water at any time before the said first Day of December one thousand Seven hundred and Eighty four[5] and that every Person who hath not taken the Oath or affirmation of Allegiance to this State required to be taken by an Act intituled "an act to oblige the free Male Inhabitants of this State above a certain age to give assurances of Allegiance to the same and for other purposes" and shall not take the same before the first day of [May][3] next and who shall fail to produce to the Assessors in his hundred a Certificate of his having taken such Oath or affirmation shall pay [treble][3] the several Rates and Taxes imposed by this and the above recited Act for such property and Tithables hereby subject to taxation as he shall be owner of, or shall be in his Family, which several Rates and Taxes hereby imposed shall be assessed, Collected accounted for and applied in the same manner as the Rates and Taxes imposed by the aforesaid recited act is directed.[6] And for forming some Rule for the direction of the Commissioners and Assessors. It is further enacted that the several Commissioners in each County shall before the Day to be appointed for the Assessors to enter on their Office, call together at some convenient place within their respective Counties the Several Assessors of the same who shall consult together and form some general mode which they shall pursue in Rating the several articles of Taxation.[7] Provided always that there shall not be more than sixteen Assessors appointed in any one County.[8] And be it further enacted that where a Recovery shall be had against any Sherif or Collector for failure in the payment of the Monies arising from the Rates or Taxes imposed by this or the above recited act, he shall be accountable in Damages at the Rate of Twenty Percentum Perannum for all Monies which he shall so fail to pay. And Whereas by the above Recited act the Treasurer is restrained from paying the Quota of this Commonwealth required by the general Congress till the Accounts of this State against the United States are settled which may be attended with bad consequences, Be it enacted that the said Treasurer is hereby empowered and required to pay the said full quota when it shall be demanded, any thing in the said Act to the Contrary notwithstanding. And be it further enacted that the Court of each county shall at their Court to be held in the Month of April or May one thousand Seven hundred and Seventy Nine and in each of the five following Years take Bond with Sufficient security of the Sherif or Collector in a Penalty equal at least to what may be the whole amount of the Taxes imposed by this and the above recited Act in the Judgment of the Court of the County using the best means in their Power to inform themselves of such amount. And be it further enacted that no Person hereafter elected a Commissioner being a Member of either House of Assembly shall be subject to the Penalty imposed on those who refuse to act but the acceptance of the Office of a Commissioner shall vacate the Seat of any Person so accepting in either house of Assembly: [And Whereas by the said act intituled "an act for raising a supply of money for Public exigencies" it was enacted that the Commissioners for the several Counties after examining adjusting and certifying the Accounts of the Collection with their respective Sherifs and making the proper deductions for allowances to themselves the Clerks and the Assessors should enter the same in their Book and Transmit to the Treasurer a Copy of such entry and it may be necessary for the future information of the general Assembly that the said entries and copies thereof transmitted be made in a more special and distinct form that so the amount of the Assessment on the several species of Taxable property may be separately and distinctly known and also the amount of the additional Taxes paid by Nonjurors. Be it further enacted that the said entry and Copy transmitted shall in future during the continuance of the said Act be formed into Seven different Columns in one of which shall be stated the amount of the Assessment on landed property, in another that on Slaves, in another that on plate, in another that on Coin, in another that on Paper currency exclusive of loan office Certificates, in another that on Stocks, and in another that on the residuum of taxable Articles which sums Stated in the said Columns shall include a single Taxation only on Nonjurors, and that separate and a part from this shall be stated in like manner the amount of the additional Taxes paid by such Nonjurors; and at the foot of the whole shall be stated in separate articles also, the deductions for allowances to themselves, to the Clerks, and to the whole Assessors which Copy so made out they shall transmit immediately to the board of Auditors instead of that by the said act directed to be transmitted to the Treasurer for enabling them to call upon the Sherif for the ballance due and to state to the succeeding Assembly a General account in like distinct manner of the amount of the Assessment on the said Taxable Articles respectively in the several Counties.][9] Whereas by the Treaty of

Commerce entered into between his most Christian Majesty the King of France and the United States of America it is amongst other things stipulated that every commodity to be exported from any of the said States to the French West Indies Islands shall be free from any duty or impost. And Whereas by the before recited act a Tax or duty of Ten Shillings is laid on every hogshead of Tobacco to be exported from this Commonwealth Be it therefore enacted that all Tobacco cleared out at any of the naval offices of this Commonwealth to be exported to any of the West India Islands belonging to his Most Christian Majesty shall be and they are hereby exempted from any duty or Tax imposed thereon by the said Act any thing therein contained to the contrary thereof notwithstanding. And Whereas many good People of this Commonwealth who are well affected to the Cause of their Country were prevented taking the Oath of Allegiance by the Negligence of the Magistrates whereby they have been subjected to the Penalty of a double Tax as prescribed by an Act requiring all the Free Male Inhabitants of this State to give assurance of Fidelity and Allegiance to the same, Be it therefore enacted that all and every Person or Persons who hath or have been so subjected to the payment of a Double Rate or Tax as aforesaid by means aforesaid and shall make it appear to the Commissioners of their respective Counties that they have since taken the Oath Prescribed by Law, and that they now are and always have been true and faithful friends to the cause of liberty, and their Country shall be Reimbursed all such sums of Money by them paid over and above their just Tax and the same shall be deducted out of their Taxes for the Succeeding Year by the Collectors of their Respective Counties upon Certificate being had from the Commissioners of their said Counties for that purpose. And the said Commissioners are hereby directed to hold a Court or Courts for the purposes above mentioned and shall give notice of the same within their said Counties as often as they shall think fit and necessary so that the said Court or Courts are held between the time of Passing this Act and the first Day of [July next].[8] And it is further enacted that so much of the aforesaid Recited act as comes within the purview and meaning of this Act be, and the same is hereby repealed.

MS (Vi); three pages in clerk's hand. This MS is virtually the same as the Act as adopted, the text of which is in Hening, IX, 547-52, the chief difference in the two (aside from that indicated in note 8, below) being that blank spaces were left in MS as indicated in notes below and were filled by amendment in the House. These amendments are listed on ten pages endorsed "Amendments to the

Supply Bill"; some of these amendments are in a clerk's hand, others in Edmund Randolph's hand, and two, as indicated below in notes 7 and 9, are in TJ's hand. Another MS (Vi), consisting of three pages and representing the text as originally introduced, is endorsed in the hand of Edmund Pendleton: "A Bill To amend an Act intituled 'an Act for raising a Supply of Money for public exigencies'" and docketed by Randolph: "Novr. 4. 1778. read first time. Nov. 5. read 2d. time & comd. to whole on Thursday." Accompanying this MS are seven pages of amendments endorsed: "Rough amendmts. to Supply Bill." The principal variations between these two MS states of the text of the Bill are indicated in the textual notes.

This Bill, whose principal aim was just the reverse of the unwarranted optimism expressed in the preamble to the Supply Bill passed at the preceding session (q.v. under 20 May 1778; see also Harrell, *Loyalism in Virginia*, p. 66-112), was, like its predecessors, subject to considerable debate, especially over the perennial question of a fair and equitable mode of assessment of value. TJ was not in the House when the Bill was ordered to be brought in on 14 Oct. 1778 or when it was introduced on 4 Nov. by Tyler and committed to the committee of the whole. He took his seat on 30 Nov., and on 2 Dec. the Bill was taken up, being debated and amended during the next two weeks. In this debate TJ took part, as the amendments offered by him indicate (JHD, Oct. 1778, 1827 edn., p. 11, 42, 45, 95, 111, 112). ORDINARY LICENCE: i.e., a license permitting the operation of an ordinary, or tavern.

1 See Bill Providing a Supply, &c., under date of 20 May 1778, where the belief had been expressed that taxes raised by the supply bill of Jan. 1778 (Hening, IX, 349-68) would be "more than sufficient to answer the purposes expressed in the said act."

2 The words "and greater evils . . . is pursued" are in both MSS but were deleted by amendment and are not in the Act as adopted.

3 A blank occurs in MS at this point; square brackets are supplied, and word or words inserted are drawn from text of Act as adopted.

4 In May 1778 TJ had endeavored to substitute a poll tax for the ad valorem levy on slaves, but his amendment had been defeated (see Bill under date of 20 May 1778). The MS of Bill as introduced by Tyler on 4 Nov. included the following: "And be it further enacted that a Poll Tax of   for all Slaves above the age of seven & under the age of sixty years and Mulatto Servants shall be paid by the Owners or proprietors thereof . . ." but this was struck out and the previously adopted *ad valorem* system retained.

5 The following additional words are in the Act at this point: "to be paid by the importer."

6 The MS of Bill as originally introduced provided only the following taxes as compared with the list in the amended Bill and in the Act: (1) an unspecified rate on every £100 valuation on "All Manors Messuages Lands and Tenements"; (2) a similar rate on horses and mules; (3) an unspecified rate on every wheel on all riding carriages, on every ordinary and every marriage license, and on money. The increase in the amount of levies and the number of objects taxed reflects the rapidly growing disparity between the amounts of paper money issued and the funds raised by taxation for its redemption. The report of the committee of the whole of 13 Dec. 1777 had recommended an even longer list of taxable objects; but the House declined to permit taxation of dogs (JHD, Oct. 1777, 1827 edn., p. 77-8).

7 The Bill as introduced attempted to bring about both uniformity and fairness in procedures by which property in lands was assessed. The method proposed in that MS was to divide "all Lands to the Eastward of the Allegheny Mountains except Lotts or Tenements in Cities or Towns . . . in three different classes": (1) "Rich Lands"; (2) "Lands of a middling value"; and (3) "the meaner or inferior Lands." Lands in each of these categories were in turn to be classified in one of three groups—lands "of first second and third Quality." In each of these nine subdivisions, the Bill would have provided a stated maximum valuation per acre excluding "any extraordinary Buildings or improvements thereon." Lands "on the west side of the Allegheney Mountains except Lots in Towns" were to be similarly classified and maximum evaluations established, but varying from the eastern evaluations. Although the Bill as amended and the Act as adopted restated the substance of the purpose of this section of the Bill as introduced—"for establishing some general Rule for the direction of the Assessors"—their final terms

did not provide any such uniform policy, but merely directed the commissioners of the tax in each county to "form some general mode"—general mode, that is, within the limits of each county.

The question is one that has vexed legislators long before and since the debates on the Virginia supply bills of 1778, but TJ, as might have been expected, tried to solve the problem by innovation. He introduced, but failed to gain acceptance of, the following amendment for that purpose:

"Whereas many doubts have arisen among the Commissioners and assessors of the tax on the construction of the act of General assembly passed in the year 1777 intituled 'an act for raising a supply of money for publick exigencies' and also on one other act passed in the year 1778. intituled 'an act to amend an act intituled an act for raising a supply of money for publick exigencies' some apprehending that they should value lands at the rates at which they would sell in gold and silver, and not at what they would sell in paper bills of credit of this Commonwealth or of Congress; others that they should value them as they would sell were all or a great part of the lands within the commonwealth, or within a county to be offered to sale at one time, and not at the sum at which they would sell if exposed to sale in moderate quantities as happens in the ordinary course of things; and others that, as the legislature had by the latter act only trebled the tax laid in the former, they intended thereby that no more than three times as much money should be raised, and of course that the valuation of the present year should be the same as it was the last without any regard to the rise in the price of property since that time; all which constructions are contrary to the intention of the said acts: and in consequence of such differences of construction very great inequalities have arisen in the rates at which property of equal value has been assessed in different counties during the present year:

"Be it therefore enacted by the General assembly that forthwith on the receipt of this act the Commissioners of the tax for the several counties and corporations shall call together their respective assessors to meet at their court house at as short a day as may be in the present year, and in the subsequent years during the continuance of this act at such time as by the said first mentioned act is directed; and being there assembled, the said assessors shall take an oath or make affirmation as follows 'I do swear (or affirm) that I will when called on by the commissioners of the tax for my county, truly, candidly, and without reserve declare the worth of the several kinds of lands within my county or corporation, as they would sell according to my own opinion if exposed to sale for ready money in paper bills of credit of this Commonwealth or of Congress, so help me god.' which oath or affirmation may be administered by any one of the Commissioners. The said Commissioners shall then proceed to describe the lands of their county in so many general classes not exceeding six as their different natures or kinds may require, and shall call on each assessor singly to declare under the obligation of his oath or affirmation what he thinks each several kind of the said lands would sell for by the acre if exposed to sale in moderate quantities according to the usual course of things, for ready money in paper bills of credit of this commonwealth or of Congress; which several opinions, together with their own they shall state in writing for each kind of land separately, and shall add together the several sums at which the same kind of land is rated by the different commissioners and assessors, and then divide the aggregate sum by the number of persons whose opinions were stated, and shall take the quotient or result, or such sum nearthereto as to avoid the difficulty of fractions may be approved by a majority of the said commissioners and assessors, as the average price of such kind of land; and so shall proceed to deduce an average price for every other kind into which they shall have classed the lands of their county, as before directed. But lots of land in towns and ferry landings and mines of coal or metal, shall not be included within any of the said general classes, but shall, as well as mills and other extraordinary buildings be valued by the assessors within whose bounds they are as they would sell if exposed to sale for ready money in paper bills of credit of this commonwealth or of Congress. The said assessors shall then instead of the oath or affirmation appointed to be taken by the first mentioned act, take the following oath or affirmation to be administered by any one of the Commissioners 'I do swear (or affirm) that I will to the best of my skill and judgment, in the several parcels of land within the bounds of my assessment estimate the quantity of each kind thereof as classed or described by the commissioners of the tax for my county, that I will assess the same at the legal pound rate according to the average value of the same kind of lands settled by the commissioners and assessors of my county: that I will faithfully justly and impartially assess the pound rate imposed by law on all other property liable thereto within my hundred, according to the plain meaning of the several acts of assembly under which I act as they appear to my judgment; that I will spare none for favour or affection and none aggrieve for hatred malice or illwill, but in all things do my duty of an assessor honestly, impartially and to the best of my abilities: so help me god.' And if any assessor were not present at the said meeting, the said oath last stated shall be afterwards administered to him by some one of the Commissioners or any Justice of the peace of the county or corporation and before he shall proceed to make his assessments. The said Assessors shall then proceed to the assessment of their hundred; in the course of which if they shall differ in opinion as to the value of any parcel of land or of other property the medium between their two opinions shall be taken as the true value.

"And the same inequalities having arisen in the assessment of slaves in the several counties, and it being supposed that the assessment on this kind of property may be rendered much more equal by way of poll tax so settled as to bear the proportion of one and a half per cent to their average value."

This was a more ingenious and less artificial plan to obtain uniformity and fairness in evaluations of property than that proposed in the Bill as introduced, but it, too, failed to convince the legislators and the varying interpretations on the part of different county commissioners of the tax no doubt continued.

8 The following paragraph, not in either MS of the Bill, is found in the Act as adopted: "And whereas, by the restraint of the number of assessors in this act, their business may be greatly increased, and the provision made by the before recited act for their trouble be inadequate to their services, *Be it enacted*, That it may and shall be lawful for the commissioners in each county to settle what satisfaction shall be made to each assessor for his extraordinary trouble, so as such allowance shall not be more than five pounds above what is allowed by the said recited act."

9 All of the passage enclosed in brackets (supplied) was written by TJ on one of the pages of amendments; this amendment offered by him was adopted without change.

To John Hancock

HONORABLE SIR Albemarle in Virginia Octob. 19. 1778.

In a late conversation with Mr. T. Adams since his return from Congress I find, what indeed might have been well supposed that the state of the Continental finances was not the most flourishing. The establishment of banks in Europe for the purpose of maintaining our credit there, as well as here, and by that means of enlarging our supplies by way of loan may perhaps meet with the attention of Congress. As it is probable this cannot be done to a sufficient extent in any one place in Europe, the procuring credit in several places tho' to no great amount in any one of them, will answer the same end. An acquaintance with two Italian gentlemen who have settled in my neighborhood has been the means of my becoming acquainted with some facts which may perhaps be of some use to the general cause. The Grand duke of Tuscany by great oeconomy and a particular attention to the affairs of his treasury has I understand a very large sum in ready money which it is thought he would readily put out to interest, more especially if it was proposed not to carry it out of his state, but to invest it in necessaries there. Having also established at his own expence public manufactures for the employment of his poor, it is said he has immense magazines of these which he would without doubt gladly furnish on credit. The Genoese are among the richest people in Europe. Being principally commercial they make great sums of money, which their sumptuary laws put it out of their power to expand. The consequence is that for a long time they have put their money into the banks of Europe for 3 and 3½ per cent. They have immense sums in the London bank, the state of which has for some time alarmed them: and nothing has prevented their drawing it out but the impossibility of disposing of it elsewhere. Were they indeed to go pretty generally on the plan of selling out, it is probable they must sell to considerable loss, yet the high interest we pay would make amends for that, more especially when they contemplate the certain loss of their principal at no very distant period if suffered to remain there. There seems therefore reason to hope we might do something clever with them, which would be doubly beneficial by supplying our wants, and perhaps rendering our Enemies bankrupt by sudden and large calls on them. I throw out these things for your contemplation. If they can be wrought into any public good I know you will do it. Should Congress think them worth an essay, they will probably think it wisest to negotiate at first in a covered way, and not put their credit to the hazard of an affrontive refusal, till they see a disposition to accept their terms. One of the gentlemen of whom I spoke above (Mr. Mazzei) is I think more likely to negotiate this matter to our advantage than perhaps a native alone. He possesses first rate abilities, is pretty well acquainted with the European courts, and particularly those abovementioned, is a native of Tuscany with good connections and I have seen certain proofs of the Grand duke's personal regard for him. He has been a zealous whig from the beginning and I think may be relied on perfectly in point of integrity. He is very sanguine in his expeditions[1] of the services he could render us on this occasion and would undertake it on a very moderate appointment. This, if Congress were to adopt the plan at all, they would order as they please: he thinks £600 sterl. would enable him to continue there a twelvemonth within which time it might be effected. I think the sum which would be hazarded of little consideration when compared with the benefits hoped for.

I have taken the liberty of troubling you with this information, finding there are few others now remaining at Congress of my former acquaintance, and none for whom I have greater esteem. A love for the General cause makes me hazard it for the general service. We have nothing here interesting or worthy your knolege. I shall therefore conclude not dealing in compliments, for it is none when I assure you I am with high esteem Your most obedt. humble servt., TH: JEFFERSON

Facsimile (NN) from the original RC at one time in the possession of Moses Polock, Philadelphia. RC, now missing, sold in Polock Sale at Henkels', Philadelphia, 9 Mch. 1904, lot 1125. Addressed: "The Honble. John Hancock esq. of the Massachusets delegation Philadelphia"; the last word is corrected in another hand to "Boston."

TWO ITALIAN GENTLEMEN: Charles Bellini and Phillip Mazzei; see TJ to John Adams, 21 Aug. 1777, and references there.

[1] Thus in facsimile; an error (by the engraver?) for "expectations."

Bill to Amend the Act Establishing a General Court

[27 October 1778]

[Be it enacted by the general Assembly][1] That instead of the Days heretofore set apart for the Trial of Criminal Causes in the General Court held in the months of March and October the said Court shall at the Commencement of the said Terms enter upon the Trial thereof as null those for capitol offences as others setting apart the four first Days, for that Purpose, but the Judges may direct the Clerk at any Time before his Docket be made out and subpœnas issued for witnesses, to appropriate a longer or shorter Time to such Business and to those days so set apart no other Causes shall be docketed and all Process issued either from the County Courts or the General Court in those Causes shall be returnable to the first Day of the next succeeding Session.[2]

That all Indictments Presentments Informations Actions and Suits which now are or which were on the twelfth Day of April 1774[3] depending in any Court within this Commonwealth in the Name or on Behalf of George the Third King of Great Britain and or in the Names of any Persons on Behalf of themselves and the said King, shall, where Trials have not been already had be carried on in the Name of the Commonwealth or in the Names of such Persons and the Commonwealth, instead of the said King in the same Manner as if they had been found made entered or commenced since the Establishment of the said Commonwealth.[4] That all

Appeals depending against the said King shall be carried on against the Commonwealth instead of the said King, and all Bonds and Recognizances entered into to the said King shall operate as if given to the Commonwealth and in Cases of Breaches thereof Suits or Prosecutions may be carried on in the Name of the Commonwealth.[5] That where Trials have been had, and Judgments given in the Name or on Behalf of the said King or in the Names of any other Persons on Behalf of themselves and the said King and not satisfied the same shall inure to the commonwealth instead of the said King and Executions may thereupon issue accordingly but no Time shall bar the Commonwealth of Execution. That all Indictments Presentments Informations Actions and Suits in the Name or on Behalf of the said King or in the Name of any Persons on Behalf of themselves and the said King and all appeals against the said King which may have been discontinued or abated in any Court within this Commonwealth on Account of the Abolition of regal Government shall be forthwith revived redocketed and carried on in the Manner before directed. And all Judgments for or against the Commonwealth shall be the same as would have been entered for or against the King had no Revolution in Government taken Place.[6]

That any Persons who shall be charged with a Capital Offence and not tried at the second Session after their Examination in the County Court and after Petition to the General Court for Trial shall be acquitted and discharged of such Offence unless good Cause be shewn for postponing their Trials but if they be not tried at the third Session they shall be for ever acquitted and discharged of such offence.[7]

That when any Criminal shall by the General Court be continued to a succeeding Session for Trial the Sherif of the County in which the Crime is alledged to have been committed shall summon twelve good and able Freeholders of his County every one of whom shall be possessed of a visible Estate over and above his Debts of at least the Value of   to serve as a venire upon such Trial and all veniremen shall hereafter be summoned by the high Sherif and Qualified as before is mentioned otherwise they shall be incapable of serving.[8]

That the Clerk of the Court in which any Criminal is examined shall issue subpœnas for witnesses either against or on Behalf of such Criminal returnable to the first Day of the then next General Court and such witnesses being legally summoned and failing to appear shall be fined in a sum not exceeding[9]

MS (Vi); in clerk's hand, containing alterations in the hand of TJ. This text is referred to below, for the sake of clarity, as MS (1). Another MS (Vi); in an unidentified hand; endorsed: "A Bill to amend an act, intituled 'an act for establishing a general court,' and other purposes." Docketed in hand of Edmund Randolph: "Octr. 27. 1778. read first time. Octr. 28. 1778. read second time & to be committed to whole on ⟨*Monday next*⟩ Thursday se'ennight." This text is referred to below as MS (2). The Act as adopted, which agrees precisely with the text of MS (1) except as indicated below, is in Hening, IX, 473-4.

Although MS (2) was the Bill that was introduced and MS (1) represents the amendment offered to it, the latter was in effect an entire new Bill and was adopted. The initial stages of the legislative history of MS (2) are indicated in the docketing quoted above; between 5 Nov. and 13 Dec. consideration of the Bill as introduced by Terry was postponed no less than ten times. This may possibly have been due to the fact that TJ was absent from the House until 30 Nov.: his colleagues, knowing the leading part he had taken in drafting the judiciary bills, may have deferred action on this amending Act until his arrival. This supposition is given weight by the fact that MS (1), which bears alterations in his hand, was, on 18 Dec., offered as an amendment in substitution for the Terry Bill and was adopted by the House on 19 Dec.: the Senate agreed to this "amendment" or substitute Bill the same day (JHD, Oct. 1778, 1827 edn., p. 29, 32, 46, 51, 56, 67, 76, 81, 90, 94, 100, 108, 110, 112, 124-5, 126). It is probable that TJ was not the author of the Bill as introduced by Terry or of the substitute embraced in MS (1), though, as indicated in note 2, below, he certainly was instrumental in keeping the latter from interfering with an Act passed at the previous session.

[1] MS (1) contained no enacting clause, having been offered as an amendment to MS (2) as introduced by Terry. Enacting clause has been taken from MS (2); square brackets supplied.

[2] MS (2) does not contain a paragraph corresponding to the foregoing. As originally drafted in MS (1), this paragraph provided that at the March and October terms the first four days should be set aside for the trial of criminal causes and at the June and December terms the first three days should be devoted to the same purpose. This would have had the effect of amending an Act passed at the May 1778 session, the object of which was to create two additional terms, to be held in June and December, for the purpose of trying criminal causes only (see Bill to Enable Judges of the General Court to Hold Two Additional Sessions, under date of 27 May 1778; Hening, IX, 460-1); this Act of May 1778 provided, however, that treasons, felonies, misdemeanors, and other commonwealth pleas should continue to be cognizable at the March and October terms as theretofore. MS (1) as originally drawn, therefore, would have had the effect of making other than criminal causes cognizable at the June and December terms; this apparently was unacceptable to TJ and he therefore struck out the proviso relating to these two terms, interlined the necessary changes, and caused the paragraph to read as above and as in the Act as adopted. By this alteration he left the June and December terms to serve their oyer and terminer functions as contemplated by the Act of May 1778. In view of this, it is likely that TJ was not the author of MS (1); conversely, the change that he made in MS (1) to safeguard the object of the Act of May 1778 is further evidence that he was probably the author of that Act.

[3] The words "the twelfth" and "of April 1774" are in TJ's hand. The corresponding section of MS (2) reads "the day of July 1776."

[4] MS (2) agrees in substance with the foregoing, but there were important variations in phraseology and MS (2) was also broader in scope. It provided that in the case of all indictments, presentments, informations, and prosecutions standing in the name of the king and entered "before the day of July 1776" and still undetermined, the judges of any court having jurisdiction of such might "proceed to Tryal, judgment and execution thereon in the same manner, as it would have proceeded had the present revolution in Government not taken place." MS (2) also contained a further proviso that "where trials have already been had and judgments obtained, or executions awarded in any such indictment, presentment, information or prosecution, the same shall be as valid and binding as though the said revolution had not taken place."

[5] In the corresponding proviso, MS (2) has the following: "All appeals wherein

the said King was a defendant shall be carried on against the commonwealth according to the forms of law used against him. And all bonds and recognizances given to the said King shall operate as if given to the commonwealth."

[6] In the section corresponding to the foregoing, MS (2) has the following: "If any indictment presentment, information, prosecution, appeal against the said King, scire facias, or other action or suit, hath already abated by judgment of any court on account of the abolition of regal government here, the same shall be forthwith reinstated, and carried on to trial, judgment, and execution.

"And in case of judgment being pronounced in favour of a defendant in any of the modes of prosecution abovementioned the same entry (except where the said King is defendant) shall be made against the commonwealth as would otherwise have been made against the said King; and where judgment should have been given in favour of the said King, the same entry shall be made, as if the process had originated in the name of the commonwealth."

MS (2) also has, following the above section, these three sections not in MS (1) or in Act as adopted: "And be it further enacted that where the plaintiff in any petition for lapsed land, now depending and undetermined, makes good his pretentions, the judgment shall be that the land petitioned for is vested in the commonwealth, that it be certified to the Governour or chief Magistrate, that such plaintiff is the first petitioner, and hath pursued his petition with effect; who upon such certificate is hereby impowered to act therein in the same manner as the Governor of the King of Great Britain formerly acted under the laws of Virginia. And the general court shall hear such petitions at their sessions in June and December.

"And be it further enacted that instead of the 6th. day, all criminal process in the General court shall be returnable to the first Monday in each of the March and October sessions; and the court shall proceed on the said first monday to the trial of criminals.

"If the whole number summoned for a grand Inquest should not appear, it may be compleated with bystanders, qualified as the law directs. And for reasons appearing to the court, any one or more of the grand jury may be withdrawn, even after it be sworn, and another or others substituted in his or their stead."

[7] In the section corresponding to the foregoing, MS (2) has the following: "And if a person committed to the publick Gaol for trial in the General court shall not be tried at the second term after commitment, and after petition offered for trial, such person shall be for ever discharged and acquitted of the offence for which he or she may have been committed, unless by affidavit, or otherwise, good cause be shewn for not bringing him or her to trial; and if such person be not tried at the third term after commitment, and after petition offered for trial, he or she shall be discharged and acquitted, any plea allegation or affidavit notwithstanding."

MS (2) also has the following section not in MS (1) or in the Act as adopted: "And the General court shall have power at the end of each term to settle a proper allowance for the services of the assistant clerks, the sherif of York, crier and tipstaff in attending the said court; and the treasurer for the time being is hereby required to pay any sum or sums of money which may be drawn for by them, for the purpose aforesaid; and shall have been first entered in the auditors books."

[8] This and the following paragraph, which have been struck out in MS (1), are not in MS (2) or in the Act as adopted, probably having been deleted by amendment.

[9] The text ends thus abruptly.

To George Wythe

DEAR SIR Monticello Nov. 1. 1778.

I have got thro' the bill 'for proportioning crimes and punishments in cases heretofore capital,' and now inclose it to you with a request that you will be so good as scrupulously to examine and correct it, that it may be presented to our committee with as few defects as possible. In it's style I have aimed at accuracy, brevity and simplicity, preserving however the very words of the established law, wherever their meaning had been sanctioned by judicial decisions, or rendered technical by usage. The same matter if couched in the modern statutory language, with all it's tautologies, redundancies and circumlocutions would have spread itself over many pages, and been unintelligible to those whom it most concerns. Indeed I wished to exhibit a sample of reformation in the barbarous style into which modern statutes have degenerated from their antient simplicity. And I must pray you to be as watchful over what I have not said as what is said; for the omissions of this bill have all their positive meaning. I have thought it better to drop in silence the laws we mean to discontinue, and let them be swept away by the general negative words of this, than to detail them in clauses of express repeal. By the side of the text I have written the notes I made, as I went along, for the benefit of my own memory. They may serve to draw your attention to questions to which the expressions or the omissions of the text may give rise. The extracts from the Anglo-Saxon laws, the sources of the Common law, I wrote in their original for my own satisfaction; but I have added Latin, or literal English translations. From the time of Canute to that of the Magna charta, you know, the text of our statutes is preserved to us in Latin only, and some old French.

I have strictly observed the scale of punishments settled by the Committee, without being entirely satisfied with it. The lex talionis, altho' a restitution of the Common law, to the simplicity of which we have generally found it so advantageous to return will be revolting to the humanised feelings of modern times. An eye for an eye, and a hand for a hand will exhibit spectacles in execution whose moral effect would be questionable; and even the membrum pro membro of Bracton or the punishment of the offending member, altho' long authorised by our law, for the same offence in a slave, has you know been not long since repealed in conformity with public sentiment. This needs reconsideration.

I have heard little of the proceedings of the Assembly, and do not expect to be with you till about the close of the month. In the mean time present me respectfully to Mrs. Wythe and accept assurances of the affectionate esteem and respect of Dear Sir Your friend & servt,

TH: JEFFERSON

RC? (DLC). The MS has the appearance of being the letter sent rather than a draft. A retained fair copy, signed, is in TJ's commonplace book with binding title "Law Treaties" in MHi. Enclosure: see below.

For TJ's BILL FOR PROPORTIONING CRIMES AND PUNISHMENTS, enclosed in the present letter, see Bill No. 64, Report of the Committee of Revisors, 18 June 1779. For TJ's objections to MODERN STATUTORY LANGUAGE, see also his Autobiography (Ford, I, 61) and his letter to Joseph C. Cabell, 9 Sep. 1817.

Bill for Giving the Members of the General Assembly an Adequate Allowance

[12 December 1778]

Whereas it is just that the members of General assembly, delegated by the people to transact for them the legislative business, should, while attending that business, have their reasonable sustenance defrayed, dedicating to the public service their time and labors freely and without account: and it is also expedient that the public councils should not be deprived of the aid of good and able men, who might be deterred from entering into them by the insufficiency of their private fortunes to bear the extraordinary expences they must necessarily incur:

And it being inconsistent with the principles of civil liberty, and contrary to the natural rights of the other members of the society, that any body of men therein should have authority to enlarge their own powers, prerogatives, or emoluments without restraint, the said General assembly cannot at their own will increase the allowance which their members are to draw from the public treasury for their expences while on assembly; but to enable them so to do, an application to the body of the people has become necessary:

And such application having been accordingly made to the freeholders of the several counties, and they having thereupon consented that the said allowance shall be enlarged, and authorized and instructed their members to enlarge the same for themselves and the members of all future assemblies, to   pounds[1] of nett tobacco by the day for attendance on assembly, and to   ℔s[2] of like tobacco for every mile they must necessarily travel going to or from the same, together with their ferriages, to be paid in money out of the public treasury at such rate as shall be estimated by the court of appeals[3] at their session next before the meeting of every session of assembly, governing themselves in the said estimate by the worth of the said tobacco, and the competence of the same to defray the necessary expences of travelling and attendance:

Be it therefore enacted by the General assembly by express authority and instruction from the body of the people that the allowance to the several members of the present and of all future general assemblies shall be of pounds[1] of tobacco by the day for attendance on the said assemblies, ℔s[2] of the like tobacco for every mile they must necessarily travel going to or from the same, together with their ferriages; to be paid to them in money out of the public treasury at such rate as shall be estimated by the court of appeals[3] at their session next before the meeting of each respective session of assembly, governing themselves in the said estimate by the worth of the said tobacco and the competence of the same to defray the necessary expences of travelling and attendance.

MS (Vi); in TJ's hand. Endorsed by him: "A Bill for giving the members of the General assembly an adequate allowance for their services." Docketed by Edmund Randolph: "Decr. 12. 1778. Read the first time. Decr. 14. read second & comd. to whole to morrow. Decr. 18. To be engd. & printed." Broadside, printed as ordered, entitled: "An Act for giving the members of the General Assembly an adequate allowance for their services." (This broadside is not recorded in the standard bibliographies.) The latter is attached to the MS copy of the Report of the Committee of Revisors, 18 June 1779 (Vi), where the words "An Act" are crossed out and "A Bill" inserted by hand.

On 8 Dec. 1778 the Committee on Propositions and Grievances brought in several resolutions, the first of which was to the effect that that part of the remonstrances of the freeholders of Halifax and Prince William counties praying for a repeal of the Act of the previous session granting an increase in allowance to members of the General Assembly (Hening, IX, 466-7, an Act which provided a salary of twenty shillings per day while attending, plus the same rate per diem while traveling to and from the Assembly, and ferriage costs) was reasonable. The House laid this resolution on the table but immediately thereafter appointed a committee of six, of which TJ was chairman, to bring in a Bill "for giving the members of the General Assembly an adequate allowance for their services." The Bill was introduced by George Mason on 12 Dec.; on 14 Dec. it was read the second time and committed to the committee of the whole, where it was debated on 15, 17, and 18 Dec. and amended. On the last date the House ordered the Bill engrossed and, in accordance with the broad philosophy stated in the preamble, directed 175 copies to be printed for the use of members of both houses. Members were directed to "consult with their constituents, during the recess of Assembly, on the justice and expediency of passing the bill . . . and procure from them instructions whether or not the said bill shall be passed" (JHD, Oct. 1778, 1827 edn., p. 104, 111, 112, 117, 121, 123). At the next session the delegates reported the views of their constituents, which were favorable to the increase, and on 25 May 1779 the House appointed a committee to bring in a Bill; TJ was a member of this committee. The Bill, identical to the one that TJ had drawn up the previous session, was reported the same day. It was passed promptly, without amendment, and agreed to by the Senate on 1 June (same, May 1779, p. 21, 23, 26, 27, 29). The Act as adopted is in Hening, X, 29-30.

1 The broadside (and, of course, the Act as adopted) reads: "fifty pounds."

2 The broadside (and the Act as adopted) reads: "two pounds."

3 This was amended on 18 Dec. 1778 to read (as it does in the broadside and in the Act): "by the grand jury at the session of the General Court next before."

From John Hook

SIR New London [Bedford County, Virginia] Janry 5 1779

I am sorrey to be under the Needcessity of troubleing you with a Matter that is of little consequence to you or any one at Present but my self, but as I have been imposed on and have no Prospect of redress but from you I hope you will consider my circumstance as a sufficient appoligy. In October last your overseear Zach Morris was offering for sale three Hhds of Your Tobo on James River at the Plantation where Walter Mousley was lately oversear for you. He said he was directed by the Steward Mr. Garth to dispose of them in order to discharge the taxes. They were offerd to me at 15£ ℔ 100—and each Hhd. said to weight 1000 11 Neat and hf a bushell of Salt besides for the use of the Plantation. Mr. Morris said he was instructed to warrent their Passing the Inspection but urged that they were Prized by A Man of skill and Experience and one reputed for being an Honest Man and further that the reason why those three was directed to be sold before any others was that you had sold the Plantation where they lay. I became a Purchasser and on examining the Tobacco find it to be trash in quallity and one Hhd. to appearance half destroyd by wet; were you to see the Tobacco I'm certain you would conclude with me that it was Prized more with a design to impose upon a Purchasser in the way I have been then with any expectation of its ever Passing the Inspection; I have further to observe to you that at the time I paid Mr. Garth the Money for the Tobacco (in Presence of Zach. Morris the 29th of Novr.) I at that time had heard of one Hhd. of the Tobacco being damaged by a leak falling on it and told Mr. Garth hereof, also that if there was any considerable damage on it and if it should appear that it was in that condition at the time I made the Purchass, I should consider it as your loss, as Mr. Morris had assured me at that time when makeing the Purchass, that it was in a good tight barn where it could not get any damage; I then Immagind the damage was triffeling from its being represented as a drop that had run down the Prize beem and from a jealousey that Mr. Garth and Mr. Morris might immagin that I wanted to Put off Payment of the Purchass Money, to put it out of their Power to say this, I Paid the Money without more to do. Mr. Garth urged that he was acting for you and that as Mr. Morris had sold the Tobacco as it stood, he consider'd it out of his Power to do any thing in it. As I am now circumstanced in this bargain there is but few men that I would apply to for any redress in this way but as I consider you as a Gentleman of extensive and liberall Notions of justice and above takeing advantage of my Credulity I hope you will direct an enquiry to be made herein and that I may be redressed. If you shall consider me intitled to this I would recommend Mr. Winston and Mr. Innis to consider of this matter with any judges of Tobacco you think fit to appoint. Mr. Morris is removed to Amelia but I will have his deposition taken to Produce to the gentlemen who is chosen to determin herein.

If agreeable to you I will take three Hogsheads at your Forrest Plantation in lue of them and whatever they weigh over the three thousand I will Pay the Current Price for at the time they are Inspected and will have them Waggon'd down, at my Expence as soon as the Weather will Permitt and as £93. 18. 0 has been Paid to Mousley in consideration of his share in the Tobacco by order of Mr. M. I shall be willing to reimburse you herein in case you think the same cannot be recoverd of Mousley. Shall be much obliged to you for your answer and am with due respect. I mention this that you may not be embarrased in discussing the equity of this Purposall.

Dft (Felix Hargrett, New York City, 1944). Scored-out words and sentences have not been noted here.

PRIZE BEEM: probably the handle bar or beam of a tobacco prize, used to compress hands of tobacco firmly in the hogshead. An eighteenth-century drawing of a tobacco prize is to be found in William Tatham's *An Historical and Practical Essay on the Culture and Commerce of Tobacco*, London, 1800, reproduced in Louis Morton's *Robert Carter of Nomini Hall*, Williamsburg, 1945 (information from A. Pierce Middleton, Williamsburg).

From Edward Rutledge

MY DEAR JEFFERSON Charles Town Feby: 12. 1779

As there is a probability that the Gentlemen who bear this letter will arrive in Virginia when you have condescended to come down from above and interest yourselves in Human Affairs; I could not but take the Liberty of introducing them and the Business with which they are commissioned to your Attention. They go to represent to your Commonwealth, the Situation of this State and of Georgia, which is now reduced to the Condition of a Conquer'd Province. It would take me more Time than I could possibly bestow (as I write this on a sick bed) to mention the Circumstances in which we are, and the Occasion; I can only say at Present that they go, for what we very much require, the Assistance of Virginia, and that you would do a very essential piece of Service to this Country, and (if it could possibly have weight) to your Friend, should you exert yourself in favour of their Commission. But you know the Benefit which we shall receive will be increased or lessen'd by Expedition or delay. I am my dear Sir with Sincere affection your Friend, E: RUTLEDGE

RC (DLC).

To George Wythe

DEAR SIR Forest March. 1. 1779.

Since I left you I have reflected on the bill for regulating the practising of attornies, and of our omitting to continue the practitioners at the county and General courts separate. I think the bar of the general court a proper and an excellent nursery for future judges if it be so regulated as that science may be encouraged and may live there. But this can never be if an inundation of insects is permitted to come from the county courts and consume the harvest. These people traversing the counties seeing the clients frequently at their own courts or perhaps at their own houses must of necessity pick up all the business. The convenience of frequently seeing their counsel without going from home cannot be withstood by the country people. Men of science then (if there were to be any) would only be employed as auxiliary counsel in difficult cases. But can they live by that? Certainly not. The present members of that kind therefore must turn marauder[s] in the county courts; and in future none will have leisure to acquire science. I should therefore be for excluding the county court attorneys, or rather for taking the General court lawyers from the incessant drudgery of the county courts and confining them to their studies that they may qualify themselves [as] well to support their clients as to become worthy successors of the bench. I hope to see the time when the election of Judges of the supreme courts shall be restrained to the bars of the General court and high court of chancery, for when I speak of the former above, I mean to include the latter. I should even in our present bills have no objections to inserting such a restriction to take place seven or fourteen years hence. Adieu. TH: JEFFERSON

RC (DLC). For the BILL in question, see Report of the Committee of Revisors, 18 June 1779, Bill No. 97.

From Richard Henry Lee

DEAR SIR Philadelphia March 15. 1779

I have not been unmindful of the small commission you gave me to procure the song and receipt for you. I once had these, but they are mislaid so that I could not find them when I returned home, from Williamsburg, or they should have been sent from thence. I have here applied to Mr. Peters for the one, and to Mrs. Shippen for the other and I have hopes of getting them both. I send you herewith a small pamphlet containing a collection of such papers and proceedings as clearly defeats the calumny of the British Commissioners charging this war to our ambition, when the Tyranny and avarice of the British Court most indubitably produced and has continued it.

That our enemies will not get aid from any power in Europe to carry on the war against us is very certain and the probability is great that Spain will speedily join in the war with France against England. Yet such is the temper of the British Court that it seems clear to me that nothing but the severest gripes of adversity and the last necessity can inspire wisdom and moderation. They certainly mean another campaign, a last effort; [as] Georgia and South Carolina, with the frontiers and sea coasts appear to be their objects at present. Whether Gen. Clinton will take the field or not must depend on the succors he shall receive and the strength of our army. The flatte[ring] royal visits that are industriously made to the Nobil[ity] and gentry of England may possibly give such energy to the militia as to enable the sending a small reenforcement from their national troops to Gen. Cli[nton.] With our present prospects every nerve should be strained to make our Army strong. By being prepared we shall have a moral certainty of defeating the designs of our enemies the next campaign, which will in my opinion put a glorious period to the war. I am with much esteem and affection yours, RICHARD HENRY LEE

RC (DLC); Tr (PPAP). The enclosure was a pamphlet issued by Congress entitled *Observations on the American Revolution*, Phila.: Styner and Cist, 1779 (Evans 16625; see R. H. Lee to TJ, 3 May 1779; JCC, XV, 1452).

MR. PETERS: Probably Richard Peters, secretary of the Board of War (DAB). MRS. SHIPPEN was Alice Lee Shippen, sister of R. H. Lee.

To Patrick Henry

SIR[1] Albemarle Mar. 27. 1779

A report prevailing here that in consequence of some powers from Congress the Governor and council have it in contemplation to remove the Convention troops either wholly or in part from their present situation, I take the liberty of troubling you[2] with some observations on that subject. The reputation and interests of our country in general may be[3] affected by such[4] a measure. It would therefore hardly be deemed an indecent liberty in the most private citizen to[5] offer his thoughts to the consideration of the executive. The locality of my situation particularly in the neighborhood of the present barracks and the public relation in which I stand with the people among whom they are situated, together with a confidence which a personal knowlege of the members of the executive[6] gives me, that they will be glad of information from any quarter on a subject interesting to the public, induce me to hope that they[7] will acquit me of impropriety in the present representation.

By an article in the convention of Saratoga[8] it is stipulated on the part of the United States that the officers shall not be separated from their men. I suppose the term officers includes *general* as well as *regimental* officers. As there are General officers then who command all the troops, no part of them can be separated from these officers, without a violation of the article: they cannot of course be separated from one another unless the same General officer could be in different places at the same time. It is true the article adds 'as far as circumstances will admit.'[9] This was a necessary qualification; because in no place in America I suppose could there have been found quarters for both officers and men together, those for the officers to be according to their rank. So far then as the circumstances of the place where they should be quartered should render a separation necessary in order to procure quarters for the officers, according to their rank, the article admits that separation. And these are the circumstances which must have been under the contemplation of the parties both of whom and all the world beside who are ultimate judges in this case would still understand that they were to be as near in the environs of the camp, as convenient quarters could be procured and not that the qualification of the article destroyed the article itself and laid it wholly at our discretion. Congress indeed have admitted of this separation: but are they so far lords of right and wrong as that our consciences may be quiet with their dispensation? Or is the case amended by saying they leave it optional in the Governor and council to separate the troops or not? At the same time that it exculpates not them, it is drawing the Governor and council into a participation in the breach of faith. If indeed it is only proposed that a separation of the troops shall be referred to the consent of their officers; that is a very different matter. Having carefully avoided conversation with them on public subjects I can not say of my own knowledge how they would relish such a proposition. I have heard from others that they will chuse to undergo any thing together rather than to be separated: and that they will remonstrate against it in the strongest terms. The executive therefore, if voluntary agents in this measure,[10] must be drawn into a paper war with them, the more disagreeable as it seems that faith and reason will be on the other side. As an American I cannot help feeling a most thorough mortification that our Congress should have permitted an infraction of our public honour; as a citizen of Virginia I cannot help hoping and[11] confiding that our supreme Executive, whose acts will be considered as the acts of the Commonwealth, estimate that honour too highly [to][12] make it's infraction their own act. I may be permitted to hope then that if any removal[13] takes place it will be a general one: and as it is said to be left to the Governor and council to determine on this, I am satisfied, that suppressing[14] every other consideration, and weighing the matter dispassionately, they will determine upon this sole question. Is it for the benefit of those for whom they act that the Convention troops should be removed from among them? Under the head of interest these circumstances viz. the expence of building barracks said to have been £25,000: and of removing the troops backwards and forwards, amounting to I know not how much, are not to be pretermitted merely because they are Continental expences; for we are a part of the Continent. We must pay a shilling of every dollar wasted.[15] But the sums of money which by these troops or on their account are brought into and expended in this state, are a great and local advantage. This can require no proof. If at the conclusion of the war for instance our share of the Continental debt should be 20 millions of dollars, or say that we are called on to furnish an annual quota of 2,400,000 dollars to Congress to be raised by tax, it is obvious that we should raise these given sums with greater or less ease in proportion to the greater or less quantity of money found in circulation among us. I expect that our circulating money is increased by the presence of these troops at the rate of 30,000 dollars[16] a week at the least.[17] I have heard indeed that an objection arises to their being kept within this state from the information of the Comissary that they cannot be subsisted here. In attending to the information of that office it should be borne in mind that the county of King William and it's vicinities are one thing, the territory of Virginia another. If the troops could be fed upon long letters I beleive the gentleman at the head of that department in this country would be the best commissary upon earth. But till I see him determined to act, not to write, to sacrifice[18] his domestic ease to the duties of his appointment and apply to the resources of this[19] country wheresoever they are to be had, I must entertain a different opinion of him. I am mistaken if for the animal subsistence of the troops hitherto we are not principally indebted to the genius and exertions of Hawkins during the very short time he lived after his appointment to that department by your board. His eye immediately pervaded[20] the whole state, it was reduced at once to a regular machine, to a system, and the whole put into movement and animation by the fiat of a comprehensive mind. If the commonwealth of Virginia cannot furnish these troops with bread I would ask of the commissariate, Which of the thirteen is now become the grain colony? If we are in danger of famine from the addition of 4000 mouths, what is become of that surplus of bread the exportation of which used to feed the West Indies and Eastern states and fill the colony with hard money? When I urge the sufficiency of this state however to subsist these troops I beg to be understood as having in contemplation the quantity of provisions necessary for their real use and not as calculating what is to be lost by the wanton waste, mismanagement and carelessness of those employed about it. If magazines of beef and pork are suffered to rot by slovenly butchering or for want of timely provision of salt, if quantities of flour are exposed in open waggons to pillage and destruction; and if when laid up in the Continental stores it is still to be embezzled and sold by the commissaries entrusted with the keeping of it the land of Egypt itself would be insufficient for their supply and their removal will be necessary not to a more plentiful country but to more able and honest commissaries. Perhaps the magnitude of this question and it's relation to the whole state may render it worth while to await[21] the opinion of the national council which is now to meet within a few weeks. There is no danger of distress in the mean time as the commissaries affirm they have a great sufficiency of provisions for some time to come. Should the measure of removing them into another State be adopted, and carried into execution before the meeting of assembly no disapprobation of theirs will bring them back, because they will then be in the power of others who will hardly give them up.

Want of information what may be the precise measure proposed by the Governor and council obliges me to shift my ground and take up the subject in every possible form. Perhaps they have not thought to remove the troops out of this state altogether, but to some other part of it. Here the objections arising from the expences of removal and of building new barracks recur: As to animal food, it may be driven to one part of the country as easily as to another: that circumstance therefore may be thrown out of the question. As to bread I suppose they will require about 40, or 45000 bushels of grain a year. The place to which it is to be brought to them is about the center of the state. Besides that the country round about is fertile. All the grain made in the counties adjacent to any kind of navigation may be brought by water to within 12 miles of the spot. For these 12 miles waggons must be employed, I suppose half a dozen will be a plenty. Perhaps this part of the expence might have been saved had the barracks been built on the water. But it is not sufficient to justify their being abandoned now they are built and waggonage indeed seems to the commissariate an article not worth œconomising. For they kill meat at Richmond, Fredsbgh and I suppose at other places and waggon it to the barracks instead of driving it alive, but when they purchase flour in the upper counties they contrive a wanton and studied circuity of waggonage. To mention only one fact, they have bought quantities of flour for these troops in Cumberland, have ordered it to be waggoned down to Manchester[22] and waggoned thence to the Barracks. This fact happened to fall within my own knolege. I doubt not there are many more such, in order either to produce their total removal or to run up the expences of the present situation and satisfy Congress that the nearer they are brought to the Commissary's own bed the cheaper they will be subsisted. The grain made in the Western counties may be brought partly in waggons as conveniantly to this as to any other place, perhaps more so on account of it's vicinity to one of the best passes through the blue ridge, and partly by water as it is near James river to the navigation of which ten counties are adjacent above the falls. When I said that the grain might be brought hither from all the counties of the state adjacent to navigation, I did not mean to say it would be proper to bring it from all of them. On the contrary I think commissary[23] should be instructed after the next harvest not to send one bushel of grain to the barracks from below the falls of the rivers or from the Northern counties.

The counties on tide waters are accessible to the calls for our own army. Their supplies ought therefore to be husbanded for them. The counties in the Northern parts of the state are not only within reach for our own Grand army but peculiarly necessary for the support of Mackintosh's army, or for the support of any other western expedition that the uncertain conduct of the Indians should render necessary, insomuch that if the supplies of that quarter should be misapplied to any other purpose it would destroy in embryo every exertion either for particular or general safety there. The counties above the tide waters in the middle and Southern and Western parts of the country are not accessible to calls for either of those purposes, but at such an expence of transportation as the articles would not bear. Here then is a great feild whose supplies of bread cannot be carried to our army, or rather which will raise no supplies of bread because there is no body to eat them. Was it not then wise in Congress to remove to that feild 4000 idle mouths who must otherwise have interfered with the pasture of our own troops? And if they are removed to any other part of the country will it not defeat this wise purpose. The mills on the waters of James river above the falls open to canoe navigation are very many. Some of them are of great note as manufacturers. The Barracks are surrounded by mills. There are 5 or 6 round about Charlottesville. Any two or three of the whole might in the course of the winter manufacture flour sufficient for the year. To say the worst then of this situation it is but 12 miles wrong.

The safe custody of these troops is another circumstance worthy consideration. Equally removed from the access of an Eastern or Western enemy central to the whole state so that should they attempt an eruption in any direction they must pass through a great extent of hostile country, in a neighborhood thickly inhabited by a robust and hardy people zealous in the American cause, acquainted with the use of arms and the defiles and passes by which they must issue, it should seem that in this point of view no place could have been better chosen.

Their health is also of importance. I would not endeavor to shew that their lives are valuable to us, because it would suppose a possibility that humanity was kicked out of doors in America and interest only attended to. The barracks occupy the top and brow of a very high hill (you have been untruly told they were in a bottom). They are free from fog, have four springs which seem to be plentiful, one within 20 yds. of the picket, 2 within 50 yards, and another within 250 and they propose to sink wells within the picquet. Of

4000 people it should be expected according to the ordinary calculations that one should die every day. Yet in the space of near 3 months there have been but 4[24] deaths among them. 2 infants under three weeks[25] old, two others by apoplexy. The officers tell me, the troops were never before so healthy since they were embodied.

But is an enemy so execrable that tho in captivity his wishes and comforts are to be disregarded and even crossed? I think not. It is for the benefit of mankind to mitigate the horrors of war as much as possible. The practice therefore of modern nations of treating captive enemies with politeness and generosity is not only delightful in contemplation but really interesting to all the world, friends foes and neutrals. Let us apply this. The officers after considerable hardships have all procured quarters comfortable and satisfactory to them. In order to do this they were obliged in many instances to hire houses for a year certain and at such exorbitant rents as were sufficient to tempt independent owners to go out of them and shift as they could. These houses in most cases were much out of repair. They have repaired them at a considerable expence. One of the General officers has taken a place for two years, advanced the rent for the whole time and been obliged moreover to erect additional buildings for the accomodation of part of his family for which there was not room in the house rented. Independent of the brick work, for the carpentry of these additional buildings I know he is to pay 1500 dollars. The same gentleman to my knolege also has paid to one person 3670 dollars for different articles to fix himself commodiously. They have generally laid in their stocks of grain and other provision, for it is well known that officers do not live on their rations, they have purchased cows, sheep &c., set in to farming, prepared their gardens, and have a prospect of comfort and quiet before them. To turn to the soldiers, the environs of the barracks are delightful. The ground cleared, laid off into hundreds of gardens each inclosed in it's separate paling, these well prepared, and exhibiting a fine appearance.[26] General Riedezel alone laid out upwards of 200£[27] in garden seeds for the German troops only.[28] Judge what an extent of ground these seeds would cover. There is little doubt that their own gardens will furnish them a great abundance of vegetables through the year. Their poultry, pigeons[29] and other preparations[30] of that kind present to the mind an idea of a company of farmers rather than of a camp of soldiers.[31] In addition to the barracks built for them by the publick and now very comfortable they have built great numbers for themselves in such messes[32] as fancied each other: and the whole corps both officers and men seem now[33] happy and satisfied with their situation. Having thus found the art of rendering captivity itself comfortable, and carried it into execution at their own great expence and labor, their spirits sustained by the prospect of gratifications rising before their eyes, does not every sentiment of humanity revolt against the proposition of stripping them of all this and removing them into new situations where from the advanced season of the year no preparations can be made for carrying themselves comfortably through the heats of summer, and when it is known that the necessary advances for the conveniencies already provided have exhausted their funds and left them unable to make the like exertions anew.

Again view this matter as it may regard appearances.[34] A body of troops after staying a twelvemonth at Boston are ordered to take a march of 700 miles to Virginia where it is said they may be plentifully subsisted. As soon as they are there they are ordered on some other march because in Virginia it is said they cannot be subsisted. Indifferent nations will charge this either to ignorance or to whim and caprice; the parties interested to cruelty. They now view the proposition in [that light] and it is said there is a general and firm persuasion among them that they were [marched from Boston with no other purpose than to harass and destroy them with eternal marches.][35]

There could not have been a more unlucky concurrence of circumstances than when these troops first came. The barracks unfinished for want of labourers, the worst spell of weather ever known within the memory of man, no stores of bread laid in, the roads by the weather and number of waggons soon rendered impassable; not only the troops themselves were greatly disappointed, but the people in the neighborhood alarmed at the consequences which a total failure of provision might have produced. In this worst state of things their situation was seen by many and disseminated thro' the country so as to occasion a general dissatisfaction, which even seised the minds of reasonable men [who][36] if not infected with the contagion must have foreseen that the prospect must brighten and that great advantages to the people must necessarily arise. It has accordingly so happened. The planters being more generally sellers than buyers have felt the benefit[37] of their presence in the most vital part about them their purses and are now sensible of it's source. I have too good an opinion of their love of order to beleive that a removal of these troops would produce any irregular proofs of their disapprobation, but I am well assured it would be extremely odious[38] to them.

To conclude. The separation of these troops would be a breach of public faith, therefore I suppose it impossible. If they are removed to another state, it is the fault of the commissaries; if they are removed to any other part of the state it is the fault of the commissaries; and in both cases, the public interest and public security suffer, the comfortable and plentiful subsistence of our own army is lessened, the health of the troops neglected, their wishes crossed and their comforts torn from them, the character of whim and caprice or, what is worse, of cruelty fixed on us as a nation, and to crown the whole our own people disgusted with such a proceeding.

I have thus taken the liberty of representing to you the facts and the reasons which seem to militate against the separation or removal of these troops. I am sensible however that the same object may appear to different persons in very different lights. What I have urged as reasons may to sounder minds be apparent fallacies. I hope they will appear at least so plausible as to excuse the interposition of Your Excellency's most obedt. & most humble servt.

Dft (DLC). Fragmentary fair copy by TJ (DLC), consisting of first paragraph and part of second only. The Dft is one of the most difficult texts to decipher in the whole body of TJ's papers, because of the extensive additions and substitutions between the lines and in the margins. This fact and the vigor of TJ's language give evidence of the seriousness, not to say indignation, with which he viewed this matter. The more significant of the several hundred alterations made by TJ in composing this important letter are recorded in the textual notes below.

The REPORT concerning removal of THE CONVENTION TROOPS arose from official apprehensions that this body of some 4,000 British and German troops could be neither adequately provisioned nor guarded in their encampment in Albemarle co. These troops consisted of the remainder of the army surrendered upon convention at Saratoga, 17 Oct. 1777, who at the beginning of 1779 had reached an encampment prepared for them on Ivy Creek a few miles north of Charlottesville; the site is still known as The Barracks. Though technically interned, the troops were in effect prisoners of war. The officers rented houses in the vicinity and settled down for a long stay which was of great advantage to the social life of the neighborhood, as TJ well knew, for he made lasting friendships among the foreign officers. For a concise history of the Convention Troops, see A. J. Wall, "The Story of the Convention Army," NYHS, *Quart. Bull.*, XI (1927-1928), 67-99, with facsimiles, maps, views, and portraits; the fullest contemporary source, though not a trustworthy one, is *Travels through the Interior Parts of America*, London, 1789 (reprinted Boston and N.Y., 1923), by Thomas Anburey, an officer in Burgoyne's army. For TJ's relations with the officers and their families, see Randall, *Life*, I, 232-7, and Kimball, *Jefferson: War and Peace*, p. 33-45. He was doubtless prompted to write the present letter, on which he lavished the utmost pains, by hearing that the Virginia Council had pointed out to Congress the difficulty, if not impossibility, of provisioning the interned army; see JCC, XIII, 190, 216; see also the deliberations of Council in April on the problem of guarding the army against desertion or revolt (*Va. Council Jour.*, II, 254-5). THE COMMISSARY whose delinquencies TJ reflects on has not been identified with perfect certainty, though it may have been Col. William Finnie, deputy quartermaster general of the Southern Department, of whom there were official complaints in June (TJ to Theodorick Bland, 18 June 1779). His predecessor, John HAWKINS, whose conduct TJ praises, had been appointed Continental purchasing officer in Apr. 1778 but had died a few weeks afterward (*Va. Council Jour.*, II, 114, 139). Gaps in the minutes of Council prevent knowledge of Council's action on TJ's letter, but Congress disapproved removal, conditions at the encampment improved, and the Convention troops remained near Charlottesville until British operations in the South compelled their removal in Oct. 1780 (Wall, as cited above, p. 94-5).

1 Substituted for "May it please your Excellency."

2 Substituted for "your excellency."

3 "deeply" deleted.

4 Lost in margin of draft; supplied from the partial fair copy.

5 "become an intermediator" deleted.

6 This phrase substituted for "your excellency."

7 Substituted for "you."

8 Deleted at this point is the following parenthetical phrase: "(if I recollect it rightly, for I have no copy of it)."

9 Deleted at this point is the following: "Congress have not yet declared that Convention to be annulled. Will not a palpable breach of it then fix upon us the imputation of enormous want of faith in our public contracts and [. . .] it justly? Can the citizens of America acquiesce under such an imputation on their character, or will they not rather animadvert on and disavow it? If Congress should have declared the convention null (which they may have done, tho' I have not heard of it)."

10 Partial fair copy ends at this point.

11 "surely" deleted.

12 TJ first wrote "will be careful to avoid making" and in substituting the present phrase omitted the sign of the infinitive "to."

13 "at all" deleted.

14 Substituted for "smothering."

15 Deleted at this point is the following: "Nor should it be answered that our enemies are to pay this: I suppose that according to the usage of nations they are to pay for nothing but their subsistence."

16 TJ first wrote "£30,000."

17 Deleted at this point is the following: "Perhaps the magnitude of this question and it's general concern to the whole state might render it worth while to ask counsel from the General assembly which is now to sit within 6 weeks and there can be no danger arising within that time from a want of provision."

18 "the enjoiment of" deleted.

19 "great" deleted.

20 Substituted for "expanded itself over."

21 Substituted for "take."

22 "ferried from there to Richmond" deleted.

23 Thus in draft. No doubt meant to be pluralized, but neglected by TJ in revising this sentence, which originally read: "On the contrary a commissary should be displaced who after the next harvest should send one bushel of wheat from below the falls of the rivers."

24 TJ first wrote "three."

25 TJ first wrote "days."

26 Substituted for "as promising a prospect as can be conceived."

27 TJ first wrote "£300."

28 Substituted for "most of which he gave to the soldiers."

29 "house pigs" deleted.

30 Substituted for "provisions."

31 This sentence originally concluded as follows: "raise the idea of a well governed farm."

32 Substituted for "companies."

33 "perfectly" deleted.

34 Substituted for "our character."

35 This whole paragraph is written lengthwise in the margin and is now partly lost in the mounting sheet; matter in brackets supplied from Ford's text.

36 Lost in the margin; supplied from Ford.

37 Substituted for "blessing."

38 Substituted for "disagreeable."

To George Rogers Clark

SIR Williams[burg, March or April 1779]

Your letter and verba[l message] by Mr. St. Vrain was received today; your m[essage will be?] attended to. Much solicitude will be felt for the result of your expedition to the Wabash; it will at least delay their expedition to our frontier Settlements; and if Successful, have an important bearing ultimately in Establishing our North Western boundary. I am Sir your Mo. obt. [. . .]

TH: JEFFERSON

Tr (WHi). In an unidentified hand but with conjectural readings supplied in the hand of Lyman C. Draper, who added this memorandum respecting date and provenance: "T Jefferson to G R Clark. Evidently Clark wrote to Jefferson just before setting out from Kaskaskia on his Vincennes Expedition, Feb. 3d 1779. . . . This from Col. [Geo.] Hancock, Louisville, who showed me the original. L. C. D."

Clark had written Patrick Henry on 3 Feb. 1779, the day before he left Kaskaskia on his famous march against Vincennes, determined to "Risque the whole on a Single Battle" (*George Rogers Clark Papers, 1771-1781*, p. 98). Probably he wrote TJ about the same time, but his letter is missing. He was not heard from again until his letter of 29 Apr. 1779, q.v., reached Williamsburg after TJ had become governor. TJ's reply to Clark's missing letter, with its significant final clause, was apparently first printed in *Col. George Rogers Clark's Sketch of His Campaign in the Illinois in 1778-9*, ed. Henry Pirtle (*Ohio Valley Historical Series*, No. 3), Cincinnati, 1869, p. 2, note, without source and with the comment that the original is mutilated. It has been quoted by several historians since, but it was omitted by James from the *George Rogers Clark Papers*, and there would be serious doubt of its authenticity if Draper had not authenticated the transcript from which we print.

From Samuel Stanhope Smith

SIR [March? 1779].

I have had a transient view of a general scheme of education for this state, which I am informed was so far approved by the last Assembly as to be submitted to the consideration of the people and referred to a future session. The nature of the design must recommend it to every lover of learning and of his country; the idea was greatly imagined; and the whole plan bears an impression of the wisdom of antiquity, when legislation and philosophy were always connected, and but different parts of the same sage characters. I entertain no doubt of its importance and utility; but whether it be practicable in the present state of opinions and parties in this country is a more dubious point. It is that which has induced me a stranger to address a letter to you, who are reputed to be the author of the plan; whose rank and character at least must give you a principal share in carrying it into effect. I foresee that the chief obstacle to its execution will arise from the variety of religious sentiments that exist in the state. The expence that will unavoidably attend it ought not to create the least difficulty in the breast of a wise legislator. It is applying money to its most valuable and important use. The opposition of parties will create a barrier of a different kind. Each solicitous for their own preservation and jealous of their antagonists, will be very scrupulous with regard to the character and *profession* of the teacher to whom they are going to intrust their children. In many places the public master will be deserted by half his hundred, and a rival opposed to him in the same neighbourhood. And the present disposition of the people is such as to render it dangerous to attempt to compel them to abide by the choice which the state may make for them in their schools, more than in their churches; or to contribute to support a man whose services they do not use. However, this difficulty might be considerably alleviated in the hundred schools by a few precautions, if matters were reconciled in the higher schools or academies, and in the university. Whatever party enjoys the preeminence in these will insensibly gain upon the others, and soon acquire the government of the state. This contest will chiefly lie betwixt the Presbyterians and the Episcopalians. The Baptists and Methodists content themselves with other kinds of illuminations than are afforded by human science. In the scheme, I observe that *William & Mary* is to be the university; and her visitors and professors will enjoy the power of appointing the academical and other masters, and of prescribing the system of education. Be assured Sir, that while she continues under her present influence, the proposal will alarm the whole body of Presbyterians. In their view it will be erecting a noble fabric upon too contracted a bottom, and they will oppose it. It will be insufficient to say that in the present dearth of capable professors, the learned among them may possibly find some place. The security is not precise and well ascertained. The jealousy of parties is eager eyed, and can espy dangers under very handsome appearances. The partialities of sects indeed ought to have no place in a system of liberal education. They are the disgrace of science and would to Heaven it were possible utterly to banish them from the society of men. But such is our misfortune; they exist; and they exist in considerable force. A direct attack upon them, or even the most oblique, where it is discerned, serves only to inflame an evil that might be palliated, if not effectually cured by generous and candid measures. The very name of party, altho a man should be as far from believing the peculiar dogmas of his own sect, as of that which he opposes for its sake; yet the *name* is apt to inflame his passions, to produce a blind and perverse zeal for his partizans, and to plant round him eyes of jealousy, and points of steel. How few are possessed of that cool and philosophic temper, and that confinement of sentiment that is necessary to overcome this unhappy influence! And these few are usually the men who are the least trusted by their own faction. I said the Presbyterians as a separate sect would oppose the intrusting another sect with the election of their masters and professors, and with the power of prescribing their forms of education. They are a numerous body, and not destitute of learning, whose concurrence may be found necessary on the present occasion, and whose opposition may embarrass, if not disconcert any *general* scheme of education wherein they are neglected, and likely to be undermined. Good God! What suspicions, what animosities divide the disciples of a religion whose ruling maxim is charity and love! It is time to heal these divisions, as well for the honour of religion, as in order to promote the noblest literary design to which this or any other country has given birth. Difference of external forms and names will always preserve the same distrustful, narrow, and contentious spirit, equally detrimental to religion and to learning. It will indeed excite the emulation of the antagonists; but it will direct that emulation too much to the defence of their characteristic peculiarities, and thus in reality contract the free spirit and the sphere of science, and substitute bigotry and prejudice in the room of true philosophy. Each will endeavour to defeat a system of education in which the other enjoys the superiority. Whereas if they were united under one denomination their efforts, instead of being divided and opposed, would concenter on one object, and concur in advancing the same important enterprize. My extreme love of peace, of that benevolence which my religion recommends, and of enlarged and liberal inquiry in matters of science, makes me wish for a union, at least of the two capital sects of christians [in] this state. And this appears to me to be the most favourable moment in which such a design could be proposed. Nor do I think it by any means impracticable if one party will descend a little from that pride and insolence; and the other relax somewhat of that rigour and austerity that have hitherto characterized them. This I conceive would be an effectual measure, and indeed the only one, to give effect [to] this new literary system. If you should think it feasible, [or that] it would in any degree promote the object you have in view my small influence on one of the parties, and my utmost exertions shall be at your service. But till

I know your opinion of it, I shall say no more upon the subject. I have no personal interest that I know of in making the proposal. In my present situation my honour, in the common acceptation of that word, and my interest seem rather to oppose it. However when religion, learning, or my country's good require my aid, I would not wish to occupy a place that would be injurious to either. I have no ambition to become the leader of a sect. And I may add to this that I do not expect to continue in Virginia long enough to reap any advantage by the change, were any to be gained. But it would make me happy before I go, to contribute to the success of so salutary a project. If you approve of my opinion, I shall hope by some means to know it. If not, I beg that it may remain a secret with you and that whatever judgment you may pass upon the judiciousness and propriety of my present interposition, you would, at least attribute it to good motives; for such alone have influenced Sir, yr. mo. hbl. servt.,

SAML. S SMITH

RC (ViWC). Addressed: "Thomas Jefferson Esqr. Favd. by Mr. C: Wingfield." Endorsed in TJ's hand.

This important and recently discovered letter is a critique by the then rector of Hampden-Sydney Academy (later Hampden-Sydney College), who was to become an eminent leader in the Presbyterian Church, a philosopher of some reputation, and 7th president of the College of New Jersey at Princeton, of TJ's GENERAL SCHEME OF EDUCATION for Virginia, which had been introduced in the House of Delegates on 16 Dec. 1778 as a "bill for the more general diffusion of knowledge" and which is printed below as Bill No. 79 in the Revisal of the Laws, 18 June 1779, q.v. Though on 18 Dec. 1778 the public printer was ordered "forthwith to print and forward four copies of the said act to each county," it is very doubtful that the Bill was printed (JHD, Oct. 1778, 1827 edn., p. 117, 120). No copy has been found; Samuel Smith had apparently not seen one when he next wrote TJ (19 Apr. 1779, q.v.), and neither had Edmund Pendleton when he discussed the subject in his letter to TJ of 11 May. Dr. E. G. Swem is of the opinion that, since Purdie had difficulty in securing paper, he could not print every item ordered (Swem, "Va. Bibliog.," II, p. 1064; also a communication to the editors, 5 Oct. 1949). IT WOULD MAKE ME HAPPY BEFORE I GO: Smith went north on a visit soon afterward and before the end of the year was appointed professor of moral philosophy at Princeton; Smith still lacks a biographer, but there is a good recent account of his career by Samuel H. Monk in *The Lives of Eighteen From Princeton*, ed. Willard Thorp, Princeton, 1946, p. 86-110.

From George Mason

DEAR SIR Gunston-Hall, April 3rd. 1779.

The Indiana Company, I hear, are preparing to defend their Claim, under the Indian Purchase; which is to come before the Assembly, on the third Monday in May next; and will of Course, I suppose, desire to be heard at the Bar of the House: if it will be agreeable to You to answer the Arguments of their Counsel, I will undertake to open the Matter, on Behalf of the Commonwealth.

The Treaty with the six Nations of Indians at Lancaster in 1744, with the Deed then obtain'd from them, and also the Treaty at Logs-Town in 1752, with the Deed of Confirmation then obtained, will I apprehend be very material: after endeavouring in vain, by every Means in my Power, to procure them, I have now applyed, by Letter, to Mr. Waller; and beg'd the Favour of him, if he knows in what Office they were lodged or recorded, to procure me either the Originals, or authenticated Copys, against the meeting of the Assembly; as You will probably see him before I shall, I entreat You to remind him of it. Perhaps our Friend Mr. Wythe can inform You how they are to be got.

I have, since I came up from the last Session, drawn over again the two Bills for establishing a Land-Office, and for adjusting and setling the Claims to unpatented Lands under the former Government &c. in which I have provided for some Omissions, and Difficultys in the Execution; but have made no material Alterations in the plan which You and I had agreed on in the Bills in Janry. 1778, except one, in the Land-Office Bill; which I will submit to Your Consideration, when we meet, and be governed in it entirely by Your Opinion. I have not in these Bills taken any Notice of Escheats;[1] if You think that Subject may be more properly provided for in the Land-Office Bill, than by a separate Bill, I must beg the Favour of You to consider it, and draw a Clause for the Purpose before the Assembly meets; for I think it will be best to push these Laws in the next Session: they have been too long delayed already, to the great Loss of the Public; and the Confusion among the People in the back Country will be every Day encreasing, until Laws are made to settle the present, and remove the Cause of future Disputes. Having lived always in the Northern Neck, I am altogether unacquainted with the Mode of Proceeding in the Case of Escheats, under the former Government.

I wish You also to consider what will be a proper Price to fix the Purchase Money of the back Lands at; there will be great Variety of Opinion upon the Subject. I have been thinking of 25£ or 30.£ Per hund. acres; which I am of Opinion they will readily sell for. On the other Side are some Remarks on the Reasonableness of the Demand. I have been so roughly handled by the Gout this Winter (having had two Fits since I came from the Assembly, the last a most dangerous one in my Stomach) that I believe I shou'd have resolved to quit all public Business; had I not, just before, given my Word to some of my Constituents, that I wou'd serve them another Year.

I beg my Compliments to Your Lady; and am, dear Sir, Your affecte. Friend & Servt., G. MASON

ENCLOSURE

The ancient Terms of granting Lands under the Crown.

	Curry.
Composition 10/ Ster: ℔ hund: Acres, at 25 ℔ Ct., Exchange	0..12..6.
Annual Quitrent 2/ Ster: 2/6 Curry.; which being Part of the Consideration, & now abolished, is estimated low at 20 Years Purchase	2..10..0.
	3.. 2..6.
Suppose the present Depreciation, from Gold & Silver, to be eight for one, which is the lowest it can be called, it is now as easy to pay eight Shillings, as formerly one.	8.
	£25.. 0..0.

But the legal Par of Exchange has been raised from 25. to 33.⅓ ℔ Ct. Composition of 10/ Ster: is then	0..13..4.
Quitrent of 2/ Ster: 2/8 Curry., at 20 Year's Purchase	2..13..4.
	3.. 6..8.
	8.
	£26..13..4.

I saw the new Instructions from the Crown to Ld. Dunmore in 1774, to grant no Lands in future, under 50/ Ster: ℔ hund. Acres, & a Quitrent of a Ha'penny Ster: Per Acre.

	Curry.
Composition, or Purchase-Money 50/ Ster: at 33.⅓d. Exchange	3.. 6..8.
Quitrent 4/2 Ster: 5/6.½ Curry., at 20 Years Purchase	5..10.10.
	8..17..6.
	8.
So that, had the old Government continued, Lands wou'd now cost the Taker-up, a Sum Per hund. Acres, equal in our present Money to	£71.. 0..0.

But it may be said that our Money will appreciate
So will the back Lands.

There is a Circumstance too in this kind of Purchase, different from all others; for tho' the Payment is substantial and real to the State, it is, in some Measure, nominal to the Payer; who with the very Money he is purchasing an Estate for his Posterity is discharging them of so much in Taxes; which must otherwise, one Day or other, come out of their other Property.

RC (DLC). Addressed: "Thomas Jefferson Esqr." Enclosure printed herewith.

For the background of the matters discussed in this letter, see Bills for Adjusting and Settling the Titles of Claimers to Unpatented Lands and for Establishing a Land Office printed above under 8-14 Jan. 1778.

[1] TJ drew the Bill concerning Escheats (q.v., 4 June 1779).

From William Phillips

Blenheim Sunday Evening April 11th. 1779

Major General Phillips sends his Compliments to Mr. and Mrs. Jefferson, requests the favour of their company at dinner on Thursday next at Two o'clock to meet General and Madame de Reidesel. Major General Phillips hopes Miss Jefferson will be permitted to be of the party to meet the young Ladies from Collè.

RC (DLC).

Maj. Gen. William Phillips was the ranking officer of the Convention Army; while in Albemarle co. he lived at Edward Carter's house, Blenheim, which still stands (DNB; Rawlings, *Ante-Bellum Charlottesville*, p. 9). The REIDESEL family (Maj. Gen. Friederich Adolph, Baron von Riedesel, commander of the Brunswick troops in British service, the Baroness Frederika von Riedesel, and their three young daughters) were established at COLLE, Philip Mazzei's house and farm near Monticello, where they lived upon an ample scale; see Riedesel's *Memoirs, Letters and Journals . . .*, transl. W. L. Stone, Albany, 1868, II, 66ff.; and Mme. Riedesel's *Letters and Journals*, ed. W. L. Stone, Albany, 1867, p. 143ff. MISS JEFFERSON: Martha, TJ's eldest child, born 1772.

From William Phillips

Monday April 12th. 1779

Majr. Genl. Phillips sends his compliments to Mr. Jefferson. He would with much pleasure wait on Mr. Jefferson next Wednesday, but is engaged for that day at dinner with his family at General Reidesel's.

RC (DLC).

From Samuel Stanhope Smith

Sir — Hampden-Sydney April 19th 1779

I beg your pardon for having writen to you prematurely. I confess I had never seen the printed bill, and having waited for it a long time, I began to be afraid that negligent printer would not publish it before the next session of Assembly. I am much indebted to you for the obliging pains you have taken to inform me of its nature and design. I was mistaken with regard to the appointment of teachers particularly in the grammar schools, and utterly unacquainted with the new regulations proposed to be introduced into the College of Wm. & Mary. It is difficult however to persuade a very considerable part of the state that that institution can ever be delivered from the influence of party; and that, being the principal hope of a Church already greatly mortified to have fallen from absolute power, every effort will not be exerted to retain it in its former channel. To prevent if possible this collision of parties, and to preclude the unhappy effects their mutual jealousies might have upon this, and every similar bill, was my chief motive in proposing a coalition of the principal religious sects, and as many others as were willing to unite upon the same catholic foundation. I had no idea of a legal establishment; and I conceive that the civil constitution might erect such barriers against it as should be impassable by ecclesiastical ambition. The reasons for a public religion have always appeared to me inconclusive. If christianity is of divine original it will support itself or forfeit its pretensions; and upon this principle it first undertook to disciple the world. And if there be no religion of divine authority except the religion of nature, the state may well be contented to leave men in the condition which the Diety himself hath left them with regard to his worship, and permit every man to be his own interpreter of that natural law. I was in hopes that the enlightened sentiments of the present age had dispelled the gloomy spirit of bigottry, that formerly accuminated the minds of men so much against each other to the great disgrace of religion; especially when interest, and the spirit of party were out of the question. Interest I expected to preclude by destroying the hope of establishments; and party by a union under one denomination. And when united, I hoped that their endeavours would concur, without being divided and weakened by mean distrusts and jealousies, in advancing the generous schemes of education proposed by the Assembly. I am aware, however, that the speculations of the closet are often very wide of the sentiments and manners of actual life. But I foresee a contest betwixt these parties, if they are to continue separate, from which I hope to withdraw before it commences. It is not to be expected that a sect elated by customary dominion will resign her interest and her superiority without the most obstinate struggle. And I am well informed that a gentleman in the judicial department, of no inconsiderable influence, and merit in other respects, has actually digested a system of religious laws, and prepared his liturgies &c. to be brought before the legislature at a convenient time, and by a party to be regularly formed for the engagement, against men undisciplined and unprepared to meet them. So that till something definitive be done upon the subject of religion, I am still of opinion that distrust will combat this bill; because the intire direction of the College is too great an acquisition to be easily resigned to any party. And such an acquisition will infallibly follow an establishment, if that should unfortunately take place after having settled by law this general system of education. If this matter as well decided upon any plan, I think the reform introduced into the College by the second bill, if the Assembly will adopt it, and resolutely take the direction of that institution into their own hands, will remove a capital objection against the authority of her Visitors. Yet, is not the situation of the College inconvenient? Will not the Visitors generally be appointed in the neighbouring Counties for the ease of meeting to transact their business? Are they not by their situation and their prejudices more liable to religious partialities than those in the middle Counties of the state? Would not the place of the College be better altered not only on that account, but for the health of the students, and the convenience of the people? Would not two universities by their emulation have a favourable influence on learning? In prescribing a system of education, would it not be better for the Assembly to take it more immediately under their own direction? Whatever partialities may be feared to infect a College or a few Visitors, the people always confide in their own representatives more than in such particular bodies of men, and such fears do not regard them in so great a degree. Indeed the annual appointment of Visitors will make every such matter ultimately rest in the Assembly. But in my opinion it would give more authority to the system of education and be more satisfactory to the public, if it were compiled by a select body of men appointed for that *particular* purpose, out of different denominations, subject to the review of the Assembly, and finally enacted by it. There might be regular periods appointed when this system should be subject to a revision, and any alterations in it proposed and enacted in the same manner. You however are much the best judge of this subject. I confide intirely in your known liberality of sentiment. And while I continue in Virginia shall to the utmost of my power promote your intentions with those men on whom I have any influence even if they should indirectly have an aspect somewhat unfavourable to the party to which I am thought to belong. For it is better that one sect should suffer a little than that the general interests of learning should be injured. I am obliged to you for the polite manner in which you promise me an answer; but I expect to be in Pennsilvania and the Jerseys till the middle of June, and therefore cannot have the pleasure of receiving it before the Session of Assembly. I am, Sir, with great respect, your Mo. hbl. servt.,

SAML S SMITH

RC (ViWC). Without indication of addressee, but manifestly a reply to TJ's (missing) answer to Smith's letter printed above at the end of March 1779, q.v.

TJ's most unfortunately missing answer to Smith's earlier letter evidently described the whole plan of educational reform which the Committee of Revisors had in mind, including THE NEW REGULATIONS PROPOSED TO BE INTRODUCED INTO THE COLLEGE OF WM. & MARY, i.e., Bill No. 80 in the Revision of the Laws, 18 June 1779, q.v. The GENTLEMAN IN THE JUDICIAL DEPARTMENT who had a different plan has not been identified.

To Richard Henry Lee

DEAR SIR Monticello Apr. 21. 1779.

Among the convention prisoners in this neighborhood is a Baron de Geismar of the Germans, brigade-major to Genl. Gall, whose situation I would wish to make you acquainted with. He is the only son of a German nobleman, and has I beleive an only sister; his Father, now 70 years of age, if living; and excessively anxious to see him before his death: his patrimonial expectations in danger of being transferred to others in the weak state of his father, or perhaps plundered in case of his death; the footing on which he stands with his prince such as might give him reason to hope for promotion were he on the spot, but every thing of that kind certain of passing by him as long as he is absent. Under these circumstances captivity is peculiarly injurious to him, and he petitions Congress to exchange him if possible, or otherwise permit him to return home on any parole they will prescribe. I am satisfied he will carry with him no dispositions to injure us; and his personal merit, with which I am become intimately acquainted, entitles him to every indulgence consistent with the indispensable rules of Congress. I take the liberty of recommending his request to your sollicitation, as from a knolege of the man I am become interested in his happiness; whatever you can do for him will be considered as a peculiar obligation on Dr. Sir, Your friend & servt., TH: JEFFERSON

RC (NjSum). Addressed: "The Honble. Richard Henry Lee esq. of the Virginia delegation Philadelphia." Endorsed: "April 21. 1779 Thos. Jefferson Esqr." Tr (ViU).

BARON DE GEISMAR: For TJ's subsequent relations with this young officer of the Hesse Hanau regiment, see Kimball, *Jefferson: War and Peace*, p. 40-5; see also Lee's answer to TJ, 22 May 1779.

George Rogers Clark to Patrick Henry

Dr. Sir Kaskaskias Illinois Apl: 29th. 1779

A few days ago I received certain intelligence of William Morris my express to you being killed near the falls of Ohio news truly disagreeable to me as I fear many of my letters will fall into the hands of the Enemy at Detroit altho some of them as I learn were found in the woods torn in pieces. I do not doubt but before the receipt of this you will he[ar] of my late success against Governor Hamilton at post St. Vincenne. That gentleman with a body of men possessed himself of that post on the 15th. of December last repaired the fortifications for a repository and in the spring means to attack this place which he made no doubt of carrying, where he was to be joined by 200 Indians from Mechetemachinoi and 500 cherokees chiccasaws and other nations. With this body he was to penetrate up the Ohio to Fort Pitt, sweaping Kentuckey on his way having light brass Cannon for the purpose, joined on his way by all the Indians that could be got to him. He made no doubt but that he could force all West Augusta. This expedition was ordered by the commander in cheif of Canada. Destruction seemed to hover over us from every quarter detached parties of the Enemy in the neighbourhood every day but afraid to attack. I ordered Majr. Bowman to evacuate the fort at the Cohas and join me immediately which he did. Having not received a scrape of a pen from you for near twelve months I could see but little probability of keeping possession of the country as my number of men was too small [to] stand a seige and my situation too remote to call for assistance. I made all the preparations I possibly could for the attack and was necessitated to set fire to some of the houses in Town to clear them out of the way, but in the height of the hurry a Spanish merchant who had been at St. Vincenne arrived and gave the following intelligence. That Mr. Hamilton had weakened himself by sending his Indians against the Frontiers and to block up the Ohio; that he had not more than eighty men in garrison three pieces of Cannon and some swivils mounted that he intended to attack this place as soon as the winter opened and made no doubt of clearing the western waters by the fall. My situation and circumstances induced me to fall on the resolution of attacking him before he could collect his

Indians again. I was sensible the resolution was as desperate as my situation but I saw no other probability of securing the country. I immediately dispatched of a small galley which I had fitted up mounting two four pounders and four swivils with a company of men and necessary stores on board with orders to force her way if possible and station herself a few miles below the Enemy suffer nothing to pass her and wait for further orders. In the mean time I marched across the country with 130 men being all I could raise after leaving this place garrisoned by the militia. The inhabitants of the country behaved exceedingly well. Numbers of young men turned out on the expedition and every other one embodied to guard the different towns. I marched the 7th of February altho so small a body it took me 16 days on the route. The inclemency of the season high waters &c. seemed to threaten the loss of the expedition. When within three leagues of the Enemy it took us five days to cross the drowned lands of the Wawbash river having to wade often upwards of two leagues to our breast in water. Had not the weather been warm we must have perished. But on the evening of the 23d we got on dry land in sight of the Enemy and at seven Oclock made the attack before they knew any thing of us. The Town immediately surrendered with joy and assisted in the seige. Th[ere] was a continual fire on both sides for eighteen hours. I had no expectation of gaining the fort until the arrival of my artillery. The moon setting about one oclock I had an intrenchment thrown up in rifle shot of their strongest battery and poured such showers of well directed balls into their post that we silenced two pieces of Cannon in 15 minutes without getting a man hurt. Governor Hamilton and myself had on the following day several conferences but did not agree until the evening when he agreed to surrender the garrison (79 in number) prisoners of war with considerable stores. I got only one man wounded not being able to lose many I made them secure themselves well. Seven badly wounded in the fort thro' the ports. In the height of this action an Indian party that had been to war and taken two prisoners came in not knowing of us. Hearing of them I dispatched a party to give them battle in the commons and got nine of them with the two prisoners which proved to be Frenchmen. Hearing of a convoy of goods from Detroit I sent a party of 60 men in armed boats well mounted with swivils to meet them before they should receive any intelligence. They met the Convoy 40 leagues up the river and made a prize of the whole taking 40 prisoners and about £10,000 worth of goods and provisions also the mail from Canada to Governor Hamilton no news of importance. But what crowned the general joy was the arrival of William Morris my express to you with your letters which gave general satisfaction. The Soldiery being made sensible of the gratitude of their country for their services were so much elated that they would have attempted the reduction of Detroit had I have ordered them. Having more prisoners than I knew what to do with I was necessitated to discharge a greater part of them on parole. Mr. Hamilton his principal officers and a few soldiers I have sent to Kentuckey under convoy of Capt. Williams in order to be conducted to you: After dispatching Morris with letters to you treating with the neighbouring Indians &c. I returned to this place leaving a sufficient garrison at St. Vincenne. During my absence, Capt. Robert George who now commands the company formerly Capt. Willing['s] had returned from new Orleans which greatly added to our strength. It gave great satisfaction to the inhabitants when acquainted with the protection which was given them, the alliance with France &c. I am impatient for the arrival of Colo. Montgomery but have heard nothing of him lately. By your instructions to me I find you put no confidence in Genl. Mckintosh's taking Detroit as you encourage me to attempt it if possible. It has been twice in power. Had I been able to raise only 500 men when I first arrived in the country, lastly when I was at St. Vincenne could I have secured my prisoners and only had 300 good men I should have attempted it and since learn there could have been no doubt of success as by some gentlemen lately from that post we are informed that the Town and country kept three days in feasting and diversions on hearing of my success against Mr. Hamilton and was so certain of my embracing the fair opportunity of possessing myself of that post that the merchants and others provided many necessaries for us on our arrival the garrison consisting of only eighty men not daring to stop their diversions. They are now completing a new fort and I fear too strong for any force I shall ever be able to raise in this country. We are proud to hear congress intends putting her forces on the frontiers under your direction. A small army from Pittsburgh conducted with spirit may easily take Detroit and put an end to the Indian war. Those Indians who are active against us are the six nations part of the Shawnese the Meamonies and about half the chesaweys Ottawas Iowaa's and Poutawatimas nations bordering on the Lakes. Those nations who have treated with me have behaved since very well to wit, the Peankishaws Kicapoues Oreaottenaws of the Waubash river, the Kaskias, Perrians Mechigamies, Foxes, Socks, opays Illinois and poues nations of the Mississispi and Illinois rivers. Part of the chessaways have also treated and are peaceable. I continually keep agents among them to watch their motions and keep them peaceably inclined. Many of the cherokees chiccasaws and their confederates are I fear ill disposed. It would be well if Colo. Montgomery should give them a dressing as he comes down the Tenissee. There can be no peace expected from many nations while the English are at Detroit. I strongly suspect they will turn their arms against the Illinois as they will be encouraged. I shall always be on my guard watching every opportunity to take the advantage of the Enemy and if I am ever able to muster six or seven hundred men I shall give them a shorter distance to come and fight me than at this place. There is one circumstance very distressing which is that of our money's being discredited to all intents and purposes by the great number of traders who come here in my absence each out bidding the other giving prices unknown in this country by 500 ℔ cent by which the people conceived it to be of no value and both French and Spaniards refused to take a farthing of it. Provision is three times the price it was two months past and to be got by no other means than my own bonds goods or force. Several merchants are now advancing considerable sums of their own property rather than the service should suffer by which I am sensible they must suffer greatly unless some method is taken to raise the credit of our coin or a fund sent to Orleans for the payment of the expences of this place which would at once reduce the price of every species of provisions money being of little service to them unless it would pass at the posts they trade at. I mentioned to you my drawing some Bills on Mr. Pollock in new Orleans. As I had no money with me he would accept the Bills but had not money to pay them off tho the sums were trifling so that we have little credit to expect from that quarter. I shall take every step I possibly can for laying up a sufficient quantity of provisions and hope you will immediately send me an express with your instructions. Public expences in this country have hitherto been very low and may still continue so if a correspondence is fixed at New Orleans for payment of expences in this country or gold and silver sent. I am glad to hear of Colo. Todds appointment. I think Government has taken the only step they could have done to make this country flourish and be of service to them. No other regulation could have suited the people. The last account I had of Colo. Rogers was his being in new Orleans with six of his men, the rest he left at the Spanish Ozack above the Natches. I shall immedeately send him some provisions as I learn he is in great want. I doubt he will not be able to get his goods up the River except in Spanish bottoms. One Regiment would be able to clear the Mississippi and do great damage to the British interest in Florida and by properly conducting themselves might perhaps gain the affection of the people so as to raise sufficient force to give a shock to Pensacola. Our alliance with France has entirely devoted this people to our interest. I have sent several copies of the articles to Detroit and do not doubt but they will answer the desired effect. Your instructions I shall pay implicit regard to and hope to conduct myself in such a manner as to do honour to my country.

I am with the greatest respect your hbl. servant, G R CLARK

P. S. I understand there is a considerable quantity of Cannon ball at Pittsburg. We are much in want of four and six pound ball. I hope you will immediately order some down.

Tr (DLC) of an enclosure sent in TJ's letter to Washington, 19 June 1779.

Though addressed to Gov. Henry, Clark's dispatch (the second he had sent) relating the capture of Fort Sackville at Vincennes, 25 Feb. 1779, was received by TJ early in June. On GOVERNOR HAMILTON (Henry Hamilton, Lt. Gov. of Detroit), see TJ to Theodorick Bland, 8 June 1779, and references there. YOUR LETTERS: Henry to Clark, 15 and 16 Dec. 1778 (*George Rogers Clark Papers, 1771-1781*, p. 87-9). COLO. TODDS APPOINTMENT: As county lieutenant of Illinois co., established by an Act of this session of the Assembly (Hening, IX, 552-5).

To Gabriel Jones

DEAR SIR Monticello, April 29th, 1779.

By Mrs. Harvey I enclose to you the principal and interest of the money you were so kind as to lend me some years ago. It furnishes me also with an occasion of acknowledging, with this, the many other obligations under which you have laid me, of which I shall always be proud to shew a due sense, whenever opportunity shall offer.

I am, Dear Sir, with much esteem, Your friend and servt.,

TH: JEFFERSON

MS not located. Printed from the Richmond *Recorder*, 4 June 1803, where it appears, together with a statement by Jones, as part of a serial attack by James T. Callender on the President.

The Callender-Jones charge, first made in the *Recorder* for 8 Dec. 1802, was that TJ, having borrowed £50 in 1773, dishonorably attempted to pay back the debt and interest in depreciated paper money. Two relevant entries will be found in TJ's Account Book under 29 Sep. 1773 and 28 Apr. 1779. Jones refused this mode of payment, and TJ later repaid the loan in hard money while minister to France. What Jones and Callender regarded as a very nefarious act on TJ's part was perfectly legal, and anyway Jones eventually got his money back; but personal vilification was Callender's specialty, and all was grist to his mill. Over the signature "Timoleon" an answer to Callender's charge was promptly published in the Richmond *Examiner* and reprinted in the *National Intelligencer*, 1 July 1803: it points out that TJ repaid the debt in hard money as soon as hard money became available after Jones' refusal of paper money. Another answer, signed "Veritas" and believed to have been written by Philip Grymes, was printed and circulated as an address "To Gabriel Jones," 20 July 1803 (2-page leaflet without imprint, DLC: Broadsides Collection). "Veritas" declared that Jones had suppressed a material fact, namely, that Mrs. Harvie had given Jones, along with TJ's letter, a verbal message, to the effect that TJ would make payment in hard money as soon as possible if Jones declined accepting paper money. The remainder of Grymes' address is a violent attack on Jones' ethics as lawyer and citizen. TJ Editorial Files contain evidence that, so late as 1949, the Callender-Jones charge, in fancifully adumbrated form, was still being repeated as family legend.

To William Phillips

[April? 1779]

I should have been very happy to have seen you yesterday as I shall be at all times when you can make it convenient to call on us. The great cause which divides our countries is not to be decided by individual animosities. The harmony of private societies cannot weaken national efforts. To contribute by neighborly intercourse and attentions to make others happy is the shortest and surest way of being happy ourselves. As these sentiments seem to have directed your conduct, we should be as unwise as illiberal were we not to preserve the same temper of mind. It is my wish therefore particularly as I am pleased to see it yours that we keep up the intercourse which has begun between our families.

I am to thank you for your kind offer in the close of your letter. We have hitherto been supplied in a tolerable degree with those things which are most necessary. I should hardly be able to reconcile it to myself to encroach on those stores provided for your own comfort and that of those with you.

The orders you desire with respect to the bricks shall be given. I am &c.

Dft (MoSHi), attached to Phillips' letter to TJ, 18 June 1779. Corrections made by TJ in the course of composition are not noted here.

Quite probably TJ's first letter to Phillips; the letter to which it is a reply is missing.

From Richard Henry Lee

Dear Sir Philadelphia May the 3d. 1779

Always attentive to your commands, I have obtained here, and now inclose you the song and the receipt you desired. I once had both of them at home, but they are mislaid among a mass of papers, so that I could find neither previous to my leaving Chantilly, or your request would then have been complied with. I hope you have received the pamphlet I sent you some weeks ago entitled "Observations on the American revolution" containing a collection of the most material congress papers with a few remarks interspersed, in order to shew in one comprehensive view the progress of our glorious revolution, and to rectify some false representations of the British Commissioners. This pamphlet was sent by an Express that came here from Mr. Harvey, and returned to Williamsburg, with intention to follow Mr. Harvey to Albemarle if he found him not at the former of these places. I wish it were in my power to entertain you with news, but we are here as void of that as if profound peace reigned thro' out the world. We have not heard from Europe for four months and altho there then seemed a disposition in many Powers to restore the general tranquility, yet all were industriously preparing for war, and some being actually engaged, the fate of millions hung in doubtful ballance.

The armies here continue quiet within their quarters. That of the enemy by their late embarkation of nine regiments, rendered too weak for taking the field, must content itself with holding N. York as the Gibralter of N. America. If we can baffle the Southern invasion, it [is] clear to me that the game will be presently up with our enemies, and that they will be compelled by inevitable necessity to be content with the loss of thirteen flourishing states. A very fit consequence of the foolish and wicked attempt to reduce to slavery so many free useful, and affectionate friends. I hope that when you and my other friends consider all things, that you will not blame me for send[ing] my resignation to the Assembly. I am realy injured in my health by such continued, close application; and a long neglected numerous family demands some attention. Add to these, that persecuted as I have been by the united voice of toryism, peculation, faction, envy, m[alice] and all uncharitableness, nothing but the certain prospect of doing essential service to my country can compensate for the injuries I receive. It would content me indeed to sacrifice every considerat[ion] to the public good that would result from such persons as yourse[lf,] Mr. Wythe,

Mr. Mason and some others being in Congress. I would wi[th] persevering ardor press thro every difficulty in conjunction with such Associates. I am informed that Colo. Blackburn intends to propose a bi[ll] this Session for the relief of Landlords. I should suppose that the wisd[om] and justice of the Legislature can and will devise some remedy for the [relief] of this class of people among us. I am one, who have the misfortune to [see] myself and family nearly ruined by the retrospective effect of our law. Almost the whole of my landed estate was rented out some years before [the] war for low cash rents, and under the faith of existing law which secur[ed] me specie for my rents. The vast sums of paper money that have been issued (this being now a tender for the discharge of rents growing from old contracts) and the consequent depreciation, has well nigh effected an entire transfer of my estate to my Tenants. This year Sir, the rents of 4000 acres of fine Land will not buy me 20 barrels of Corn! I am very far from desiring that the law should place these contracts litterally as they were, but substantially so, if it seems just that they should be. When the Tenant agreed to pay me £6. for an hund. acres rent he could not sell his Tobo. for more than 16 or 18 shillings an hundred. Now he sells his Tobo. for £10 and 12 per Cent. It does not appear to me that the public good can be concerned in thus transfering the property of Landlords to their Tenants. But public justice demands that the true meaning and genuine spirit of contracts should be complied with. It appears to me that an Act of Commutation might set this business right by directing the payment in produce at the prevailing price of such produce when the Contracts were made, leaving this to be settled by the Courts annually as they formerly did in the case of exchange. I well know your love of justice to be such that your approbation will be given to any proper plan for doing right in the premisses. For my own part, I am willing to suffer every thing rather than injure the public cause, but in the present state of things I can see no possibility of public injury from thus rendering private justice. I am with much esteem and regard dear Sir your most obedient and very humble Servant,

Richard Henry Lee

RC (DLC). Enclosures missing.

The SONG and RECEIPT, which Lee secured from Mr. Peters and Mrs. Shippen (R. H. Lee to TJ, 15 Mch. 1779) have not been identified. Lee's RESIGNATION from Congress was read in the House of Delegates on 15 May 1779 (JHD, May 1779, 1827 edn., p. 9). The INJURIES Lee suffered were occasioned by Silas Deane's attacks on his brothers William and Arthur, which were widely published in America in Jan. 1779 (R. H. Lee, *Letters*, II, 1-26). No bill was passed in the Virginia General Assembly for the adjustment and settlement of CONTRACTS in depreciated paper money until the session of Nov. 1781 (Hening, X, 471-4).

From William Fleming

DEAR SIR Philadelphia, 10th May, 1779.

I wish it were in my power to write you satisfactorily on the state of our public affairs. My residence here is of too short a date to enable to form a proper judgment of them. There are matters of great concern now before congress, of which I am not at liberty to speak freely, tho' I am of opinion we may have peace on honorable and advantageous terms, in the course of the ensuing winter. We have pretty certain intelligence that a considerable reinforcement (the N. York papers of the 1st. of May say 8000 men) will be sent over immediately; and if so there will, no doubt, be an active campaign, which it is generally supposed will be chiefly confined to the southern states, where we are the most vulnerable—and from thence the enemy can more easily withdraw their troops to the West Indies, if occasion should require it.

I beg I may not be put in nomination at the ensuing election of delegates to serve in congress; as I find it next to impossible for me to serve longer than til August, should my country be disposed to continue me here; for besides my own loss of time; and the long separation from my family, my expences are so enormous that I find my fortune quite insufficient to support them. I am in private lodgings, with only a servant and two horses, which are in the continental stable, and I live as frugal as possible, notwithstanding which it costs me, at least, 25£ a week, over and above my wages. If our assembly do not determine to support their delegates in congress, they will shortly find that none of those of small fortunes will be able to continue here long enough to make themselves acquainted with the business they come to transact, so as to render them essential service; for I think I already discover men here who have local views, highly detrimental to the general good of the union.

Beef is from 12 to 15/ a pound, butter 20/, good lamb 20 dollars a quarter, and every thing else proportionably dear, and rising daily. From hence you may form some idea of what the dec[ent] support of your delegates will require. I wish not to put a shilling of public money in my pocket, and as the necessaries of life are daily rising, and what would now be an adequate allowance will not be so a month hence, I think it would be better for the delegates [to] render an account of their expences, and let them be paid by the treasurer. No man who could not be trusted to render a just account deserves a seat in congress.

You will pardon the liberty I have taken of mentioning this

subject to you. I did it from a conviction that you will do what you think right on the occasion.

I beg the favor of a line when you have a leisure half hour. I shall remember your weeping willow, & am Yr. affct. friend & servt,
WM. FLEMING

May 11th

I closed my letter yesterday morning, thinking it was post day, but have since been better informed; and as the paper of this day contains the latest advices we have, I inclose it for your amusement. Genl. Washington in a letter to Congress, dated the 7th is somewhat more particular than the paper respecting the embarkation from N. York. He says he received a letter from Genl. Maxwell, who is near Amboy, the 5th. instant, informing "that that day there sailed from N. York about 4 or 5000 troops, chiefly Brittish, supposed either for Georgia or the West Indies, and said to be commanded by generals Vaughan and Leslie." The same day he received a letter from Colo. Ford, stationed in the neighbourhood of Maxwell, with an account "that the same day (the 5th.) 27 square rigged vessels and 12 or 14 sloops and schooners put to sea, and steered S.E. 'til out of sight."—That by a prisoner from N. York he was informed that the *report* there was, that between 6 and 7000 troops were embarked (He sailed with them to the watering place) that there was a vast number of light horse [on] board; and the fleet was very full of men—their destination unknown to the officers, who were very anxious to be informed whether they were going. Their conjectures were various—some for Georgia, some for Maryland, and some for Rh: Island. And that Genl. Clinton was said to be on board—but that Genl. Washington thinks highly improbable. The General thinks, from the number of vessels, that the whole embarkation cannot exceed 4000 men.

We are just informed (by report) that two large French merchantmen, full of dry goods, are taken off the Cape of Delaware, and carried into N. York. Adieu.

RC (DLC). Addressed: "Thomas Jefferson esquire in Wmsburg." Franked: "Free Wm. Fleming."

Fleming presented his credentials to Congress on 28 Apr. (JCC, XIV, 527). By an Act of the General Assembly in Oct. 1778, the ALLOWANCE to members in Congress had been increased from ten to fifteen dollars per day (Hening, IX, 388-9, 558). Before Fleming's letter could have reached TJ, the latter had, on 17 May, introduced a Bill for the Annual Appointment of Delegates in Congress, which set the allowance for delegates at forty dollars a day. The Bill was agreed to by both Houses on 25 May 1779 (Bill No. 10 in Report of the Committee of Revisors, 18 June 1779). By the same law, the term of service was extended from 11 Aug. to 1 Nov. 1779. In Oct. 1779, a new act was passed further increasing the allowance of members in Congress and reducing their number to five (Hening, X, 163-4).

From Edmund Pendleton

DR. SIR Edmundsbury May 11. 1779.

The difficulty of conveying letters across the Countrey and some hopes of seing you in the City the first of April, are but poor, and yet they are the only Palliatives I can offer, for having so long delayed Acknowledging the receipt of your favor of Decemr. 18th.

I immediately wrote to our friend W. to be informed if any thing had happen'd, or passed between you and him, which made it necessary for me to attend further to the work of Revisal, contrary to what had been agreed between Us, that you should settle our diversity of Opinion upon the Bills he had prepared, as well as mine, which he chose to consider by himself, and Point out for your Examination any alterations he judged proper, and then they were to be fairly transcribed as well as yours, which we had before gone through, and reported. I let him know I was ready to attend him at any time, if such Occurrence had made it necessary; he answered that no Alteration was made in that plan and I was satisfied.

I find you have discarded all my Forms of Executions; perhaps it might be wrong to meddle with the Subject in that Partial manner, but would it not be an useful part of our Work to revise the Register and Publish a sett of forms which would be Intelligent to commonsense and adapted to our Circumstances. We have had sad blundering among the Clerks, and shall have worse, now that they will not have a Mr. Waller at their head to apply to in cases of difficulty.

I thank you for the friendly Interest you take in my health and happiness, and cordially assure you I feel mutually for yours, and for the like reasons respecting my friend and my Countrey. You hurt those feelings when you sometimes speak of retiring. You are too young to Ask that happy quietus from the Public, and should at least postpone it 'til you have taught the rising Generation, the forms as well as the Substantial principles of legislation. A Correspondence with you will give me much pleasure. I have liesure enough for it, and if you can point out a medium through which the letters may be conveyed, and satisfie me that it will not Interrupt your more importanant calls, I will certainly provoke you to it.

I have been impatient to se what you call your Quixotism for the diffusion of knowledge, a passion raised by it's title and its being yours. I desired Mr. Purdie to send me ½ a dozen of them at my expence, but he failed, nor have I been able to get a sight of one, if sent to the County. I am willing however my Representatives should Adopt, if they approve it, as well as pass a law to give themselves such Wages as will at least Answer their expences. I fear the Rockbridge Deputies want to be Satisfied that your Bill encourages a *Presbeterian*, not a *liberal* Education. Present my Complts. to Mrs. Jefferson when you se her, whom, as well as the little ones, I hope you left Well. Adieu, My freind,

EDMD. PENDLETON

Pray think of our poor Serjeant. He is a good one and has attended now 3 Courts decently dressed and received Nothing.

RC (DLC).

TJ's letter of 18 Dec. has not been located. YOUR QUIXOTISM FOR THE DIFFUSION OF KNOWLEDGE: TJ's Bill for the More General Diffusion of Knowledge (Report of the Committee of Revisors, 18 June 1779, Bill No. 79).

From William Fleming

DEAR SIR Philadelphia, 22d. May 1779.

I promised myself the satisfaction of receiving letters from some of my friends by the express who brought the distressing account of the enemy's success at Portsmouth, but I have not received a letter from Virginia since my arrival here, except from Mrs. Fleming.

I am apprehensive the enemy will commit great ravages before an effectual check can be given to their progress, as the dispersed situation of our militia, and their want of arms and accoutrements will greatly retard their operations, be them ever so spirited and active.

From the best observations I have been able to make, our great concerns wear a very gloomy aspect, owing principally to the rapid and excessive depreciation of our money, which is almost beyond conception; and the misfortune is, the mischief is daily increasing, and no man can see where it will stop; and I am persuaded if something effectual is not speedily done, it will in a short time cease to be current at all. Should that happen, the disbanding our army must inevitably be the consequence. When I came here, the 27th of April, the difference between paper and gold was sixteen for one, and I was yesterday told by a member of congress that 75£ a peice is now given for half Joes. Provisions, and all kinds of goods rise in proportion to the depreciation of the paper money. Add to all this that our credit with foreigners is sinking a pace, and the enemy in possession of most of our ports to the southward of Rhode Island; which will consequently increase the difficulty of procuring cloaths for our soldiers, and military stores, should the war be continued, which is a thing not at all improbable, but will, in my apprehension, depend in a great measure on Congress.

I am of opinion the enemy have pretty well lost sight of conquering America by arms; for instead of drawing their force to a point, and making an effort against our grand army, it seems to be their plan to carry on a kind of piratical war in detached parties, by burning our towns, plundering our sea coasts, and distressing individuals; besides endeavouring, by every artifice in their power, to destroy the little credit left of our paper money, to sow dissentions and create divisions among us, and, if possible, to wean a party from the alliance with France and, that being effected, to offer independence to America on her entering into a treaty, offensive and defensive with G. Britain. These are my conjectures—whether well or ill founded time perhaps may discover.

Genl. Thompson, and several other officers of rank, are just arriv'd from N. York on parole. The enemy there are about 7000 strong, including American recruits, of which they have a great proportion. They have received no reinforcements from Europe this spring.

I think we have little to fear but from the depreciation of our money; and from that source we have, in my opinion, much to fear. There are between 130 and 140 millions of dollars now in circulation; and congress, to make one bold effort to restore its sinking credit, yesterday passed an act to call on the states for their respective quotas of 45 millions of dollars, by the first day of next January; and this (if it can be effected) will not answer the end, without the aid of a foreign loan; for unless some such measure can be speedily adopted, the emissions between this and the first day of January, must greatly exceed 45 millions of dollars. The demand appears large, and doubtless it is so; but the very critical situation of our affairs seems to make it not only expedient, but absolutely necessary; and I am hopeful a plentiful crop this year will enable our people to pay it without making sale of much of their property, besides the produce of their lands, and many will pay it with less than a fourth of that produce. On those who have no land it will fall the lightest. An address from congress to the people of each state, shewing the situation of their affairs, and the necessity for the measure, will accompany the requisition. What cannot be raised by taxes must I suppose, be borrowed; but in my opinion, the less of the latter the better. I believe most of the states to the northward of Virginia will raise their whole proportion by taxes; and if Virginia (instead of laying high taxes, now the produce of her lands are high) should give too much into the scheme of borrowing, she will have the greatest part of her enormous debt to pay with interest when (the money having in a great measure recovered its credit) her commodities will have fallen many hundred per cent; and the consequence will be that your speculating harpies, who have large sums of money in their hands, will carefully lay it up, as soon as they see its credit established, to purchase your lands and negroes at an under value.

Our great misfortune is, that the bulk of the people, thro'out the states, seem to have lost sight of the great object for which we had recourse to arms, and to have turned their thoughts soley to accumulating *ideal* wealth, and preying upon the necessities of their fellow citizens.

I have heard much, but seen very little, of patriotism and public virtue: If there is any remains of it in America, this is the season for calling it forth, and for it's utmost exertions.

France has done generous things for us, to which she was not bound by treaty, and if we will but be firm and united, all may yet be well.

It is of the utmost consequence that the confederation be speedily ratified. It would in a great degree give force and energy to the proceedings of congress, and defeat the hope our enemy entertains of dividing us. Maryland is the only state that now refuses to accede tho' many of the states have acceded on condition that all the rest come into the confederation. The Maryland delegates, a few days ago delivered in, to congress, an instruction from their assembly on the subject; and a very extraordinary, indecent performance it is. A copy will be sent by the express to our assembly for their consideration, and I hope we shall be favoured with a proper comment upon it.

I am afraid I have trespassed on your patience by dwelling on so melancholy a subject, but I thought it necessary to say something on what appears to me to be the state of our affairs, and having entered on the subject, could not well say less. When I speak of facts, what I say I know to be true. The rest are mere conjectures I have ventured to make from particular circumstances which have occurred.

We are just informed, by report, of some horrid depredations of the enemy, which, if true, I hope will rouse the spirit of our people, as their conduct in 76 did that of the people of Jersey.

We have a report from different quarters, that Colo. G. R. Clarke has made prisoner the Governor of Detroit (one Hamilton) with about 34 [ ] privates, who are now on their way to Wmsburgh. I am with great esteem, Dr Sr Yr. affect. friend & servt,

WM. FLEMING

RC (DLC). Tr (PPAP).

From Richard Henry Lee

DEAR SIR Philadelphia May 22. 1779

I have paid due attention to your favor of April the 21st., and I believe there would have been no difficulty in obtaining what is desired for Baron de Geismar had not the enemy created the difficulties that do exist. They absolutely refuse to admit partial exchanges, and they have lately proposed such unfair terms for general exchange that nothing can be done in either of these ways. They will not allow one of our Officers to come out on parole, if like permission be granted to one of theirs, as appeared in the case of Major de Passeren [of] the Regiment of Hesse Hanau. Upon consideration of this matter with your friend Mr. Peters, who is one of the Board of War, we conclude the way to put this matter into the best train will be for the Baron to apply to the British Commander in Chief for this parole exchange, and write to Gen. Knip-hausen to support the request. That these letters be sent here to the Board of War, and they will immediately forward them thro the Commissioner of Prisoners expressing their willingness to gratify the Baron. An objection is raised here to gratifying this Officer without receiving something like an equivalent from the enemy, as tending to encourage their obstinacy in refusing a general exchange on terms of fair equality, by which our captive Of[ficers suffer?].[1]

We have no news here but what comes from Virginia. All good men are waiting with anxious expectation to hear that our Countrymen have given these wicked Invaders cause to repent of their undertaking.

We have been told that Colo. Hamilton of Detroit is our prisoner, made so by the brave Colo. Clarke. I wish it may be true, and I hope the Prisoner will be well secured, because his enmity to us, his activity and influence among the Indians are equal and all very great. My respects to Mr. Wythe and my other friends. I am dear Sir yours sincerely,

RICHARD HENRY LEE

RC (DLC).

There was much discussion of Geismar's application to return on parole to Germany; see note in Burnett, *Letters of Members*, IV, 225.

1 Partly lost in margin, but quite evidently Lee omitted one or more words, perhaps in copying.

Bill for the Removal of the Seat of Government of Virginia

[*Williamsburg, 29 May 1779.*] This Bill is substantially the same as that drawn by TJ in 1776 and summarily rejected on its first reading (q.v., under date of 11 Nov. 1776). TJ had made the proposal in 1776 because of the exposure of Williamsburg to an invading enemy and also because of its inconvenient distance from the western inhabitants; by 1779 danger of invasion was great and the power of the western delegates had grown; hence removal farther to the west was both imperative and a foregone conclusion (see TJ's Autobiography, Ford, I, 55). In all of TJ's drafts of the Bill, the location of the new seat of government was left blank; the House in 1779, in one of the few amendments made to his Bill, inserted the name of Richmond, the growing town in Henrico county at the head of tidewater. When, on 25 May 1779, the House appointed a committee to bring in a Bill, TJ was not a member. He was added to the committee on 28 May, and his draft was reported the next day by Harvie (JHD, May 1779, 1827 edn., p. 25, 26, 27, 28, 33, 34, 36). It is clear that he was added to the committee because he had retained the rough draft of his 1776 Bill and was ready. He revised this rough draft (the revisions noted below prove that this was done at the time he was added to the committee), made a fair copy of it, and presented it to the committee. This fair copy contained some deletions, perhaps made in committee.

The Bill in 1776 provided for six squares allocated to public buildings as follows: (1) for the capitol to house the General Assembly; (2) for the "General Courthouse" to house the various courts, juries, &c.; (3) for three buildings to house the clerks of courts, the land office, and the public jail; (4) and (5) for the governor; and (6) for a public market. When TJ revised the rough draft of his 1776 Bill on 28-29 May 1779, he allowed the uses of the first three squares to stand virtually unchanged, but he revised the provisions for the last three by deleting the passage concerning them from the rough draft and interlining the following: "On one other of the said squares shall be built a house to be called the State house which shall contain two apartments for the use of the Council of state and it's clerks, two others for the use of the Board of war and it's clerk, two others for the use of the board of trade and it's clerk, two others for the use of the board of Auditors and it's clerk, two others for the use of the Treasurer, and two others for the land office, with necessary entries passages and stairways; on one other of the said squares shall be built a palace for the use of the Govr. of this Commonw. for the time being, with proper apartments and offices: to which shall appertain also one other of the said squares and the street intervening: and the remaining square shall be appropriated to the use of ⟨*an Exchange and*⟩ a public market." This revision proves that TJ revised his 1776 rough draft in May 1779 for the committee, since the boards of war and of trade had been established only a few days before the committee was appointed (Report of Committee of Revisors, Bills No. 8 and 9, 18 June 1779). For some reason, TJ deleted this revised statement of purpose of the last three squares even after he had drawn off a fair copy of the Bill, for over the passage quoted he pasted a slip of paper on which was written still another version—the one accepted by the committee and by the House: "One other of the said squares shall be reserved for the purpose of building thereon hereafter a house for the several executive boards and offices to be held in. Two others with the intervening street shall be reserved for the use of the governor of this commonwealth for the time being to be built on hereafter" (the last five words were deleted in the House by amendment). There were a number of other changes made in TJ's fair copy of the Bill, but these were of minor importance and may have been made either by him or by the committee. The Act as adopted contained two important additions not to be found in any of TJ's drafts or in the MS Bill reported by the committee and therefore inserted by amendment. The first of these provided that, because of the "just and necessary war this commonwealth is at present engaged in, the difficulties of procuring the materials for building, and the high price for labour," there should be built "some proper and temporary buildings for the sitting of the general assembly, the courts of justice, and the several boards." (For details, see TJ's instructions to Thomas Whiting, 26 June 1779, and enclosure.) The second provided that the county jail of Henrico should be enlarged to accommodate the purposes of a public jail until a more commodious one could be built and that the directors of public buildings could not draw upon the treasury for any sum exceeding £20,000 (TJ's draft in 1776 had stipulated £6,000), nor could they let any contracts for the public buildings on the six squares until further provision should be made by the General Assembly (Hening, X, 88-9). For TJ's continued efforts in respect to the planning of the new seat of government and his drawings for the Capitol, see Fiske Kimball, "Jefferson and the Public Buildings of Virginia," *Huntington Library Quarterly*, XII (1949), 115-20 and 303-10. Kimball concludes that "Jefferson had arrived at the fundamental scheme of the Capitol before he ever left America and long before he met Clérisseau, the French architect who helped him with the model."

MS (DLC), in TJ's hand, with alterations as described above. MS (Vi), in clerk's hand, docketed in the hand of Edmund Randolph: "May 29. 1779. first reading & to be read again on Monday. Commd. to Thursday 3d. June 1779. . . . gone thro' & to be reported tomorrow. June 4th. 79. repd. agd. to & ordered to be engrossed." Dft (DLC) in TJ's hand; this is the rough draft of TJ's 1776 Bill, referred to above, which he revised 28-29 May 1779. The Act as adopted is in Hening, X, 85-9.

Bill Amending Act for Fixing the Allowance of Members of the General Assembly

[31 May 1779]

Whereas by an act intituled 'an act for fixing the allowance of the members of general assembly' passed at this present session by authority from the body of the people it was provided that the said allowances should be of 50. pounds of neat tobacco by the day for attendance on assembly, two pounds of the like tobacco for every mile they must necessarily travel going to or from the same, together with their ferriages to be paid to them in money out of the public treasury, at such rate as shall be estimated by the grand jury at the session of the General court next before the meeting of each respective session of assembly, governing themselves in the said estimate by the worth of the said tobacco and the competence of the same to defray the necessary expenses of traveling and attendance; but no mode was pointed out for estimating the said tobacco for the present session: Be it therefore enacted that the grand jury which shall be sworn at the first session of the General court after the passing of this act shall make the said estimate as well for the present as for any session which may ensue; and such estimation being made it shall be lawful for [the several] members to receive paiment of the same of the Treasurer for their attendance at [and traveling to and] from the present session and their ferriages, observing the forms heretofore prescribed by law.

No [person] shall heretoforward be capable of serving on any grand jury in the general court while he shall be a member of either house of assembly, or a candidate for a seat therein.

The grand [juries of] the general court shall be sworn by the clerk to make the estimate directed by the said act honestly impartially and according to the plain intention of the said act; and if they shall differ in opinion as to the price at which the said tobacco shall be estimated, the sum at which every of the said jurors estimates it shall be distinctly noted in writing and the whole added together, and the amount thereof divided by the number of those who shall have given in their estimate, and the quotient or average value which shall result from this operation or such other sum near thereto as to avoid fractions shall be approved by a majority of them shall be the estimate at which the said allowances shall be paid.

MS (Vi); in TJ's hand, endorsed by him: "A Bill for paying the wages of the members of the present session of assembly." Docketed by Edmund Randolph: "May 31. 1769. [i.e., 1779] first reading. June 1. To be engd. Engrossed."

MS faded; words in square brackets have been supplied from text in Hening, x, 104-5.

This Bill, to cover an omission in the Bill passed by the House on 29 May (same, p. 29-30; see also Bill providing allowances, &c., 12 Dec. 1778), was obviously drafted during TJ's last hours in the House. Introduced on 31 May, it was passed by the House on 2 June and agreed to next day by the Senate, being amended by neither (JHD, May 1779, 1827 edn., p. 26, 28, 29, 30, 33).

Bill for Allowing Salaries to Certain Officers of Government

[May 1779]

Be it enacted by the General assembly that from the 1st day of Jan. which shall be in the year of our lord 17— there shall be paid the following salaries to the officers of government herein after named, viz.

to the Governor	153,000 ℔ of nett tobo. by the year
to each of the judges of the High Court of Chancery, General court and court of Admiralty	60,000 ℔ of like tobo. by the year
to the Speaker of the House of Delegates the same as to the said Judges by the year	
to the Speaker of the Senate	30,000 ℔ of like tobo. by the year
to each member of the council of state for every day he shall attend in council	200 ℔ of tobo.
to each member of the board of Trade for every day he shall attend the board	150 ℔
to each of the Auditors and to the Treasurer the same as to the Judges	
to the Attorney General	30,000 ℔ of nett tobo. by the year
to the Clerk of the council	40,000 ℔ of like tobo. by the year
to the clerk of foreign Correspondence	30,000 ℔ of like tobo. by the year

to the clerk of accounts in the Auditors' office 20,000 ℔ of like tobo. by the year
to the copying clerk in the same office 10,000 ℔ of like tobo. by the year
and to the printer of the Commission ℔ of like tobo. by the year

which tobo. shall be rated in money by the joint vote of the two houses of assembly at the first session of every General assembly taking into their consideration as well the market price of the said tobo. as the expences to be concurred by the said officers: and according to such rate the salaries for the ensuing year shall be paid out of the public treasury by quarterly paiments to the said officers of government respectively.

Dft (DLC); in TJ's hand, written on the blank portion of a note addressed to "Col. Jefferson" by a Mr. Foster declining an invitation and dated "Thursday Morn. 11 O C[lock]." Title of Bill is at top of recto in TJ's hand and worded as in caption above.

On 16 Dec. 1777 TJ was appointed member of a committee to bring in a bill "for giving proper salaries to certain officers of government." It is not certain what part he had in the drafting of that Bill, but it is certain that the Act then passed (24 Jan. 1778; Hening, IX, 435) could not have been the present Bill, since (1) the 1778 Bill provided for payment of salaries in dollars, and (2) the present Bill provides for officers not in existence in Jan. 1778: the clerkship of foreign correspondence was not established until May 1778 and the Board of Trade was not created until May 1779. Since TJ became Governor on 2 June 1779, the present Bill, therefore, could only have been introduced at the session of May 1779 and after the Board of Trade was created (its Bill was introduced by TJ on 12 May 1779; see Bill No. 9, Report of Committee of Revisors, 18 June 1779). There was an Act passed at the May 1779 session "giving salaries to certain officers of government" (Hening, X, 118), but it provided for payment in dollars and also provided for members of both the Board of Trade and the Board of War. Salaries were not paid in tobacco until after the enactment of the Act of May 1780 (same, p. 278-9), an Act whose salaries were less liberal than those provided by TJ. It is possible that he drafted the Bill in May 1779, intending to submit it to the House, and then was prevented from doing so because of his election as governor. His own salary on entering office was at the rate of £4,500 per annum (same, p. 118); this was increased by the Act of Oct. 1779 to £7,500 (same, p. 219); at the session of May 1780 the governor was granted—instead of the 153,000 pounds of tobacco called for by TJ's draft Bill—a salary of 60,000 pounds (same, p. 278).

Bill for Lessening the Evils of Securityship

[Before June 1779?]

Whereas the laws permitting one person to become bound for another have been found in experience to be of more harm than help to the citizens of this commonwealth, by encouraging merchants and others to extend credits beyond the abilities of their debtors to pay, by giving fatal facilities to thoughtless and unprincipled spendthrifts to continue their extravagant courses till they have not only exhausted beyond recovery their own means of paiment and future subsistence, but expended the fortunes of their friends and relations also, and by overwhelming in the end good men and their families, victims of their own benevolence and of the avarice and dissipation of others: for lessening these evils therefore ⟨*by rendering the act of securityship a more solemn warning to the parties*⟩

The General assembly does enact as follows.[1]

No person shall *hereafter* be able, *within the limits or jurisdiction of this commonwealth*, to make his person or property liable for the debt duty, default or undertaking of another; except [for lands by a mortgage and?] the personal chattels whereof he is in possession, nor these otherwise than by a delivery of them in pledge to the creditor.[2]

Where the laws require security or bail from executors, administrators, guardians, defendants in any plea, recognisors, public officers, or any others whatsoever, a sufficient mortgage of lands or in the case of defendants and recognisors a sufficient delivery of sufficient moveable goods in pledge, to the sheriff or coroner as the case may be, and their successors, for the commonwealth or the creditor shall hereafter be required.

The Judgment respondendum which shall be taken out of the Chancery for foreclosing the right of redeeming the property mortgaged or pledged under this act, shall give notice that, on some day to be named in the subpoena at the will of the plaintiff, not less than month after service of the same and a copy of the bill left with the defendant, the court will be moved for a decree of foreclosure and sale; on which day, or as soon after as may be, the court shall, with or without the appearance, answer or other pleading of the defendant, hear and decide the cause on the bill and other pleadings and exhibits, the depositions and vivâ voce testimony, according to substantial justice, but without delay or indulgence; and if they find cause of foreclosure, shall decree a sale of the lands mortgaged or of the moveable goods pawned within months after the date of the decree.

In like manner a bill for redemption of the lands mortgaged, or action for the detainer of the pawn shall be heard and decided on a day to be named in the subpoena or writ, with equal circumstances of justice and dispatch.

All acts done in evasion of this law shall be void, and not merely voidable.

PrC (DLC); in TJ's hand. The title is worded as in caption and is in TJ's hand at top of page. There is no indication of date, and it is uncertain when TJ drew this Bill. Several possibilities suggest themselves: (1) it may have been drawn during the normal course of his legislative activity in order to remedy an obvious evil; (2) it may have been prepared during the course of TJ's work for the Committee of Revisors and not incorporated, for one reason or another, in their Report; (3) it may have been drawn by TJ sometime after his legislative career had closed and perhaps given to James Madison, for example, to introduce; or (4) it may have been drawn by TJ late in life after his own disastrous experience in becoming security for the debts of another person. Since this is a letterpress copy, it is very unlikely that the Bill was drawn so early as 1779; yet, with several possibilities suggesting themselves, the editors have placed the document at the close of TJ's Virginia legislative career since that seems the earliest possible date at which it could have been drawn.

At the Oct. 1786 session an Act was adopted whose preamble bore a remarkable similarity to the preamble of TJ's Bill: "Whereas many persons have been reduced from affluence to poverty, by securityships, and it frequently happens that the security or securitys upon bonds or other obligations, their heirs, executors, or administrators, have been compelled to pay the whole, or the greater part of the debt due upon such bonds or obligations, and in many cases have not been able, by the insolvency of the principal or principals, or a tardy administration of justice, to recover from them or their representatives, the whole or any part of the amount of such debts, whereby the said securities have been involved in great inconveniences, and often times in manifest ruin. . . ." This Act enabled securities so involved to obtain judgment by motion against principals or their heirs, &c. (Hening, XII, 268-70). This, however, was very far from prohibiting securityship except under certain conditions, as was done in this Bill.

1 This form of enacting clause seems never to have been employed by TJ during his legislative career from 1776 to 1779. His usual form following a preamble was: "Be it therefore enacted by the General Assembly."

2 The letterpress copy is mutilated at the critical part of this paragraph, i.e., in the exception to the general prohibition. The words "lands by a mortgage" are clearly discernible, but it is not certain whether these words were struck out, since the words "the personal chattels whereof he is in possession, nor these otherwise than" are interlined. From the context of the Bill, however, it seems clear that the exception amounted to this: property in lands could not be offered in securityships except by mortgage, and property in personal chattels except by pledge. In the margin TJ wrote the following: "[. . .] securityships in common transactions between individuals, endorsements of bills of exchange, &c. for executors, administrators, guardians public officers for defendants, in bail common or special, for prison bounds, or replevin by recognisance for the peace, behavior &c." It is not certain just where this marginal matter was supposed to be inserted in the Bill. The letterpress copy is so poor that no caret, if one ever existed, can be discerned.

Message Accepting Election as Governor

Gentlemen [2 June 1779]

The honour which the General Assembly have been pleased to confer on me, by calling me to the high office of Governour of this commonwealth, demands my most grateful acknowledgments, which I desire through you Gentlemen, to tender to them with the utmost respect. In a virtuous and free state, no rewards can be so pleasing to sensible minds, as those which include the approbation of our fellow citizens. My great pain is, lest my poor endeavours should fall short of the kind expectations of my country; so far as impartiality, assiduous attention, and sincere affection to the great American cause, shall enable me to fulfil the duties of any appointment, so far I may, with confidence undertake; for all beyond, I must rely on the wise counsels of the General Assembly, and of those whom they have appointed for my aid in those duties. To you, Gentlemen, I return my particular thanks, for the polite terms in which you have been pleased to notify the will of the General Assembly.

MS not located. Text from *Va. Gaz.* (D & N), 5 June 1779. TJ is here replying to a message brought by a joint committee of both houses of the Assembly.

On 1 June the two houses of the Assembly in joint session took two ballots to elect a successor to Gov. Henry. The result of the first ballot was:

For Thomas Jefferson 55
For John Page 38
For Thomas Nelson 32

"But neither of the persons ballotted for having a majority of both Houses, the House proceeded to ballot between Thomas Jefferson Esq., and the Hon. John Page, who stand foremost." The result was:

For Jefferson 67
For Page 61

(See JHD, May 1779, 1827 edn., p. 29.)

From John Page

MY DEAR JEFFERSON Wmsburg June the 2d. 1779

I would have waited on you to congratulate you on your Appointment yesterday had I not been under an Engagement to return Home with Mazzei. I attended at your Lodgings today as soon as our Board adjourned, but you were not at Home. I am unhappily obliged to be at Gloster Court tomorrow, and therefore think it proper, notwithstanding our Intimacy and Friendship, to inform you of this; lest till I can have the Pleasure of conversing freely with you, you might be induced to suspect that I am influenced by some low dirty feelings and avoid seeing you to conceal that Embarasment which might be the Result of them. I can assure you However that I have such Confidence in your good Opinion of my Heart that were it not for the World who may put a wrong Construction on my Conduct I should scarcely trouble you with this Apology. I sincerely wish you all Happiness and will do every thing in my Power to make your Administration easy and agreeable to you. As soon as Mrs. Jefferson comes to Town Mrs. Page will wait on her. I am Yrs., JOHN PAGE

RC (DLC). Addressed: "To His Excellcy. Thos. Jefferson Esqr. Governour of Virginia." (TJ used the address leaf for his draft answer to Page, 3 June.)

To John Page

DEAR PAGE [Williamsburg, 3 June 1779]

I received your letter by Mr. Jamieson. It had given me much pain that the zeal of our respective friends should ever have placed you and me in the situation of competitors. I was comforted however with the reflection that it was their competition, not ours, and that the difference of the numbers which decided between us, was too insignificant to give you a pain or me a pleasure [had] our dispositions towards each other been such as to have admitted those sensations. I know you too well to need an apology for any thing you do, and hope you will for ever be assured of this; and as to the constructions of the world, they would only have added one to [the many sig]ns for which they [are] to go to the devil. As this is the first, so I hope it will be the last instance of ceremony between us. A desire to see my family which is in Charles [City] carries me thither tomorrow, and I shall not return till Monday. Mrs. Jefferson I beleive will not come short[ly] to [town.] When she does however she has too much [value] for [Mrs.] Page not to consider her acquaintance as a principal among those circumstances which are to reconcile her to her situation. A knolege of her sentiments on this subject renders me safe in undertaking that she shall do her equal part in cultivating a friendly intercourse. Be pleased to present my compliments to her & add this to the assurances I have ever given you [that I am] Dr. Page Your affectionate friend.

Dft (DLC) written on the blank side of the address leaf of Page's letter to TJ, 2 June. RC, dated 3 June 1779, sold in Manning Sale, Anderson Galleries, 19-20 Jan. 1926, has not been located.

The date of this letter is wrongly given by TJR, HAW, and L & B as 22 Jan. 1779; Ford (II, 187) conjectures the more nearly correct date of June 1779 and prints a complete text; the others are docked of several sentences. TJ went to visit his family at The Forest, CHARLES CITY on Friday, 4 June, and returned on Monday, 7 June; see his ferriage expenses in Account Book under those dates. For the background of this letter, see TJ's Message of 2 June and Page's letter to TJ, same date.

Bill concerning Escheats and Forfeitures from British Subjects

[4 June 1779]

Whereas during the connection which subsisted between the now United states of America and the other parts of the British empire, and their subjection to one common prince the inhabitants of either part had all the rights of natural born subjects in the other and so might lawfully take and hold real property, and transmit the same by descent to their heirs in fee simple, which could not be done by mere aliens; and the inhabitants on each part had accordingly acquired real property in the other: and in like manner had acquired personal property which by their common laws might be possessed by any other than an alien ennemy and transmitted to executors and administrators: but when by the tyrannies of that prince, and the open hostilities committed by his armies and subjects inhabitants of the other parts of his dominions on the good people of the said United states they were obliged to wage war in defence of their rights and finally to separate themselves from the rest of the British empire to renounce all subjection to their common prince and to become sovereign and independant states the said inhabitants of the other parts of the British empire became aliens and ennemies to the said states and as such incapable of holding the property, real or personal so acquired therein and so much thereof as was within this commonwealth became by the laws vested in the commonwealth.

Nevertheless the general assembly tho provoked by the example of their enemi[es] to a departure from that generosity which so honourably distinguishes the civilized nations of the present age yet desirous to conduct themselves with moderation and temper by an act passed at their session in the year 1777 took measures for preventing what had been the property of British subjects within this commonwealth from waste and destruction by putting the same into the hands and under the management of commissioners appointed for that purpose that so it might be in their power if reasonable at a future day to re[sto]re to the former proprietors the full value thereof:

And whereas it is found that the said property is liable to be lost, wasted and impaired without greater attention in the officers of government than is consistent with the discharge of their public duties and that from the advanced price at which the same would now sell it may be most for the benefit of the former owners, if the same should be restored to them hereafter or to the public if not so restored that the sale thereof should take place at this time and the proceeds be lodged in the public treasury subject to the future direction of the legislature:

Be it therefore enacted by the General assembly that so much of the act beforementioned as may be supposed to have suspended the operation of the laws of escheat and forfeiture shall be hereby repealed and that all the property real and personal within the commonwealth belonging at this time to any British subject or which did belong to any British subject at the time such escheat or forfeiture may have taken place shall be deemed to be vested in the commonwealth the said[1] real estate, by way of escheat and the said personal estate by forfeiture:

The Governor with the advice of council so far as their information will enable them and the commissioners of the tax within their several counties aided by their assessors shall forthwith institute proper proceedings of escheat and forfeiture for all such property real and personal in which they shall be advised and assisted by the several attornies for the commonwealth.

Where any office in the cases beforementioned shall be found for the commonwealth and returned to the General court it shall remain there but one month for the claim of any pretending right to the estate; and if within that time no such claim be made, or being made if it be found and discussed for the commonwealth, the title of the owner to such estate real or personal shall be for ever barred, but may be afterwards asserted as to the money proceeding from the sale thereof with equal force and advantage as might have been to the thing itself; and such further proceedings shall be had for making sale, of the[2] lands so found, in parcels not greater than 400 acres (to be described by the commissioners hereafter mentioned and measured and marked by metes and bounds by a surveyor where they shall think it necessary)[3] and of the other property as in other cases of escheat and forfeiture; save only that the Governor with advice of council for every such sale shall appoint two commissioners to superintend and controul the proceedings of the said escheator, which commissioners shall be sworn to use their best endeavors to have the estate to which their trust extends sold to the best advantage. The said sales shall be for ready money to be paid to the Escheator, who shall retain thereof[4] five per centum for his trouble. His certificate of such paiment in the case of lands and of the person purchasing, to the register of the land office shall entitle the purchaser to a grant of the said lands.[5] If the said Escheator shall fail to pay the said money into the hands of the treasurer within a reasonable [time] after any such sale (which reasonable time shall be accounted one day for every 20 miles such sale was distant from the public treasury and [twenty] days of grace in addition thereto he shall pay interest thereon from the time of the said sale at the rate of 20 per centum per annum; and moreover it shall be lawful for the auditors on the last day but one [of] any general court, or at any court to be held for the county wherein such property was sold, after the expiration of the time allowed for paiment to obtain judgment on motion against such Escheator his heirs executors and administrators for the principal sum and such interest together with costs. And for the information of the auditors the commissioners of the sale shall immediately on such sale certify to whom and for how much such sale was made and transmit such certificate by some safe and early conveyance to the Auditors which certificate shall be legal evidence against such Escheator. The Auditors shall allow the commissioners so appointed the expences of the surveys by them directed and made, and other their reasonable expences and such compensation for their trouble as to them shall seem proper. Where the commissioners shall be of opinion that it will be more to the interest of the owner or public that possession of such property real or personal should be retained for finishing and removing a crop or other purpose it shall be lawful for them to stay the possession as it now is until the day of[6] giving notice of such their intention at the time of the sale.

And for preventing doubts who shall be deemed British subjects within the meaning of this act it is hereby declared and enacted that (1.) all persons, subjects of his Britannic majesty who on the[7] day of April in the year 1775, when hostilities were commenced at Lexington between the United states of America and the other parts of the British empire, were resident or following their vocations in any part of the world other than the said United states and have not since either entered into public employment of the said states, or joined the same and by overt act adhered to them; and (2.) all such subjects, inhabitants of any of the said United states as were out of the said states on the same day, and have since by overt act adhered to the enemies of the said states; and (3.) all inhabitants of the said states who after the same day and before the commencement of the act of General assembly intituled 'an act declaring what shall be treason' departed from the said states and joined the subjects of his Britannic majesty of their own free will, or who by any county court within this commonwealth were declared to be British subjects within the meaning and operation of the resolution of the General assembly of[8] and the governor's proclamation founded thereon; shall be deemed British subjects within the intention of this act.

But this act shall not extend to debts due to British subjects and paiable into the loan office according to the act of General assembly for sequestering British property; nor take effect [on the property of such British subjects as are infants, femes covertes, or of insane mind, who within one year after their disability removed and hostilities suspended between his Britannic majesty and the United states shall become citizens of any of the said states; nor][9] on any lots of land within the town of Richmond as the limits of the said town now are, or shall be at the time of the inquest found, which by the directors of the public buildings shall be included within the squares appropriated for such buildings further than that an office shall be found as to such lots of land and the estimated value [there]of be disposed of hereafter as the price would have been by this act had they been exposed to public sale; nor on any other such lots within the same town[10] as shall by the said directors be declared proper for the public use until buildings be erected on the squares beforementioned[11] and so long as they shall be [applied] to such public use.

MS (Vi); in TJ's hand. Endorsed by him: "A Bill concerning escheats & forfeitures from British subjects." Docketed: "To be engrossed. Engrossed." MS is much faded and the parts in square brackets (except where otherwise noted) have been supplied from text in Hening, X, 66-71. Accompanying this is a MS (also Vi), in the hand of John Beckley, headed: "Amendments to the Bill concerning Escheats & forfeitures from British subjects." Ford (II, 182-6) prints this Bill, but confuses its legislative history with that of the Bill Concerning Escheators (Hening, X, 115-17; see also Bill No. 24, Report of Committee of Revisors, 18 June 1779), a bill which was also passed at this session.

On 4 June 1779 a committee composed of Charles Carter, Mason, Henry, Baker, Lyne, Thomas Hite, Munford, and Page was ordered to bring in a Bill providing for the sale of all real and personal property owned by enemy aliens. This Bill was reported by Harvie (not a member of the committee) on 19 June; it passed the first two readings the same day and was committed to the committee of the whole; on 22 June it was debated by the committee and several amendments offered; on 23 June it was read the third time and passed, being carried to the Senate by Carter (JHD, May 1779, 1827 edn., p. 35, 59, 61, 62). TJ may have drafted the Bill before the session began (see George Mason to TJ, 3 Apr. 1779); since he became governor on 2 June, he was obliged to entrust the measure to his colleague from Albemarle, John Harvie.

It is to be noted that TJ, in the preamble to this Act, does not rest its justification upon the recommendation of the Continental Congress of 27 Nov. 1777 that real and personal estates of disloyal persons be seized and sold and the proceeds converted into Continental Loan Office certificates (JCC, IX, 971). Van Tyne, *Loyalists*, appendixes B and C, contains an analysis of legislation against the loyalists in various states. In some states confiscation was effected through acts of attainder, but Virginia passed only one such act during the Revolution—that against Josiah Philips, which TJ drew. Instead, sequestration was effected, as in the case of confiscation of property in England, under the customary process of *office found.* This was a process of inquiry, or inquest by virtue of office, held by the sovereign's sheriff, coroner, or escheator to determine the validity of the sovereign's title to the personal or real property involved (Tucker, *Blackstone*, 1803, II, 60). It is interesting to observe that TJ, whose legislative reforms generally were in advance of those undertaken by other states, should in this instance have been the only one to advance such a traditional legal concept to effect confiscation. It is impossible to determine how much property of loyalists was sold under this law; the auditor's accounts from 1779 to 1795 show a total of £3,041,167; "With the exception of £13,126, this money was paid to the commonwealth prior to 1782 in depreciated paper currency; the benefits to the state were small" (Harrell, *Loyalism in Virginia*, 1926, p. 84-98). Not all of this property was sold. The clauses at the conclusion of TJ's Bill concerning lots in Richmond show that escheated real estate there was to have title confirmed in the commonwealth through process of *office found* and the lots used for such purposes as the state might direct. Under this clause, the property of James McDowell was set apart for the auditor's office; that of French Crawford for the treasurer's office; that of Ninian Minzies was leased to Penet, Windel, & Company as a repair shop for the ordnance department; and, until the completion of the capitol in 1789, the General Assembly met in a house that had belonged to Cunningham and Company (same, p. 99). With materials scarce and building costs high, this use of loyalist property by the state was one that resulted in considerable benefit to the commonwealth. Yet neither the sequestration of debts due British subjects nor the confiscation of loyalists' property had the effect that TJ expected of stabilizing state finances and of halting the rapid inflation of the paper money.

1 The first of the amendments noted above altered this to read, as it does in the Act: "the lands, slaves, and other real estate." This, of course, involved deleting the second "said" also. This and the following amendments were keyed to TJ's MS Bill by page and line references; all but the last few of these marginal numerals were in his hand, indicating that he, though governor, sat in the House during debates.

2 Act as adopted reads: "right, title, claim, and interest, legal and equitable, of any British subject in and to the lands so found."

3 Act as adopted reads: "and in and to the other party as in other cases of escheat."

4 Act as adopted reads: "three per centum on the first thousand pounds arising from the sale of any such estate, and one and a half per centum on the remainder for his trouble."

5 The Act as adopted adds the following at this point: "free and fully exonerated from all the rights, title, claim, and interest, legal and equitable, of any British subject thereto; and also from the right, title, claim, and interest of all and every person whatsoever, by or under any deed of mortgage, the equity of redemption whereof had not been foreclosed at the time of the sale, but such mortgages [thus in Hening, x, 68, but correctly given as *mortgagees* in MS list of amendments noted above], their heirs or assigns, may nevertheless afterwards assert their claim and title to the money proceeding from the sale thereof, with equal force and advantage as they might have done to the land itself before such sale."

6 Act reads "sixth day of December next," and the following was added by amendment at this point: "and in such cases postpone the sale of the slaves, tools, and other personal property, necessary for their subsistence, and making the said crop, until the said sixth day of December. The money for which such property was sold being paid into the publick treasury, and all expenses allowed and deductions made, the balance thereof shall be extended in nett tobacco, at the market price as the same shall be estimat on oath by the grand jury of the succeeding general court, and such balance of tobacco shall be considered in future as the true measure of retribution to be made to the individuals interested; if retribution be made, and in such case shall be repaid to them by the publick in quantity and kind. The duties which, under this act, are to be performed by an escheator in the several counties of this commonwealth, not being within the territory commonly called the Northern Neck, shall in the counties within that territory be performed by the sheriff of such counties respectively, which sheriff shall have the same powers, be entitled to the same allowances, and subject to the same penalties, conditions, and legal proceedings as escheators are in the other counties." The exception concerning British property in the Northern Neck may have been inserted at the suggestion of George Mason.

7 TJ evidently did not remember the exact date of the battle of Lexington; the Act reads "nineteenth."

8 Act reads: "of the nineteenth day of December, 1776, for enforcing the statute staple"; the words "and the governor's proclamation founded thereon" were deleted by amendment.

9 The words within square brackets (supplied) were deleted by amendment.

10 The Act as adopted reads: "whether held in severalty by any British subject or subjects, or by a citizen or citizens and a British subject or subjects, as joint tenants or tenants in common, which shall by the said directors."

11 The remainder of this sentence ("and so long . . . public use") was deleted by amendment and the following added: "except that an office shall be found as to the interest of any British subject in such lots, and such interest estimated by the same jury which found the office, and at the same time, as also the interest therein of any citizen who is joint tenant or tenant in common with such British subject, and the value of the interest of such citizen shall be paid to him, in like manner as is directed in the case of squares of ground appropriated to the publick buildings by an act passed at this present session of assembly, entitled, 'An act for the removal of the seat of government,' and the value of the interest of any such British subject shall be disposed of hereafter as the price would have been by this act, had they been exposed to publick sale, and the property in such lots shall be vested in the commonwealth; provided that the estates real and personal of such British subjects who have wives, widows, or children, residing within this state, shall be appropriated as follows: Such estates where there is a widow and no children, shall be subject to the widow's dower; where a wife and no child, to the like claim; but where a wife and child, or child and no wife, the whole of the estate belonging to such British subject shall be without the perview of this act. The residue of any estate not appropriated as hereby directed, shall be subject to the dispositions of this act."

Evan Shelby to Patrick Henry

SIR — Washington [County, Virginia] June 4. 1779

Since my last which I had the honor to address to your Excellency some of the Chiefs of the peaceable Towns of the Cherokee Nation of Indians came into Fort P Henry where they discovered some talks which I herewith send you, Some short time since I received a Letter from the Chiefs of Chickamogga accompanied with one other from Oconastota the great Warrior of Chota with orders to dispatch them to your Excy which I also send you by Express. It gives me real Satisfaction to find by the Contents of those Letters and other Circumstances that those people are reduced to a Sense of their Duty and a Willingness to treat for peace with the united States which I flatter myself will ease us in some measure from the Calamities incident to an Indian War.

I am informed that the Chiefs of the Chickamoga Towns have since my departure from that place discharged all the white people and Traders from amongst them who came from Mobille, or had connexions with the British party and from the purport of their Letters it Seems they depend soly on the State of Virga. for Goods. I would therefore beg leave to offer it as my opinion that if some necessary Goods could be provided for them it might answer a good end. I am &c., EVAN SHELBY

Tr (DLC: PCC, No. 71, I). In a clerk's hand and endorsed by Charles Thomson as enclosure No. 3 in TJ to John Jay, 19 June 1779. Copies of three other enclosures (originally accompanying Shelby's letter to Henry) were forwarded at the same time to Jay and are so endorsed by Thomson; they are: (1) message from the Chickamauga Chiefs, dated at Shelby's headquarters, Fort Patrick Henry on the Holston, 21 May 1779; (2) a similar message from The Great Warrior (i.e., the Cherokee chief Oconastota), dated Chuckamogge, 22 May 1779; and (3) transcript of the talks between The Raven and Hanging Maw, "Chiefs of the peaceable Towns of the Cherokees," on the one part, and Col. Shelby and Maj. Joseph Martin, Virginia agent to the Cherokees, on the other part, at Fort Patrick Henry, 22 May 1779. Another Tr (DLC).

Shelby's letter and its interesting enclosures (apparently unpublished) were received by TJ as Gov. Henry's successor, and he promptly transmitted copies to Pres. Jay and Gen. Washington (see letters of 19 June 1779). An account of Evan Shelby's punitive expedition against the hostile Chickamauga Indians in the Holston region, who were believed to have been incited by Gov. Hamilton of Detroit and his agents, will be found in J. G. M. Ramsey, *Annals of Tennessee*, Phila., 1853, p. 186-9.

To Benjamin Harrison

[*Williamsburg*, *7 June 1779*. A. L. S., 1 p., Henkels Catalogue No. 906 (Hampton L. Carson Sale, 26 Oct. 1904), pt. II, suppl., lot 2262. Not located. See note on TJ's letter to Harrison, 8 June 1779, the text of which refers to this letter.]

To Theodorick Bland

SIR Williamsburg June 8th. 1779.

Your letter to Governor Henry of the 1st. instant came safe to hand yesterday and I immediately laid it before the Council. It gave them pain to hesitate on my request from General Phillips whose polite conduct has disposed them to every indulgence consistent with the duties of their appointment. The indiscriminate murther of men, Women and children with the usual circumstances of barbarity practised by the Indian savages, was the particular task of Governor Hamilton's employment, and if any thing could have aggravated the acceptance of such an office and have made him personally answerable in a high degree it was that eager Spirit with which he is said to have executed it and which if the representations before the Council are to be credited seems to have shewn that his own feelings and disposition were in union with his employment. The truth of these representations will be the subject of their inquiry shortly, and the treatment of Governor Hamilton will be mild or otherwise as his conduct shall appear to merit. On a dispasionate examination we trust it must furnish a contemplation rather pleasing to the generous Soldier to see his honourable bravery respected even by those against whom it happens to be inlisted, and discriminated from the cruel and cowardly warfare of the savage, whose object in war is to extinguish human nature. I am Sir, &c,

TH: JEFFERSON

Tr, including the signature, transmitted to Congress (DLC: PCC, No. 57). RC (sold at Anderson Galleries, Sale of 20-1 Jan. 1916, lot 304, and now not located) was transmitted by Bland to Gen. Phillips in a letter dated 28 June 1779 (Dft owned by Lloyd W. Smith, Madison, N.J., 1946; clerk's copy transmitted to Congress, DLC: PCC, No. 57).

Bland's LETTER TO GOVERNOR HENRY of 1 June 1779 has not been found. It resulted from an appeal to Phillips by Henry HAMILTON, formerly lieutenant-governor of Detroit and commander of the British force at Vincennes that had surrendered to George Rogers Clark, 25 Feb. 1779. Hamilton had been sent back to Virginia with other captured officers, and his case was to prove troublesome to TJ throughout nearly the whole of his governorship. For Hamilton represented to the Virginians the bloody and merciless savagery of frontier warfare; his repute is epitomized in George Rogers Clark's phrase for him: "the Famous Hair Buyer General" (Clark to Patrick Henry, 3 Feb. 1779; *Clark Papers*, *1771-1781*, p. 97). Hamilton has since found defenders among both American and Canadian historians, but once he had been apprehended, the Virginia government took no chances on his possible escape and responded without enthusiasm to proposals for his exchange. He was regarded as a captive of the State of Virginia, and his status as such was firmly supported by both Congress and the Commander in Chief. Hamilton's own narrative of his captivity (same, p. 196) states that he was marched from Chesterfield Courthouse on 15 June, "an Officer having a written order under the hand of the Governor of the Province Thomas Jefferson for taking me in Irons to Williamsburgh." (The original of this order has not been found.) Hamilton had earlier written to Phillips to intercede in his behalf; Phillips' answer, dated 29 May 1779, was enclosed in a letter to Bland of the same date, and both were forwarded to Gov. Henry in Bland's missing letter of 1 June; copies of Phillips' two letters are in DLC: PCC, No. 57; that to Bland is printed in *Bland Papers*, I, 130-1. On 15 June Hamilton wrote Phillips to thank him for his efforts and to say that he was on his way to Williamsburg, handcuffed to another prisoner and therefore unable to write in detail (copy in DLC: PCC, No. 57). By the time Hamilton arrived in the capital, the REPRESENTATIONS BEFORE THE COUNCIL and THEIR INQUIRY, mentioned by TJ in the present letter, had been completed, and the results were shortly published; see the Council's Order of 16 June 1779, below. Hamilton's Report on his expedition from Detroit, his captivity in Virginia, and exchange in Mch. 1781 is printed in *Clark Papers*, *1771-1781*, p. 174-207; it was written in London and bears the date 6 July 1781. Hamilton's conduct as commander of British-allied Indian forces on the northwest frontier has been discussed frequently; the official Virginia view is set forth in Burk-Girardin, *Hist. of Va.*, IV, 353ff.; for modern opinions see especially Prof. James' Introduction to the *Clark Papers*, *1771-1781*, p. xxxvi ff. (unfavorable); N. V. Russell, "The Indian Policy of Henry Hamilton," *Canadian Hist. Rev.*, XI (1930), 20-37 (favorable); and Milo M. Quaife, ed., *The Capture of Old Vincennes*, Indianapolis, 1927, in the Introduction to which Quaife declares Hamilton "a brave and high-minded soldier" and his principal accuser, John Dodge, a conscienceless rascal (p. xix, xxi). Copies of Gen. Phillips' correspondence relating to the Hamilton case are in the Continental Congress Papers, No. 57 ("Convention Troops"), p. 349-418. Photostats and originals of important papers of Henry Hamilton are in the Clements Library; see Peckham, *Guide to Manuscript Collections in the Clements Library*, p. 127-8.

To William Fleming

DEAR FLEMING Williamsburgh June 8. 1779.

I received your letter and have now to thank you for it. Some resolutions of Congress came to hand yesterday desiring an authentic state to be sent them of the cruelties said to have been committed by the enemy during their late invasion. The council had already taken measures to obtain such a state. Tho' so near the scene where these barbarities are said to have been committed I am not able yet to decide within myself whether there were such or not. The testimony on both sides is such as if heard separately could not admit a moment's suspension of our faith.

We have lately been extremely disturbed to find a pretty general opinion prevailing that peace and the independance of the thirteen states are now within our power, and that Congress have hesitations on the subject, and delay entering on the consideration. It has even been said that their conduct on this head has been so dissatisfactory to the French minister that he thinks of returning to his own country, ostensibly for better health, but in truth through disgust. Such an event would be deplored here as the most dreadful calamity. It was in contemplation of some gentlemen who conferred on the subject to propose the re-establishment of our committees of correspondence; others thought this too slow for the emergency and that plenipotentiary deputies should be sent to satisfy the mind of the French minister, and to set on foot proper measures for procuring the genuine sense of the several states. The whole however subsided on a supposition that the information might not be true, and that our delegates in Congress would think no obligations of secrecy under which they may have been laid sufficient to restrain them from informing their constituents of any proceedings which may involve the fate of their freedom and independance. It would surely be better to carry on a ten years war some time hence than to continue the present an unnecessary moment.

Our land office I think will be opened; the sale of British property take place, and our tax bill put on a better footing. These measures I hope will put our finances into a better way and enable us to cooperate with our sister states in reducing the enormous sums of money in circulation. Every other remedy is nonsensical quackery. The house of delegates have passed a bill for removing the seat of government to Richmond. It hesitates with the Senate. We have established a board of war and a board of trade. I hear from your quarter that Genl. Sullivan is marching with a large army against the Indians. If he succeeds it will be the first instance of a great army doing any thing against Indians and his laurels will be greater. We have ever found that chosen corps of men fit for the service of the woods, going against them with rapidity, and by surprize, have been most sucesful. I beleive that our Colo. Clarke if we could properly reinforce him would be more likely to succeed against those within his reach than Genl. Macintosh's regular method of proceeding. I shall hope to hear from you often. I put no name to this letter, because letters have miscarried, and if it goes safely you know the hand.

RC (The Rosenbach Co., Philadelphia, 1946); unsigned. Endorsed: "Letter T. Jefferson."

To Conrad Alexandre Gérard

SIR Wmsburg June 8th 1779.

The General Assembly of Virginia at their first Session which was held after the conclusion of the Treaties of Alliance and Commerce between his most Christian Majesty and the American Congress, tho' seeing that fortunate event in all its importance, yet omitted to give it their particular approbation, entertaining a daily hope that the Confederation of the united States would be acceded to by all the parties, and that the Ratification of their Congress would then be the most proper and complete confirmation, and the most satisfactory to the Mind of their great and good Ally. But as that has not yet taken place they have now thought it their Duty no longer to pretermit their particular Sense of it and so far as their Interests and powers extend, to declare it obligatory; and have accordingly instructed me to communicate to the Minister of his most Christian Majesty resident at Philadelphia their Note of ratification; which I now have the honor to inclose to you. I obey their Commands with the greater pleasure because I know the grateful Sense which the Individual Members of that Body and the Citizens of this Commonwealth in general entertain of those Treaties, the high Value they set on them, and the disposition they have to convince you in every future instance that Nothing in their power shall be wanting to remove from your mind every cause of dissatisfaction which may at any time arise and to render these Treaties as lasting as to them they have been Safe honourable and pleasing.

I have the Honor to be with the most profound respect Your Excellency's Most Obedt. & mo: hble Servt., TH: JEFFERSON

ENCLOSURE

In General Assembly
friday the 4th June 1779.

Resolved nemine contradicente, that the treaties of alliance and commerce entered into between His Most Christian Majesty of France, on the one part, and the Congress of the United States of America, on behalf of the said States on the other part, ought to be ratified and confirmed so far as is in the power of this Commonwealth, and the same are accordingly hereby ratified, confirmed and declared binding on this Commonwealth.

Resolved, that the Governor be desired to notify to the Minister of His Most Christian Majesty, resident at Philadelphia, the above ratification under the Seal of the Commonwealth.

Archibald Cary, Speaker of the Senate
Benjamin Harrison, Speaker of the House of Delegates

Test:
J. Beckley, Clerk of the Senate.
Edmund Randolph, Clerk of the house of delegates.

Virginia to wit

In pursuance of the resolutions of the two Houses of Assembly, I hereby notify their joint ratification of the treaties of Alliance and Commerce entered into between his most Christian Majesty of France on the one part and the Congress of the United States on the other part, as expressed in their resolutions of June 4th 1779. and in testimony thereof have caused the Seal of the Commonwealth to be affixed hereto. Given under my hand this 7th day of June in the Year of Our Lord 1779.

TH: JEFFERSON
Governor of the Commonwealth of Virginia

RC (Arch. Aff. Etr., Paris, Corr. Pol., E-U, Suppl., vol. 1); in a clerk's hand and signed by TJ. Endorsed: "rep." Enclosure (same location, following letter of transmittal): Virginia General Assembly, Resolution of 4 June 1779, engrossed, sealed, and signed on parchment. Both papers were enclosed in a dispatch from Gérard to Vergennes, 22 June 1779, printed in Gérard, *Despatches and Instructions*, p. 740-3. Locations of other copies of these papers in the Archives of the Ministry of Foreign Affairs are given in the same, p. 741, note 6.

The Treaty with France was approved unanimously by the House of Delegates on 2 June and by the Senate on 4 June (JHD, May 1779, 1827 edn., p. 32, 34). The satisfaction of Gérard in this step by Virginia is expressed in Gérard's reply of 22 June and in his dispatch to Vergennes, mentioned above; see also Fleming to TJ, 22 June 1779.

To Benjamin Harrison

SIR In Council June 8. 1779.

Since receiving the resolutions of Congress calling for an additional sum of money, which I had the honor of transmitting to you yesterday, the inclosed address relating to the same subject, with the letter accompanying it has come to hand. I take the liberty through you of communicating it to the General assembly, and am Sir with the greatest esteem Your most obedient & most humble servant, TH: JEFFERSON

RC (ViW). Addressed in an unidentified hand to Harrison as Speaker. Endorsed: "Govrs. letter June 10. 1779. inclosing address to people as to taxation." Enclosure: see explanatory note.

RESOLUTIONS OF CONGRESS: These were the additional state quotas voted on 21 May (copy transmitted by Charles Thomson to TJ is in Vi); see entry for TJ's missing letter to Harrison of 7 June, above. THE INCLOSED ADDRESS: Doubtless a copy of the *Address to the Inhabitants of the United States of America* (Evans 16636) drafted by John Dickinson, agreed upon in Congress, 26 May, and ordered printed (JCC, XIV, 649-57). The House of Delegates ordered the Address to be printed in *Va. Gaz.* (JHD, May 1779, 1827 edn., p. 39).

To Charles de Klauman

In council June 12. 1779.

Capt. de Klauman being already sufficiently authorized to inspect and state the quantity and condition of all military stores within this commonwealth and to require necessary aid from the proper officers, I have only to desire that he will in every instance take from the officer in whose custody any ordnance arms, or other military stores are a certificate thereof signed by such officer; and where any such articles may not be in the custody of a particular officer, Capt. Klaumann is desired to certify under his own hand what and where they are. TH: JEFFERSON

RC (Vi).

De Klauman, a Danish volunteer officer, later transmitted the present document to the House of Delegates in support of a petition, 12 May 1780 (MS in Vi), requesting payment for his services, which was granted. For his report as a result of the present authorization, see below, 17 July 1779.

From Theodorick Bland

SR Charlotteville June 14th 1779

Having been inform'd that since your Excellencys Appointment to the Government of this Commonwealth your residence will be chiefly, if not entirely at the seat of Government, You will pardon me if (tempted by the perpetual view of your delightfull Seat from my lowly and I may say Dirty Cottage) I should venture to ask a preference should you be disposed to permit any other than your own family to Occupy it. Mrs. Bland who is and has been for some time with me Joins me in Congratulation and in paying her respects to your Excellency and Mrs. Jefferson and in wishing you both all possible earthly filicity, In the High Station wherein the Voice of your Country has so honorably Placed you and be assured sir that we are not less happy in hearing of your appointment than we are sensible of the loss we personally sustain, in the absence of yourself and Lady from our Society at this place, and at the same time that we cannot help rejoicing in common with the rest of our Country at the one, we must for ourselves lament the other. I have the Honor to be with the greatest Sincerity Sr. Yr most obedt. & very hbl Svt,

THEODK. BLAND

RC (DLC). It does not appear that anything came of Bland's application to rent Monticello; see TJ to Bland, 18 June 1779.

From John Jay

SIR — Philadelphia 16th June 1779

Copies of two Acts of Congress of the 14th Inst. are herewith enclosed. One recommending to the States to exempt Drivers of Waggons from Militia duties while in Service. The other for ascertaining their wages.

I have the honor to be with great Respect Your Excellency's Most obedt. Servant.

FC (DLC: PCC, No. 14) of a circular to several governors from the President of Congress. A copy, signed by Charles Thomson, of the first resolution enclosed is in Vi, with TJ's endorsement of date on verso. Both resolutions are printed in JCC, XIV, 726-7.

Order of Virginia Council Placing Henry Hamilton and Others in Irons

In COUNCIL, *June* 16, 1779.

THE Board proceeded to the consideration of the letters of Colonel Clarke, and other papers relating to Henry Hamilton, Esq; who has acted some years past as Lieutenant Governour of the settlement at and about Detroit, and commandant of the British garrison there, under Sir Guy Carleton as Governour in Chief; Philip Dejean, Justice of the Peace for Detroit, and William Lamothe, Captain of volunteers, prisoners of war, taken in the county of Illinois.

They find that Governour Hamilton has executed the task of inciting the Indians to perpetrate their accustomed cruelties on the citizens of these states, without distinction of age, sex, or condition, with an eagerness and activity which evince that the general nature of his charge harmonized with his particular disposition; they should have been satisfied from the other testimony adduced that these enormities were committed by savages acting under his commission, but the number of proclamations which, at different times were left in houses, the inhabitants of which were killed or carried away by the Indians, one of which proclamations, under the hand and Seal of Governor Hamilton, is in possession of the Board, puts this fact beyond doubt. At the time of his captivity it appears, that he had sent considerable detachments of Indians against the frontier settlements of the[1] states, and had actually appointed a great council of Indians to meet him at the mouth of the Tanissee, to concert the operations of this present campaign. They find that his treatment of our citizens and soldiers, captivated and carried within the limits of his command, has been cruel and inhumane;[2] that in the case of John Dodge, a citizen of these states, which has been particularly stated to this Board, he loaded him with irons, threw him into a dungeon, without bedding, without straw, without fire, in the dead of winter and severe climate of Detroit; that in that state he harrassed and wasted him, with incessant expectations of death; that when the rigours of his situation had brought him so low that death seemed likely to withdraw him from their power, he was taken out and attended to till somewhat mended, and then again, before he had recovered abilities to walk, was returned to his dungeon, in which a hole was cut seven inches square only, for the admission of air, and the same load of irons again put on him; that appearing again to be in imminent danger of being lost to them, he was a second time taken from his dungeon, in which he had lain from January to June, with the intermission beforementioned of a few weeks only; that Governour Hamilton gave standing rewards for scalps, but offered none for prisoners, which induced the Indians, after making their captives carry their baggage into the neighbourhood of the fort, there to put them to death, and carry in their scalps to the Governour, who welcomed their return and successes by a discharge of cannon; that when a prisoner brought alive, and destined to death by the Indians, the fire already kindled and himself bound to the stake, was dexterously withdrawn and secreted from them by the humanity of a fellow prisoner; a large reward was offered for the discovery of the victim, which having tempted a servant to betray his concealment, the present prisoner Dejean being sent with a party of soldiers, surrounded the house, took and threw into jail the unhappy victim, and his deliverer, where the former soon expired under the perpetual assurances of Dejean, that he was to be again restored into the hands of the savages, and the latter when enlarged was bitterly and illiberally reprimanded and threatened by Governour Hamilton.

It appears to them that the prisoner Dejean, was on all occasions the willing and cordial instrument of Governour Hamilton, acting both as judge and keeper of the jail, and instigating and urging him by malicious insinuations and untruths, to increase rather than relax his severities, heightening the cruelty of his orders by the manner of executing them; offering at one time a reward to one prisoner to be the hangman of another, threatening his life on refusal, and taking from his prisoners the little property their opportunities enabled them to acquire.

It appears that the prisoner Lamothe, was a Captain of the volunteer scalping parties of Indians and whites, who went out, from time to time, under general orders, to spare neither men, women, nor children.

From this detail of circumstances which arose in a few cases only, coming accidentally to the knowledge of the Board, they think themselves authorized to presume by fair deduction what would be the horrid history of the sufferings of the many who have expired under their miseries (which therefore will remain for ever untold) or who have[3] escaped from them, are yet too remote and too much dispersed to bring together their well grounded accusations against these prisoners.

They have seen that the conduct of the British officers, civil and military, has in its general tenor, through the whole course of this war, been savage and unprecedented among civilized nations; that our officers and soldiers taken by them have been loaded with irons, consigned to loathsome and crouded jails, dungeons, and prison ships; supplied often with no food, generally with too little for the sustenance of nature, and that little sometimes unsound and unwholesome, whereby so many of them have perished that captivity and miserable death have with them been almost synonimous; that they have been transported beyond seas where their fate is out of the reach of our enquiry, have been compelled to take arms against their country, and by a new refinement in cruelty to become the murtherers of their own brethren.

Their prisoners with us have, on the other hand, been treated with moderation and humanity; they have been fed on all occasions with wholesome and plentiful food, lodged comfortably, suffered to go at large within extensive tracts of country, treated with liberal hospitality permitted to live in the families of our citizens, to labour for themselves, to acquire and to enjoy property, and finally to participate of the principal benefits of society while privileged from all its burthens.

Reviewing this contrast which cannot be denied by our enemies themselves in a single point, which has now been kept up during four years of unremitted war, a term long enough to produce well founded despair that our moderation may ever lead them into the practice of humanity, called on by that justice which we owe to those who are fighting the battles of their country, to deal out at length miseries to their enemies, measure for measure, and to distress the feelings of mankind by exhibiting to them spectacles of severe retaliation, where we had long and vainly endeavoured to introduce an emulation in kindness; happily possessed by the fortune of war of some of those very individuals, who having distinguished themselves personally in this line of cruel conduct, are fit subjects to begin on with the work of retaliation, this Board has resolved to advise the Governour that the said Henry Hamilton, Philip Dejean, and William Lamothe, prisoners of war, be put into irons, confined in the dungeon of the publick jail, debarred the use of pen, ink, and paper, and excluded all converse except with their keeper. And the Governour orders accordingly. (*A Copy*)

Attest ARCHIBALD BLAIR, C.C.

Broadside (DLC: PCC, No. 71, I), bearing imprint at foot of text: "Williamsburg: Printed by John Dixon and Thomas Nicolson"; Evans 16657; Swem, "Va. Bibliog.," 7190. This copy, enclosed in TJ's letter to Pres. Jay, 19 June 1779, has several small corrections, in an unidentified hand, which are indicated in the textual notes below. Another copy of the Order was sent to Washington in TJ's letter of 19 June 1779; PrC in clerk's hand is in DLC: TJ Papers, misdated 18 (for 16) June. A MS copy in an unidentified hand is in the Phillips correspondence, DLC: PCC, No. 57; "Taken from the Virginia Gazette of Saturday June 19th. 1779"; this item, however, does not appear in the issue of the *Va. Gaz.* (D & N) for that date. It may have been printed in *Va. Gaz.* (C & D) on 19 June, but no copy of this issue is now known to be extant.

This Order, marked conspicuously by TJ's traits of style, was to bring about a long controversy between the government of Virginia and the British command on the status and treatment of Henry Hamilton; see note on TJ to Bland, 8 June 1779. THE LETTERS OF COLONEL CLARKE: The principal letter meant is that from G. R. Clark to Gov. Henry, Kaskaskias, 29 Apr. 1779 (printed under that date, above), reporting the capture of Hamilton at Vincennes; Clark's letter was published in *Va. Gaz.* (D & N), 26 June 1779. Concerning PHILIP DEJEAN and WILLIAM LAMOTHE (Guillaume La Mothe, variously spelled), French partisans who served with Hamilton, see *Clark Papers, 1771-1781*, index, and Ill. Hist. Libr., *Colls.*, V, index, for various references; both accepted paroles in October of this year, and Dejean joined the Americans in the West. ONE OF WHICH PROCLAMATIONS: "An Address to the inhabitants of Illinois, by Henry Hamilton, Lieutenant Governour of Detroit and its dependencies, &c., &c., found among Mr. Hamilton's papers," printed in *Va. Gaz.* (D & H), 26 June 1779; printed from a copy in Draper MSS in *Clark Papers, 1771-1781*, p. 95-7. The "Address" is dated 29 Dec. 1778 (hence had been issued at Fort Sackville, Vincennes) and was "Translated [from the French] by order of the Board" (i.e., the Virginia Council) by Charles Bellini, "Clk. of Foreign Correspondence." The text recites the preparations made "to expel the rebels" from the Illinois country—these preparations being plans for Indian raids on an extensive scale. JOHN DODGE, Indian trader and border adventurer, had been captured in 1776 and carried to Detroit and Quebec, whence he escaped late in 1778; he capitalized on his experiences by publishing *A Narrative of the Capture and Treatment of John Dodge, by the English at Detroit*, Phila., 1779 (also in Almon's *Remembrancer* for 1779, p. 73-81), a very lurid account which probably closely corresponds with the testimony he gave before the Virginia Council during their investigation of Hamilton's conduct. The value of his testimony must be weighed in the light of a private statement he made at this time: "I am going to Williamsburg in a few days to prosecute Hamilton and that Rascal Dejean Lamotte, likewise Hominay Hay. They will all be hanged without redemption, and the Lord have mercy on their Souls" (to Philip Boyle, 13 July 1779, *Kaskaskia Records*, ed. C. W. Alvord, Ill. Hist. Libr., *Colls.*, V, 104-5). Dodge later abused his office as Indian agent by terrorizing and plundering the French inhabitants of the Illinois country; see *Kaskaskia Records*, passim, also *Cahokia Records*, ed. C. W. Alvord, Ill. Hist. Libr., *Colls.*, II, Introduction and passim. It seems clear that the Governor and Council accepted the testimony of a well-informed but thoroughly disreputable witness. The conduct of Hamilton and his confederates, as related by Dodge and seemingly confirmed by documentary evidence, shocked TJ, whose earlier feeling and general policy toward enemy captives was extremely generous and humane—a fact freely acknowledged by Phillips himself (see Phillips to TJ, 5 July 1779).

1 Corrected by hand to "these."

2 Corrected by hand to "inhuman."

3 Corrected by hand to "having."

Inventory of Furniture in the Governor's Palace

An Inventory of household furniture in the palace taken the 16h. June 1779

1 blue & white China Tureen
6 Do. Do. Do. Dishes
11 red & white Do. Do.
13 blue & white Do. Plates
28 red & white Do. Do.
1 china Teapot creampot & 3 Sausors
1 large red & white china Bowl
2 blue & white butter Boats
1 Queens china Dish. 1 Do. Tureen
6 delf Coffee Cups 6 delf plates & 1 water bottle
1 Glass Salver 13 wine glasses 11 Cyder Do.
4 Glass Quart Decanters
1 Japan bread Basket plate basket
1 Do. plate warmer
2 pr. french plate candle sticks 1 do. Snuffer stand.
1 pr. Silver Salts
2 small Mahogany Waiters
1 small floor Cloth
1 Walnut writing desk
½ Doz Mahogany Chairs hair bottoms
10 Do. leather Bottoms
1 Doz Hair Do.
3 Mahogany four feet dining tables
1 marble Sideboard. 16 Scripture prints
2 Doz Mahogany Chairs hair bottoms
2 Do. Elbow
4 Mahogany & 2 Walnut 4 foot dining tables
18 Do. Chairs & 2 Elbow with hair bottoms
2 Do. pembrook Tables 2 Walnut chairs
1 Looking glass gilt frame
1 Chimney Glass
12 prints 8 old fashioned mahogany Chairs
1 large oval Walnut Table. 1 Walnut desk
1 Mahogany Tea table. 9 old fashioned mahogany Ch[airs]
1 Elbow Do.
1 wash bason stand 1 mahogany Chest-draws

1 Mahogany dressing Table. 6 Do. Chairs
5 Do. old fashioned Chairs
1 large old fashioned looking Glass
12 mahogany chairs. 6 Elbow Chairs covered wh. crimson damask
1 mahogany Card table
1 mahogany pembroke. 1 Do. Tea Table
1 Large looking Glass gilt frame
1 Japan Tea Kitchen
7 Walnut Chairs
1 4 foot Walnut Table
1 pair hand Irons & 1 poker
12 mahogany Chairs check bottoms & 1 Elbow Do.
1 Do. Chest-Draws
1 wash bason stand
1 looking Glass. 2 mahogany Book Cases
1 Chimney Glass. guilt fram
10 Globe Lamps
4 Beds 4 bolsters & 2 pillows
4 Bedsteads 1 sett green worsted bed Curtains wanting vallons, top and head-piece[1]
6 Leather water Buckets. 9 Lamps
1 pr. racks. 1 hand Iron 1 Spit
5 prints
1 four foot Walnut Table

Signed WM. GOODSON
H HARWOOD
June 16. 79.

MS (DLC); in an unidentified hand. Docketed in another hand: "Copy Inventory of Articles at Palace."

An inventory of the furniture in the governor's palace was made early in 1776 (*Va. Council Jour.*, II, 425), and at various times during Gov. Henry's administration additional articles of furniture were purchased for the palace by the State (*Va. Council Jour.*, I, 121, 142, 218, 280). The present inventory was evidently made after Patrick Henry had vacated the palace and was then turned over to TJ, who carefully checked it. On the leaf bearing the endorsement, there is the following notation in TJ's hand: "things omitted. 2. delft wash basons. 4. blankets." See also correction by TJ, footnote 1, below. There exists also (DLC: TJ Papers, 3: 492) a copy of a receipt signed by Patrick Henry, 29 May 1779, for a list of articles purchased for the Palace, which probably accompanied the inventory.

[1] The words from "wanting" are interlined in TJ's hand.

To Benjamin Harrison

[*Williamsburg, 17? June 1779.* JHD, May 1779, 1827 edn., p. 52 (17 June): "The Speaker laid before the House, a letter from the

Governor, enclosing several papers and stating sundry matters for the consideration of the General Assembly. . . ." Not located.]

To Richard Henry Lee

DEAR SIR Williamsburgh June 17 1779

I received your letter and kind congratulations for which I return you my thanks. In a virtuous government, and more especially in times like these, public offices are, what they should be, burthens to those appointed to them which it would be wrong to decline, though foreseen to bring with them intense labor and great private loss. I am also still to thank you for a former favor enclosing a song and receipt.

We have little new here. Colo. Clarke's expedition against St. Vincent's you know of. His prisoners are arrived at Chesterfeild, and three of them brought to this place to be severely dealt with. The enclosed paper will explain that matter. We have 300 men under Colo. Bowman in the Shawanee country, of whom we hope to receive good account. The destruction of the villages of the seceding Cherokees at Chuckamogga, and taking their goods &c. has brought them to sue for peace but the happiest stroke was the burning 20,000 bushels of corn collected there for the use of the expeditions which were to have been adopted at the great council. Governor Hamilton had called at the mouth of the Tanissee, as mentioned in the within paper.

It is a cruel thought that when we feel ourselves standing on the firmest ground in every respect, the cursed arts of our secret enemies combining with other causes, should effect, by depreciating our money, what the open arms of a powerful enemy could not. What is to be done? Taxation is become of no account, for it is foreseen that notwithstanding it's increased amount there will still be a greater deficiency than ever. I own I see no assured hope but in peace or a plentiful loan of hard money.

I shall be obliged by your letters when convenient to you to write. I never was a punctual correspondent to any person, as I must own to my shame. Perhaps my present office will put it more out of my power. However as it may sometimes furnish me with matter which may induce me to hope my letters may be worth sending, I may venture to say you shall hear from me whenever I can get over the twofold difficulty of many letters of absolute necessity to write, and an innate aversion to that kind of business.

I am Dr. Sir Your friend & servt., TH: JEFFERSON

RC (PPAP). Addressed: "Richard Henry Lee esq. Westmoreland." Enclosure: Order of Virginia Council, 16 June 1779, printed above. Text is badly faded and has been collated with the early printed text in R. H. Lee, *Memoir and Corr. of R. H. Lee*, II, 189.

YOUR LETTER: Missing. A SONG AND RECEIPT: See Lee to TJ, 3 May 1779.

To Theodorick Bland

SIR Williamsburg, June 18th, 1779.

Yours of the 14th inst., came to hand this day. * * * with respect to Col. Finnie, as a continental officer, [we decline med]-dling with his conduct; being yourself in the continental service, [we] take it for granted, that if he fails in his duty you will [put] him under a proper train of enquiry. His assurances to us are fair; one thing only I am to inform you, that however true it may be that he is without money, it is no just excuse for failing to do any thing for the public service, because that was never permitted by the executive here, to be on sufferance for want of money. He never applied in vain, and we still are, as we ever have been, ready to lend him (as a continental officer) any monies, which the due discharge of his office may call [for,] * * * * and politeness at the [least] hardly permits them to suppose the duties of the [post can be as] well discharged by any other, as by yourself. But your health for that very reason is the more to be taken care of. You will please to permit Capt. Bertling and Lieutenant Campbell to pass by land to the lower ferry of the Chickahominy, [where the Flag] lies, and finally settle the business, on which she came, according [to the rules] usual in their service. I inclose you the reasons, which have induced the council to [act] with such rigor with Governor Hamilton and the others there. It is impossible for any generous man to disapprove his sentence. I am, sir, with much [respect,] your most obedient and most humble servant, &c.

MS not located; text from *Bland Papers*, I, 138-9. The asterisks and square brackets are in the printed text. Enclosure: Order of Virginia Council, 16 June 1779, printed above.

YOURS OF THE 14TH INST.: If the present letter is a reply to Bland's letter of the 14th (see above), its passages commenting upon Bland's application for the use of Monticello during TJ's absence must have been among the omissions indicated by the use of asterisks. On the case of GOVERNOR HAMILTON, see TJ to Bland, 8 June, and references there. THE FLAG: a vessel bearing a flag of truce; concerning the BUSINESS ON WHICH SHE CAME see TJ to William Phillips, 25 June 1779.

To the Continental Board of War

SIR Williamsburgh June 18. 1779.

Inclosed you will receive the information you formerly desired on the subject of the barracks ordered to be built at Frederick. Some difference will appear between the report of some gentlemen formerly appointed for that purpose and Colo. Smith's letter; which difference however may be accounted for by their different dates. It is with concern we find that the continent is likely to lose by the inconsiderate omission of Colo. Kennedy to take security from the undertaker. Upon thorough enquiry into the best measures which may now be pursued, and from gentlemen in whom we confide, we would take the liberty of recommending, that Mr. Hobday the undertaker be immediately prosecuted for not complying with his contract that the whole management be put into the hands of gentlemen near the place who may be relied on to have the work executed on the best terms possible, for we must observe for a very obvious reason that no one will undertake it for a fixed sum, and that you send a proper plan for the barracks, as we learn that egregious blunders in this way would have been committed had the former contract been complied with. Our only object in having Hobday sued is that an execution may be levied on the timber brought into place which seems to be all the property he has, and will be of worth in the execution of the work; and lest any delay should put it in his power to withdraw this we have recommended to your deputy paymaster here to authorize a suit against him immediately without awaiting your orders, which suit by our laws will be determined at the first court of the county after the expiration of ten days from the service of the writ. We recommend Colo. John Smith and Isaac Zane as proper persons for your full confidence in engaging this work on the best terms. From a knowledge of the country in which this building is to be erected we would advise you strongly to build of stone rather than wood. It will cost as little, perhaps less, in the outset as we are assured on good testimony. The stone is not half a mile distant, the spot itself abounding with limestone, the timber prepared fit for cutting into joists, boards &c. and whenever the determination of the war shall render the building useless for barracks, it will reimburse you in some degree by sale, rent or otherwise. This is submitted altogether to your consideration. You formerly expressed a wish that the executive of this state should ease you of this troublesome business. They then declined it, in hopes that the channel into which you had put it would have had the work effected without trouble to you or them. Seeing now the unlucky turn it has taken and sensible that the common cause will be aided by the assistance of the executive in every state, where a business is become intricate and involved so as to require more of the time of the General council than ought to be so employed, they are willing to take up this matter and have the old contract settled as well as they can and the work carried into execution for you, if you think your distance or other occupations may prevent your being able to take better care of it. In this they will await your orders, and if you confide it to them, expect you shall be particular in your directions as to the plan, of what materials it shall be built and other circumstances of weight.

Among the prisoners taken at Detroit by Colo. Clarke, were some whose conduct seemed to call for severe treatment. I do myself the honour to inclose you a copy of our resolutions on that subject, containing the reasons of our severity. I have the honour to be Sir Your most obedient & most humble servt.,

TH: JEFFERSON

RC (DLC: PCC, No. 147, III). Endorsed: "Govr. Jefferson relative to the Barracks intended to have been built at Winchester." Enclosure: Order of Virginia Council, 16 June 1779, printed above.

This letter was read in Congress on 30 June and returned to the Board of War to "take order thereon" (JCC, XIV, 786). Col. John SMITH, of Hackwood Hall near Winchester, was county lieutenant and member of the House of Delegates for Frederick (Cartmell, *Shenandoah Valley Pioneers*, p. 296); his LETTER has not been found.

Thomas Jefferson and George Wythe to Benjamin Harrison

SIR Williamsburg, June 18, 1779.

The committee appointed in pursuance of an act of General Assembly passed in 1776, intituled "An act for the revision of the laws," have according to the requisitions of the said act gone through that work, and prepared 126 bills, the titles of which are stated in the inclosed catalogue. Some of these bills have been presented to the House of Delegates in the course of the present session two or three of them delivered to members of that House at their request to be presented, the rest are in the two bundles which accompany this; these we take the liberty through you of presenting to the General Assembly.

In the course of this work we were unfortunately deprived of the assistance and abilities of two of our associates appointed by the General Assembly, of the onc by death, of the other by resignation. As the plan of the work had been settled, and agreeable to that plan it was in a considerable degree carried into execution before that loss, we did not exercise the powers given us by the act, of filling up the places by new appointments, being desirous that the plan agreed on by members who were specially appointed by the Assembly, might not be liable to alteration from others who might not equally possess their confidence, it has therefore been executed by the three remaining members, one of whom being prevented from putting his signature hereto, by the great distance of his residence from this city, has by letter authorized us to declare his concurrence in the report.

We have the honor to be with the utmost respect, Sir, Your most obedient And most humble servants, T. JEFFERSON, G. WYTHE.

No MS located. Printed from *Report of the Committee of Revisors Appointed by the General Assembly of Virginia in MDCCLXXVI*, Richmond, 1784, p. 3.

The revised code of laws for Virginia prepared by TJ, Wythe, and Pendleton in pursuance of the Act for the Revision of the Laws, printed above under date of 15 Oct. 1776, was transmitted with this letter and is printed *in extenso* immediately following the present document.

THE REVISAL OF THE LAWS

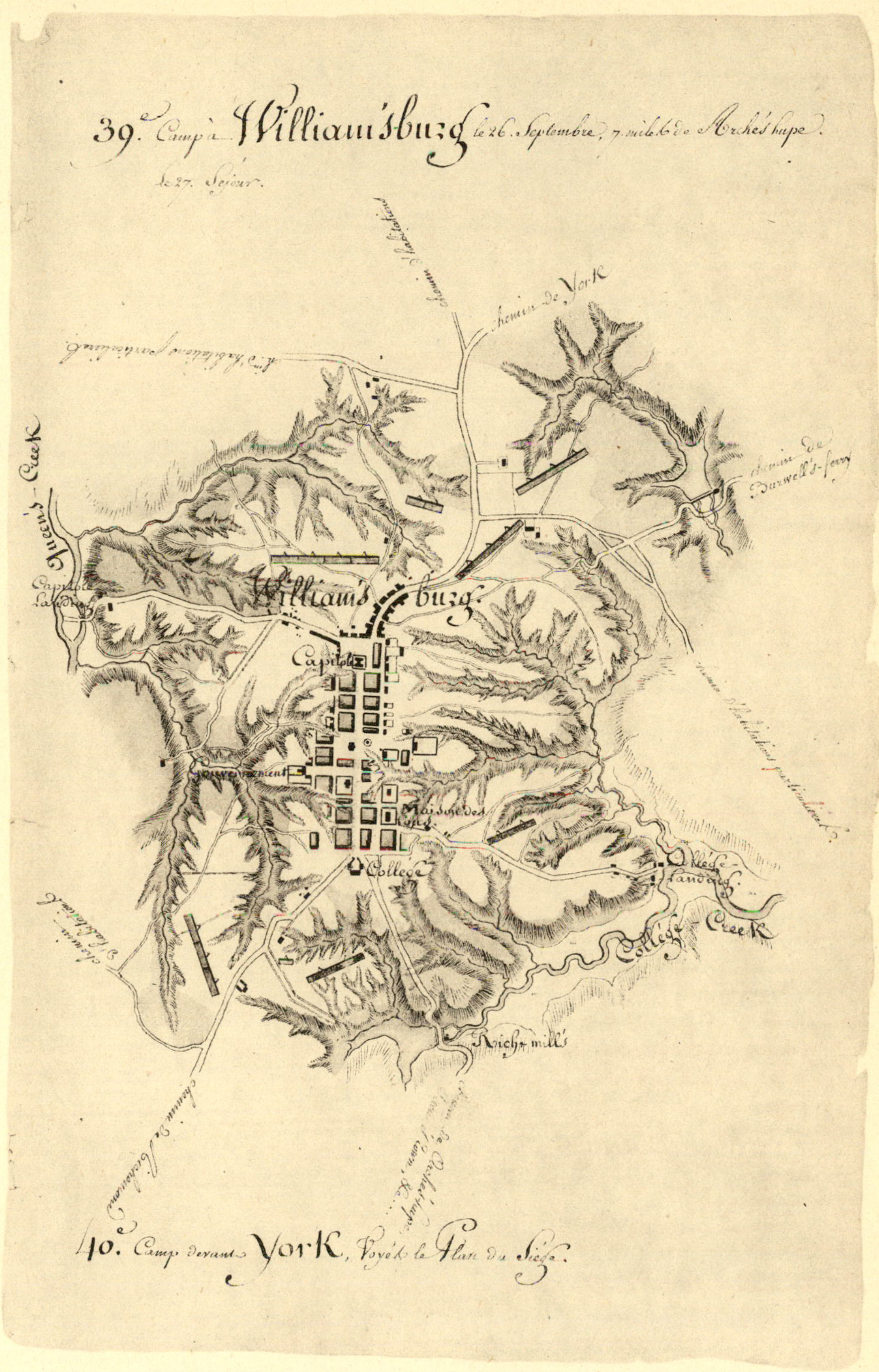

Plan of Williamsburg and the Surrounding Country in 1781

REPORT

OF THE

COMMITTEE of REVISORS

APPOINTED BY THE

GENERAL ASSEMBLY

of *VIRGINIA*

In MDCCLXXVI.

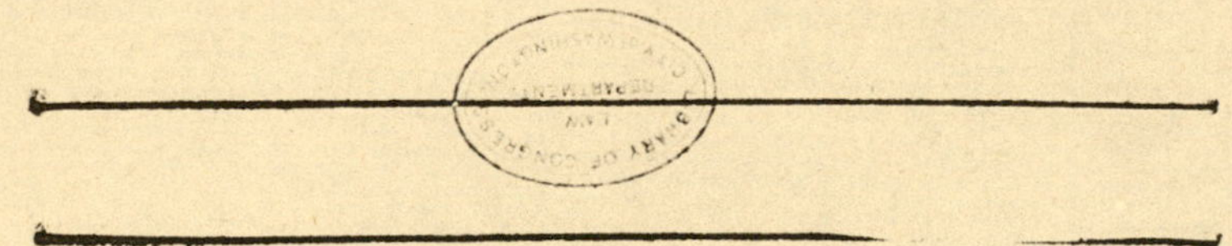

PUBLISHED BY *ORDER*

OF THE

GENERAL ASSEMBLY,

AND

PRINTED BY DIXON & HOLT,

In the CITY of RICHMOND,

NOVEMBER, MDCCLXXXIV.

Titlepage of Jefferson's Copy of the *Report of the Committee of Revisors*

A BILL *for eſtabliſhing* RELIGIOUS FREEDOM, *printed for the conſideration of the* PEOPLE.

WELL aware that the opinions and belief of men depend not on their own will, but follow involuntarily the evidence propoſed to their minds, that Almighty God hath created the mind free, and manifeſted his Supreme will that free it ſhall remain, by making it altogether inſuſceptible of reſtraint: That all attempts to influence it by temporal puniſhments or burthens, or by civil incapacitations, tend only to beget habits of hypocriſy and meanneſs, and are a departure from the plan of the holy author of our religion, who being Lord both of body and mind, yet choſe not to propagate it by coercions on either, as was in his Almighty power to do, but to extend it by its influence on reaſon alone: That the impious preſumption of legiſlators and rulers, civil as well as eccleſiaſtical, who, being themſelves but fallible and uninſpired men, have aſſumed dominion over the faith of others, ſetting up their own opinions and modes of thinking, as the only true and infallible, and as ſuch, endeavouring to impoſe them on others, hath eſtabliſhed and maintained falſe religions over the greateſt part of the world, and through all time: That to compel a man to furniſh contributions of money for the propagation of opinions which he diſbelieves and abhors, is ſinful and tyrannical: That even the forcing him to ſupport this or that teacher of his own religious perſuaſion, is depriving him of the comfortable liberty of giving his contributions to the particular paſtor whoſe morals he would make his pattern, and whoſe powers he feels moſt perſuaſive to righteouſneſs, and is withdrawing from the Miniſtry thoſe temporal rewards which, proceeding from an approbation of their perſonal conduct, are an additional incitement to earneſt and unremitting labour for the inſtruction of mankind: That our civil rights have no dependance on our religious opinions, any more than on our opinions in phyſicks or geometry: That therefore the porſcribing any citizen as unworthy the publick confidence, by laying upon him an incapacity of being called to offices of truſt and emolument, unleſs he profeſs or renounce this or that religious opinion, is depriving him injuriouſly of thoſe privileges and advantages to which, in common with his fellow citizens he has a natural right: That it tends alſo to corrupt the principles of that very religion it is meant to encourage, by bribing with a monopoly of wordly honours and emoluments, thoſe who will externally ~~profeſs and~~ conform to it: That though indeed theſe are criminal who do not withſtand ſuch temptation, yet neither are thoſe innocent who lay the bait in their way: That the opinions of men are not the object of civil government, nor under its juriſdiction: That to ſuffer the civil Magiſtrate to intrude his powers into the field of opinion, and to reſtrain the profeſſion or propagation of principles on ſuppoſition of their ill tendency, is a dangerous fallacy, which at once deſtroys all religious liberty; becauſe he being of courſe Judge of that tendency will make his own opinions the rule of judgment, and approve or condemn the ſentiments of others only as they ſhall ſquare with, or differ from his own: That it is time enough for the rightful purpoſes of civil government for its officers to interfere when principles break out into overtacts againſt peace and good order: And finally, that truth is great and will prevail if left to herſelf; that ſhe is the proper and ſufficient antagoniſt to errour, and has nothing to fear from the conflict, unleſs by human interpoſition, diſarmed of her natural weapons, free argument and debate; errours ceaſing to be dangerous when it is permitted freely to contradict them

WE the General Aſſembly of *Virginia* do enact, that no man ſhall be compelled to frequent or ſupport any religous Worſhip place or Miniſtry whatſoever, nor ſhall be enforced, reſtrained, moleſted, or burthened in his body or goods, nor ſhall otherwiſe ſuffer on account of his religious opinions or belief, but that all men ſhall be free to profeſs, and by argument to maintain their opinions in matters of religion, and that the ſame ſhall in no wiſe diminiſh, enlarge, or affect their civil capacities.

AND though we well know that this Aſſembly, elected by the people for the ordinary purpoſes of legiſlation only, have no power to reſtrain the acts of ſucceeding Aſſemblies, conſtituted with powers equal to our own, and that therefore to declare this act irrevocable would be of no effect in law; yet we are free to declare, and do declare, that the rights hereby aſſerted are of the natural rights of mankind, and that if any act ſhall be hereafter paſſed to repeal the preſent, or to narrow its operation, ſuch act will be an infringement of natural right.

Earliest Printed Text of the Bill for Establishing Religious Freedom

I. Crimes whose punishment extends to Life.

1. High treason. Death by hanging.
   Forfeiture of lands & goods to Commwth.
2. Petty Treason. Death by hanging
   Dissection.
   Forfeitre of half lands & goods to representatives of person killed.
3. Murder. 1. by poyson. Death by poyson.
   Forfeitre of one half as before.
   2. in Duel. Death by hanging
   gibbeting, if the challenger.
   Forfeitre of one half as before unless the challenger fell, then to Commw.
   3. any other way. Death by hanging
   Forfeitre of half as before.
4. Manslaur. 2d offence is murder.

II. Crimes whose punishment goes to Limb.

1. Rape. } Castration.
2. Sodomy. }
3. Maiming } Retaliation.
4. Disfiguring } Forfeiture of half to sufferer.

III. Crimes punisheable by Labor &c.

1. Manslaur. 1st offence. Labor VII. years.
   Forfeitre of half as before.
2. Counterfeiting. Labor VI. years.
   Forfeit whole to Commw.
3. Arson. } Labor V. years.
4. Asportn of vessels } Reparation threefold
5. Robbery } Labor IV. years
6. Burglary } Reparation. double.
7. Housebreaking } Labor III years
8. Horse stealing } Reparation.
9. Grand Larceny. Labor II. years
   Reparation
   pillory ½ an hour.
10. Petty Larceny. Labor I. year.
    Reparation
    pillory ¼ of an hour
11. Witchcraft &c. Ducking
    15. stripes.
12. Excusable homicide. nothing.
13. Suicide. nothing
14. Apostacy. Heresy. nothing.

Jefferson's Outline for His Bill for Proportioning Crimes and Punishments

The Revisal of the Laws 1776-1786

I. PLAN AGREED UPON BY THE COMMITTEE OF REVISORS AT FREDERICKSBURG [13 JANUARY 1777]

II. CATALOGUE OF BILLS PREPARED BY THE COMMITTEE OF REVISORS

III. BILLS REPORTED BY THE COMMITTEE OF REVISORS, 18 JUNE 1779

IV. APPENDIX

1. BILL DECLARING WHEN LAWS SHALL BE IN FORCE
2. JEFFERSON'S NOTES OF ENGLISH STATUTES
3. JEFFERSON'S NOTES OF ACTS OF ASSEMBLY ADOPTED OCTOBER 1777 AND MAY 1778
4. OUTLINE OF BILL FOR PROPORTIONING CRIMES AND PUNISHMENTS, &c.
5. MEMORANDUM BY JEFFERSON ON BILLS TO BE DRAFTED

EDITORIAL NOTE

It is an extremely difficult task to bring into proper focus, to say nothing of fully encompassing, the far-reaching revision of the laws that Jefferson and other leading Virginians embarked upon in the autumn of 1776. This is chiefly because the revision of the laws itself never came into focus. It was a long-drawn-out movement, ending in something of an anti-climax, and never became embodied in a single enactment as in the case of earlier or later revisions in Virginia and in other states. However important for the whole future of society its Bill for Establishing Religious Freedom may have been, the revision as a whole has, for the most part, faded into obscurity against the background of ordinary legislation in the decade from 1776 to 1786, with an occasional landmark standing out in bold relief. There is no single identifiable entity that can be called the Revision of the Laws as there is, for example, in the so-called Chancellors' Revisal of 1785 or the revision approved in 1792.

This resulted partly from its purpose, which was not that of forming a collection of laws then in force but of reforming the entire structure of law so as to strip it of all vestiges of its earlier monarchical aspects and to bring it into conformity with republican principles. If Jefferson and his colleagues had been content merely to collect the body of law then in force, no doubt the General Assembly would have approved in 1779 what it actually did approve in 1792. But this would have been executing the task of compilers, not that of legislators, and Jefferson, Pendleton, Wythe, Mason, and others apparently never entertained the idea of making a mere collection of the laws. Certainly Jefferson never did. The failure of the Virginia Convention of 1776 to adopt his proposed Constitution undoubtedly emphasized the need he felt for reform of the laws. For his Constitution had included some provisions that he later incorporated in legislative bills that he thought would form "a system by which every fibre would be eradicated of antient or future aristocracy; and a foundation laid for a government truly republican"

(Autobiography, Ford, I, 68). But he no doubt would have proposed a general overhauling of the legal system as an urgent necessity even if his Constitution had been wholly adopted, for he understood the distinction between fundamental and statutory law and knew that the former could not and should not embrace the detailed provisions of the latter. Certainly Jefferson's historic decision in the early days of October 1776 to remain in Virginia rather than accept the mission to France was largely determined by his zeal to remake the legal structure of the commonwealth and to remold it both in form and substance so as to coincide more nearly with the leading principles of the Revolution. "I knew," he wrote in his Autobiography, "that our legislation under the regal government had many very vicious points which urgently required reformation, and I thought I could be of more use in forwarding that work. I therefore retired from my seat in Congress on the 2d. of Sep., resigned it, and took my place in the legislature of my state" (same, p. 48).

Yet the failure of the revision of the laws to come into focus and to be adequately appraised has resulted from the method as well as the intent of its leading architect. Jefferson, who was unquestionably the principal advocate of the idea of reform, was possessed of a sense of urgency that would not permit a single approach toward the goal. As an active legislator, enmeshed from 1776 to 1779 in the details of day-to-day law-making and its inevitable turmoil of political maneuverings, Jefferson was obliged to be alert to the possibility that any legislative calendar might bring forth bills proposed by adherents of the old order. This ever-present tendency to preserve the status quo or to project the nature of colonial institutions into the future required constant vigilance on his part. But important as this was in the time and energies it consumed, the daily hacking away at laws advocated by conservatives was not reform; it was merely the negative strategy of holding ground that had already been gained. Jefferson's achievement as legislator in the years 1776 to 1779 was more positive and proceeded on a two-fold method.

The first was a singlehanded effort to hasten the new era of republicanism by the drafting of legislative bills on particular subjects—courts of justice, entails, the established church, importation of slaves, naturalization, &c. On these and many other subjects it is safe to say that Jefferson was, as author or chief advocate, responsible for the introduction and adoption of more bills than any other single member of the General Assembly in the years 1776 to 1779. In the variety of subjects touched upon, in the quantity of bills drafted, and in the unity of purpose behind all of this legislative activity, his accomplishment in this period was astonishing. He was in himself a veritable legislative drafting bureau. Often his bills were introduced by others; equally as often he seems to have had himself appointed to committees in order that he might give effect to some of his own legislation by inserting it in or attaching it to the bills of others. But, however his bills were introduced or however important some of them were, Jefferson realized that these were "the details of reformation only . . . points of legislation prominent in character and principle, urgent, and indicative of the strength of the general pulse of reformation" (same, I, 57). Despite the fact that this piecemeal approach to reform resulted in legislative achievements greater than he recalled and more extensive than biographers have recognized, Jefferson realized that a broader, more systematic revision of the laws was necessary.

His second approach, therefore, sprang from the conviction, as he later expressed it, "that our whole code must be reviewed, adapted to our republican form of government, and, now that we had no negatives of Councils, Governors, and Kings to restrain us from doing right, it should be corrected, in all it's parts, with a single eye to reason, and the good of those for whose government it was framed. Early therefore in the session of 76, to which I returned, I moved and presented a bill for the revision of the laws" (same, I, 57-8). Under the broad terms of this Act a Committee of Revisors carried on the work of systematic reform, submitting its report on 18 June 1779. This Report of the Committee of Revisors comes nearer than anything else to representing a concrete revisal of the laws executed under Jefferson's leadership. Yet many bills included in this Report were, for one reason or another, deemed to be of such urgency or importance that they were lifted from it, introduced, and in some instances enacted in advance of the submission of the full Report. Others were singled out for similar action in the years following. Despite this selective treatment of its bills, the proposed revision as a whole was brought forward for consideration at the October 1785 session. At that time about a third of the bills were enacted, though all that were adopted were suspended in operation until 1 January 1787 so that the remainder of the Report could be considered at the next session and, if approved, the entire revisal put into effect as a unit. Only a few of the bills that were held over for the October 1786 session were adopted and the revisal was never put into effect as a unit. In 1785 Jefferson was in France and the sponsorship of the reform rested upon James Madison. Some of the radical measures proposed in the Report met with strong opposition. Then a new committee was set to work, not with the object of reforming but of collecting and publishing the laws in one source. By 1786, in legislation as in other fields of political endeavor, "the general pulse of reformation" was far weaker than it had been in 1776.

Because of these facts, the landmarks of the revision that have been emphasized are chiefly those that Jefferson himself remembered and singled out for emphasis. He left several appraisals of the revision. The most nearly contemporary account—that in *Notes on Virginia*—contains the longest list of "the most remarkable alterations" that had been proposed by the Committee of Revisors (same, III, 242-55). It is also a fairly accurate index of what Jefferson considered his most important contributions to the work of revision, since most of the bills listed were those that he drew. In 1785, before the Report of the Committee of Revisors was even brought up, Jefferson wrote to G. K. van Hogendorp a very depreciatory comment on the revisal: "It contains not more than three or four laws which could strike the attention of a foreigner. . . .

The only merit of this work is that it may remove from our book shelves about twenty folio volumes of statutes, retaining all the parts of them which either their own merit or the established system of laws required" (letter dated 13 October 1785). But by far the most dramatic and most famous comment was that made by Jefferson in his Autobiography. Here he discussed the bills that he introduced separately as well as those that formed his part of the revisal, an account which concluded with this sweeping estimate of purpose and accomplishment: "I considered 4 of these bills, passed or reported, as forming a system by which every fibre would be eradicated of antient or future aristocracy; and a foundation laid for a government truly republican. The repeal of the laws of entail would prevent the accumulation and perpetuation of wealth in select families, and preserve the soil of the country from being daily more and more absorbed in Mortmain. The abolition of primogeniture, and equal partition of inheritances removed the feudal and unnatural distinctions which made one member of every family rich, and all the rest poor, substituting equal partition, the best of all Agrarian laws. The restoration of the rights of conscience relieved the people from taxation for the support of a religion not theirs; for the establishment was truly of the religion of the rich, the dissenting sects being entirely composed of the less wealthy people; and these, by the bill for a general education, would be qualified to understand their rights, to maintain them, and to exercise with intelligence their parts in self-government: and all this would be effected without the violation of a single natural right of any one individual citizen" (Ford, I, 68-9).

This dramatic summation by the chief architect of the revision undoubtedly played its part in throwing the foothills into deeper shadow once the peaks had been singled out. But the total work of revision extending over a full decade would have been obscured even without such an emphasis upon some of its parts. For there were other factors involved in addition to those of purpose, method, and timing indicated above. First of all, there is apparently no manuscript extant for the entire Report of the Committee of Revisors. Apparently no complete manuscript of the Report was submitted to the General Assembly even when Jefferson and Wythe, with Pendleton's concurrence, addressed their letter to Benjamin Harrison on 18 June 1779, for that letter, after explaining that "Some of these bills have been presented to the House of Delegates in the course of the present session two or three of them delivered to members of that House at their request to be presented," explicitly stated that "*the rest are in the two bundles which accompany this*" (italics supplied). Second, the *Report of the Committee of Revisors*, a printed text of ninety-six pages issued under authority of the General Assembly, is the only approximately complete text of the work of the Committee of Revisors existing in any form. Even this cannot be regarded as a complete text of the bills prepared by the Committee. For it lacks the text of Bill No. 15, which must have been among "the two bundles" submitted in 1779 but which, being a wartime measure, had served its purpose so that by 1784 there was no need to print it. Also, the Committee originally prepared at least 128 bills, but during the first week of June 1779 and undoubtedly while preparing "the two bundles" for transmittal, TJ struck two from the list; these were bills "for establishing a loan office" and "for regulating the inspection of tobacco" (see Document II in this series, notes 6 and 12). Furthermore, the *Report of the Committee of Revisors* is, except for specialists, a rare and inaccessible text of the most interesting and significant legal reforms attempted during the Revolutionary era. No complete publication or reproduction of the bills included in it has been made available heretofore. Finally, even a full and correct reprinting of this pamphlet would be very far from presenting a full account of the reform of the law attempted by Jefferson and his colleagues. To represent the scope of the revision fully it would be necessary to trace at least three difficult and tedious stages: (1) the law as it stood before the Committee of Revisors began work; (2) the alterations that the Committee proposed; and (3) the extent to which these alterations were adopted by the General Assembly. Even in so detailed a work as the present, such an analysis, in documentary form, would not be feasible and probably not desirable. That kind of appraisal must await investigation and evaluation by the legal historian.

Meanwhile, for the purposes of this work it has been deemed essential to present at least the full texts of all bills drafted by the Committee of Revisors, so far as texts can be found. This has been done in the following pages. In many cases a bill as proposed by the Committee has been compared with the law which it reenacted or altered; in many other cases—some of them of the highest importance—this has not been possible because no prototype existed, as, for example, in the Bill for Establishing Religious Freedom or the Bill for Proportioning Crimes and Punishments. In all cases, however, the extent to which the General Assembly accepted or rejected the terms of the bills proposed by the Committee has been noted through a comparison of the text of the bill as proposed with that of the act as adopted.

This has never been done before, though in a few notable instances the difference between what was proposed and what was accepted has been commented upon. However, even in respect to the most famous of all bills in the Report—that concerning religious freedom—the exact nature of the differences has not been indicated and has possibly been misunderstood (see Hening, XII, 84, where the opinion is given that the "variations . . . render the style less elegant, though the sense is not affected"; but see Malone, *Jefferson*, I, 279, for a more correct opinion). A comparison of texts of this Bill also brings out the surprising fact that the text most widely accepted by the general public and by scholars as the Act for Establishing Religious Freedom is neither the text of the Bill as drafted nor of the Act as adopted, but a variant of the two which, for some unknown reason, Jefferson made in 1786 and published under a title that induced subsequent generations to accept it as the text of the Act as adopted. This timeless declaration of intellectual freedom is here presented (either through a full text, a facsimile reproduction, or textual annotation) in the following forms: (1) as originally printed in 1779 and distributed "for the consideration of the people"; (2) as printed in the *Report of the Committee of Re-*

visors; (3) as amended by the General Assembly and enacted into law in 1785; and (4) as the Act of Assembly was "amended" by Jefferson himself in 1786 and printed separately in France and also in various editions of *Notes on Virginia* (see Bill No. 82 and notes thereto).

In the absence of a better and more complete text for all of the bills, the editors have been obliged to use that of the *Report of the Committee of Revisors* as printed in 1784. Whenever possible this has been supplemented and corrected by such manuscript fragments as remain. Curiously, the manuscript notes, memoranda, and drafts that Jefferson left concerning the bills that he introduced individually in the years 1776 to 1779 are far more extensive than those that deal with the work of the Committee of Revisors. We have no manuscript text of the Bill for Establishing Religious Freedom. The *Report* is the sole text for Jefferson's bills concerning education (Bills No. 79, 80, 81). It is ironic that these bills setting forth Jefferson's system of public education should exist only in a poorly printed text and that the Bill for Proportioning Crimes and Punishments, which was never adopted and which in many respects was a harshly reactionary piece of legislation, should be preserved in two self-consciously precious and meticulously drafted manuscripts.

It was remarked above that no complete publication or reproduction of the *Report of the Committee of Revisors* has been made available heretofore. Insofar as this may be taken to imply that the *Report* is included in full in this volume, this statement needs qualification. What is here included is both more and less than the printed pamphlet which is the only approximately complete text of the Report of the Committee of Revisors. That pamphlet—specifically, Jefferson's annotated copy of it now in the Library of Congress—is employed here only as the basic source of the texts of 126 of the 128 bills prepared by the Committee of Revisors. As such, and in order to indicate precisely what is omitted from it, the *Report* requires description.

This printed pamphlet took its origin from a resolution adopted by the House of Delegates 29 May 1784 and concurred in by the Senate 2 June 1784: "Whereas, in pursuance of an act, entitled 'an act, for the revision of the laws,' a revisal of the laws of this Commonwealth has been executed with great labor and care, and reported to the General Assembly by the committee appointed for the said purpose: and whereas, it is highly expedient that the said revisal should as early as possible undergo the consideration; and if approved, receive the sanction of the Legislature: and whereas, it is necessary for that purpose, and moreover for the purpose of affording to the citizens at large, an opportunity of examining and considering a work which proposes such various and material changes in our legal code, that the same should be printed, and copies thereof diffused throughout the community: *Resolved*, That the clerk of this House, be empowered and directed to make out a complete set of the bills contained in the said revisal, as originally reported; and after the same shall have been inspected and approved by the members of the committee of Revisal, or any two of them, to cause five hundred copies thereof to be forthwith printed; that of the copies, when printed, one shall be delivered to each member of the General Assembly, of the Executive, of the General Court, of the Courts of Chancery and Admiralty, to the Attorney General, and to each of the delegates representing this State in Congress; and that the residue of the said copies be distributed throughout the several counties by the Executive, in such manner as they shall judge most conducive to the end proposed" (JHD, May 1784, 1828 edn., p. 26-7, 31; the resolution also directed that the unspecified sum of money necessary for carrying this into effect "be advanced by the treasurer, on warrant from the auditors, out of the first unappropriated money which shall come into his hands").

Two observations on this resolution are pertinent. First, it was an unusual procedure, for in other instances (e.g., those of 1769, 1792, 1819) it was not deemed necessary to print the revisals and distribute them to the people in advance of legislative action. It seems obvious that the reason for doing this in the case of the Report of the Committee of Revisors was that theirs was regarded as "a work which proposes such various and material changes in our legal code," whereas other revisals, being mere collections or codifications, did not attempt general reforms. Second, this resolution directed the clerk of the House (Jefferson's protégé John Beckley) "to make out a *complete set of the bills contained in the said revisal*, *as originally reported*." The phrase "as originally reported" meant, obviously, the bills as reported by Jefferson and Wythe on 18 June 1779; it also meant, certainly, *all* of the bills that had been reported at that time. For the Report by Jefferson and Wythe on 18 June 1779 was, in fact, the first and only report made; and the printed pamphlet contains, with the exception of Bill No. 15 noted above, the entire text of all the bills reported by the Committee of Revisors. But, as the letter from Jefferson and Wythe clearly shows, the Committee of Revisors did not on 18 June 1779 transmit *all* of the texts of bills that had been drafted; they merely transmitted "*the rest* . . . in the two bundles which accompany this." This remnant could not have included more than 116 of the total of 126 bills and probably included at most not more than 113; for several bills were selected from the whole and introduced separately before Wythe and Jefferson reported "the rest," or were left in the hands of members to be so introduced. Of these, ten bills were enacted into law and several others (e.g., Bills No. 5, 6, 92) were introduced at the May 1779 session but failed to be adopted. These facts suggest, if indeed they do not prove, that in 1784 the clerk of the House obtained access to a manuscript copy of the entire revisal or perhaps to fair copies of the separate parts of the work allocated to Jefferson, Pendleton, and Wythe. With Jefferson in Paris and Pendleton in semi-retirement, it is plausible to assume that Beckley obtained his full text from Wythe. But the most that can be said with certainty is that he could not have relied upon "the bills . . . as originally reported"; otherwise the pamphlet he produced would not have been as complete as it was and as the General Assembly's resolution had required it to be.

It should also be noted that Beckley was directed by this resolution to have his complete text "inspected and approved by the members of the committee of Revisal, or any two of them." Pendleton's part of this duty was probably delegated to Wythe, just as he had in 1779 authorized Jefferson and Wythe to "declare his concurrence in the report." Jefferson was unavailable for this task of inspecting and approving the text. Though Beckley may have relied upon Wythe for the copy of the whole text and for examining and approving it for publication, he alone had the legal duty "to cause it to be printed." His execution of that duty leaves much to be desired. The proofreading of the printed text was slovenly: punctuation and spelling are often erroneous. Most of these lapses have been corrected silently, though much of the spelling and punctuation has been allowed to stand for lack of a manuscript copy, a text as enacted into law, or other valid standard of comparison (a good example of the difference between a bill as Jefferson wrote it and as it was mangled by clerks or by proofreaders occurs in the middle of Bill No. 80, for which there exists a fragment of Jefferson's draft).

This *Report of the Committee of Revisors Appointed by the General Assembly of Virginia in MDCCLXXVI* was printed by Dixon & Holt in Richmond in November 1784 (see facsimile of title-page in this volume). It consists of ninety-six pages in two numbered sequences (p. [1]-6, 1-90). The following items are included in the preliminary pages of the *Report* but are not reprinted here for obvious reasons: (1) the full text of the 1776 Act for the revision of the laws, which Jefferson wrote and the Bill for which is printed above under date of 15 Oct. 1776 (see Hening, IX, 175-7); (2) the resolution of the General Assembly of 5 Nov. 1776 appointing the Committee of Revisors, attested by Beckley and by John Pendleton, clerk of the Senate; (3) extract from the Journal of the House of Delegates of 18 June 1779, certified by Beckley, giving the text of the letter of the same date from Jefferson and Wythe to the Speaker of the House; and (4) a copy of the resolution of 1 June 1784 (quoted above), certified by Beckley and William Drew, clerk of the Senate. This preliminary section of the *Report* also includes the following: (1) a complete catalogue by title of all the 126 bills prepared by the Committee of Revisors (p. 4-5; this catalogue is printed below as Document II); and (2) a memorandum which may have been prepared by Wythe or Pendleton: "N.B. George Mason, Esq; one of the Committee of Revisors declined to act; Thomas Ludwell Lee, Esq, another of the same Committee died without having taken any part in the business; and the three remaining Gentlemen, to wit: Thomas Jefferson, Edmund Pendleton, and George Wythe, Esquires, performed the present work."

The remainder of the pamphlet consists (p. 1-90) of the complete texts (with the exception of Bill No. 15) of the 126 bills. These are here presented in full (including the text of Bill No. 15) as Document III in the present series, though occasionally a manuscript text has been employed when available. There are, however, the following departures from the manner of presentation of the bills in the pamphlet: (1) the

Report follows parliamentary use by citing the bills as "chapter I," "chap. II," "chap. XXXVIII," &c.; in the following pages, though the title of each bill follows that in the *Report* literally, this method of citing by chapter has been rejected and, instead, each title is given its appropriate arabic numeral; (2) all of the bills in the *Report*, even those that consist of a single sentence or paragraph, have numbered sections. (It may be noted here that, although the Journals of the House of Delegates for 31 Oct. 1785 refer to the *printed* bills then introduced, many of the titles there cited vary considerably from the titles given in the *Report*; some of these were obviously clerks' errors, but others varied so much as to make it certain that either different texts had been used or the printed titles in the *Report* were altered; see Bills No. 24, 43, 44, 59, 74, 80, 95, 106, 115.) Paragraph divisions in the following pages are the same as those of the *Report*, but section numbers have been omitted.

In view of these omissions and additions, the documents printed here cannot be regarded as a reprinting of the *Report of the Committee of Revisors*: that pamphlet is employed only as the basis of Documents II and III in the present series. But, while these volumes contain all of the matter in the *Report*, much that is not included in that pamphlet is presented in this series—for example, the various items included in Documents I and IV, below.

THERE can be no doubt that Jefferson was nominally and actually the leading figure in the revisal. Madison's comment in 1826 on both the revisal and Jefferson's share in it is the comment of one who, next to Jefferson himself, felt the deepest concern for this reform: "The revised Code, in which he had a masterly share, exacted perhaps the most severe of his public labours. It consisted of 126 Bills comprizing and recasting the whole Statutory Code British and Colonial then admitted to be in force or proper to be adopted, and some of the most important articles of the unwritten law, with original laws on particular subjects; the whole adapted to the Independent and Republican form of Government. The work tho' not enacted in the mass as was contemplated has been a mine of Legislative wealth; and a Model also of Statutory Composition, containing not a single superfluous word, and preferring always words and phrases of a meaning fixed as much as possible by oracular treaties or solemn adjudications" (Madison to S. H. Smith, 4 Nov. 1826, DLC: Madison Papers). As author of the Bill for Revision of the Laws, as chairman of the Committee of Revisors, and as proponent of the chief landmarks of liberal legislation during this period, Jefferson was indubitably the primary spokesman for reform.

The Bill for the Revision of the Laws was adopted 24 October 1776. On 5 November following, the House of Delegates proceeded to nominate a "committee to revise the laws." The "several gentlemen . . . nominated" by the House were the following: Edmund Pendleton, George Wythe, Thomas Jefferson, Peter Lyons, Edmund Randolph, Thompson Mason, Richard Parker, Thomas Ludwell Lee, George Mason, John Blair, Paul Carrington, William Ellzey, Jack Power, and John Bannister (apparently the nominations were made in this order, according to a MS: Vi, in the hand of John Tazewell). The Senate made its nominations the same day; the lists of nominees were exchanged by the two houses; each house balloted on the combined lists; and a committee of tellers of the House "reported that they had met a committee from the Senate, in the conference room, and had jointly with them examined the ballot boxes, and that the majority was in favour of Thomas Jefferson, Edmund Pendleton, George Wythe, George Mason, and Thomas Ludwell Lee, Esquires" (JHD, Oct. 1776, 1828 edn., p. 41). To be chosen, at the age of thirty-three, head of so important a committee and in competition with some of the finest legal minds in America indicates that the suffrage of his colleagues in the legislature agrees with all other surviving evidence as to his leadership and fitness for this work of reform.

The Committee, under Jefferson's chairmanship, met at Fredericksburg on 13 January 1777 "to settle the plan of operation and to distribute the work" (Autobiography, Ford, I, 58). Under the Act of 1776 the Committee had "full power and authority to revise, alter, amend, repeal, or introduce all or any" of the laws of the state, though the work of the Committee would not have the force of law, in any of its parts, until duly passed by the General Assembly (Hening, IX, 177). Under this broad authority the Committee defined its own scope and intent. The first question to be settled, Jefferson stated in his Autobiography, was "whether we should propose to abolish the whole existing system of laws, and prepare a new and complete Institute, or preserve the general system, and only modify it to the present state of things. Mr. Pendleton, contrary to his usual disposition in favor of antient things, was for the former proposition, in which he was joined by Mr. Lee. To this it was objected that to abrogate our whole system would be a bold measure, and probably far beyond the views of the legislature; that they had been in the practice of revising from time to time, the laws of the colony, omitting the expired, the repealed and the obsolete, amending only those retained, and probably meant we should now do the same, only including the British statutes as well as our own: that to compose a new Institute like those of Justinian and Bracton, or that of Blackstone, which was the model proposed by Mr. Pendleton, would be an arduous undertaking, of vast research, of great consideration and judgment; and when reduced to a text, every word of that text, from the imperfection of human language, and it's incompetence to express distinctly every shade of idea, would become a subject of question and chicanery until settled by repeated adjudications; that this would involve us for ages in litigation, and render property uncertain until, like the statutes of old, every word had been tried, and settled by numerous decisions, and by new volumes of reports and commentaries; and that no one of us probably would undertake such a work, which, to be systematical, must be the work of one hand" (Autobiography, Ford, I, 58-9). Jefferson described the plan in concise terms in *Notes on Virginia*: "The common law of England . . . is made the basis of the work. It was thought dangerous to attempt to reduce it to a text: it was therefore left to be collected from the usual monuments of it.

Necessary alterations in that, and so much of the whole body of the British statutes, and of acts of assembly, as were thought proper to be retained, were digested into 126 new acts, in which simplicity of style was aimed at, as far as was safe" (Ford, III, 243; see Document I in this series, below).

This description is so similar to the one by Madison in 1826 (quoted above) as to suggest that he relied upon *Notes on Virginia.* If so, he was led astray by Jefferson's broad generalization that "so much of the whole body of the British statutes, and of acts of assembly, as were thought proper to be retained, were digested into 126 new acts." The actual scope of the revision seems to lie somewhere between the two extremes of a complete codification or institute advocated by Pendleton and a compilation of laws in force, "omitting the expired, the repealed and the obsolete," that the majority of the Committee, according to Jefferson's remembered account, agreed upon. Its scope was also much less comprehensive than Jefferson asserted in *Notes on Virginia* and Madison repeated in 1826. For the revisal omitted much besides the expired, the repealed, and the obsolete; it omitted, for example, the Declaration of Rights and the Constitution of 1776; it omitted the fundamentally important land laws, and it particularly failed to carry out the land reforms agreed upon (see Document I, below), probably because some of these had been defeated when the Act of 1779 for establishing a land office was adopted; it omitted several whole categories of legislation without defining precise Acts (see Bill No. 126, below); and, as shown in some of Jefferson's few surviving memoranda, there were many specific Acts that were intended to be excepted in the repealing Bill (see Document IV, 3, note 1, below). While the revisal, therefore, did not succeed in "recasting the whole Statutory Code British and Colonial," it did go "far beyond the views of the legislature" if those views comprehended a mere collection of laws in force. For in addition to Jefferson's great new bills on education and religion, the Committee of Revisors so drastically altered many existing laws as to amount to the proposal of wholly new legislation (e.g., Bill No. 86 concerning marriages). As the notes to many of the bills show, the Committee proposed reforms not heretofore recognized and in more than one instance the revisal even assaulted the deeply-entrenched county court system (see Bill No. 95). The General Assembly that in 1784 adopted the resolution to print the *Report of the Committee of Revisors* was well aware that this revisal was not a mere imitation of those that had been made before the Revolution but was indeed a work "which proposes . . . various and material changes in our legal code."

THE SCOPE of the work agreed upon, the Committee next attacked the problem of allocating different parts of the revisal to the different members of the Committee. "When we proceeded to the distribution of the work," Jefferson later recalled, "Mr. Mason excused himself as, being no lawyer, he felt himself unqualified for the work, and he resigned soon after. Mr. Lee excused himself on the same ground, and died, indeed, in a short time. The other two gentlemen, therefore, and myself divided the work among us. The common law and statutes to the 4 James I. (when our separate legislature was established) were assigned to me; the British statutes from that period to the present day, to Mr. Wythe; and the Virginia laws to Mr. Pendleton" (Autobiography, Ford, I, 59). In *Notes on Virginia* Jefferson wrote that "the rule, in our courts of judicature was, that the common law of England, and the general statutes previous to the 4th of James, were in force here; but that no subsequent statutes were, *unless we were named in them*, said the judges and other partisans of the crown, but *named or not named*, said those who reflected freely" (Ford, III, 238). The allocation to George Wythe of that part of English statutory law subsequent to 1607 would seem to indicate that the Committee proceeded under the customary rule.

But this account of the allocation of duties does not square with the only contemporary account of the plan agreed upon that apparently has survived (Document I, below). In that document the first period, dealing with English statutes down to 25 Henry VIII, was assigned to Jefferson; the second, presumably including both English statutes and Acts of Assembly down to the Revolution [of 1688?], to Pendleton; the third, also presumably English statutes and Acts of Assembly from that time down to "the present Day," to Wythe; the fourth, that part of Virginia law not in the first three divisions, plus land law and criminal law, to Mason; and the fifth, property in slaves and the laws of other colonies, to Lee. While this is probably the division of labor that prevailed at the beginning, Lee's death and Mason's resignation caused a redistribution and the ultimate plan worked out may have approximated what Jefferson remembered. It seems clear that most of the work that fell to Lee and Mason was taken over by Jefferson; certainly he did those parts dealing with slavery and criminal law. It is also certain that in addition to this agreement upon the general scope of the plan and distribution of tasks, the Committee, at Jefferson's solicitation, settled "the leading principles" of the law of descents and the criminal law (see notes to Bills No. 20 and 64, below).

In carrying out his part of this plan, Jefferson attempted a reform in style as well as substance. With respect to the older laws, he retained the time-honored phraseology, thinking it wise "not to vary the diction of the antient statutes by modernizing it, nor to give rise to new questions by new expressions" (see, for example, Bill No. 26 concerning mortmain and Bill No. 72 forbidding and punishing affrays). But in dealing with later statutes, though the Committee had agreed to make as few changes as possible except to remedy "Diction . . . obsolete or redundant" (see Document I in this series, below), Jefferson thought it would be useful "in all new draughts, to reform the style of the later British statutes, and of our own acts of Assembly, which, from their verbosity, their endless tautologies, their involutions of case within case, and parenthesis within parenthesis, and their multiplied efforts at certainty by *saids* and *aforesaids*, by *ors* and by *ands*, to make them more plain, do really render them more perplexed and incomprehensible, not only to common readers, but to the lawyers themselves" (Autobiography, Ford, I, 61).

Certainly simplicity, brevity, and directness were among the primary rules of drafting agreed upon by the Committee. These rules, such as "not to include Matters of different Natures" and "not to insert an unnecessary word, nor omit a useful one" (Document I, below), no doubt gave point to each of the bills and enabled the Committee to encompass its great task within a remarkably brief space. But the rules involved disadvantages for the historian if not for the contemporary legislator. For example, except in a few instances (and these were chiefly in the reform bills written by Jefferson) all preambles in existing statutes were omitted, presumably because they were neither necessary nor useful additions to their respective acts. But such preambles, by the occasional vigor of denunciation or by explanation of acts legislated against, are of first importance to the historian.

The Committee, Jefferson later wrote, "were employed in this work from that time to Feb. 1779, when we met at Williamsburg, that is to say, Mr. Pendleton, Mr. Wythe, & myself, and meeting day by day, we examined critically our several parts, sentence by sentence, scrutinizing and amending until we had agreed on the whole. We then returned home, had fair copies made of our several parts, which were reported to the General Assembly June 18. 1779. by Mr. Wythe and myself, Mr. Pendleton's residence being distant, and he having authorized us by letter to declare his approbation" (Autobiography, Ford, I, 61; it is clear, as has been pointed out by Mr. David J. Mays, Richmond, Virginia, in a communication to the editors of 19 June 1950, that Jefferson was in error in thinking that Pendleton had attended the meeting of February 1779; see, for example, Pendleton's letter to Jefferson of 11 May 1779).

The fair copies that were made of the three separate divisions are not known to be extant. There is, however, as noted above, one manuscript of a part of the revisal in the University of Virginia that requires some explanation. Its provenance and nature are not fully established, but some facts about it are known and others are deducible. First, it was once a part of the estate of Dr. Joshua I. Cohen (1801-1870) and was sold in 1930, being given to the University of Virginia shortly thereafter (American Art-Anderson Galleries, 15 Jan. 1930, lot 83; communication from Francis L. Berkeley, Jr., 24 Feb. 1950). The MS consists, first, of a four-page list in Jefferson's hand, headed: "A Catalogue of bills prepared by the Commee for the revision of the laws" (see notes to Document II in this series, below). Second, following this there are copies of sixty-six of the 126 bills. These bills are written in various clerks' hands and on several varieties and sizes of paper, Jefferson's numbered "Catalogue of bills prepared" being the smallest sheet used. The MS is not as complete as it once was; certainly a part of its last bill is missing (see Bill No. 124, below) and Bills No. 125 and 126 may possibly have been included in it originally. Also, at the beginning of the MS (Bills No. 1, 2, 3, 4, 6, 7, 12, 13, and 16), each bill is written on a separate sheet or sheets, in hands of different clerks, and on different kinds and sizes of paper. But all of those bills included in the MS from No. 17 to No. 124 are written continuously, a new bill following immediately after another wherever the latter ends on the page, though in a few instances toward the end of the MS a fresh start was made at the top of the succeeding page even when this meant leaving considerable blank space. The MS, diverse in character as some of its elements are, seems separable into two parts: the nine individual, docketed bills in the first part, and the fifty-seven more or less continuous bills in the second part. As explained under Document II, the "Catalogue of bills" in Jefferson's hand has the crossed-out original numbering of the bills, and also the new sequence of numbers made necessary by his dropping from the list Bill No. 13 providing for a loan office and the renumbering of Bills No. 14 to 127 to accord with the present Bills No. 13 to 126. Now the sixty-six bills in the MS are numbered according to this renumbered sequence, most of these numbers being in clerks' hands, some in Wythe's hand, and a few in Jefferson's hand. As shown in notes 9 and 13 to Document II in this series, the original Bill No. 13 was rejected and the renumbering of the list was done after 1 June 1779. Hence the bills in this MS were numbered after 1 June 1779 and probably at the time Jefferson and Wythe were preparing the "two bundles" of bills they submitted on 18 June. But does this mean that the MS was itself the "two bundles" of bills submitted 18 June? Obviously not. For the letter of the Committee of that date proves that each of the bills submitted was separable from the mass—some had been introduced, some had been left with members, and "the rest" was submitted with the letter of 18 June. The "rest" presumably was also made up of bills prepared in separate form. Moreover, the "Catalogue of bills" that accompanied "the rest" was not the same as that catalogue in Jefferson's hand which is attached to the MS but a clerk's copy made from it. Other supporting evidence will appear below.

Hence it appears that this MS must have been the copy of one or more of the three parts of the revision. Clearly it is not the part or parts that the Committee in February 1779 "examined critically . . . sentence by sentence, scrutinizing and amending," for both the nine separate bills and the fifty-seven continuous bills are fair copies; occasional corrections have been made (one being in Wythe's hand), but these are all corrections of copyists' errors, not the Committee's alterations. The MS, therefore, is one or more of the three fair copies of the parts of the revision that Jefferson said were made after the Committee returned home from its February 1779 meeting. It cannot be the fair copies of all three parts since the whole consists of only sixty-six bills. It must contain all or most of George Wythe's part, for all of the bills that are known certainly to have been prepared by him (Bills No. 6, 35, 89, 92, 93, 108; see Document IV, Parts 3 and 4, in the present series) are in this MS. What, then, is it?

This MS, clearly, contributes most to the answer to this question not by what it includes but by what it omits. An analysis of its omissions involves an examination of another interesting and puzzling aspect of the "Catalogue of bills" in Jefferson's hand which accompanies the MS. Suffixed to forty-nine of the titles in this catalogue are alphabetical and numerical designations that, for some purpose, Jefferson set down. To make that purpose more apparent, these devices are given in full as follows (though they are arranged alphabetically here, whereas in the notes to Document II they are placed numerically to accord with the different bills to which each refers; also Jefferson's period after each letter and number is here omitted): A1, C1, C2, D3, E3, E4, F2, F4, G2, G4, H3, H4, I3 (bis), J4, K1, L2, M3, N1, Q4, R2, S3, T2, U3, V1, V2, W3, Z3, CC3, FF1, FF4, HH2, LL1, LL4, MM2, NN3, PP1, PP3, RR1, RR3, SS3, TT1, UU1, UU3, VV1, VV2, VV4, and WW3.

The first and most obvious meaning to be attached to these devices is that they were employed by Jefferson to designate gatherings of sheets on which bills were written, that these sheets were folded in fours, that, since the signatures ran from A1 to WW3, there were at least forty-nine such gatherings, and that each occupied four pages. That is to say, Jefferson was here referring to a manuscript of at least 196 pages in length. Second, this manuscript must have been the *whole* of the manuscript of the revisal and not one or two of its three parts. This can be demonstrated by the fact that N1 refers to the relatively short Bill No. 125, which at most could not fill more than four pages and which was certainly far too short to occupy the gap of fifteen pages between N1 and Q4 (two Bills, Nos. 73 and 94, provide a convenient gauge, for both fall on one page, I3, and the two represent about half the length of Bill No. 125). The most obvious conclusion from this is that Jefferson's signature designations refer to the whole of the three corrected and amended parts made at the February 1779 meeting, though it is possible also that this could have been a fair copy of the whole.

But what is most important about these signature designations is that they point the way to the task of defining that part of the revision for which Jefferson was responsible. Two significant facts at once become apparent. First, not one of the bills whose title is thus designated is to be found in the MS described above. Second (with two exceptions, Bills No. 98 and 119), *all* of the bills that are certainly known to have been prepared for the revision by Jefferson are included in the forty-nine bills bearing these signature designations. It seems certain therefore that these designations must refer to the part for which Jefferson was responsible and, in consequence, the MS must contain most of the remainder—that is, either one or both of the parts assigned to Wythe and Pendleton. The two exceptions noted (Bills No. 98 and 119) do not invalidate the premise or the proof; they merely suggest that Jefferson may have prepared—and in these two instances did prepare—more of the total of 126 bills than were designated. Both of the bills in question, incidentally, refer to oaths and are closely related; for one of them there exists one of the few MSS of any part of the revisal in Jefferson's hand. It is quite possible, therefore, that they were drawn after the MS to which Jefferson's signature designations refer and therefore were not physically a part of it; hence there could have been no occasion to place such a designation after the titles to Bills No. 98 and 119.

The above observations find further support in another striking fact.

In what seems to be the earlier of the two MSS of the Bill for Proportioning Crimes and Punishments, Jefferson at one point wrote the following: "See sheet F.3.b." This particular designation does not appear on the "Catalogue of bills prepared" and it may in fact refer only to a sheet of notes rather than to the drafts of bills. But the use by Jefferson of such a designation in connection with the drafting of one of his own bills and its close identity with the nature of the signature designations listed above would certainly seem to reinforce and lend plausibility to the supposition here advanced.

If this supposition and the evidence on which it rests are valid, then for the first time it becomes possible to attempt a demarcation of most, if not the whole, of that part of the revision for which Jefferson was responsible. According to this interpretation of the meaning of the signature devices, Jefferson drew Bills No. 8, 9, 10, 11, 14, 15, 19, 20, 24, 26, 27, 28, 29, 30, 31, 32, 37, 40, 46, 48, 51, 52, 55, 56, 57, 58, 64, 66, 67, 68, 70, 71, 72, 73, 74, 75, 76, 79, 80, 81, 82, 83, 84, 94, 110, 112, 113, 121, and 125, together with the exceptions noted above, 98 and 119, or a total of fifty-one Bills. These, added to the sixty-six in the MS described above, leave only nine unaccounted for. It is known that Pendleton, though he assisted in the work, had a minor share and that Jefferson and Wythe bore the brunt of the labor. But Pendleton certainly prepared more than nine bills. Also, the MS described above is mutilated at the end and may indeed have become separated from some of the individual bills at its beginning. Hence it seems obvious that that MS must have contained all or most of the parts by Wythe and Pendleton. (The editors are indebted to Mr. David J. Mays, Richmond, Virginia, for calling their attention to a letter in the University of Virginia written by Pendleton to Richard Henry Lee, 8 November 1777, in which he said: "I hear nothing from the Assembly whom I propose to Viset the latter end of next week, with my Part of the Revised Laws"; this indicates that Pendleton had completed his part of the statutes in a few months, much of which required redrafting perhaps because Pendleton, who may have misunderstood what the Committee desired, had preserved the redundant legal phraseology of the laws; communication to the editors, 19 June 1950.)

This, of course, should not be taken to mean that Jefferson wrote only those bills listed above. What is meant to be suggested by that list is that it is the part that Jefferson prepared for the revision. Many of the bills of which he was the author were adopted in the years 1776 to 1779; these, in many instances, fell in the parts assigned to Wythe or Pendleton, as for example the court bills (e.g., it is established that Jefferson wrote the Bills for the Court of Appeals and the Admiralty Court, but in the work on the revisal these—Bills No. 92 and 93—fell in the part assigned to Wythe). Conversely, we know that Jefferson had much to do with bills that are by this analysis ascribed to Wythe and Pendleton. For example, on the important matter of writs Jefferson took the English statute of 13 Edward I, chapter 24, reduced it to a single sentence, proposed to reenact it in full force in Virginia, and had a bill copied by his clerk to be added to the revisal. Subsequently, however, he decided not to make this a separate bill but to incorporate it in one of the bills already prepared; it is to be found, therefore, at the beginning of Bill No. 102, which probably was prepared by Wythe. This, incidentally, is a good instance of the manner in which "Statutes British and Colonial" were compressed and also of the fact that the revisal proposed to enact a vast amount of legislative matter that does not explicitly appear in its pages.

MORE could be ascertained about the division of labor and methods of work if the corrected parts and notes had been preserved. It is much to be regretted and probably will remain an inexplicable mystery that no one of the MSS of the revisal that would be the most illuminating documents concerning the Committee's methods of work—that is, the drafts of the three separate parts that the Committee "examined critically . . . sentence by sentence, scrutinizing and amending"—has ever come to light. It is understandable why those corrected drafts of Pendleton's and Wythe's parts should be lost, but it is surprising indeed that Jefferson's own papers, which he preserved with such high regard for the purposes and uses of history, should not contain full notes, memoranda, corrected drafts, and fair copies of his greatest and most sustained legislative effort. From a fragment showing Jefferson's classification and shelf arrangement of his personal archives, it appears that he had carefully preserved "Draughts, Notes &c. relating to Revised Code" (MS owned in 1947 by the late Roger W. Barrett, Chicago). Only a paltry remnant of this rich source remains.

Those few bills that were lifted from the "two bundles" transmitted by the Committee of Revisors and were introduced separately at the session of May 1779 may have been selected by Jefferson himself, though the letter of transmittal suggests that this was done at the request of some members. There were ten of these bills passed at that session (Nos. 8, 9, 10, 15, 24, 55, 65, 93, 98, and 119). Others, as indicated above, were acted upon separately after 1779 (such as Nos. 5, 6, 59, 78, and 96). In *Notes on Virginia* Jefferson expressed the belief that the Report as a whole probably would "not be taken up till a restoration of peace shall leave to the legislature leisure to go through such a work" (Ford, III, 242-3). But peace apparently brought neither leisure nor inclination to consider the revisal of 1779; that of 1769 was to be the starting point. Precisely four years after that Report was submitted, the General Assembly instructed "the Executive to cause the several acts . . . subsequent in date to the revisal in the year 1769, and the ordinances of Convention which are now in force, to be collected into one code, with a proper index, and marginal notes, to be revised and examined by any two judges of the High Court of Chancery" (JHD, May 1783, 1828 edn., p. 53). At the same time the House authorized the printing of sufficient copies of this revisal to supply all branches of government. This resolution resulted in the compilation of the laws and ordinances passed between 1769 and 1785, and published in 1785, commonly referred to as The Chancellors' Revisal. Meanwhile, however, Madison pressed for action upon the more inclusive code that the Committee of Revisors had brought in. At the October 1785 session, as Jefferson expressed it, "by the unwearied exertions of Mr.

Madison, in opposition to the endless quibbles, chicaneries, perversions, vexations and delays of lawyers and demi-lawyers, most of the bills were passed by the legislature, with little alteration" (Autobiography, Ford, I, 62). This, however, is a generalized recollection that requires modification: it exaggerates the opposition of the legislature and the number of bills approved and minimizes the alterations such bills underwent. The legislature was slow to take up the revisal, but its action in 1785-1786 indicated that its attitude was neither that of indifference nor of hostility. The bills that it selected for approval or for opposition showed that, as legislatures go, its examination of the bills was constructively critical and even discriminating. Shortly after the presentation of the bills in October 1785 Madison wrote to Washington that the "House have engaged with some alacrity in the consideration of the Revised Code. . . . The present temper promises an adoption of it in substance. The greatest danger arises from its length compared with the patience of the members. If it is persisted in it must exclude several matters which are of moment, but I hope only for the present Assembly" (11 Nov. 1785; Madison, *Writings*, ed. Hunt, II, 192).

On 31 October 1785 Madison introduced one hundred and eighteen of the bills reported by the Committee of Revisors. The eight bills omitted from the whole (Nos. 7, 8, 9, 15, 16, 18, 30, and 36) that Madison presented were excluded because they had had effect, or had been repealed, or were of a temporary nature. The bills were taken up in order and little opposition was met with until Bill No. 64 for Proportioning Crimes and Punishments came up. This, as might have been expected, proved to be a stumbling block. Only thirty-five of the bills presented by Madison were adopted at this session, though, under the influence of urgent petitions, the legislature did select out of the remainder the greatest of all for adoption—that concerning religious freedom (see Madison to TJ, 22 Jan. 1786). Some of these were, indeed, passed with little alteration; others were changed greatly. "We have got thro' a great part of the revisal and might by this time have been at the end of it had the time wasted in disputing whether it could be finished at this Session been spent in forwarding the work. As it is we must content ourselves with passing a few more of the important bills, leaving the residue for our Successors of the next year. As none of the bills passed are to be in force till Jany. 1787, and the residue unpassed will probably be least disputable in their nature, this expedient, though little eligible, is not inadmissible" (Madison to Washington, 9 Dec. 1785, *Writings*, ed. Hunt, II, 199).

The bills that were not acted upon were held over until the October 1786 session and at that time, again under the sponsorship of Madison, twenty-three of them were adopted. These were Bills No. 66, 69, 71-76, 84, 87, 97, 103-106, 108-115. By this time, however, it was clear that the General Assembly had no intention of acting upon the revisal as a whole, though the Report continued to be a legislative mine from which particular items were extracted from time to time; for example, Bills No. 100, 121, and 122 were passed in 1789, and that part of Bill No. 79—Jefferson's famous Bill on education—which pertained to aldermen was incorporated in the Act of 1796, though this scarcely touched the substantial elements of his plan. The Chancellors' Revisal had been compiled, providing a useful compendium of laws still in force between 1769 and 1785, and, on 25 December 1786, a Bill was ordered to be brought in "for completing the revision of the laws." This Bill was introduced by Madison two days later and, after being amended by both houses, was passed on 2 January 1787 (JHD, Oct. 1786, 1828 edn., p. 123-6, 134-5, 137, 151). In order to salvage as much of the work of the Committee of Revisors as possible, Madison proposed that, instead of having the legislature continue its consideration of the revisal, a committee of three be appointed to consider such of the bills reported by the Committee of Revisors as had not been enacted, to examine them with a view to making such alterations as might be necessary due to "change of circumstances or otherwise," and to report at the next session. Madison explained the necessity for this move in his letter to Jefferson of 15 February 1787—conditions had changed since 1779, many of the bills needed amendment, and the repealing Bill (No. 126) could not safely be passed "before the operation of the various amendments, &c. made by the Assembly could be leisurely examined by competent Judges." Madison had also written Pendleton a few days earlier that several circumstances had convinced him "that if the work was put within the reach of the next assembly, there would be danger not only of its being left in a mutilated state, but of its being lost altogether" (9 Jan. 1787, *Writings*, ed. Hunt, II, 304-06); in the letter to Jefferson he had explained more candidly that there "was good reason to suspect Mr. Henry who will certainly be then a member."

The new Committee of Revisors was authorized under the law passed in consequence of Madison's motion to consider all Acts passed since the revisal of 1779 and, in the words of the Act of 1776, "to revise, alter, amend, repeal or introduce all or any of the said laws." At the same time, all of the twenty-three Acts passed at the October 1786 session were suspended until 1 July 1787 (Hening, XII, 409-11). But Madison's loyal efforts to salvage the heroic work of his friend Jefferson and to thwart "Mr. Henry" and the next session of the legislature proved of no avail. He had, before making the move, told Jefferson that he would have "no hesitation at this policy if I saw a chance of getting a Committee equal to the work of compleating the Revision. Mr. Pendleton is too far gone to take any part in it. Mr. Wythe I suppose will not decline any duty which may be imposed on him, but it seems almost cruel to tax his patriotic zeal any farther. Mr. Blair is the only remaining character in which full confidence could be placed" (see under date of 4 Dec. 1786). A month after this was written the General Assembly elected Edmund Pendleton, George Wythe, and John Blair as the new Committee of Revisors who were to carry out the purpose of this Act. But misfortune again dogged the steps of the revisal. Neither Pendleton, Wythe, nor Blair was a member of the General Assembly that had elected them to do the work; possibly they were not consulted before being elected to perform this task. Pendleton was in semi-retirement, save for his work as president of the Court of Appeals. Wythe, as Madison's letter implies, had labored heroically on the revisal of 1776-1779 and had just helped complete The Chancellors' Revisal of 1785. Possibly both were disappointed that their labors of a decade earlier had been so long neglected. Whatever the cause, nothing whatever seems to have been done under this Act. Another Act calling for a revisal of the laws, passed in 1789, asserted that "the great number of laws of this Commonwealth, dispersed as they are through many different volumes, renders it often questionable which of them are in force; copies of those laws are procured with difficulty, and only at high prices; and so many of them have been repealed, wholly or in part, were temporary and have expired; were occasional, and have had their effect; were private or local, or have been reenacted in substance, in the laws, taken from the report of the revisors . . . that scarce a third of them concern the public at large" (Hening, XIII, 8-9). The Act then appointed a committee of eight to execute this law. The committee was an able and distinguished one, including as it did St. George Tucker, Edmund Randolph, James Innes, John Taylor, and John Marshall. But again nothing resulted. At the October 1790 session another Act was passed appointing Edmund Pendleton, Henry Tazewell, St. George Tucker, Joseph Prentis, Arthur Lee, and William Nelson, Jr., a committee to effect a general revision of the laws, with specific directions to ascertain what British statutes there were, if any, that were appropriate but had not yet been enacted in Virginia; to ascertain what general laws should be continued and what discontinued, &c. (same, XIII, 130-1). This Act finally brought about a comprehensive revision, the results being adopted at the October session 1792. The Revised Code of 1792 was then authorized to be published and was issued in Richmond in 1795 by Augustine Davis. It contained all of the general laws in force that had been adopted down to and including the session of October 1794 (see *The Code of Virginia*, Richmond, 1849, p. vi). It included among these laws many that had been reported by the Committee of Revisors in 1779 and adopted in 1785-1786 or earlier, but none that had failed of adoption.

At last Virginia had produced a comprehensive revisal of the laws of the commonwealth. It was narrower in scope and less elevated in purpose than that which Jefferson and his colleagues had attempted, but, at least in respect to legislative approval, its accomplishment was more complete. Yet none of its Acts, and none passed in that era, could match in timelessness and in continuing influence one Bill of the revisal of 1779 that alone would justify the great effort at reform and compensate for the frustration which that effort met with—Jefferson's declaration of intellectual and spiritual independence in his Bill for Establishing Religious Freedom.

In the preceding comments and throughout the notes to Documents I-IV in this series, any citation given as *Report* is to be understood as meaning the pamphlet issued in 1784 under the title *Report of the Committee of Revisors Appointed by the General Assembly of Virginia in MDCCLXXVI*; and any reference to the Report is to be understood as meaning the Report of the Committee of Revisors as submitted on 18 June 1779.

I. Plan Agreed upon by the Committee of Revisors at Fredericksburg

[13 January 1777]

The Common Law not to be medled with, except where Alterations are necessary.

The Statutes to be revised and digested, alterations proper for us to be made; the Diction, where obsolete or redundant, to be reformed; but otherwise to undergo as few Changes as possible.

The Acts of the English Common-wealth to be examined.

The Statutes to be divided into Periods: the Acts of Assembly, made on the same Subject, to be incorporated into them.

The Laws of the other Colonies to be examined, and any good ones to be adopted.

General Rules in Drawing

Provisoes &c. which wou'd do only what the Law wou'd do without them, to be omitted.

Bills to be short; not to include Matters of different Natures; not to insert an unnecessary word, nor omit a useful one.

Laws to be made on the Spur of the present Occasion, and all innovating Laws, to be limited in their Duration.

Criminal Law.

Treason and Murder (and no other Crime) to be punished with Death, by hanging and Forfeiture; saving Dower.

Petty-treason, Parricide, Saticide; the Body to be delivered over to Surgeons to be anatomized.

Manslaughter to be punished by Forfeiture and Labour.

Suicide not to incur Forfeiture, but considered as a Disease.

Justifiable Homicide not to be punished at all.

Rape, Sodomy, Bestiality to be punished by Castration.

Other Crimes punishable by Forfeiture, Fine, Labour in public-works, such as mines, Gallies, Saltworks, Dock-Yards, Founderies, and public manufactories.

The Benefit of Clergy, and the actual Cautery to be abolished.

Protection, Comfort &c. by a Parent, Child, or wife not to be deemed misprision of Treason.

Corruption of Blood to be abolished in all Cases.

Standing mute on Trial to amount to plea of not guilty, and the Court to proceed to Trial, and punishment (if guilty) or Acquittal (if innocent) in same manner as if the criminal had pleaded not guilty.

The Act which makes Concealment by the Mother of the Death of her bastard Child amount to Evidence of her having murdered it to be repealed.

New Trials to be allowed in Criminal Cases (in favour of the Criminal) during the Term or Session, for good Cause shewn to the Judges.

Whether Pardons shall be allowed or not, in any Instance, the Committee having not yet determined, defer to be consider'd at the next meeting.

The Lands to which an Intestate had Title in fee to descend in parcenary to Males and Females, in equal Portions.

Descents. The Course of Descent to be as follows.

First to the Children or their Descendants.

If there be no Children or their Descendants to the Father.

If no Father, then to the Mother, Brothers and Sisters equally, or the Descendants of Brothers and Sisters.

If neither Father nor mother then to Brothers and Sisters, and their Descendants.

If there be neither Father, Mother, Brothers nor Sisters, then to divide the Lands into moieties; one of them for the Paternal, the other for the Maternal Relations, to go to each in the following order.

First to the Grandfather

If no Grandfather then to Grandmother, Uncles and Aunts, and Descendants of Uncles and Aunts.

If neither Grandfather nor Grandmother, then to Uncles and Aunts, and their Descendants.

If no Uncles nor Aunts, nor their Descendants, then to Great Grandfather.

If no Great Grandfather, then to Great Grandmother, with Granduncles and Aunts and their Descendants.

If neither Great Grandfather nor mother to Great Uncles and Aunts and their Descendants.

And so of the rest.

Relations of the half Blood to have half a Share with those in equal Degree of the whole Blood; but to take the whole, when nearest in Degree to the Deceased.

Representation to be admitted to any Degree of Descendants.

The Person last entitled (i.e. the Decedent) to be considered as if He had been the Purchaser, without Regard to Seisin, or the Rule "Paterna paternis, Materna maternis."

To share per Stirpes, in every Instance, and not per Capita.

Advancement from the same Ancestor, in his Life-time, to be brought into Hotchpot.

Conveyance by Deed or will to a Person, without words of Limitation shewing a less Estate intended, to carry a fee simple.

Widows to have Dower as heretofore. Dower.

The Distribution of personal Estate to be made conformable to the Division of Lands, except the widow's part; which is to be as heretofore. Distribution.

Executions to be first levied on personal Chattels; if the Sherif can find none, then on Slaves; if he can find no Slaves, then on Lands; if the Sherif levies on Lands or Slaves, for want of personal Chattels, and the Party before Sale produces to him such Chattels sufficient, He shall release the Lands or Slaves: so also where Slaves alone are seised &c. Executions

Execution not to be against the Body, unless Estate concealed; and against Estate made more easy.

In Suit for the Debt of a Testator or Intestate, the Heir and Executor or Administrator shall be join'd. Debt

Sureties (except for Guardians Executors or Administrators) if not sued within seven Years, to be discharged of the Suretyship. Sureties

The Tenure of Lands to be of the Common-wealth by Fealty. Land Law.

Quit-rents to be abolished.

Survivorship among Joint-tenants not to take Place.

Unappropriated Lands to be entered for with Surveyor. New Grants.

No man allowed to enter for more than 400 Acres in any one County.

The Breadth of Surveys to be at least one third it's length, unless hindered by adjacent Lines, watercourses or impassable Swamps.

Entries to be surveyed as formerly, and works return'd to Land-Office.

No orders of Governor and Council for Land.

Grants to be signed by Governor, to express the Conditions of Fidelity, and Improvement. No right money for Lands to be required.

Lands irregularly obtained to be liable to Caveat.

Caveats to be entered in Land-Office, but tried before General Court; the Facts by a Jury.

Improvements to be the same as by Acts of 1713.C.3. and 1720.C.3.

Lands not improved to be lapsed on Petition.

Petitions for lapsed Lands triable before General Court by Jury.

Real Actions. Lands to be recovered by one uniform rational Action.

New Trial to be allowed, at Discretion of Judges.

As many Coparceners as will may join in Action: so the Demandant may join as many as He will Defendants.

The First Period in the Division of the Statutes, to end with 25th.H.8th.

The Second to end at the Revolution.

The third to come down to the present Day.

A fourth part to consist of the residuary Part of the Virginia Laws, not taken up in either of the three first parts; to which is added the criminal Law, and Land-Law.

The fifth Part to be the Regulation of Property in Slaves, and their Condition, and also the Examination of the Laws of the other Colonies.

Alotment of the Parts, to each Member, on the other side.

T. Jefferson to undertake the first Part, with the Law of Descents.

E. Pendleton the second.

G. Wythe the third.

G. Mason the fourth; but if He finds it too much, the other Gentlemen will take off his Hands any Part He pleases.

T. Lee the fifth Part.

MS (Vi); four numbered pages, entirely in the hand of George Mason. Endorsed by him: "Plan setled by the Committee of Revisors, in Fredericksburg January 1777."

This document apparently has not been printed in full heretofore. It is summarized and extracts from it printed in Rowland, *Mason*, I, 276-7, but the opinion there expressed that "It is evident from this paper that George Mason had no small share in sketching the plan of revision" needs modification insofar as it implies that this plan was drawn by Mason. It appears, on the contrary, that this "Plan setled by the Committee of Revisors" should be regarded as an aide-memoire representing conclusions arrived at through deliberations of the Committee, rather than as a plan written in whole or in part by any one person. Each of the members of the Committee probably kept a copy of this aide-memoire, but none seems to have survived except that in Mason's handwriting. Certainly TJ's recollections in later life are so precise and agree with so much of this document as to suggest that he too had an aide-memoire (e.g., see notes to Bills No. 20 and 64). It is impossible to say what parts, if any, were original contributions by any given member of the Committee of Revisors, but in such of the "General Rules in Drawing" as "not to insert an unnecessary word, nor omit a useful one," the object is certainly one on which TJ had positive views.

Not all parts of this plan were embodied in the Bills reported 18 June 1779. The agreement here recorded concerning the land law, though its basic terms were incorporated in the Bills for Establishing a Land Office and for Adjusting and Settling Titles (q.v., under date of 8-14 Jan. 1778), and though some of those terms were nullified by the Act of 1779 establishing a land office, was not put in the form of a Bill by the Committee, or at least was not reported.

II. Catalogue of Bills Prepared by the Committee of Revisors

A CATALOGUE *of* BILLS *prepared by the Committee for the revision of the laws.*

1. A Bill To arrange the counties into Senatorial districts.
2. Concerning the election of members of General Assembly.[1]
3. Empowering one of the Privy Council to officiate in certain cases as Lieutenant Governor.
4. To empower the Governor with advice of the Privy Council to lay embargoes.
5. For regulating and disciplining the militia.[2]
6. Making provision against invasions and insurrections.
7. Giving certain powers to the Governor and Council for a limitted time.
8. Establishing a board of war.[3]
9. Establishing a board of trade.[4]
10. For the annual appointment of Delegates to Congress.[5]
11. For establishing a board of Auditors.
12. For appointing a Treasurer.
13. For appointing Naval Officers.[6]
14. For the appointment of Clerks to the Governor and Council.
15. For the enlistment of soldiers, sailors, and marines.[7]
16. For apprehending deserters and preventing the loss of arms and other things delivered to soldiers.[8]
17. Concerning seamen.
18. For supplying the public with lead.
19. For establishing cross posts.[9]
20. Directing the course of descents.
21. Concerning wills, the distribution of intestates estates, and the duty of Executors and Administrators.
22. For regulating conveyances.
23. Securing the rights derived from grants to aliens.
24. Concerning escheators.[10]
25. To prevent frauds and perjuries.
26. Of mortmain.
27. Concerning dower and jointure of widows.
28. For preservation of the estates of ideots and lunatics.

29. A Bill Providing that wrongful alienations of lands shall be void so far as they be wrongful.
30. For amending the act intituled an act for raising a supply of money for public exigencies.
31. For levying county rates.
32. For support of the poor.[11]
33. For ascertaining and collecting certain officers fees.
34. Declaring bills of credit to be equal to gold and silver coin of the same denominations.
35. To prevent the circulation of private bank notes.
36. For withholding British property to indemnify citizens who may suffer by confiscation and to prevent succour to the enemy thereby.
37. To prevent lossess by pirates and enemies on the high seas.
38. For preservation of vessels wrecked or in distress and of their crews and cargoes.
39. Concerning strays.
40. For restitution of stolen goods.
41. For preventing infection of the horned cattle.
42. For improving the breed of horses.
43. For preserving the breed of deer.[12]
44. For preventing frauds by the dealers in certain commodities.
45. For licensing and regulating taverns.
46. Concerning public roads.
47. Establishing public ferries.
48. Concerning mill-dams and other obstructions of water courses.
49. For unlading ballast and burial of dead bodies from on board ships.
50. Concerning public store-houses.
51. Concerning slaves.
52. Concerning servants.
53. For apprehending and securing runaways.
54. Declaring what persons shall be deemed mulattoes.
55. Declaring who shall be deemed citizens of this commonwealth.[13]
56. Concerning aliens.
57. Declaring that none shall be condemned without trial and that justice shall not be sold or deferred.
58. Directing what prisoners shall be let to bail.

59. A Bill For granting writs of habeas corpus.

60. Concerning guardians, infants, masters, and apprentices.

61. To enable guardians and committees to perform certain acts for the benefit of those who are under their care.

62. For the restraint, maintenance and cure of persons not sound in mind.

63. For registering births and deaths.

64. For proportioning crimes and punishments in cases heretofore capital.

65. For punishing persons guilty of certain forgeries.[14]

66. Concerning treasons, felonies and other offences committed out of the jurisdiction of this commonwealth.

67. Concerning truces, safe conducts, passports, licenses, and letters of marque.

68. For the employment, government, and support of malefactors condemned to labor for the commonwealth.

69. To encourage the apprehending of horse-stealers.

70. For preserving the privileges of Ambassadors.

71. For the suppression and punishment of riots, routs, and unlawful assemblies.

72. Forbidding and punishing affrays.

73. Against conspirators.

74. Against conveying or taking pretensed titles.

75. To punish bribery and extortion.

76. Prescribing the punishments of those who sell unwholesome meat or drink.

77. To prevent the spreading of the small-pox.

78. For compelling vessels and persons coming and goods brought from infected places to perform quarentine.

79. For the more general diffusion of knowledge.

80. For amending the constitution of the college of William and Mary and substituting more certain revenues for its support.

81. For establishing a public library.

82. For establishing religious freedom.[15]

83. For saving the property of the church heretofore by law established.[16]

84. For punishing disturbers of religious worship and sabbath breakers.

85. A Bill For appointing days of public fasting and thanksgiving.

86. Annulling marriages prohibited by the levitical law and appointing the mode of solemnizing lawful marriage.

87. Against usury.

88. To prevent gaming.[17]

89. To prevent forestalling, regrating, and engrossing and sale by auction.

90. Constituting the High Court of Chancery.

91. Constituting the General Court.

92. Constituting the Court of Admiralty.[18]

93. Constituting the Court of Appeals.[18]

94. For constituting Courts Marshall.[19]

95. For constituting Justices of the Peace.

96. Concerning sheriffs.

97. For licensing council, attornies at law and proctors.

98. Prescribing the oath of fidelity and the oaths of certain public officers.[20]

99. To prevent the sale of public offices.

100. Directing the method of proceeding upon impeachments.

101. For regulating proceedings in courts of equity.

102. For regulating proceedings in courts of common law.

103. Directing the method of proceeding against, and trying free persons charged with certain crimes.

104. Directing the method of trying slaves charged with treason or felony.

105. For reforming the method of proceeding in writs of right.

106. Concerning partitions and joint rights.

107. For the speedy determination of suits wherein foreigners are parties.

108. For speedy recovery of money due from certain persons to the public.

109. For recovering demands of small value in a summary way.

110. Providing that actions popular, prosecuted by collusion, shall be no bar to those which be pursued with good faith.

111. For preventing vexatious and malicious prosecutions, and moderating amercements.

112. A Bill Providing a mean to help and speed poor persons in their suits.
113. Providing that an infant may sue by[21] his next friend.
114. Declaring when the death of persons absenting themselves shall be presumed.
115. Prescribing a method of protesting inland bills of exchange and allowing assignees of obligations to bring actions thereupon in their own names.
116. For limitation of actions.
117. For granting attachments against the estates of debtors removing privately or absconding.[22]
118. Concerning inquests.
119. Permitting those who will not take oaths to be otherwise qualified.[23]
120. For regulating the commencement of the year and the computation of time.
121. Allowing a bill of exceptions to be sealed.
122. For enforcing performance of awards made by rule of court.
123. Concerning executions.
124. Concerning rents and distresses.
125. Providing remedy and punishment in cases of forcible entries and detainers.
126. Repealing certain acts of Parliament and of General Assembly.

Report, p. 4-5; marginal notations in TJ's hand as indicated below in note 1. Also, there are two MS copies, referred to where necessary in the notes below as MS (1) and MS (2), as follows: (1) MS (Vi); six pages. This is a clerk's copy, but the title and all numbers are in TJ's hand, as well as the marginal and other additions noted below. This, obviously, is the copy which John Beckley employed in 1784 in preparing the *Report.* MS is endorsed in a clerk's hand: "A List of Bills prepared by the Committee ⟨*for the Revision of the Laws*⟩ of Revisors. 1778." Despite this date, this MS was drawn up during the session of May 1779, probably between 1 June and 5 June, as the notes below indicate. (2) MS (ViU), four pages, entirely in TJ's hand. This MS catalogue accompanies the MS of the sixty-five bills described in Editorial Note above. Also, as indicated by the notes below, this MS was annotated by TJ at the May 1779 session, and, as indicated in note 6, below, MS (1) was obviously copied from MS (2). These two MSS agree with the text of the catalogue as printed in the *Report*, except for the differences noted below.

1 *Report*, p. 4, has a check mark (√) preceding the title of this and the following bills, after each of which TJ wrote "passd." except that, after Bill No. 32, he wrote "passd. with great alterns.": Nos. 3, 12, 14, 17, 20, 21, 22, 24, 25, 27, 28, 29, 32, 35, 37, 39, 40, 41, 42, 45, 48, 49, 51, 52, 53, 54, 56, 57, 58, 60, 61, and 62. These notations were obviously made some time after the close of the Oct. 1785 session and before that of Oct. 1786; for all of the 33 bills checked and noted by TJ were passed at the Oct. 1785 session. Surprisingly, TJ failed to check the only other bills passed at the Oct. 1785 session: No. 46

and No. 82, the latter being the Bill for Establishing Religious Freedom.

2 Both MSS have in the margin the following notation by TJ: "delivd. to a member." (See letter of TJ and Wythe to Speaker of House, 18 June 1779.) This Bill was brought in but not passed in 1779.

3 Both MSS have the following in TJ's hand in the margin: "passd." Bill was presented by TJ 8 May 1779. MS (2) has the following after the title: "V.V.1." It also has a similar device affixed to each of the titles of bills indicated by the numbers in parentheses: (9):V.V.2; (10):U.U.3; (11):F.F.4; (14):W.W.3; (15):V.V.4; (19):R.R.3; (20):A.1; (24):L.2; (26):R.2.; (27):K.1.; (28):-V.1.; (29):J.4.; (30):U.U.1.; (31):-P.P.1.; (32):P.P.3.; (37):F.4.; (40):-U.3.; (46):N.N.3; (48):M.M.2.; (51):-T.T.1.; (52):S.S.3.; (55):G.2.; (56):-G.4.; (57):C.2.; (58):Q.4.; (64):Z.3.; (66):F.2.; (67):E.4.; (68):F.F.1.; (70):E.3.; (71):V.2.; (72):W.3.; (73):I.3.; (74):H.4.; (75):M.3.; (76):-H.3.; (79):H.H.2.; (80):C.C.3.; (81):-R.R.1.; (82):L.L.1.; (83):L.L.4.; (84):-D.3.; (94):I.3.; (110):C.1.; (112):-S.3.; (113):T.2.; (121):M.1.; (125):-N.1.

4 Both MSS have the following in TJ's hand in the margin: "passd." Bill was presented by TJ 12 May 1779.

5 Both MSS have the following in TJ's hand in the margin: "passd." Bill was presented by TJ 17 May 1779.

6 MS (2) has the following deleted at this point: "13. for establishing a loan office. [Act 1778. c. 9.]." This, of course, meant that originally MS (2) had a total of 127 Bills (actually 128; see note 12, below). TJ had already numbered each of these from 1 to 127; consequently, after he had made this deletion, he renumbered Bills No. 14 to 127 to accord with Nos. 13 to 126 as given in *Report* and in MS (1). Since there was no such deletion or renumbering in MS (1), it is obvious that it was copied from MS (2).

7 MS (1) has the following in TJ's hand in the margin: "passd." Bill presented by TJ 21 May 1779.

8 MS (2) originally read: "to discourage desertion . . ." but this was altered by TJ to read as above.

9 MS (1) has the following in TJ's hand: "presentd." Bill was presented by TJ 18 May 1779, passed by the House 26 May, and rejected by the Senate 5 June. This marginal note must, therefore, have been made before 5 June 1779; see note 13, below.

10 MS (1) has "presentd" in TJ's hand. This Bill was presented 27 May.

11 This title is in TJ's hand in MS (1). The clerk had mistakenly added it to the preceding title, causing that to read "for levying county rates for support of the poor."

12 MS (2) has the deleted title of another Bill following this one: "for regulating the inspection of tobacco." There is no number prefixed to this deleted title; hence the deletion was made *before* the numbering from 1 to 127 as indicated in note 6 above, whereas the deletion described in that note was made *after* the numbering. Since, as indicated in note 13 below, this renumbering was done after the marginalia were written, it follows that these two Bills were struck from the list by TJ somewhere around 1-5 June (see notes 6 and 9, above). The titles of Bills No. 17, 25, 53, 62, and 104 were interlined in MS (2) by TJ; this may possibly mean that he decided to add them to the Report of the Committee of Revisors just as, at the last moment, he decided to strike two from the list.

13 TJ added the following in margin of MS (2): "delivd. to a member." This Bill was turned over to George Mason on 1 June 1779 (see notes to Bill No. 55) when TJ became governor. Now, in every case except this and one other (see note 15, below), the renumbering described in note 6, above, was done by crossing out the old number and writing the new number in front of it. This resulted in a column of crossed-out numbers preceded by a parallel column of new numbers. In the case of Bill No. 55, however, TJ made the change by superimposing the new number on the old. This was obviously done to allow room in the margin for the words "delivd. to a member," for the word "member" falls in the middle of the space that would have been occupied by the new number "55" if it had been placed as all others. From this it follows, of course, that the words "delivd. to a member" were already there before TJ renumbered the bills. Now these marginal notes were written not earlier than 1 June or later than 5 June 1779 (see note 9, above). Hence bills described in notes 6 and 12, above, were clearly struck from the Report by TJ (possibly in consultation with George Wythe) during the first week of June 1779 and just before the

two men submitted their shortened list of bills to the General Assembly. For MS (1) was copied from MS (2) before any numbering had been made on the latter and after two of these titles had been struck from it. TJ then prefixed the correct and final numbers 1 to 126 to the titles of MS (1).

14 MS (2) has the following in the margin: "brought in." The Bill was introduced 26 May 1779 and passed 14 June.

15 The words "delivd to a member" are written in the margin of MS (2), the word "member" being written in a minuscule hand beneath the new number "82" (see note 13, above). Bill was introduced on 13 June 1779 (see notes to Bill No. 82).

16 The words "delivd to a member" are written in the margin of MS (2) but the new number "83" was superimposed on the old and the marginal phrase placed as in the instance described in note 13, above. This was introduced by John Harvie 13 June 1779, but it did not get beyond the first reading (see notes to Bill No. 83).

17 The word "passd." is written in margin of MS (2). This Act was not passed until the Oct. 1779 session (see notes to Bill No. 88). This notation must have been made by TJ, therefore, at a later date than the others referred to above.

18 The word "passed" is written in margin of MS (2). Bill No. 93 was passed 26 June 1779. The Bill for Establishing a Court of Admiralty was passed in 1776 and TJ's marginal note obviously refers to that.

19 TJ wrote "Marshall" in MS (2); it was so copied in MS (1) and thus printed in *Report*.

20 The word "passed" is written in margin of MS (2). Bill No. 98 was passed 1 June 1779.

21 In MS (2) TJ first wrote "prochain ami" and then deleted the phrase.

22 Following this title in MS (2) is another, deleted and unnumbered as in the instance described in note 12, above. This deleted title reads: "for enforcing performance of awards made by rule of court," which of course is the same as the title of Bill No. 122.

23 The word "passed" is written in the margin of both MSS. Bill No. 119 was introduced by TJ 29 May and it was passed 1 June 1779.

III. Bills Reported by the Committee of Revisors

1. A Bill to Arrange the Counties into Senatorial Districts

Be it enacted by the General Assembly that the districts, for which Senators are to be chosen to serve in General Assembly, shall be those which are herein after described, that is to say, the counties of Accomack and Northampton, one district; the counties of Princess Ann, Norfolk, and Nansemond, one other district; the counties of Isle-of-wight, Surry, and Prince George, one other district; the counties of Dinwiddie, Southampton, and Sussex, one other district; the counties of Brunswick, Lunenburg, and Mecklenburg, one other district; the counties of Charlotte, Halifax, and Prince Edward, one other district; the counties of Chesterfield, Amelia, Cumberland, and Powhatan, one other district; the counties of Buckingham, Albemarle, Amherst, and Fluvanna, one other district; the counties of Pittsylvania, Bedford, and Henry, one other district; the counties of Botetourt, Montgomery, Washington, and Kentucky, one other district; the counties of Elizabeth City, Warwick, and York, one other district; the counties of Charles City, James City, and New Kent, one other district; the counties of Henrico, Goochland, and Louisa, one other district; the counties of Hanover, and Caroline, one other district; the counties of Ohio, Yohogania, Monongalia, and Shenando, one other district; the counties of Gloucester, and Middlesex, one other district; the counties of Essex, King William, and King and Queen, one other district; the counties of Lancaster, Richmond, and Northumberland, one other district; the counties of Westmoreland, Stafford, and King George, one other district; the counties of Spotsylvania, Orange, and Culpeper, one other district; the counties of Prince William, and Fairfax, one other district; the counties of Loudoun, and Fauquier, one other district; the counties of Frederick, Berkeley, and Hampshire, one other district; and the counties of Augusta, Rockingham, Greenbrier, and Rockbridge, one other district.

Report, p. 1. MS (ViU); clerk's copy.

It is strange that this Bill was not adopted, since it was merely a revision of the ordinance of 1776 that divided the sixty-two counties into twenty-four districts (Hening, IX, 128-30). This Bill omits Fincastle, East Augusta, and West Augusta and includes the following that were not in the ordinance of 1776: Powhatan, Fluvanna, Henry, Montgomery, Washington, Kentucky, Ohio, Yohogania, Monongalia, Shenandoah, Augusta, Rockingham, Greenbrier, and Rockbridge. Presumably the arrangement of the counties in districts met with objection in the Senate, for, after the Bill was introduced on 31 Oct. 1785 and passed by the House, it was referred to the Senate and no further action was taken on it (JHD, Oct. 1785, 1828 edn.,

p. 12-15, 40, 47). The Chancellors' Revisal of 1785 repeats the ordinance of 1776 as enacted, including the names of obsolete counties and omitting those that had been erected since 1776. It was not until the passage of the Act of 1792 that the twenty-four districts required by the Constitution of 1776 were redefined so as to account for all of the existing counties (Shepherd, I, 7-8).

2. A Bill concerning the Election of Members of General Assembly

Be it enacted by the General Assembly, that the Delegates for the several counties, and the City of Williamsburg and Borough of Norfolk, and the six Senators for one of the four classes of districts, in the room of those who will annually be displaced, shall be chosen, in the manner hereafter directed, on the first Monday of September in every year, and shall meet together, and with the remaining Senators, on the first Monday of October then next following in General Assembly, at the place the last preceeding General Assembly shall have sat in or adjourned to, unless such place be in possession of a public enemy, or infected with the plague or smallpox, in which case they shall meet at such other place as the Governor with advice of the Council shall appoint and notify by proclamation.[1]

Every male citizen[2] of this commonwealth, aged twenty one years, other than such as have refused to give assurance of fidelity to the commonwealth, being possessed, or whose tenant for years, at will or at sufferance is possessed of twenty five acres of land, with a house, the superficial content of the foundation whereof is twelve feet square, or equal to that quantity, and a plantation thereon, or fifty acres of unimproved land, or a lot or part of a lot of land in a city or town established by act of General Assembly with a house thereon, of the like superficial content or quantity, having in such land an estate of freehold at the least, and, unless the title shall have come to him by descent, devise, marriage or marriage settlement, having been so possessed six months, and no other person, shall be qualified to vote for Delegates to serve in General Assembly for the county, city or borough respectively in which the land lieth. If the fifty acres of land, being one entire parcel, lie in several counties, the holder shall vote in that county wherein the greater part of the land lieth only, and if the twenty five acres of land, being one entire parcel, be in several counties, the holder shall vote in that county wherein the house standeth only. In right of land holden by parceners, jointenants or tenants in common but one vote shall be given by all the holders capable of voting, who shall be present and agree to vote for the same candidate or candidates, unless the quantity of land, in case partition had been made thereof, be sufficient to entitle every holder present to vote separately, or unless some one or more of the holders may lawfully vote in right of another estate or estates in the same county, in which case the others may vote if holding solely they might have voted.

Every person having such a freehold in the City of Williamsburg or Borough of Norfolk as will qualify him to vote for Delegates to represent the county, and also every freeman[3] aged twenty one years, being a citizen of the commonwealth, and not having refused to give assurance of fidelity, who shall be a housekeeper, and shall have resided for six months in the said city or borough, and shall be possessed of a visible estate of the value of fifty pounds at the least, or shall actually have served as an apprentice to some trade within the said city or borough for the term of five years, and shall have obtained a certificate of such service from the Court of Hustings under the common seal of the city or borough, and no other, shall be qualified to vote for a Delegate to represent the city or borough respectively in General Assembly. Every person qualified as aforesaid to vote for Delegates, not being an Alderman or Assessor of the public taxes nor otherwise disqualified,[4] shall be capable of being elected a Delegate for the county, city, or borough, or Senator for the district in which he resides. No person who shall have served as a member of the Legislature for seven years in the whole shall be afterwards compellable to serve therein. Any elector qualified according to this act failing to attend any annual election of Delegates, or of a Senator, and, if a poll be taken, to give, or offer to give his vote shall pay a double portion[5] of all such levies and taxes as shall be assessed and levied in his county the ensuing year, unless being required by the Assessors of his hundred, who ought in such case to call upon him to make his excuse, he shall satisfy them; or they shall otherwise know that his failure was occasioned by grievous sickness, infirmity, or necessary absence in discharge of a public duty elsewhere;[6] and for enabling them to discover who did and who did not vote, the clerk of every county court shall deliver to the Aldermen of his county, before their meeting to appoint Assessors, a copy of the poll books taken at the preceeding election of Delegates, and the Aldermen shall deliver so much thereof to the Assessors of the several hundreds as may be requisite for their information.[7] Every elector going to, abiding at, and returning from an election, shall be privileged from arrests one day for every twenty miles he shall necessarily travel, exclusive of the day of election; and any process against such elector executed during such privilege shall be void. Upon the election of a Senator, and also of a Delegate or Delegates when the election of such Delegate or Delegates cannot be determined by view, the sheriff, or in his absence, the under sheriff of the county, or the Mayor of the city or borough, shall in presence of the candidates, or their agents, cause the poll to be taken in the court-house, or if that be in a town infected with any contagious disease, or be in danger of an attack from a public enemy, at some other place according to these directions: He shall appoint such and so many writers as he shall think fit, who shall respectively take an oath, to be administered by him, or make solemn affirmation that they will take the poll faithfully and impartially. He shall deliver a poll book to each writer, who by ruling lines thereon, having made as many columns as there shall be candidates, shall enter the name of each candidate in a distinct column at the head thereof, and under his name in the same column the name of every elector who shall vote for that candidate; and after the names of all the electors who will give their votes (proclamation having been made three times at the door of the court house by the officer requiring those who had not been polled to come in and give their votes) shall have been thus entered he shall conclude the poll, and declare the candidates for whom the greatest number of votes shall appear to have been given to be elected; or if the greatest number of votes for several candidates shall be equal with one, another may declare which of the candidates he will elect. If the numbers of votes for several persons to be a Senator be equal, and the votes of the returning officers be equal also, it shall be decided by a lot taken by the said returning officers at their meeting, which shall be the seventh day after the day of election at such place as shall be appointed by the last Senator of the district then surviving.[8] No elector shall be admitted to poll a second time at one and the same election, although at the first time he shall have given but a single vote. If the electors who appear be so numerous that they cannot all be polled before sunsetting; or if by rain or rise of water courses many of the electors may have been hindered from attending, the sheriff or under sheriff may, by request of one or more of the candidates or their agents, adjourn the proceeding on the poll until the next day; and so from day to day through the week[9] if the same cause continue, giving public notice thereof by proclamation at the door of the court-house, and shall on the last day of election conclude the poll according to the directions aforesaid. On complaint to either House of Assembly of an undue election or return of any member to their house, such house shall forthwith appoint some day for trying the same as shortly as shall be consistent with fair enquiry; but not within less than fourteen days after such complaint lodged; whereof notice shall be given by the Speaker to the party against whom the complaint is if he be absent; which day of trial may be lengthened from time to time on good cause shewn to the house and notice to the absent party. [On the day appointed for the trial, the petitioners, their counsel and agents shall be called to the bar of the house, and the door being then locked, the names of all the members present shall be put into six boxes or glasses, and the Speaker shall draw one name out of each by regular rotation, to be noted by the clerk as they are drawn, until the number drawn shall be forty nine if the complaint be before the House of Delegates, or nine if before the Senate. If, among those drawn, there be the name of any member who is a party to the said complaint, or who shall have voted in the election, he shall be set aside; and if any other member whose name is drawn shall shew good cause against his being put on the trial, he shall be excused, and in their stead others shall be drawn to make up the number before specified: it shall be lawful for the petitioners to name one other member present, and the sitting member another, to be of the committee, who may for the like causes be set aside or excused, and the party permitted to name another so often as it shall happen, or on their failure to nominate, the number shall be made up by drawing; which being done the door shall be opened, lists of the names drawn shall then be given to the parties, their agents, or counsel, who, with the clerk of the house, shall forthwith withdraw and strike off one alternately (the petitioners first beginning) until the number be reduced to thirteen if the matter be before the House of Delegates, or five if before the Senate; which thirteen or five, as the case shall be, together with the two members named by the parties, shall be a select committee to try the said complaint, and shall forthwith take the following oath to be administered, in presence of the house, by the Speaker. "You shall swear that well and truly, according to the best of your skill and judgment and the evidence which shall be given, you will try the complaint which has been lodged by   against   that you will nothing say or do therein, or leave unsaid or undone, for envy, hatred, malice, love, fear or reward, but you shall try and determine the same truly and according to law. So help you God." The said committee being sworn and not yet departed the house shall fix the time and place of their meeting, which time shall be within twenty four hours. They shall at their first meeting choose their chairman from among the members whose names were drawn by lot, and in case of an equality of votes, the vote of the member first drawn shall be decisive. The said committee shall have power to send for persons, papers and records, to administer oaths by their chairman, examine witnesses and to determine finally on the said complaint; and such determination shall report to the house to be by them carried into execution; they shall not adjourn themselves without leave of the house for any longer time than from day to day, nor do business but when all their members are attending; if they shall fail to meet within one hour after the time appointed, they shall adjourn and report the same to the house with the cause thereof, and the names of the absentees, who shall be subject to the censure or punishment of the house, unless they shew cause of unavoidable necessity for their failure; if there shall fail to be a committee for three several appointments successively, they shall be thereby dissolved, their past proceedings void, and another committee shall be chosen in the same way, and to proceed in the like manner as is herein before directed for the original committee, and so as often as the like case shall happen.][10] If any person sworn before the said committee shall give, or withhold, any evidence under such circumstances as would have constituted the same to be perjury, if done in presence of a court of record, the same shall be deemed perjury.

If upon any such trial it shall appear that equal numbers of qualified electors shall have voted for the petitioner and the sitting member; and the officer who conducted the election shall swear or solemnly affirm that if such equality had appeared at the election he would have declared the petitioner elected, such petitioner shall be deemed duly elected; and his name, instead of the name of the sitting member which shall be erased, shall be inserted in the certificate or return. No elector shall be polled before he shall have declared, if required to do so by any candidate or his agent, in what right he offers to vote and shall have taken an oath, which the officer conducting the election shall administer, or made a solemn affirmation in this form: "I do swear [or do solemnly affirm][11] that I do in my conscience believe myself to be duly qualified to vote for Delegates to serve in General Assembly for the county of according to the act of General Assembly, intituled, an act

"[12] of which oath or affirmation a

note shall be made in the poll book opposite and referring to the name of the person swearing or affirming.

The making such oath or affirmation falsely shall be perjury. The names of electors offering to be polled, but refusing to make such oath or affirmation, shall be entered on the poll books in separate lists with the names of the candidates for whom they voted, and shall be added to the poll if upon a scrutiny the votes be justified. The officer who shall conduct the election shall within twenty days afterwards deliver to the clerk of his county court or court of his city or borough the poll books to be by him preserved and recorded, and shall in the meantime suffer any candidate or elector, at his own expence, to take a copy thereof.[13]

The sheriff or under sheriff shall certify the election of Delegates in this form or to this effect: "Be it known to all to whom these presents shall come, that I sheriff [or deputy of sheriff] of the county of in my full county, held at the court-house thereof [or at] on the day of in the year of our Lord by the electors of my said county, qualified according to law, caused to be chosen two Delegates for my said county, namely, and to represent the same in General Assembly. Given under my hand and seal the day and year aforesaid."

The Mayor of a city or borough entituled to particular representation shall certify the election of a Delegate in this form or to this effect: "Be it known to all to whom these presents shall come, that I Mayor of the city [or borough] of at the court-house of [or at] in the said city [or borough] on the day of in the year of our Lord by the electors of the said city [or borough] qualified according to law caused to be chosen a Delegate for the said city [or borough] namely, to represent the same in General Assembly. Given under my hand and seal the day and year aforesaid."

The sheriffs or under sheriffs of the several counties of a district shall certify the election of a Senator in this form or to this effect: "Be it known to all to whom these presents shall come, that we sheriff [or deputy of sheriff] of the county of , sheriff [or deputy of sheriff] of the county of and sheriff [or deputy of sheriff] of the county of in our full counties, held at the court-houses thereof [or at] respectively, on the day of in the year of our Lord by the electors of our said respective counties, qualified according to law, caused to be chosen a Senator for the district composed of the said counties, namely, to represent the same in General Assembly. Given under our hands and seals the day and year aforesaid." The officers directed to make such certificates of elections as aforesaid, shall cause them to be delivered, those of Delegates, to the clerk of the House of Delegates, and those of Senators to the clerk of the Senate, one day at least before the succeeding session of General Assembly. For election of a Delegate or Senator, when a vacancy shall happen, a writ or writs shall be issued by the Speaker of that House whereof he was a member, but if the vacancy be occasioned by acceptance of an office, the writ or writs shall not be issued without the special order of the House; and the officer to whom such writ shall be directed, so soon after the receipt thereof as he may be able, shall dispatch messengers to[14] give the electors notice thereof, as well as of the time and place of election, and shall cause the election to be made in the manner herein before prescribed, and shall have the same power of adjourning the proceeding upon the poll, as in case of a general election. The return of such writ for electing a Delegate or Delegates shall be in this form or to this effect: Upon the writ shall be endorsed these or the like words: "The execution of this writ appears in a schedule hereunto annexed;" and on another paper annexed to the writ shall be written, if the writ be for election of a Delegate for a county, these or the like words: "By virtue of this writ to me directed, in my full county held at the court-house thereof [or at] on the day of in the year of our Lord by the electors of my said county qualified according to law I caused to be chosen a Delegate [or two delegates] for my said county, namely, to represent the same in General Assembly. Given under my hand and seal the day and year aforesaid;" and if the writ be for the election of a Delegate for a city or borough, these or the like words: "By virtue of this writ to me directed at the court-house of the city of [or borough of] [or at in the borough of] on the day of in the year of our Lord by the electors of the said city [or borough] qualified according to law, I caused to be chosen a Delegate for the said city [or borough] namely to represent the same in General Assembly. Given under my hand and seal the day and year aforesaid." And the return of the writs for electing a Senator shall be in this form or to this effect: Upon each writ shall be endorsed these or the like words: "The execution of this writ appears in a schedule hereunto annexed;" and on another paper connecting the several writs together shall be written these or the like words: "By virtue of these writs to us directed, in our full counties held at the court-houses thereof, respectively [or at] on the day of in the year of our Lord by the electors of our said respective counties, qualified according to law, we caused to be chosen a Senator for the district composed of our said counties, namely to represent the same in General Assembly. Given under our hands and seals the day and year aforesaid."

And the officers conducting the elections shall make their said returns to the General Assembly, if it be sitting immediately, or if it be not sitting, one day at least before the time to which the writ shall be returnable. A sheriff, under sheriff, or Mayor, refusing to take the poll when he shall be required by a candidate or elector, or taking it in other manner than is herein before prescribed, or making a false certificate or return of the election of a member or members to serve in the General Assembly, or neglecting to cause the certificate or return of such election to be made to such clerk, and at or before such time as is herein before directed, shall forfeit and pay one hundred pounds; and neglecting to deliver the poll books to the clerk of the court, to whom, and before the expiration of the time within which they are herein before directed to be delivered, or refusing to suffer any candidate or elector, at his own expence, to take a copy of the poll books, shall forfeit and pay ;[15] which penalties may be recovered with costs in actions of debt, by any person who will sue for the same; one half to his own use and the other half to the use of the commonwealth. A[16] person hereafter to be elected to serve in General Assembly who shall directly or indirectly give or agree to give to any elector or pretended elector, money, meat, drink, or other reward, in order to be elected, or for having been elected, for such or any other county, city, or borough, shall be expelled and disabled to be re-elected during the term of three years.

The privilege of members of the General Assembly shall continue during every session, and one day before and after for every twenty miles they must necessarily travel to and from home, and in the meantime process in which they are parties shall be suspended, without abatement or discontinuance: If any person taken in execution be delivered by privilege of either House of General Assembly, so soon as such privilege ceaseth, the plaintiff, his executors, or administrators may sue out a new execution against him.[17]

If a sufficient number of the members of General Assembly, or of either House thereof, to adjourn from day to day, shall not meet at any time when they ought, the Governor, by proclamation with advice of the Council, may prorogue the General Assembly, or adjourn the deficient House, from day to day, until a sufficient number shall convene, and their acts and proceedings afterwards shall be as valid as if there had been no such interruption. But a Delegate or Senator shall loose all the wages he would otherwise have been entitled to, if he shall depart from the General Assembly before it be adjourned without license from the Speaker and other members of the House whereof he is a member first entered on the journal; yet any member of either House taken so sick during his attendance in General Assembly, or in his journey thither, as that he shall be unable to come to or sit in the House, shall receive wages for every day of the session he shall be so disabled, in the same manner as if he had sat in the House. If on the day appointed for the meeting of any General Assembly, or at any other time during the session, a sufficient number of the members thereof to proceed to business do not attend for that purpose, every absent Delegate or Senator shall, besides losing his wages during absence, forfeit and pay to the use of the commonwealth ;[18] such forfeiture to be recovered by prosecution to be instituted in the General Court by order of such House; and on the trial of such prosecution no excuse for non attendance, other than those before mentioned, shall be admitted by the jury; and if it be alledged that the defendant did attend such house, on any of the days during which they could not do business for want of members, the proof of such attendance shall rest on him. The General Assembly may during a session, or at the end thereof, adjourn to any other place than that where they shall then be sitting. Every act of the General Assembly hereafter to be made, shall commence and be in force from the passing thereof, unless in the act itself another day for the commencement thereof be particularly mentioned; and in the former case the day of passing thereof shall be noted next after the title.[19]

Report, p. 1-4. MS (ViU); clerk's copy. Probably drawn by TJ or Wythe, since there is in DLC: TJ Papers, 236: 42327-8, a four-page MS in the hand of George Mason endorsed: "Remarks upon the Mode of regulating the Elections of Members of the General Assembly." This MS is referred to below as Mason MS. Text of Act as adopted is in Hening, XII, 120-9.

Bill was presented by Madison 31 Oct. 1785. The House passed it, apparently without amendment, but the Senate offered numerous amendments, some of which the House accepted and others rejected (JHD, Oct. 1785, 1828 edn., p. 12-15, 40, 47, 94, 97, 98, 100, 133). The principal differences between the Bill and the Act as adopted are indicated below.

1 Act as adopted provided that elections should be held during court days in April and meeting of Assembly be convened third Monday in October. On this point Mason MS has the following:

"The Month of March will be preferable to April for the following reasons. The Elections in April preventing the Assembly's sitting in that month, tho' the Emergency be ever so great, may produce much Inconvenience, as the active Season of the Year, and the opening the Campaign in time of War, is then approaching; this might be provided against, by holding the Elections, thro' out the Country, on the same Day; but there are some considerable objections to such a Regulation, particularly the Danger of Insurrection of the Slaves, or disaffected. By law, the Assembly is always to meet on the first Monday in May, and the Elections, being the respective County Court Days in April, many of them fall so late in the month, as to prevent the Members of distant Counties attending early in the Session, to the great Delay of public Business.

"The People, being wearied with too frequent Elections, seldom meet to chuse the Commissioners of the Tax, who are therefore generally appointed by the County Courts; this, growing into precedent, may encroach upon one of the fundamental, and most important principles of the Constitution. If the Election of Commissioners of the Tax, and all other annual Elections were fixed to the time of chusing the Members of the Assembly, it wou'd more deeply engage the public Attention, occasion a fuller meeting, and the People wou'd be in the habitual Exercise of one of their most essential Rights and privileges; but if the Election of the Commissioners of the Tax was changed from March to April, it wou'd delay and impede the Execution of the Assessment, in many Particulars."

[2] The Act as adopted reads: "(other than free negroes or mulattoes)."

[3] The Act as adopted reads: "except as before excepted."

[4] The Act as adopted omits the passage: "not being an Alderman . . . otherwise disqualified."

[5] The Act as adopted reads: "one fourth of his portion."

This severe legislative penalty for refusal to vote can, in all probability, be traced to George Mason. For on this point the Mason MS has the following: "The Members of the late Assemblys have been the nominal, rather than the real Representatives of the people; many of them have been the Choice of a Handful, a Neighbourhood, or a Junto. An ignorant or obscure Man may have considerable Influence within a narrow Circle; but it will seldom extend thro' a County; unfortunately Elections are now so little attended to, that a factious, bawling Fellow, who will make a noise four or five miles around him, and prevail upon his party to attend, may carry an Election against a Man of ten times his weight and Influence in the County, and men of modesty and merit are discouraged from offering themselves; this is the true Cause why we have seen our late Assemblies filled with men so unequal to the Office: a Law therefore which wou'd bring the Body of the People to attend, and vote at their County Elections, wou'd be of the greatest Importance to the State. It is presumed some such Regulations as the following may effect it.

"Let two or three Justices of the Peace, taking an Oath of Impartiality, superintend the Election, and be empowered to judge of the Qualifications of the Voters, upon the Spot; for as we have now annual Elections, there will seldom or ever be a disputed Election brought before the Assembly. [Ed. note: see the elaborate provisions in this Bill, below, concerning disputed elections and the manner of resolving such disputes—provisions which were struck out when the Bill was enacted into law.]

"Let all the Freeholders, resident within the County, be obliged, under a certain penalty, to attend and vote at their County Election, unless they send such a reasonable Excuse, in writing, for their Absence, as shall be approved by the Judges of the Election; let such Excuses as the Judges have approved be certified, and filed, together with a Copy of the Poll, in the Clerk's Office of the County; or let the names of the Absentees, whose Excuses have been admitted, be added at the Foot of the Poll, and certified by the said Judges.

"Let the Sherif, if the said Judges shall see just Cause, adjourn the Election, from Day to Day; and where it shall appear upon closing the Poll, that ⟨*less than two thirds*⟩ a Majority of the Freeholders, resident within the County, have not voted, let such County remain unrepresented until the next annual Election, and the Sherif make his Return accordingly to the General Assembly.

"In Order to ascertain the Number of Freeholders resident within the County, and carry the Law into due Execution

"Let the Assessors annually, with their Assessment, return to the Commissioners of the Tax, an exact List of the Names of all the Freeholders resident within their respective Hundreds and from these returns let the Commissioners make out an alphabetical List of all the Freeholders resident within their County, to be return'd certified under their Hands, to the Clerk's Office; a Copy of which List, with a Copy of the last poll, and a List of the Names of the Absentees whose Excuses have been admitted, to be returned, by the Clerk of the County, to the next Court after every General Election, such Court imediatly to appoint two of their Members to examine these Returns, and from them to make out a List of the Delinquents, to be delivered to the Attorney for the Commonwealth, who shou'd be directed by the Court to commence Suits against them. As the County's Representation will be suspended from the Fault of these Delinquents, their Fines shou'd be applied to the use of the County, rather than to the use of the Commonwealth.

"That the two Houses of Assembly may have authentic Information of, and proper Command of their own Members, the Sherif, besides the Certificate he delivers to each Member, shou'd make regular Returns to the Assembly."

6 The Act as adopted omits the following: "unless being required . . . duty elsewhere."

7 The Act as adopted provides that the sheriff or other officer taking the poll shall deliver a copy of the poll within ten days to the clerk of the county, who is required to deliver it to the next grand jury, this jury to be charged by the presiding magistrate to make a presentment of all qualified persons who refused to vote; the sheriff of the county was also required by the Act to deliver to the grand jury for their information a list of landholders in the county, under penalty of £50 for failure to do so (Hening, XII, 122).

8 The Act as adopted reads: "which shall be within twenty days after the last day of election, at such place as shall be appointed by the returning officer of the first county in which such election shall be, who is hereby commanded forthwith to give notice to the returning officers."

9 The Act as adopted reads: "for four days (Sundays excluded)."

10 The elaborate procedure provided for in the passage enclosed within square brackets (supplied) was struck out and, instead, the Act as adopted provided that the committee of privileges and elections should take cognizance of disputed elections before proceeding to any other business and the House (or Senate) would merely confirm or disagree with the findings of the committee.

11 Square brackets are in *Report* here and elsewhere throughout the Bill, except for the square brackets supplied at the place indicated in note 10.

12 The blank space after the word "act" also appears in the Act as adopted.

13 The substance of this sentence is incorporated in the Act as adopted at the point indicated by note 7.

14 The preceding three words are omitted in the Act as adopted and the following inserted after the words "place of election": "by advertisement to be affixed at four of the most convenient places in the county."

15 The Act as adopted reads: "fifty pounds."

16 The Act as adopted reads: "Any."

17 The Act as adopted reads: "ceaseth, he shall return himself a prisoner in execution or be liable to an escape."

18 The Act as adopted reads: "ten pounds."

19 The Act as adopted has an additional clause putting it in force 1 Jan. 1787. The general rule here enacted for putting an Act into effect prevailed over the alternative proposed by George Mason (see Document IV, 1, below).

3. A Bill Empowering One of the Privy Council to Officiate in Certain Cases as Lieutenant Governor

Be it enacted by the General Assembly, that if the Governor and President of the Privy Council shall die, or otherwise become unable to perform his duty, in the recess of the General Assembly, the Privy Councillor whose name stands next in the list of their appointments shall officiate as Lieutenant Governor, until the vacancy be supplied, or the disability cease. And, in the absence of the Governor, such intended absence having been previously notified to them by him and entered on their journals, or in the like absence of the President and upon the like notification, if any business, to be transacted at the Council Board, necessarily require dispatch before he can attend it, the Council may proceed without him, and in either case the act shall be as valid as if he had been present.

Report, p. 4. MS (ViU); clerk's copy. Bill was presented by Madison 31 Oct. 1785, passed by House 22 Nov., and approved by Senate 25 Nov. (JHD, Oct. 1785, 1828 edn., p. 12-15, 40, 47, 56, 132). This Bill reenacts, in different and briefer form, the Act of 1776 (Hening, IX, 212).

4. A Bill Empowering the Governor, with Advice of the Privy Council, to Lay Embargoes

Be it enacted by the General Assembly, that it shall be lawful for the Governor, with advice of the Privy Council, whenever, before the next session of General Assembly, they shall judge it to be for the good of the commonwealth, by his proclamation, published in the Virginia Gazette, to prohibit, during such time, to be therein limitted, as they shall think the exigency will probably continue; the exportation, by land or water, of wheat, and Indian corn, and the flour or meal thereof, and rice, barley, rye, oats, pease, or other pulse, potatoes, beef, pork, and bacon, or any, or either, of them, except such as, by his leave, and special order, with the advice aforesaid, shall be allowed to be exported, for supplying the army or navy of the United American States, or their allies, or for relieving any of the said states, represented, by the Executive powers thereof, to be distressed for want of provisions. If any such prohibited commodity be loaded in a vessel, more than what is necessary for sustenance of the crew thereof in the voyage, or in a cart, waggon, or other vehicle, for exportation, after the owner or master of the vessel, or the owner or driver of the vehicle, shall have notice of the embargo, or, having been loaded before such notice, shall not, in convenient time afterwards, be unloaded, and so remain, until the embargo shall expire, or be revoked, such vessel, with its rigging, apparel, and whole cargo; or such vehicle, with its team and whole load, or the value thereof, shall be forfeited; one half, to the use of the commonwealth, and the other, to the use of him who will sue, and may be recovered, by information; the former, in the

Court of Admiralty, and the latter in the court of common law. During such embargo, the chief commanding officer of any fort, or ship of the commonwealth, is hereby empowered, and any other person, by warrant of a justice, to be granted when affidavit shall be made that there is cause to suspect an illicit exportation to be intended, may with a sheriff, or constable, be empowered, to search for such prohibited articles, and seize them, with the vessel or vehicle wherein they shall be found, and the residue of the loading thereof; and no action shall be maintainable for damages, occasioned by such seizure of commodities, permitted by order of the Governor to be exported, unless such order shall have been produced and shewn to the person making the seizure, at that time, or before. The master of every vessel, before it be cleared out, during the continuance of an embargo, shall enter into bond, with sufficient surety, in the penalty of five thousand pounds, payable to the Governor, with condition, that none of the commodities prohibited shall be carried in the said vessel, more than such as are sufficient to sustain the crew thereof in the voyage; or that the commodities on board, if they shall have been loaded by such order of the Governor as aforesaid, shall be carried to the place destined by the said order, and there delivered; but such bond shall be void, if no action thereupon be commenced within one year after a breach of the condition shall happen.

Report, p. 4. MS (ViU); clerk's copy.

Bill presented by Madison 31 Oct. 1785 and committed to the committee of the whole, but no further action was taken (JHD, Oct. 1785, 1828 edn., p. 12-15). This Bill is substantially the same as the Act authorizing the Governor and Council to lay an embargo for a limited time, passed at the Oct. 1778 session and continued thereafter at each session until its repeal at the Nov. 1781 session (Hening, IX, 530-2; X, 105, 140, 306, 376, 423, 443). There were, however, some differences between the Act and this Bill, chief of which are the following: (1) the Bill omitted the preamble to the Act, which read: "Whereas divers persons for their own private lucre, transport out of this state into parts beyond the seas, wheat, Indian corn, and other provisions, when the same may be greatly wanted for the relief of the inhabitants of this state and support of our army and navy and those of our allies. And whereas no person or persons hath or have been hitherto invested by the legislature of this commonwealth, by whom alone it can be done, with power to lay an embargo on provisions, except wheat, Indian corn, and other grain, when necessary and expedient for the good of the same, *Be it therefore enacted . . .*"; (2) the Act was always limited, in its various continuing Acts, to the end of the next session of the Assembly; the Bill carried no such limitation; and (3) the Act specified only "beef, pork, bacon, wheat, Indian corn, pease, or other grain or flour . . . or any other provisions." Both the Act and the Bill carried the same penalties; and both made exceptions for the army and navy of the United States and of allies, but the Act did not include the proviso "for relieving any of the said states, represented, by the Executive powers thereof, to be distressed for want of provisions."

5. A Bill for Regulating and Disciplining the Militia

For[1] forming the citizens of this commonwealth into a militia and disciplining the same for defence thereof, be it enacted by the General Assembly of the commonwealth of Virginia, that all free male persons, hired servants and apprentices,[2] between the ages of 16 and 50 years (except the Governor and members of the Council of State, members of the American Congress, Judges of the Superior Courts, Speakers of the two Houses, the Treasurer, Attorney General, Commissioners of the navy, Auditors, Clerks of the Council of state,[3] of the Houses of Assembly and of the Navy Board, all Ministers of the Gospel, licensed to preach according to the rules of their sect, who shall have previously taken, before the court of their county, an oath of fidelity to the commonwealth, the Presidents, Professors, and students of the College of William and Mary, and Academy of Hampden-Sidney, post-masters, keepers of the public jail and public hospital, millers, except in the counties of Accomack and Northampton, persons concerned in iron or lead works, inspectors of tobacco, quakers and menonists, and military officers or soldiers, whether continental or colonial,[4] all of whom are exempted from the obligations of this act) shall, by the commanding officer of the county in which they reside, be inrolled and formed into companies of not less than 32, nor more than 68 rank and file; and these companies shall again be formed into battalions of not more than 1000 nor less than 500 men, if there be so many in the county; the free mulattoes in the said companies or battalions shall be employed as drummers, fifers, or pioneers.

Each company shall be commanded by a Captain, two Lieutenants and an Ensign; each battalion by a Colonel, Lieutenant Colonel and Major, who shall take precedence and command of each other according to rank and seniority, and the whole by a County Lieutenant, shall be resident within their county, and, before they enter on the execution of their office, shall, in presence of the court of the same county, take the following oath: "I   do swear that I will be faithful and true to the commonwealth of Virginia, of which I profess myself to be a citizen, and that I will faithfully and justly execute the office of a   in the militia of the county of   according to the best of my skill and judgment: So help me God."

There shall be a private muster of every company once in every month, except the months of December and January,[5] at such convenient time and place as the Captain, or next commanding officer, shall appoint; and a general muster in each county, at the courthouse of the same,[6] on a convenient day in the months of April and October in every year, to be appointed by the County Lieutenant or other commanding officer,[7] Every officer and soldier shall appear at his respective musterfield, by 11 o'clock in the forenoon, armed or accoutred as follows; the County Lieutenant, Colonels, Lieutenant Colonels, and Majors, with a sword; every Captain and Lieutenant with a firelock and bayonet, a cartouch box, a sword, and three charges of powder and ball; every ensign with a sword; every serjeant with a sword and halbard; every private with a rifle and tomahawk, or common firelock and bayonet, with a pouch and horn, or a cartouch or cartridge box, and with three charges of powder and ball; and moreover each of the said officers and soldiers shall constantly keep one pound of powder and four pounds of ball to be produced whenever called for by his commanding officer.[8] If any soldier be certified to the court-martial to be so poor that he cannot purchase such arms, the said court shall cause them to be procured at the expence of the public, to be reimbursed out of the fines on the delinquents of the county; which arms shall be delivered to such poor person, to be used at musters, but shall continue the property of the county; and if any soldier shall sell such arms, the seller and purchaser shall each of them forfeit the sum of six pounds; and on the death of such poor soldier, or his removal out of the county, such arms shall be delivered to his Captain, who shall make report thereof to the next court-martial, and deliver the same to such other poor soldier as they shall order.[9]

Each Captain shall at every muster, either by himself or some sworn officer, note down the delinquencies occurring in his company, and make return thereof to the next court-martial: But where any person is disabled by sickness from attending, the Captain, or commanding officer, being satisfied thereof by testimony on oath, which he is hereby enabled to administer, on the spot, shall not note down such non-attendance.

Every officer and soldier shall be allowed six months, after his appointment, or enrollment, to provide such arms or accoutrements as he has not at the time.

All arms and ammunition, of the militia, shall be exempted from executions and distresses at all times; and their persons from arrest, in civil cases, while going to, continuing at, or returning from any muster or Court-Martial.

Each Captain shall appoint a drummer and fifer to his company, and also shall provide a drum, fife, and colors, and halbards[10] for the same, at the public expence, to be reimbursed out of the fines on the delinquents of his county.

An adjutant[11] shall be appointed, by the court-martial of each county, to attend all musters general and private, and instruct the officers and soldiers in military duty: He shall continue in office till the next court-martial, and have an allowance by the said court, not exceeding the rate of fifty pounds a year, to be paid out of the fines, or, if they be not sufficient, the deficiency to be supplied by the Justices of the same county, in their next county levy, on certificate from the court-martial of such deficiency.

Every Captain or next commanding officer, shall, at every general muster, make up and report to his County Lieutenant a state of the company last assigned to him, noting therein such as are dead, removed or exempted, and adding the names of such persons not already enrolled as are within the extent of his company and ought to be enrolled; and also of all quakers and menonists, within the same extent, not yet divided into tenths;[12] and on failure to make such report shall forfeit five pounds.

For failing to qualify himself, to a commission, at the first or second court, which shall be held after accepting the same, every officer shall forfeit five pounds; for failing to enroll the militia or to appoint a general muster, the County Lieutenant, or if he be absent on necessary business, the next commanding officer shall forfeit one hundred pounds; for not appointing a private muster, the Captain, or next commanding officer, shall pay forty shillings; for failing to appear at any general muster, properly armed, or at any court-martial, every County-Lieutenant and field officer shall pay ten pounds; for failing to appear at any court-martial, every Captain shall pay forty shillings; for failing to appear at any general or private muster, properly armed or accoutred, every Captain shall forfeit forty shillings, every lieutenant or ensign, twenty shillings, and every soldier five shillings; for not returning to the next court-martial a true list of the delinquencies in his company, every Captain, or commanding officer for the time, shall forfeit ten pounds;[13] which penalties, where incurred by infants, shall be paid by the parent or guardian; and, where incurred by servants, shall be paid by the master, who, if such delinquency were without his influence or direction, may retain so much out of the hire of such servant.[14]

If any officer, when on duty, shall, misbehave, he may be put under arrest, for the day, by his commanding officer, and the next court-martial, if required, shall enquire into such misbehavior and either censure the same or make report thereof to the Governor and Council, who, if the cause be sufficient, shall thereupon degrade such officer. If any soldier, at any muster, shall refuse to obey the command of his officer, or shall behave himself refactorily or mutinously, or misbehave himself at a court-martial, the commanding officer,[15] may, in like manner, put him under arrest, for the day, or may cause him to be bound neck and heels for any time not exceeding five minutes. If any by-stander interrupt, molest or insult any officer or soldier, while on duty, at any general or private muster, or misbehave before any court-martial, the commanding officer, or court-martial, may put him under a arrest for the day.

The County-Lieutenant, Field-Officers, and Captains, or the greater part of them, whereof the County-Lieutenant, or a Field Officer, shall be one, shall hold a court-martial at the court-house of their county,[16] on the day following their general muster; having first taken the following oath: "I do swear that as a member of this court-martial I will do equal right and justice to all men according to law: So help me God." Which oath shall be administered, to the presiding officer, by the next in command: and then by such presiding officer to the other members. The said court may adjourn from day to day, and shall have power to exempt all persons enrolled, whom, from age or inability, they may adjudge incapable of service; and shall also enquire, by testimony on oath, which the clerk is hereby enabled to administer, into all delinquencies against this act, which shall have happened since the last court-martial; and, where no reasonable excuse for the same is made appear to them, shall give judgment for the penalties thereto annexed. But if it shall appear to the next court-martial, that any person fined for any such delinquency was unable to attend the court, by which he was fined, and had reasonable excuse for the delinquency, such fine shall be remitted.

The said court shall have power to appoint a clerk to enter and preserve their proceedings, to whom the president shall administer an oath truly and faithfully to execute the duties of his office; and may also appoint a provost martial to attend on the said court for the preservation of order and good behavior; and either by themselves, or any of their members, by their order, may appoint one or more persons to collect all fines, with an adequate allowance out of the same for their trouble: who shall have power to distrain for the same, and failing, or refusing, without reasonable cause, to make such collection, after having undertaken it, shall be held accountable for the same, each in his proper person and of his proper estate, to be recovered before any court of record, by action to be brought in the name of the court martial: And if after collecting the same he shall refuse to pay them, to the order of the said court-martial, he shall be subject to pay the double thereof on motion in any court of record and ten days previous notice given him of such motion;[17] and the said court-martial shall also appoint some person, not being a member of the said court, to be their burser, who shall receive, from the collector, all fines by him collected, and all sums of money recovered from him; and who before he enters on the execution of his office, shall give bond with sufficient security, payable to the members of the said court and their successors, for the due payment of all such monies which shall come to his hands. And if any burser shall fail, or delay, to account with the said court, or to apply the money, in his hands, as by them directed, after deducting at the rate of five per centum for his own trouble, on motion made in any court of record, by any person authorised to receive money from him; or by any other, by order of the said court-martial, judgment shall be given, and execution awarded, for the sums so unpaid or unaccounted for, together with the costs of the motion; the defendants having first had ten days notice of such motion.

All fines imposed by this act shall be appropriated in the first place to the payment of the salaries and allowances to the adjutant, clerk, provost martial, collectors and burser; then to reimbursing the public treasury for any arms purchased for the poor soldiers, of such county, and for drums, fifes, and colors, bought for the several companies; and if any surplus remain it shall be laid out by the court-martial in establishing and furnishing, for the use of their county, a magazine of small arms, field-pieces, ammunition, and such other military stores as may be useful in case of invasion or insurrection.[18]

All other acts and ordinances, so far as they relate to regulating and disciplining the militia of the several counties, are hereby repealed.[19]

This act shall be read, to every company of the militia, by order of the Captain or next commanding officer thereof, at the first muster next succeeding every general muster, on penalty of five pounds for every omission.

Report, p. 4-6. No MS of this Bill, as introduced in 1777, has been found. See Bill No. 6, below, which TJ introduced the same day that this one was brought in, 10 May 1777; both Bills were based on the ordinance of 1775 (Hening, IX, 9-35) and both, in fact, were embodied in one Bill when finally enacted into law in 1784 and again in 1785 (same, XI, 476-94; XII, 9-24).

III. BILL NO. 5

On 9 May 1777 TJ was appointed a member to bring in a Bill for regulating and disciplining the militia; he introduced the Bill 10 May; and during the next month it was amended by both the House and the Senate (JHD, May 1777, 1827 edn., p. 6-7, 12, 14, 20, 36, 58-9, 62, 68, 70, 72). The text here presented (Bill No. 5) follows the text of the Act of 1777 (Hening, IX, 267-74) except as indicated in the notes below. The Act of May 1777 (same, IX, 313-14), which provided for regulating and disciplining the militia of the city of Williamsburg and the borough of Norfolk by incorporating the students, professors, and others liable to militia duty in a special category, but subject to the same regulations, orders, and penalties as set forth in the general militia Act passed at the same session, was disregarded in Bill No. 5, thereby making the exemption of professors and students absolute; the special Act relating to Williamsburg and Norfolk was incorporated in the Act of 1784 (same, XI, 494). The latter Act, as indicated in the notes below, elaborated the militia law and incorporated many of the lessons learned during the Revolution; such as that Steuben's plan of discipline should be followed in training the militia; it also embraced much of Bill No. 5 as here presented and also of Bill No. 6. For the treatment of Bill No. 5 by the General Assembly in 1785, see notes to Bill No. 6.

1 The Acts of 1784 and 1785 include a preamble which indicates in part why the Act of 1777 and Bills No. 5 and 6 of the Committee of Revisors were considered inadequate: "the defence and safety of the commonwealth depend upon having its citizens properly armed and taught the knowledge of military duty, and the different laws heretofore enacted being found inadequate to such purposes, and in order that the same may be formed into one plain and regular system" (same, XI, 476; XII, 9).

2 The Acts of 1784 and 1785 omit the phrase "hired servants and apprentices" and alter the age limits to 18 and 50 years respectively.

3 The Act of 1777 does not include the following exemptions allowed by Bill No. 5: clerks of the houses of assembly, the presidents, professors, and students of the College of William and Mary and of Hampden-Sidney, inspectors of tobacco, Quakers, and Menonists. The Act of 1777 includes the following not in Bill No. 5: clerks of the treasury and persons solely employed in manufacturing firearms. The Acts of 1784 and 1785 enlarged the exemptions by the addition of auditors and their clerks, the solicitor general and his clerks, clerks of the treasury, the register of the land office, the deputy-register, and clerks of the register, custom house officers; it excluded clerks of the houses of assembly and of the navy board, Quakers and Menonists. The exclusion of Quakers and Menonists from the Acts of 1777, 1784, and 1785 is an indication of TJ's authorship of Bill No. 5; see note 2 to Bill No. 6.

4 The Act of 1777 reads "whether of the continent or this commonwealth"; the use of the word "colonial" here and elsewhere in Bill No. 5 may be another indication of TJ's authorship, since Bill No. 6, which TJ drew, also used the inappropriate word "colonial."

5 The Act of 1777 reads: "January and February"; the Act of 1784 provided that each company should muster once in every three months, each regiment in March or April, and a general muster be held in October or November.

6 The Act of 1777 reads: "at a convenient place, near the centre of the county."

7 The Act of 1777 provided for an elaborate manner of giving notice of muster days, through the regular chain of command from the county lieutenant down to the individual militiaman. This proviso was not incorporated in Bill No. 5, but was included and elaborated in the Acts of 1784 and 1785.

8 The terms of the Acts of 1784 and 1785 respecting arms reflect some of the lessons learned during the Revolution: captains, lieutenants, and ensigns were to carry swords and espontoons; non-commissioned officers and privates, "a good clean musket," carrying an ounce ball and having a barrel three feet eight inches long, twenty cartridges, a knapsack, a canteen, a pound of good powder and four pounds of lead, "including twenty blind cartridges"; each sergeant was required to carry a pair of molds for casting musket balls; and the counties westward of the Blue Ridge were not required to be armed with muskets but might bear rifles instead. The Act of 1777 had provided that non-commissioned officers and privates should carry a rifle and tomahawk or a "good firelock and bayonet."

[9] The Act of 1777 includes at this point a provision for penalizing poor soldiers and others guilty of carrying arms out of the county; this was also included in Act of 1784. The omission of this provision from Bill No. 5, together with those described in notes 7, above, and 18, below, is another indication that, in drawing this Bill in 1779, TJ may have depended upon an original bill drafted by him in 1777.

[10] The Act of 1777 omits the words "and halbards."

[11] The Act of 1777 reads: "One or more adjutants."

[12] The words "and also of all quakers . . . not yet divided into tenths" were not included in the Act of 1777.

[13] The Act of 1777 adds the following at this point: "Every officer failing to furnish himself with one pound of powder shall forfeit and pay ten shillings, and the same for failing to furnish himself with four pounds of ball; and every soldier failing therein shall likewise be liable for the same penalties."

[14] The Act of 1777 adds the following at this point: "or be compensated by farther service, to be ascertained by the county court."

[15] The Act of 1777 adds: "or court martial."

[16] The Act of 1777 adds: "or at, or convenient to, the place where the general muster shall be."

[17] Instead of the foregoing, the Act of 1777 provides authority for collection of fines by the sheriff.

[18] The Act of 1777 includes a section at this point requiring small details of officers and men to make monthly inspections of "all negro quarters, and other places suspected of entertaining unlawful assemblies of slaves, servants, or other disorderly persons . . . or any others strolling about from one plantation to another, without a pass. . . ." The Act of 1784 also included such a provision; see notes 7 and 9, above.

[19] The Act of 1777 includes the following at this point: "*Provided*, nothing in this act shall be construed to alter or change any thing contained in the general constitution or form of government, or to disqualify any militia officers heretofore appointed from acting by virtue of such commissions respectively; *and provided also*, that any court martial, which shall be held by virtue of this act, shall hear and determine any delinquency committed or done before the passing thereof, according to the laws in force at the time of the commission of the offence." See note 17 to Bill No. 6.

6. A Bill Making Provision against Invasions and Insurrections

For making provision against invasions and insurrections, and laying the burthen thereof equally on all: Be it enacted by the General Assembly, that the division of the militia of each county into ten parts, [made under the laws heretofore in force, shall be][1] kept up in the following manner: The commanding officer of every county, within one month after every general muster, shall enroll, under some Captain, such persons, not before enrolled, as ought to make a part of the militia, who, together with those before enrolled, and not yet formed into tenths[2] shall, by such Captain, at his first muster after receiving the same, be divided into ten equal parts, as nearly as may be, each part to be distinguished by fair and equal lot, by numbers from one to ten, and when so distinguished to be added to and made part of the division of the militia of such county already distinguished by the same number. And where any person subject to such allottment, shall not attend, or shall refuse to draw for himself, the Captain shall cause his lot to be drawn for him, by some other in presence of the company; [and as soon as such division shall be made, the Captain shall make return thereof to the commanding officer of the county. For failing to make such division, or return the same, the Captain shall forfeit ten pounds to be assessed by the court-martial of his county.] When any officer of the militia shall receive notice of any invasion or insurrection within his own county, he shall immediately give intelligence thereof to the commanding officer of the county, and if the urgency of the case requires it, he shall forthwith raise the militia under his special command, and proceed to oppose the enemy or insurgents. The commanding officer of the county, on receiving notice thereof, shall immediately, if the case will admit delay, or the danger be greater than the force of his own militia may be able to encounter, communicate the same to the Governor by express, for which purpose he may impress boats, men, and horses, and may also notify it to any militia officer of the adjacent counties, to be by him forwarded to his commanding officer; and in the meantime, if it be urgent, shall raise such part of his own militia as the case shall require and admit. The commanding officer of any adjacent county, receiving the notice so forwarded, shall immediately raise such part of his militia[3] as the circumstances of the case may require, and order them to the assistance of such adjacent county; but any officer thinking[4] the case of too small consequence to require these proceedings, may call a council of war, to consist of a majority of his Field-Officers and Captains, [or of a Field-Officer and of five Captains at the least,] and take their advice whether any, and what force, shall be raised or sent, or whether they may wait the Governor's orders. The Governor, on receiving such intelligence, may, with advice of the Council of State, cause to be embodied and marched, to oppose such invasion or insurrection, such numbers of the militia as may be needful, and from such counties as will suit the exigency of the case, and, if the corps consists of three or more battalions may appoint a general officer [or officers, as the case may require,] to take command thereof. The several divisions of the militia of any county shall be called into duty by regular rotation from the first to the tenth; and every person failing to attend when called on, or to send an able bodied man in his room, shall, unless there be good excuse, be considered as a deserter, and suffer accordingly. Any able bodied volunteers who will enter into the service shall be accepted instead of so many of the divisions of the militia called for, [or of the particular person in whose room they may offer to serve;] but if the invasion or insurrection be so near and pressing as not to allow the delay of calling the division or divisions next in turn, the commanding officer may call on such part of the militia as shall be most convenient to continue in duty till such division or divisions can come to supply their places. The soldiers of such militia, if not well armed and provided with ammunition, shall be furnished with the arms and ammunition of the county, and any deficiency in these may be supplied from the public magazines, or if the case admit not that delay, by impressing arms and ammunition of private property; which ammunition, so far as not used, and arms, shall be duly returned, as soon as they may be spared: And any person embezzling any such public or private arms, or not delivering them up when required by his commanding officer, shall, on his warrant, be committed to prison without bail or mainprize, there to remain till he deliver or make full satisfaction for the same, [unless he be sooner discharged by the court of his county.] The commanding officer shall appoint such officers of the militia as he shall think most proper to command the men called out by divisions, in the following proportions: If there be called into duty not more than twenty, nor less than fifteen, he shall appoint one ensign and one serjeant to command them. If not more than thirty, or under twenty men,[5] a Lieutenant, an ensign, and two serjeants. If not more than fifty men,[6] a Captain-Lieutenant, ensign, and three serjeants. If sixty eight men,[7] a Captain, two Lieutenants, an ensign, and four serjeants. And [if not more than one hundred and fifty, nor less than one hundred, a Major shall command. If more than one hundred and fifty, and not exceeding two hundred and fifty, a Lieutenant-Colonel shall command, and have under him a Major, with the proper number of Captains and other officers. A Colonel to command any number of men not exceeding five hundred, nor under two hundred and fifty. A County Lieutenant to command any number of men above five hundred, and not exceeding a battallion.][8] A distinct list of the names and numbers of officers and soldiers sent on duty, and of all persons impressed, with the time they served, attested, on oath, by the officer commanding such party, shall be certified by the commanding officer of the county to the [Auditors of Public Accounts to be by them examined and certified to the Treasurer, for payment of what may be justly due.][9]

Any officer resigning his commission on being called into duty by the Governor, or his commanding officer, shall be sent on the same duty as a private, and shall moreover, suffer punishment as for disobedience of command. The commanding officer of the corps marching to oppose any invasion or insurrection, or any commissioned officer, by warrant under the hand of such commander, may, for the necessary use of such corps or for the transportation of them across waters, or of their baggage by land or water, impress provisions, vessels with their furniture, hands, waggons, carts, horses, oxen, utensils for intrenching, smiths, wheel-wrights, carpenters, or other artificers, and arms in the case before directed. Such necessaries, or the use of them by the day, shall be previously appraised by two persons chosen, the one by such officer, and the other by the person interested, or both by the officer, if the person interested shall refuse to name one, [or cannot readily be called upon] and duly sworn by the said officer, who is hereby, empowered to administer the oath. Such officer shall give a receipt or a certificate of every particular impressed, of its appraised value, and of the purpose for which it was impressed. And if any article impressed shall [be lost, or] receive damage, while in public service, such [loss and] damage shall be enquired of, and estimated by two men chosen and sworn in the same manner. [The said certificates shall be transmitted to the Auditors, to be by them certified and paid in manner herein before directed.][10] All persons drawn into actual service, [or impressed] by virtue of this act, shall be exempted in their persons and property from civil process, and all proceedings against them in civil suits shall be stayed during their continuance in service. When any corps or detachment of militia shall be on duty with any corps or detachment of [regulars belonging to the continent or this commonwealth,][11] or both of them, the continental officer shall take command of [officers of the commonwealth][12] of the same rank, and these again of militia officers of the same rank, [and all militia officers of the same rank shall take command according to seniority, and if their commissions be of equal date, then their rank shall be decided by lot; a County-Lieutenant, when acting in concert with regulars taking rank as a Colonel.] The commanding officer of each of the counties of Elizabeth City, Princess Anne, Norfolk,[13] Northampton, and Accomack, with permission from the Governor, may appoint any number of men not exceeding six, in each [of the former counties, and in the two latter not more than ten men,] to keep a constant looking out to seaward, by night and by day, who discovering any vessels appearing to belong to an enemy, or to purpose landing or hostility, shall immediately give notice thereof to some militia officer of the county. [And the Lieutenant, or next commanding officer of the several counties on the western frontier, with the like permission, shall be empowered to appoint any number of proper persons not exceeding ten, in any one county, to act as scouts for discovering the approach of the Indians, or any other enemy on the frontiers; who, on such discovery, shall immediately give notice thereof to some militia officer of the county,] whereon such course shall be pursued as is before directed in case of an invasion or insurrection. The pay of all officers and soldiers of the militia, from the time they leave their homes by order of their commanding officer till they return to them again, and of all look-outs [or scouts,] shall be the same as shall have been allowed by the last regulations of General Assembly to regulars of the same rank or degree. Messengers shall be allowed, by the Auditors of Public Accounts, according to the nature of their service. Any militia officer receiving notice of an invasion or insurrection, or of the approach of any vessel with hostile purpose, and not forwarding the same to his commanding officer, shall forfeit, if a Field-Officer, one hundred pounds; if a Captain or subaltern, fifty pounds; and any commanding officer of a county receiving such notice, and not raising part of his militia, nor taking the advice of his council of war, two hundred pounds. [Such forfeitures to be recovered,] with costs, by action of debt, in the name of the [other members of the said court-martial, or the survivors of them][14] before any court of record, and appropriated to the same use as the fines imposed by the court-martial of his county. Any officer or soldier guilty of mutiny, desertion, or disobedience of command, absence from duty or quarters neglect of guard, or cowardice, shall be punished at the discretion of a court-martial, by degrading, cashiering, drumming out of the army,[15] fine not exceeding two months pay, imprisonment not exceeding one month.[16] Such court-martial, [which the commanding officer is hereby empowered to order,] shall be constituted of militia officers only, of the rank of Captains or higher, and shall consist of seven members at the least, whereof one shall be a County-Lieutenant or Field-Officer: [Provided that if two or more companies, without a Field-Officer, should be called out to duty, the senior officer, may appoint a court-martial, to consist of one Captain and three or more commissioned officers, whose sentence, not extending to amercement or imprisonment, being confirmed by the commanding officer, not being a member of the court, shall be put in execution;] each of whom shall take the following oath: "I do swear, that I will well and truly try, and impartially determine the cause of the prisoner now to be tried, according to the act of Assembly, for providing against invasions and insurrections. So help me God." Which oath shall be administered to the presiding officer by the next in command, and then by such presiding officer to the other members. The said court shall also appoint a clerk to enter and preserve their proceedings, to whom the president shall administer an oath, truly and faithfully to execute the duties of his office. [And such clerk shall be paid such compensation for his service as shall be judged reasonable by the court-martial, out of the fines imposed by this act; the fines to be collected by the sheriff, as in the militia law, except such as can be retained out of the pay of the delinquent.] All persons called to give evidence shall take the usual oath of evidence, to be administered by the clerk of the court. If in any case the offender be not arrested before the corps of militia on duty be discharged, or cannot be tried for want of members sufficient to make a court, he shall be subject to be tried after by the court martial of his county. [The Governor with the advice of the Council of State, may, and he is hereby authorised and desired, to appoint one or more fit and able persons to act as quarter-masters to the militia drawn into actual service, whose duty it shall be to provide, in due time, all things necessary for their accommodation. And such quarter-masters shall have power, and they are hereby strictly enjoined, to inspect and examine all provisions dealt out by any comissary or contractor to such militia, and make report to the Governor, from time to time, of the quality thereof. And the said quarter-masters shall, for their services, receive such allowance as to the Governor and Council may appear reasonable. The commanding officer of any detachment of militia drawn out into actual service shall, if necessary, appoint a commissary, or contractor, to procure provisions for the said detachment. Such commissary, upon complaint to a court-martial, to be composed of the officers of the corps, may, by judgement of such court-martial, be removed for misconduct. Every commissary or contractor appointed by virtue of this act shall obtain a certificate of his service from the commanding officer of the detachment for which he served, on producing which to the Governor and Council he shall be entitled to such reward as they think fit.][17]

This act shall be read to every company of the militia by order of the Captain, or next commanding officer, twice in every year,[18] on penalty of five pounds for every omission.

Report, p. 6-8. MS (Vi) in TJ's hand endorsed: "3. A Bill for providing against invasions & insurrections." Also docketed, partly in hand of John Tazewell: "In the House of Delegates. A Bill for providing against invasions and Insurrections. May 1777. to be engrossed." Accompanying this MS is a list of amendments to TJ's Bill, in the hand of Tazewell; most of these are indicated in textual notes below. This MS is not to be confused with MS (ViU), which is the clerk's copy described in Editorial Note, above. The Act as adopted in 1777 is in Hening, IX, 291-7.

On 9 May 1777 TJ was appointed a member of a committee to bring in a Bill on this subject; he reported the Bill next day, when it was read the first time; in the course of the next month it was amended by both the House and Senate (JHD, May 1777, 1827 edn., p. 6-8, 20, 24, 56, 70-2). Bill No. 6 is the same text as the Act of 1777, except as indicated in the notes below; in one instance TJ did not include in this Bill a significant clause that had been in the Act of 1777 (note 17, below); nor did this Bill take account of the amending Act of 1778 (note 16, below). The Bill here presented was not adopted, though the general militia Act of Oct. 1784, which repealed all preceding Acts pertaining to the subject, incorporated many of the provisions set forth in Bills No. 5 and 6 (Hening, XI, 476-94). On 31 Oct. 1785 Madison presented this and the preceding Bill. Earlier, the House had received a petition protesting against the Act of 1784 as being "in several instances repugnant to the principles of the constitution." In response to this petition a Bill repealing part of the Act of 1784 was introduced but failed of passage. Instead a bill "to amend and reduce into one Act, the several laws 'for regulating and disciplining the militia, and guarding against invasions and insurrections'" was introduced and, after being amended by both houses, was adopted (JHD, Oct. 1785, 1828 edn., p. 7, 8, 12-15, 34, 73, 75, 91, 93, 117, 125, 127, 129, 135-7, 144; Hening, XII, 9-24).

1 Matter within square brackets (supplied) here and elsewhere in the text is not in TJ's MS Bill of 1777 but is in the Act of 1777. MS at this point reads: "directed by a former ordinance shall be completed and kept up"; Act of 1777 reads: "directed by an ordinance of general convention shall be completed and kept up." The ordinance referred to is that of 1775 concerning the militia (Hening, IX, 9-35, at p. 27ff.).

2 At this point the MS included the phrase "and with such Quakers and Menonists as are not formed into tenths." This was deleted by amendment.

3 MS read: "not exceeding two thirds," but this was deleted by amendment.

4 MS read: "any of the said commanding officers, if he think"; this was altered by amendment to read as above and in the Act.

5 MS read: "25 men," but this was altered by amendment to read as above and in the Act.

6 MS read: "40 men," altered by amendment to read as above and in the Act.

7 MS read: "50 men," altered by amendment to read as above and in the Act.

8 The passage in square brackets was substituted by amendment for the following in MS: "and so in proportion for every greater number; adding, if there be several companies, such feild officers as may be requisite."

9 The passage in square brackets was substituted by amendment for the following in MS: "next General Assembly."

10 The passage in square brackets was substituted by amendment for the following in MS: "and shall be made good by the public."

11 The passage in square brackets was substituted by amendment for the following in MS: "Colonial regulars or Continental troops."

12 The passage in square brackets was substituted by amendment for the following in MS: "the Colonial regulars."

13 "Norfolk" does not appear in MS.

14 The passage in square brackets was substituted by amendment for the following in MS: "Commonwealth."

15 The following in MS was deleted by amendment: "whipping not exceeding 20 lashes."

16 An amending Act of May, 1778, stated that it had been found by experience that the fine inflicted on any officer or soldier guilty of mutiny, desertion, &c., was by no means sufficient to deter the defaulters; hence the amending Act provided that the court martial could inflict any fine "they shall determine reasonable," so long as it did not exceed six months' pay (Hening, IX, 458).

17 MS and the Act as adopted contain at this point the following: "All other acts and ordinances so far as they make provision against invasions and insurrections are hereby repealed"; the Act also contains the following proviso, but the MS does not: "Provided, that noth-

ing in this act shall be construed to alter or change anything contained in the general form or constitution of this government."

18 The following in MS was deleted by amendment: "that is to say, at their first muster next succeeding every general muster in his county."

7. A Bill Giving Certain Powers to the Governor and Council for a Limitted Time

Whereas the present war between America and Great-Britain was undertaken for defence of the common rights of the American States, and it is therefore just that each of them, when in danger, should be aided by the joint exertions of all; and as on any invasion of this commonwealth in particular, we should hope for and expect necessary aids of militia from our neighboring sister states, so it is incumbent on us to yeild the same assistance to them under the like circumstances;[1] and the laws heretofore empowering the Governor and Council to send aids of militia to such states[2] will expire[3] at the end of this present session of Assembly.

Be it therefore enacted by the General Assembly that on the invasion, or reasonable apprehension of an invasion of[4] any sister state,[5] and application from Congress, or from the Legislative or Executive powers of such state for aids of militia, it shall be lawful for the Governor, with the advice of the Council of State, to order to their assistance such corps of the militia, from any of the counties of this commonwealth, as the exigence of the case may require or admit, having regard, in such orders, to the convenience and vicinity of such counties to the place invaded, their internal security and the imminence of the danger; and moreover to appoint such General, Field, and Staff Officers as may be requisite to command, attend and provide for the same, to have them furnished with necessaries for travelling and camp uses, and such arms, ammunition, and accoutrements, as may be called for, if the same can be procured and spared from this commonwealth. And to answer the expences hereof in the first instance, the Governor with the advice of Council[6] is empowered[7] to draw for any sums of money necessary to carry these purposes into effect, on the Treasurer of this commonwealth, who shall pay the said draughts[8] and keep a separate and distinct account thereof, in order that the same may be reimbursed to the commonwealth.

Such militia while on duty shall be subject to the continental rules and articles of discipline and government;[9] save only that all courts-martial, whether general or regimental, which shall be holden on any of them, shall consist of their own officers only.

This act shall be in force till the end of the next session of General Assembly only, and no longer.

Report, p. 8. MS (Vi) in TJ's hand, endorsed partly in his hand (the deleted portion in TJ's hand being indicated by angle brackets), followed by the substituted title in another hand: "A Bill ⟨*empowering the Governor to send aids of militia to our sister states when invaded*⟩ for giving certain powers to the Governor and council." Also docketed, partly in the hand of John Tazewell: "Jan: 13. 1778. Read the first time. Jan: 14: Read the second time & commd. to be ingrossed." This MS is not to be confused with MS (ViU), which is the clerk's copy described in Editorial Note, above.

On 6 Nov. 1777 the committee on courts of justice was ordered to bring in a Bill on this subject: the Bill was introduced by Fleming on 13 Jan.; on 21 Jan. it was amended by the committee of the whole; the next day it was passed by the House and agreed to by the Senate (JHD, Oct. 1777, 1827 edn., p. 15, 113, 114, 124-6). At the sessions of May and Oct. 1778 and May 1779 the Act of 1777 was continued from session to session (Hening, IX, 428-9, 462, 477-8; X, 106). The continuing Act of Oct. 1778 added certain other powers authorizing the Governor and Council to appoint justices of the peace in certain cases (death, refusal to act, and removal out of the county) and to remove justices from office for proved misconduct; these additional powers were continued, but that portion of the Act of 1777 respecting the use of the militia was allowed to expire with the continuing Act of May 1779, being superseded by enlarged emergency powers granted to the Governor by other Acts (Chancellors' Revisal, p. 81; Hening, X, 309-15, 336-9, 413-16; the first of these superseding Acts was passed May 1780, the second Oct. 1780, and the third May 1781). Except as indicated below, the MS Bill, the Act of 1777, and Bill No. 7 are identical.

1 The word "circumstances" is underscored in MS, with the number "6" written in the margin corresponding to the number of the line, as if an amendment to the MS Bill had been intended; but the Act as adopted corresponds to the reading above.

2 The laws referred to are the ordinance of May 1776 and its continuing Acts of Oct. 1776 and May 1777 (Hening, IX, 119-22, 178, 309). The ordinance of May 1776 and its continuing Acts gave the Governor and Council a general power "to direct such military movements and operations as . . . will be necessary for the safety and security of the commonwealth." It is significant that this general power, which under a broad construction could be regarded as authorizing the sending of militia out of the state, was made explicit under TJ's Bill of 1777.

3 MS read originally "have expired," and TJ altered it to read as above.

4 The words "or reasonable apprehension of an invasion of" are not in MS Bill or in Act of 1777 as adopted.

5 MS reads: "of any adjacent or neighboring state," but this was amended to read as above, which corresponds to the wording of the Act of 1777.

6 The words "with the advice of Council" do not appear in MS or in Act of 1777.

7 MS read originally "authorised," and TJ altered it to read as above.

8 MS and Act of 1777 read: "who is hereby authorised to pay the same out of any public money in his hands."

9 MS read originally "but shall be subject and shall be tried," but these words were deleted by TJ.

8. A Bill Establishing a Board of War

Be it enacted by the General Assembly that a Board of War shall be constituted to consist of five persons, to be chosen by joint ballot of both Houses of Assembly, at the first session of every Assembly, and to continue in office until the next choice shall be made. But any member may be removed within that time by joint vote of both Houses, and thereupon, as also on the death, resignation or refusal to act, of any member, they shall proceed to chuse another to act in his stead and during his term, and if either of these events happen during the recess of Assembly, the Governor and Council may appoint some person to act in the said office until the end of the next session of Assembly:[1] Any three of the members may proceed to business, and he who is first in the nomination shall preside.

The duty of the said board shall be to superintend and manage, subject to the direction and controul of the Governor with advice of the Council, all matters and things within the department of war, and all persons holding offices or performing duties within that department: All their resolutions, proceedings and orders, before they are carried into execution, shall be signed by the Governor: The said board shall depute by rotation, unless they can otherwise agree, some one of their members to visit and personally examine and report, once in every two months at the least, the condition of the military stores and provisions in the several magazines.[2]

They shall sit at such places, and in such apartments, as the Governor with advice of the Council shall direct: And if at any time they shall be separated and occasion for their meeting shall arise, the Governor shall have power to call them together: They shall have authority from time to time to appoint a Commissioner of the Navy and also their own clerk; which clerk shall take an oath to keep secret all such matters as they shall direct to be kept secret;[3] the said oath may be administered by any member of the board.

Report, p. 8. See Note on Bill No. 9.

This Bill was introduced by TJ separately at the session of May 1779; it is substantially the same as the Act then adopted (JHD, May 1779, 1827 edn., p. 6-8, 10; Hening, X, 17-18); the principal differences are indicated below. This Act was repealed by an Act of May 1780 which, "for the purpose of introducing œconomy into all the various departments of government, and for conducting the publick business with the greatest expedition," established in place of the boards of war and trade a commercial agent, a commissioner of the navy, and a commissioner of the war office, appointed by the governor with advice of the council and under direction of both (same, X, 291-2; see also "an act to regulate the department of the war office," adopted May 1781, same, p. 426-9).

1 The Act includes at this point the requirement that the members take an oath of fidelity and also an oath of office, the terms of the latter being specified in the Act.

2 The Act also gives the board authority to appoint a commissary of prisoners.

3 The Act required both the commissioner of the navy and the clerk of the board to take an oath of office and also an oath of secrecy.

9. A Bill Establishing a Board of Trade

Be it enacted by the General Assembly that a Board of Trade shall be constituted to consist of three persons, not exercising commerce on their private account, to be chosen by joint ballot of both Houses of Assembly, at the first session of every Assembly, and to continue in office until the next choice shall be made: But any member may be removed within that time by joint vote of both Houses, and thereupon, as also on the death, resignation, or refusal to act of any member, they shall proceed to chuse another in his stead; or if such death, resignation, or refusal happen during the recess of Assembly, the Governor and Council may appoint some person to act in the said office until the end of the next session of Assembly:[1] Any two of the said members may proceed to business.

The duty of the said board shall be to see to the procuring, by importation or otherwise, all military stores, clothing, accoutrements, utensils, materials and necessaries which shall be required by the Governor with advice of the Council, for the public use, or for the use of the officers, soldiers, sailors and marines raised under the laws of this commonwealth; taking care to send for such additional quantities as may provide against total disappointments happening by capture or otherwise:[2] To make payment for the same in money, or by remittance of commodities or bills of exchange to be purchased by them for that purpose, or of specie or bullion; to have them stored and safely kept until called for by the Governor and Council or Board of War: To superintend and direct all persons and things employed in or about the said business:[3] [To license proper pilots for the ports within this commonwealth, without which license no person shall act as pilot; to deprive them for misbehavior and to regulate their fees from time to time: They shall deliver to every such pilot on his application an attested list of the fees which he may take and notify to him from time to time all alterations made therein; which list and notifications he shall constantly carry with him when in the execution of his office, and produce it if required to the person making payment of his fees on pain of deprivation of his license: If he shall demand any greater fees, he shall in like manner be deprived of his license; and if when required by the master of any vessel belonging to this commonwealth or any citizen thereof or to any other state in amity with this commonwealth or any of its subjects or citizens, he shall refuse to conduct such vessel to any port within his license, he shall be deprived of his license and forfeit his vessel:][4] All the proceedings of the said board, before they are carried into execution, shall be submitted to the Governor and Council for their approbation, amendment or negative.

The Governor with advice of Council shall notify from time to time to the Board of Auditors, the sums of money which may be necessary for the purposes before mentioned, who shall thereupon give their warrant or warrants, on the Treasurer, for the advance of such monies to be regularly debited and accounted for in due time.

The said board shall sit at such place and in such apartments as the Governor with advice of Council shall direct: And if at any time they shall be separated and occasion for their meeting shall arise, the Governor shall have power to call them together: They shall from time to time appoint their own clerk,[5] who shall take an oath to keep secret all such matters as they shall direct to be kept secret; which oath may be administered by any member of the board.

Report, p. 9.

This Bill was introduced by TJ separately at the session of May 1779; it is substantially the same as the Act then adopted, the principal differences being indicated below (JHD, May 1779, 1827 edn., p. 6-8, 10, 13, 14; Hening, X, 15-16). TJ very probably drew this Bill (see Document IV, 3, note 8, below) and Bill No. 8, since he introduced both, but no MS of either has been found. The Act of May 1779 was repealed by an Act of May 1780 (same, X, 291-2).

1 The Act includes at this point the requirement that the members take an oath of fidelity and also an oath of office, the terms of the latter being specified.

2 The Act adds the following authorization at this point: "to procure salt, and cards for manufacturing cotton and wool, and distribute the same properly among the people of this commonwealth, at such prices only, as will reimburse the publick; where cargoes shall contain a considerable proportion of the articles before mentioned, together with others not wanting for the publick use, and the same can only be bought by wholesale, or may be so bought to better account, to purchase the said cargoes, and to sell again as diffusive as possible, such parts of them as are not so wanting."

3 The Act adds the following authorization at this point: "to superintend the publick manufactories of all articles, which by this act they are required to provide, to fit out, purchase, or charter vessels of burthen, or of dispatch necessary for fulfilling the purposes of this act, or for carrying or procuring advices for government."

4 The passage within square brackets (supplied) is not included in the Act.

5 The Act adds the following at this point: "or clerks."

10. A Bill for the Annual Appointment of Delegates to Congress, and of a Member for the Committee of the States

Be it enacted by the General Assembly, that at the first session of every General Assembly there shall be chosen by joint ballot of both Houses, seven persons to act as Delegates for this commonwealth in General Congress, from the first Monday in November next ensuing, the said election for the term of one year.

Four of the said Delegates at the least, shall be always at Congress during its sessions, the majority of those present shall give the vote of this commonwealth, provided there be present three at the least; otherwise they shall give no vote. If they shall not by agreement among themselves, to be stated in writing, otherwise settle the portions of the year during which each member shall attend, so as to keep up a constant attendance of four at the least, then they shall serve as follows, to wit:

The first member in the nomination shall serve during the months of November, December, January, February, June, July and August.

The second, during the months of January, February, March, April, May, September and October.

The third, during the months of November, December, March, April, May, September and October.

The fourth, during the months of November, December, January, February, June, July and August.

The fifth, during the months of February, March, April, July, August, September and October.

The sixth, during the months of November, December, January, May, June, July and August.

And the seventh, during the months of March, April, May, June, September and October.

No member shall be capable of being a Delegate for more than three years in any term of six years.[1]

So soon as it shall be decided on the ballot, who are to be Delegates for the ensuing year, the two Houses, shall proceed to chuse, in like manner, by joint ballot, one of the said Delegates, to be a member of the committee of the states for this commonwealth during the same year, who shall reside during the recess of Congress wherever they shall have appointed the said committee to sit.[2]

Any of the said Delegates, or the said member of the committee of the states, shall be subject to be removed at any time within the year, by the joint vote of both Houses, and thereon, or in case of the death, resignation, or refusal to act, of any such Delegate, or member, they shall proceed to chuse another, to serve in his stead, and during his term.[3]

The reasonable expences for sustenance and travelling, of the said Delegates and member of the committee of states, and of their wives, and children accompanying them, shall be paid or advanced by the Treasurer, at whatever place Congress or the said committee shall be sitting, the account thereof to be made up of general heads only, to be proved to the Auditors, by the oath of the member, or by other vouchers at his election; or any such member preferring the same, may be entitled to receive, in like manner, and in lieu thereof, from the Treasurer, the sum of dollars for every day he shall be at Congress, or the said committee, and half a dollar for every mile travelling to, or returning from the same with his ferriages.[4]

If any person holding any office under the laws of this commonwealth, Legislative, Executive, or Judiciary, be appointed a Delegate to Congress, or member of the committee of the states, such office shall not thereby be vacated.[5]

The Delegates to Congress to be chosen during the present session of Assembly in lieu of those who have resigned, or shall resign, together with those remaining in office, shall be continued until the first Monday in November next, and shall be subject to the same rules of voting, and entitled to the same allowances as are before stated, in case of the members to be annually chosen.

Report, p. 9-10. No MS of this Bill, other than its predecessor of 1777 which was unquestionably drawn by TJ, has been found, but his authorship may be safely assumed from the following facts: (1) he introduced it; (2) he had drawn up a resolution while in Congress respecting qualifications of delegates (q.v., ca. 1 July 1776); (3) he drew the controversial Bill for Regulating the Appointment of Delegates to the Continental Congress (q.v., 12 May 1777; Hening, IX, 299).

On 17 May 1779 TJ presented the Bill; it was read the second time and amended by the House 18 May; on 25 May the Senate amended the Bill further and, after a conference, the House agreed to the Senate amendments (JHD, May 1779, 1827 edn., p. 9, 11, 13, 20-2; Hening, X, 74-5; see also Fleming to TJ, 10-11 May 1779). Bill agrees with the Act of May 1779 except as noted below. This Bill was also introduced in the House by Madison on 31 Oct. 1785 but was superseded by another which was adopted under the title "An act to provide for the appointment of delegates . . . until the first Monday in November next" (JHD, Oct. 1785, 1828 edn., p. 12-15, 34, 35, 36, 37, 39; Hening, XII, 26-7).

1 The Act adds at this point: "taking into account as well the past as future time."

2 This paragraph does not appear in the Act, probably having been deleted by amendment.

3 The Act adds at this point: "and each of the said delegates shall receive from the treasurer the sum of forty dollars for every day he shall be at congress, or for attending the committee of the states, and a dollar for every mile travelling to, or returning from either, with his ferriages." The Act, however, omits the words "or the said member of the committee of the states" and "or member" as given in the above paragraph of Bill No. 10, deletions which necessarily followed from that indicated above in note 2.

4 This paragraph is omitted from the Act. However, at the Oct. 1779 session an Act was passed stating that the Act of the preceding session had been "found inconvenient and not to answer the end proposed"; this Act reduced the number of delegates from seven to five; made it possible for one person to cast the state's vote or a majority if more than one delegate were in attendance; allowed delegates "the expense for such part of their families as they may severally incline to keep with them, provisions for necessary servants and horses, not exceeding

three servants and four horses for each; pay for house-rent and fuel, and also the farther sum of twenty dollars to each delegate for every day they shall be in congress"; in providing for family expenses in line with the above section of Bill No. 10, though differing considerably from it, the Act of Oct. 1779 enjoined delegates always to "keep in remembrance that œconomy is expected from them by their country" and required in consequence an accounting for housekeeping expenses (Hening, x, 163-4).

5 The Act of Oct. 1779 repealed that part of this paragraph which permitted a delegate to hold state office, declaring that such office-holder could not remain in a state office during his term in Congress. In May 1783, however, the legislature specifically declared that appointment to Congress would vacate a seat held in the General Assembly by the appointee (same, xi, 249-50).

11. A Bill Establishing a Board of Auditors

Be it enacted by the General Assembly that there shall be a standing Board of Auditors for Public Accounts, to consist of three persons to be chosen from time to time, as vacancies shall happen, by joint ballot of both Houses of Assembly, and to continue in office until removed by the joint vote of both the said Houses; and where any person so appointed shall refuse to act, resign, or die, during the recess of Assembly, it shall be lawful for the Governor with advice of the Council of state, to appoint some other fit and able person to act in his stead, until the next meeting of the General Assembly. The Auditors so appointed shall not be capable of acting until they shall have taken the oath of fidelity to the commonwealth, and also an oath impartially and honestly to execute the duties of their office; which oaths, during the sessions of the High Court of Chancery, shall be taken before the said court, and during their vacation shall be taken before some judge thereof, and by him shall be certified to his next succeeding court and entered of record: Any two of the said Auditors so qualified, shall have power to proceed to business. The Auditors now in office, by virtue of former appointments, shall continue to act and be considered to all future intents and purposes as if they had been appointed by virtue of this act. The said Board of Auditors are authorised and required to state and keep an exact account of all articles of debit or credit hereafter to arise between this commonwealth and the United States of America, or any of them, or any other state, to raise and keep accounts with all officers of civil government who are intitled to receive from the public treasury salaries or wages fixed by law: To enquire into all legal expenditures for the army, navy, or militia of this commonwealth, and on requisition from the Governor, with the advice of Council, to give their warrant on the Treasurer for the advance of monies for such purposes, debiting therewith the person to whom it is confided, and calling him in due time to render account of the application thereof: To examine all demands for the hire of horses, waggons, or other things employed, or impressed by authority of law, for the public service, or for the worth thereof, or injury done thereto, where the thing impressed has been consumed, lost, destroyed, or damaged in such service: To make just allowances to expresses employed by the Governor and Council, the Boards of War or Trade, or our Delegates in Congress, or sent on the public service to the Governor and Council, or to any Indian nation, the Governor and Council certifying there was good reason for sending such express, or to scouts, and to look outs, or any others doing services to the public, for which they are intitled in law to receive payment, and no person particularly authorised to ascertain the quantum of such payment: To allow annual pensions to officers, soldiers, sailors, and marines, of the army or navy raised by any act of General Assembly and disabled in the service, and to the widows of those slain or dying therein, as also sums in gross for their immediate relief, proportioning the same with impartiality and discretion to the nature of every case; such sums in gross however, to be given but once to any one person, and not to exceed one year's pay, and such annual pension not to exceed full pay: To enter in account all draughts on the Treasurer for money by the Governor and Council for the public service: To certify such entry to the Treasurer for payment, and to audit in due time the expenditure thereof: To give warrants on the Treasurer for the payment or advance of wages to our Delegates in Congress, debiting each Delegate respectively with the warrant given in his name, and requiring account thereof to be rendered within three months after the expiration of his appointment: To audit all accounts for wages due to the members of the General Assembly for attendance therein, or for their travelling allowances, such attendance and allowances being previously entered with the clerk of the House, of which such member is, in separate books to be kept for that purpose and to lie during the session on the table of the House, and being certified by the said clerk, to be so entered; and to audit accounts for salaries or wages to the officers and attendants of the two Houses: To settle the expences of sending for the members of either House by special messengers: Of providing robes for the Speakers and clerks of both Houses, maces, lights, fuel, blank books, parchment, paper, and other articles necessary for the use of either House, or of the Governor and Council, the Boards of War or Trade, Treasurer, Register, or the Superior Courts of

Justice, while on duty in the capitol or in their offices: To audit all accounts for building or repairing houses or other articles of public property, such buildings or repairs being authorised by act of Assembly, or the previous vote of the two Houses of Assembly: To examine all claims for the support of prisoners where the public is chargeable with such support, or for the removal of any such to the prison of the General Court, or for the guard of criminals, or for jurors or witnesses attending their trials, or witnesses for the commonwealth attending a court of justice, or judicial officer in any other case; or for slaves executed by judgment of common law for any crime, or legally put to death under process of outlawry: To call for annually, and to examine the accounts of expenditures for the public trade, the public hospital, and for all works undertaken and carried on, at the public expence, by authority from the Legislature, and to enter the same in separate accounts: To enquire into all demands for bounties, or premiums payable by law, out of the public treasury, for the encouragement of particular manufacturers: Of bringing to justice public offenders: Of destroying noxious animals, or of any other matter: To examine and enter in account of all other demands, for money on the Treasurer, made under authority of any law heretofore passed, or hereafter to be passed: To settle the accounts of all public debtors, and of all collectors of any revenue or tax levied by act of General Assembly and payable to the Treasurer; or of any monies due to the public: To call upon such debtors or collectors to render account at proper times, and on their failure so to do, to instruct the Attorney General to institute proceedings at law for compelling them to justice, and though it should appear on trial that the defendant oweth no balance to the public, yet his having failed to render account to the Auditors and to take them in his quietus, shall subject him to the payment of all costs incurred by such proceedings, as well to himself as to the commonwealth: To require information on oath from any person, party or privy, of matters relative to any account under their examination and material for their information: To administer such oath where the party is attending, and where absent to take out a commission from the High Court of Chancery directed to any Justice of the Peace, to take his examination on interrogatories to be stated by them; whereon any such settlement a balance shall appear due to the public, to certify the same under their own hands to the Treasurer and hold the party charged therewith till he shall produce to them the Treasurer's receipt for the same, on which they shall give him a quietus, debit the Treasurer therewith, and certify such debits to the next committee of Assembly appointed to settle the Treasurer's accounts; and where such balance is due from the public to certify it in like manner to the Treasurer, and debit the party with such certificate: To enter in proper accounts all loan office certificates hereafter to be given, and endorse on such certificates that they are entered in the said Auditors office, without which endorsement no such certificate shall be valid: To require counsel of the Attorney General on all doubts in matters of law relative to the duties of their office: To state and keep all the accounts coming under their examination, specially against each person, so as to shew the amount of all warrants and certificates given on the Treasurer, for what service or article of public expence they were given, or where they have been, for money advanced, to whom it was advanced, and for what purpose, and to preserve the vouchers in due order: And also to raise general accounts shewing the amount of the expenditures for the army, the navy, the militia, the public trade, the public works and manufactories of every kind, of pensions, claims, and all other expences of government, each stated in a collective view, under its separate and proper head, and to lay before the Assembly annually the said general accounts together with an account of all balances due to and from the public as nearly as they shall be able.

And it is farther enacted, that it shall not be lawful for the Treasurer to pay or receive any money on account of the public but on warrant or certificate from the Board of Auditors, unless in cases where any future act of Assembly shall in express words, and not by inference or implication only, declare that in that particular case it is to be understood as the intention, that the claim specified by such act shall not be audited in the regular course, save only that the salaries of the said Auditors, together with the accounts for the expences of their office for fuel, blank books, paper, presses for the preservation of their books and papers, and other implements necessary for the use of their office, shall be examined and certified for payment to the Treasurer by the Governor and Council. The said Auditors shall be allowed a clerk of accounts and an assistant clerk, to be appointed by themselves from time to time at their will, who, before entering on the exercise of their office, shall take the like oath and in like manner as is before directed for the said Auditors to take. Where the Auditors acting according to their discretion and judgment shall disallow or abate any article of demand against the commonwealth, and any person shall think himself agrieved thereby, he shall be at liberty to petition the High Court of Chancery or the General Court, according to the nature of his case, for redress, and such court shall proceed to do right thereon, and a like petition shall be allowed in all other cases to any other person who is intitled to demand against the commonwealth any right in law or equity.

Report, p. 10-11.

With certain exceptions, Bill No. 11 is a restatement of the Act adopted Oct. 1778 "for establishing a board of Auditors for publick accounts," which in turn repealed an Act of 1776 for a similar purpose and greatly enlarged the powers of the board of auditors as created in 1776 (Hening, IX, 245-7, 536-40; JHD, Oct. 1778, 1827 edn., p. 94, 95, 98, 105, 107, 111). Most of the differences between the Act of 1778 and Bill No. 11 were minor, but one was of some importance since it concerned a subject that had consumed a great part of the attention of the legislature since 1776—that is, the proviso in the Bill granting the board authority to allow pensions to men disabled in military service or to the widows of those killed in such service.

Bill No. 11 was presented by Madison 31 Oct. 1785. It passed the second reading and was referred to the committee of the whole. On 28 Nov., however, another bill to amend the Act of 1778 was ordered to be brought in. It was introduced on 1 Dec., was amended by both houses, and, on 10 Jan. 1786, was passed under the new title "An act for the reform of certain public Boards." This Act dealt not only with the duties of the auditors but also with those of the solicitor and the treasurer (same, Oct. 1785, 1828 edn., p. 12-15, 59, 68, 119, 129, 130, 136, 142; Hening, XII, 106-9). This did not alter in any important way the authority granted by the Act of 1778; its chief purpose was to make specific allocations of authority to each of the three auditors. One auditor was charged with the duty of stating and balancing all accounts up to 31 Dec. 1785; another was authorized to examine, settle, and audit all claims and accounts as provided for by the Act of 1778; and the other was required to open a new set of books of account as of 1 Jan. 1786, in which "every public fund created by the laws of appropriation, by way of debt and credit, shewing the annual product and application of each, and the balance thereof, on the last day of December in every year" should be stated, together with the public account against the treasurer and against sheriffs, escheators, clerks of the different counties, &c. In short, the reform effected by this Act was one of administration, not of authority; hence the alterations in the authority of the board of auditors proposed by Bill No. 11, including the extensive delegation of power over pension grants, were not adopted and apparently no further action was taken on the Bill.

12. A Bill concerning the Public Treasurer

Be it enacted by the General Assembly, that the public Treasurer may continue in office, without re-election, until the end of the session of General Assembly next after one year from the time of his appointment shall have expired. On his first election, before he shall have power to act, he shall give bond to the Governor, with sureties, to be approved by the Council of State, in the penalty of four hundred thousand pounds, payable to the commonwealth, with condition, that he will faithfully account for all monies and other things, which shall come to his hands in virtue of his office, and perform all other duties thereof; and shall take an oath to the same purpose, and give assurance of fidelity to the commonwealth, before some court of record, or before a judge or justice thereof, the administration of which oaths, or the certificate thereof, shall be recorded in such court. When the office shall become vacant, during the recess of the General Assembly, the Governor, with advice of the Council of State, shall appoint a successor, to act until such time as he or another shall be legally elected. Upon a motion, made to the General Court, by a succeeding Treasurer, on behalf of the commonwealth, whereof more than ten days notice in writing shall have been given to the obligors, judgment may be awarded for the penalty of the said bond, to be discharged by payment of so much as a jury, to be empanneled instantly, for trial of the issue, if an issue be joined, or to enquire of damages, if the defendants make default, shall find to be due by breach of the condition aforesaid, with costs. The Treasurer, in books provided at the public expence, shall state the accounts of money by him received for public taxes and impositions, and paid in pursuance of acts and votes of General Assembly, in such a manner as that the neat produce of the whole revenue, as well as of every branch thereof, and the amount of disbursements in discharge of the several demands may distinctly appear; and lay the said accounts, from time to time, and all his other transactions, before the General Assembly. And if he divert or misapply any part of the public treasure, being convicted thereof upon such prosecution as is before prescribed, he shall not only be adjudged to pay double the money so found to have been diverted or misapplied, to the use of the commonwealth, but shall be thereby rendered incapable of any office of public trust.

Report, p. 11. MS (ViU); clerk's copy. Text of Act as adopted is in Hening, XII, 130-1.

Bill No. 12, in different and briefer terms, restates the Act of Oct. 1776 (Hening, IX, 199-201). It was presented by Madison 31 Oct. 1785, passed by the House 22 Nov., and approved by the Senate 25 Nov. (JHD, Oct. 1785, 1828 edn., p. 12-15, 40, 47, 55). This Bill was adopted without alteration save for the addition of a final clause putting it into effect 1 Jan. 1787.

13. A Bill for Appointing Naval Officers

Be it enacted by the General Assembly, that the districts of the naval officers shall remain as they have been heretofore laid off, that is to say, two for James river, one below and the other above Kyth's or Lawn's creek; one for Elizabeth river; one for South-Quay; one for York river; one for Rappahannock river; one for South-Potowmack, and one for each of the counties of Accomack and Northampton. Every future Naval Officer shall be appointed by commission of the Governor, and, before he act, shall enter into bond, with sufficient surety, before the Governor, in the penalty of five thousand pounds, with condition for the faithful execution of his office, and shall give assurance of fidelity to the commonwealth, and take the oath of office in some court of record, or before a Judge of the High Court of Chancery or General Court, who shall certify the same to the court he is a member of to be there recorded.

Every Naval Officer shall give a permit to any master of a vessel requiring it to lade within the district of such officer those goods which may be lawfully exported; inserting in the permit the name and burthen of the vessel, with such descriptions by her construction and rigging as distinguish her from others, the place where she was built, and the names of the master and owner, with the place of abode of the latter, and specifying the cargo which may be put on board; and having taken bond of the master, with sufficient surety, in the penalty of one thousand pounds, if the burthen be equal to, or less than, one hundred tons, or of two thousand pounds, if the burthen be greater, with condition that the cargo so to be laded, shall not be carried to any place whither it ought not by law to be carried; and that the master shall, within eighteen months thence next following, produce to the said officer or his successor a signed and sealed certificate of some chief magistrate of the place where the cargo shall be delivered, or of two creditable merchants residing there, that the cargo had been so delivered. The officer to whom such certificate shall be produced shall immediately cancel the bond: And if no action be commenced within one year after a breach of the condition, if any shall happen, the bond, after that time, shall be of no force. The Naval Officer shall give a permit, at the like request, to any master of a vessel importing goods into the district of the said officer to carry them, unless they shall have been imported contrary to law, to any place within the commonwealth and there deliver them; and the master breaking bulk or disposing of any part of the cargo without having obtained such permit, shall forfeit and pay   Before either of those permits shall be given, the officer shall take bond of the master, with sufficient surety, in the penalty of   if the burthen of the vessel be one hundred tons or less,   if greater than one hundred tons and not less than two hundred tons, or   if greater than two hundred tons, with condition that such vessel shall not depart the commonwealth, with goods prohibited to be exported by any embargo, during the continuance of such embargo. And before any such permit as aforesaid, shall be given, the officer shall also take bond of the master in the penalty of two hundred pounds, with condition that he will not crop, or cut the bulge or draw the staves of any tobacco cask put on board of his vessel, or otherwise abuse or injure such cask, or knowingly suffer it to be done. A Naval Officer suspecting or being informed of a fraud, unlawful concealment, or false report of a cargo, may examine upon oath, the mate, boatswain or any other of the seamen belonging to the vessel within his district, or any other person, not punishable for the offence, touching the fact. A Naval Officer, or person deputed by him, taking a bribe, directly, or indirectly; or conniving at a false or illegal entry, shall forfeit   and be disabled to hold his office or any office or employment of the same kind. No vessel shall be cleared out before the master of her shall make oath, or produce an authentic certificate, that the goods laden for exportation had been shipped according to law; and the Naval Officer clearing out a vessel otherwise shall forfeit   And any Naval Officer may go on board of a vessel within his district in order to search for goods laden contrary to law, and discovering any such may seize them, and bring them on shore, and the goods shall be forfeited. Every Naval Officer shall write down in a book, to be kept for that purpose, the entries and clearances of vessels, at his office, with accounts of their cargoes, and deliver copies thereof, every three months, to the Governor.

Report, p. 11-12. MS (ViU); clerk's copy.

Bill was presented by Madison 31 Oct. 1785, read the second time, and committed to the committee of the whole (JHD, Oct. 1785, 1828 edn., p. 12-15). It was not brought in with the remaining Bills of the revisal that Madison presented in Oct. 1786 and apparently no further action was taken on it. This is probably due to the fact that the Bill was a partial and inadequate coverage of the general maritime and customs regulations enacted at various times. The Act for appointing naval officers, passed at the Oct. 1776 session, was enlarged, amended, and continued at the sessions of May 1779 and May 1780. At the session of May 1783 these and several other special Acts pertaining to customs and maritime regulations were reduced to one Act (Hening, IX, 184-91; X, 122-3, 304-6; XI, 258-64).

14. A Bill for the Appointment of Clerks to the Governor and Council

Be it enacted by the General Assembly that the Governor and Council shall have power to appoint, from time to time, as they shall be wanting, a drawing clerk, a copying clerk, and a clerk of foreign correspondence, who shall each of them take an oath to be administered by any member of the board, to keep secret all such matters as they shall direct them to keep secret: Which clerks shall be removable at their will.

Report, p. 12. Probably drawn by TJ (see Document IV, 3, note 7).

This Bill supersedes the Bill to appoint a clerkship of foreign correspondence (q.v., under 18 May 1778). It was presented by Madison 31 Oct. 1785, passed by the House 22 Nov., and approved by the Senate 25 Nov. (JHD, Oct. 1785, 1828 edn., p. 12-15, 40, 47, 55, 132). The Act as adopted is identical with the Bill as proposed save for the addition of a final clause putting it into effect 1 Jan. 1787.

15. A Bill for the Enlistment of Soldiers, Sailors and Marines

Be it enacted by the General Assembly that every able bodied freeman who will enlist[1] to serve during the continuance of the present war among the troops of this commonwealth either at home or in the Continental army as he shall be directed, or as a sailor or marine on board the armed vessels of this commonwealth shall receive so much money as with the continental bounty if he be put on that service shall make up seven hundred and fifty[2] dollars, and the pay and rations allowed to the like soldiers sailors or marines in the continental service to begin from the day of his enlistment: he shall also be furnished at the public expence with a coat waistcoat pair of overalls[3] two shirts, a pair of shoes and a hat to be delivered at the place of rendezvous, and with the like articles every year after during his service, to be delivered at his station, in lieu of such of those articles as are allowed by congress; which articles so allowed by congress shall be received by proper officers to be appointed by the Governor with advise of council, and applied to the discharge of the engagements of this act, or otherwise to the use of this commonwealth as the Governor with advice of the Council shall direct. At the end of the war every of the said sailors soldiers and marines shall be entitled to a grant of one hundred[2] acres of any unappropriated land, within this commonwealth,[4] which they shall locate according to the directions of the laws; for which no purchase money shall be acquired on behalf of the commonwealth: such of them as shall be disabled in the service and the widows of those slain or dying therein, shall be entitled to immediate releif and also to annual pensions as provided in one act of General Assembly passed at the last session entituled "an act for establishing a board of auditors for public accounts."

Officers, soldiers, sailors and marines during their continuance in the service shall be exempted from all taxation in their persons.

Officers, soldiers, sailors and marines raised under the Laws of this commonwealth, shall, during their continuance in the service, be furnished by the agent or commissary of stores on behalf of this commonwealth at the principal encampments, with the following articles at the rates herein stated, to wit, Oznabrigs at one shilling and six pence by the Yard, coarse hats at seven shillings and six pence each, coarse shoes at eight shillings by the pair, coarse yarn hose at five shillings by the pair, rum or brandy at ten shillings by the gallon, whiskey at five shillings by the Gallon, brown sugar at one shilling[2] by the pound, coffee at two shillings and sixpence[2] by the pound and such other imported articles as may be necessary for them at one hundred and twenty per centum advance on their Costs at the European port whence they shall have been imported: and if they shall have been purchased on behalf of the public after their exportation from any European port so that their costs at such port shall not be known, their costs there shall be estimated by such agent or commissary as nearly as he shall be able, and they shall be vended at the same advance on that estimation.[5]

All general Officers of the army being citizens of this commonwealth, and all field officers, captains and subalterns commanding in the battalions of this commonwealth on Continental establishment or serving in the battalions raised for the immediate defence of this state who shall serve henceforward or from the time of their being commissioned until the end of the war[6] and all such officers who have or shall become supernumerary on the reduction of any of the said battalions and shall again enter into the said service whenever required so to do, in the same or any higher rank and continue therein until the end of the war,[7] shall be entitled to half pay during life, to commence from the determination of their command.

The field officers of every County shall from time to time during the continuance of the present war appoint one or more persons such as in their judgments are best fitted to the purpose of recruiting soldiers, sailors and marines under this act, who shall be removeable at their will. Every recruiting officer shall from time to time give notice of the men enlisted by him to the Governor who with the advice of council shall appoint such time and place within this commonwealth for their rendezvous as shall be convenient, and an officer then and there to review and receive them; to which place of rendezvous the said recruiting officer shall conduct them and in the mean time from their enlistment till their review shall have the same powers over them as if he were their proper commanding officer. For every man who shall be reviewed and received by the officer appointed for that purpose the officer recruiting him shall receive one hundred and fifty[2] dollars to be paid on certificate of such review and receipt from the board of war to the Auditors and their warrant on the Treasurer.

The board of war shall cause accounts to be raised with every county in which each shall have credit for the men so recruited by their officers and received by the officer of review: and whensoever afterwards it shall become necessary for the public exigencies to call for any greater number of regular troops than shall have been raised under this act, the number of all those raised under this act shall be added to the number to be called for and the quota of the aggregate number being settled for each county in proportion to their militia, where it shall appear that any County has furnished under this act a number equal to such their quota, they shall not be subject to furnish any part of those then called for, and where they shall have furnished a part of such quota, they shall be subject to furnish so many only of those as shall make up their deficiency.[8]

The bounties and other allowances given by this act to officers, soldiers, sailors, and marines shall be deemed in lieu of those of the same kind given by any act of assembly, ordinance, or resolution of Congress heretofore passed.[9]

MS (Vi), in clerk's hand, with several alterations in hand of TJ. Docketed: "A Bill ⟨*for the enlistment of*⟩ concerning officers, soldiers, sailors & marines. May 21st. 1779. first reading. 22d. comd. to whole on Wednesday next. Engrossed." The deletion in the title just quoted was made by TJ, who interlined the words "concerning officers" as a substitution for those struck out. This is perhaps explained by TJ's attitude toward dependence upon volunteers (see TJ to R. H. Lee, 5 June 1778). Accompanying MS of the Bill is a one-page list of amendments offered in the House. The Bill is not printed in *Report*, p. 12, but instead, under the same title as given above, is the following: "This was a bill designed to answer a temporary and occasional purpose during the war, and was incorporated into a law in the May session 1779. . . . It is now expired and was deemed unnecessary to be here inserted." The Act as adopted at the session of May 1779 is in Hening, x, 23-7; the major differences between the Act and the Bill as reported by TJ are indicated in the notes below.

On 21 May 1779 TJ was appointed head of a committee to bring in a "bill concerning officers, soldiers, sailors and marines"; he reported it the same day. These facts show that the Bill was already in the corrected state as described above when the committee was appointed. The Bill was amended by both the House and the Senate and finally agreed to 16 June (JHD, May 1779, 1827 edn., p. 16-17, 25-7, 45, 50, 51).

1 The Act as adopted also included those who had previously enlisted for a specified term that was unexpired and who were willing to reenlist for the duration of the war.

2 The figures were inserted by amendment to the Bill at this and other points, the MS having blank spaces for this purpose.

3 The word "breeches" was deleted in MS and "overalls" interlined in TJ's hand.

4 At this point the Act as adopted includes a proviso that commanding officers are to be entitled to the same quantity of lands as allowed to officers of

equivalent rank in Virginia regiments on the continental establishment.

[5] At this point the Act as adopted includes the following proviso: "that every of the said officers shall, in any one year, be entitled to receive . . . the following articles of imported dry goods, to wit: Six yards of cloth, seven quarters of a yard wide, with trimmings for a suit of clothes, stuff for six summer vests and breeches, linen for six shirts, cambrick for ruffles to them, and buttons, six stocks, three pair of silk, and three pair of thread hose, six handkerchiefs, two pair of good shoes, and one hat, and no more." Considering the enormous difficulties being experienced in obtaining essential materials for the conduct of the war (see, for example, notes to Bill No. 89, below), it is fairly certain that the amendment entitling officers to silk stockings and cambric ruffles was not one proposed by TJ.

[6] The Act as adopted extends the half-pay-for-life provision to chaplains, physicians, surgeons, and surgeons' mates.

[7] The proviso concerning supernumerary officers was inserted in MS in TJ's hand.

[8] Following this point there are, in the Act as adopted, several provisions not found in MS of the Bill: (1) authorization of the raising of a troop of horse for the defense of Illinois county; this possibly was suggested by TJ (see his comment on the raising of such troops vis-à-vis the problem of depending on volunteers in his letter to R. H. Lee, 5 June 1778); (2) the granting of land bounties of 200 acres to each of those volunteers who were with Clark in the Illinois country; and (3) authorization for the raising of four troops of horse for the defense of the eastern part of the commonwealth.

[9] This paragraph of the Bill is in TJ's hand.

16. A Bill for Apprehending Deserters, and Preventing the Loss of Arms and Other Things Delivered to Soldiers

Be it enacted by the General Assembly, that the commanding officer of the militia of every county, shall appoint persons to search for soldiers and seamen who shall have deserted from the army or navy of the United American States, or of this commonwealth; and the said searchers shall apprehend every such deserter, by them discovered, or person, for good cause, suspected to be such, and carry him before some neighboring Justice of the Peace, who shall cause the man so apprehended, if he appears by his confession, the testimony of witnesses, or other proof, to be a deserter, to be conveyed and delivered to the commanding officer in such army or navy at the nearest post or station, if that be within the distance of fifty miles, or, if the distance be greater, to be committed to the jail of the county, there to be detained until he can be so delivered, or shall give sufficient security to return to the army or navy, and give notice of the commitment, by advertising it four times in the Virginia Gazette. He who shall convey such deserter, producing a receipt for him from the officer to whom he shall have been delivered, or from the keeper of the jail to which he shall have been committed, with a certificate of the said justice ascertaining the number of miles he must necessarily travel in performing that duty, and returning, shall receive, for his trouble and expence, from the

Treasurer one dollar for every such mile. And any person, not appointed a searcher as aforesaid, may apprehend such deserter, and bring him before a justice, who shall thereupon proceed in the manner before prescribed, and producing a certificate thereof from the said justice, shall receive ten dollars from the said Treasurer. Whosoever shall harbor or entertain such deserter, more than twenty four hours, knowing or suspecting him to be so, and not discovering to a justice or searcher; or shall buy, or, without special authority, receive in exchange, or otherwise, or detain, from any soldier or deserter his wearing apparel, arms, furniture, or accoutrements, or any part of them, or purchase them from any other, not empowered to dispose of them, shall forfeit, for either offence, five pounds, and, moreover, for the latter, the value of the things bought, received, or detained; one half of which forfeiture shall be to the use of the commonwealth, and the other to the use of the informer.

Report, p. 12-13. MS (ViU); clerk's copy.

This Bill, being of a temporary nature, was not considered in 1785 by the General Assembly. It is similar to the Act of May 1777 entitled "An Act to discourage Desertion, and to punish persons harbouring or entertaining Deserters," the preamble of which stated: "Whereas many soldiers employed in the service of the United States of America, and others in the service of this state, desert their respective duties, to the great prejudice of the service, and ill example of others. . . ." (Hening, IX, 289-90).

17. A Bill concerning Seamen

Be it enacted by the General Assembly, that every seaman, whose habitation is within this commonwealth, not less than eighteen nor more than fifty years old, capable of sea service, and willing to serve in the ships or vessels of the commonwealth, may give in a ticket containing his christian name, surname, and proper addition, with his age, and the place of his habitation, and the time when the ticket shall be delivered to any Naval Officer, who shall transmit it to the Board of Trade, to be by them entered in a register. Promotions to commission and warrant officers in the navy becoming vacant, shall be made and adjusted according to the order following: Seamen registered and actually serving shall be preferred to all others, and of the former those who shall have served a longer to such as shall have served a shorter time, and if the times of service shall have been equal, they whose tickets shall be of prior to them whose tickets shall be of posterior dates; and if the merits of the competitors shall be equal in those respects the preference shall be decided by lot. Every registered seaman, actually serving in the navy, disabled by age, or wounds, so as that he can be no longer useful there, and not being in a condition to maintain himself comfortably, nor having been promoted to any commission or warrant office, or to the office of master, mate, boatswain, gunner, carpenter, purser, or surgeon, obtaining a certificate thereof from the captain, master, and surgeon, of the ship, or vessel, on board of which he had served, under their hands and seals, shall receive from the Treasurer the sum of [1] every year during his life: And the widow of every registered seaman, serving on board of a ship or vessel of war, slain, or drowned, in the service, if he was not in such a condition, and had not been promoted to such office, as aforesaid, obtaining the like certificate therof, shall receive from the Treasurer the sum of [2] every year during her life. But a registered seaman, withdrawing himself from the service of the commonwealth, in the time of actual war, and not repairing on board one of the ships or vessels thereof, within thirty days after he shall have been required so to do by any officer of the navy, unless detained by sickness, to be proved by the oaths of two witnesses, shall have no benefit by this act. And out of the wages due or becoming due to every seaman serving on board a ship or vessel belonging to the commonwealth, or any citizen thereof, and used in sea voyages, six pence, per month, shall be paid by the commander thereof, if she be a ship or vessel of war, public, or private, to the Treasurer, or if she be a merchantile ship or vessel, to the Naval Officer of the port where she shall be entered inward or cleared outward, who shall discover the number, wages and time of service of all persons belonging to the ship or vessel, by examining the commander of her, upon oath, or affirmation, and account for what he shall receive to the Treasurer, and the money, so to be collected, shall be applied towards reimbursing the annuities to disabled registered seamen, and to the widows of those who shall be slain or drowned in the public service. Boys of the age of ten years, or upwards, who shall beg for alms, or who, or whose parents are, or shall be chargeable to any county, may, by the Aldermen[3] of the county wherein they inhabit, be bound apprentices, by indentures, to owners or masters of ships, or vessels, used in sea voyages, and belonging to any ports within the commonwealth, until they shall attain to the ages of twenty one years, respectively, in every one of which indentures the age of the boy, to be ascertained by the register of births, or, not being entered therein, by the adjudication of the Aldermen,[3] shall be inserted, with a covenant, on the part of the master, that he will provide sufficient food and convenient raiment and lodging for his apprentice, and employ him in the sea service, and in such offices as appertain thereto, and, moreover, deliver to him a suit of clothes suitable to the season, to wit: a coat, waistcoat, pair of breeches, two pair of stockings, a pair of shoes, and a hat, with a blanket. And every owner or master of a ship or vessel, used in sea voyages, and belonging to a port within the commonwealth, shall be obliged to take one of such apprentices, not being under thirteen or above seventeen years of age, nor being deficient in health and strength of body, if the ship or vessel be of the burthen of thirty and not more than fifty tuns; another for the next fifty tons of her burthen, and one more for every hundred her burthen shall exceed one hundred tons; and refusing so to do, if he shall be required, unless he shall have an equal number of other apprentices, shall forfeit ten pounds, to be recovered, with costs, in an action of debt, by him who will sue, one half to his own use, and the other half to the use of the county wherein the boy shall inhabit. The apprentice so bound shall be clothed, if it be necessary, and conveyed to the port his master shall belong to, at the expence of the county, from which he shall be sent. The clerks of the courts shall transmit the names of the masters and apprentices, with the ages of the latter, and the times when they shall be bound, to the Board of Trade,[4] to be entered by them in their register; and the apprentices, after they shall have been eighteen years old, shall be deemed registered seamen, entitled to the benefit of this act, in like manner, as if they had voluntarily given in tickets. The county court, nearest to a port in which an apprentice, bound by virtue of this act, or otherwise, shall serve or ought to serve on board of a ship or vessel, shall, at any time, when they shall be sitting, receive and hear a complaint made to them by him of hard or ill usage, or breach of covenant, and redress the complainant, if he shall appear to have justly complained, prescribing milder and better treatment for the future, ordering an action to be commenced against the master, or removing the apprentice and binding him to another master, as it may seem right and expedient. Any Alderman[5] may, by warrant, under his hand and seal, cause any able bodied man, who not having wherewithal to maintain himself, shall be found loitering, and shall leave a wife or children, without means for their subsistance, whereby they may become burthensome to their county, or shall wander abroad, without betaking himself to some honest employment, or shall go about begging, to be apprehended and brought before him, and, if he shall, upon examination of himself, or by the testimony of others, appear to be within this description, the Alderman,[5] by his warrant, may cause such vagrant to be sent and delivered on board one of the ships of war of the commonwealth, there to serve as a seaman, during the term of eighteen months. An agreement in writing shall be made between the master or commander and seamen, not being his apprentices, of every ship or vessel, belonging to any port of the commonwealth, and bound to parts beyond sea and be signed by both parties and by the seamen, within three days after they shall have shipped and entered themselves, respectively, declaring the voyage to be performed, and ascertaining the wages, either by the month, or for the run, to be paid to every seaman; and any such master or commander, proceeding on the voyage, before that agreement shall be made and signed, shall forfeit the sum of five pounds, for every seaman, who shall not have signed it, carried out in the vessel, to be recovered, with costs, by information, and to be paid to the Treasurer, for the same purpose as the six pence, per month, out of the wages of seamen. Any seaman, who shall have signed such agreement, absenting himself from the ship or vessel, without leave of the master, or other officer having charge of her, shall forfeit, for every day's absence, the pay of two days, and refusing to proceed on the voyage, or deserting from the ship or vessel, shall forfeit the wages then due. But seamen shall not be deprived, by the agreement, of any remedy for their wages which they might have lawfully pursued, before this act; and in any suit between them and the master it shall be incumbent upon him to exhibit the agreement, if it shall be requisite, and they shall not lose or suffer any thing by his suppression of it, or failure to produce it. The master or commander of any ship or vessel, arriving from beyond sea, into a port of the commonwealth, shall, within thirty days after she shall be entered at the naval office, unless there shall have been a covenant to the contrary, or at the time of discharging the seamen, which ever shall first happen, pay the wages due to every seaman, if he shall demand them, after deducting what may, by virtue of this act, be withheld, or, refusing so to do, shall pay to him, over and above the wages detained, the further sum of twenty shillings, to be recovered with the other demand. A seaman, who shall belong to a ship or vessel, travelling by land, and having no certificate of his discharge, signed by the master or commander, or a pass or order, with the like signature, or that of some other officer of the ship or vessel, unless he shall be going to a proper place to seek redress of any grievance, shall be deemed a deserter, and may be apprehended by any person, and brought before a Justice of the Peace, and shall be, by his warrant, returned, through the hands of constables, one taking him from another, and conveying him to the next; and for this service the master or commander, if the seaman shall not have been discharged, shall pay to the person who shall apprehend him, ten shillings, and to the constables one shilling for every mile they shall conduct him, to be proportioned amongst them by the number of miles they shall respectively go, in the most direct way; to ascertain which a certificate of the whole distance, from the place where he was apprehended, to the port the ship or vessel shall be at, shall be endorsed by the Justice of the Peace on his warrant; and if the master or commander shall refuse to pay the money to the persons entitled to it, or to others authorised by their orders to receive it, the Naval Officer of the port, with whom the warrant and orders shall be left, shall not clear the ship or vessel out, before it shall be paid to him, for their use, unless the master or commander shall make it appear, by the oath of himself, or of some other, on board, that the seaman had not been returned, or had been discharged, before he was apprehended; and the master or commander paying the money may deduct it out of the wages becoming due to the seaman. A constable wilfully or negligently suffering a seaman, not being discharged from his ship or vessel, who shall have been committed by warrant of a Justice of the Peace to his custody, to escape, unless he shall recover him, and proceed to deliver him as the warrant required, shall, upon complaint made to a Justice of the Peace, which he shall be summoned to answer, pay the rewards due to the person who apprehended the seaman, and to the constables by whom he had before been conducted, and shall moreover pay the sum of [6] to the master or commander of the ship or vessel, to be recovered, with costs, by petition to the county, city, or borough court. A person concealing a deserted seaman, or entertaining any seaman, not going to a proper place to seek redress of any grievance, nor being employed in the proper business of his office,[7] shall pay the sum of [8] to the master or commander of the ship or vessel, to which he shall belong, to be recovered, with costs. The master or commander of a ship or vessel, who shall entertain, employ, or hire a seaman, belonging to a ship or vessel, owned by a citizen of the commonwealth, before he shall have been discharged, shall pay to the owner the sum of twenty pounds, to be recovered, with costs, by action of debt. Two Justices of the Peace may hear a complaint made to them of any mutinous or refractory behavior in a seaman or waterman, and, causing the parties to appear before them, at a convenient time, in some place near the ship or vessel they shall belong to, with their witnesses, may adjudge the accused, if he shall be proved to have stricken, or to have offered to strike the master, or other superior officer, or to have threatened to do any bodily hurt to him, or to have preremptorily refused, without just cause, to obey his commands, to forfeit to the owner such part of the wages due to the seaman or waterman as will make reasonable amends for the injury and damage, not exceeding the sum of five pounds; and if satisfaction cannot be obtained by other means, may award execution for the amount of the forfeiture, or so much thereof as shall exceed the wages due, against his goods and chattles. But seamen or watermen shall not be obliged to serve on board of any ship or vessel, if such sufficient wholesome victuals and drink, and convenient accommodations, as are customary in the merchant service, shall not be provided for and allowed to them. A master, who shall correct immoderately, or maim a seaman under his command, may be brought before any Justice of the Peace, by his warrant, and be compelled to give security for his good behavior, and shall moreover be liable to the action of the party injured for damages. The master or commander of a ship or vessel, who shall put and leave on shore any sick or disabled seaman, not entitled to his discharge by their contract, without providing for his cure and maintenance, shall forfeit ten[9] pounds, to be recovered, with costs, by action of debt, one half to him who will sue, to his own use, and the other half to the use of the county, in which the seaman shall be left, and applied towards his cure and maintenance. The master or commander of a ship or vessel, discharging a seaman from his service, shall sign and deliver to him a certificate thereof, and refusing so to do, when it shall be required, shall pay the sum of five pounds to the seaman, to be recovered, with costs, by action of debt.

Report, p. 13-14. Text of Act as adopted is in Hening, XII, 131-7.

Bill presented by Madison 31 Oct. 1785, passed by House 22 Nov., amended by Senate and finally agreed to by House 19 Dec. (JHD, Oct. 1785, 1828 edn., p. 12-15, 40, 47, 95, 98). This Bill departs in many particulars from the Act of the same title of 1748 and its amending Act of 1772 (Hening, VI, 24-8; Chancellors' Revisal, p. 24). The Act as adopted follows the text of the Bill here presented except for the addition of a final clause putting it in force 1 Jan. 1787, and except for several other variations, the more important of which are noted below.

1 The Act reads: "fifteen pounds."

2 The Act reads: "eight pounds."

3 The Act reads: "court" instead of "Aldermen."

4 The Act reads: "executive" instead of "Board of Trade."

[5] The Act reads: "justice" instead of "alderman."

[6] The Act reads: "five pounds."

[7] The words "or entertaining . . . of his office" are omitted from the Act.

[8] The Act reads: "three pounds."

[9] The Act reads: "twenty pounds."

18. A Bill for Supplying the Public with Lead

Be it enacted by the General Assembly, that the Governor, with advice of the Council, from time to time, may hire or purchase, so many laborers to work in the lead mines, in the county of Montgomery, as may be beneficially employed therein, for the use of the public, and put them, with the others already there, under the direction of a manager. Of the lead produced from the said mines so much as may be spared, without danger of detriment to the commonwealth, shall be disposed of to the United States of America, or any of them, and what they want not may be sold to others. A reasonable annual rent shall be paid to the proprietors of the land in which the mines are opened, to be adjusted between the said proprietors and the Governor, with advice of the Council. But the said mines, if the proprietors will undertake, at their own charges, to work them, and engage to deliver one hundred tons of lead, every year, to the use of the public, at the price of   by the ton, and give satisfactory assurance that the contract shall be performed, shall be resigned to the said proprietors, and shall not be resumed so long as that engagement shall be punctually observed and fulfilled. All expences incurred in the execution of this act shall be defrayed in like manner as other public debts and accounts thereof, as well as of the disposition of the lead, shall be orderly kept, and laid before the General Assembly, whenever it shall be required.

Report, p. 14.

This Bill restates, though in different language, the Act of 1776 which authorized the governor to operate "certain lead mines in the county of Montgomery, formerly Fincastle, belonging to the hon. William Byrd, esq. and the estates of John Robinson and John Chiswell, esquires" or to contract with the owners to operate such mines on assurance that the latter would deliver to the state one hundred tons annually at £33 6s. 8d. per ton (Hening, IX, 237-8). Since this Act was in the nature of temporary legislation, Bill No. 18 was not considered by the General Assembly in 1785.

19. A Bill for Establishing Cross Posts

For the more general diffusion of public intelligence among the citizens of this commonwealth and the maintenance of correspondence between friends and merchants, be it enacted by the General

Assembly, that across the post road, which is, or shall be hereafter established through this commonwealth, by Congress, according to the powers with which they are invested by the confederating states of America, there shall be established postriders on or near to the following lines, to wit:

One from the mouth of Potowmack up the same to the confluence of and the south branch thereof to its head, and thence to the Monongahalia and down the same to Fort Pitt.

One other from the mouth of Rappahannock up the same and the Hedgeman branch to the head thereof, and thence to Winchester.

One other from the mouth of York river up the same and up Pamunkey, the north Anna and Terry's run, thence to and up the Rapidan and Conway to its head and thence northwestwardly to the North mountain.

One other from the mouth of James river up the same to the mouth of Appamatox, there to be branched into two, one of them to go up Appamatox to its head, the other up James river to the confluence of the Rivanna and Fluvanna, there again to be branched into two, one of them to proceed up the Rivanna to Charlottsville, thence to Staunton, the Warm Springs and Greenbrier; and the other up the Fluvanna to Carter's creek and thence to the lead mines.

One other from South Quay to Nottoway river, there to be branched into two, one of them to go up Nottoway river to its head, the other to and up Roanoke river to the confluence of Staunton and Dan, there to be branched again into two, one of them to proceed up Staunton river to its head, and the other along Dan river and the county line to their last intersection and then to Holston river.

The general postmaster shall from time to time determine on the roads along which the said riders shall pass, having regard in such determination to those which are best, most direct, through the thickest settlements and coinciding most nearly with the lines before described.

The said riders shall perform the journey assigned them, from stage to stage, forwards and backwards, once in every week, and between such hours as shall be prescribed to them by the postmaster general, giving and taking way bills for the more certain proof thereof; and to enable them to do this, all ferry keepers shall give them passage at their ferries as soon as required, gratis, and in preference to all other passengers.

There shall moreover be established, for the same purposes, a boat, to pass and repass weekly, between Cherrystone's, on the Eastern shore, and the town of York.

The public printer for the time being, or if there be more than one, then such one of them as the Governor and Council shall appoint, shall be postmaster general, with power to appoint deputy postmasters, so many and at such stages as shall be requisite, which deputies shall employ riders with their horses, from stage to stage, and a boat and master in the case before directed, on such wages as shall be directed by their principal; and in all things appertaining to their office shall follow his instructions.

The masters and agents of the said office shall have the sole and exclusive right of taking and conveying all letters and packets passing through any part of this commonwealth, except such as shall be conveyed by the masters and agents of the continental post office along the post road established by Congress as before recited; such as shall be passing from any place to the next post road or stage; such as shall be sent by the carriers of goods along with and concerning the said goods; such as are sent by any private friend without fee in their way of journey or travel, or by any messenger express, employed for the particular occasion; and except also commissions, warrants, affidavits, process or proceedings or the returns thereof issuing from the Legislative, Executive, or Judiciary departments in this commonwealth.

The said masters and deputies may lawfully take for the post of any single letter twenty miles, six pence, and so in proportion for any greater distance, and for a double, treble or other letter; for the post of every printed news-paper, twenty miles, one penny, and so in proportion for any greater distance: And for the post of every packet of writs, deeds, or other things, twenty miles, one shilling and six pence for every ounce weight, and so in proportion for any greater distance. All fractions whereby such letters or packets, or the post thereof shall exceed any integral number of the said distances, weights, or sheets being to be counted as an additional integral number; and any distance less than twenty miles as an integer; which postage shall be paid at the stage where the letter, news-paper or packet is last delivered, unless any person shall chuse to pay the same earlier, and on failure of payment, at or before the last stage, such letter, paper or packet may be detained by the master or agent until payment. But acts and journals of Assembly sent into the counties by order of either House, and letters to and from the Governor or any of the public boards shall be carried by the riders ex officio and free of postage.

The said postmaster general in determining the postroads, settling the stages and hours, appointing, continuing, removing and instructing postmasters, shall be subject to the controul of the Governor with the advice of Council. He shall also annually, at such time as the Auditors shall direct, make up a full and fair account, on oath, of the expences of the institution, and also of the postages received, stating therein every article specially, and lay the same before the Auditors, and on their certificate shall pay to, or receive from the Treasurer, any balance appearing due thereon. It shall be also lawful for the Auditors, on the application of the postmaster general, to give their warrant on the Treasurer for the advance of such sums as they shall think reasonable and necessary for carrying on the execution of this act, charging the same to the postmaster general and requiring account of the expenditure thereof at their next settlement. The deputy postmasters shall be obliged, in like manner, to render account, on oath, to their principal whenever called on by him, and to pay to him any balance remaining in their hands: And on failure either of the principal, or of any deputy postmaster to render account, or pay any balance in their hands as before required, it shall be lawful for a Court of Justice on motion, and ten days previous notice to give judgment for such balance, or if it be for failure to render account, then to give such judgment or judgments as have been usual in actions or writs of account and to issue execution accordingly.

Report, p. 15.

This Bill, whose object of promoting a "more general diffusion of public intelligence" has the earmarks of TJ's influence, was undoubtedly written by him (see Document IV, 2, note 3). It was, in fact, brought in by TJ as a separate Bill on 18 May 1779. It passed the second reading the next day, was amended 25 May, and passed by the House on 26 May. From 27 May until 5 June it was debated by the Senate and then rejected (JHD, May 1779, 1827 edn., p. 7, 13, 14, 21, 23; *Journal of the Senate of Virginia*, May 1779, Richmond, 1828, p. 17-26). It was brought in again by Randolph at the Oct. 1779 session but was again rejected; on 31 Oct. 1785 Madison presented it as a part of the *Report of the Committee of Revisors*, but no further action was taken on it (JHD, Oct. 1779, 1827 edn., p. 13, 24; same, Oct. 1785, 1828 edn., p. 12-15).

20. A Bill Directing the Course of Descents

Be it enacted by the General Assembly, that henceforth when any person having title to any real estate of inheritance, shall die intestate as to such estate, it shall descend and pass in parcenery[1] to his kindred male and female in the following course: that is to say:

To his children or their descendants, if any there be:

If there be no children, nor their descendants, then to his father:

If there be no father, then to his mother, brothers and sisters and their descendants, or such of them as there be:

If there be no mother, nor brother, nor sister, nor their descendants, then the inheritance shall be divided into two moieties, one of which shall go to the paternal, the other to the maternal kindred, in the following course, that is to say:

First to the grandfather.

If there be no grandfather, then to the grandmother, uncles and aunts on the same side, and their descendants, or such of them as there be:

If there be no grandmother, uncle nor aunt, nor their descendants, then to the great-grandfathers, or great-grandfather if there be but one:

If there be no great grandfather, then to the great-grandmothers, or great-grandmother if there be but one, and the brothers and sisters of the grandfathers and grandmothers, and their descendants, or such of them as there be:

And so on in other cases without end; passing to the nearest lineal male ancestors; and for the want of them to the lineal female ancestors in the same degree, and the descendants of such, male and female lineal ancestors, or to such of them as there be.

But no right in the inheritance shall accrue to any persons whatever, other than to children of the intestate, unless they be in being and capable in law to take as heirs at the time of the intestates death.

And where for want of issue of the intestate, and of father, mother, brothers and sisters and their descendants, the inheritance is before directed to go by moieties to the paternal and maternal kindred, if there should be no such kindred on the one part, the whole shall go to the other part: And if there be no kindred either on the one part or the other, the whole shall go to the wife or husband of the intestate. And if the wife or husband be dead, it shall go to her or his kindred, in the like course as if such wife or husband had survived the intestate and then died, entitled to the estate.

And in the cases before-mentioned where the inheritance is directed to pass to the ascending and collateral kindred of the intestate, if part of such collaterals be of the whole blood to the intestate, and other part of the half blood only, those of the half blood shall inherit only half so much as those of the whole blood: But if all be of the half blood, they shall have whole portions, only giving to the ascendants (if there be any) double portions.

And where the children of the intestate, or his mother, brothers, and sisters, or his grandmother, uncles, and aunts, or any of his female lineal ancestors living, with the children of his deceased lineal ancestors male and female in the same degree come into the partition, they shall take per capita, that is to say, by persons; and where a part of them being dead, and a part living, the issue of those dead have right to partition, such issue shall take per stirpes or by stocks, that is to say, the share of their deceased parent.

And where any of the children of the intestate, or their issue, shall have received from the intestate in his life time any real estate by way of advancement, and shall chuse to come into partition with the other parceners, such advancement shall be brought into hotchpot with the estate descended.

In making title by descent it shall be no bar to a demandant that any ancestor through whom he derives his descent from the intestate, is or hath been an alien. Bastards also shall be capable of inheriting or of transmitting inheritance on the part of their mother, in like manner as if they had been lawfully begotten of such mother.

Where a man having by a woman one or more children, shall afterwards intermarry with such woman, such child or children if recognized by him shall be thereby legitimated. The issue also of marriages deemed null in law shall nevertheless be legitimate.

Report, p. 16. The text of the Act as adopted is in Hening, XII, 138-40.

The Bill was presented by Madison on 31 Oct. 1785, passed by the House on 22 Nov., and agreed to by the Senate 30 Nov. (JHD, Oct. 1785, 1828 edn., p. 12-15, 40, 47, 67, 132). The Bill as proposed by the Committee of Revisors was adopted without alteration, save for the addition of a final clause providing that the Act should be in force beginning 1 Jan. 1787. TJ regarded this reform in the rules of descent as being among the most important parts of the revision of the laws; indeed, this subject headed the list of "the most remarkable alterations proposed" that he drew up in *Notes on Virginia*. The important departure provided for in this Bill was that the lands of any person dying intestate should "be divisible equally among all his children, or other representatives, in equal degree" (Ford, III, 243). The degrees of legal consanguinity and other parts of the law of descents as here set forth were agreed upon by the Committee of Revisors (see Document I, above). This was at TJ's request, though, in view of his opposition to primogeniture and his provision for coparceny in his proposed Constitution, it is obvious that he took the lead in making the proposed change. His remembered statement in the Autobiography is explicit on this point: "As the law of Descents, and the criminal law fell of course within my portion, I wished the committee to settle the leading principles of these, as a guide for me in framing them. And, with respect to the first, I proposed to abolish the law of primogeniture, and to make real estate descendible in parcenary to the next of kin, as personal property is by the statute of distribution. Mr. Pendleton wished to preserve the right of primogeniture, but seeing at once that that could not prevail, he proposed we should adopt the Hebrew principle, and give a double portion to the elder son. I observed that if the eldest son could eat twice as much, or do double work, it might be a natural evidence of his right to a double portion; but being on a par in his powers and wants, with his brothers and sisters, he should be on a par also in the partition of the patrimony, and such was the decision of the other members" (Autobiography, Ford, I, 59). For the 1748 Act governing distribution of intestate estates, which set forth the law of descents as it stood prior to the Revolution, see Hening, V, 444-8.

[1] The Act of 1785, as given in Hening, XII, 138, has an erroneous reading: "parency."

21. A Bill concerning Wills; the Distribution of Intestate's Estates; and the Duty of Executors and Administrators

Be it enacted by the General Assembly that every person aged twenty one years or upwards, being of sound mind, and not a married woman, shall have power at his will and pleasure, by last will and testament, in writing, to devise all the estate, right, title, and interest, in possession, reversion, or remainder, which he hath, or at the time of his death shall have, of, in, or to lands, tenements, or hereditaments, or annuities, or rents charged upon or issuing out of them; so as such last will and testament be signed by the testator, or by some other person in his presence, and by his direction, and moreover, if not wholly written by himself, be attested by two or more credible witnesses subscribing their names in his presence.

Saving to the widows of testators their dower in such lands, tenements, rents, or annuities, according to the laws, which shall not be prejudiced by any devise thereof.

No devise so made, or any clause thereof, shall be revocable but by the testator's destroying, cancelling, or obliterating the same, or causing it to be done in his presence, or by a subsequent will, codicil, or declaration in writing, made as aforesaid. But every last will and testament, made when the testator had no child living, wherein any child he might have is not provided for or mentioned, if, at the time of his death he leave a child, or leave his wife enseint of a child which shall be born, shall have no effect during the life of such after born child, and shall be void unless the child die without having been married, or before he or she shall have attained the age of twenty one years. When a testator shall leave children born, and his wife enseint, the posthumous child, if it be unprovided for by settlement, and be neither provided for nor disinherited, but only pretermitted by the last will and testament, shall succeed to the same portion of the father's estate as such child would have been intitled to, if the father had died intestate; towards raising which portion, the devisees and legatees shall contribute proportionably out of the parts devised and bequeathed to them by the same will and testament.

No person under the age of eighteen years shall be capable of disposing of his chattels by will.

No nuncupative will, shall be established unless it be made in the time of the last sickness of the deceased, at his habitation, or where he hath resided for ten days next preceeding, except where the deceased is taken sick from home, and dies before he returns to such habitation; nor where the value exceeds ten pounds unless it be proved by two witnesses that the testator called on some person present to take notice or bear testimony that such is his will, or words of the like import.

After six months have elapsed from the time of speaking the pretended testamentary words, no testimony shall be received to prove a nuncupative will, unless the testimony, or the substance thereof, shall have been committed to writing within six days after making the will.

No will in writing, or any devise therein of chattels, shall be revoked by a subsequent will, codicil, or declaration, unless the same be in writing.

Any soldier in actual military service, or any mariner or seaman being at sea, may dispose of his chattels as he might heretofore have done.

If any person shall subscribe his name as a witness to a will wherein any bequest is given to him, if the will may be not otherwise proved, the bequest shall be void, and such witness shall be allowed and compellable to appear and give testimony on the residue of the will in like manner as if no such bequest had been made. But if such witness would be entitled to any share of the testator's estate, in case the will were not established, so much of his said share shall be saved to him as shall not exceed the value of the legacy bequeathed him.

The several county courts shall have power to hear and determine all causes, matters, suits and controversies, testamentary, arising within their respective jurisdictions, and to examine and take the proof of wills, and grant certificates thereof according to the methods and rules following, that is to say: If any testator shall have a mansion house or known place of residence, his will shall be proved in the court of the county wherein such mansion house or place of residence is: If he hath no such place of residence, and lands be devised in the will, it shall be proved in the court of the county wherein the lands lie, or in one of them, where there shall be lands in several counties: And if he hath no such known place of residence, and there be no lands devised, then the will may be proved either in the county where the testator shall die, or that wherein his estate, or the greater part thereof shall be, or such will may in any case be proved in the General Court.

When any will shall be exhibited to be proved, the court having jurisdiction as aforesaid, may proceed immediately to receive the proof thereof, and grant a certificate of such probat: If however any person interested shall within seven years afterwards appear, and by his bill in Chancery contest the validity of the will, an issue shall be made up, whether the writing produced be the will of the testator or not, which shall be tried by a jury, whose verdict shall be final between the parties; saving to the court a power of granting a new trial for good cause, as in other trials; but no such party appearing within that time, the probat shall be forever binding.

In all such trials by jury, the certificate of the oath of the witnesses, at the time of the first probat, shall be admitted as evidence, to have such weight as the jury shall think it deserves.

No nuncupative will shall be proved within fourteen days after the death of the testator, nor until his widow, if any, and next of kin have been summoned to contest the same if they please.

If the General Court or any county court, having jurisdiction as aforesaid, shall be informed that any person hath the will of a testator in his custody, such court may summon such person, and by a proper process compel him to produce the same.

If the executors named in any will shall all refuse the executorship, or being required to give security, as herein after-mentioned, shall refuse, or fail to give the same, which shall amount to a refusal of the executorship, in either case, the court having jurisdiction as aforesaid, may receive the proof of the will and grant a certificate for obtaining letters of administration with the same annexed, to the person to whom administration would have been granted if there had been no will of the deceased.

Before granting a certificate of the probat of any will, the Executor or administrator with the will annexed, as the case shall be, shall in open court take the following oath, to wit: "You shall swear that this writing contains the true last will of the within named as far as you know or believe; and that you will well and truly perform the same, by paying first his debts, and then the legacies contained in the said will, as far as his goods, chattels and credits will extend and the law charge you; and that you will make a true and perfect inventory of all the said goods, chattels and credits, as also a just account when thereto required." And shall also give bond in such penalty as will be equal to the full value of the estate at the least, and with such security as shall be approved of by the court, with the following condition, to wit: "The condition of this obligation is, that if the said executor of the last will and testament [or administrator, with the will annexed, of all the goods, chattels and credits][1] of deceased, do make a true and perfect inventory of all and singular the goods, chattels and credits of the said deceased, which have or shall come to the hands, possession or knowlege of the said or into the hands or possession of any other person or persons for , and the same so made do exhibit into the court at such time as shall be thereto required by the said court; and the same goods, chattels and credits do well and truly administer according to law; and make a just and true account of actings and doings therein, when thereunto required by the said court; and further do well and truly pay and deliver all the legacies contained and specified in the said will, as far as the said goods, chattels and credits will extend according to the value thereof, and as the law shall charge ; then this obligation to be void, or else to remain in full force."

Which bond shall be payable to the Judges or Justices sitting in court and their successors, and shall not become void upon the first recovery, but may be put in suit and prosecuted from time to time, by, and at the costs of any party injured, by a breach thereof, until the whole penalty be recovered thereupon.

But where any testator shall leave visible estate, more than sufficient to pay all his debts, and by will shall direct that his executors shall not be obliged to give security, in that case no security shall be required, unless the court shall see cause from their own knowledge or the suggestions of creditors or legatees, to suspect the executors of fraud, or that the testator's personal estate will not be sufficient to discharge all his debts, and shall require security, when the same shall be given, before a certificate shall be granted, notwithstanding any directions to the contrary in the testator's will.

The power of executors over their testator's estates before probat of the will, is not hereby restrained, but shall continue as heretofore.

During any contest about a will, or in the absence of executors, or whenever the court, from any other cause, shall judge it convenient, they may appoint any person or persons to collect and preserve the estate of any decedent, until a probat of his will, or administration of his estate, be granted, taking bond and security for collecting the estate, making an inventory thereof, and safe keeping and delivering up the same, when required, to the executors or administrators.

When any widow shall not be satisfied with the provision made for her by the will of her husband, she may within one year from the time of his death, before the General Court or court of the county, having jurisdiction of the probat of his will as aforesaid, or by deed, executed in the presence of two or more credible witnesses, declare that she will not take or accept the provision made for her by such will, or any part thereof, and renounce all benefit which she might claim by the same will; and thereupon such widow shall be intitled to one third part of the slaves whereof her husband died possessed, which she shall hold during her life, and at her death they and their increase shall go to such person or persons to whom they would have passed and gone if such declaration had not been made; and she shall moreover be entitled to such share of his other personal estate as if he had died intestate, to hold to her as her absolute property; but every widow not making a declaration within the time aforesaid, shall have no more of her husband's slaves or personal estate than is given her by his will.[2]

All original wills shall be recorded and shall also remain in the clerk's office of the court wherein they are respectively proved, except during such time as they may be in any superior court, having been removed thither for inspection by certiorari, or otherwise, after which they shall be returned to the said office.

When any person shall die intestate as to his goods and chattels or any part thereof, after funerals, debts and just expences paid, if there be no child, one moiety, or, if there be a child or children, one third of the surplus shall go to the wife, but she shall have no more than the use for her life of such slaves as shall be in her share, and the residue of the surplus, and after the wife's death, the slaves in her share, or if there be no wife, then the whole of such surplus shall be distributed in the same proportions, and to the same persons as lands are directed to descend in and by an act of General Assembly, intitled, "An act directing the course of descents." Nothing in this act contained shall be understood so as to compel the husband to make distribution of the personal estate of his wife dying intestate. Where any children of the intestate, or their issue, shall have received from the intestate, in his life time, any personal estate by way of advancement, and shall chuse to come into the distribution with the other persons intitled, such advancement shall be brought into hotchpot with the distributable surplus.[3]

The General Court and the several county courts respectively, shall have the like jurisdiction to hear and determine the right of administration of the estates of persons dying intestate, as is herein beforementioned as to the proof of wills, in respect to the intestate's place of residence, or death, or where the estate shall lie, and shall grant certificates, for obtaining such administration, to the representatives who apply for the same, preferring, first the husband or wife, and then such others as are next intitled to distribution, or one or more of them as the court shall judge will best manage and improve the estate.

If no such person applies for administration within thirty days from the death of an intestate, the court may grant administration to any creditor or creditors who apply for the same, or to any other person the court shall in their discretion think fit: But if any will shall afterwards be produced and proved by executors, or the wife or other distributee, who shall not have before refused, shall apply for the administration, the same shall be granted, in like manner as if the former had not been obtained.

Before granting a certificate for the administration of any estate, the person or persons to whom the same is granted, shall in open court take the following oath, to wit: "You shall swear that deceased, died without any will, as far as you know or believe, and that you will well and truly administer all and singular the goods, chattels and credits of the said deceased, and pay his debts as far as his goods, chattels and credits will extend and the law require you; and that you will make a true and perfect inventory of all the said goods, chattels and credits, as also a just account when thereunto required. So help you God." And shall also give bond in a penalty at least equal to the value of the estate, and with such security as shall be approved of by the court, with the following condition, to wit: "The condition of this obligation is, that if the said administrator of the goods, chattels and credits of deceased, do make a true and perfect inventory of all and singular, the goods, chattels and credits of the said deceased, which have or shall come to the hands, possession or knowledge of the said or into the hands or possession of any other person or persons for ; and the same so made, do exhibit into the court when he shall be thereto required by the said court; and such goods, chattels and credits do well and truly administer according to law; and further do make a just and true account of his actings and doings therein, when thereto required by the said court: And all the rest of the said goods, chattels and credits which shall be found remaining upon the account of the said administrator, the same being first examined and allowed by the Justices of the said court, for the time being, shall deliver and pay unto such persons respectively, as are intitled to the same by law. And if it shall hereafter appear that any last will and testament was made by the deceased, and the same be proved in court, and the executor obtain a certificate of the probat thereof, and the said do in such case, being required, render and deliver up his letters of administration, then this obligation to be void, or else to remain in full force," which bond shall be payable to the sitting Justices and their successors, and may be put in suit and prosecuted, in like manner as is before directed in the case of bonds to be given by executors or administrators with the will annexed.

But no security for an executor or administrator shall be chargable beyond the assets of the testator or intestate, by reason of any omission or mistake in pleading or false pleading of such executors or administrator.

If any court shall grant a certificate for obtaining administration of the estate of any person deceased, without taking good security for the same, as aforesaid, to be judged of according to the apparent circumstances of the security when taken, and not from subsequent accidents or discoveries thereof, the Justices of such court then sitting, shall be answerable to the person or persons injured, for all loss or damage occasioned by the not requiring any, or by the taking insufficient security, recoverable, with costs, by action on the case, in any court of record.

When securities for executors or administrators conceive themselves in danger of suffering thereby, and petition the court for relief, the court shall summon the executor or administrator, and make such order or decree thereupon to relieve and secure the petitioners, by counter security, or otherwise, as to them shall seem just and equitable.

All certificates of probat, or of administration, attested by the clerk, shall enable the executor or administrator to act, and may be produced or given in evidence in any court within this commonwealth, and be as effectual as a probat or letters of administration made out in due form; nevertheless the clerks of the courts shall, when required by any executor or administrator, make out such probat or letters, in due form, in the name of the first Justice of the court, which probat or letters shall be signed by such Justice, and sealed with the county seal, if the will be proved in a county court, or with the seal of the commonwealth if proved in the General Court.

The clerk of every county court shall half yearly, in the months of April and October, return to the clerk of the General Court, a list of all certificates granted in his court for probats and administrations, within the preceeding half year, in this form [date of certificate][1] [name of testator or intestate][1] [names of securities][1] [penalty of bond][1] which lists, together with such certificates as are granted in the General Court, shall be entered by the clerk of the General Court, alphabetically, in books for that purpose.

Every court granting a certificate for a probat or administration shall nominate three or more appraisers in every county, where any of the personal estate of the decedent shall be, who being sworn, before a Justice of Peace for that purpose, shall truly and justly, to the best of their judgment, view and appraise all the personal estate to them produced; and shall return such appraisement under their hands to the court ordering the same; which appraisement, if signed by the executor or administrator, may be considered as an inventory of such part of the estate as had theretofore come to his hands.

Inventories and appraisements may be given in evidence in any suit, by or against the executor or administrator, but shall not be conclusive for or against him if other testimony be given that the estate was really worth, or was bona fide, sold for more or less than the appraisement.

Each appraiser shall be intitled to thirty pounds of tobacco, per day, for his attendance, to be paid by the executor or administrator and charged to the estate.

Executors and administrators, whether it be necessary for payment of debts, or not, shall as soon as convenient, after they are qualified, sell at public sale all such goods of their testator or intestate, specific legacies excepted, or are liable to perish, be consumed, or rendered worse by keeping, giving such credit as they shall judge best and the circumstances of the estate will admit of, taking bond and good security of the purchasers, and shall account for such goods according to the sales. If more be sold than will pay the debts and expences, the executor or administrator may assign the bonds for the surplus to those intitled to the estate, and be discharged as to so much.

If such perishable goods be not sufficient for paying the debts and expences, the executor or administrator shall proceed in the next place to sell the other personal estate, disposing of the slaves last, until the debts and expences be all paid, having regard to the privilege of specific legacies.

Nevertheless if the testator direct his estate not to be appraised it shall be sufficient to return an inventory thereof only, and if he direct his estate not to be sold, the same shall be preserved in specie, unless a sale be necessary for the payment of debts.

The dead victuals and liquors which at the death of any testator or intestate shall have been laid in for consumption in his family, shall not be sold by the executor or administrator, but shall remain for the use of such family without account thereof to be made: If however, before its final consumption, any child shall leave the family, such child shall have a right to carry with him an equal share of what shall then be on hand. Any live stock which may be necessary for the food of the family may also be killed for that use, at any time before the sale, division, or distribution of the estate.

The sale and conveyance of land devised to be sold, shall be made by the executors or such of them as shall undertake the execution of the will, if no other person be thereby appointed for that purpose, or if the person so appointed shall refuse to perform the trust, or die before he shall have completed it.

If any person shall die after the first day of March, the servants and slaves of which he was possessed, whether held for life or for other interest, and which were employed in making a crop, shall be continued on the plantations in the occupation of the decedent until the last day of December following, and then delivered to those who shall have a right to demand the same; and their crops shall be assets in the hands of the executors or administrators, subject to debts, legacies and distribution, the levies and taxes, their tools, the expence of feeding them and their families to that time, and delivering them well clothed, being first deducted: And if such servants or slaves be held by the testator or intestate for his life only, in that case the executor or administrator shall be obliged to deliver to those who are intitled in remainder or reversion, three barrels of Indian corn for every such servant or slave, old and young, to be allowed in their accounts of administration. If a testator or intestate shall die after the first day of March, all the emblements of his lands, which shall be severed before the said thirty first day of December following, shall in like manner be assets in the hands of his executor or administrator; but all such emblements growing on the lands on that day, or at the time of the death of the testator or intestate, if that event happen after the thirty first day of December and before the first day of March, shall pass with the land to the heir, devisee, reversioner or remainder man.

If there be tenant for life of lands or slaves let or hired to another, at the death of such tenant for life, if that event happen after the first day of March, the lessee, or person hiring shall hold the lands and slaves until the last day of December following, paying rent or hire to that time, and in the case of slaves delivering them well clothed.

The rent of land or hire of slaves shall be apportioned between the executor or administrator of him who having a freehold, or other uncertain estate in the land, and the use for life or for other uncertain term in the slaves, shall die before the rent or hire become due, and him who shall succeed to the land, and slaves, as heir, devisee, or person in reversion or remainder, unless, in the case of a devisee, the contrary be directed by the testator.

The appointment of a debtor executor shall in no case be deemed an extinguishment of the debt unless it be so directed in the will.

No distribution shall be made of an intestate's estate until nine months after his death, nor shall an administrator be compelled to make distribution at any time, until bond and security be given by the person intitled to distribution, to refund due proportions of any debts or demands which may afterwards appear against the intestate, and the costs attending the recovery of such debts.

Executors and administrators shall be allowed in their accounts all reasonable charges and disbursements which they shall lay out and expend in the funeral of the deceased and other their administration; and in extraordinary cases may be allowed such recompence for their personal trouble, as the court, on passing their accounts, shall judge reasonable.

The executors or administrators of a guardian, of a committee, or of any other person who shall have been chargeable with, or accountable for the estate of a ward, an ideot, or a lunatic, or the estate of a dead person committed to their testator or intestate by a court of record, shall pay so much as shall be due from their testator or intestate to the ward, ideot, or lunatic, or to the legatees or persons intitled to distribution, before any proper debt of their testator or intestate.

Where any person shall die seized of lands held for life of another, such person may by his or her last will and testament, in writing, made and proved as is herein before directed, for the devise of lands, devise of his interest in such lands, which shall, if necessary, be assets in the hands of such devisee. And if no such devise be made, such lands for the residue of the term, shall be assets in the hands of the heir, if it shall come to him by reason of a special occupancy, in the same manner as lands descending in fee simple, and if there shall be no special occupant, it shall go to the executors or administrators of the person so dying seized, and be assets in their hands, subject to debts, legacies and distribution.

Executors or administrators may sue or be sued upon all judgments, bonds or other specialties, bills, notes or other writings of their testators or intestates, whether the executors or administrators be or be not named in such instruments, and also upon all their personal contracts.

Actions of trespass may be maintained by or against executors or administrators for any goods taken and carried away in the lifetime of the testator or intestate; and the damages recovered shall be in the one case for the benefit of the estate, and in the other out of the assets.

Executors of executors shall do and perform all things in the execution of the will of the first testator, which shall remain undone at the death of the first executor; and shall and may sue or be sued in all things respecting the estate, in the same manner as such first executor could or might have sued or been sued.

If all the executors named in any last will shall refuse to undertake the executorship, or being required to give security, shall refuse to give, or be unable to procure the same, and no person will apply for administration with the will annexed: Or if no person will apply for administration of the goods and chattels of any intestate, it shall be lawful for the General Court, or county court having jurisdiction of such probat or administration as herein before mentioned, after the expiration of three months from the death of the testator or intestate, to order the sheriff of the county to take the estate into his possession and make sale of so much thereof, by public auction, as the payment of debts shall make necessary, or as shall be perishable, or be directed by will to be sold: And all sales and conveyances, bona fide, made by the sheriff, or his deputies, in consequence of such order, shall be as effectual to the purchasers, as if they had been made by the testator or intestate in his lifetime. The estate shall be sold upon such credit as the court shall direct, and upon public notice previously given, the purchasers giving bond and good security for payment according to the limited time of credit. The sheriff may sue, if necessary, for the recovery of debts, or of goods and chattels, and shall make a true and perfect inventory of the whole estate, and an account of sales, and shall return the same, together with the bonds, to the court by whom he was ordered to sell without delay, who shall first direct the payment of such debts as shall be proved before them, and proportion the assets amongst the creditors without regard to the dignity of debts, where there shall not be sufficient to pay the whole; and then order the surplus, if any, to the legatees or next of kin to the decedent, according to the directions of the will or of this act. Whereupon the sheriff, or deputy, shall assign the bonds and deliver the estate remaining unsold to the creditors, or others, according to such order, retaining nevertheless his commissions, which shall be the same upon the estate by him sold, as is allowed for goods taken in execution; and where the whole estate is not sold, he shall moreover be allowed his reasonable expences and disbursements in the care of the part unsold.

All sales and conveyances of lands heretofore bona fide made by a sheriff, under an order of court, where the lands had been devised to be sold, and the executors had refused to act, are hereby confirmed and made effectual against all persons claiming under the testator.

Report, p. 16-20. Text of Act as adopted in 1785 is in Hening, XII, 140-54.

This Bill, which restates and alters the law of wills and estates as enacted in 1711 (Hening, IV, 12-25) and 1748 (same, V, 444-8, 454-67), was presented 31 Oct. 1785 by Madison and was passed by the House on 24 Nov. The Senate accepted it with several amendments, some of which the House agreed to, others amended, and still others rejected; the Senate insisted on some of its amendments but the House was adamant, whereupon the Senate yielded on 8 Dec. (JHD, Oct. 1785, 1828 edn., p. 12-15, 48, 53, 73, 75, 76, 133). The Act as adopted was substantially the same as that proposed by the Committee of Revisors. One exception is noted below; others were: (1) wherever in the Bill reference is made to county courts and their jurisdiction over wills, administration of estates, &c., the Act reads "county, city, or corporation courts" or some equivalent phraseology; (2) the Act includes a final clause putting it in force 1 Jan. 1787.

[1] Brackets in text.

[2] Following this point the Act includes two sections not in the Bill as proposed: the first provides that if any widow possessed of slaves as of the dower of her husband should remove such slaves from the state without the consent of the person holding a reversionary interest in the estate, she would forfeit not only the slaves but also "all other the dower which she holds of the endowment of her husband's estate," both being forfeited to the one having a reversionary interest; and the second provides that if a widow married to a husband who should remove or permit the removal of such slaves from the state, the reversioner could take possession of the estate held by the husband in right of his wife's dower.

[3] This point was agreed upon by the Committee of Revisors at its meeting in Fredericksburg (see Document I in this series, above).

22. A Bill for Regulating Conveyances

Be it enacted by the General Assembly, that no estate of inheritance, or freehold, or for a term of more than five years, in lands or tenements, shall be conveyed from one to another, unless the conveyance be declared by writing, sealed and delivered; nor shall such conveyance be good against a purchaser, for valuable consideration, not having notice thereof, or any creditor, unless the same writing be acknowledged by him who shall have sealed and delivered it, or be proved by three witnesses, to be his act, before the General Court, or before the court of that county,[1] in which the land conveyed, or some part thereof, lieth, or in the manner herein after directed, within eight months after the time of sealing and delivering, and be lodged with the clerk of such court, to be there recorded. No covenant or agreement, made in consideration of marriage, shall be good against a purchaser, for valuable consideration, not having notice thereof, or any creditor, unless the same covenant or agreement be acknowledged by the party bound thereby, or be proved by three witnesses, to be his act; if land be charged before the General Court, or the court of that county in which the land, or part thereof, lieth, or if personal estate only be settled or covenanted, or agreed to be paid or settled, before the court of that county, in which such party shall dwell, or in the manner herein after directed, within eight months after the covenant or agreement made, and be lodged with the clerk of such court, to be there recorded. If the party, who shall sign and seal any such writing, reside not in Virginia, the acknowledgement by such party, or the proof by the number of witnesses requisite, of the sealing and delivering of the writing, before any court of law, or the mayor, or other chief magistrate, of any city, town, or corporation, of the country[3] in which the party shall dwell, certified by such court, or mayor, or chief magistrate, in the manner such acts are usually authenticated by them, and offered to the proper court to be recorded, within eighteen months after the sealing and delivering, shall be as effectual as if it had been in the last mentioned court. When husband and wife shall have sealed and delivered a writing, purporting to be a conveyance of any estate or interest, if she appear in court, and, being examined, privily, and apart from her husband, by one of the Judges thereof, shall declare to him, that she did freely and willingly seal and deliver the said writing, to be then shewn and explained to her, and wishes not to retract it, and shall, before the said court, acknowledge the said writing, again shewn to her, to be her act; or if before two Justices of the Peace of that county, in which she dwelleth, if her dwelling be in America,[2] who may be empowered by commission, to be issued by the clerk of the court wherein the writing ought to be recorded, to examine her privily, and take her acknowledgement, the wife, being examined privily and apart from her husband, by those commissioners, shall declare, that she willingly signed and sealed the said writing, to be then shewn and explained to her by them, and consenteth, that it may be recorded, and the said commissioners shall return, with the commission, and thereunto annexed, a certificate, under their hands and seals, of such privy examination by them, and of such declaration made and consent yeilded by her; in either case the said writing, acknowledged also by the husband, or proved by witnesses to be his act, and recorded, together with such her privy examination and acknowledgement, before the court, or together with such commission and certificate, shall not only be sufficient to convey or release any right of dower, thereby intended to be conveyed or released, but be as effectual, for every other purpose, as if she were an unmarried woman. If the dwelling of the wife be not in America,[2] the commission, to examine her privily, and take her acknowledgement, shall be directed to any two Judges or Justices of any court of law, or to the mayor, or other chief magistrate, of any city, town, or corporation, of the country,[3] in which the wife shall dwell, and may be executed by them, in the same manner as a commission directed to two Justices, in America;[2] and the certificate of the Judges or Justices of such court, or the certificate of such mayor or chief magistrate, authenticated in the form, and with the solemnity, by them used in other acts, shall be as effectual as the like certificate of the Justices in America.[2] No part of the four years, next after the twelfth day of April, one thousand seven hundred and seventy four, shall be accounted in the time, within which any deed or conveyance ought to be acknowledged or proved.[4] The clerk of every court shall record all writings, acknowledged or proved before such court, or certified to have been acknowledged, or proved, in manner before prescribed, together with the commissions for privily examining and taking the acknowledgements of married women, and all endorsements on such writings, and plots, schedules, and other papers, thereto annexed, by entering them, word for word, in well bound books, to be carefully preserved, and afterwards redeliver them to the parties intitled to them; and shall moreover make a docket of all such writings, containing the dates thereof, and of the acknowledgements and probats, the names, surnames, and additions, of the parties thereto, in alphabetical order, and the quantities and situations of land, numbers and names of slaves, and descriptions of personal estate, conveyed thereby; and the clerk of every county court shall transmit such docket, made by him, to the clerk of the General Court, in every March[5] and October term, to be recorded by him. Every estate in lands or slaves, which on the day of [6] in the year of our Lord one thousand seven hundred and seventy six, was an estate in fee-tail, shall be deemed, from that time to have been, and, from thence forward, to continue, an estate in fee-simple; and every estate in lands, which since hath been limited, or hereafter shall be limited, so that, as the law aforetime was, such estate would have been an estate-tail, shall also be deemed to have been, and to continue, an estate in fee-simple: And all estates, which, before the said day of [6] one thousand seven hundred and seventy six, by the law, if it remained unaltered, would have been estates in fee-tail, and which, now, by virtue of this act, are and will be estates in fee-simple, shall, from that time, and henceforth, be discharged of the conditions annexed thereto by the common law, restraining alienations before the donee should have issues; so that the donees, or persons, in whom the conditional fees vested, or shall vest, had, and shall have, the same power over the same estates, as if they were pure and absolute fees. Every estate in lands, which shall hereafter be granted, conveyed, or devised to one, although other words, heretofore necessary to transfer an estate of inheritance, be not added, shall be deemed a fee-simple; if a less estate be not limited, by express words, or do not appear to have been granted, conveyed, or devised, by construction, or operation of law. Where an estate hath been, or shall be, by any conveyance limited, in remainder, to the son or daughter, or to the use of the son or daughter, of any person, to be begotten, such son or daughter, born after the decease of his or her father, shall take the estate, in the same manner, as if he or she had been born in the lifetime of the father, although no estate shall have been conveyed to support the contingent remainder after his death. By deed of bargain and sale, or by deeds of lease and release, or by covenant to stand seized to use, or deed operating by way of covenant to stand seized to use, the possession of the bargainer, releaser, or covenanter, shall be deemed heretofore to have been, and hereafter to be transferred to the bargainee, relessee, or person intitled to the use, for the estate or interest which such person hath, or shall have in the use, as perfectly, as if such bargainee, relessee, or person intitled to the use, had been enfeoffed with livery of seisin, of the land, intended to be conveyed by such deed or covenant. Estates of every kind, holden or possessed in trust, shall be subject to like debts and charges of the persons, to whose use, or for whose benefit, they were, or shall be, respectively, holden or possessed, as they would have been subject to, if those persons had owned the like interest in the things holden or possessed, as they own or shall own in the uses or trusts thereof. Where any person, to whose use, or in trust for whose benefit, another is or shall be seized of lands, tenements, or hereditaments, hath, or shall have, such inheritance in the use or trust, as that, if it had been a legal right, the husband or wife of such person would thereof have been intitled to curtesy or dower, such husband or wife shall have and hold, and may by the remedy proper in similar cases, recover curtesy or dower of such lands, tenements, or hereditaments. Grants of rents, or of reversions, or remainders, shall be good and effectual, without attornments of the tenants; but no tenant, who, before notice of the grant, shall have paid the rent to the grantor, shall suffer any damage thereby. The attornment of a tenant, to any stranger, shall be void, unless it be, with consent of the landlord of such tenant, or pursuant to, or in consequence of the judgement of a court of law, or the order or decree of a court of equity.

Report, p. 20-1. Text of Act as adopted is in Hening, XII, 154-8.

Bill presented by Madison 31 Oct. 1785, passed by House 24 Nov., and amended by Senate on 5 Dec.; House accepted Senate amendment same day (JHD, Oct. 1785, 1828 edn., p. 12-15, 48, 53, 72, 132). Text of Act as adopted agrees with Bill proposed by Committee of Revisors except for the principal differences noted below and for the addition of a final clause putting Act into effect 1 Jan. 1787. For the Acts of 1734 and 1748 regulating conveyances, see Hening, IV, 397-402; V, 408-31.

1 The Act adds the words "city, or corporation" at this point.

2 The Act reads: "United States of America."

3 The Act as given in Hening, XII, 156, reads, erroneously, "county."

4 The words "no part of the . . . acknowledged or proved" are not in the Act.

5 The Act reads: "April."

6 The Act reads: "seventh day of October"; i.e., the date of the opening of the General Assembly of Oct. 1776 at which TJ's Bill abolishing entails was passed.

23. A Bill Securing the Rights Derived from Grants to Aliens

Be it enacted by the General Assembly, that those citizens who heretofore were aliens, and had not been naturalized, shall be deemed to have been able to hold the lands, tenements, or hereditaments granted to them by the crown, or conveyed to them by others, so that all who deriving the rights and titles they claim under such grants or conveyances, either by color of hereditary succession or by purchase, are with good faith and by lawful means in possession of such lands, tenements, or hereditaments, shall, and may continue to hold, or who being out of possession had been deforced by wrong, or kept out by fraud, may recover the same lands, tenements, or hereditaments, in like manner, and by like remedies, as they might have held or recovered the same if they, to whom the grants or conveyances were made, had been citizens of the commonwealth, or had been such as were formerly called natural born subjects.

Report, p. 21-2. MS (ViU); clerk's copy.

Bill was presented by Madison on 31 Oct. 1785, read twice and committed to a committee of the whole, but no further action was taken on it (JHD, Oct. 1785, 1828 edn., p. 12-15). See Act of 1776 on this subject (Hening, IX, 207-10).

24. A Bill concerning Escheators

Be it enacted by the General Assembly, that there shall be one escheator commissioned in every county, by the Governor on recommendation from the court of the same county, who shall execute his office in proper person, and not by deputy, and shall, before the court of the county, be bound in the penalty of 1000 l. with security to be approved by the same court, duly to perform the duties of his said office.

The said escheator shall sit in convenient and open places, and shall take his inquests of fit persons, who shall be returned and empanelled by the sheriff of the county, and shall suffer every person to give evidence, openly, in their presence, to such inquest; and the said inquisition, so taken, shall be, by indentures to be made between the said escheator and them of the inquest, whereof the counterpart, sealed by the escheator, shall remain in the possession of the first person that shall be sworn in the said jury, and by him shall be returned to the court of the same county there to be recorded; and the other part, sealed by the jurors, shall, by the escheator, be sent into the General Court within one month after the inquest taken. And if it be found for the commonwealth, and there shall be any man that will make claim to the lands he shall be heard without delay on a traverse to the office, monstrans de droit or petition of right; and the said lands, or tenements, shall be committed to him, if he, shew good evidence of his right and title to hold, until the right shall be found and discussed for the commonwealth or for the party, finding sufficient surety to prosecute his suit with effect, and to render and pay to the commonwealth the yearly value of the lands, if the right be discussed for the commonwealth.

No lands nor tenements, seized into the hands of this commonwealth upon such inquests taken before escheators, shall be in any wise granted, nor to farm let, to any, if it be not to him or them which claim as is aforesaid, till the same inquests and verdicts be fully returned into the General Court, nor within six months after the same return, but shall intirely and continually remain in the hands of the escheators, who shall answer to the commonwealth the issues and profits yearly coming of the said lands and tenements, without doing waste or destruction.

If no person, within the six months before mentioned, make claim to the lands or tenements so seized, or claim being so made, if it be found and discussed for the commonwealth, the clerk of the General Court, shall, within one month thereafter, certify [to the escheator of the county, wherein the lands lie, that no claim hath been made, or that being made, it hath been discussed for the commonwealth, which escheator shall thereupon proceed to make sale of the land, for the benefit of the commonwealth, to him who will give the most, after one month's public notice of the time and place of doing the same, and shall certify the purchaser and price to the Register of the Land-Office, who, on receiving a certificate that such price hath been paid into the treasury, shall have a grant executed to the purchaser in such manner as by law directed in the case of unappropriated lands.][1]

Where any person holds lands, or tenements, for term of years, or hath any rent, common, office, fee, or other profit apprender of any estate of freehold, or for years, or otherwise out of such lands or tenements which shall not be found in such office or inquisition, such person shall hold and enjoy his lease, interest, rent, common, office, fee and profit apprender in manner as if no such office or inquisition had been found, or as if such lease, interest, rent, common, office, or profit apprender had been found in such inquisition. Also if one person or more be found heir by office or inquisition, in one county, and another person be found heir to the same person, in another county, or if any person be untruly found lunatic, ideot, or dead, or where it shall be untruly found that any person attainted of treason, or felony, is seized of any lands, tenements, or hereditaments, at the time of such treason or felony committed, or at any time after, whereunto any other person hath any just title or interest of any estate of freehold, the person grieved by such office or inquisition may have his traverse or monstrans de droit to the same, without being driven to any petition of right and proceed to trial therein, and have like remedy and restitution upon his title found or judged for him therein, as in other cases of traverse upon untrue inquisition found.

Report, p. 22. Text of Act as adopted in 1785 is in Hening, XII, 158-60. A MS fragment (Vi) of this Bill has been preserved; it is partly in a clerk's hand and partly in TJ's hand, as indicated below. On its verso is the MS draft in TJ's hand of the Bill for Providing a Supply (q.v., under 20 May 1778). Also, MS (ViU); clerk's copy.

TJ was ordered to bring in a Bill on this subject 27 May 1779; presented it the same day; read 2d time 28 May and committed to the committee for courts of justice, who reported the Bill on 11 June with an amendment which was agreed to by the House; read 3d time and passed on 12 June; approved by Senate with amendments which were agreed to by House on 16 June (JHD, May 1779, 1827 edn., p. 23, 25, 26, 43, 44, 50). Bill as amended and adopted in 1779 is in Hening, X, 115-17. The Bill as reported by the Committee of Revisors was again presented by Madison 31 Oct. 1785, passed without alteration by House 25 Nov., and approved by Senate 3 Dec. (JHD, Oct. 1785, 1828 edn., p. 12-15, 48, 55, 70, 132). The amendments made in 1779 by the committee for courts of justice and by the Senate can be determined by comparing the text in Hening, X, 115-17 with this text. The principal amendment, probably made by the committee for courts of justice, excepted the counties of the Northern Neck, by permitting the sheriffs of these counties to perform the duties of an escheator. See also Bill concerning Escheats and Forfeitures from British Subjects, 4 June 1779. Act of 1785 concerning Escheators was repealed at the session of Oct. 1786 (Hening, XII, 411).

[1] The passage in square brackets (supplied) is that part of the MS fragment described above which is in TJ's hand.

25. A Bill to Prevent Frauds and Perjuries

Be it enacted by the General Assembly, that no action shall be brought, whereby to charge any executor or administrator upon any special promise, to answer any debt or damages out of his own estate; or whereby to charge the defendant upon any special promise to answer for the debt, default or miscarriage of another person, or to charge any person upon any agreement made upon consideration of marriage; or upon any contract for the sale of lands, tenements or hereditaments, or the making any lease thereof for a longer term than one year; or upon any agreement which is not to be performed within the space of one year from the making thereof, unless the promise or agreement, upon which such action shall be brought, or some memorandum or note thereof, shall be in writing, and signed by the party to be charged therewith, or some other person by him thereunto lawfully authorised.

Every gift, grant, or conveyance of lands, tenements, hereditaments, goods or chattels, or of any rent, common or profit out of the same, by writing or otherwise, and every bond, suit, judgment or execution, had or made, and contrived of malice, fraud, covin, collusion, or guile, to the intent or purpose to delay, hinder or defraud creditors of their just and lawful actions, suits, debts, accounts, damages, penalties, or forfeitures, or to defraud or deceive those who shall purchase the same lands, tenements, or hereditaments, or any rent, profit or commodity out of them, shall be from henceforth deemed and taken (only as against the person or persons, his, her, or their heirs, successors, executors, administrators, or assigns, and every of them whose debts, suits, demands, estates or interests, by such guileful and covinous devices and practices, as is aforesaid, shall or might be in any wise disturbed, hindered, delayed or defrauded) to be clearly and utterly void, any pretence, color, feigned consideration, expressing of use, or any other matter or thing to the contrary notwithstanding. And moreover if a conveyance be of goods and chattles, and be not on consideration deemed valuable in law, it shall be taken to be fraudulent within this act, unless the same be by will duly proved and recorded, or by deed in writing acknowledged or proved, if the same deed include lands also, in such manner as conveyances of land are by law directed to be acknowledged or proved, or if it be of goods and chattels only, then acknowledged or proved by two witnesses in the General Court or court of the county wherein one of the parties live, within eight months after the execution thereof; or unless possession shall really and bona fide remain with the donee. And in like manner where any loan of goods and chattels shall be pretended to have been made to any person with whom, or those claiming under him, possession shall have remained by the space of five years, without demand made and pursued by due process at law on the part of the pretended lender, or where any reservation or limitation shall be pretended to have been made of a use or property by way of condition, reversion, remainder or otherwise, in goods and chattels, the possession whereof shall have remained in another as aforesaid, the same shall be taken, as to the creditors and purchasers of the persons aforesaid so remaining in possession, to be fraudelent within this act, and that the absolute property is with the possession; unless such loan, reservation or limitation of use or property were declared by will or by deed in writing proved and recorded as aforesaid.

This act shall not extend to any estate or interest in any lands, goods, or chattels, or any rents common or profit out of the same, which shall be upon good consideration and bona fide, lawfully conveyed or assured to any person or persons, bodies politic or corporate.

Report, p. 22-3. Text of Act as adopted is in Hening, XII, 160-2.

Bill was presented by Madison 31 Oct. 1785, passed by House 25 Nov., and approved by Senate 5 Dec. (JHD, Oct. 1785, 1828 edn., p. 12-15, 48, 55, 72, 132). Text of Act follows that of Bill except in the addition of a clause putting it into effect 1 Jan. 1787.

26. A Bill of Mortmain

Be it enacted by the General Assembly that no person presume to convey by deed, will, or otherwise any lands or slaves, or the use of them, or under the color of any such conveyance to receive of any man, or by any other craft or ingenuity to appropriate to himself any lands or slaves, or the use of them, whereby such lands or slaves, or the use thereof may any wise come into mortmain. And if any body politic do implead any and the party impleaded maketh default whereby he ought to lose the lands or slaves after the default made, it shall be enquired by the country whether the plaintiff had right in the thing demanded or no; and if it be found that the plaintiff had right in his demand, the judgment shall pass with him, and he shall recover; and if he hath no right it shall be taken to be amortised.

And in all these cases the thing amortised shall incur, the one moiety to the commonwealth, and the other moiety to him who will demand the same with good faith, as well for himself as for the commonwealth, or the whole shall incur to the commonwealth if it be first demanded on that behalf.

Report, p. 23.

Bill presented by Madison and committed to a committee of the whole, read twice 31 Oct. 1785, but no further action was taken on it (JHD, Oct. 1785, 1828 edn., p. 12-15). The later English statutes of mortmain, upon which TJ based this Bill (e.g., 9 Geo.II,c.36), were intended to prevent great accumulation of wealth in the hands of perpetual corporations.

27. A Bill concerning the Dower and Jointures of Widows

Be it enacted by the General Assembly, that a widow after the death of her husband, shall tarry in the mansion house of her husband and the plantation thereto belonging, rent free, until her dower shall be assigned her. And if she be thereof in the meantime deforced, she shall have a vicontiel writ in the nature of the writ de quarentinâ habendâ, directed to the sheriff, whereupon such proceedings and speed shall be used as hath or might have been used on the said writ of quarentine.

Whosoever shall deforce widows of their dowers of the lands whereof their husbands died seized, or of such mansion-house or plantation, if the same widows after shall recover by plea, they that be convicted of such wrongful deforcement shall yeild damages to the same widows, that is to say, the value of the whole dower to them belonging from the time of the death of their husbands unto the day that the said widows by judgment have recovered seisin of their dower.

In a writ of dower called 'unde nihil habet' the writ shall not abate by the exception of the tenant, because the demandant hath received her dower of another man before her writ purchased, unless he can shew that the dower, so received, was in satisfaction of her right of dower in the lands whereof she demands dower.

In case where the husband being impleaded for land by default, the woman after his death demanding her dower shall be heard. And if it be alledged against her that her husband lost the land whereof the dower is demanded, by judgment, whereby she ought not to have dower, and then it be enquired by what judgment, and it be found that it was by default, whereupon the tenant must answer, then it behoveth the tenant to answer further, and to shew that he had right and hath in the foresaid land according to the form of the writ, that the tenant before purchased against the husband: And if he can shew that the husband of such wife had no right in the lands, nor any other but he that holdeth them, the tenant shall go quit, and the wife shall recover nothing of her dower; which thing if he cannot shew, the wife shall recover her dower.

And where sometime it chanceth that a woman not having a right to demand dower, the heir being within age, doth purchase a writ of dower against a guardian, and the guardian endoweth the woman by favor, or maketh default, or by collusion defendeth the plea so faintly, whereby the woman is awarded her dower, in prejudice of the heir, it is provided that the heir, when he cometh to full age, shall have an action to demand the seisen of his ancestor against such a woman, like as he should have against any other deforcer. Yet so that the woman shall have her exception saved against the demandant, to shew that she had right to her dower, which if she can shew, she shall go quit and retain her dower, and if not the heir shall recover his demand. In like manner the woman shall be aided if the heir or any other do implead her for her dower, if she lose her dower by default, in which case the default shall not be so prejudicial to her, but that she shall recover her dower, if she have right thereto, and she shall have this writ. "Command A. that justly, &c. he render to B. who was the wife of F. so much land with the appurtenances in C. which she claims to be her reasonable dower, or of her reasonable dower, and that the aforesaid A. deforceth her &c." and to this writ the tenant shall have his exception, to shew that she had no right to be endowed; which if he can verify, he shall go quit, if not, the woman shall recover the land whereof she was endowed before.

Also widows may bequeath the crop of their ground as well of their dowers as of other their lands and tenements.

But if a wife willingly leave her husband and go away and continue with her adulterer, she shall be barred forever of action to demand her dower that she ought to have of her husband's lands, if she be convict thereupon, except that her husband willingly and without coercion reconcile her and suffer her to dwell with him, in which case she shall be restored to her action.

Also if any estate be conveyed by deed or will, either expressly or by averment, for the jointure of the wife, in lieu of her dower, to take effect in her own possession immediately on the death of her husband, and to continue during her life at the least, determinable by such acts only as would forfeit her dower at the common law, such conveyance shall bar her dower of the residue of the lands, tenements or hereditaments which at any time were her said husband's.

But if the said conveyance were before the marriage and during the infancy of the feme, and the guardian hath not expressed his approbation thereof by becoming a party to the same conveyance,[1] or if it were made after the marriage, in either case the widow may, at her election, wave such jointure and demand her dower.

When any conveyance intended to be in lieu of dower, shall, through any defect, fail to be a legal bar thereto, and the widow, availing herself of such defect, shall demand her dower, the estate and interest conveyed to such widow with intention to bar her dower shall thereupon cease and determine.

If a widow be lawfully expulsed or evicted from her jointure, or any part thereof, without any fraud or covin, by lawful entry or action, she shall be endowed of as much of the residue of her husband's lands, tenements, or hereditaments, whereof she was before dowable, as the same lands, tenements, or hereditaments, so evicted and expulsed shall amount or extend unto.

Report, p. 23-4. Text of the Act as adopted is in Hening, XII, 162-5.

Bill was presented by Madison 31 Oct. 1785, passed by the House on 29 Nov., and approved by the Senate without amendment on 6 Dec. (JHD, Oct. 1785, 1828 edn., p. 12-15, 48, 62, 74, 133). The Bill was adopted precisely as proposed by the Committee of Revisors except for the addition of a final clause putting the Act into effect 1 Jan. 1787 and except for the omission noted below.

1 The words "and the guardian . . . to the same conveyance" are not in the Act as adopted.

28. A Bill for the Preservation of the Estates of Ideots and Lunatics

Be it enacted by the General Assembly that the lands, tenements and chattels, of ideots and lunatics, shall be safely kept without waste and destruction, and they and their household shall live and be maintained competently with the profits of the same, and the residue, besides their sustentation, shall be kept for their use, to be delivered unto them when they come to right mind: And if they die in such estate their lands shall be rendered to the right heirs and their chattels be distributed.

Report, p. 24. Text of Act as adopted is in Hening, XII, 165.

Bill was presented by Madison 31 Oct. 1785, passed by House 26 Nov., and approved by Senate 29 Nov. (JHD, Oct. 1785, 1828 edn., p. 12-15, 51, 58, 63, 132). Act as adopted differs from Bill as proposed only in the addition of a clause putting it into effect 1 Jan. 1787. See Bill No. 62, below; see also the terms of the Act of 1769 concerning the treatment of mentally incompetent persons having estates (Hening, VIII, 380-1).

29. A Bill Providing that Wrongful Alienations of Lands Shall Be Void So Far as They Be Wrongful

Be it enacted by the General Assembly, that all alienations and warranties of lands, tenements and hereditaments made by any purporting to pass or assure a greater right or estate than such person may lawfully pass or assure, shall operate as alienations or warranties of so much of the right and estate in such lands, tenements, or hereditaments as such person might lawfully convey; but shall not pass or bar the residue of the said right or estate purported to be conveyed or assured.

But if the deed of the alienor doth mention that he and his heirs be bound to warranty, and if any heritage descend to the demandant of the side of the alienor, then he shall be barred for the value of the heritage that is to him descended. And if in time after any heritage descend to him by the same alienor, then shall the tenant recover against him of the seisin warranted by a judicial writ, that shall issue out of the rolls of the Justices, before whom the plea was pleaded; to resummon his warranty, as before hath been done in cases where the warrantor cometh into the court, saying, that nothing descended from him by whose deed he is vouched.

Report, p. 24. Text of Act as adopted is in Hening, XII, 166.

Bill presented by Madison 31 Oct. 1785, passed by the House 26 Nov., and approved by Senate 5 Dec. (JHD, Oct. 1785, 1828 edn., p. 12-15, 51, 58, 72, 133). Text of Bill does not differ from Act save in the addition of a final clause putting it into effect 1 Jan. 1785.

30. A Bill for Amending an Act, Intitled, "An Act for Raising a Supply of Money for Public Exigencies"

Be it enacted by the General Assembly, that so much of one act passed in the year of our Lord 1777, and intitled, "An act for raising a supply of money for public exigencies," as directs that during the continuance thereof, the freeholders and house-keepers shall meet together and chuse commissioners of the tax for their county, and that the said commissioners of the tax shall lay off their county, city, or borough, into hundreds, shall be repealed, and that the Aldermen to be chosen annually by direction of one act of this present General Assembly, intitled "An act for the more general diffusion of knowledge," shall perform the duties heretofore required of the said commissioners of the tax, and shall have the same powers, be liable to the same penalties, and to all intents and purposes, as well of the beforementioned act as of any other, stand in the place of the said commissioners.

Report, p. 24.

Bill No. 30 was not presented by Madison in 1785 and its fate was obviously determined by the legislative action respecting Bill No. 79, below. TJ was probably the author of Bill No. 30, since its terms were made necessary by his Bill concerning education.

31. A Bill for Levying County Rates

Be it enacted by the General Assembly, that the Justices of every county, at some court, to be held for their county, between the last day of April and second Tuesday in July, in every year, shall make up in their minutes an account of all expences incurred by the said court, under authority of law, and remaining unpaid, stating therein the sums due, for what, and to whom due, and all credits owing to the said county, and certify the balance to the Aldermen of their county. The said Aldermen shall meet together, at the court-house of their county, at some time between the said second Tuesday in July, and the first day of August next following, and by taxation of the persons and property in their county, according to the mode of assessment prescribed by the law which shall then be in force for raising money for the public exigencies, shall make provision for raising the said balance, and shall, on or before the said first day of August, deliver to the collector of the public taxes, a list of the persons chargeable with the county rate, and the sum to be paid by each for his county rate; and also a list of the credits owing to them on behalf of their county, and of the persons from whom due: Which collector shall give bond with responsible security for the discharge of his duty herein, and shall collect the credits and county rates in the same time, and with the same powers, for the same commission, and subject to the same fines, forfeitures, and prosecutions, as in the case of public taxes. The said court shall also, before the said first day of August annually, deliver to the said collector a copy of such their account, who shall proceed, so soon as his collection shall have enabled him to pay off the demands of the several creditors therein stated. And if he shall fail so to do, and also to settle his accounts with the court of his said county, on or before the first day of November following, it shall be lawful for the said court, on the motion of any creditor unpaid, ten days previous notice of such motion having been given, to render judgment against such collector for the amount of the claim and costs; or if the failure were to account, then of their own motion to render such judgment or judgments as are usual in actions on writs of account, and thereon to award execution, unless the claim shall not exceed twenty five shillings, in which case it shall be determinable before a Justice of the Peace in like manner.

Report, p. 24-5. This Bill was drawn by TJ; see Document IV, 5 in the present series.

Bill presented by Madison 31 Oct. 1785, passed by House, and referred to the Senate 26 Nov.; apparently no further action was taken on it (JHD, Oct. 1785, 1828 edn., p. 12-15, 51, 58). See the 1777 Act for laying a county levy (Hening, IX, 369-71).

32. A Bill for Support of the Poor

Be it enacted by the General Assembly, that the Aldermen of every county wherein such provision, as is herein after required for setting the poor of the county to work, shall not have been made, shall, so soon as conveniently may be, purchase the inheritance, or procure a lease, of one hundred acres of land, or any less quantity that is sufficient for the purpose intended, in the county, and thereon cause a house to be built, if a proper one be not there already, and kept in repair, and shall cause all persons in their county, who are maintained thereby, or who seek relief therefrom, to be put into such house, to be there maintained and employed in such work as they shall be able to perform; and may also, by their warrant, apprehend and send to the same place all persons found wandering and begging alms, in the county, other than seamen, who having been shipwrecked or discharged from vessels they had belonged to, and returning to their habitations, or going to some port to seek employment, and not loitering on the way thither, or abiding in port and offering to be employed, shall ask subsistance on their journey, or until any be willing to employ them, and shall put such beggar to work for any time not exceeding twenty days. And the said Aldermen shall hire some discreet man to oversee those who shall come or be put into such work-house, and shall, from time to time, ordain rules for his conduct, and for the government, employment, and correction of the persons subject to him, restraining him from correcting any of them with more stripes than ten, at one time, or for one offence. And in order to keep them at work shall provide wool, cotton, flax, hemp and other materials, with the tools and implements necessary for the manufacture thereof. And the said Aldermen shall meet together, at the court-house of their county, at some time between the second Tuesday in July and the first day of August in every year, and by taxation of the persons and property, in their county, according to the mode of assessment prescribed by the law which shall be then in force, for raising money for the public exigencies, shall raise competent sums of money for the necessary relief of such poor, lame, impotent, blind, and other inhabitants of the county as are not able to maintain themselves. And also for the putting out the poor children apprentices, as well as for defraying the expences of putting so much of this act in execution as relates to setting the poor to work and keeping them so employed; they shall moreover on or before the first day of August annually, make up in their minutes an exact account of the persons to, and for whom, such monies are to be paid, the purposes for which and the particular sums; a copy of which they shall, on or before the same day, deliver to the collector of the public tax, together with a list of the persons chargeable with the poor rates, and the sums to be paid by each for his poor rate, and also a list of the debts due to them on behalf of their county: which collector shall give bond with responsible security for the discharge of his duty herein; and shall collect the said debts and poor rates in the same time, with the same powers, for the same commission, and subject to the same fines, forfeitures, and prosecutions as in the case of public taxes. The said collector shall proceed, so soon as his collection shall have enabled him, to pay the several sums as shall be specially directed in the account rendered him: and if he shall fail so to do, and also to settle his account with the Aldermen, on or before the first day of November following, it shall be lawful for the court of the county, on the motion of the said Aldermen, or of the person to whom any sum of money is directed to be paid, ten days previous notice of such motion having been given, to render judgment against such collector for the sum and costs; or if it be for failure to account, then to render such judgment or judgments as are usual in actions on writs of account, and thereon to award execution, unless the sum shall not exceed twenty five shillings, in which case it shall be determinable before a Justice of the Peace, in like manner. And at such annual meeting, and at other times when they shall think proper, the said Aldermen shall cause the overseer of the poor to render account of the persons under his care, the produce of their labor, and the disposition of such produce, and of all other things committed to his care, or belonging to his office, and apply the profits arising from their work towards defraying the expences of their maintenance. The Aldermen shall register in a book, to be provided at the expence of the county, and transmitted to their successors, the names of all persons who receive relief from the county, entering the times they were admitted, and stating the reasons of their admissions. When a person shall have resided twelve months in a county, without any intermediate change of habitation, such residence shall be deemed a settlement in that county, of such person, and those of his children who remain a part of his family. A bastard child shall be deemed a settled inhabitant of that county in which, at the birth, the mother was settled. Any person acknowledged by the Aldermen of a county to be a settled inhabitant thereof, producing a certificate of such acknowledgement, signed by the said Aldermen, and delivering the certificate to the Aldermen of another county, wherein he shall not have such leasehold, or greater estate as is herein after mentioned, shall be adjudged to continue a settled inhabitant of the former county, which shall reimburse all expences incurred by the latter, for his maintenance, or curing, or attempting to cure him of any disease he may labor under, to be recovered, in case of refusal to repay them, in an action on the case, brought by the Aldermen of one county against those of the other. A widow shall be adjudged a settled inhabitant of that county in which her husband shall have gained a settlement, although his death happen before she shall have resided there twelve months: But if he had no settlement any where, she shall be considered with respect to her settlement as if she were an unmarried woman. A person holding any estate of freehold, in lands or possessing an estate, for one or more years, in lands, and coming to dwell in the county wherein such lands lie, shall have the same right to remain there as if he had been a settled inhabitant thereof. When a settled inhabitant of any county, or one who according to this act is deemed such, shall leave it, and the Aldermen, or any two of them, in any other county, in which he shall come to dwell, or abide, if he have not therein such estate as aforesaid, or do not give security to indemnify the county, and shall be apprehensive he will become chargeable to their county, they may, by their warrant, cause such emigrant to be removed to the county whereof he was a settled inhabitant, and delivered to one of the Aldermen thereof; and if he be unable to travel immediately, the Alderman who signed the warrant, shall, at the charge of their county, provide for his maintenance and cure, until he shall recover strength and health sufficient for the journey, the expence of which removal shall be reimbursed, and may be recovered in the same manner as those of the maintenance and cure are before directed to be. Any Alderman refusing to receive a settled parishioner, so removed, shall be himself answerable for his maintenance and cure, in like manner as his county is declared to be. All able bodied persons not having wherewithal to maintain themselves, who shall waste their time in idle and dissolute courses, or shall loiter or wander abroad, refusing to work for reasonable wages, or to betake themselves to some honest and lawful calling, or who shall desert wives or children, without so providing for them as that they shall not become chargeable to a county, shall be deemed vagabonds, and shall be sent, by order of an Alderman, to the poor house, there to be kept to labor during such time as shall be limited by the order, not exceeding thirty days; or if he be a settled inhabitant of another county, shall, by warrant of the said Alderman, be conveyed, by constable to constable, to some Alderman of such other county, who shall, by his order, send him to the proper poor house, to be there kept to labor as aforesaid; unless, in either of the cases, the vagabond shall give surety for his good behavior, and that he shall betake himself to some honest and lawful calling for twelve months; from which order the party thereby condemned may appeal to the county court, who, if the order be affirmed, shall award him to pay the costs. The assessors of the several hundreds, in every county, shall be aiding and assisting to their Aldermen, in the execution of this act, by giving information of such persons, within their respective hundreds, as ought to be supported by the county; and of these who shall come from any other county, where they had a settled residence, to dwell within their hundred, and be likely to become chargeable, by apprehending, and carrying before the said Aldermen, any person found wandering or begging within their hundred, or coming within the description of a vagabond before given; and by dispensing, according to the instructions of the said Aldermen, any reliefs which may, by them, be deposited with such assessors for the use of the poor of their hundred. The Aldermen of every county and their successors shall have power to call upon the former vestrymen of any parish which, or any part of which, is within their county, to render account of the expenditure of all money, or tobacco, by them received, and to pay into their hands any balance, or their due proportion of any balance, which may remain, to be applied to the lessening of the poor rates, and on failure may maintain proper actions in law, or equity, against them for enforcing the same.

Report, p. 25-6. MS (DLC); in hand of Edmund Pendleton. Endorsed: "concerning the Poor & Vagabonds. 1 Geo.2. c.1."

The MS Bill described above represents Pendleton's redrafting of the 1755 Act for employing and better maintaining the poor (Hening, VI, 475-8). Pendleton adhered closely to the Act of 1755, which placed the care of the poor in the hands of the vestry of each parish. He omitted, however, the harsh final clause of that Act, which required all persons receiving relief to wear a badge "upon the shoulder of the right sleeve of his or her uppermost garment, in an open and visible manner . . . with the name of the parish to which he or she belongs, cut either in blue, red, or green cloth"; the vestry was empowered to punish violations of this requirement by curtailing or suspending the allowance to the person or by imposing a whipping.

The alterations made in Pendleton's Bill were probably by TJ, since control of the poor was transferred to the aldermen of the county, officials created under TJ's Bill for the More General Diffusion of Knowledge (see Bill No. 79, below). The major differences between Pendleton's Bill and the Bill as proposed by the Committee were (1) transference of jurisdiction from the vestry to the aldermen; (2) establishment of more regular procedures for handling accounts, &c.; and (3) extension of the Bill to cover the "poor, lame, impotent, blind, and other inhabitants of the county as are not able to maintain themselves."

As noted by TJ (Document II, note 1, above), this Bill was "passd. with great alterns." The fact is that the Act as adopted was the product of two bills, and it owed less to the Bill proposed by the Committee than to one that had been ordered to be brought in on 27 Oct. 1785 to provide for the poor of the various parishes. On 31 Oct. Madison presented, along with others, the Bill prepared by the Committee of Revisors; on 3 Nov. Braxton reported the bill that had been previously ordered to be prepared. The latter was read the second time on 4 Nov. and committed to the committee of the whole. On 28 Nov. the committee of the whole was discharged from proceeding on the bill and it was recommitted to a special committee. The committee reported this bill with amendments on 6 Dec. and it was again recommitted. It was further amended, and on 22 Dec. it was finally agreed to by the House and ordered to be engrossed; it was passed by the House the next day, amended by the Senate on 29 Dec., and the Senate's amendments approved by the House 30 Dec. (JHD, Oct. 1785, 1828 edn., p. 9, 12-15, 21, 22, 60, 74, 104, 105, 118, 119, 148). Since the House took no action on the Committee's Bill subsequent to its second reading on 31 Oct., it is clear that the two recommitments were for the purpose of combining the two bills. The main features of the bill introduced by Braxton were: (1) each county court was directed to lay off the county into convenient districts; (2) in each of these districts the freeholders and housekeepers were to elect three overseers of the poor who were to serve three years; (3) the overseers were directed to meet each year and assess levies on the tithables of the county for the support of "the poor, lame, impotent, blind," &c.; (4) they were required to make monthly returns to the court of the poor orphans and, at the court's direction, to bind out such orphans as apprentices (Hening, XII, 27-30). The provisions of the Act calling for annual returns of the poor, accounting for and paying obligations, and collecting levies were substantially the same as those set forth in the Committee's Bill.

33. A Bill for Ascertaining the Salaries and Fees of Certain Officers

Be it enacted by the General Assembly, that the salaries and fees, ascertained by the table hereunto annexed, shall be paid to the officers therein mentioned, the salaries out of the public treasury, and the fees by the persons for whom the services, opposite to which the fees are extended, shall be respectively performed. The clerk, or register, of every court, shall, within six months after the commencement of this act, set up, and continually afterwards keep, one fair and correct copy of the said table, or so much thereof as concerns the officers of such court, in some part of the room the court shall sit in, and another in his own office, visible to persons resorting thither; and if he omit this, he shall be amerced. Before one shall be compellable to pay any such of the said fees, as by virtue of this act distress may be made for, an account thereof shall be produced and delivered to him, signed by the officer, specifying distinctly every article, in words at length, with the particular fee charged for it. Such account of a surveyor, clerk, register, sheriff or marshall being put into the hands of that sheriff, in whose county the debtor dwelleth, or the services shall have been performed, before the twentieth day of January, the said sheriff shall collect the fees so charged; and, if, when they shall have been demanded by him, they be not paid before the tenth day of April then next following, he shall distrain sufficient of the debtor's goods, and sell them in the same manner as goods taken in execution by writ of fieri facias, to discharge the said account; and he may retain, to his own use, a proportion, equal to six in the hundred, of the fees so collected or levied by him: And if he refuse, or neglect, to account for, or pay, the balance, before the last day of May, then next following, to the officer intitled to it; or, if he dwell in another county, to such agent as he shall empower to receive it, such officer may recover the same, with damages, to be assessed by a jury, and costs, against the sheriff, or his representative, by motion to the court of that county whereof he is or was a sheriff; or, if the officer be clerk of the High Court of Chancery, or General Court, or register of the Court of Admiralty, either to the General Court, or the said county court, ten days notice having been given to the defendant of the time when such motion would be made: And upon a judgment in such motion, the plaintiff may sue out the like execution as may be taken out upon a judgment in an action for debt or damages; and if the execution be a fieri facias, the clerk issuing it shall endorse thereon "that no security shall be taken," which the officer it shall be directed to shall obey. No suit to recover any such fees, for which distress may be made, shall be maintained before the account thereof shall have been put into the hands of such sheriff, as aforesaid, and he shall have made a return thereupon, that the debtor had no goods whereof he could make distress in his bailiwic, unless the books of the office shall have been destroyed by fire, or some other accident. No office copy taken out by or for either party, of a writing filed on behalf of himself, if he recover costs, shall be taxed, in the bill of costs, against his adversary, nor shall more than one fee be charged for entering the attornies on each side in any suit. If an officer, for whose fees distress may be made, exact or take a greater fee than what is allowed by this act, or take any fee for service not performed, he shall make amends, to the party injured, by payment of   times so much as the fee exacted or taken shall exceed the legal fee, or as the fee unearned shall amount to, and may, nevertheless, be criminally prosecuted for the extortion.

TABLE mentioned and referred to in the Act for ascertaining the Salaries and Fees of certain Officers.

OFFICERS. Their salaries by the year, and after that rate for a less time, in pounds of current money.

Governor.

Members of the Privy Council. To be distributed amongst them in proportion to the numbers of days they shall respectively attend, or, being in the proper place for that purpose, shall be hindered by sickness from attending, the Board.

Every Member of the American Congress.

Speaker of the Senate, besides daily wages in session.

Speaker of the House of Delegates, besides daily wages in session.

Public Treasurer.

Each of the Auditors for Public Accounts.

Commissioners of the Navy, to be distributed amongst them in like proportion as the salary to Members of the Privy Council.

Clerk of the Privy Council.

Clerk of the Auditors for Public Accounts.

Clerk assistant of the same.

Clerk of the Commissioners of the Navy.

Clerk assistant of the same.

Every Judge of the High Court of Chancery, General Court, and Court of Admiralty.

Clerk of the High Court of Chancery, besides his fees.

for services performed.	fees				
	pounds	shillings	pence	of current money, or, if the debtor chuse it	pounds of tobacco
CLERK of the court of appeals, equity, or common law, and register of the court of admiralty.					
For recording the acknowledgement or probate of a conveyance or other deed.					
For a dedimus potestatem to take the acknowledgement of a married woman, party to a conveyance.					
For recording the return of commissioners impowered to take such acknowledgement.					
For recording the probate of a testament, or last will.					
For a commission of administration.					
For entering a suit in a docket, to be charged once only.					
For a subpœna, writ, summons, citation, or other process, original, mesne, or judicial, in any case civil or criminal.					
For entering the return of such process.					
For a petition to recover a demand of less value than five pounds, with a copy of the writing, specifying the demand, and the summons thereupon.					
For entering the appearance of either party in a suit, personally, or by attorney, or proctor, to be charged once only.					
For entering a warrant of attorney.					
For filing a bail-bond for appearance.					
For entering a recognizance of special bail in court, or taken in the country.					

	fees				
	pounds	shillings	pence	of current money, or, if the debtor chuse it	pounds of tobacco
For entering the undertaking of one becoming bound for another, as surety for payment of costs.					
For filing a bill, declaration, libel, claim, petition and appeal, answer, plea, demurrer, replication, rejoinder, or other pleading or written allegation of either party, in any suit.					
For filing papers intended as exhibits in such suit.					
For a dedimus potestatem to take the examinations of witnesses.					
For filing the return thereof.					
For every rule given in court or in the office.					
For every order of court in any suit.					
For entering the continuance of a suit by special order of the court.					
For every thing done, during a trial by jury, from the calling, till the discharging them.					
For entering a decree, judgment, or sentence, interlocutory or final.					
For taxing costs.					
For a bond given by an executor, or administrator, or sheriff, or upon entering or lodging an appeal, or upon issuing a certiorari, a writ of error, an injunction, or a ne exeat.					
For every twenty words contained in the record of any conveyance or deed, with the papers thereunto annexed, except such as a particular fee is before allowed for the recording of, or in the record of any letter of attorney, bond, testament, or last will, inventory, account, report, or ar-					

	fees				
	pounds	shillings	pence	of current money, or, if the debtor chuse it	pounds of tobacco
bitrament; or in the record of proceedings and exhibits filed in any suit; or contained in the copy of any such record, writing, or exhibit; four arithmetical figures being computed as one word.					
For a search, if the writing searched for be not found, or a copy thereof be not taken.					
SHERIFF or MARSHALL.					
For an inquisition taken in the country.					
For summoning the jurors when no inquisition shall be taken, if not through his default.					
For serving and returning any process to summon, attach, or arrest one, or distrein his estate, and either delivering to him a copy of the process, or taking him in custody, or taking bond for his appearance, as the law may require in the case.					
A writ of scire facias.					
A writ of exigi facias.					
An order of court.					
A subpœna in chancery.					
A summons or subpœna to testify.					
A writ of dower or partition.					
A declaration in ejectment, if on one tenant.					
if more than one, for each.					
The warrant of a Justice of the Peace.					
For returning upon any process that the party is not found, or hath nothing in the bailiwick of the sheriff by which he could make known.					

	fees				
	pounds	shillings	pence	of current money, or, if the debtor chuse it	pounds of tobacco
For committing one to prison, and releasing him.					
For summoning and impannelling a jury charged in court.					
For every day he shall attend a surveyor, with jurors, or without them, in the country, by writ, or by order of court.					
For returning nulla bona, or a devastavit.					
For every day a prisoner in his custody shall be maintained by him.					
For returning, and doing execution by virtue of, a writ of levari facias, fieri facias, or any writ of attachment in nature thereof, or by virtue of a sentence of the Court of Admiralty.					
If the debt or damages and costs recovered, or the proceeds of the subject condemned to be sold, be not more than one hundred pounds, for every twenty shillings.		1			
If more than one hundred pounds, and less than four thousand eight hundred and fifty pounds, for the first hundred pounds.	5				
And for every fifty shillings above one hundred pounds.		1			
And if equal to, or more than, four thousand eight hundred and fifty pounds.	100				
If the debt or damages be tobacco the fees for making or levying such debt or damages, shall be paid in money, and shall be adjusted by the foregoing rules, every thousand pounds weight					

	fees				
	pounds	shillings	pence	of current money, or, if the debtor chuse it	pounds of tobacco
of tobacco being estimated at ten pounds of money.					
For returning, and doing execution by virtue of, a writ of capias ad satisfaciendum, the same proportion of the debt, or damages, and costs, appearing by the writ to be due, as in the preceeding paragraph; unless the defendant shall be discharged by taking the oath of an insolvent debtor, or because no security is given for the prison fees; in the former of which cases the sheriff shall be intitled to the proportion aforesaid of what the debtor's effects, contained in the schedule delivered in by him, shall amount to when sold or recovered; and in the other case to fees for the commitment and releasement of the prisoner, and the allowance for his maintenance in jail only.					
For returning, and doing execution of, a writ of habere facias seisinam, or habere facias possessionem, or to make partition, and assign the purparties.					
For putting one in the stocks.					
in the pillory.					
Whipping one.					
For every mile he shall necessarily travel in prosecution of any business he is by law directed to transact out of his county.					
For summoning and attending the Justices of his county for examination of one charged with treason or felony.					

	fees				
	pounds	shillings	pence	of current money, or, if the debtor chuse it	pounds of tobacco
For summoning a jury to try such prisoner.					
For every day he shall attend the General Court on such trial.					
For executing one condemned to die.					
CORONER.					
For an inquisition taken on view of the body of a dead person, to be paid out of the estate of the deceased, if any, or else by the county.					
For any other service the same fees as the sheriff is intitled to for the like.					
JAILOR.					
CONSTABLE.					
For serving a warrant.					
summoning a witness.					
a Coroner's inquest.					
putting one in the stocks.					
serving an execution.					
For every mile he shall necessarily travel in removing one and returning, besides ferriages.					
COUNCELLOR, or ATTORNEY AT LAW, or PROCTOR.					
For prosecuting or defending a suit in the High Court of Chancery, or in the General Court when the title or boundaries of land shall be in question, or in the Court of Admiralty.					
any other suit in the General Court.					
For an opinion given by one practising in the High Court of Chancery or General Court.					
For prosecuting and defending a					

fees	pounds	shillings	pence	of current money, or, if the debtor chuse it	pounds of tobacco
petition for a demand of less value than five pounds.					
any other suit in the court of the county, city or borough; or for advice by one practising in such court one half so much as one practising in the High Court of Chancery or General Court is hereby intitled to in the like case.					
SURVEYOR OF LAND.					
For the survey of a tract of land, and a certificate of the survey, with a plot protracted by the true meridian, and determining the variation thereof, towards the east or west, from the magnetical meridian, delineating the waters and mentioning the marked trees, and other notable objects which occur in, coincide with, or are adjacent to, every line, with their distances from one another, and from such line, and casting up the content of the area, if such content be less than four hundred acres, not being a lot in a town, or laid off for a mill.					
if the content be more than four hundred acres, besides that fee, for every hundred acres of such surplus.					
For surveying a lot in town.					
an acre of land laid off for a mill.					
For every pole of a single line, or of several lines, not inclosing a space, or any part of such line or lines, in the surveying whereof his progress shall be hindered by another.					

	fees				
	pounds	shillings	pence	of current money, or, if the debtor chuse it	pounds of tobacco
For joining together the plots of several parcels of land, which are contiguous and making one plot of the whole.					
NAVAL-OFFICER.					
For entering a vessel of fifty tons burthen or under.		10			
above fifty and under one hundred tons.		15			
of one hundred tons or more.	1	10			
taking a bond.		2	6		
giving a permit to break bulk and to load.		2	6		
a bill of health.		5			
a bill of stores, to be granted during an embargo on provisions, and not otherwise.		2	6		
a certificate for imported goods removed out of one district to another after they shall have been landed, to be paid to the officer from whose district the goods shall be carried.		2	6		
For authenticating a register.					
For attesting a transfer.					
performing the duty of a ballast master where there is no such officer the same that he would have been intitled to.					
BALLAST MASTER.					
For every day he shall attend the delivery of ballast, to be paid before a certificate thereof be given.					

Report, p. 26-9. MS (ViU); clerk's copy.

Bill presented by Madison on 31 Oct. 1785, passed its second reading, and was committed to a committee of the whole (JHD, Oct. 1785, 1828 edn., p. 12-15). No further action was taken on Bill proposed by Committee of Revisors. On 22 Nov. Madison presented a new bill to revive the Act of 1745 for the better regulating and collecting of certain officers' fees. This new bill was amended and passed by the House 16 Jan. 1786, being approved by the Senate the next day (JHD, Oct. 1785, 1828 edn., p. 49, 50, 136, 141, 143, 145, 148). The Act of

1745 is in Hening, v, 326-44, and the reviving Act of 1785 in Hening, XII, 91-2. The latter neither fixed the amounts of fees nor made any provision concerning officers' salaries; its methods for collecting fees by the county sheriffs were similar to those provided in Bill No. 33 but not so explicit (see also the Act of 1777 and its amending Act of 1778, Hening, IX, 368-9, 528-30).

34. A Bill Declaring Bills of Credit to Be Equal to Gold and Silver Coin of the Same Denominations

Be it enacted by the General Assembly, that the bills of credit emitted by the American Congress, so long as they continue current by the same authority, and the like bills emitted by act of General Assembly, may be paid in discharge of all demands due in money, every four pence, contained in the denominations of the said bills, being computed equal to three pence of sterling money, or of the lawful money of England, and to four pence of the lawful money of this commonwealth: And a tender of any sum in such bills, or in bills of credit emitted or to be emitted by acts of General Assembly, to any creditor, or to the factor or agent of a creditor residing in foreign parts, with whom the contract, by which the debt or demand arose, was made, or to any other person authorised to receive the same, shall be as effectual as a tender of the like sum in gold or silver coin of the legal standard, according to the proportions aforesaid, or as a tender to the creditor himself.

Report, p. 29. MS (ViU); clerk's copy.

In May 1777 the General Assembly passed an Act making bills of credit issued by Congress or by the state legal tender, stipulated penalties for refusal to accept such at an equal rate with gold or silver, provided that a tender of payment and refusal to accept in bills of credit would amount to an extinguishment of interest, and established the rate of exchange for debts payable in sterling at 33⅓% (Hening, IX, 297-8). In May 1779 that part of the Act making it a penal offense to ask more for an article in paper money than in gold or silver was repealed (same, X, p. 125). The purpose of Bill No. 34 in the Report of the Committee of Revisors, in briefer form, is substantially to reenact the Act of May 1777. The Bill was presented by Madison 31 Oct. 1785, but apparently no further action was taken on it (JHD, Oct. 1785, 1828 edn., p. 12-15). Another bill touching upon exchange is of particular interest in view of the fact that the general sequestration Act of 1777 provided that debts due British subjects from citizens of Virginia could be paid into the loan office; i.e., that sterling debts could be paid in Virginia bills of credit (Hening, IX, 377-80; see above under date of 13 Jan. 1778). This was a bill for settling the rate of exchange and mode of judgments on foreign debts; TJ was a member of the committee appointed 19 May 1779 to prepare it. It was brought in 15 June and passed its second reading, but was ordered to be postponed to the next session (JHD, May 1779, 1827 edn., p. 14, 49, 50). The MS (Vi) is entirely in George Mason's hand and is as follows:

"Whereas many Merchants in Great Britain and other parts beyond the Seas, having Effects or Property within this Commonwealth, unjustly indebted to the Citizens of this and other of the united American States, in considerable Sums of Sterling Money, and in other Money of the Denomination of forreign Countrys, and have since the Year one thousand seven hundred and seventy five, protested, or may hereafter protest their Bills for the same, with Design to discharge such Debts here, at the nominal Rate of Current Money, in it's depreciated Value; and it is necessary that some just and certain Mode of discharging such Debts shou'd be established, to prevent the Disputes and Difficulties, which may otherwise arise: Be it therefore enacted by the General Assembly, that in any Suit which shall be commenced and depending, in any Court of Record within this Commonwealth, for the Recovery of Money due upon any Bill of Exchange, which hath been, or shall be drawn and protested, from and after the first Day of January in the Year one thousand seven hundred and seventy six, or for any Debt due from a Merchant or Subject of Great Britain, or any other forreign Country to any Citizen of this or any other of the United States, wherein the Plaintiff or Plaintiffs shall recover, such Court shall have Power, and are hereby directed, to render Judgment for so much Sterling Money, or other Money of the Denomination of any forreign Country (as the Case may be) as shall appear to be justly due, and by Rule, to be entered at the foot of their Judgment, in such Suit, to order such Judgment to be discharged, or levyed in Current Money, at such Difference of Exchange as they shall think just, having Regard therein to the true Value or Rate (at the time of such Judgment) of good Bills of Exchange drawn on the Country, or Place, where such Debt became due; any Law, Usage, or Custom, to the contrary thereof, in anywise, notwithstanding."

35. A Bill to Prevent the Circulation of Private Bank Notes

Be it enacted by the General Assembly, that it shall not be lawful for any person to offer in payment a[1] bank bill, or note for money, payable to bearer, and whosoever shall offend herein shall not only forfeit, to the informer, ten times the value of the sum mentioned in such bill or note, but may be apprehended by warrant of a Justice, and, upon due proof of the fact made to him, or[2] upon his own acknowledgement[3] thereof, be bound to the good behavior, and[4] if he afterwards offend in the like manner it shall be deemed a breach of the condition of the recognisance.[5]

Report, p. 29. MS (ViU); clerk's copy. Text of Act as adopted is in Hening, XII, 166-7. This Bill was evidently drawn by Wythe (see Document IV, 3, note 4, below).

Bill was presented by Madison 31 Oct. 1785, amended and passed by the House 29 Nov., and approved by the Senate 3 Dec. (JHD, Oct. 1785, 1828 edn., p. 12-15, 51, 62, 70, 132). Text of Act as adopted agrees with Bill as proposed save as noted below. See the 1777 Act to prevent the circulation of private bank notes (Hening, IX, 431-2).

1 The Act adds the word "private" at this point.

2 The Act substitutes "and" for "or."

3 Both MS and *Report* read, erroneously, "knowledge" for "acknowledgement."

4 The Act substitutes "or" for "and."

5 The Act has a final clause putting it into effect 1 Jan. 1787.

36. A Bill for Withholding British Property, to Indemnify Citizens Who May Suffer by Confiscation and to Prevent Succour to the Enemy Thereby

For securing to the citizens of this commonwealth an indemnification out of the property of British subjects here, in case the sovereign of the latter should confiscate the property of the former in his dominions, as well as to prevent that accession of strength which the enemy might derive by withdrawing their property from hence: Be it enacted by the General Assembly, that the lands, slaves, stocks, implements of husbandry, and other estate, except what is otherwise herein after provided for, within this commonwealth, of British subjects, shall be sequestered, and remain in possession of the commissioners heretofore for that purpose appointed, or be put into the possession of such as shall be from time to time, appointed, by the Governor, with advice of the Council of State. The said commissioners shall have power, and are required, to place and keep the said estates under the management and direction of proper agents, stewards, or overseers, and dispose of the produce thereof, and to demand, receive, and, by actions in the names of the proprietors, recover monies and other things which are and shall become due to them, and, after defraying the expences incurred in the management of the said estates, and applying so much of the profits thereof, as the Governor, with the advice aforesaid, shall judge reasonable, and direct to be allowed, towards maintaining the wives and children, if any there be residing here, of the proprietors, pay the balances of such profits and receipts into the loan-office of this commonwealth, taking certificates in the proprietors names, and delivering the certificates, and annually rendering accounts of their respective transactions to the Governor, who, with the advice aforesaid, may cause the said accounts to be adjusted, and in the names of the proprietors, recover any arrears from the commissioners, and pay the same into the said loan-office.

A citizen of the commonwealth, who is debtor to a British subject, may lodge the money due, or any part thereof, in the said loan-office, accounting sixteen pence of the lawful money of the commonwealth, or two-ninths of a dollar in bills of credit there current, equal to twelve pence of any such debt payable in the lawful money of England, taking a certificate payable to the creditor, with an endorsement thereon of the debtor's name, signed by the commissioner of the office, and delivering the same to the Governor, whose receipt shall discharge the debt, wholly or partly as the case may be. A state of all which matters shall be laid before the General Assembly, whenever they shall require it. If a citizen of the commonwealth, being a coparcener, jointenant, or tenant in common, with a British subject, bring a writ de partitione facienda in the General Court, or a suit for a partition by bill in equity, if that be the proper remedy in the High Court of Chancery, service of the process, against the tenant or defendant, upon the commissioner, for his estate, personally, shall be seemed equivalent to service upon the party himself, and be as effectual to all purposes, save that if the partition thereupon made be without title, or unequal, which the commissioner shall endeavor to prevent, entering into the defence, or answering, and contesting the matter, for the tenant or defendant, and at his costs, the tenant or defendant shall not be concluded by the partition, unless the purparty assigned or allotted to the demandant or plaintiff shall be afterwards sold to a purchaser for valuable consideration, bona fide paid or agreed to be paid, in which case the tenant or defendant shall have redress against the demandant or plaintiff, or his representatives, when the General Assembly shall hereafter allow suit to be brought for that purpose.

Suits between British subjects only, demandants or plaintiffs, and citizens of the commonwealth, tenants or defendants, which have not been, or shall not be, discontinued by acts of the parties, or abated by death, shall stand continued in the same condition as they were in on the twelfth day of April, in the year of our Lord one thousand seven hundred and seventy four; and in suits between subjects and citizens, joint demandants or plaintiffs, and citizens, tenants or defendants, execution, as to the parts recovered on behalf of the subjects, shall be suspended, until further provision be made in the cases of both those classes: And in suits between such citizens only, demandants or plaintiffs, and subjects only, or citizens and subjects jointly, tenants or defendants, the benefit of new trials or rehearings, with future Legislative permission and direction, if it be then judged reasonable, shall be saved to the latter.

Report, p. 29-30. MS (ViU); clerk's copy.

This Bill was not presented by Madison in 1785, for obvious reasons. The Bill restated, in different form, most of the terms of the Bill for Sequestering British Property, &c. (see above, under date of 13 Jan. 1778). At the Oct. 1784 session in compliance with Article VI of the Treaty of Paris, an Act was passed providing that there should be no confiscations in future, but expressly safeguarding suits commenced prior to the ratification of the Treaty (Hening, XI, 446). In view of this, the terms of Bill No. 36 were clearly obsolete in 1785.

37. A Bill to Prevent Losses by Pirates, Enemies, and Others on the High Seas

Be it enacted by the General Assembly, that when any ship[1] of this commonwealth shall have been defended against pirates or enemies and brought to her port of delivery, and in making such defence any of the officers or seamen shall have been killed or wounded, the Judges of the Admiralty, on the petition of the master or seamen; shall call unto them four or more good and substantial merchants, and by advice with them, shall levy on the respective adventurers and owners of the ship and goods, by process out of the said court, such sums of money as themselves and the said merchants, by plurality of voices, shall judge reasonable, not exceeding two pounds per cent. of the freight, ship, and goods, according to the first cost of the goods, and shall distribute the same among the captain, master, officers and seamen of the ship, and the widows and children of the slain, proportioning the same, according to their best judgment, and having special regard to the said widows and children and to such as shall have been wounded. And if the commander, master, or other officer, or any seaman or mariner, in any vessel, carrying guns and arms, shall not, when attacked by any pirate, or enemy, fight and endeavor to defend themselves and their vessel, or shall utter any words to discourage the other mariners from defending the same, and by reason thereof the said vessel shall fall into the hands of such pirate, or enemy, such offender shall forfeit all wages due to him, to the owner and shall suffer imprisonment, at the discretion of a jury, if in their opinion such vessel might have been saved by a defence.

If any combination shall be set on foot for running away with or destroying any vessel, or the goods and merchandizes therein laden, the captain, commander or master, on due proof thereof, shall give a reward of fifty dollars, if the vessel be of one hundred tons or under, and seventy five dollars if of greater burthen, to such person as shall first make discovery thereof: Payment to be made at the port where the wages of the seamen ought next to be paid, and to be reimbursed as in other cases of salvage.[2]

Report, p. 30. Text of Act as adopted is in Hening, XII, 167-8.

Bill was presented by Madison 31 Oct. 1785, passed by House on 28 Nov., amended by Senate 30 Nov., and Senate's amendment agreed to by House 1 Dec. (JHD, Oct. 1785, 1828 edn., p. 12-15, 51, 59, 67, 68, 132). Text of Act as adopted agrees with Bill as proposed except as indicated below. See the Act of 1699 concerning losses by pirates (Hening, III, 176-9, and note).

[1] Here and elsewhere in the Act the words "or other vessel" are added.

[2] The Act includes a final clause putting it into effect 1 Jan. 1787.

38. A Bill for Preservation of Vessels Wrecked, or in Distress, and of Their Crews and Cargoes

Be it enacted by the General Assembly, that a person descrying a vessel wrecked, or in peril, or goods belonging to her in danger of being lost, shall immediately give notice thereof, to some neighbouring Justice of the Peace, or the Naval-Officer of the next port: And a Justice of the Peace descrying, or being informed of such vessel or goods, shall forthwith call together, to assist in the preservation thereof, so many men as he shall think necessary, who shall, without delay, attend accordingly: And for the same purpose the master or chief officer, of every vessel, near the other, having the like knowledge, or information that the latter is in distress, shall send his boats and hands, so many as can be spared. The persons so assembled shall obey the orders of the master or chief officer of the vessel in distress, or, if he be not present, of the Justice of the Peace, or, in his absence of the Naval-Officer. To all, who shall have assisted on such occasion, reasonable satisfaction shall be made, the quantum whereof, as well as the proportions among the claimants if the parties disagree, shall be adjusted by the Court of Admiralty. And in the meantime the goods preserved, or so much of them as may be sufficient, shall remain in the hands of the Justice of the Peace, or Naval-Officer, who shall sign an account of them, and deliver it, with a receipt, to the master or chief officer of the vessel in distress, or, if he be not there to some other Justice of the Peace. Whoever shall refuse, or wilfully neglect, to perform the duty, by this act enjoined, shall be amerced, and moreover may be compelled, in an action on the case, to be brought against him by any suffering party, to make reparation for such damage sustained as it shall be judged might have been prevented by performance. If no person authorised to take charge of the things saved from the wreck be present, the Justice of the Peace, or Naval-Officer, having provided for the security thereof, shall, so soon as may be, report the matter to the Court of Admiralty, who shall thereupon give such directions, as they think proper, for defraying the salvage, selling the perishable goods, and the safekeeping of the others, to be restored with the money raised by such sale, to him, who within one year and a day, shall claim and prove his property before the said court, and if within that time no such claimant appear, the things so preserved, by order of the said court, shall be sold to the highest bidders, and the proceeds, after deducting incidental expences, together with the proceeds of the perishable goods put into the public treasury, for the use of the commonwealth, to be, nevertheless, restored to him who shall at any time afterwards prove his property before the said court and produce their allowance of his claim.

Every citizen of this commonwealth commanding and navigating a vessel shall assist any other vessel met with, or descried by him at sea, or elsewhere, in distress, and relieve the crew thereof, if he be desired, so far as it can be done consistently with the safety of his own vessel and crew: and if he refuse, or wilfully neglect, to give such assistance and relief, shall be subject to the like action, as other persons, by virtue of this act, are subject to for refusal or neglect; and if any of the distressed crew perish through such inhumanity shall be likewise amerced.

Report, p. 30. MS (ViU); clerk's copy.

Bill presented by Madison 31 Oct. 1785, read twice, and committed to a committee of the whole, but no further action was taken on it (JHD, Oct. 1785, 1828 edn., p. 12-15). This was due, obviously, to the fact that in May 1782 the General Assembly had passed a much more comprehensive Act concerning wrecks (Hening, XI, 51-4). By this Act the governor was empowered to appoint two commissioners of wrecks in each of the counties bordering on the ocean or on the bay; their jurisdiction and the other terms of this Act extended not only to wrecks but also to vessels stranded or in danger—in short, the Act of 1782 provided, in very rudimentary form, for a sort of coast guard service, whereas the Bill proposed by the Committee of Revisors was concerned with safeguarding property in vessels or cargoes after such vessels had been wrecked.

39. A Bill concerning Estrays

Be it enacted by the General Assembly, that it shall be lawful for any person, by himself, or his agent, to take up any estray on his own land; and having taken it, he, or his agent, shall forthwith give information thereof to some Justice of the Peace, for the said county, who shall thereupon issue his warrant to three disinterested freeholders, of the neighbourhood, commanding them, having been first duly sworn, to view and appraise such estray and certify the valuation under their hands; together with a particular description of the kind, marks, brand, stature, color, and age; which certificate shall, by the Justice, be transmitted to the clerk of the county court, within twenty days, and by such clerk entered in a book to be kept for that purpose; for which he may demand and take ten pounds of tobacco to be paid down by the taker-up.

The clerk shall moreover cause a copy of every such certificate to be publicly affixed at the door of his court-house on two several court days next after he receive the same, for which, and a certificate thereof, he shall receive the like fee as for entering the same in the book.

If the valuation shall be under twenty shillings, and no owner shall appear until notice shall have been twice published as aforesaid, the property shall then be vested in the owner of the land on which such estray was taken; and if the valuation shall exceed twenty shillings, such owner shall, within one month after the appraisement, send to the public printer a copy of the certificate, to be advertised three times in the Virginia Gazette with notice of the place where such estray is, for which the printer may demand four shillings for each estray; and if no owner appears to claim such estray within a year and a day after the publication, the property shall, from thenceforth, be vested in the owner of the lands whereon it was taken. But the former owner, in either case, may, at any time within five years afterwards, upon proving his property, demand and recover the valuation money, deducting therefrom the clerk and printer's fees, and five shillings for every horse or head of neat cattle, and one shilling for each other beast.

If any person shall take up a boat or other vessel adrift, he shall in like manner make application to a Justice of one of the adjacent counties, for his warrant to have the same valued and described by her kind, burthen and built, and shall proceed in all other respects, and have the same benefit as before directed in the case of estrays.[1]

Report, p. 31. MS (ViU); clerk's copy. Text of Act as adopted is in Hening, XII, 168-70.

Bill was presented by Madison 31 Oct. 1785, passed by the House on 28 Nov., and approved by the Senate 12 Dec. with an amendment which was accepted the same day by the House (JHD, Oct. 1785, 1828 edn., p. 12-15, 51, 59, 88, 133). Text of Act as adopted agrees with Bill as proposed save as noted below. See the 1769 Act concerning estrays (Hening, VIII, 354).

[1] The Act has, in addition to a clause putting it into effect 1 Jan. 1787, the following proviso: "*Provided always*, That if after notice published as aforesaid, any estray shall happen to die, or by any casualty get out of the possession of the person who took the same up, without his or her default, such taker up shall not be answerable for the same, or for the valuation thereof; nor shall any taker up be answerable for any boat or other vessel lost as aforesaid."

40. A Bill for Restitution of Stolen Goods

Be it enacted by the General Assembly, that if any felon do rob or take away any money, or goods, or chattels, from any of the citizens of this commonwealth,[1] from their person or otherwise, within this commonwealth and thereof the said felon be indicted, and after arraigned of the same felony, and found guilty thereof, or otherwise attainted by reason of evidence given by the party so robbed, or owner of the said money, goods, or chattels, or by any other by their procurement, that then the party so robbed, or owner, shall be restored to his said money, goods and chattels: And that the Justices before whom any such felon shall be found guilty, or otherwise attainted by reason of evidence given by the party so robbed, or owner, or by any other by their procurement have power by this present act, to award, from time to time, writs of restitution for the said money, goods and chattels.[2]

Report, p. 31. Text of Act as adopted is in Hening, XII, 170.

Bill presented by Madison 31 Oct. 1785, passed by House 29 Nov., amended by Senate 5 Dec., and amendments approved by House same day (JHD, Oct. 1785, 1828 edn., p. 12-15, 51, 62, 72, 132). Act as adopted agrees with Bill as proposed save as indicated below.

[1] The Act adds: "or from any person travelling through or making a temporary stay within the same."

[2] The Act includes a final clause putting it into effect 1 Jan. 1787.

41. A Bill for Preventing Infection of the Horned Cattle

Be it enacted by the General Assembly, that the driving of cattle into, or through, the commonwealth, or any part thereof, if it be not to remove them from one plantation to another of the same owner, or to be used at his house, shall be deemed a nuisance, unless the driver shall produce to any freeholder of a county, wherein the drove is passing, who shall require it, a bill of health, signed by some Justice of the commonwealth, containing the number of the drove, with descriptions of the cattle by their sexes, flesh marks and ear marks, or brands, and certifying them to be free from distemper; or, notwithstanding he may produce such bill of health, unless he shall forthwith obtain another, at the like requisition, if any such freeholder make affidavit, before a Justice, that he hath cause to suspect some of the cattle to be distempered. Such bill of health shall not be given, in either case, before two disinterested freeholders appointed by warrant of a Justice, shall have viewed the cattle and reported them to be free from distemper. A freeholder refusing to obey such warrant shall be amerced.[1] If the cattle appear, by the report, to be distempered, the owner may impound them; and if he refuse to do so, or if he suffer them to escape from the pound before a Justice shall have certified that they may be removed without annoying others, the same Justice, or some other, to whom information shall be given of the fact, shall, by his order, cause them to be slaughtered; and their carcases, with the hides on, but so cut or mangled that none may be tempted to take them up and flay them, to be buried four feet deep. Those who shall be employed in executing such order shall receive five shillings for every head so buried, to be paid by the county wherein it shall happen; and every one appointed by the order who shall refuse or neglect to execute it, shall be amerced.[2] Every one shall so restrain his distempered cattle, or such as are under his care, as that they may not go at large off the land to which they belong; and when they die shall bury them with their hides in manner aforesaid, and knowingly offending in either of those instances shall be amerced.[3]

Report, p. 31. MS (ViU); clerk's copy. Text of the Act as adopted is in Hening, XII, 171-2.

Bill presented by Madison 31 Oct. 1785, passed by House 30 Nov., amended by Senate 7 Dec., and amendment accepted by House the next day (JHD, Oct. 1785, 1828 edn., p. 12-15, 51, 65, 75, 76, 133). Act as adopted agrees with Bill as proposed save for differences indicated below. See Act of 1766 for preserving the breed of cattle (Hening, VIII, 245-50).

1 The Act adds: "by the justice granting such warrant, in any sum not exceeding twenty five shillings."

2 The Act adds: "in the sum of five shillings for every head so ordered to be buried."

3 The Act adds: "in the sum of twenty shillings for every head they shall neglect so to bury." The Act has an additional clause putting it into effect 1 Jan. 1787.

42. A Bill for Improving the Breed of Horses

Be it enacted by the General Assembly, that no person shall suffer a stoned horse, of the age of two years, whereof he is owner, or hath the keeping, to run at large, out of the inclosed ground of the owner or keeper; and whosoever shall wilfully or negligently do so, after having been admonished to confine such horse, shall forfeit and pay five pounds, to him who will sue for it, and double that sum for any such transgression after one conviction; and if, after a second conviction, the same horse be found so running at large, it shall be lawful for the person who will take him up to retain him to his own use.

Report, p. 31. MS (ViU); clerk's copy. Text of Act as adopted is in Hening, XII, 172.

Bill presented by Madison 31 Oct. 1785, passed by House 29 Nov., and approved by Senate 3 Dec. (JHD, Oct. 1785, 1828 edn., p. 12-15, 51, 62, 70, 132). Act as adopted agrees with Bill as proposed save in the addition of a clause putting it into effect 1 Jan. 1787. This Bill is a revision of the 1748 Act to restrain the keeping too great a number of horses and mares, and for amending the breed (Hening, VI, 118-20). The preamble of the Act of 1748 stated that "the keeping too many horses or mares, by persons who have no freehold . . . and suffer the same to run at large upon the lands of other persons, is not only prejudicial to the breed of horses, but also to the stocks of cattle, and sheep, of the freeholders of this colony."

43. A Bill for Preservation of Deer

Be it enacted by the General Assembly, that it shall not be lawful for any person to kill, hunt, or course any wild deer whatever, not being more than twelve months old, or in any year called bissextile or leap year; or to kill, hunt or course in any other year, a wild buck, after the first day of December, and before the first day of August, or a wild doe, between the first day of January, and the first day of October following, unless such deer, at the time, be found within the inclosed land of such person, or be wanted for food, on the westside of the Alleghany ridge of mountains. Whosoever shall offend against this act, shall forfeit and pay, for every deer by him unlawfully killed, twenty shillings, one half thereof to the use of the commonwealth, and the other half to the informer; and moreover, shall be bound to their good behaviour; and, if, within twelve months after the date of the recognizance he shall bear a gun out of his inclosed ground, unless whilst performing military duty, it shall be deemed a breach of the recognizance, and be good cause to bind him a new, and every such bearing of a gun shall be a breach of the new recognizance and cause to bind him again.

Report, p. 32. MS (ViU); clerk's copy.

Bill was presented by Madison on 31 Oct. 1785, read twice, and committed to whole House, but no further action was taken on it (JHD, Oct. 1785, 1828 edn., p. 12-15). See the Act of 1738 on this subject and its amending Act of 1772 (Hening, V, 60-3; VIII, 591-4). These early conservation measures were made necessary, as stated in the preamble to the amending Act of 1772, by reason of "many idle people making a practice, in severe frozen weather, and deep snows, to destroy deer, in great numbers, with dogs, so that the whole breed is likely to be destroyed in the inhabited parts of the colony." This Act forbade the killing of any deer from 1772 to 1 Aug. 1776 and provided severe penalties for violations, including fines and whippings.

44. A Bill for Preventing Frauds by the Dealers in Flour, Beef, Pork, Tar, Pitch and Turpentine

Be it enacted by the General Assembly, that flour, beef, pork, tar, pitch and turpentine, before they be shipped for exportation, or sold, or bartered, shall be inspected, and the vessels containing them shall be stamped, in the manner herein after directed, by one of the persons whom the county courts shall appoint, residing in their respective counties, and not being owners of merchant mills, or employed in them, nor dealing in any of the commodities subject to their examination; which appointment shall be made, with open doors, in August or September, annually, or at such other time as it may be necessarily required. The inspector, having in the court of his county given assurance of his fidelity to the commonwealth, and taken an oath to execute his office faithfully and impartially, shall attend at such time and place as the owner of the commodity shall appoint; such place, if the commodity be brought from any other state, being a public landing; and the inspector, if he judge the commodity inspected to be of such quality, and it be packed, or filled, preserved, and secured, in such manner as are herein after described, shall stamp on the vessel containing it the letter V, the initial letters of his county's name, and his own christian name, and his Sur-name at length, and the letter F, if it be fine flour, or the letters S F, if superfine, and L, if it be large, or S, if it be small pork; and if it be tar, pitch, or turpentine, shall mark it so as to distinguish the species, and moreover if it be turpentine, shall mark it so as to distinguish whether it be dipped or scraped, or a mixture of both, and shall also mark on every vessel the nett weight or gauge, and give a certificate thereof accordingly to the owner; and may demand for every vessel, if it contain flour, three halfpence, if beef, or pork, six pence, and if tar, pitch, or turpentine, two pence. Whosoever shall deal in any of those commodities, after he shall have been appointed inspector thereof, during the time he shall continue in office, otherwise than in selling the immediate production of his estate, which shall be examined by another inspector, if necessary, or in buying for the consumption of his own family, or for the use of such estate; and every inspector guilty of any breach of duty, either by refusing or wilfully neglecting to perform his office, or by stamping any vessel contrary to the directions of this act, shall be amerced. A person making wheat flour for exportation shall take an oath, which a Justice shall administer and certify, that such flour is clean, pure, or not a mixture of different species, and merchantable, as the deponent believes; and such certificate being produced to the inspector, the flour, if it appear to him, after examination, to deserve that character, shall, in his presence, be packed; those parcels of it which are of different degrees of fineness, separately, in casks made of seasoned timber, clear of sap, and bound with good hoops securely nailed or pinned. Every cask in which beef or pork shall be packed for exportation, or sale, shall be made of seasoned white oak staves and heading clear of sap, and five eighths of an inch thick, and bound with hoops securely nailed or pegged, and shall be light and contain two hundred and twenty pounds weight, at least, of clean, sound, fat meat, well pickled, with salt strewed between the layers; and not more than two heads shall be in one and the same cask of pork. And every cask of tar, pitch, or turpentine, shall be made of staves of equal lengths, and not less than three fourths of an inch thick, and heading not less than three fourths of an inch, nor more than one inch and an half thick, and both clear of sap; shall be well bound with good hoops two thirds of its length; shall have the bulge and each head circular; and shall contain thirty two gallons and an half, wine measure, at least. Whosoever shall alter or counterfeit the stamp or certificate of an inspector shall be amerced, and imprisoned: And whosoever shall sell or barter flour, beef, pork, tar, pitch, or turpentine, not stamped as aforesaid shall be amerced. The cooper setting up, or other person selling, casks for the reception of the commodities before enumerated, shall make or dispose of such only as are of the materials and capacities respectively required by this act, with his name branded thereon, and, if he do otherwise, he shall forfeit and pay to the informer two shillings and six pence for every cask defective in any such requisites or unbranded. The owner of a merchant mill or bake-house, with a branding instrument, a description of which shall be recorded in the court of his county, shall impress on every cask of bread or flour, there manufactored for sale or exportation, before it be removed from thence, either the initial letter of his Christian name, and his Sur-name at length, or the name of the mill; he shall also mark, on such cask, the tare thereof, and when he shall deliver bread or flour, he shall give a manifest or invoice thereof: And if he neglect or refuse to perform what is hereby enjoined, he shall forfeit and pay to the informer for every cask so delivered, if it be unbranded, or untared, one shilling; or if false tared fifty shillings; and for refusing to give the manifest or invoice forty shillings. Weights and measures at all merchant mills and bake-houses shall be examined once in every year, by persons to be appointed by the county court, and adjusted by the legal standard; and the owners who shall deal by weights and measures not so examined and adjusted shall be amerced. The driver of a carriage, or skipper of a vessel, conveying bread or flour, to be shipped for exportation, shall cover it so that it receive no damage from the weather, and if he neglect to provide and make use of sufficient covering for the purpose, he shall forfeit, one shilling, to the informer, for every cask of bread or flour so conveyed. The seller or exporter of any of the commodities before enumerated shall take an oath, to be administered and certified by a Justice at the time of delivering them for exportation, that they are the same which are mentioned in the certificates of the inspectors corresponding with them; and that the deponent doth not know nor believe them to have been embezzled, or altered, or otherwise diminished than by unavoidable shrinkage; and no vessel having such commodities on board shall be cleared out before the certificate of such oath, as well as the inspector's certificates shall be produced to the Naval-Officer. A Justice shall grant a warrant to any person requiring it, impowering the sheriff, in the day time, to search for any of the said commodities suspected to be shipped for exportation, uninspected or unstamped, affidavit having been first made that there is a good cause for such suspicion; and every cask or other vessel containing any such commodity, so shipped contrary to law, whether discovered by the search, or otherwise proved to be so, may be seized, and shall be forfeited to the use of the informer.

Report, p. 32-3. MS (ViU); clerk's copy.

Bill presented by Madison 31 Oct. 1785, read twice, and committed to a committee of the whole, but no further action was taken (JHD, Oct. 1785, 1828 edn., p. 12-15). See the 1776 Act for the inspection of pork, beef, flour, tar, pitch, &c. (Hening, IX, 250-7).

45. A Bill for Licensing and Regulating Taverns

Be it enacted by the General Assembly, that it shall not be lawful for any one to keep a tavern, before they shall have obtained a license for that purpose, from the court of the county in which the tavern is, or, if it be in Williamsburg, from the court of that city;[1] and if any one, without such authority, open a tavern, or sell, by retail, wine, beer, cyder, or rum, brandy, or other spiritous liquor, or a mixture thereof, to be drunk in the place where it shall be sold,[2] such offence shall be deemed a breach of good behaviour:[3] Which license shall be granted only to such as the court shall think able to provide for the accommodation of travellers, and in such places as are most convenient for them, and shall be in force one year, and from the end thereof until the next session. If guests, or others, play at any game, contrary to law, in a tavern, and the keeper thereof shall not endeavor to hinder them, and if they persist, to give information of the offence, within one month thereafter, to the court, or two Justices of the Peace, his license shall be revoked by the court, unless, being summoned to shew cause to the contrary, he appear, and prove such facts as induce them to believe, not only he did not know of, but moreover that he had no reason to suspect such playing. The prices to be paid for diet, liquors, lodging, provender, stablage, and pasture, at taverns, shall be rated, once a year, by the court, of which rates a copy, within one month afterwards, as they shall be set, or from time to time, altered, attested by the clerk of the peace,[4] shall be set up by every keeper of a tavern, exposed in some public room thereof, not more than six feet above the floor; and so long as he neglect this, after the month, he shall have no right to demand any price for a rated article. Neither shall the keeper of a tavern recover more than [5] for liquors sold, within the space of a year, to one person, residing less than twenty miles from such tavern, and drunk, or sold to be drunk, in the place where it is kept; and a written contract, or bond, or other specialty, for payment, delivery, or security, of money, or other thing, or for performance of any work or service, whereof the whole or any part shall have become due for liquors so sold, shall be void.[6]

Report, p. 33. MS (ViU); clerk's copy. Text of Act as adopted is in Hening, XII, 173-4.

Bill presented by Madison 31 Oct. 1785, passed by House 30 Nov., amended by Senate 8 Dec. House amended one of Senate amendments and refused to accept others; Senate did not insist upon these (JHD, Oct. 1785, 1828 edn., p. 12-15, 51, 65, 76, 78). Text of Act as adopted agrees with Bill as proposed save for the differences noted below. See Act of 1748 for regulating ordinaries (Hening, VI, 71-6).

1 Instead of the words "from the court of the county . . . of that city," the phrase "from the court authorized to grant the same" is employed in the Act.

2 The Act, following more closely the Act of 1748 for regulating ordinaries, adds at this point: "or in any booth, arbour, or stall" (see Hening, VI, 73).

3 The Act adds the following: "and he or she so offending, shall moreover forfeit and pay the sum of ten pounds current money, to be applied towards lessening the county levy."

4 The older phrase "clerk of the peace" is replaced in the Act by "clerk of the court."

5 The Act reads: "twenty-five shillings."

6 The Act includes an additional clause putting it into effect 1 Jan. 1787.

46. A Bill concerning Public Roads

Be it enacted by the General Assembly, that where any person or persons shall make application, to any county court, to have a new road opened, or a former one altered, within their county, for the convenience of travelling to their county court-house, to any public ware-house, landing, ferry, mill, lead or iron works, or to the seat of government, they shall appoint three or more fit and able persons, to be sworn before a Justice of the Peace, to view the ground along which such road is proposed to be conducted, and to report to them truly and impartially, the conveniencies and inconveniencies which will result, as well to individuals, as to the public, if such way shall be opened; and where the application is to alter a former road, they shall also view the former road, and report, in like manner, the comparative conveniencies and inconveniencies thereof.

Upon the return of the said viewers, if the court shall be of opinion that the road applied for will be convenient, they shall order summonses to be issued to the proprietors and tenants of the lands through which the same is proposed to be conducted, if they be found within the county, and if not, then to their agents therein, if any they have, to shew cause why such road should not be opened; upon the return of which summons, if any proprietor or tenant, so desire, the said court shall order their clerk to issue a writ, in the nature of a writ of ad quod damnum, to be directed to the sheriff, commanding him to summon and empannel twelve able and discreet freeholders of the vicinage, no ways related to any party, to meet at some certain place, on the grounds through which the said road is proposed to be conducted, and on a certain day, to be named by the court, and inserted in the said writ, of which notice shall be given by the sheriff to the said proprietors or tenants, or their agents, as before directed, if they were not present, in court, at the time of the order made: Which freeholders taking nothing (on pain of being discharged from the inquest and immediately imprisoned by the sheriff) either of meat or drink, from any person whatever, from the time they shall come to the said place until their inquest sealed shall be charged by the said sheriff impartially, and to the best of their skill and judgment to view the lands through which the said road is proposed to be conducted, and say to what damage it will be of to the several and respective proprietors and tenants who desired such writ, taking into estimation, as well the use of the lands, to be laid open for such road, as the additional fencing which will thereby be rendered necessary; and if the said inquest cannot be completed in one day, the sheriff shall adjourn the said jurors, from day to day, until the same be completed. Which inquest, sealed by the said jurors, together with the writ, shall be returned to the court, who thereupon, as well as upon other evidence, shall proceed to consider whether all circumstances weighed, it be better that the said road shall be opened; and if they be of opinion that the same shall be opened, they shall levy on their county, at their next levy to be laid, the damages so found, and the costs of the inquest, and direct them to be paid to those respectively entitled thereto. But if they shall be of opinion the said road ought not to be opened, the costs of such inquest shall be adjudged against the party applying for the said road. But it shall not be lawful for any court to order a road to be opened through any lot of land, in any town, without the consent of the owner and tenant thereof.

The several courts shall also divide all the public roads into precincts, and as often as it shall be necessary, appoint a surveyor over every precinct, whose duty it shall be to superintend the road in his precinct, and see that the same be cleared and kept in good repair; which surveyor shall continue in office until another shall be appointed, by the said court, in his stead.

All male labouring persons of the age of sixteen years or more, except such as are masters of two or more male labouring slaves of the age of sixteen years or more, shall be appointed by the court, to work on some public road; for every person so appointed, who, when required by the surveyor placed over him, shall, without legal cause or disability, fail to attend with proper tools for clearing the road, or shall refuse to work when there, or to find some other person equally able to work in his room, the sum of [1] for every day's offence, shall be paid by himself, if he be a freeman of full age; if an infant, then by his parent, guardian, or master, and if a slave or servant, then by his overseer, if he be under one, or otherwise by his master.

The clerk of every county court, shall, within ten days after the appointment of any surveyor of a road, deliver a copy of the order to the sheriff of the county under the penalty of fifteen shillings, and the sheriff, within fifteen days after the receipt of such order, shall deliver the same to the surveyor under the penalty of fifteen shillings. And each clerk shall moreover, once in every year, fix up, in the court-house, a list of the names and precincts of all the surveyors of roads in his county, under the penalty of fifty shillings for every neglect.

Every surveyor of a road shall cause the same to be constantly kept well cleared and smoothed, and thirty feet wide at the least, and at the fork or crossing of every public road shall cause to be erected and kept in repair, from time to time, a stone, or otherwise an index on a post or tree, with plain inscriptions thereon, in large letters, directing to the most noted place to which each of the said roads shall lead, and may take stone or wood, for that purpose, from any adjoining land: And for the expence of setting up and inscribing such stones, posts or indexes, and keeping them in repair, the surveyor shall be reimbursed by the county court in their next succeeding levy; and where bridges and causeys are necessary, the surveyor shall cause them to be made twelve feet broad at the least, convenient and safe, and shall keep the same in repair; and for that purpose may cut and take, from the lands of any person adjoining, such and so much timber, earth, or stone, as may be necessary; the same being first viewed and valued by two honest house-keepers appointed and sworn, for that purpose, by a Justice of Peace, unless the owner shall freely give such timber, stone or earth for that use; but where a road leads through a city or town, the surveyor shall not take any timber, stone or earth, from any lot within the town, without the permission of the owner, but shall take the same from the lands nigh or adjacent to the said town, where it will do the least injury to the proprietor; and where the assistance of wheel carriages is necessary for making or repairing any causey, any Justice of Peace may issue his warrant, under his hand and seal, for impowering the surveyor to impress such necessary carriages, draught horses, or oxen, with their gear and driver belonging to any person, who, or their servants or slaves, are appointed to work on the road, and appointing two honest house-keepers, who, being sworn, shall value, by the day, the use of such carriages, draught horses, oxen and driver: Which valuation, with a certificate from the surveyor how many days the said things were imployed in the work, shall intitle the owner to an allowance for the same in the next county levy. And in the like manner shall the owner of timber, stone or earth taken for bridges or causeys, be intitled to the valuation thereof in the next county levy, upon a certificate from the two house-keepers who value the same. Every surveyor of a road, who fails to do his duty as aforesaid, shall forfeit fifteen shillings for every offence.

Where a bridge or causey shall be necessary, and the surveyor with his assistants cannot make or maintain the same, the court of the county are impowered and required to contract for the building and repairing such bridge or causey, and to levy the charge thereof in their county levy. And where such bridge or causey shall be necessary from one county to another, the court of each county shall join in the agreement for building and repairing the same, and the charge shall be defrayed by both counties, in proportion to the public tax or assessment paid by each. Upon every such contract or agreement, bond and security shall be given by the undertaker, payable to the Governor, and his successors, for the use of the county, or counties, as the case shall be, with condition for performing the same; and may be prosecuted, at the costs, and for the benefit of the county or counties, or any person sustaining a loss by the breach thereof, as often as it shall happen, until the whole penalty of the bond shall be paid. And all such contracts, made by county courts, or others appointed by them, shall be available and binding upon the Justices and their successors, so as to intitle the undertaker to his stipulated reward in the county levy; or to a recovery thereof, with costs, by action of debt against the Justices refusing to levy the same.

When the Justices of one county shall judge a bridge or causey over any place, between them and another county, to be necessary, they shall notify the same to the Justices of such other county, and require them to appoint three persons, to meet at the said place, on a certain day, to be named by the court requiring the same, to confer with three others, to be appointed by the said requiring court, and agree on the manner and condition of executing the same: Which six persons, or so many of them as meet, being not fewer than three, shall have power to agree on the manner and conditions of doing the said work, and to see that the same be done: And if the court so required shall fail to appoint persons to act on their behalf, or to do what on their part should be done towards executing and paying for the said work, the Justices of the court which made the requisition shall apply to the General Court for a writ of mandamus, to be directed to the Justices of the other court, commanding them to do what on their part they ought to have done and have failed to do, or to signify to them cause to the contrary thereof; upon the return of which writ, the General Court, if they shall be of opinion that the work is unnecessary, or that other sufficient cause is returned, shall quash the writ, or if they think otherwise, shall cause such further proceedings to be had as are usual in other cases of mandamus issuing from the said court: And the like method of proceeding, by way of mandamus, shall be used where the Justices of one county shall think it necessary to open a road, to their county line, for the convenience of passing to some public place in another, and the Justices of such other shall refuse to continue the road through their county.

If any person shall fell a tree into a public road, or into any stream of water whereon there shall be any public bridge, and shall not remove the same within forty eight hours, or shall kill, or fell, a tree within the distance of fifteen[2] feet from the road, or shall cut, pull up, destroy, or deface, any stone or post erected for the direction of travellers, or the indexes, or inscriptions thereon, it shall be deemed a nuisance.

Every free man, of full age, so offending, or the parent, master or owner of every child, apprentice, servant or slave, so offending, with his or her knowledge, shall forfeit and pay ten pounds for every offence. And where any fence shall be made across a public road, the owner or tenant of the land, shall pay ten shillings for every twenty four hours the same shall be continued.

The owner or occupier of every dam, over which a public road passes, shall constantly keep such dam in repair, at least twelve feet wide, at the top, through the whole length thereof, and shall keep and maintain a bridge of like breadth, with strong rails on each side thereof, over the pier head, flood-gates, or any waste cut through or round the dam, under the penalty of ten shillings for every twenty four hours failure: But where a milldam shall be carried away, or destroyed, by tempest or accident, the owner or occupier thereof shall not be liable to the said penalties, from thenceforth, until one month after such mill shall have been so repaired as to have ground one bushel of grain for toll.

All the penalties in this act, not otherwise directed, shall be one moiety to the informer, and the other to the use of the county, recoverable, with costs, on warrant, petition, or action, as the case may be. Any Justice, who upon his own view, shall discover a road, bridge, causey or milldam, as aforesaid, out of repair, shall issue a warrant against the surveyor or other delinquent; and if no reasonable excuse be made for such default, may give judgment for the penalty, and costs, not exceeding twenty five shillings; or such offenders may be presented by the grand juries; in all which cases of conviction, on view of a Justice or presentment, or on private informations to Justices where there shall be no evidence to convict the offender but the informers own oath, the whole penalties shall be to the use of the county towards lessening the levy thereof, and shall be annually collected and accounted for by the sheriff in the same manner as county levies; and to enable the sheriff to make such collection, every Justice immediately, on conviction of any offender where the penalty is to be to the county, shall certify the same to the clerk of his county court, who shall yearly, before the first day of March, deliver to the sheriff a list of all the offenders so certified, and of all others convicted in court, within one year preceeding of any offence against this act.

Provided that prosecutions for any offence herein mentioned, shall be commenced within six months after the offence committed, and not after.[3]

Report, p. 33-5. Text of Act as adopted is in Hening, XII, 174-80. This Bill was prepared by TJ; see Document IV, Part 5 in the present series.

It is possible that TJ intended, and may indeed have prepared, a road bill aimed at a reform of existing methods, for he mentioned such a bill in *Notes on Virginia.* Concerning this, Madison wrote TJ on 19 June 1786: "I observe that in your analysis of the Revisal, p. 251 of your notes, a Bill is mentioned for consigning our roads to undertakers, instead of the present vicious plan of repairing them. No such provision is comprized in the Road bill reported and printed [i.e., Bill No. 46]. If it be any where in existence I wish you could put me on the means of getting a sight of it. I conceive such a reform to be essential and that the Legislature would adopt it, if presented in a well digested form." But no MS of such a road bill has been found.

Bill was presented by Madison 31 Oct. 1785, passed by House 30 Nov., and approved by Senate 5 Jan. 1786 (JHD, Oct. 1785, 1828 edn., p. 12-15, 51, 65, 129, 144). Text of Act as adopted agrees with Bill as proposed save as indicated below. This Act was essentially a restatement and modification of the 1748 Act concerning highways, mill dams, and bridges (Hening, VI, 64-9).

1 The Act reads: "seven shillings and six pence."

2 The Act reads: "fifty"; the Act of 1748 read "sixty."

3 The Act has an additional clause putting it into effect 1 Jan. 1787.

47. A Bill for Establishing Public Ferries

Be it enacted by the General Assembly, that ferries be constantly kept, at the places hereafter mentioned, and at the rates annexed to each ferry; that is to say.

Over the BAY of CHESAPEAK.

	For a Man.		Horse.	
From George Wilson Spooner's to Cedar Point in Maryland,	2	6	2	6
From Robert Lovel's to Maryland,	2	6	2	6
From William Tyler's to Cedar Point,	2	6	2	6
From Hoes to ditto,	2	0	2	0
From Lawrence Washington's to the opposite shore above or below Nanjamy creek,	2	6	2	6
From Boyd's Hole to the same place,	2	6	2	6
From Cook's, in Stafford, to Kennedy's, in Maryland,	2	0	2	0
From George Brett's, in Prince William, to Chamberlayne's, in Maryland,	1	6	1	6
From Triplett's land, below Quantico creek, to Brooks's, in Maryland,	1	6	1	6
From Posey's, in Fairfax, to Marshall's, in Maryland,	1	0	1	0
From Hereford's, in Doeg's Neck, to the lower side of Pamunky creek, Maryland,	1	0	1	0
From William Clifton's to Wallis's in Maryland,	1	0	1	0
From Hugh West's to Frazier's or Addison's, in Maryland,	1	0	1	0
From Hunting creek ware-house landing to the same place,	1	0	1	0
From Floyd's to Powell's,	0	6	0	6
Over the river Occoquan at Colchester,	0	3	0	3
Over Nominy in Westmoreland,	0	4	0	4
Over Mattox in Westmoreland,	0	3	0	3
From Mason's, opposite to Rock creek, over to Maryland,	0	4	0	4
From the Earl of Tankerville's, in Loudoun, over to Maryland,	0	8	0	8
From Philip Noland's, in Loudoun, over to Maryland,	0	8	0	8

	For a Man.		Horse.	
From Swearingham's, in Frederick, to his land in Maryland,	0	3¾	0	3¾
From Harper's to his land in Maryland,	0	3¾	0	3¾
From Foreman's, in Frederick, to the opposite shore,	0	3¾	0	3¾
From Awbrey's, in Loudoun, to Hook's, in Maryland,	0	3¾	0	3¾
From Watkins's, opposite to Canagochego creek, to Wade's in Maryland,	0	3	0	3
From the land of Abraham Shepherd, in the county of Berkely, over Potowmack, to the land of Thomas Swearingen in Maryland.	0	3	0	3
From Russell's land on Shenandoah to the fork or over the main river,	0	3	0	3
From Kersey's landing, on Burwell's land, to the land of Col. Landon Carter,	0	3¾	0	3¾
From Gersham Key's land to the land of William Fairfax, Esq; his heirs,	0	3¾	0	3¾
At Williams's Gap, from the land of Lord Fairfax to the land of Ralph Wormley, Esq.	0	3¾	0	3¾
From Samuel Earles's to Lord Fairfax's,	0	3	0	3

On RAPPAHANNOCK River and its Branches.

From Whiting's to Gilbert's,	2	0	2	0
From Urbanna to Chetwood's,	2	0	2	0
to Locust Point on the land of Ralph Wormeley, Esq.	0	3	0	3
From the lower side of Parrot's creek to Teague's creek,	1	6	1	6
From Byrd's to Williams's,	1	3	1	3
Over Piscataway creek in Essex county,	0	3	0	3
Over Rappahannock creek in Richmond county,	0	3	0	3
From the landing of Archibald Ritchie, in Tappahannock town, to the causey opposite thereto,	1	0	1	0
From Ley's land to Robinson's,	0	6	0	6
From the public landing at Leed's town to the causey opposite,	0	6	0	6
From Tankersley's to the usual place,	0	4	0	4
From the public landing in Port Royal to Gibson's ware-house landing,	0	4	0	4

	For a Man.		Horse.	
From the public landing in Port Royal across Rappahannock to the lands of Francis Conway to be kept by James Bowie the younger and his heirs, so long as they shall keep the same well,	0	3¾	0	3¾
From Roy's ware-house landing to Gibson's ware-house landing,	0	4	0	4
From Kay's landing to Skinner's,	0	4	0	4
From Taliaferro's landing to Berry's,	0	4	0	4
From Doniphan's landing to Battaile's,	0	3	0	3
From Casson's landing to Conway's,	0	3	0	3
From the warf at Newpost to Ball's landing,	0	3	0	3
From Johnston's plantation, in Spotsylvania, to Washington's, in King George,	0	3	0	3
From Fredericksburg ware-house landing to Hunter's landing,	0	3	0	3
From Falmounth landing to the land of Francis Thornton,	0	3	0	3
From Germanna over the Rappidan,	0	3	0	3
At Philemon Cavenangh's ford,	0	3	0	3
From Branham's over the Rappidan to Moore's,	0	3	0	3

On PIANKETANK River.

From Seaton's to the opposite shore,	0	6	0	6
From Turk's to the opposite shore	0	3¾	0	3¾

On YORK River and its Branches.

From York town to Gloucester town,	0	7½	0	7½
From Cappahosick to Scimino,	1	3	1	3
From the brick house to Dudley's	1	0	0	10½
From West Point to Dudley's,	0	6	0	6
From Fleet's to Fox's,	0	7½	0	7½
From William Frazier's to the causey opposite,	0	6	0	6
From Mantapike on the land of Col. George Brooke, to the causey on the land of William Frazier,	0	6	0	6
From Waller's to Walkerton,	0	3¾	0	3¾
From Temple's landing to the opposite shore,	0	3	0	3
From the brick house to We[st] Point,	0	9	0	9
From Sweet Hall to Claiborne Gooches, if the causey be not kept in repair,	0	6	0	6

	For a Man.		Horse.	
From the land of John Watkins, in New Kent, to the land of Thomas Claiborne's heirs, in King William,	0	6	0	6
From Chamberlayne's to Williams's,	0	6	0	6
From the land of George Webb, Esq. to the opposite landing,	0	6	0	6
From Blackwell's to King's,	0	3	0	3
From Taylor's land to the land of Thomas Nelson, Esq.	0	3	0	3

On JAMES River and its Branches.

From Hampton to Sewil's Point,	3	0	3	0
to Brook's Point,	0	3	0	3
to Norfolk, or Nansemond town,	7	6	7	6
or if more than a single man and horse,	5	0	5	0
From Mulbery Island Point, in Warwick, to Cocket's, in Isle of Wight,	1	3	1	3
From Norfolk town to Crawford's or Sawyer's Point,	0	6	0	6
From Crawford's to Powder Point,	0	4	0	4
From William Hodsden's, over Pagan creek, to Smithfield,	0	4	0	4
From Charles Fulgham's to Smithfield,	0	6	0	6
From Cockfield's Point to Robert Peale's near Sleepy Hole,	0	6	0	6
From Jeremiah Godwin's, over the Western branch, to James Benn's,	0	4	0	4
From Benjamin Bascomb's, over Bennet's creek, to James Buxton's,	0	4	0	4
From John Reid's, over the Western branch, to Jeremiah Godwin's,	0	3	0	3
From the land of Riddick, in Suffolk, to Jordon's,	0	4	0	4
From Col. Lewis Burwell's landing to Fort Point on Hog Island,	1	3	1	3
From the College Landing to Hog Island,	2	6	2	6
From James Town to Swan's Point,	0	7½	0	7½
to Cobham,	0	7½	0	7½
On Chickhominy at the usual place,	0	6	0	6
From Cole's to William's,	0	3¾	0	3¾

	For a Man.		Horse.	
From Delony's to Edloe's,	0	7½	0	7½
From Westover to Maycox or Coggin's Point,	0	7½	0	7½
From City Point to Bermuda Hundred,	1	0	1	0
From Bermuda Hundred to Shirley,	0	6	0	6
From Hood's, in Prince George, to Minge's land in Wyanoke,	0	7½	0	7½
From Kennan's to Maye's, on Appamatox river,	0	3¾	0	3¾
From Henry Batte's land, in Chesterfield, to Bolling's land,	0	3	0	3
From the land William Pride, over Persie's Stile creek, to the land of Peter Baugh,	0	3	0	3
to William Pride's land in Prince George county,	0	2	0	2
From Bolling's Point over Appamatox river,	0	2	0	2
From Charles Woodson's, in Henrico, to Tarlton Woodson's, Chesterfield,	0	4	0	4
From the land of Henry Batte to the Glebe land, Varina,	0	3¾	0	3¾
From Charles Ellis's to Daniel Weldon's,	0	3	0	3
From the ware-house landing at Warwick to the land of Moseley,	0	3	0	3
From the land of Patrick Coutt's, deceased, in Richmond town to Manchester town,	0	4	0	4
From the upper landing in Beverley town to the land of Britton				
From the land of Stephen Woodson to the Menacon town,	0	3	0	3
From the land of Bennett Goode to the land of Col. John Fleming's heirs,	0	3	0	3
From the land of Tucker Woodson to the land of Paul Micheux,	0	3	0	3
From the land of Richard Moseby to the land of Tarlton Fleming's heirs,	0	3	0	3
From the land of John Woodson below the mouth of Willis's creek, to his land on the opposite side of the river,	0	3	0	3
From the point of the fork of the Fluvanna and Rivanna rivers, across the Fluvanna to the lands of Philip Mayo,	0	3	0	3
From the same point, across the Rivanna, to the lands of Samuel Martin,	0	2	0	2

	For a Man.		Horse.	
From the said lands of Samuel Martin to the said land of Philip Mayo,	0	3	0	3
From the lands of John Harvie, across the Rivanna, to the land of Martin Key,	0	3	0	3
From the lands of William Cannon, across the Fluvanna, to the lands of Walter King,	0	3	0	3
From the land of John Nicholas, Esq; over the Slate river,	0	3	0	3
From the land of John Scott, over the Fluvanna, to the lands of Randolph Jefferson,	0	3	0	3
From the land of Nicholas Davies, near the mouth of Battery creek, in the county of Bedford, over the Fluvanna, to his land opposite,	0	6	0	6
From the lands of Benjamin Howard to the lands of Neil Campbell,	0	3	0	3
From William Cabell's, over Rockfish, to Benjamin Howard's land,	0	2	0	2
From Thomas Joplin's, on Rockfish, to the opposite shore,	0	3	0	3
From Joseph Cabell's land to the land of William Cabell opposite,	0	3	0	3
From John Cabell's land, over the Fluvanna, to the opposite shore,	0	3	0	3
From the north side of the Fluvanna to William Megginson's,	0	3	0	3
From the land of Cabell, at the mouth of Swan's creek, over the Fluvanna, to the land of Samuel Spencer, or across the river,	0	3	0	3
From Edward Lynch's to Edward Moorman's land,	0	3	0	3
From the lands of Henry Trent, across the Fluvanna, to the lands of Nicholas Davies,	0	3	0	3
From the lands of Nicholas Davies, over the Fluvanna, to his lands on the opposite side,	0	3	0	3
From George Stovall's land, over the Fluvanna, to his land opposite,	0	3	0	3
From the land of William Crow to the land of Andrew Boyd,	0	3	0	3
From the land of John Buchannon's heirs to their land opposite,	0	3	0	3

	For a Man.		Horse.	
From Branches over James river to the opposite shore,	0	3	0	3
From the land of Jacob Micheaux to the land of Thomas Atkins,	0	3	0	3
From the land of William Ingles, over New river, to the opposite shore,	0	3	0	3
From the lands of Jacob Bousman, across the Monongala, to Pittsburg,	0	4½	0	4½

On NOTTOWAY River.

From Thomas Drew's land to Dr. Brown's,	0	3	0	3
From Bolton's to Simmons's land,	0	3	0	3

On ROANOAKE River and its Branches.

From Jefferson's in Mecklenburg to the opposite shore,	0	4	0	4
From Anderson's to Taylor's land,	0	3	0	3
From Wagstaff's to Palmer's	0	3	0	3
From Samuel Jones's to Frederick Jones's	0	3	0	3
From Fox's to Blanton's,	0	3	0	3
From Harwood's to Royster's,	0	3	0	3
From William Black's to the opposite shore,	0	4	0	4
From Wade's, over Staunton, to the opposite shore,	0	3	0	3
From the land of John Ward, over Staunton, to his land opposite in the county of Bedford,	0	6	0	6
From Hunt's land to Abney's,	0	4	0	4
From Booker's to the opposite shore,	0	3	0	3
From Blanks's to Bruas's,	0	3	0	3
From Cobb's to the opposite shore,	0	3	0	3
From James Steward's to Thomas Steward's,	0	3	0	3
From Barksdale's to James Hunt's,	0	3	0	3
From Simms's to Randolph's,	0	3	0	3
From Cargill's to Foushee's,	0	3	0	3
From the land of John Owen's, in the county of Pittsylvania, over Dan river to the land of Sylvester Adams,	0	6	0	6
From Margaret Boyd's, over Dan river, to her land opposite,	0	3	0	3
From Col. Nathaniel Terry's to Fuqua's,	0	3	0	3

	For a Man.	Horse.
From Dix's to Green's	0 3	0 3
From Miller's to Legrand's,	0 3	0 3
From Jones's to Seldon's,	0 3	0 3
From Coles's to Joseph Fuqua's,	0 3	0 3
From the land of David Brandon, over Dan river, to the land of John Lawson,	0 3	0 3
From the land of John Boyd, over Dan river, to the land of Patrick Boyd.	0 3	0 3
From the land of James Devore, in the county of Yohogania, over Monongalia, to the land of Joseph Parkerson,		

And that ferries be kept, opposite to all the places hereby appointed, across the rivers Rappahannock, Piankatank, York, James and Nottoway below the falls thereof; and the several county courts are impowered to appoint opposite ferries, where they shall judge it necessary, at all other places herein appointed, above the falls of the said rivers, or across any branches thereof; also on such parts of the rivers Potowmack and Roanoake, or their branches, as have places hereby established for ferries, where both sides are within this commonwealth; and the several keepers of such opposite ferries shall be intitled to the rates of ferriage herein allowed at the place, and be subject to all the regulations of this act. But this shall not extend to any ferry which by a former law is vested on both sides in any person or persons: All which ferries shall remain subject to the regulations of the several acts of Assembly, by which they were respectively established.

And for the transportation of wheel carriages, tobacco, or live stocks, at either of the ferries hereby, or hereafter to be established; the ferry keepers may respectively demand the rates following, to wit:

For every coach, chariot, or waggon, and the driver, the same as for six horses.

For every four wheeled chaise, or phæton, and the driver, or cart, as for four horses.

For every two wheeled riding carriage as for two horses.

For every hogshead of tobacco, or head of neat cattle, as for one horse.

For every sheep, goat, or lamb, one fifth part of the ferriage of one horse.

For every hog one fourth part of the ferriage of one horse.

If any ferry keeper shall demand and take from a passenger a greater rate than is herein allowed for ferriage, he or she shall forfeit, for every offence, the sum over charged, and ten shillings, to the party grieved, recoverable, with costs, before any Justice of the Peace in the county where the offence shall be committed.[1]

The several county courts are hereby empowered to appoint a ferry over any river or creek, within their respective counties, where they shall judge the same convenient, and settle the rate of ferriage, and may contract with the keeper of such ferry, or of any public ferry, within the county, for setting over the militia, on muster days, and to make an allowance for the same, in their county levy.

The said courts are also impowered and required to order and direct what boat or boats, and the number of hands which shall be kept at each ferry, appointed, or to be appointed, within their respective counties; and the owner of the land from whence the ferry is, or shall be, shall, within from the commencement of this act, give bond, with security, in the penalty of payable to the Justices of the said court, and their successors, with condition, that he or she will duly cause such ferry to be kept, according to law, and give immediate dispatch to all passengers, public messengers and expresses when required. And if such owner shall fail to give security, within the time aforesaid, and, being summoned to appear at the county court, shall fail to appear, or appearing, shall refuse, or be unable, to procure such security, the court shall have power, upon the application of any other person, to order the sheriff to summon a jury of twelve good and lawful men, to meet at the ferry landing; who, being sworn by the sheriff or under sheriff attending, shall view and value an acre of land, to be laid off convenient to include the landing; and as little prejudicial as may be to the owner, and return their inquisition to the next court; and thereupon, unless the proprietor shall then appear, enter into bond with security as aforesaid, and pay down the costs of the proceedings, the court may grant the ferry to the petitioner, upon his giving such security, and paying down to the proprietor the valuation of the acre of land, of which the petitioner shall be from thenceforth seized in fee simple.[2]

All expresses, sent by the Governor, or Commander in Chief, to any person or persons, on public business, or sent to the Governor, by the General Congress, the Commander in Chief of the American army, or Commanding Officer of any detachment thereof, or of any militia of this state, in actual service; or by any Field Officer of the militia, to the Governor, or to the Commanding Officer of the militia, in an adjacent county, to give intelligence of an invasion, or insurrection, or of the approach of an enemy, shall be deemed public expresses, and ferry free, in case the dispatches, by such express, be directed, for public service, and such direction be signed by the person sending the same.

All the men, attending public ferries, shall be free from county and public levies, from attendance at musters, clearing highways, impressments and other service of a like nature; and every ferry keeper shall be intitled to a license for keeping ordinary, at his ferry, upon application to the county court, notwithstanding there may be a sufficient number of other ordinaries in the county.

If any person, other than a ferry keeper, shall, for reward, set any person or persons, carriages, horses, or stocks, over any river, or creek, whereon ferries are or shall be established, he or she so offending, shall forfeit and pay five pounds, for every offence, to the ferry keeper nearest to the place where the offence shall be committed, to be recovered, with costs, by action of debt, or information, in any court of record, wherein the same is cognizable; neither shall any person, for reward, set any person, carriage, horses, or stocks, over the Bay of Chesapeak, from Northampton county, or from Accomack county, other than the inhabitants thereof to York, Hampton, or Norfolk towns, or any other place, adjacent thereto, under the like penalty, to the keeper of the ferry from Hungar's to the said towns, to be recovered as aforesaid.

The Justices of the county of Surry, at the charge of the county, shall cause to be constantly kept and maintained a bridge, over Hog Island creek; for the convenience of passing to and from the ferry at Fort Point, on that Island, under the penalty of one thousand pounds of tobacco, upon every Justice neglecting, or refusing, to keep and maintain such bridge in sufficient repair.

Report, p. 35-8. MS (ViU); clerk's copy.

Bill presented by Madison 31 Oct. 1785; it was read the first and second times the same day. No further action was taken on it. This Bill was a modification and restatement of the Act of 1748 for the settlement and regulation of ferries and for dispatch of public expresses (Hening, VI, 13-23). It apparently included all of the public ferries established by the General Assembly up to the time the Committee of Revisors reported, together with general regulations concerning ferries and ferry-keepers as based on the Act of 1748. But, instead of acting upon this Bill, the House passed another which was limited merely to the authorization of new ferries not already established; most of these were on the Kentucky and Ohio rivers and other "western waters" (JHD, Oct. 1785, 1828 edn., p. 12-15, 116, 119, 122, 125, 128, 144; the Act for establishing several new ferries is in Hening, XII, 83-4).

[1] This paragraph, with minor variations, appears in the 1748 Act and also in the Act of Oct. 1785 which replaced the Committee's Bill.

[2] The passage "and if such owner shall fail to give security . . . shall be from thenceforth seized in fee simple" does not appear in the 1748 Act.

48. A Bill concerning Mill Dams and Other Obstructions of Water Courses

Be it enacted by the General Assembly, that when any person owning lands on one side of any watercourse the bed whereof belongeth to himself, or to the commonwealth, and desiring to build a water grist mill on such lands, and to erect a dam across the same, for working the said mill, shall not himself have the fee simple property in the lands on the opposite side thereof, against which he would abutt his said dam, he shall make application for a writ of ad quod damnum to the court of the county wherein the lands proposed for the abuttment are, having given ten days previous notice to the proprietor thereof, if he be to be found in the county, and if not, then to his agent therein, if any he hath, which court shall thereupon order their clerk to issue such writ, to be directed to the sheriff commanding him to summon and impannel twelve fit persons, to meet upon the lands so proposed for the abuttment, on a certain day, to be named by the court and inserted in the said writ, of which notice shall be given by the sheriff to the said proprietor, or his agent, as before directed, if neither of them were present in court at the time of the order made; which freeholders, taken, shall be charged, by the said sheriff, impartially and to the best of their skill and judgment, to view the said lands so proposed for an abuttment, and to locate and circumscribe by certain metes and bounds one acre thereof, having due regard therein to the interests of both parties, and to appraise the same according to its true value; to examine the lands above and below, of the property of others, which may probably be overflowed, and say to what damage it will be of to the several proprietors, and whether the mansion house, of any such proprietor, or the offices, curtilage, or garden thereunto immediately belonging, or orchards, will be overflowed; to enquire whether and in what degree fish of passage and ordinary navigation will be obstructed, whether by any and by what means such obstruction may be prevented; and whether, in their opinion, the health of the neighbours will be annoyed by the stagnation of the waters. And the inquest so made and sealed, by the said jurors, together with the writ, shall be returned, by the said sheriff, to the succeeding court; who shall thereupon order summonses to be issued to the several persons, proprietors or tenants, of the lands so located, or found liable to damage, if they be to be found within the county; and if not, then to their agents therein, if any they have, to shew cause why the party applying should not have leave to build the said mill and dam. And in like manner if the person proposing to build such mill and dam shall have the fee simple property in the lands on both sides the stream, yet application shall be made to the court of the county, wherein the mill house will stand, for a writ to examine, as aforesaid, what lands may be overflowed, and say to what damage it will be of to the several proprietors, and whether the mansion house, of any such proprietor, or the offices, curtilage, or garden, thereto immediately belonging, or orchards, will be overflowed; also whether and in what degree fish of passage and ordinary navigation will be obstructed thereby, whether by any and by what means such obstruction may be prevented: and whether in their opinion the health of the neighbours will be annoyed by the stagnation of waters: Which writ shall be directed, executed, and returned as prescribed in the former case. And if on such inquest, or on other evidence, it shall appear, to the court, that the mansion house, of any proprietor, or the offices, curtilage, or garden, thereto immediately belonging, or orchards, will be overflowed, or the health of the neighbours be annoyed they shall not give leave to build the said mill and dam, but if none of these injuries are likely to ensue, they shall then proceed to consider whether, all circumstances weighed, it be reasonable that such leave should be given, and shall give or not give it accordingly: And if given, they shall lay the party applying under such conditions for preventing the obstruction, if any there will be, of fish of passage, and ordinary navigation as to them shall seem right.

And if the party applying obtain leave to build the said mill and dam, he shall upon paying respectively, to the several parties intitled, the value of the acre located, and the damages which the jurors find will be done by overflowing the lands above or below, become seized in fee simple of the said acre of land. But if he shall not, within one year thereafter, begin to build the said mill and finish the same in three years, and afterwards continue it in good repair for public use, or in case the said mill or dam be destroyed, if he shall not begin to rebuild it within one year after such destruction, and finish it within three years, the said acre of land shall revert to the former proprietor and his heirs; unless at the time of such destruction of the said mill or dam the owner thereof be an infant, feme covert, imprisoned, or of unsound mind, in which case he shall be allowed the same terms for beginning and completing the said mill or dam after such disability removed.

The inquest of the said jurors nevertheless, or opinion of the court, shall not bar any prosecution, or action, which any person would have had in law, had this act never been made, other than for such injuries as were actually foreseen and estimated by the said jury.

It shall be lawful for the owner, or tenant, of any such mill, or of any other grist mill, to take for toll one eighth part, and no more, of all grain of which the remaining part shall be ground into meal, and one sixteenth part, and no more, of that the remainder of which shall be ground into hominy or malt.

No owner or tenant, of any mill, not having fifty acres of land adjoining thereto shall keep any swine uninclosed at such mill, on pain that the same shall be liable to be taken and converted to his own use, by the proprietor or tenant of any adjacent lands, or by any other person authorised by them.

Where the owner of any mill, now standing or licensed to be built, hath by any act of Assembly been compelled to make locks, slopes, or openings for navigation or the passage of fish, the same shall be continued under the conditions imposed by such act, and shall be deemed sufficient in law so long as the dam now standing or building shall remain: But it shall not be lawful to rebuild such dam in future but on enquiry by jury into the obstructions of fish and navigation and the means of preventing the same, and the final order of the court, to be applied for and conducted in the manner before directed in other cases.

It shall not be lawful for any person to erect, or fix, in any water-course, any dam, hedge, weir, seine, drag, or other stoppage whereby navigation, or the passage of fish, may be obstructed, save only for the purpose of working some machine or engine useful to the public, in which cases the same proceedings shall be had, as are before directed, in the case of a water grist mill, or for the purpose of a water grist mill before provided for: And where any such are now standing, or shall hereafter be erected, or fixed, the owner, or tenant, of the lands adjacent thereto (whether the same were erected or fixed by himself or another) shall cause it to be abated. And whoso offendeth herein shall be deemed guilty of a nuisance.

The bed of all tide waters within the low water mark shall be vested in the commonwealth, and shall not be granted to any, except such part thereof as shall be capable of being reclaimed from the water, and shall be actually reclaimed by the grantee within three years after the passing of this act; in all cases of grants heretofore made, and in all cases of future grants within three years after the date thereof. And the channel of all other watercourses, capable of being navigated by any loaded craft, great or small, shall be open to the citizens of this commonwealth, for the purpose of navigation, notwithstanding the bed thereof shall have been granted to any.[1]

Report, p. 38-9. Text of Act as adopted is in Hening, XII, 187-90.

Bill presented by Madison 31 Oct. 1785, amended and passed by House 29 Nov. and 1 Dec., approved by Senate 5 Dec. (JHD, Oct. 1785, 1828 edn., p. 12-15, 54, 64, 68, 71, 132). Text of Act as adopted agrees with Bill as proposed except for the difference indicated below and for the addition of a final clause putting the Act into effect 1 Jan. 1787. See the 1748 Act concerning water mills (Hening, VI, 55-60).

[1] This paragraph is not in the Act as adopted.

49. A Bill for Unlading Ballast and Burial of Dead Bodies from on Board Ships

Be it enacted by the General Assembly, that the court of every county, adjacent to any navigable river or creek, shall from time to time, as vacancies happen, appoint one or more ballast masters, residing near to the places where vessels usually ride in such river or creek, to be overseers and directors of the delivery and unloading of ballast from on board any ship or vessel within a certain district, to be by them ascertained.

Every ballast master so appointed, upon receiving notice from the master or chief officer, on board of any ship or vessel within his district, that ballast is to be discharged from such vessel shall go on board the same and attend until the whole ballast is delivered, which he shall see brought on shore and laid at some convenient place near the vessel, where it may not obstruct navigation nor be washed into the channel; shall thereupon give such master or officer a certificate that the ballast hath been duly unladen from such vessel.[1]

Every ballast master failing to do his duty, according to this act, shall forfeit twenty pounds for each default, in which case, or if there be no ballast master, the naval officer of the district, shall, under the like penalty, perform the same duty.

Every master or chief officer of a ship, or vessel, having ballast to unlade, shall give notice in writing, of the time he purposes to land the same, to the ballast master of the district; and shall produce to the naval officer, at the time of his clearing out, a certificate of his having unladen his ballast according to this act: And if any master or chief officer, on board of any ship or vessel, shall presume to land or cast over board any ballast therefrom, without giving such notice, or contrary to the orders he shall receive from the ballast master of the district, or shall fail to produce a certificate, of his having duly landed his ballast, to the naval officer, at the time of his clearing out, he shall forfeit fifty pounds for every offence or failure; and, in any suit to be brought for the said penalty, the clerk shall indorse on the writ, that bail is to be required, and the court may rule the defendant to give special bail if they see cause so to do.

When any person shall die on board of any ship or vessel, within this state, the master thereof shall cause the dead body to be brought on shore and there buried, at least four feet deep above high water mark, or be subject to the penalty of fifty pounds; in any suit for which, the defendant may be ruled to give special bail, and the clerk shall indorse on the writ that bail is required.[2]

Report, p. 39. MS (ViU); clerk's copy. Text of Act as adopted is in Hening, XII, 180-1.

Bill was presented by Madison 31 Oct. 1785, amended 29 Nov., and passed by House 1 Dec.; amended by Senate 16 Dec.; Senate amendment agreed to by House 19 Dec. (JHD, Oct. 1785, 1828 edn., p. 12-15, 54, 64, 68, 95, 98, 133). Text of Act as adopted agrees with Bill as proposed save as indicated below. See the 1748 Act for preventing frauds in the customs (Hening, VI, 98-101).

[1] The Act adds the following at this point: "for which service he shall receive five shillings per day, to be paid by the master or chief officer to whom such certificate is granted."

[2] The Act contains a final clause putting it into effect 1 Jan. 1787.

50. A Bill concerning Public Store-Houses

Be it enacted by the General Assembly, that the courts of the respective counties, situate upon any navigable river or creek, may appoint any place or places within the county, which to them shall appear convenient and necessary, for the lading and unlading of goods or merchandise, which, together with such as have been heretofore so appointed shall be deemed public landings: And where sufficient store-houses are not already built at, or convenient to such landings, the courts shall order such house or houses to be erected by the proprietor of the land, at his expence, for the commodious reception and safe keeping of all goods and merchandise brought thither by land or water, which shall be accordingly built by such proprietor, within twelve months after the order made, and shall be accounted public store-houses.

If the proprietor of any store-house, heretofore established, shall refuse to suffer the same to be used for that purpose; or if the owner of any land on which a public store-house shall be ordered to be built, shall fail to build the same, within a year after such order, or shall refuse to do it; in either case it shall be lawful for the court, and they are hereby required to order the sheriff to summon a jury of freeholders, to meet at the place appointed for such store-house, who, being sworn by such sheriff, shall value and lay off half an acre of land, whereon to build a store-house, or on which the house already built shall stand, as the case shall be, and return their inquisition to the court, there to be recorded; and thereupon it shall be lawful for the court to give liberty to any other person to build, or keep, such store-house, and upon such person's paying down the valuation to the owner, he shall be, from thenceforth, seized in fee of the said half acre of land, so long as he, his heirs, or assigns, shall keep and maintain such convenient store-house thereon, as the court shall from time to time direct, but on his failing therein the land shall revert to the former proprietor, or his heirs, or pass to such other person as shall undertake, with the approbation of the court, to build and maintain such store-house. But it shall not be lawful for the jury so to lay off the said half acre of land as to include the mansion house of the proprietor, or the offices, curtilage, or garden, thereunto immediately belonging, or orchards.

No owner or tenant of any such half acre of land, not having fifty acres adjoining, shall keep thereon any swine, uninclosed, on pain that the same shall be liable to be taken and converted to his own use by the proprietor or tenant of any adjacent lands, or by any other person authorised by them.

The proprietor shall constantly keep and maintain such store-house in repair, for the reception of all goods and merchandise brought to the same, and shall be intitled to the following rates and prices of storage, to be paid before the removal or delivery of the goods, that is to say; for every hogshead of tobacco brought to a store-house, above the falls of any river, eight pence; for every cask containing sixty gallons, and every bale or parcel of goods of the like or greater bulk, one shilling for the first day, or any time not exceeding three months, and one penny for every month above three; for every cask under sixty gallons, and every bale or parcel of the like or less bulk than such a cask, six pence; and one penny as aforesaid; for salt, or grain, not packed in casks, after the rate of one penny a bushel for the first day or three months, and a farthing a bushel for every month after the said three; and for every bar or pig of iron one half penny.

Every parcel of salt or grain brought loose, shall be kept, in separate heaps, unmixed with any other, and the whole delivered as received; save that there shall be an allowance to the store-house keeper for any loss which may happen by dissolution, rats or other unavoidable accident, not exceeding five per centum for the first three months, and one per centum for every month it shall lie above three, so as that the whole be not more than ten per centum. If any person, not being the proprietor or keeper of a public store-house, shall demand or receive storage, or other reward, for goods landed or lodged within one mile of a public store-house on the same side of the river or creek, he shall forfeit five pounds for every offence to the owner or keeper of the nearest public store-house, to be recovered with costs.

Every proprietor of a public store-house, who, or whose agent, shall refuse to take in any goods or merchandise, brought to such house, shall be liable to the action of the party grieved for all damages sustained by such refusal.

The owner or keeper of every store-house shall, at the time of his receiving any goods or merchandise therein, give a receipt for the same in writing, wherein shall be mentioned the marks, numbers and condition of each parcel of such goods; and shall enter the same fairly in a book to be kept for that purpose, to which all persons concerned may have recourse at any time: And every such owner or keeper refusing or failing to make such entry, to give such receipt, or to give a copy of such entry when required (for which copy he may receive six pence and no more) shall forfeit twenty shillings for every failure or refusal, recoverable with costs before a Justice of Peace.

Report, p. 39-40. MS (ViU); clerk's copy.

Bill presented 31 Oct. 1785 by Madison, read twice and committed to a committee of the whole, but no further action was taken on it (JHD, Oct. 1785, 1828 edn., p. 12-15). This Bill was a simplified restatement of the 1748 Act for appointing public storehouses and ascertaining the prices of storage (Hening, VI, 60-4).

51. A Bill concerning Slaves

Be it enacted by the General Assembly, that no persons shall, henceforth, be slaves within this commonwealth, except such as were so on the first day of this present session of Assembly, and the descendants of the females of them.

Negroes and mulattoes[1] which shall hereafter be brought into this commonwealth and kept therein one whole year, together, or so long at different times as shall amount to one year, shall be free.

[But if they shall not depart the commonwealth within one year thereafter they shall be out of the protection of the laws.

Those which shall come into this commonwealth of their own accord shall be out of the protection of the laws; save only such as being seafaring persons and navigating vessels hither, shall not leave the same while here more than twenty four hours together.

It shall not be lawful for any person to emancipate a slave but by deed executed, proved and recorded as is required by law in the case of a conveyance of goods and chattels, on consideration not deemed valuable in law, or by last will and testament, and with the free consent of such slave, expressed in presence of the court of the county wherein he resides: And if such slave, so emancipated, shall not within one year thereafter, depart the commonwealth, he shall be out of the protection of the laws. All conditions, restrictions and limitations annexed to any act of emancipation shall be void from the time such emancipation is to take place.

If any white woman shall have a child by a negro or mulatto, she and her child shall depart the commonwealth within one year thereafter. If they fail so to do, the woman shall be out of the protection of the laws, and the child shall be bound out by the Aldermen of the county, in like manner as poor orphans are by law directed to be, and within one year after its term of service expired shall depart the commonwealth, or on failure so to do, shall be out of the protection of the laws.

Where any of the persons before described shall be disabled from departing the commonwealth by grievous sickness, the protection of the law shall be continued to him until such disability be removed: And if the county shall in the mean time, incur any expence in taking care of him, as of other county poor, the Aldermen shall be intitled to recover the same from his former master, if he had one, his heirs, executors and administrators.][2]

No negro or mulatto shall be a witness except in pleas of the commonwealth against negroes or mullatoes, or in civil pleas wherein negroes or mulattoes alone shall be parties.

No slave shall go from the tenements of his master, or other person with whom he lives, without a pass, or some letter or token whereby it may appear that he is proceeding by authority from his master, employer, or overseer: If he does, it shall be lawful for any person to apprehend and carry him before a Justice of the Peace, to be by his order punished with stripes, or not, in his discretion.

No slave shall keep any arms whatever, nor pass, unless with written orders from his master or employer, or in his company, with arms from one place to another. Arms in possession of a slave contrary to this prohibition shall be forfeited to him who will seize them.

Riots, routs, unlawful assemblies, trespasses and seditious speeches by a negro or mulatto shall be punished with stripes at the discretion of a Justice of the Peace; and he who will may apprehend and carry him before such Justice.[3]

Report, p. 40. Text of Act as adopted is in Hening, XII, 182-3. This Bill was prepared by TJ; see Document IV, Part 5 in the present series.

Bill presented by Madison 31 Oct. 1785, amended 29 Nov., and passed by House 5 Dec.; amended by Senate 8 Dec., and Senate amendments accepted by House 9 Dec. (JHD, Oct. 1785, 1828 edn., p. 12-15, 54, 64, 71, 78, 79, 133). In his Autobiography, TJ stated that "The bill on the subject of slaves was a mere digest of the existing laws respecting them, without any intimation of a plan for a future and general emancipation. It was thought better that this should be kept back, and attempted only by way of amendment, whenever the bill should be brought on. The principles of the amendment, however, were agreed on, that is to say, the freedom of all born after a certain day, and deportation at a proper age. But it was found that the public mind would not yet bear the proposition. . ." (Ford, I, 67-8). If this emancipation amendment was reduced to writing, no manuscript or other record of it has yet come to light; in the more detailed account of this suppressed amendment as given in *Notes on Virginia*, TJ indicated that such an amendment had been reduced to writing. Among the "remarkable alterations proposed" in the revision, TJ listed that of the emancipation "of all slaves born after passing the act." To this he quickly added, however, that "The bill reported by the revisers does not itself contain this proposition; but an amendment containing it was prepared, to be offered to the legislature whenever the bill should be taken up, and further directing, that they should continue with their parents to a certain age, then be brought up, at the public expence, to tillage, arts, or sciences, according to their geniusses, till the females should be eighteen, and the males twenty-one years of age, when they should be colonized to such place as the circumstances of the time should render most proper, sending them out with arms, implements of houshold and of the handicraft arts, seeds, pairs of the useful domestic animals, &c. to declare them a free and independant people, and extend to them our alliance and protection, till they shall have acquired strength; and to send vessels at the same time to other parts of the world for an equal number of white inhabitants; to induce whom to migrate hither, proper encouragements were to be proposed" (Ford, III, 243-4). This detailed account was followed by a lengthy explanation of TJ's reasons for displacing blacks by whites, the essence of which is reduced to "the real distinctions which nature has made" between the two races. Though the amendment as described by TJ was undoubtedly in advance of the sentiment of the day, it is equally certain that he was firmly convinced then, as later, that (1) the natural differences were indeed such as to create separate and distinct races; that (2) making "allowances for the difference of condition, of education, of conversation," the Negroes were an inferior race ("The improvement of the blacks in body and mind, in the first instance of their mixture with the whites, has been observed by every one, and proves that their inferiority is not the effect merely of their condition of life"); that (3) the two races, because of historic and "Deep rooted prejudices entertained by the whites" and "ten thousand recollections, by the blacks, of the injuries they have sustained," could never live in freedom and in harmony together under the same government, and, if it were attempted, would "produce convulsions, which will probably never end but in the extermination of the one or the other race"; and finally, that (4) colonization in some form appeared to be the only alternative, since ultimately freedom for the slave was a foregone conclusion. These were propositions to which TJ adhered with undeviating conviction throughout life (same, 244-7).

While the suppressed amendment that he outlined was undoubtedly in advance of general sentiment, the arguments that he employed to justify it probably reflected prevalent liberal views and the Bill as proposed lagged behind. It was far less liberal even than the legislature would accept, preserving as it did some of the harshest and most inhumane features of the colonial slave code. These the legislature of 1785 would not tolerate. Though TJ endeavored to view this problem with the reasoned humanity that characterized his liberal thought in almost all other realms, he was, on this issue, inflexible in opinion and conservative in legislation. The chief extenuating circumstance that can be advanced in defense of the Bill's cruel penalties providing for outlawry in many cases is the supposition that the Committee never expected the Bill to be adopted as proposed.

But the Bill shows that it was not in fact a "mere digest of the existing laws" respecting slaves. Its first clause provided that none should henceforth be slaves in Virginia "except such as were so on the first day of this present session of Assembly, *and the descendants of the females of them.*" The first part of this clause is substantially of the same purport as TJ's suppressed amendment; the second part continues the institution of slavery on a narrower base by limiting the increase to the descendants of female slaves then in Virginia. This, together with the remainder of the Bill, by its drastic penalties imposed on free blacks for remaining in the state after manumission and on those daring to immigrate, supports the view that what was intended here was not merely a decoy Bill to be killed by amendment but a definite proposal for a system of gradual emancipation, the anticipated decline being brought about by failure to replenish the stock through importation and by manumission on the part of individual owners. When the legislature accepted this first clause of the Committee's Bill and threw out many of its complementary parts prohibiting free blacks to remain in or enter the state, it may have acted partly in opposition to the inhumane penalties of the Bill, and partly in the belief that the future of slavery should not be so narrowly limited.

The principal differences between the Act as adopted and the Bill as proposed are indicated in the notes below. See the Act for the better government of Negroes, mulattoes, and Indians, 1748 (Hening, VI, 104-12), and another Act for the better government of servants and slaves, 1753 (same, 356-69).

1 The Act reads: "slaves" instead of "Negroes and mulattoes."

2 The paragraphs enclosed in square brackets (supplied) are not in the Act as adopted.

3 Following this point the Act includes three sections not in the Bill: the first provides that the provisions of the Act do not extend (1) to those of other states who remove to Virginia in order to become citizens and who take an oath that this is not done for the purpose of evading the laws against the importation of slaves or for the purpose of selling slaves and that the one taking the oath has not imported slaves from Africa or the West Indies since 1 Nov. 1778; (2) to those claiming slaves by descent, marriage, or devise; (3) to a citizen of Virginia owning slaves in other states and bringing them to the state; (4) to travelers and transients. The second section prohibits trading with slaves without the consent of the master or overseer, under penalty of four times the value of the item sold or bought and also under penalty of a forfeit of £5 to any person suing for it, recoverable as other debts, or thirty-nine lashes at the public whipping post (taken from the Act of 1753, Hening, VI, p. 359-60). The third section provides that the Act is to go into effect 1 Jan. 1787.

52. A Bill concerning Servants

Be it enacted by the General Assembly, that all white persons, not being citizens of any of the confederating states of America, who shall come into this commonwealth under contract to serve another in any trade, or occupation, shall be compellable to perform such contract specifically during the term thereof, or during so much of the same as shall not exceed seven years. Infants under the age of fourteen years, brought in under the like contract, entered into with the consent of their father or guardian, shall serve till their age of twenty one years only, or for such shorter term as the said contract shall have fixed.

The said servants shall be provided, by their master, with wholesome and sufficient food, clothing and lodging; and at the end of their service, if they shall not have contracted for any reward, other than transportation, food, clothing and lodging, shall receive from him one new and complete suit of clothing, suited to the season of the year, to wit, a coat, waistcoat, pair of breeches and shoes, two pair of stockings, two shirts, a hat and blanket.

The benefit of the said contract of service shall be assignable by the master to any person to whom the servant shall, in the presence of a Justice of the Peace, freely consent that it shall be assigned, the said Justice attesting such free consent in writing; and shall also pass to the executors, administrators, and legatees of the master.

Any such servant being lazy, disorderly, guilty of misbehaviour to his master or in his master's family, shall be corrected by stripes on order from the court[1] of the county wherein he resides, or refusing to work shall be compelled thereto in like manner; and moreover shall serve two days for every one he shall have so refused to serve, or shall otherwise have lost without sufficient justification. All necessary expences incurred by any master for apprehending and bringing home any absconding servant shall be repaid by further service after such rates as the court[2] shall direct; unless such servant shall give security, to be approved of by the court, for repayment in money within six months after he shall be free from service, and shall accordingly pay the same.

If any master shall fail in the duties prescribed by this act, or shall be guilty of injurious demeanor towards his servant it shall be redressed on motion by the court[2] of the county wherein the servant resides, by immediate discharge from service, if the injury were gross, or by a specific order for a change in his demeanor, and a discharge from service if such order be disobeyed.

All contracts between master and servant during the time of service shall be void.

Report, p. 41. Text of Act as adopted is in Hening, XII, 190-1.

Bill presented by Madison 31 Oct. 1785, passed by the House 1 Dec., amended by the Senate, and amendment agreed to by House 9 Dec. (JHD, Oct. 1785, 1828 edn., p. 12-15, 64, 68, 78, 133). The text of Act as adopted agrees with Bill as proposed except for differences noted below and except for addition of a final clause putting it into effect 1 Jan. 1787. See the Act of 1753 for the better government of servants and slaves (Hening, VI, 356-69).

[1] Act reads: "from a justice of the county, city, or corporation"; this of course simplified the procedure for the master and made it easier to obtain permission to correct a servant.

[2] The Act reads: "court of the county, city, or corporation."

53. A Bill for Apprehending and Securing Runaways

Be it enacted by the General Assembly, that any person may apprehend a servant or slave, suspected to be a runaway, and carry him before a Justice of Peace, who, if to him the servant or slave appear, by the oath of the apprehender, to be a runaway, shall give a certificate of such oath, and the distance, in his opinion, between the place where the runaway was apprehended and that from whence he fled; and the apprehender shall thereupon carry the runaway to the last mentioned place, or deliver him to the owner, or some other authorised to receive him, and shall be intitled to   and   [1] for every mile of such distance as he shall necessarily carry him, to be paid by the owner. The runaway, if the owner be not known, or reside not in the commonwealth, shall be, by warrant of the Justice, committed to the jail of his county, the keeper whereof shall forthwith cause an advertisement, with a description of the runaway's person and wearing apparel, to be set up at the door of the court-house, and of every church in his county within ten miles. If the owner claim not within two months thereafter, the sheriff shall publish a like advertisement in the Virginia Gazette for three months; and shall hire the runaway out during such time and for such wages as his county court shall approve, having put an iron collar, stamped with the letter F, round his neck, and out of the wages pay the reward for apprehending, and the expences incurred on his account; but he shall deliver the runaway, even before the time expire, and pay the balance of the wages received, if any, to him who shall claim, and who, having proved before the court of some county,[2] that he had lost such an one as was described in the advertisement, and having there given security to indemnify the sheriff, shall produce the clerk's certificate of such proof made and security given, prove, by his own or another's oath, the runaway, when shewn to him, to be the same that was so lost, and pay so much as the expences aforesaid shall exceed the wages. The runaway being a slave, after the end of one year from the last advertisement, shall be sold, and the proceeds of the sale, with the balance of the wages, paid to the public Treasurer, for the use of the owner, proving his property at any future time, or, otherwise, for the use of the commonwealth. If the runaway die in jail the expences shall be defrayed by the public. The runaway, if he shall have crossed the Bay of Chesapeak, shall be delivered to the sheriff of some county, bounded thereby, who shall transport him to the other side, and cause him to be put into the hands of a constable, to be, by constable to constable, conveyed to the owner, who shall pay to the sheriff [3] and to the constable [4] for every mile he shall necessarily travel in performing this duty.[5]

Report, p. 41. MS (ViU); clerk's copy. Text of Act as adopted is in Hening, XII, 192-3.

Bill was presented by Madison 31 Oct. 1785, passed by the House 1 Dec., amended by Senate 17 Dec., and Senate amendment agreed to by House 19 Dec. (JHD, Oct. 1785, 1828 edn., p. 12-15, 64, 68, 97, 98). Text of Act as adopted agrees with Bill as proposed by Committee save as indicated below. See the Acts of 1753 and 1765 concerning runaways (Hening, VI, 363-8; VIII, 135-6).

1 The Act reads: "ten shillings and one shilling."

2 The Act adds at this point: "or a justice of the peace of the county in which such runaway is confined."

3 The Act reads: "five pounds."

4 The Act reads: "one shilling."

5 An additional clause appears in the Act putting it into effect 1 Jan. 1787.

54. A Bill Declaring What Persons Shall Be Deemed Mulattoes

Be it enacted by the General Assembly, that every person, of whose grandfathers or grandmothers any one is, or shall have been, a negro, although all his other progenitors, except that descending from the negro, shall have been white persons, shall be deemed a mulatto; and so every person, who shall have one fourth part or more of negro blood, shall, in like manner be deemed a mulatto.

Report, p. 41. MS (ViU); clerk's copy. Text of Act as adopted is in Hening, XII, 184.

Bill was presented by Madison 31 Oct. 1785, passed by House 2 Dec., and approved by Senate 5 Dec. (JHD, Oct. 1785, 1828 edn., p. 12-15, 64, 69, 71, 132). Text of Act as adopted is identical with Bill as proposed, save in the addition of a final clause putting it into effect 1 Jan. 1787. See Act of 1705 on the subject of eligibility for office (Hening, III, 252).

55. A Bill Declaring Who Shall Be Deemed Citizens of This Commonwealth

Be[1] it enacted by the General Assembly, that all white persons born within the territory of this commonwealth and all who have resided therein two years next before the passing of this act, and all who shall hereafter migrate into the same;[2] and shall before any court of record give satisfactory proof by their own oath or affirmation, that they intend to reside therein, and moreover shall give assurance of fidelity to the commonwealth; and all infants wheresoever born, whose father, if living, or otherwise, whose mother was, a citizen at the time of their birth, or who migrate hither, their father, if living, or otherwise their mother becoming a citizen, or who migrate hither without father or mother, shall be deemed citizens of this commonwealth, until they relinquish that character in manner as herein after expressed: And all others not being citizens of any the United States of America, shall be deemed aliens. The clerk of the court shall enter such oath of record, and give the person taking the same a certificate thereof, for which he shall receive the fee of one dollar. And in order to preserve to the citizens of this commonwealth, that natural right, which all men have of relinquishing the country, in which birth, or other accident may have thrown them, and, seeking subsistance and happiness wheresoever they may be able, or may hope to find them: And to declare unequivocably what circumstances shall be deemed evidence of an intention in any citizen to exercise that right, it is enacted and declared, that whensoever any citizen of this commonwealth, shall by word of mouth in the presence of the court of the county, wherein he resides, or of the General Court, or by deed in writing, under his hand and seal, executed in the presence of three witnesses, and by them proved in either of the said courts, openly declare to the same court, that he relinquishes the character of a citizen, and shall depart the commonwealth; or whensoever he shall without such declaration depart the commonwealth and enter into the service of any other state, not in enmity with this, or any other of the United States of America, or do any act whereby he shall become a subject or citizen of such state,[3] such person shall be considered as having exercised his natural right of expatriating himself, and shall be deemed no citizen of this commonwealth from the time of his departure. The free white inhabitants of every of the states, parties to the American confederation, paupers, vagabonds and fugitives from justice excepted, shall be intitled to all rights, privileges, and immunities of free citizens in this commonwealth, and shall have free egress, and regress, to and from the same, and shall enjoy therein, all the privileges of trade, and commerce, subject to the same duties, impositions and restrictions as the citizens of this commonwealth. And if any person guilty of, or charged with treason, felony, or other high misdemeanor, in any of the said states, shall flee from justice and be found in this commonwealth, he shall, upon demand of the Governor, or Executive power of the state, from which he fled, be delivered up to be removed to the state having jurisdiction of his offence. Where any person holding property, within this commonwealth, shall be attainted within any of the said states, parties to the said confederation, of any of those crimes, which by the laws of this commonwealth shall be punishable by forfeiture of such property, the said property shall be disposed of in the same manner as it would have been if the owner thereof had been attainted of the like crime in this commonwealth.[4]

Report, p. 41-2. Text of Act as adopted is in Hening, X, 129-30.

In his Autobiography TJ stated: "Early in the session of May 79. I prepared, and obtained leave to bring in a bill, declaring who should be deemed citizens, asserting the natural right of expatriation, and prescribing the mode of exercising it. This, when I withdrew from the House, on the 1st of June following, I left in the hands of George Mason and it was passed on the 26th of that month" (Ford, I, 55-6; see also TJ to John Manners, 12 June 1817). TJ's Bill was ordered to be brought in on 4 June 1779, and Mason presented it on 14 June. It was amended on 25 June and passed by both houses the next day (JHD, May 1779, 1827 edn., p. 35, 48, 67, 68). The Bill as proposed by the Committee of Revisors agrees with the Act passed in 1779 (Hening, X, 129-30) except as indicated below. At the end of the war the question of citizenship became involved in the question of debts owed by Virginians to British merchants; petitions, letters to the *Virginia Gazette*, and pamphlets opposed the return of the British and their admission to citizenship, since, as citizens, British merchants would be in a position to bring suits and have judgments executed against real property (Harrell, *Loyalism in Virginia*, p. 133-40). At the Oct. 1783 session a compromise solution was agreed upon: TJ's citizenship Act of 1779 was repealed in an Act which, however, substantially restated its terms (Hening, XI, 322-4) and another Act was adopted prohibiting the migration of certain persons. The latter forbade the return of anyone who had been a resident in any one of the United States on 19 Apr. 1775 and had subsequently borne arms against the United States; anyone who had owned or had been part owner of a privateer operating against the United States; or anyone who had acted as a member of the board "commonly called the Board of Refugee Commissioners at New-York"; all other former residents who had been forbidden to return were allowed to do so and were given all rights of citizenship save those of voting or of holding office (same, p. 324-5).

On 31 Oct. 1785 Madison presented Bill No. 55 as proposed by the Committee of Revisors; it was read the second time and apparently not acted upon again. Instead, on 24 Dec. 1785 another bill was presented to amend and reduce to one the several Acts on this subject (JHD, Oct. 1785, 1828 edn., p. 12-15, 76, 87, 108, 111). It was not until the Oct. 1786 session, however, that such a bill was passed under the title of "An Act to explain, amend, and reduce into one act, the several acts for the admission of emigrants to the rights of citizenship, and prohibiting the migration of certain persons to this commonwealth." This Act reenacted substantially the provisions of TJ's Act of 1779 and the two Acts of 1783, but, with the exception of the specific prohibitions mentioned above, any alien taking an oath of fidelity to the state could become a citizen, though he could not vote or hold office until he had resided in the state five years and had "evinced a permanent attachment to the state" by marrying a citizen or purchasing lands valued at a minimum of £100—for alien merchants the minimum was £500 (Hening, XII, 261-5).

1 The following highly interesting preamble, which was not in the Act of 1779 or in the Bill as proposed by the Com-

mittee of Revisors, was included in the Acts of 1783 and 1786: "Whereas it is the policy of all infant states to encourage population, among other means, by an easy mode for the admission of foreigners to the rights of citizenship; yet wisdom and safety suggest the propriety of guarding against the introduction of secret enemies, and of keeping the offices of government in the hands of citizens, intimately acquainted with the spirit of the constitution; and the genius of the people, as well as permanently attached to the common interest."

2 The Act of 1779 adds: "other than alien enemies."

3 The Act of 1779 does not include the words "or whensoever he shall without such declaration . . . of such state."

4 The three final provisos of the Act of 1779—(1) equal rights, privileges, and immunities for the citizens of other states; (2) recognition of the right of extradition; and (3) forfeiture under bills of attainder—are not included in the Act of 1783 or in the Act of Oct. 1786 which specifically repealed the Act of 1779.

56. A Bill concerning Aliens

Be it enacted by the General Assembly, that all manner of aliens, of whatsoever nation or country they be, being in amity with the United States of America, together with their families, agents and servants whom they bring, shall be welcome, and freely may come within the commonwealth and there be conversant to merchandise and tarry, or travel, as long as them liketh, and they bear themselves well and with their families, agents and servants whom they bring and their goods shall be suffered peaceably to return into their proper country or elsewhere, without disturbance or impeachment of any.[1]

In case that war arise betwixt the United States of America, and any foreign state, the merchants and people of such state, their families, agents and servants aforesaid, found in this commonwealth, at the beginning of the war, shall not be attached, either in their body or goods, because of such war, but shall be warned by proclamation from the Governor, taking thereon the advice of the Council of State, that they shall depart the commonwealth with their families, agents and servants aforesaid, and their goods, freely, within forty days after the proclamation made and published. In the meantime they shall not be impeached, nor let of their passage, or of making their profit of the same merchandises if they will sell them. And in case that for default of wind, or of ship, or for sickness, or for other evident cause they cannot depart the commonwealth within so short a time, then they shall have other forty days, or so much more as the necessity of their affairs may require, and the Governor and Council may think it safe to allow, and in the meantime may sell their merchandise as afore is said.

But if before their departure credible intelligence shall be brought to the Governor, that the merchants or people of any of the American States[2] be evil treated in the land making war against us, then they shall be attached without harm of body, or goods, until the truth of the matter be certainly known unto the Governor and Council of State: And if the merchants and people of the American States[2] be well treated there, theirs shall be likewise with us: And if otherwise, theirs shall be treated, or demeaned, within the commonwealth, in the manner, form, and condition, as the merchants or people of the American States[2] be treated, or demeaned, in the land making war against us.

Report, p. 42. Text of Act as adopted is in Hening, XII, 184-5.

Bill presented by Madison 31 Oct. 1785, amended 29 Nov., passed by House 2 Dec., and approved by Senate 5 Dec. (JHD, Oct. 1785, 1828 edn., p. 12-15, 64, 69, 71, 132). This Bill, obviously, is based on one of the English statutes TJ had in mind when he wrote that he "thought it material not to vary the diction of the antient statutes by modernizing it, nor to give rise to new questions by new expressions" (Autobiography, Ford, I, 60). With one important exception, together with the usual clause for putting the law in force 1 Jan. 1787, the text of the Act as adopted agrees with the Bill as drawn by the Committee.

1 This paragraph, except for the enacting clause, is not in the Act as adopted, no doubt having been deleted by amendment because of the prevalent feeling of hostility toward former Loyalists (see Harrell, *Loyalism in Virginia*, p. 57-9, 140).

2 The Act reads: "United States."

57. A Bill Declaring that None Shall Be Condemned without Trial, and that Justice Shall Not Be Sold or Deferred

Be it enacted by the General Assembly, that no freeman shall be taken or imprisoned, or be disseised of his freehold, or liberties, or free customs, or be outlawed, or exiled, or any otherwise destroyed, nor shall the commonwealth pass upon him, nor condemn him but by lawful judgment of his peers, or by the laws of the land. Justice or right shall not be sold, denied or deferred to no man.[1]

Report, p. 42. Text of Act as adopted is in Hening, XII, 186.

Bill presented by Madison 31 Oct. 1785, passed by House 2 Dec., amended by Senate 5 Dec., and amendment agreed to by House same day (JHD, Oct. 1785, 1828 edn., p. 12-15, 64, 69, 72, 133). The text of this Bill providing for the ancient right of trial by jury is based upon Magna Carta and was adopted as proposed except for the addition of a clause putting it in effect 1 Jan. 1787 and except for the grammatical correction noted below; TJ must have employed a very early text containing this double negative expression.

1 Act reads: "to any man."

58. A Bill Directing What Prisoners Shall Be Let to Bail

For ascertaining in what cases persons apprehended on suspicion of felony shall, or shall not, be admitted to bail, Be it enacted by the General Assembly that those shall be let to bail who are apprehended for any crime not punishable in life or limb: And if the crime be so punishable, but only a light suspicion of guilt fall on the party he shall in like manner, be bailable: But if the crime be punishable in life or limb, or if it be manslaughter, and there be good cause to believe the party guilty thereof, he shall not be admitted to bail.

No person shall be bailed after conviction of any felony.

If any Justice let any go at large, on bail, who is not bailable, or refuse to admit to bail any who have right to be so admitted, after they shall have offered sufficient bail; or require excessive bail, he shall be punished by imprisonment and amercement[1] at the discretion of a jury.

Report, p. 42-3. Text of Act as adopted is in Hening, XII, 185-6.

Bill was presented by Madison 31 Oct. 1785, amended 29 Nov., passed by House 2 Dec., and approved by Senate 5 Dec. (JHD, Oct. 1785, 1828 edn., p. 12-15, 64, 69, 72, 132). Except for the usual clause putting the Act into effect 1 Jan. 1787 and except for the difference noted below, the Bill as proposed and the Act as adopted are the same.

[1] The Act reads: "he shall be amerced at the discretion of a jury."

59. A Bill Directing the Mode of Suing Out and Prosecuting Writs of Habeas Corpus

Be it enacted by the General Assembly, that whensoever a habeas corpus shall be served, by delivering it to the officer or other person to whom it is directed; or by leaving it at the jail or prison in which the party suing it out is detained; unless the warrant of committment plainly and specially express the same to have been for treason or felony; if the charges of bringing the prisoner, to be ascertained by the Court or Judge who awarded the writ, and thereon endorsed, not exceeding twelve pence per mile, be paid or tendered, and security[1] to pay the charges of carrying him back, in case he be remanded, and that he will not escape by the way, be given by his own or any other person's bond;[2] the officer or his deputy within three days after such service, or, if the prisoner is to be brought more than twenty miles, within so many days more as will be equal to one day, for every twenty miles of such further distance, shall make return of the writ and bring the body of the prisoner, or cause it to be brought, before the proper Judge or

Judges according to the command thereof, and shall then likewise certify the true causes of his detainer or imprisonment:[3] Every such writ shall be signed by him who awards it; and if any person shall be, or stand committed or detained as aforesaid, for any crime, unless it be for treason or felony[4] plainly expressed in the warrant of committment in the vacation time, the prisoner, not being convict, or in execution by legal process, or any one on his behalf may appeal and complain to any Judge of the High Court of Chancery,[5] or General Court, who at the request of such prisoner, or other person on his behalf, attested by two witnesses present at the delivery thereof, is hereby authorised, upon view of a copy of the warrant of committment, or detainer; or otherwise, upon affidavit made, that such copy was denied[6] to be given by him in whose custody the prisoner is detained, to award and grant a habeas corpus, under the seal of the said court, to be directed to the officer in whose custody the party committed or detained shall be returnable immediately before the said Judge, or any other Judge of one of the said courts; and upon service thereof, as aforesaid, the officer, or his deputy, in whose custody the party is so committed or detained, shall, within the times before respectively limitted, bring the prisoner before the court, or one of the Judges thereof, before whom the writ is made returnable; or in case of his absence before any other of them, with the return of the writ and the true causes of the committment and detainer; and thereupon the Judge, before whom the prisoner shall be brought, shall, within two days thereafter discharge him from imprisonment, taking his recognizance, with surety, in any sum according to the discretion of the Judge, having regard to the circumstances of the prisoner and nature of the offence, for his appearance in the General Court the term following, or in some other court where the offence is properly cognizable, as the case shall require;[7] and then shall certify the said writ with the return thereof and the said recognizance into the said court, where such appearance is to be made, unless it shall appear to the Judge that the party so committed is detained upon a legal process, order or warrant, out of some court that hath jurisdiction of criminal matters; or by some warrant signed and sealed, with the hand and seal of any of the said Judges, or some Justice of the Peace, for such matters, or offences, for the which, by the law, the prisoner is not bailable: If any person shall have wilfully neglected, by the space of two terms after his imprisonment, to pray a habeas corpus for his enlargement, such writ shall not be granted to him, in vacation, in pursuance of this act. Any officer neglecting or refusing to make the return aforesaid, or to bring the body of the prisoner, according to the command of the writ within the time aforesaid, or not delivering a true copy of the warrant of committment and detainer within six hours after demand thereof made, to the prisoner, or person demanding it on his behalf, which copy the officer, or his deputy, is hereby required to deliver; shall forfeit to the prisoner one hundred pounds,[8] to recover which, the right of action shall not cease by the death of either or both the parties. No person who shall have been delivered upon a habeas corpus, shall afterwards be imprisoned or committed for the same offence, otherwise than by the order or process of the court wherein he shall be bound by recognizance to appear, or of some other court having jurisdiction of the cause.[9]

A citizen of this commonwealth committed to prison, in custody of an officer, for any criminal matter, shall not be removed from thence into the custody of another officer,[10] unless it be by habeas corpus, or some other legal writs; or where the prisoner shall be delivered to the constable or another inferior officer, to be carried to some common jail, or shall be sent by warrant of an Alderman to some common work-house; or shall be removed from one place to another within the same county, in order to his discharge, or trial, in due course of law; or in case of sudden fire or infection, or other necessity; or where the prisoner shall be charged by affidavit with treason or felony, alledged to be done in any of the other United States of America, in which last case he shall be sent thither, in custody, by order of the General Court, or warrant of Judges[11] thereof, in vacation time, or may be bound by recognizance with sureties before them to appear there, whichsoever shall seem most proper, if the said court or Judges, upon consideration of the matter, shall think he ought to be put upon his trial.[12] Any person as aforesaid may move for, and obtain, his habeas corpus, as well out of the High Court of Chancery, as out of the General Court, and if any Judge of either of the said courts, in the vacation time, upon view of the copy of the warrant of committment, or detainer, or upon affidavit made that such copy was denied as aforesaid, shall refuse any writ of habeas corpus by this act required to be granted, being moved for as aforesaid, such Judge shall be liable to the action of the party grieved.[13]

Report, p. 43. MS (ViU); clerk's copy. Text of Act as adopted in 1784 is in Hening, XI, 408-10. There is also a closely-related draft of a Bill on this subject in DLC: TJ Papers, 236: 42275-6; this is a clerk's copy, endorsed "Concerning Writs of Habeas Corpus," but it has several corrections and interlineations in TJ's hand. There is some evidence that this is a Bill that TJ brought up separately rather than being an early draft of the Bill concerning writs of habeas corpus that was intended for the Committee of Revisors; it is more comprehensive than either the proviso that TJ wrote into his 1776 Bill for Establishing a General Court (q.v., Vol. 1, p. 636, 644, esp. note 33) or the text of Bill No. 59. This MS is referred to below as MS Bill.

Bill No. 59 was brought up separately at the May 1784 session, passed by the House 21 June, and by the Senate 26 June, with several amendments to which the House agreed the same day (JHD, May 1784, 1828 edn., p. 30, 38, 39, 66, 69, 81). The principal differences between the Act as adopted, MS Bill, and Bill No. 59 are indicated below. (MS Bill differs greatly in phraseology even in those passages in which its substance agrees with Bill No. 59.) Despite the Act of 1784, Madison brought up Bill No. 59 on 31 Oct. 1785, when it was read twice and committed to the committee of the whole, but no further action was taken on it (JHD, Oct. 1785, 1828 edn., p. 12-15).

1 Act of 1784 reads: "sufficient security."

2 The preceding eight words are not in Act of 1784.

3 The preceding passage, or rather its equivalent, respecting the manner of issuing and making return on a writ of habeas corpus is in another part of MS Bill, rather than at the beginning; in this passage TJ altered "twenty miles" to "twenty five miles."

4 MS Bill, in the corresponding part, reads: "Treason or Murder."

5 MS Bill merely reads: "upon application to the General Court in term time or to one or more of the Judges thereof in vacation."

6 Act reads "desired"; MS Bill reads "had been demanded of him by whom the Prisoner is detained."

7 Instead of the words "and thereupon the judge . . . case shall require," MS Bill has the following: "And thereupon the said Court, or Judge or Judges, *within two days after* such return made and delivered shall proceed to examine whether the cause of such commitment appearing upon the said return be just and legal or not and shall thereupon do what to justice shall appertain either by delivering bailing or remanding the Prisoner." The italicized words are underscored in MS Bill and the words "immediately on" are interlined above them in TJ's hand. This clearly indicates that this was an alteration made by amendment, and therefore MS Bill must have been introduced as a separate piece of legislation some time during TJ's legislative career.

8 MS Bill reads, following this point: "to be recovered with costs by action of debt or Information in any Court of Record."

9 At this point MS Bill adds the following: "And if any other person contrary to this Act shall knowingly commit or procure to be committed or imprisoned any person so discharged, for the same offence, or be aiding or assisting therein, he shall forfeit to the Party grieved five hundred Pounds to be recovered as aforesaid."

10 MS Bill reads: "he shall not be removed to another prison but by writ of Habeas Corpus; unless it be where the prisoner is directed to be conveyed from Constable to Constable, or to some work house . . . under penalty of one hundred pounds to the Prisoner removed, to be paid by the Person signing a Warrant for such removal, and if none such, then by the Officer or other person removing the Prisoner to be recovered as aforesaid." The words "unless it be" are in TJ's hand.

11 The Act reads: "any two judges."

12 The passage "or where the prisoner shall be charged . . . put upon his trial" is not in MS Bill, but it contains, instead, the following: "But if any person resident within this Commonwealth shall have committed any Capital Offence in any other State in America, where he ought to be tried for the same, such person may be sent in Custody to such other State, there to receive his trial for such Offence, in such manner as shall be settled by the Laws of this and the other States without incurring the Penalties of this Act."

13 The preceding sentence is not in MS Bill, but it contains the following not in Bill No. 59: "No citizen of this Commonwealth resident therein, shall or may be sent Prisoner to any other State in America or beyond sea, under pain of forfeiting to the Person so sent a Prisoner double damages and costs to be recovered by Action of False Imprisonment in any Court of Record, against the Person conveying him and every other person who shall sign any War-

rant or order for the same, or be aiding, assisting or advising therein, or any or either of them. . . . All prosecutions for the Penalties hereby inflicted shall be commenced within two years after the Offence committed and not after."

60. A Bill concerning Guardians, Infants, Masters, and Apprentices

Be it enacted by the General Assembly, that any father, even if he be not twenty one years old, may, by deed, or last will and testament, either of them being executed in presence of two creditable witnesses, grant or devise the custody and tuition of his child, which had never been married, although it be not born, during any part of the infancy of such child, to whomsoever he will; and such grant or devise, heretofore or hereafter to be made, shall give the grantee or devisee the same power over the person of the child, as a guardian in common socage hath, and authorise him, by action of ravishment of ward, or trespass, to recover the child, with damages for the wrongful taking or detaining him or her, for his or her use, and, for the same use, to undertake the care and management, and receive the profits, of the wards estate real and personal, and prosecute and maintain any such action, and suits, concerning the same, as a guardian in common socage may do. The High Court of Chancery, generally, and the court of every county in chancery, within the limits of their jurisdiction, shall have power from time to time, to controul guardians, and hear and determine all matters between them and their wards: To require security of any guardian in socage, or statutory guardian, when that caution shall seem necessary for prevention of any damage his ward may suffer, by neglect, mismanagement, or malversation; and, if the security be refused, or delayed, or if such guardian appear to have been guilty of a flagrant abuse of trust, to displace him, and appoint another in his stead, and to give such directions, and make such rules and orders, as they shall think fit, for the government, maintenance, and education of wards, and preservation of their estates, and for the conduct of guardians. Every court appointing a guardian shall take bond of him, with sufficient surety, for the faithful execution of his office, and if any court omit this duty, or take such surety as shall not satisfy them of his sufficiency, which may be done as well by the surety's affidavit as otherwise, the ward, by an action on the case against the Judges or Justices, so making default, may recover so much of the damages which the guardian and surety shall be answerable for as these shall be unable to pay. If any guardian refuse, or be unable, to give the surety required of him, the court may put the estate into the hands of a curator, the fittest they can prevail upon to undertake the care of it, to be accountable to them; and in that case shall not be sponsible for his ability. Every guardian or curator, to be appointed by any court, shall, at the term or session next afterwards, deliver into such court an inventory upon oath, of all the estate which he shall have received, to be entered of record, in a separate book, and such guardian or curator, and every guardian heretofore so appointed, shall exhibit to such court, once in every year, which if it be a county court, shall be in August, or at the next session, if there be none in that month; or oftener, if he be specially required, accounts upon oath,[1] of the produce of the estate, of the sales and disposition of that produce and of the disbursements; which accounts shall be examined by the court, or by such persons as the court shall refer them to, and, being found and certified, or reported to be properly and fairly stated, and the articles thereof to be justified by the vouchers, and the report, in case of a reference, being approved and confirmed by the court, shall, with such certificate or confirmation, be entered of record in the book aforesaid: And if any article of such accounts, at any time afterwards, be excepted to by the ward or his representative, it shall be incumbent on him to prove or shew the falsity or injustice thereof, unless notice, on his behalf, shall have been given, at the time of passing the accounts, that such article would be excepted to, and a memorandum of that notice shall have been entered on record or desired to be entered. The court at any time when they shall know or have cause to suspect, that the surety of a guardian is failing, may require and compel such guardian to give supplemental security, or, if he refuse or neglect to do so, may displace him. A guardian who shall not deliver in such inventory and render such accounts as aforesaid, shall, by order of the court to which he is amenable, be summoned, and if he remain in default, be compelled to perform his duty, or be displaced, for which purpose the summons or other process from a county court may be directed to, and shall be executed by the sheriff, of any other county, wherein the guardian may be found; and every Judge or Justice of the court sitting therein, at any time during the term or session, in which the process ought to have been ordered, if it be not ordered accordingly, shall be amerced. If the disbursements of the guardian, being suitable to the estate and circumstances of the ward, shall exceed the profits of his estate, in any year, the balance, with the allowance of the court, may be debited in the account of a succeeding year; and a balance appearing on the contrary side may be put out to interest for the benefit of the ward, upon such securities as the court shall approve; or the guardian, if it remain in his hands, shall account for the interest, to be computed from the time his accounts were or ought to have been passed. If any surety for a guardian, by petition to the court before whom they were bound, setting forth, that he apprehends himself to be in danger of suffering thereby, shall pray that he may be relieved, the court, after a summons to answer the petition shall have been served upon the guardian, or a copy of such summons shall have been left at the place of his usual abode, shall order him to give counter security, or to deliver the ward's estate into the hands of the surety or some other; in that case taking sufficient security, or may make such other order for relief of the petitioner as to them shall seem just. The estate of a guardian, not under a specific lien, shall after his death be liable for whatsoever may be due from him on account of his guardianship to his ward, before any other debt due from such guardian. Every orphan, who hath no estate or not sufficient for a maintenance out of the profits, shall by order of the court of the county in which he or she [shall have resided twelve months next preceeding be sent to the school of the hundred for three years; if he or she shall not before have been there, or if he or she shall have been there a part of the said term, then for so long a time as shall complete the said term; and, during attendance on the said school, shall be clothed and boarded so far as his or her own estate will not extend in the like manner as is provided by law for the support of other poor; after which he or she shall][2] be bound apprentice until the age of twenty one years if a boy; or of eighteen years, if a girl, to some master or mistress, who shall covenant to teach the apprentice some art, trade, or business, to be particularised in the indenture,[3] and to pay to him or her three pounds and ten shillings at the expiration of the time. Any guardian may, with the approbation of that court in which his appointment shall be recorded, and not otherwise, bind his ward apprentice to such person, for learning such art, or trade, and with such covenants on the part of the master or mistress, as the said court shall direct; and any such apprentice, with the like approbation, or any apprentice bound by his father may with the approbation of the court of that county in which the father shall reside, after he shall be sixteen years of age, agree to serve until he shall be twenty-four years of age, and such agreement entered on record shall bind him.

The court of every county, city, or borough, shall at all times, receive the complaints of apprentices or hired servants, being citizens of any one of the confederating States of America, who reside within the jurisdiction of such court, against their masters or mistresses, alledging undeserved or immoderate correction, insufficient allowance of food, raiment, or lodging, or want of instruction, and may hear and determine such cases in a summary way, making such orders thereupon as in their judgment will relieve the party injured in future, or removing the apprentices and binding them to other masters or mistresses when it shall seem necessary: and may also in the same manner hear and determine complaints of masters or mistresses against their apprentices or hired servants, for desertion, without good cause, and may oblige the latter, for loss thereby occasioned, to make retribution by further services after expiration of the times for which they had been bound.[4]

Report, p. 43-4. MS (ViU); clerk's copy. Text of Act as adopted is in Hening, XII, 194-8.

Bill presented by Madison 31 Oct. 1785, passed by House 3 Dec., and amended by Senate and referred back to House 7 Dec. On 8 Dec. some of Senate amendments were accepted by House, others amended, and others rejected; the Senate agreed on 9 Dec. (JHD, Oct. 1785, 1828 edn., p. 12-15, 64, 70, 76, 78, 133). This Bill fell within the portion of the work of revision allotted to Pendleton; see 1748 Act for the better management and security of orphans (Hening, V, 449-54). But, as indicated in note 2 below, TJ must have inserted the provision for the elementary schooling of orphans in order to bring this part of the Bill into conformity with his Bill for the More General Diffusion of Knowledge. Except as noted below, the text of the Act as adopted agrees with that of the Bill as proposed by the Committee.

1 The words "upon oath" are not in the Act.

2 The words enclosed in square brackets (supplied) are not in the Act, having been deleted by amendment and the word "resides" substituted therefor. This proviso for educating orphans at public expense was probably written into the Bill by TJ.

3 The Act adds at this point: "as also reading and writing, and if a boy, common arithmetic, including the rule of three." This amendment preserved the existing practice of placing responsibility for the elementary schooling of an apprentice upon the master, a necessary consequence of the rejection of public responsibility as indicated in note 2.

4 The Act as adopted includes the following additional sections not in the Bill: (1) the courts of hustings in the cities of Williamsburg and Richmond and borough of Norfolk and all other incorporated towns were to have the same power as given in this Act to county courts; (2) the Act was to be put in force 1 Jan. 1787.

61. A Bill to Enable Guardians and Committees to Perform Certain Acts for the Benefit of Those Who Are under Their Care

Be it enacted by the General Assembly, that where any person under the age of twenty-one years, or of unsound mind, is, or shall be seized or possessed of any land, tenements, or hereditaments, in trust, or by way of mortgage, the guardian of the one, or committee of the other,[1] by order of the High Court of Chancery, made upon the petition of one or more of the parties interested, and after hearing them all may execute any such deed, or perform any other such act, as the trustee or mortgagee, if he were of full age, or of sane mind, respectively might have executed or performed; and such deed or other act shall be as valid, except that he shall not be bound by a warranty or other covenant contained in the deed. Also the said court may in like manner empower such guardian or committee to make, or take, a surrender of a former lease, and to take, or make, a new lease, as the case may require and as it shall seem most for the advantage of the infant, ideot, or lunatic, out of whose estate any fine that may be advanced and all other just expences that may be incurred in order to obtain a new lease to him, shall be reimbursed, and the new lease shall not be only chargeable with such fine and expences, but shall remain subject to all incumbrances which the lease surrendered would have been subject to.

Report, p. 44-5. MS (ViU); clerk's copy. Text of the Act as adopted is in Hening, XII, 193-4.

Bill was presented by Madison 31 Oct. 1785, amended 29 Nov., passed by House 5 Dec., and approved by Senate the next day (JHD, Oct. 1785, 1828 edn., p. 12-15, 64, 71, 74, 133). Text of Act as adopted agrees with Bill as proposed except for additional clause putting it into effect 1 Jan. 1787 and except as noted below.

[1] The Act adds at this point: "(which committee shall be appointed by the high court of chancery)."

62. A Bill for the Restraint, Maintenance, and Cure of Persons not Sound in Mind

Be it enacted by the General Assembly, that the present directors of the hospital for reception of persons of unsound minds, and their successors, to be chosen when vacancies happen, by joint ballot of both Houses of General Assembly, are hereby constituted a body politic and corporate, to have perpetual continuance, by the name of the Directors of the Hospital, for the maintenance and cure of persons of unsound minds; and by that name may sue and be sued and may, and shall have, and use a common seal; and are enabled to take and hold any estate real and personal, given, or to be given, to the said hospital, or to themselves for the use thereof, so as the annual revenue, or income, of such donations exceed not five[1] hundred pounds, any law or statute to the contrary notwithstanding: and shall, and may, so often as it shall be necessary, choose a president to continue in office until his death, resignation, or removal. And the said directors, or any seven of them, the president being one, shall, from time to time, ordain regulations for the government of the said hospital, and appoint a keeper and[2] matron thereof, with nurses and guards, when they shall be necessary, and provide for the accommodation, maintenance, and cure of the patients remaining and to be received therein. By warrant to be directed to the sheriff, a Justice of Peace may order to be brought before him any person whose mind, from his own observation, or the information of others, he shall suspect to be unsound and with two other Justices who, at his request, shall associate with him, shall inquire into the state of such person's mind; and the said Justices shall write down as well what shall appear to themselves, as what shall be testified by witnesses, touching the supposed insanity; and, if two of them adjudge the party to be such a one as ought to be confined in the hospital, and some friend will not become bound, with surety, to restrain, and take proper care of him or her, until the cause for confinement shall cease, the said Justices, or two of them, shall order the insane to be removed to the said hospital, and there received, and, for that end direct a warrant to the sheriff, and a mittimus to the said keeper, transmitting therewith to the latter the examinations of the witnesses, and a relation of such facts as the said Justices shall think pertinent to the subject, to be laid before the directors. The said keeper, immediately after the person removed shall be delivered to him, the receipt of whom he shall acknowledge in a writing signed by him, and given to the sheriff, shall inform the president thereof, who shall require his colleagues to meet so soon as may be; and at such meeting, which shall not be unnecessarily delayed, the directors, if having considered the case, they concur in opinion with the Justices, shall register the insane as a patient; but they may, at any time afterwards, deliver him or her to a friend becoming bound to restrain, and take care of him or her, in the same manner as the Justices might have done. If the directors differ in opinion from the Justices, they shall report the matter to the High Court of Chancery, who shall thereupon award the writ de idiota inquirendo, directed to the sheriff of that county, from whence the person supposed to be insane shall have been removed, and such person shall be put into the custody of the said sheriff, and remain there until the inquisition be taken and returned, and then shall be enlarged, or registered, as the said court shall order. The court of a county, city, or borough, shall refer it to three Justices to examine into the state of mind of an infant child, or ward, in their county, city, or borough, suggested to such court, by the parent or guardian, to be insane, and upon the report of the said Justices, if the suggestion appear to be true, shall order such insane to be removed, in the manner before directed, to the hospital, where he or she shall be received and registered. The expences of maintaining and endeavouring to cure a registered insane shall be reimbursed out of his estate, if any such there be, and in case of an infant, not an orphan, shall be repaid by the parent,[3] and may be recovered by an action commenced and prosecuted in the names of the directors, who shall account for what shall thus come to their hands. Accounts of expences incurred in execution of this act, as well as for repairing the hospital, and other necessary incidental works and services, shall be audited and discharged in the same manner as other public accounts. The directors shall enlarge every person confined in the hospital, who shall appear to them to be perfectly cured of insanity, and give such person a certificate thereof. A person registered in the hospital, shall, nevertheless, during the time of his or her confinement there, be deemed an inhabitant of that county in which was his or her legal settlement at the time of his or her removal to the hospital.[4]

Report, p. 45. MS (ViU); clerk's copy. Text of Act as adopted is in Hening, XII, 198-200.

Bill was presented by Madison 31 Oct. 1785, amended 20 Dec. and passed by the House 22 Dec., and approved by the Senate 29 Dec. (JHD, Oct. 1785, 1828 edn., p. 12-15, 74-5, 100, 102, 117, 133). The text of the Act as adopted agrees with Bill as proposed by the Committee except as noted below. See the Act of 1769 making provision for the support of persons of unsound mind (Hening, VIII, 378-81); this Act was continued by an Act of Oct. 1776 (same, IX, 173).

1 This was increased to £1000 by the Act as adopted.

2 The Act reads: "or."

3 The Act adds the following at this point: "if of sufficient ability to support such infant, to be adjudged of and certified by the court of the county where such parent resides."

4 The Act has a final clause putting it into effect 1 Jan. 1787.

63. A Bill for Registering Births and Deaths

Be it enacted by the General Assembly, that notice, in writing, of the birth, and time of the birth, of every child shall be given to the Assessors of the public taxes of the hundred, wherein the birth shall have been, at the time of making the assessment next after such birth, by the father, or, if he be dead or unknown, by the mother of the child, in case such mother be a free woman; or, if she be a servant or slave, by her master or mistress, or the overseer or other person having the care of her; in which writing the sex of the child shall be distinguished, with the name and surname of each parent, if it be not a slave; and if it be the child of a servant, with the name and surname of the master or mistress also; but, if it be the child of a slave, with the name and surname of the master or mistress only: And the master or mistress of a family, and the overseer or other person having under his care a family of servants, or slaves, shall give the like notice of every death, and time of the death, which shall happen in such family, adding in the description the name of the deceased, within the same time as is limited for giving, and to the same persons as are appointed to take, the notices of births. Which writings shall be transmitted by such Assessors, together with the notice of the like events in their own families, to the clerk of the peace of the county in which the hundred lieth, and be by him registered. Any person neglecting the duty enjoined by this act shall make amends for the default in this manner; the parent, master, mistress, overseer, or manager, shall be taxed, in the public assessment next afterwards, the sum of five shillings for every birth, or death, whereof notice shall not have been given, and the Assessor or clerk of the peace shall be amerced.

Report, p. 45. MS (ViU); clerk's copy. Bill presented by Madison 31 Oct. 1785, amended 20 Dec., and passed by the House on 21 Dec., when it was referred to the Senate. Apparently no further action was taken on it (JHD, Oct. 1785, 1828 edn., p. 12-15, 74-5, 100, 101-2). See the Act of 1713 (Hening, IV, 42-5).

64. A Bill for Proportioning Crimes and Punishments in Cases Heretofore Capital

Whereas it frequently happens that wicked and dissolute men resigning themselves to the dominion of inordinate passions, commit violations on the lives, liberties and property of others, and, the secure enjoyment of these having principally induced men to enter into society, government would be defective in it's principal purpose[1] were it not to restrain such criminal acts, by inflicting due punishments on those who perpetrate them; but it appears at the same time equally deducible from the purposes of society that a member thereof, committing an inferior injury, does not wholly forfiet the protection of his fellow citizens, but, after suffering a[2] punishment in proportion to his offence is entitled to their protection from all greater pain, so that it becomes a duty in the legislature to arrange in a proper scale the crimes which it may be necessary for them to repress, and to adjust thereto a corresponding gradation of punishments.

And whereas the reformation of offenders, tho' an object worthy the attention of the laws, is not effected at all by capital punishments, which exterminate instead of reforming, and should be the last melancholy resource against those whose existence is become inconsistent with the safety of their fellow citizens, which also weaken the state by cutting off so many who, if reformed, might be restored sound members to society, who, even under a course of correction, might be rendered useful in various labors for the public, and would be living and long continued spectacles to deter others from committing the like offences.

And forasmuch the experience of all ages and countries hath shewn that cruel and sanguinary laws defeat their own purpose by engaging the benevolence of mankind to withold prosecutions, to smother testimony, or to listen to it with bias,[3] when, if the punishment were only proportioned to the injury, men would feel it their inclination as well as their duty to see the laws observed.[4]

For rendering crimes and punishments therefore more proportionate to each other: Be it enacted by the General assembly that no crime shall be henceforth punished by deprivation of life or *limb except those hereinafter ordained to be so punished.

If a man do levy war† against the Commonwealth[5] or be adherent 25.E.3st.5.c.2.
to the enemies of the commonwealth‡[6] giving to them aid or[7] comfort in the commonwealth, or elsewhere, and thereof be convicted
of open deed, by the evidence of two sufficient[8] witnesses, or his 7.W.3.c.3.§.2.

* This takes away the punishment of cutting off the hand of a person striking another, or drawing his sword in one of the Superior courts of justice. Stamf. P.C. 38. 33.H.8 c.12. In an earlier stage of the Common law it was death. Gif hwa ʒefeohte on Cyninʒes huse, sy he scyldiʒ ealles his yrfes, & sy on Cyninʒes dome hwæþer he lif aʒe ðe naʒe: si quis in regis domo pugnet, perdat omnem suam haereditatem, et in regis sit arbitrio, possideat vitam an non possideat. Ll.Inae.6. Gif hwa on Cyninʒes healle ʒefeohte, oþþe his wæpne ʒebrede, & hine mon ʒefo, sy þæt on Cyninʒes dome swa deaþ, swa lif, swa he him forʒyfan wille: si quis in aula regia pugnet, vel arma sua extrahat et capiatur, sit in regis arbitrio tam mors quam vita, sicut ei condonare voluerit. Ll.Alfr.7. Gif hwa on cyninʒes hirede ʒefeohte, ðoliʒe ðæs lifes, buton se cyninʒ him ʒearian wille: si quis in regia dimicat, perdat vitam, nisi rex hoc illi condonare velit. Ll.Cnuti.56. 4.Blackst.125.

† Tho' the crime of an accomplice in treason is not here described, yet Ld. Coke says the partaking and maintaining a treason herein described makes him a principal in that treason; it being a rule that in treason all are principals. 3.Inst. 138. 2.Inst.590. 1.H.6.5.

‡ These words in the Eng. statute narrow it's operation. A man adhering to the enemies of the commonwealth, in a foreign country, would certainly not be guilty of treason with us, if these words be retained. The convictions of treason of that kind in England have been under that branch of the statute which makes the compassing the king's death treason. Foster.196.197. But as we omit that branch, we must by other means reach this flagrant case.

own voluntary confession, the said cases, and ¶no others, shall be adjudged treasons which extend to the commonwealth, and the person so convicted shall suffer death by §hanging, and shall forfiet his lands and goods to the Commonwealth.

If any person commit Petty treason, or a husband murder his wife, a *parent his child, or a child his parent, he shall suffer death by hanging, and his body be delivered to Anatomists to be dissected.

Whosoever committeth murder by poisoning shall suffer death by poison.

Whosoever committeth murder by way of duel, shall suffer

¶ The statute 25.E.3. directs all other cases of treasons to await the opinion of parliament. This has the effect of negative words excluding all other treasons. As we drop that part of the statute we must, by negative words prevent an inundation of Common law treasons. I strike out the word 'it' therefore, and insert 'the said cases and no others.' Qu. how far those negative words may affect the case of accomplices abovementioned? Tho' if their case was within the statute so as that it needed not await the opinion of parliament, it should seem to be also within our act, so as not to be ousted by the negative words.

§ This implies 'by the neck.' See 2. Hawk.444. notes n.o.

* By the statute 21.Jac.1.c.27. and act. assembly 1710.c.12. concealment by the mother of the death of a bastard child is made murder. In justification of this it is said that shame is a feeling which operates so strongly on the mind as frequently to induce the mother of such a child to murther it, in order to conceal her disgrace. The act of concealment therefore proves she was influenced by shame, and that influence produces a presumption that she murthered the child. The effect of this law then is to make what in it's nature is only presumptive evidence of a murder, conclusive of that fact. To this I answer 1. So many children die before, or soon after birth, that to presume all those murdered, who are found dead, is a presumption which will lead us oftener wrong than right, and consequently would shed more blood than it would save. 2. If the child were born dead, the mother would naturally chuse rather to conceal it, in hopes of still keeping a good character in the neighborhood. So that the act of concealment is far from proving the guilt of murder on the mother. 3. If shame be a powerful affection of the mind, is not parental love also? Is it not the strongest affection known? Is it not greater than even that of self-preservation? While we draw presumptions from shame, one affection of the mind, against the life of the prisoner, should we not give some weight to presumptions from parental love, an affection at least as strong, in favor of life? If concealment of the fact is a presumptive evidence of murther, so strong as to overbalance all other evidence that may possibly be produced to take way the presumption, why not trust the force of this incontestable presumption to the jury, who are, in a regular course, to hear presumptive, as well as positive testimony? If the presumption, arising from the act of concealment, may be destroyed by proof positive or circumstantial to the contrary, why should the legislature preclude that contrary proof? Obj. the crime is difficult to prove, being usually committed in secret. Answ. but circumstantial proof will do, for example, marks of violence, the behavior, countenance &c. of the prisoner &c. and if conclusive proof be difficult to be obtained, shall we therefore fasten irremovably upon equivocal proof? Can we change the nature of what is contestable and make it incontestable? Can we make that conclusive which god and nature have made inconclusive? Solon made no law against parricide, supposing it impossible any one could be guilty of it; and the Persians, from the same opinion, adjudged all who killed their reputed parents to be bastards: and altho' parental, be yet stronger than filial affection, we admit saticide proved on the most equivocal testimony, whilst they rejected all proof of an act, certainly not more repugnant to nature, as of a thing impossible, unprovable. See Beccaria §.31.

death by hanging; and if he were the challenger, his body, after death, shall be gibbeted. He who removeth it from the gibbet shall be guilty of a misdemeanor; and the officer shall see that it be replaced. 25.G.2.c.37.

Whosoever shall commit murder in any other way shall suffer death by hanging.

And in all cases of Petty treason and murder one half of the lands and goods of the offender shall be forfieted to the next of kin to the person killed, and the other half descend and go to his own representatives. Save only where one shall slay the Challenger in at †duel, in which case no part of his lands or goods shall be forfieted to the kindred of the party slain, but instead thereof a moiety shall go to the Commonwealth.

The same ‡evidence shall suffice, and order and ¶course of trial be observed in cases of Petty treason as in those of §other murders.

Whosoever shall be guilty of *Manslaughter, shall for the first offence, be condemned to †hard labor for seven years, in the public works, shall forfiet one half of his lands and goods to the next of kin to the person slain; the other half to be sequestered during such term, in the hands and to the use of the Commonwealth, allowing a reasonable part of the profits for the support of his family. The second offence shall be deemed Murder.

† Qu. if the estates of both parties in a duel should not be forfieted? The deceased is equally guilty with a suicide.

‡ Qu. if these words may not be omitted? By the Common law one witness in treason was sufficient. Foster 233. Plowd.8.[a.] Mirror c.3.§.34. Waterhouse on Fortesc. de laud.252. Carth.1[44] per Holt. But Ld. Coke contra 3.inst.26. The statute 1.E.6.c.[12.] and 5.E.6.c.11. first required two witnesses in treason. The clause against high treason supra does the same as to high treason: but it seems if 1st. and 5th. E.6. are dropped Petty treason will be tried and proved as at Common law, [by] one witness. But qu. Ld. Coke being contra, whose opinion it is ever dangerous to neglect.

¶ These words are intended to take away the peremptory challenge of 35. jurors. The same words being used 1.2. Ph.&M.c.10. are deemed to have restored the peremptory challenge in high treason; and consequently are sufficient to take it away. Foster.237.

§ Petty treason is considered in law only as an aggravated murder. Foster 107.323. A pardon of all murde[rs] pardons Petty treason. 1.Hale P.C.378. see 2.H.P.C.340.342. It is also included in the word 'felony,' so that a pardo[n] of all felonies pardons petty treason. See sheet F.3.b.

* Manslaughter is punishable at law by burning in the hand, and forfieture of chattels.

† It is best, in this act, to lay down principles only, in order that it may not for ever be undergoing change: and, to carry into effect the minuter parts of it, frame a bill 'for the employment and government of felons, or malefactors condemned to labor for the Commonwealth,' which may serve, as an Appendix to this, and in which all the particulars requisite may be directed: and as experience will from time to time be pointing out amendments, these may be made without touching this fundamental act. See More's Utopia. pa.50. some good hints. Fugitives might, in such a bill, be obliged to work two days for every one they absent themselves.

And where persons, meaning to commit a ‡trespass only, or larceny, or other unlawful deed, and doing an act from which involuntary homicide hath ensued, have heretofore been adjudged guilty of manslaughter, or of murder, by transferring such their unlawful intention to an act much more penal than they could have in probable contemplation; no such case shall hereafter be deemed manslaughter, unless manslaughter was intended, nor murder, unless murder was intended.

In other cases of homicide[10] the law will not add to the miseries of the party by punishments or forfietures.¶

‡ The shooting at a wild fowl, and killing a man is homicide by misadventure. Shooting at a pullet,[9] without any design to take it away, is manslaughter; and with a design to take it away, is murder. 6.Sta.tr.222. To shoot at the poultry of another, and thereby set fire to his house, is Arson, in the opinion of some. Dalt.c.116. 1.Hale's P.C.569. contra.

¶ Beccaria.§.32. suicide. Homicides are 1. Justifiable. 2. Excusable. 3. Felonious. For the last, punishments have been already provided. The 1st. are held to be totally without guilt, or rather commendable. The 2d. is in some cases not quite unblamable. These should subject the party to marks of contrition. viz. the killing a man in defence of property; so also in defence of one's person, which is a species of excusable homicide; because altho' cases may happen where these also are commendable, yet most frequently they are done on too slight appearance of danger; as in return for a blow, kick, fillup &c. or on a person's getting into a house, not animo furandi, but perhaps Veneris causâ &c. Bracton says 'si quis furem nocturnum occiderit, ita demum impune foret, si parcere ei sine periculo suo non poterit, si autem potuit, aliter erit.' 'Item erit si quis *hamsokne* quae dicitur invasio domus, contra pacem domini regis in domo sua se defenderit, et invasor occisus fuerit; impersecutus et inultus remanebit, si ille quem invasit aliter se defendere non potuit; dicitur enim quod non est dignus habere pacem qui non vult observare eam.' L.3.c.23.§.3. 'Qui latronem occiderit, non tenetur, nocturnum vel diurnum, si aliter periculum evadere non passit; tenetur tamen si possit. Item non tenetur si per infortunium, et non animo et voluntate occidendi, nec dolus, nec culpa ejus inveniatur.' L.3.c. 36.§.1. The statute 24.H.8.c.5. is therefore merely declaratory of the Common law. See on the general subject Puffend. 2.5.§.10.11.12.16.17. Excusable homicides are by Misadventure, or in self-defence. It is the opinion of some lawyers that the Common law punished these with death, and that the statute of Marlbridge c.26. and Glocester c.9. first took away this by giving them title to a pardon, as matter of right, and a writ of restitution of their goods. See 2.Inst.148. 315. 3.Inst.55. Bracton L.3.c.4.§.2. Fleta L.1.c.23.§.14.15. 21.E.3.23. But it is believed never to have been capital. 1.H.P. C.425. 1.Hawk.75. Foster 282. 4.Bl.188. It seems doubtful also whether at Common law the party forfeited all his chattels in this case, or only paid a weregild. Foster, ubi supra, doubts, and thinks it of no consequence, as the statute of Glocester entitles the party to Royal grace, which goes as well to forfeiture as life. To me there seems no reason for calling these Excusable homicides, and the killing a man in defence of property a Justifiable homicide. The latter is less guiltless than misadventure or self-defence.

Suicide is by law punishable by forfeiture of chattels. This bill exempts it from forfeiture. The Suicide injures the state less than he who leaves it with his effects. If the latter then be not punished, the former should not. As to the example, we need not fear it's influence. Men are too much attached to life to exhibit frequent instances of depriving themselves of it. At any rate, the quasi-punishment of confiscation will not prevent it. For if one be found who can calmly determine to renounce life, who is so weary of his existence here as rather to make experiment of what is beyond the grave, can we suppose him, in such a state of mind, susceptible of influence from the losses to his family by confiscation? That men in general too disapprove of this severity is apparent from the constant practice of juries finding the suicide in a state of insanity; because they have no other way of saving the forfeiture. Let it then be done away.

Whenever sentence of death shall have been pronounced against any person for treason or murder, execution[11] shall be done on the next day but one after such sentence, unless it be Sunday, and then on the Monday following. 25.G.2.c.37. Beccaria.§.19.

Whosoever shall be guilty of §Rape *Polygamy,[12] or †Sodomy with man or woman shall be punished, if a man, by ‡castration, if a woman, by cutting thro' the cartilage of her nose a hole of one half inch diameter at the least. §13.E.1.c.34. *1.Jac.1.c.11. †25.H.8.c.6. ‡Bracton Fleta &c.

But no one shall be punished for Polygamy who shall have married after probable information of the death of his or her hus-

§ Forcible abduction of a woman having substance, is felony by 3.H.7.c.2. 3.Inst.61. 4.Bl.208. If goods be taken, it will be felony as to them without this statute: and as to the abduction of the woman, qu. if not better to leave that, and also kidnapping 4.Bl.219. to the Common law remedies, viz. fine, imprisonment, and pillory. Raym.474. 2.Show. 221. Skin.47. Comb.10. The writs of Homine replegiando, Capias in Withernam Habeas corpus, and the action of Trespass? Rape was felony at the Common law. 3.Inst.60. But see 2.Inst.181. further. For it's definition see 2.Inst.180. Bracton L.3.c.28.§.1. says the punishment of rape is 'amissio membrorum, ut sit membrum pro membro, quia virgo, cum corrumpitur, membrum amittit, et ideo corruptor puniatur in eo in quo deliquit; oculos igitur amittat propter aspectum decoris quo virginem concupivit; amittat et testiculos qui calorem stupri induxerunt. Olim quidem corruptores virginitatis et castitatis suspendebantur et eorum fautores &c. modernis tamen temporibus aliter observatur' &c. and Fleta 'solet justiciarius pro quolibet mahemio ad amissionem testiculorum veloculorum convictum condemnare, sed non sine errore, eo quod id judicium nisi in corruptione virginum tantum competebat; nam pro virginitatis corruptione solebant abscidi et meritò judicari, ut sic pro membro quod abstulit, membrum per quod deliquit amitteret, viz. testiculos, qui calorem stupri induxerunt' &c. Fleta.L.1.c. 40.§.4. 'Gif ðeow man ðeowne to nydhæmed ȝenyde, ȝebete mid his eowende': si servus servam ad stuprum coegerit, compenset hoc virga sua virili. Si quis puellam &c.' Ll.Aelfridi.25. 'Hi purgist femme per forze forfait ad les membres.' Ll.Gul.conq.19. In Dyer 304. a man was indicted and found guilty of rape on a girl of seven years old. The court 'doubted of the rape of so tender a girl; but if she had been nine years old, it would have been otherwise.' 14.Eliz. Therefore the statute 18.El.c.6. says 'for plain declaration of law be it enacted that if any person shall unlawfully and carnally know and abuse any womanchild under the age of 10. years &c. he shall suffer as a felon without allowance of clergy.' Ld. Hale however 1.P.C.630. thinks it rape independant of that statute to know carnally a girl under 12. the age of consent. Yet 4.Bl.212. seems to neglect this opinion; and as it was founded on the words of 3.E.1.c.13. and this is with us omitted, the offence of carnally knowing a girl under 12. or 10. years of age will not be distinguished from that of any other.

* Polygamy was not penal till the statute 1.Jac. The law contented itself with the nullity of the act. 4.Bl.163. 3.Inst.88.

† Buggery is twofold. 1. with mankind, 2. with beasts. Buggery is the Genus, of which Sodomy and Bestiality are the species. 12.Co.37. says 'note that Sodomy is with mankind.' But Finch's L.B.3.c.24. 'Sodomitry is a carnal copulation against nature, to wit, of man or woman in the same sex, or of either of them with beasts.' 12.Co.36. says 'it appears by the antient authorities of the law that this was felony.' Yet the 25.H.8. declares it felony, as if supposed not to be so. Britton c.9. says that Sodomites are to be burnt. F.N.B.269.b. Fleta.L.1.c.37. says 'pecorantes et Sodomitae in terra vivi confodiantur.' The Mirror makes it treason. Bestiality can never make any progress; it cannot therefore be injurious to society in any great degree, which is the true measure of criminality in foro civili, and will ever be properly and severely punished by universal derision. It may therefore be omitted. It was antiently punished with death as it has been latterly. Ll.Aelfrid.31. and 25H.8.c.6. See Beccaria §.31. Montesq.

band or wife, or after his or her husband or wife hath absented him or herself, so that no notice of his or her being alive hath reached such person for 7. years together, or hath suffered the punishments before prescribed for rape, polygamy or sodomy.[13]

22.23.Car.2.c.1. Whosoever on purpose and of malice forethought shall maim¶ another, or shall disfigure him, by cutting out or disabling the tongue, slitting or cutting off a nose, lip or ear, branding, or otherwise, shall be maimed or disfigured in §like sort:[14] or if that cannot be for want of the same part, then as nearly as may be in some other part of at least equal value and estimation in the opinion of a jury, and moreover shall forfiet one half of his lands and goods to the sufferer.

25.E.3.st.5.c.2. Whosoever shall *counterfiet any coin current by law within this Commonwealth, or any paper bills issued in the nature of

¶ Maiming was felony at the Common law. Britton.c.25. 'mahemium autem dici poterit, ubi aliquis in aliquâ parte sui corporis læsionem acceperit, perquam affectus sit inutilis ad pugnandum: ut si manus amputetur, vel pas, oculus privatur, vel scerda de osse capitis lavetur, vel si quis dentes praecisores amiserit, vel castratus fuerit, et talis pro mahemiato poterit adjudicari.' Fleta.L.1.c.40. 'et volens que nul maheme ne soit tenus forsque de membre tollet dount home est plus feble à combatre, sicome del oyl, ou de la mayn, ou del pie, ou de la tete debruse, ou de les dentz devant.' Britton c.25. For further definitions see Bracton L.3.c.24.§.3.4. Finch L.B.3.c.12. Co.L. 126.a.b.288.a. 3.Bl.121. 4.Bl.205. Stamf. P.C.L.1.c.41. I do not find any of these definitions confine the offence to wilful and malicious definitions of it. 22.23.Car. 2.c.1. called the Coventry act has the words 'on purpose and of malice forethought.' Nor does the Common law prescribe the same punishment for disfiguring as for maiming.

§ The punishment was by retaliation. 'Et come ascun appele serra de tele felonie atteint et attende jugement, si soit le jugement tiel que il perde autiel membre come il avera tollet al pleintyfe. Et si la pleynte soit faite de femme que avera tollet a home ses membres, en tiel cas perdra la femme la une meyn par jugement, come le membre dount ele avera trespasse.' Britton.c.25. Fleta.B.1.c.40. Ll.Aelfr.19.40.

* By the laws of Aethelstan and Canute this was punished by cutting off the hand. 'ʒif se mynetere ful wurþe, slea man þa hand of, ðe he þaet ful mid worhte, & sette uppon ða mynet smiþþan': in English characters and words 'if the Minter foul [criminal][15] wert, slay the hand off, that he the foul [crime][15] with wrought, and set upon the mint-smithery.' Ll. Aethelst.14. '& se ðe ofer ðis false wyrce, ðoliʒe ðæra handa ðe he þæt false mid worhte.' 'Et si quis praeter hanc, falsam fecerit, perdat manum quacum falsam confecit.' Ll.Cnuti.8. It had been death by the Ll.Aethelredi sub fine. By those of H.1. 'si quis cum falso denario inventus fuerit—fiat justitia mea, saltem de dextro pugno et de testiculis.' Anno 1108. Operae pretium vero est audire quam severus rex fuerit in pravos. Monetarios enim fere omnes totius Angliae fecit ementulari, et manus dextras abscindi, quia monetam furtive corruperant. Wilkins ib. et anno 1125. When the Common law became settled it appears to have been punishable by death. 'Est aliud genus criminis quod sub nomine falsi continetur, et tangit coronam domini regis, et ultimum inducit supplicium, sicut de illis qui falsam fabricant monetam, et qui de re non reproba, faciunt reprobam; sicut sunt retonsores denariorum. Bract.L.3.c.3.§.2. Fleta.L.1.c.22.§.4. Ld. Hale thinks it was deemed petty treason at Common law. 1.H.P.C.220.224. The bringing in false money with *intent* to merchandise and make paiment of it is treason by 25.E.3. but the best proof of the intention is the act of passing it, and why not leave room for repentance here, as in other cases of felonies intended? 1.H.P.C.229.

money, or of certificates of loan on the credit of this Commonwealth, or of all or any of the United States of America, or any Inspectors notes for tobacco, or shall pass any such counterfieted coin, paper bills, or notes, knowing them to be counterfiet; or, for the sake of lucre, shall †diminish, case, or wash any such coin,[16] shall be condemned to hard labor six years in the public works, and shall forfiet all his lands and goods to the Commonwealth.[17]

5.El.c.11.
18.El.c.1.
8.9.W.3.c.26.
15.16.G.2.c.28.
7.Ann.c.25.

Whosoever committeth Arson shall be condemned to hard labor five years in the public works, and shall make good the loss of the sufferers threefold.‡

43.El.c.13.
Confined to 4. counties.
22.23.Car.2.c.7.
9.G.1.c.22.
9.G.3.c.29.

If any person shall within this Commonwealth, or being a citizen thereof shall without the same, wilfully destroy, or run away with any sea-vessel or goods laden on board thereof, or plunder or pilfer any wreck, he shall be condemned to hard labor five years in the public works, and shall make good the loss of the sufferers threefold.

1.Ann.St.2.c.9.
12.Ann.c.18.
4.G.1.c.12.
26.G.2.c.19.
11.12.W.3.c.7.

Whosoever committeth ¶Robbery[18] shall be condemned to hard labor four years in the public works, and shall make double reparation to the persons injured.

Whatsoever act, if committed on any Mansion house, would be

† Clipping, filing, rounding, impairing, scaling, lightening, (the words in the statutes) are included in 'diminishing': gilding, in the word 'casing'; colouring in the word 'washing,' and falsifying, or marking is 'counterfeiting.'

‡ Arson was a felony at Common law. 3.inst.66. Punished by a fine Ll.Aethelst. 6. But Ll.Cnuti.61. make it a 'scelus inexpiabile.' 'hus brec & bærnet, & open ðyfþ, & æberemorþ, & hlafordswice, æfter woruld laȝa is botleas': word for word 'house break and burnt, and open theft, and manifest murther, and lord-treachery, after world's law is bootless.' Bracton says it was punished by death. 'Si quis turbida seditione incendium fecerit nequiter et in felonia, vel ob inimicitias, vel praedandi causa, capitali puniatur poena vel sententia.' Bract.L.3.c.27. He defines it as commissible by burning 'aedes alienas.' Ib. Britton c.9. 'Ausi soit enquis de ceux que felonisement en temps de pees eient autre *blees* ou autre *mesons* ars, et ceux que serrount de ces atteyntz, soient ars issint que eux soient punys par mesme cele chose dount ilz pecherent.' Fleta.L.1.c.37. is a copy of Bracton. The Mirrour c.1.§.8. says 'Ardours sont que ardent citie, ville, maison home, maison beast, ou auters chatelx, de lour felonie en temps de pace pour haine ou vengeance.' Again c.2.§.11. pointing out the words of the appellor 'jeo dise que Sebright &c. en tiel meason ou *biens* mist le feu.' Coke 3.Inst.67. says 'the antient authors extended this felony further than houses, viz. to stacks of corn, waynes or carts of coal, wood or other goods.' He defines it as commissible not only on the inset houses, parcel of the mansion house, but to the out-set also, as barn, stable, cowhouse, sheep house, dairy-house, milhouse and the like, parcel of the mansion house. But 'burning of a barn, being no parcel of a mansion house, is no felony' unless there be corn or hay within it. Ib. the 22.23.Car.2. and 9.G.1. are the principal statutes against arson. They extend the offence beyond the Common law.

¶ Robbery was a felony at Common law. 3.Inst.65. 'Scelus inexpiabile' by the Ll.Cnuti.61. [see before in Arson.][15] It was punished with death. Britt.c.15. 'de robbours et de larouns et de semblables mesfesours, soit ausi ententivement enquis—et tauntost soient ceux robbours juges a la mort.' Fleta says 'si quis convictus fuerit de bonis viri robbatis vel asportatis ad sectam regis judicium capitale subibit.' L.1.c.39. See also Bract.L. 3.c.32.§.1.

deemed §Burglary,[19] shall be Burglary if committed on any other house; and he who is guilty of Burglary,[19] shall be condemned to hard labor four years in the public works, and shall make double reparation to the persons injured.

Whatsoever act, if committed in the night time, shall constitute the crime of Burglary, shall, if committed in the day be deemed Housebreaking*; and whosoever is guilty thereof shall be condemned to hard labor three years in the public works, and shall make reparation to the persons injured.

Whosoever shall be guilty of Horsestealing† shall be condemned to hard labor three years in the public works, and shall make reparation to the person injured.

Grand Larceny shall be where the goods stolen are of the value

§ Burglary was felony at the Common law. 3.Inst.63. It was not distinguished by antient authors, except the Mirror, from simple House-breaking, ib.65. Burglary and Housebreaking were called 'Hamsockne' 'diximus etiam de pacis violatione et de immunitatibus domus, si quis hoc in postorum fecerit ut perdat omne quod habet, et sit in regis arbitrio utrum vitam habeat. Eac we cwædon be mundbryce & be hamsocnum, se ðe hit ofer þis do, þæt he ðolie ealles ðæs ðe aʒe, & sy on cyninʒes dome hwæþer he life aʒe: and we quoth of mound-breach, and of home-seeking he who it after this do, that he dole all that he owe [owns],[15] and is in king's doom whether he life owes [owns].'[15] Ll.Eadmundi.c.6. and see Ll.Cnuti.61. 'husbrec' in notes on Arson, ante. A Burglar was also called a Burgessor. 'et soit enquis de Burgessours et sunt tenus Burgessours trestious ceux que *felonisement* en temps de pees debrusont esglises ou auter mesons, ou murs, ou portes de nos cytes, ou de nos burghes.' Britt.c.10. 'burglaria est nocturna diruptio habitaculi alicujus, vel ecclesiae, etiam murorum, portarumve civitatis aut burgi, ad feloniam aliquam perpetrandam. *Noctanter* dico, recentiores secutus; veteres enim hoc non adjungunt.' Spelm. gloss. verb. Burglaria. It was punished with death. Ib. citation from the Office of a Coroner. It may be committed in the Outset houses, as well as Inset. 3.Inst.65. Tho' not under the same roof or contiguous, provided they be within the Curtilage or Homestall. 4.Bl. 225. As by the Common law all felonies were clergiable, the statute 23.H.8.c.1. 5.E.6.c.9. and 18.El.c.7. first distinguished them by taking the clerical privilege of impunity from the principals, and 3.4.W.M.c.9. from accessories before the fact. No *statute* defines what Burglary is. The 12.Ann.c.7. decides the doubt whether, where breaking is subsequent to entry, it is Burglary. Bac. elements had affirmed, and 1.H.P.C.554. had denied it. Our bill must distinguish them by different degrees of punishment.

* At the Common law the offence of Housebreaking was not distinguished from Burglary, and neither of them from any other larceny. The Statutes at first took away clergy from Burglary, which made a leading distinction between the two offences. Later statutes however have taken clergy from so many cases of housebreaking as nearly to bring the offences together again. These are 23.H.8.c.1. 1.E.6.c.12. 5.&6.E.6.c.9. 3.&4.W.M.c.9. 39.El.c.15. 10.&11.W. 3.c.23. 12.Ann.c.7. See Barr.428. 4.Bl. 240. The circumstances which in these statutes characterise the offence seem to have been occasional and unsystematical. The houses on which Burglary may be committed, and the circumstances which constitute that crime being ascertained, it will be better to define Housebreaking by the same subjects and circumstances, and let the crimes be distinguished only by the hour at which they are committed, and the degree of punishment.

† The offence of horse-stealing seems properly distinguishable from other larcenies, here, where these animals generally run at large, the temptation is so great and frequent, and the facility of commission so remarkable. See 1.E.6. c.12. 23.E.6.c.33. 31.El.c.12.

of ‡five dollars, and whosoever shall be guilty thereof shall be forthwith put in the pillory for one half hour, shall be condemned to hard¶ labor two years in the public works, and shall make[20] reparation to the person injured.

Petty Larceny shall be where the goods stolen are of less value than five dollars; whosoever shall be guilty thereof shall be forthwith put in the pillory for a quarter of an hour, shall be condemned to hard labor one year in the public works, and shall make reparation to the person injured. 2.G.2.c.25.§.3. 7.G.3.c.50.

Robbery or Larceny of Bonds, bills obligatory, bills of exchange, or promisory notes for the paiment of money or tobacco, lottery tickets, paper bills issued in the nature of money, or of certificates of loan on the credit of this commonwealth, or of all or any of the United States of America, or Inspectors notes for tobacco, shall be punished in the same manner as robbery or larceny of the money or tobacco due on, or represented by such papers.

Buyers and Receivers of goods taken by way of robbery or larceny, knowing them to have been so taken, shall be deemed Accessaries to such robbery or larceny after the fact. 3.4.W.M.c.9.§.4. 5.Ann.c.31.§.3. 4.G.1.c.11.§.1. 1.E.2.

‡ The distinction between grand and petty larceny is very antient. At first 8d. was the sum which constituted grand larceny. Ll.Aethelst.c.1. 'ne parcatur ulli furi, qui furtum manutenens captus sit, supra 12. annos nato, et supra 8. denarios.' Afterwards, in the same king's reign it was raised to 12d. 'non parcatur alicui furi ultra 12. denarios, et ultra 12. annos nato—ut occidamus illum et capiamus omne quod possidet, et inprimis sumamus rei furto ablatae pretium ab haerede, ac dividatur postea reliquum in duas partes, una pars uxori, si munda, et facinoris conscia non sit; et residuum in duo, dimidium capiat rex, dimidium societas.' Ll.Aethelst. Wilkins p.65.

¶ Ll.Inae.c.7. 'Si quis furetur ita ut uxor ejus et infans ipsius nesciant, solvat 60. solidos poenae loco, si autem furetur testantibus omnibus haeredibus suis, *abeant omnes in servitutem.*' Ina was king of the West-Saxons, and began to reign A. C. 688. After the union of the Heptarchy, i.e. temp. Aethelst. inter 924. and 940. we find it punishable with death as above. So it was int. 1017. and 1035. viz. temp. Cnuti. Ll.Cnuti.61. cited in Notes on Arson. In the time of William the Conqueror it seems to have been made punishable by fine only. Ll.Gul.conq. apud Wilk.p.218.220. This commutation however was taken away by Ll.H.1. anno 1108. 'Si quis in furto vel latrocinio deprehensus fuisset, suspenderetur; sublata wirgildorum, id est, pecuniarae redemptionis lege.' Larceny is the felonious taking and carrying away of the personal goods of another. 1. As to the taking, the 3.4.W.M.c.9.§.5. is not additional to the Common law, but declaratory of it; because where only the care or use, and not the possession, of things is delivered, to take them was larceny at the Common law. The 33.H. 6.c.1. and 21.H.8.c.7. indeed have added to the Common law, by making it larceny in servants to convert things of his master's. But qu. if they should be imitated more than other breaches of trust in general. 2. As to the subject of larceny 4.G.2.c.32. 6.G.3.c.36.[48.] 43. El.c.7. 15.Car.2.c.2. 23.G.2.c.26. 31.G. 2.c.35. 9.G.3.c.41. 25.G.2.c.10. have extended larceny to things of various sorts either real, or fixed to the realty. But the enumeration is unsystematical and in this country, where the produce of the earth is so spontaneous, as to have rendered things of this kind scarcely a breach of civility or good manners, in the eyes of the people, qu. if it would not too much enlarge the field of criminal law? The same may be questioned of 9.G.1.c.22. 13.Car.2.c.10. 10.G.2.c.32. 5.G.3.c.14. 22.&23.Car.2.c.25. 37.E.3. c.19. making it felony to steal animals ferae naturae.

Prison breakers also shall be deemed Accessories after the fact to traitors or felons whom they enlarge from prison.§

All attempts to delude the people, or to abuse their understanding by exercise of the pretended arts of witchcraft, conjuration, inchantment, or sorcery or by pretended prophecies, shall be punished by ducking and whipping at the discretion of a jury, not exceeding 15. stripes.*

1.Ann.c.9.§.2. If the principal offender be fled, or secreted from justice, in any case not touching life or member, the Accessories may notwithstanding be prosecuted as if their principal were convicted.†

§ Breach of prison at the Common law was capital, without regard to the crime for which the party was committed. 'Cum pro criminis qualitate in carcerem recepti fuerint, conspiraverint (ut ruptis vinculis aut fracto carcere) evadant, amplius (quam causa pro qua recepti sunt exposeit) puniendi sunt, videlicet ultimo supplicio, quamvis ex eo crimine innocentes inveniantur, propter quod inducti sunt in carcerem et imparcati.' Bracton.L.3.c.9.§.4. Britt.c.11. Fleta L.1.c.26.§.4. Yet in the Y.B.Hill.1.H.7.2. Hussey says that by the opinion of Billing and Choke, and all the justices it was a felony in strangers only, but not in the prisoner himself. S.C.Fitz.abr. Coron.48. They are principal felons, not accessories. ib. Whether it was felony in the prisoner at Common law is doubted. Stam.P.C.30.b. The Mirror c.5.§.1. says 'abusion est a tener escape de prisoner, ou de bruserie del gaole pur peche mortell, car cel usage nest garrant per nul ley, ne in nul part est use forsque in cest realme, et en France, eins [mais][15] est leu garrantie de ceo faire per la ley de nature.' 2.Inst.589. the statute 1.E.2. de frangentibus prisonam restrained the judgment of life and limb for prison breaking to cases where the offence of the prisoner required such judgment.

It is not only vain, but wicked, in a legislator to frame laws in opposition to the laws of nature, and to arm them with the terrors of death. This is truly creating crimes in order to punish them. The law of nature impels every one to escape from confinement; it should not therefore be subjected to punishment. Let the legislator restrain his criminal by walls, not by parchment. As to strangers breaking prison to enlarge an offender, they should, and may be fairly considered as accessories after the fact. This bill saying nothing of the prisoner releasing himself by breach of jail, he will have the benefit of the first section of the bill, which repeals the judgment of life and death at the Common law.

* Gif wiccan, oþþe wiȝleras, mansworan, oþþe morþwyrhtan, oþþe fule afylede æbere horcwenan ahwhar on lande wurþan aȝytene, ðonne fyrsie man of earde, & clænsie ða ðeode, oþþe on earde forfare hi mid ealle, buton hi ȝeswican, & ðe deoper ȝebetan: if witches, or weirds, man-swearers, or murther-wroughters, or foul, defiled, open whore-queens ay-where in the land were gotten, then force them off earth, and cleanse the nation, or in earth forthfare them withal, buton they beseech, and deeply better. Ll.Ed.et Guthr.c.11. 'sagae, mulieres barbara factitantes sacrificia, aut pestiferi, si cui mortem intulerint, neque id inficiari poterint, capitis poena esto.' Ll.Aethelst.c.6. apud Lambard. et Ll.Aelfr.30. Ll.Cnuti.c.4. 'mesme cel jugement (d'etre ars) eyent sorcers, et sorceresses' &c. ut supra. and Fleta ut et ubi supra. 3.Inst.44. Trial of witches before Hale in 1664. The statutes 33.H.8.c.8. 5.El.c.16. and 1. Jac.1.c.12. seem to be only in confirmation of the Common law. 9.G.2.c.25. punishes them with pillory, and a year's imprisonment. 3.E.6.c.15. 5.El.c.15. punishes fond, fantastical and false prophecies, by fine and imprisonment.

† As every treason includes within it a misprision of treason, so every felony includes a misprision, or misdemeanor. 1.Hale P.C.652.708. 'licet fuerit felonia, tamen in eo continetur misprisio.' 2.R. 3.10. Both principal and accessory therefore may be proceeded against in any case, either for felony, or misprision, at the Common law. Capital cases not being mentioned here, accessories to them will of course be triable for misprisions, if the offender flies.

If any offender stand mute of obstinacy, or challenge peremptorily more of the jurors than by law he may, being first warned of the consequence thereof, the court shall proceed as if he had confessed the charge.‡ 3.E.1.c.12.

Pardon and Privilege of clergy shall henceforth be abolished, that none may be induced to injure through hope of impunity. But if the verdict be against the defendant, and the court before whom the offence is heard and determined, shall doubt that it may be untrue for defect of testimony, or other cause, they may direct a new trial to be had.¶

No attainder shall work corruption of blood in any case.[21]

In all cases of forfeiture, the widow's dower shall be saved to

‡ Whether the judgment of penance lay at Common law see 2.Inst.178. 2.H. P.C.321. 4.Bl.322. It was given on standing mute: but on challenging more than the legal number, whether that sentence, or sentence of death, is to be given, seems doubtful. 2.H.P.C.316. Qu. whether it would not be better to consider the supernumerary challenge as merely void, and to proceed in the trial? Qu. too in case of silence?

¶ 'Cum Clericus sic de crimine convictus degradetur, non sequitur alia poena pro uno delicto, vel pluribus ante degradationem perpetratis. Satis enim sufficit ei pro poena degradatio, quae est magna capitis diminutio, nisi forte convictus fuerit de *apostatia*, quia hinc primo degradetur, et postea per manum laicalem comburetur, secundum quod accidit in concilio Oxoni. celebrato a bonae memoriae S. Cantuarien. Archiepiscopo dequodam diacono, qui se apostatavit pro quadam Judaea; qui cum esset per episcopum degradatus, statim fuit igni traditus per manum laicalem.' Bract.L.3.c.9.§.2. 'Et mesme cel jugement (i.e. qu'ils soient ars) eyent sorcers, et sorceresses, et sodomites et mescreauntz apertement atteyntz.' Britt. c.9. 'Christiani autem *Apostatae*, sorti legii, et hujus modi detractari debent et comburi.' Fleta.L.1.c.37.§.2. See 3.Inst. 39. 12.Rep.92. 1.H.P.C.393. The extent of the clerical privilege at the Common law. 1. As to the crimes, seems very obscure and uncertain. It extended to no case where the judgment was not of life or limb. Note in 2.H.P.C.326. This therefore excluded it in trespass, petty larceny, or killing se defendendo. In high treason against the person of the king, it seems not to have been allowed. Note 1.H.P.C.185. Treasons therefore not against the king's person immediately, petty treasons, and felonies seem to have been the cases where it was allowed; and even of those, not for insidiatio viarum, depopulatio agrorum, or combustio domorum. The statute de Clero 25.E.3. st.3.c.4. settled the law on this head. 2. As to the persons it extended to all clerks, always, and toties quoties. 2.H. P.C.374. To Nuns also Fitz.abr.Corone. 461. 22.E.3. The clerical habit and tonsure were considered as evidence of the person being clerical. 26.Assiz.19. 20. E.2. Fitz.Corone.233. By the 9.E.4.28. b. 34.H.6.49.a.b. simple reading became the evidence. This extending impunity to a great number of laymen, and toties quoties. The Statute 4.H.7.c.13. directed that real clerks should, upon a second arraignment, produce their orders, and all others to be burnt in the hand with M. or T, on the first allowance of clergy, and not to be admitted to it a second time. A heretic, Jew, or Turk (as being incapable of orders) could not have clergy. 11.Co.rep.29.b. But a Greek or other alien, reading in a book of his own country, might. Bro.Clergie.20. So a blind man, if he could speak Latin. ib.21. qu.11.Rep.29.b. The orders entitling the party were bishop's, priest's, deacon's and subdeacon's, the inferior being reckoned Clerici in minoribus. 2.H.P.C.373. qu. however if this distinction is not founded on the statutes 23.H.8.c.1. 25. H.8.c.3?

By merely dropping all the statutes it should seem that none but clerks would be entitled to this privilege, and that they would toties quoties.

her, during her title thereto; after which it shall be disposed of as if no such saving had been.

1.Ann.c.9. The aid of Counsel, and examination of their witnesses on oath shall be allowed to defendants in criminal prosecutions.

Slaves guilty of any §offence punishable in others by labor in the public works, shall be transported to such parts in the West Indies, S. America or Africa, as the Governor shall direct, there to be continued in slavery.

§ Manslaughter, counterfeiting, Arson, Asportation of vessels, robbery, burglary, housebreaking, horsestealing, larceny.

MS (DLC); 15 pages, in TJ's hand. The text of the Bill occupies only a part of this MS, the remainder being filled by TJ's numerous citations, notes, and comments; the text occupies the left-hand column and the other matter the right. In the text as presented here, all of the notes and comments that TJ keyed to the text by means of symbols are similarly keyed, though the symbols are not identical; superscript numerals refer to the editors' textual notes. (The MS does have superscript numerals, but these are not in TJ's hand and were probably added later, perhaps by Ford [II, 203-20].) The text of this Bill is printed in *Report*, p. 46-7, but without TJ's citations, notes, or comments; it is, however, divided into numbered sections. Another MS (MHi) was written by TJ in a vellum-bound commonplace book (probably dating from the 16th century) incorrectly labeled "Law Treaties"; it bears on an inside cover, in Edmund Randolph's hand, the following: "Bought by E. Randolph of James Horrocks's estate 1764. From E. R. to Mr. Jefferson." This volume is a miscellany and includes, in addition to numerous memoranda and the text of "A Bill for proportioning crimes and punishments in cases heretofore capital," a copy of the letter from TJ to Wythe of 1 Nov. 1778 transmitting the Bill, and the text of an essay entitled "Whether Christianity is a part of the Common law?" MS (MHi) occupies 20 pages, unnumbered; but pages [17-20] have been misplaced between pages [5-8] and pages [9-12]. The two MSS of Bill No. 64 are referred to here, for the sake of clarity, as MS (DLC) and MS (MHi). It is probable that MS (DLC) is the earlier of the two, but both are so carefully wrought that they must have been preceded by one or more trial drafts. Both MSS have been collated with the text as printed in *Report*, and all important variations among the three texts are indicated in the notes below. The beautiful form of these MSS has been commented upon; Malone (I, 269-70) adjudges MS (DLC) "an extraordinarily beautiful document," and adds that TJ, for "the benefit of his own memory, . . . attached notes in Anglo-Saxon characters, in Latin, old French, and English, attesting the meticulous carefulness of his procedure. In printed versions these are naturally put at the bottom of the pages, but Jefferson himself placed them in columns, parallel with the text, after the manner of his old law book, *Coke upon Littleton*; and, as in the work of the old master, they frequently encroach upon the text. The penmanship is beautifully clear, and no other document that Jefferson ever drew better exhibits his artistry as a literary draftsman." In his letter of transmittal to Wythe, 1 Nov. 1778, TJ wrote that "the extracts from the Anglo-Saxon law, the sources of the Common law, I wrote in the original for my own satisfaction; but I have added Latin or liberal English translations." MS (DLC) employs Anglo-Saxon characters. MS (MHi) has transliterated Anglo-Saxon. The text here presented follows MS (DLC) and deals with the Anglo-Saxon passages according to the established procedure of modern editing. The editors are indebted to Professor Robert K. Root, Princeton University, for transcription of the Anglo-Saxon text of this document.

In view of the comments below it is pertinent to note that in the first part of MS (DLC) TJ spelled the word "forfeit" as he was accustomed to do; he changed suddenly to "forfiet," going back to the beginning of the MS to alter the spelling from "forfeit" to "forfiet." From that point on in MS (DLC) and throughout

MS (MHi) the word is spelled "forfiet" as if it had always been TJ's habit to do so. This may have been a sudden whim brought about by his conscious imitation of the form of old legal treatises. At any rate, it tends to prove that MS (DLC) is earlier than MS (MHi). In these MSS TJ appears also to have employed the spelling "counterfiet" for the first and only time.

The facts noted above concerning the form of the MSS are significant. Indubitably TJ did a vast amount of research in the preparation of this Bill; in the letter just cited he told Wythe that the notes accompanying the text were "made, as I went along, for the benefit of my own memory." If this were so, why were these notes arranged in such studied form, blocked out on the pages and with notes separating text occasionally? Why was it necessary to make two copies of the MS in the same form? One cannot escape the conclusion that in this exfoliation of notes and citations, drawn from classical authors and the ancient Anglo-Saxon laws, as well as such modern penologists as Beccaria, TJ was not so much creating a memory-saving device as he was yielding to the temptation to indulge in pedantic ostentation—one of the few times in his career in which his enormous learning broke through his natural modesty and reserve (compare these learned notes with the forceful memoranda set forth in Notes and Proceedings on the Disestablishment of the Church, printed under 11 Oct. 1776). This mass of notes and citations, as well as the labored and artificial imitativeness in the form of the MS, may be partly responsible for the judgment that "during the years 1776-1779, he gave more time to this bill than to all the rest together" (Malone, I, 269); actually, TJ's researches on the Case of Thomas Johnson, and his legislative labors on the court bills, the supply bills, and the land bills—to say nothing of his work on other parts of the revisal—must have severally occupied as much time as the Bill for Proportioning Crimes and Punishments. On its surface this Bill has all of the appearance of being an important and prodigious accomplishment, and both TJ's own feeling at the time and the obvious learning it required may have led to an exaggerated opinion of its importance. Yet it was less a reform than an effort to bring the penalties of the criminal law into conformity with actual practice; "cruel and sanguinary [penal] laws" of the past had defeated their own purpose "by engaging the benevolence of mankind to withold prosecutions, to smother testimony, or to listen to it with bias." The preamble to this Bill stated in superb language the enlightened ideas of Beccaria and others; but the terms of the law that TJ proposed did little more than restate generally accepted practices concerning capital offenses. In respect to crimes of mayhem, the reliance upon the *lex talionis* contrasts shockingly with the liberal thought of the age. "How this last revolting principle came to obtain our approbation," TJ wrote, "I do not remember. There remained indeed in our laws a vestige of it in a single case of a slave. . . . But the modern mind had left it far in the rear of it's advances" (Autobiography, Ford, I, 60). Even at the time of drafting the Bill, TJ felt it unwise to go beyond this vestigial remnant because the principle would be "revolting to the humanised feelings of modern times" and because the moral effect of public executions of such penalties would be questionable; he therefore urged reconsideration of this part of the Bill (TJ to George Wythe, 1 Nov. 1778). In this same communication, TJ said that he had followed "the scale of punishments settled by the Committee, without being entirely satisfied with it"; strangely, however, the only documentary evidence remaining of the plan agreed upon by the Committee contains no statement whatever in support of the principle as implemented in the Bill, though it does provide for dismemberment in the case of certain crimes (see Document I, above, and Document IV, Part 5, below, in this series).

These harsh features of the Bill undoubtedly contributed to its defeat. Madison presented it on 31 Oct. 1785, it was postponed 14 Dec. to the next session, and on 15 Dec. the committee of the whole, to which it had been referred, was discharged from further proceeding on it (JHD, Oct. 1785, 1828 edn., p. 12-15, 92, 94). Two days later Madison reported to James Monroe that this Bill "was the one at which we stuck after wading thro' the most difficult parts of it" (Madison, *Writings*, ed. Hunt, II, 205). On 1 Nov. 1786 the Bill was again brought in, read twice, referred to the committee of the whole, and amended; it was then engrossed, read the third time, and defeated (JHD, Oct. 1786, 1828 edn., p. 16-17, 67, 86, 96). While it was still in the hands of the committee Madison reported to TJ that "the bill . . . on which we were wrecked last year, has after undergoing a number of alterations, got thro' a Committee of the whole; but it has not yet been reported to the House, where it will meet with the most vigorous attack. I think the chance is rather against its final passage in that branch of the Assembly, and if it should not miscarry there, it will have another gauntlet to run through the Senate" (Madison to TJ, 4 Dec. 1786). The Bill was defeated in the House by a single vote (Madison to Washington, 24 Dec. 1786, *Writings*, ed. Hunt, II, 303). Madison, in reporting this to TJ, said that the Bill had been "altered so as to remove most of the objections as was thought," though he did not explain what alterations had taken place. He did add, however, that "The rage against Horse stealers had a great influence on the fate of the Bill. Our old bloody code is by this event fully restored. . . ." (Madison to TJ, 15 Feb. 1787).

It is possible that TJ had Bill No. 64 printed in 1779, for Philip Mazzei later asserted that, when he sailed from Virginia for Nantes in June 1779, he carried "5 of Mr. Jefferson's proposals to the Assembly relative to criminal laws" (see Mazzei to TJ, 19 Mch. 1780).

1 Note the form in which TJ here states the principal purpose which induced men to enter into society; in the case of the Declaration of Independence, "governments are instituted among men" to safeguard the natural rights of "life, liberty, and the pursuit of happiness"—a variation which has been variously interpreted (Boyd, *Declaration of Independence*, 1945, p. 3-5).

2 *Report* reads: "a suffering."

3 *Report* adds at this point: "and by producing in many instances a total dispensation and impunity under the names of pardon and privilege of clergy." MS (DLC) and MS (MHi) agree.

4 *Report* adds: "and the power of dispensation, so dangerous and mischievous, which produces crimes by holding up a hope of impunity, might totally be abolished, so that men while contemplating to perpetrate a crime would see their punishment ensuing as necessarily as effects follow their causes." MS (DLC) and MS (MHi) agree. In DLC: TJ Papers, 232: 42062 there is, in the hand of the same clerk who wrote the Bill described under Bill No. 102, note 1, below, a fragment which agrees with the reading of the *Report* as given here and in note 3, above. This fragment covers only that part of the *Report* which includes the words "to smother testimony . . . while contemplating."

5 At this point in MS (DLC) the words "in the same" appear, enclosed in a rectangle; they are bracketed in MS (MHi) but are not in *Report.*

6 At this point in MS (DLC) the words "within the same" appear, also enclosed in a rectangle; they are bracketed in MS (MHi) but are not in *Report.*

7 *Report* reads: "and."

8 *Report* adds: "and lawful."

9 I.e., and killing a man.

10 In MS (MHi) the symbol for the note referring to Beccaria is placed at this point and the note begins "See Beccaria.sect.19. Homicides are 1. Justifiable . . ."; the symbol in MS (DLC) is placed at the end of the sentence, as above, and the note begins: "Beccaria. §32 . . . turn to the last page for Notes on this paragraph." On p. 14 of MS (DLC) the note continues, as in MS (MHi), "Homicides are 1. Justifiable. . . ." (This displacement of part of the note on homicide, together with the evidence presented above in connection with the spelling "forfieture," proves that MS [MHi] was made after MS [DLC] and was probably copied from it.) In addition to this, MS (DLC) has another footnote, "Beccaria. §.19.," opposite the next paragraph of the text which TJ mistakenly copied into MS (MHi) at this point, omitting the reference to "Beccaria.§.32."

11 *Report* adds: "thereof."

12 *Report* omits: "Polygamy."

13 This paragraph is omitted in *Report.*

14 *Report* reads: "Whosoever, on purpose, shall disfigure another by cutting out or disabling the tongue, slitting or cutting off a nose, lip or ear, branding, or otherwise, or shall maim him, shall be maimed or disfigured in like sort." MS (MHi) agrees with *Report* in this passage, indicating that TJ himself made the change after he had produced MS (DLC).

15 Brackets in MS.

16 *Report* reads: "shall diminish each, or any such coin."

17 *Report* adds another section: "The making false any such paper bill, or note, shall be deemed counterfeiting."

18 *Report* reads: "a robbery."

19 *Report* reads: "a burglary."

20 Report omits: "shall."

21 This prohibition of one of the worst aspects of Bills of Attainder carries the inference that TJ considered such bills

justifiable and proper under certain circumstances, as he did later in defending his Bill of Attainder against Josiah Philips (q.v., under 28 May 1778). Yet, in the passage of this Bill defining treason and establishing its penalty, TJ employed the same phrase—"levy war against the Commonwealth"—that he employed in the Bill attainting Philips. Here, however, he requires "two sufficient witnesses" or confession to establish guilt; in the Bill of Attainder against Philips, he assumed that the legislature had power in summary form to adjudge a man guilty. It is worth noting that, as TJ was completing work on the present Bill, Philips lay under sentence of death at Williamsburg; the alterations indicated in notes 5 and 6 above may have been made by TJ with the Philips case in mind.

65. A Bill Punishing Persons Guilty of Certain Forgeries

[1]Be it enacted by the General Assembly, that he or she shall be adjudged a felon, and not have the benefit of clergy, who shall falsely make, forge, or counterfeit, or aid or assist in falsely making, forging, or counterfeiting a writing signed and directed or certified to the public Treasurer, purporting to be a warrant of the Governor or other person exercising that function, or a certificate of the Auditors for Public Accounts, to authorise the payment of money; or cause or procure such writing to be falsely made, forged or counterfeited; or present such writing, or cause or procure it to be presented, at the public treasury, knowing it to have been falsely made, forged or counterfeited, in order to receive the money, or any part of the money therein mentioned; or shall make, forge or counterfeit, or aid or assist in falsely making, forging or counterfeiting, a writing, to be offered to the Auditors for Public Accounts, as a voucher, in order to obtain their allowance of a demand, and certificate of such allowance; or cause or procure such writing to be falsely made, forged or counterfeited; or offer such writing, or cause or procure it to be offered to the said Auditors, knowing it to have been falsely made, forged or counterfeited, in order to obtain their allowance and certificate aforesaid. And he or she shall be adjuged a felon, and not have the benefit of clergy, who shall forge or counterfeit, alter or erase any bill of credit, or treasury note or loan office certificate, of the United States of America, or any, or either of them; or shall cause or procure, such bill of credit, or treasury note, or loan office certificate, to be forged or counterfeited, altered or erased; or shall aid or assist, in forging or counterfeiting, altering or erasing, such bill of credit, or treasury note, or loan office certificate; or shall pass or tender, or shall cause or procure to be passed or tendered, any such bill of credit, or treasury note, or loan office certificate in payment or exchange, knowing the same to have been forged, or counterfeited, altered or erased; or shall have in his or her custody or possession, any press, types, stamp, plate,

or other instrument necessary to be used in the fabrication of such bill of credit, or treasury note, or loan office certificate, and not actually used in some public printing-office; or any paper with or without signature, on which the characters, words and numerical figures contained in a genuine bill of credit, or treasury note, or loan office certificate, are or shall be impressed, or inscribed in like order as they are in such bill of credit, or treasury note, or loan office certificate, or any such bill of credit, treasury note, or loan office certificate, which hath been altered or erased, knowing the same to have been altered or erased, and shall not discover such press, types, stamp, plate, instrument, paper, or altered or erased bill of credit, or treasury note, or loan office certificate to two Justices of the Peace, before the last day of June, in this present year one thousand seven hundred and seventy nine, or within five days after they shall have come to his possession. When the Justices of a county, in which any such felony as is before described shall be supposed to have been done, shall have determined, upon examination, that the person charged therewith ought to be tried before the General Court, the High Sheriff, or, if he be not able to attend, the Coroner shall deliver to them a list of the names of thirty six good and lawful men, out of which twenty four shall be stricken, one after another, the Justices and the prisoner striking alternately, or if the prisoner refuse to strike the Justices striking only; and the remaining twelve men shall be summoned by the writ of venire facias for trial of the prisoner: When a Justice of Peace, before whom a person charged upon oath with any such felony as aforesaid, shall inform the Governor that he hath cause to suspect that the offender, if he should be committed to the jail of the county in which the felony was done, would be rescued (which information the Justice is required to give in writing, with secrecy and dispatch) or when a person shall be charged upon oath made before the Governor, with such felony, in either case, the Governor, with advice of the Council of State, may by his warrant, empower and order so many men as shall be judged sufficient to apprehend the person accused, and convey and commit him to any other jail, in which he shall be detained, and shall by another warrant, direct the sheriff of that county in which the last mentioned jail is, to summon the Justices thereof to meet at the court-house before the end of twenty days afterwards: And thereupon the said Justices shall proceed in the same manner as they might have proceeded if the fact alledged against the prisoner had been done in their own county. And if he be remanded, the clerk of the peace attending the said Justices, shall within twenty days afterwards certify the same to the sheriff of the county, in which the fact was done, or failing to do so, shall forfeit one hundred pounds; and the same sheriff shall summon the Justices of his county to meet at the court-house thereof within ten days after the receipt of such certificate, and then deliver to them such list as aforesaid, out of which twenty four shall be stricken, in manner before directed, any agent authorised by the prisoner striking for him, or, if no such appear, the Justices striking only; and the remaining twelve shall be summoned as jurors for trial of the prisoner, by writ of venire facias, to be issued by the clerk of the last mentioned county. Every juror summoned by virtue of any such writ of venire facias, who shall fail at the return thereof, and from that time until he be discharged, to attend the General Court, shall forfeit one hundred pounds, unless the defaulter shew good cause to the contrary having been summoned for that purpose. Any Justice of the Peace may, by his warrant, cause to be apprehended and brought before him every such person travelling in the county of the said Justice, as he shall suspect to carry forged bills of credit, or treasury notes, or loan office certificates, and search to be made in the wearing apparel and baggage of the said traveller by force, if he expose them not voluntarily. The Governor, with advice of the Council of State, may offer rewards for apprehending those who having been charged, upon oath, with any of the felonies before described, shall have fled from justice, and may draw warrants for such rewards, not exceeding one thousand pounds for any one fugitive, which shall be paid out of the public treasury.[2]

Report, p. 47-8. Text of Act as adopted is in Hening, X, 93-7.

This Bill was enacted as a separate law in 1779, which was substantially a restatement of the Act of Oct. 1778, but omitted its preamble. That preamble asserted that many counterfeiters of paper currency had escaped punishment and "this alarming evil daily increases and is become so enormous that the most fatal consequences are justly to be apprehended." The Act of Oct. 1778 also, like Bill No. 65, sought to provide remedies for the situation whereby "the unalienable privilege of trial by a jury of the vicinage, has, from the manner of summoning such juries, been abused" (Hening, IX, 541). On 23 May 1779 a Bill was ordered drawn up to guard against counterfeiting and a committee was appointed for that purpose; the next day TJ was added to the committee. The Bill was introduced on 26 May, amended by both House and Senate; House accepted Senate's amendments 18 June (JHD, May 1779, 1827 edn., p. 18, 22, 23, 44, 46, 53, 55, 62). This Bill, as originally contemplated, was probably intended only for the limited purpose indicated and summarized in the notes below. The addition of TJ to the committee suggests that he enlarged this purpose by inserting the Committee of Revisors' Bill No. 65 in the middle of the one being prepared, for this is the position that it occupies in the Act as adopted, being preceded by the part summarized in note 1 and followed by that summarized in note 2. In any case, Bill No. 65 was thus adopted without alteration.

Bill No. 65 was presented by Madison 31 Oct. 1785, postponed 14 Dec. to next session, and brought up again 1 Nov. 1786; but, since the Act of 1779 was still in force, no further action was taken upon it (JHD, Oct. 1785, 1828 edn., p. 12-15, 92; Oct. 1786, 1828 edn., p. 16-17).

1 Preceding this point the Act as adopted has a section making it a felony without benefit of clergy to steal any bill of credit, treasury note, loan office certificate of the United States or of any other state, warrant of the governor, auditors' certificate; or to present such loan certificates at any United States loan office when such certificates were known to have been stolen (Hening, X, 93).

2 Following this point the Act as adopted has a section authorizing the auditors to grant certificates to all witnesses, veniremen, and sheriffs for their attendance on criminal cases (allowing two shillings per mile for travel and £4 per day for attendance); and repealing the Act of Oct. 1778 "for more effectually guarding against counterfeiting of the bills of credit, treasury notes, and loan office certificates" (same, IX, 541-5).

66. A Bill concerning Treasons, Felonies and Other Offences Committed Out of the Jurisdiction of this Commonwealth

Be it enacted by the General Assembly, that all high treasons, misprisions and concealments of high treasons and other offences, except piracies and felonies committed by any citizen of this commonwealth, in any place out of the jurisdiction of the courts of common law of this commonwealth, and all felonies committed by citizen against citizen in any such place, other than the high seas, shall be inquired, tried, heard, determined and judged[1] before any one or more of the Judges of the High Court of Chancery, together with any two or more of the Judges of the General Court, at such time and place, within the commonwealth, as shall be limited by summons to be sent to all the Judges from the Governor after the common course of the laws of this land, used for the like offences committed within the body of a county.

The said Judges shall enquire of such offences by a grand jury of the county where the court shall sit, and upon every indictment for any such offence, such order and process shall be practised against the offenders as by the laws of this land is accustomed against those committing the like offences within the body of a county; and the trial of such offences, if denied by the offender, shall be had by twelve lawful men, inhabitants of the county where the offender was apprehended; and such as shall be convict of any such offence, shall suffer such pains, losses of lands, goods and chattels as if they had been attainted and convicted of such offence done within the body of a county.[2]

The said Judges may adjourn, from time to time, as their will, till final determination, and shall be attended by the clerk and sheriff of the General Court, which sheriff shall execute their judgment and make return thereof to the said clerk by him to be recorded together with all the proceedings.

Report, p. 48. Text of Act as adopted is in Hening, XII, 330-1.

See TJ's Bill for the Trial of Offenses Committed Out of Virginia, printed under 5 Dec. 1776. The Committee's Bill No. 66 was presented by Madison 31 Oct. 1785 and referred to the committee of the whole. On 14 Dec. action was postponed to the next session. The Bill was presented again on 1 Nov. 1786 and committed to a committee of the whole, considered and agreed to 11 Nov., read third time and recommitted 13 Nov., amended 21 Nov., and passed by the House the next day; amended by the Senate 27 Nov. and Senate amendment agreed to by the House the same day (JHD, Oct. 1785, 1828 edn., p. 12-15, 92; same, Oct. 1786, p. 16-17, 35, 36, 53, 54, 64, 127). The Act as finally adopted differs from the Bill as proposed in the manner indicated below. Operation of Act suspended until 1 July 1787 (Hening, XI, 410-11).

[1] The remainder of the Bill (with the exception noted below) was deleted by amendment and the following substituted: "by the general court, in the same manner as if the said offences had been committed within the body of a county."

[2] The words "and such as shall be convict . . . the body of a county" are included in the Act.

67. A Bill concerning Truces, Safe Conducts, Passports, Licenses and Letters of Marque

For enforcing due regard to truces, letters of safe conduct, passports, and licenses, and fixing rules for granting them, as also for granting letters of marque and reprisal, Be it enacted by the General Assembly, that letters of safe conduct, passports, and licenses, may be granted by the American Congress, by the Governor, or by any Ambassador or other public minister duly appointed by the said Congress, or from this commonwealth, or by our Delegates to the American Congress, such Ambassador, or other public minister, from this commonwealth, or Delegates being out of the commonwealth at the time, or by any military officer of the United States, or of this commonwealth, commanding in a separate department, by land or by water: which letters of safe conduct, passports, or licenses, shall express the names of the persons to whom they be granted, the name and burthen of the ship, the name of the master, and number of mariners, or attendants; and where the same are granted by the Governor they shall be under the great seal of the commonwealth, and shall be enrolled in the Chancery of record, and shall on the same paper, or parchment bear an attestation from the clerk of the chancery, that they are enrolled in his office: And where the same are granted by any Ambassador, or other public minister, Delegates, or military commander as aforesaid, from this commonwealth, copies thereof, as soon as distance and opportunity permit, shall be transmitted by such Ambassador, Delegates or commander to the Chancery for enrollment.

If any citizen of this commonwealth shall commit any trespass on the high seas, or any felony or trespass in any other place, out of the jurisdiction of the courts of common law of this commonwealth, on the person or goods of any stranger in amity, league or truce with this commonwealth, or under protection of any letters of safe conduct, passports, or licenses granted as aforesaid, or shall be accessary, before or after the fact, to any such felony, he shall suffer the same pains, losses of lands, goods and chattels, as for the like wrong committed on a citizen of this commonwealth within the same.

The said offenders having been arrested by warrant from the Governor or any Justice of the Peace (who shall immediately notify the Governor thereof) their offence shall be enquired, heard, tried, determined, and judged, by one or more of the Judges of the High Court of Chancery, together with two or more Judges of the General Court, at such time and place within the commonwealth, as shall be limited by summons to be sent to all the Judges, from the Governor with the advice of the Council of State; but if the offence be a felony and not more than three or four of the said Judges shall attend, the Governor shall join to them one or two associates to make up the number five; which associates shall be sworn, by the presiding Judge, well and truly to perform the duties of their appointment. The offender shall be indicted, arraigned and tried on evidence given viva voce in open court, or if the witnesses be not within the commonwealth, then on their depositions taken in such manner as the said court shall approve: And if found guilty, such order, process, judgment and execution shall be practised as if he had been convicted of the like offence against a citizen of this commonwealth within the same; the said Judges shall also issue process against any other to whose hands shall have come any such person or goods on which trespass was committed and shall cause delivery and restitution thereof to be made, and shall likewise levy on the estate, real and personal, of the offender and his accomplices, all costs, expences, and losses, disbursed and suffered by the party injured, together with the value of the goods taken, if they cannot be specifically restored, and they may adjourn, from time to time, at their will, till final determination, and shall be attended by the clerk and sheriff of the General Court; which sheriff shall execute their judgment and make return thereof to the said clerk by him to be registered together with all the proceedings.

If any citizen of this commonwealth feeling himself aggrieved by persons belonging to any other state in amity, league, or truce with the United States of America, shall complain to the Governor, the said Governor, calling to his assistance the Council of State, shall hear and determine of such complaint, and if the same to them appear just and the party complainant so desire, he shall make application to the American Congress, from time to time as may be proper, for letters of request to the state of the person offending, or for letters of marque and reprisal, or for such other redress as they shall think just.

And where war shall have been declared by the American Congress against any state, the Governor, with the advice of the Council of State, shall have power to issue letters of marque, under the great seal of this commonwealth, against such hostile state and the subjects thereof, to such persons, under such restrictions, and on such security, as to them shall seem expedient for the public good, and as shall likewise be consistent with the regulations which shall have been established by the American Congress.

Report, p. 48-9.
Bill presented by Madison 31 Oct. 1785 and on 14 Dec. postponed to next session, but apparently no further action was taken on it (JHD, Oct. 1785, 1828 edn., p. 12-15, 92).

68. A Bill for the Employment, Government and Support of Malefactors Condemned to Labour for the Commonwealth

Be it enacted by the General Assembly, that malefactors condemned by judgment of law to hard labour, in the public works, in punishment of their crimes, shall be employed to row in the gallies of the commonwealth, or to work in the lead mines, or on fortifications or such other hard and laborious works, for the behoof of the commonwealth, as by the Governor and Council, in their discretion, shall be directed: And during the term of their condemnation shall, at the public expence, be fed on wholesome food, shall have such lodgings as may defend them from the inclemencies of the weather, shall have their heads and beards constantly shaven, and be clothed in habits of coarse materials, uniform in color and make, and distinguished from all others used by the good citizens of this commonwealth; that so they may be marked out to public note as well while at their ordinary occupations, as when attempting to escape from the public custody.

And to the end that the opulence of the offender, or of his friends, or the indiscreet counties of individuals may not disarm the public justice, or alleviate those sufferings, which, making part of the punishment intended by the law, should be incurred equally by all, and also to render escapes more difficult, their keeper shall particularly take care that no such malefactor use or receive any clothing, other than shall be provided by the public, as is before directed; nor receive, nor have in their own keeping any weapons, arms, money, or other property, nor have attendants of their own; and all articles so prohibited to them and found in their custody, or use, shall belong to him who will seize upon and take away the same, or give information thereof to the said keeper and demand delivery to be made by him.

The sheriff of the General Court to whom the said malefactors shall be committed, in execution of their sentence, shall, from time to time, with the approbation of the Judges of the General Court, either in or out of session, appoint such and so many keepers of the said malefactors as shall be necessary, whose duty it shall be to superintend and direct their labours, provide diet, clothing, and lodging, and see to their safe custody; and in order that they may be enabled to do this, they shall have power, (using their best discretion) to inflict necessary and moderate corporal punishment on those who shall be idle, or guilty of any trespass, and to restrain in irons such as shall be incorrigible otherwise.

Every of the said keepers shall be exempted from being of the militia.

The court of the county wherein such malefactors labour, or if they be on the water, out of the body of any county, the court of any adjacent county shall have power, either ex officio, or on information against any such keeper for partiality or cruelty, to call before them such keeper, together with the material witnesses, and enquire into his conduct; and if it shall appear that he has been guilty of gross partiality or cruelty, they shall cause the said witnesses to enter into recognizance for their appearance, at as early a day as may be, before the General Court, to whom they shall represent the matter, transmitting to them the substance of the evidence given before them, together with the said recognizances for their final determination. And if the cruelty of such keeper shall require it, the said county court shall also have power to suspend him and to appoint another to exercise his office until the General Court shall take order therein. The General Court may nevertheless either on their own motion, or on complaint made by any other, take original cognizance of the misbehaviour of any keeper and remove him from his office if they see cause. They shall also, whenever it is necessary and may conveniently be done, assign some person of discretion, humanity and attention, in the neighbourhood of the place where any malefactors labour, to enquire, from time to time, into their condition and treatment, and the conduct of their keepers and to represent the same to the said court whenever it shall seem to him requisite.

If any malefactor shall escape from his keeper, or absent himself from his labour without good cause, to be judged of by the General Court, the term of his condemnation shall be lengthened two days for every one he shall be absent.

All reasonable expences incurred by authority of this act shall be laid before the Auditors and by them entered in account, and on their warrant shall be paid by the Treasurer, or the said Auditors may, on the application of the sheriff of the General Court, give their warrant on the Treasurer for the advance of such sums as they shall think reasonable and necessary, charging the same to the said sheriff and calling on him to render account of the expenditure thereof, at such times as they shall think proper.

Report, p. 49-50.

Bill was presented by Madison 31 Oct. 1785, postponed various times, and finally, on 21 Dec., was killed by being put off to 31 March 1786. It was, however, brought up again at the Oct. 1786 session, and was amended by the committee of the whole on 30 Nov. (JHD, Oct. 1785, 1828 edn., p. 12-15, 93, 94, 101; same, Oct. 1786, p. 16-17, 67). No further action was taken, this Bill being defeated along with its counterpart, the Bill for Proportioning Crimes and Punishments (Bill No. 64, above).

Of the plan set forth in this Bill TJ later wrote: "I learnt afterwards, that the substitute of hard labor in public was tried (I believe it was in Pennsylvania) without success. Exhibited as a public spectacle, with shaved heads and mean clothing, working on the high roads produced in the criminals such a prostration of character, such an abandonment of self-respect, as, instead of reforming, plunged them into the most desperate and hardened depravity of morals and character" (Autobiography, Ford, I, 63).

69. A Bill to Encourage the Apprehending of Horse Stealers

Be it enacted by the General Assembly, that whosoever shall apprehend one charged with horse stealing, if the prisoner be convicted of that crime, shall be intitled to a reward of pounds,[1] to be paid by the Treasurer, upon a certificate of the General Court, that the claimant was the apprehender, and either that he was not examined as a witness at the trial, or that the other evidence then given was sufficient, without his testimony, to convict the prisoner.

Report, p. 50. MS (ViU); clerk's copy. Text of Act as adopted is in Hening, XII, 331.

Bill was presented by Madison 31 Oct. 1785 and on 14 Dec. was postponed to the next session. At the session of Oct. 1786 it was passed with an amendment specifying the amount of the reward (JHD, Oct. 1785, 1828 edn., p. 12-15, 92; same, Oct. 1786, p. 16-17, 35, 36, 70, 127). See the 1748 "Act for preventing losses from drivers passing with horses and cattle through this colony; and for laying a duty on horses imported, and the more effectual preventing of horse-stealing" and the amending Act of 1776 (Hening, VI, 124-31; IX, 174). Operation of Act of 1786 suspended to 1 July 1787 (same, XII, 410-11).

1 The Act reads: "ten pounds."

70. A Bill for Preserving the Privileges of Ambassadors

For preserving the privileges of Ambassadors and other public ministers from other states, it is declared by the General Assembly, that all process whereby the person of any such Ambassador, or other public minister, authorised and received as such by this commonwealth, or by the Congress of the American States, in union with this commonwealth, or any his domestic servants whom he brought with him, may be arrested or their goods seized or attached, shall be void.

And it is enacted that all persons suing forth, issuing, executing, prosecuting or soliciting any such process, knowing the defendant to be an Ambassador or other public minister as aforesaid, or the domestic servant of such an one, and all who shall assault the person of any such Ambassador, or other public minister, or who shall commit any trespass on his goods, shall be deemed violators of the laws of nations and disturbers of the public repose.

The said offences shall be enquired, heard, tried, determined and judged by one or more of the Judges of the High Court of Chancery together with two or more of the Judges of the General Court, at such time and place within the commonwealth, as shall be limited by summons from the Governor, taking thereupon the advice of the Council of State; and the offender, if adjudged guilty, shall suffer such punishment by fine and imprisonment, as the said Judges shall think fit, to be inflicted; and such order, process and execution shall be practised as is agreeable to the form of the common law. The said Judges may adjourn themselves, from time to time at their will, till final determination, and shall be attended by the clerk and sheriff of the General Court; which sheriff shall execute their sentence and make return thereof to the said clerk, by him to be registered together with all the proceedings in a separate book.

And in order to ascertain what servants attending such Ambassador, or other minister, are privileged from arrest, and to make known their names, the Governor and Council, as soon as may conveniently be done after the arrival of such Ambassador, or other minister, shall take order for procuring from him an authentic roll of the names of his domestic servants whom he brought with him, a copy of which they shall deliver to the clerk of the General Court, who shall affix the same on the wall of his office, within the reach and reading of those who may resort thereto, and continue it there so long as such Ambassador, or other minister, shall remain within the commonwealth.

Report, p. 50.

Bill presented by Madison 31 Oct. 1785 and on 14 Dec. postponed to next session (JHD, Oct. 1785, 1828 edn., p. 12-15, 92). The Bill was brought up again at the Oct. 1786 session, amended by the House, passed, and referred to the Senate, where it apparently died (same, Oct. 1786, 1828 edn., p. 16-17, 40, 41). See TJ's Proclamation concerning Consuls, 30 Dec. 1779, below; TJ to Benjamin Harrison, 23 Nov. 1779; and an Act for the protection and encouragement of commerce (Hening, X, 202-3).

71. A Bill for the Suppression and Punishment of Riots, Routs, and Unlawful Assemblies

Be it enacted by the General Assembly, that if any riot, assembly or rout of people against the law, be made in any part of the commonwealth, the Justices of Peace, three, or two of them at the least, and the sheriff or under sheriff of the county where such riot, assembly or rout shall be made, shall come with the power of the county (if need be) to arrest them, and shall arrest them. And the same Justices and sheriff, or under sheriff, shall have power to record that which they shall find so done in their presence against the law, by which record such trespasses and offenders shall be convict, and shall be taken and put in the jail of the same county there to abide for so long time as shall be limited by a jury to be sworn by the Judges for that purpose, and further until they shall have paid such amercement as the same jury shall assess. And if it happen that such trespasses and offenders be departed before the coming of the said Justices and sheriff, or under sheriff, the same Justices, three or two of them, shall diligently enquire, within a month after such riot, assembly or rout of people so made, and thereof shall hear and determine according to law. And for this purpose the sheriff having a precept directed to him shall return twenty four fit persons, twelve of whom having been sworn shall enquire of the said riot, rout, or unlawful assembly, and award against those whom they shall find guilty thereof due pains by amercement and imprisonment, as before is directed; and if so many of them should not appear, those who make default shall be fined by the same Justices forty shillings[1] each; and if the default be in the sheriff or under sheriff he shall forfeit to the commonwealth twenty pounds. And if the said riot, rout or unlawful assembly be not found by the said jury by reason of any maintenance, embracery, partiality, or other misbehaviour of the said jurors, then the said Justices and the sheriff or under sheriff shall certify the whole matter and circumstances to the General Court, and also the names of the maintainers and embracers in that behalf, if any be, with their misdemeanors that they know, in order that they may be duly prosecuted, upon pain of every of the said Justices and sheriff or under sheriff to forfeit twenty pounds if they have no reasonable excuse for not certifying the same; which certificate shall be of like force as the presentment of a grand jury; and thereupon the said trespassers and offenders being put to answer, they which shall be found guilty shall be punished by imprisonment and amercement according to the discretion of a jury, as before is directed; and if the same trespassers do not appear before the General Court at the first precept, then shall be another precept directed to the sheriff of the county, to take the said trespassers and offenders, if they may be found, and to bring them, at a certain day, before the General Court; and if they cannot be found, the sheriff or under sheriff shall make proclamation in his full county next ensuing the delivery of the second precept that they shall appear before the General Court on a day named; and in case the same offenders come not as afore is said, and the proclamation made and returned, they shall be convict and attainted of the riot, assembly or rout aforesaid. And moreover the Justices of Peace in every county where such riot, assembly or rout of people shall be made, in case the same be made in their presence, or if none be present, then the Justices dwelling nighest, having notice thereof, together with the sheriff or under sheriff of the same county, shall do execution of this act, every one upon pain of a hundred pounds,[2] to be paid to the commonwealth as often as they shall be found in default of the execution of the same act.

And on such default of the Justices and sheriff or under sheriff, a commission shall go from the General Court, at the instance of the party grieved, to enquire, as well of the truth of the case and of the original matter for the party complainant, as of the default or defaults of the said Justices, sheriff or under sheriff in this behalf supposed, to be directed to sufficient and indifferent persons at the nomination of the Judges. And the said commissioners presently shall return into the General Court the inquests and matters before them in this behalf taken and found.

But no persons convicted of a riot, rout or unlawful assembly shall be imprisoned for such offence by a longer space of time than one year.

Persons legally convicted of a riot, rout, or unlawful assembly, otherwise than in the manner directed by this act, shall be punished by imprisonment and amercement at the discretion of a jury under the like limitation.

Report, p. 50-1. Text of Act as adopted is in Hening, XII, 331-3.

Bill presented 31 Oct. 1785 by Madison; on 14 Dec. action was postponed to next session (JHD, Oct. 1785, 1828 edn., p. 12-15, 92). It was brought up again at the Oct. 1786 session, was amended by both the House and the Senate, and was passed on 4 Dec. (same, Oct. 1786, p. 16-17, 40, 41, 82, 85, 127). The amendments were minor, being principally to give to a corporation the powers given under the Act to a county and to empower the sergeant of a corporation to do what the Act empowered the sheriff of a county to do. Otherwise, with the two exceptions noted below, the text of the Act as adopted and that of the Bill as proposed are identical. Operation of Act suspended until 1 July 1787 (Hening, XII, 410-11).

[1] The Act reads: "five pounds."

[2] The Act reads: "twenty pounds."

72. A Bill Forbidding and Punishing Affrays

Be it enacted by the General Assembly, that no man great nor small, of what condition soever he be, except the ministers of justice in executing the precepts of the Courts of Justice, or in executing of their office, and such as be in their company assisting them be so hardy to come before the Justices of any court, or other of their ministers of justice doing their office, with force and arms on pain to forfeit their armour to the commonwealth and their bodies to prison at the pleasure of a court, nor go nor ride armed by night nor by day, in fairs or markets or in other places in terror of the country, upon pain of being arrested and committed to prison by any Justice on his own view, or proof by others, there to abide for so long a time as a jury, to be sworn for that purpose by the said Justice, shall direct, and in like manner to forfeit his armour to the commonwealth.

But no person shall be imprisoned for such offence by a longer space of time than one month.

Report, p. 51. Text of Act as adopted is in Hening, XII, 334.

Bill presented by Madison 31 Oct. 1785 and on 14 Dec. postponed to the next session (JHD, Oct. 1785, 1828 edn., p. 12-15, 92). At the Oct. 1786 session it was passed by the House on 18 Nov. and by the Senate on 27 Nov. (same,

Oct. 1786, p. 16-17, 44, 46, 48, 64, 126). The text of the Act as adopted is identical with the Bill as proposed; its operation was suspended until 1 July 1787 (Hening, XII, 410-11). This Bill is a good example of TJ's retention of the language of early English statutes, with its archaic provision for the forfeiture of "armour," &c. It is also a good example of TJ's ability to condense the involved language of the earlier English statutes that he thought worthy of retaining in the revision (see Edward Coke, *The Third Part of the Institutes of the Laws of England*, London, 1680, ch. LXXIII, "Against going or riding armed," p. 160).

73. A Bill against Conspirators

Be it declared and enacted by the General Assembly, that conspirators be they that do confederate or bind themselves by oath, covenant, or other alliance that every of them shall aid and bear the other falsely and maliciously to move or cause to be moved any indictment[1] or information against another on the part of the commonwealth, and those who are convicted thereof at the suit of the commonwealth, shall be punished by imprisonment and amercement at the discretion of a jury.

Report, p. 51. Text of Act as adopted is in Hening, XII, 334.

Bill was presented by Madison 31 Oct. 1785 and on 14 Dec. postponed to the next session (JHD, Oct. 1785, 1828 edn., p. 12-15, 92). At the Oct. 1786 session it was brought up again, passed by the House on 18 Nov., and approved by the Senate on 27 Nov. (same, Oct. 1786, p. 16-17, 44, 46, 48, 64, 127). The text of the Act as adopted is identical with the Bill as proposed, with the exception noted below; Act was suspended until 1 July 1787 (Hening, XII, 410-11).

1 Act reads incorrectly: "enticement."

74. A Bill against Conveying or Taking Pretensed Titles

Be it enacted by the General Assembly, that no person shall convey or take, or bargain to convey or take, any pretensed title to any lands or tenements, unless the person conveying or bargaining to convey, or those under whom he claims shall have been in possession of the same, or of the reversion or remainder thereof one whole year next before. And he who offendeth herein knowingly shall forfeit the whole value of the lands or tenements; the one moiety to the commonwealth, and the other to him who will sue as well for himself as for the commonwealth.

But any person lawfully possessed of lands or tenements or of the reversion or remainder thereof, may nevertheless take or bargain to take the pretensed title of any other person, so far and so far only as it may confirm his former estate.

Report, p. 51. Text of Act as adopted is in Hening, XII, 335.

Bill was presented by Madison on 31 Oct. 1785 and on 14 Dec. was postponed to the next session (JHD, Oct. 1785, 1828 edn., p. 12-15, 92). It was brought up again at the Oct. 1786 session, was passed by the House on 18 Nov., and on 6 Dec. was approved by the Senate (same, Oct. 1786, p. 16-17, 44, 46, 48, 88, 127). Text of the Act as adopted is identical with Bill as proposed; Act was suspended until 1 July 1787 (Hening, XII, 410-11).

75. A Bill to Punish Bribery and Extortion

Be it enacted by the General Assembly, that no Treasurer, keeper of any public seal, Councillor of State, counsel for the commonwealth, Judge,[1] clerk of the peace, sheriff, coroner, escheator, nor any other officer of the commonwealth, shall in time to come take, in any form, any manner of gift, brocage, or reward for doing his office, other than is or shall be allowed by some act of General Assembly passed after the institution of the commonwealth, that is to say, after the fifteenth day of May, in the year of our Lord 1776. And he that doth shall pay unto the party grieved the treble value of that he hath received, shall be amerced and imprisoned at the discretion of a jury, and shall be discharged from his office forever; and he who will sue in the said matter shall have suit as well for the commonwealth as for himself, and the third part of the amercement.

Report, p. 51-2. Text of Act as adopted is in Hening, XII, 335-6.

Bill was presented by Madison 31 Oct. 1785 and on 14 Dec. was postponed to the next session (JHD, Oct. 1785, 1828 edn., p. 12-15, 92). It was brought up at the Oct. 1786 session, was passed by the House on 18 Nov., apparently after being amended (see below). The Senate passed the Bill with amendments on 2 Dec. The House disagreed to these amendments, the Senate insisted upon them, the House stood firm, and on 8 Dec. the Senate receded from its position (same, Oct. 1786, p. 16-17, 44, 46, 48, 82, 85, 88, 93, 95, 127). Except as indicated below, text of Act as adopted agrees with Bill as proposed; Act was suspended until 1 July 1787 (Hening, XII, 410-11).

[1] The Act adds at this point: "or attornies at law, practising either in the general court, high court of chancery, court of appeals, court of admiralty, or inferior courts."

76. A Bill Prescribing the Punishment of Those Who Sell Unwholesome Meat or Drink

Be it enacted by the General Assembly, that a butcher[1] that selleth the flesh of any animal dying, otherwise than by slaughter, or slaughtered when diseased, or a baker, brewer, or distiller,[1] who selleth unwholesome bread or drink shall, on conviction[2] the first time, be amerced; the second time he shall suffer judgment of the pillory, and the third time he shall be imprisoned and make fine; and every time after he shall be adjudged to hard labour six month in the public works.[3]

Report, p. 52. Text of Act as adopted is in Hening, XII, 336.

Bill was presented by Madison 31 Oct. 1785 and on 14 Dec. postponed to the next session (JHD, Oct. 1785, 1828 edn., p. 12-15, 92). It was brought up again at the Oct. 1786 session, was amended by the committee of the whole, to some of which amendments the House disagreed, and was passed by the House on 18 Nov. The Senate passed the Bill 27 Nov. with amendments, to which the House agreed on the same day (JHD, Oct. 1786, 1828 edn., p. 16-17, 44, 46, 48, 64, 127). Except as noted below, text of Act as adopted agrees with Bill as proposed; Act was suspended until 1 July 1787 (Hening, XII, 410-11).

1 The Act adds: "or other person."

2 The Act adds: "by the verdict of a jury."

3 It is curious that this final provision should have been allowed to stand in the Bill, in view of the fact that both Bill No. 64 and Bill No. 68, which provided penalties requiring convicted persons to labor in the public works, were rejected.

77. A Bill to Prevent the Spreading of the Small-Pox

Be it enacted by the General Assembly, that it shall not be lawful for the master or mistress of a family, of which no one was before casually infected with the small-pox, to inoculate any person at his or her house, or, if any there be infected, to inoculate one who is not of his or her family, or knowingly suffer another to do it, or bring or suffer to come an infected person thither, until such master or mistress shall have obtained consent, to perform the operation there, of the greater number of house-keepers, who dwell within two miles thereof, and whose habitations are not separated from it, by a water or marsh one quarter of a mile wide, which consent shall be declared by writing, signed, in presence of, and attested by, two witnesses. Every person, in whose house there shall be any infected with the small-pox, shall, within six hours after notice thereof, hoist a flag, of white cloth, two feet in length, and of half that breadth, on a staff erected over or near the front door case of the house, and continually keep it there exposed, until some Justice of the Peace shall certify the house, in his opinion to be free of infection. The master or mistress of a family, in whose house it will be lawful to inoculate according to this act, or the physician or practitioner undertaking the inoculation, or having the care of the patients, shall, before beginning the operation, give notice thereof, by setting up advertisements on the nearest public road, and at the nearest church, court house, tavern, and mill; and such physician or practitioner shall use the most effectual means within his power, by purifying the bodies and wearing apparel of those who shall have been under his care, to prevent infection by them, and shall deliver to every patient, when he or she shall be discharged, a certificate to that purpose, or that the person is a subject incapable of infection. A person who never had the small-pox, or upon whom the experiment of inoculation had never been made, knowingly and voluntarily going into the house, wherein one who is infected with the small-pox abideth, and returning, may, by warrant of a Justice of the Peace, due proof thereof being made before him, be apprehended, and removed to the nearest house in which inoculation is performed, and be deemed, to all intents and purposes, a regularly admitted patient there, or be confined in some other place without danger of communicating the disorder, until he may be safely enlarged; and the expences of his maintenance and cure, if he be not able to pay them, shall be defrayed by the county; and in like manner one infected with the small-pox, who shall be found strolling or wandering abroad, may be apprehended, confined, and provided for. The master or mistress of a family, who shall dwell within the limits before described, inoculating a person at his or her house, or suffering another to do it, without obtaining such consent, or giving such notice as aforesaid, or the physician or practitioner beginning to inoculate there, before such notice shall have been given, failing to perform any duty required of him by this act, or giving a false certificate, shall be amerced. Any patient, before a certificate delivered to him, or removing from the place whereat he or she shall have taken the small-pox to another habitation, or going into the company of those who never had it, or, if he be passing in a road, not retiring upon the approach of a traveller, or giving timely notice of his condition to such traveller, shall forfeit forty shillings, for every offence, to the use of the commonwealth, recoverable, if the offender be an infant, from the parent or guardian. Any person wilfully endeavouring to spread or propagate the small-pox, otherwise than by this act he lawfully may, besides the punishment or reparation for special damage he may be liable to by indictment, information, or action, shall in the meantime, be bound to the good behaviour, and any such unlawful practice afterwards shall be deemed a breach of the condition of the recognizance.

Report, p. 52.

Bill was presented by Madison on 31 Oct. 1785 and on 14 Dec. postponed to the next session. It was brought up again at the Oct. 1786 session, was committed to the committee of the whole on 1 Nov., and apparently was not acted upon further (JHD, Oct. 1785, 1828 edn., p. 12-15, 92; same, Oct. 1786, p. 16-17). See Bill concerning Inoculation for Smallpox, printed above under date of 27 Dec. 1777, and notes thereon.

78. A Bill for Compelling Vessels and Persons Coming, and Goods Brought from Infected Places, to Perform Quarantine

Be it enacted by the General Assembly, that vessels, persons, and merchandize, coming or brought into any place within this commonwealth from any other part of the world, whence the Governor, with advice of his council, shall judge it probable, that any plague, or other infectious disease, may be brought, shall be obliged to make their quarantine in such place, during such time and in such manner, as shall be directed by the Governor, by his order, in Council, notified, by proclamation, to be published in the Virginia Gazette, and, until they shall be discharged from the quarantine, no such persons or merchandize shall come, or be brought, on shore, or go, or be put on board of any other vessel in the commonwealth, but in such manner, in such cases, and by such license, as shall be permitted by the order; and the vessel and persons receiving goods out of her shall be subject to the orders concerning quarantine, and for preventing infection, which shall be made by the Governor in Council, and notified as aforesaid. The master of a vessel coming from sea, on board of which there shall be a person infected with the plague, or other pestilential disease, shall immediately make the case known to some Naval Officer, who shall send intelligence thereof, with all speed, to the Governor, that measures may be taken for support of the crew, and precautions used to prevent the spreading of the infection; and the master shall not enter into any port, but shall remain in some open road, and shall avoid, and hinder all intercourse with other vessels or persons: nor shall any of the passengers or crew go on shore, until the order of the Governor in Council shall be received by the master. Whosoever shall offend against this act, in either or any of the aforementioned instances, shall be amerced.[1] When a place shall be infected with the plague, or other pestilential disease, or when the Governor, with advice of the Council, shall have notified by proclamation, published in the Virginia Gazette, that it is judged probable the plague or other pestilential disease may be brought from any place, if a vessel from such place shall be coming into a port of the commonwealth, the Naval Officer, or person who shall be authorised to see quarantine performed, shall go off, or cause some other to go off, to the vessel, and at a convenient distance, require the commander to declare, what is his name; at what places the cargo was taken on board; at what places the vessel touched in her passage; whether any of those places were infected with the plague, or any other pestilential disease; how long the vessel had been in her passage; how many persons were on board when she set sail; whether any on board during the voyage had been infected with the plague, or other pestilential disease, and who they are; how many died in the voyage, and of what distemper; what vessels he or any of his company, with his privity, went on board of, and whether any of their company had been on board of his vessel in their voyage; and to what places those vessels belonged; and what are the contents of his lading. And if it shall appear by the examination, that the vessel ought to perform quarantine, the officers of the ships of war, and forts, and garrisons, or other officers civil or military, of the commonwealth, having notice thereof, and other persons called to their assistance, may force such vessel, by violence, and, if necessary, by firing guns at her, to go to the place appointed for quarantine. The master of a vessel, coming from a place infected with the plague, or other pestilential disease, or having any person on board so infected, who shall conceal it, or who shall not give true answers to the questions, so to be propounded to him, shall be amerced.[1] The master of a vessel, ordered to perform quarantine, when he shall be required, after his arrival at the place appointed, shall deliver to the officer, authorised to see it performed there, the bills of health and manifests he shall have received, during the voyage, with his log-book and journal; and refusing or neglecting so to do, or to repair, in convenient time after notice, to the place appointed, or escaping from thence before quarantine performed, shall be amerced.[1] Persons, ordered to perform quarantine, if they shall escape, may be compelled to return, or, if they shall attempt to escape, may be detained by the persons, who shall be authorised to see the quarantine performed, and who may employ force, and call for the assistance of others, if it be necessary, for this purpose. Any person going on board a vessel, or into a place under quarantine, without license from the superintendant thereof, may be compelled to remain there, in the same manner as he might have been, if he had been one of the crew of the vessel. A Naval Officer, or person authorised to execute an order concerning quarantine, guilty of wilful breach or neglect of duty, shall be amerced.[2] And any person embezzling, or wilfully damaging, goods performing quarantine under his direction, shall be liable to the party injured for treble the value of the damages sustained thereby. The vessel, persons and goods, after quarantine performed, certificate thereof and that they are free from infection, being given by the superintendant, shall be no further restrained by virtue of this act. A person authorised to see the quarantine performed, or a watchman upon any vessel, place, or goods, under quarantine, deserting his duty or willingly permitting a person's vessel or goods to depart, or be conveyed away, from the place, where the quarantine ought to be performed, without a lawful license, or a person, impowered to give a certificate of the performance of quarantine, knowingly giving a false certificate, shall be amerced.[3] The forfeitures inflicted by this act shall be to the use of the commonwealth, and shall be recovered, by action of debt, in which actions the defendants shall be ruled to give special bail.[4]

Report, p. 52-3. MS (ViU); clerk's copy. Text of Act as adopted is in Hening, XI, 329-31.

Earlier Acts dealing with the quarantine of vessels coming into Virginia were passed in 1722, 1766, and 1772 (Hening, IV, 99-103; VIII, 260-1, 537-8). Bill No. 78 of the revisal was passed in 1783 as a separate Act; it was ordered to be brought in on 20 Nov. 1783, was presented 24 Nov., amended by the House on 3 Dec., and passed the next day; the Senate amended it 13 Dec., which amendments were agreed to by House 15 Dec. (JHD, Oct. 1783, 1828 edn., p. 26, 31, 32, 44, 45, 59, 63). The Act as adopted and the Bill as proposed by the Committee of Revisors are the same except for the addition of a brief preamble in the Act and the other differences indicated below. Although it had already been enacted into law, the Bill was again brought up on 31 Oct. 1785 by Madison, but was postponed to the next session; it was presented at the Oct. 1786 session, but no further action was taken on it (same, Oct. 1785, p. 12-15, 92; same, Oct. 1786, p. 16-17).

1 The Act adds: "the sum of five hundred pounds."

2 The Act adds: "the sum of one thousand pounds."

3 The Act adds: "the sum of one hundred pounds."

4 The Act has an additional clause authorizing the governor in council to direct the auditors to issue warrants on the treasurer for such sums as may be necessary "for the support of the persons performing quarantine and those appointed to see it performed," to be repaid by the master or owner of the vessel at the end of quarantine.

79. A Bill for the More General Diffusion of Knowledge

Whereas it appeareth that however certain forms of government are better calculated than others to protect individuals in the free exercise of their natural rights, and are at the same time themselves better guarded against degeneracy, yet experience hath shewn, that even under the best forms, those entrusted with power have, in time, and by slow operations, perverted it into tyranny; and it is believed that the most effectual means of preventing this would be, to illuminate, as far as practicable, the minds of the people at large, and more especially to give them knowledge of those facts, which history exhibiteth, that, possessed thereby of the experience of other ages and countries, they may be enabled to know ambition under all its shapes, and prompt to exert their natural powers to defeat its purposes; And whereas it is generally true that that people will be happiest whose laws are best, and are best administered, and that laws will be wisely formed, and honestly administered, in proportion as those who form and administer them are wise and honest; whence it becomes expedient for promoting the publick happiness that those persons, whom nature hath endowed with genius and virtue, should be rendered by liberal education worthy to receive, and able to guard the sacred deposit of the rights and liberties of their fellow citizens, and that they should be called to that charge without regard to wealth, birth or other accidental condition or circumstance; but the indigence of the greater number disabling them from so educating, at their own expence, those of their children whom nature hath fitly formed and disposed to become useful instruments for the public, it is better that such should be sought for and educated at the common expence of all, than that the happiness of all should be confided to the weak or wicked:

Be it therefore enacted by the General Assembly, that in every county within this commonwealth, there shall be chosen annually, by the electors qualified to vote for Delegates, three of the most honest and able men of their county, to be called the Aldermen of the county; and that the election of the said Aldermen shall be held at the same time and place, before the same persons, and notified and conducted in the same manner as by law is directed for the annual election of Delegates for the county.

The person before whom such election is holden shall certify to the court of the said county the names of the Aldermen chosen, in order that the same may be entered of record, and shall give notice of their election to the said Aldermen within a fortnight after such election.

The said Aldermen on the first Monday in October, if it be fair, and if not, then on the next fair day, excluding Sunday, shall meet at the court-house of their county, and proceed to divide their said county into hundreds, bounding the same by water courses, mountains, or limits, to be run and marked, if they think necessary, by the county surveyor, and at the county expence, regulating the size of the said hundreds, according to the best of their discretion, so as that they may contain a convenient number of children to make up a school, and be of such convenient size that all the children within each hundred may daily attend the school to be established therein, distinguishing each hundred by a particular name; which division, with the names of the several hundreds, shall be returned to the court of the county and be entered of record, and shall remain unaltered until the increase or decrease of inhabitants shall render an alteration necessary, in the opinion of any succeeding Aldermen, and also in the opinion of the court of the county.

The electors aforesaid residing within every hundred shall meet on the third Monday in October after the first election of Aldermen, at such place, within their hundred, as the said Aldermen shall direct, notice thereof being previously given to them by such person residing within the hundred as the said Aldermen shall require who is hereby enjoined to obey such requisition, on pain of being punished by amercement and imprisonment. The electors being so assembled shall choose the most convenient place within their hundred for building a school-house. If two or more places, having a greater number of votes than any others, shall yet be equal between themselves, the Aldermen, or such of them as are not of the same hundred, on information thereof, shall decide between them. The said Aldermen shall forthwith proceed to have a school-house built at the said place, and shall see that the same be kept in repair, and, when necessary, that it be rebuilt; but whenever they shall think necessary that it be rebuilt, they shall give notice as before directed, to the electors of the hundred to meet at the said school-house, on such day as they shall appoint, to determine by vote, in the manner before directed, whether it shall be rebuilt at the same, or what other place in the hundred.

At every of these schools shall be taught reading, writing, and common arithmetick, and the books which shall be used therein for instructing the children to read shall be such as will at the same time make them acquainted with Græcian, Roman, English, and American history. At these schools all the free children, male and female, resident within the respective hundred, shall be intitled to receive tuition gratis, for the term of three years, and as much longer, at their private expence, as their parents, guardians or friends, shall think proper.

Over every ten of these schools (or such other number nearest thereto, as the number of hundreds in the county will admit, without fractional divisions) an overseer shall be appointed annually by the Aldermen at their first meeting, eminent for his learning, integrity, and fidelity to the commonwealth, whose business and duty it shall be, from time to time, to appoint a teacher to each school, who shall give assurance of fidelity to the commonwealth, and to remove him as he shall see cause; to visit every school once in every half year at the least; to examine the schollars;

see that any general plan of reading and instruction recommended by the visiters of William and Mary College shall be observed; and to superintend the conduct of the teacher in every thing relative to his school.

Every teacher shall receive a salary of by the year, which, with the expences of building and repairing the school-houses, shall be provided in such manner as other county expences are by law directed to be provided and shall also have his diet, lodging, and washing found him, to be levied in like manner, save only that such levy shall be on the inhabitants of each hundred for the board of their own teacher only.

And in order that grammar schools may be rendered convenient to the youth in every part of the commonwealth, Be it farther enacted, that on the first Monday in November, after the first appointment of overseers for the hundred schools, if fair, and if not, then on the next fair day, excluding Sunday, after the hour of one in the afternoon, the said overseers appointed for the schools in the counties of Princess Ann, Norfolk, Nansemond and Isle-of-Wight, shall meet at Nansemond court house; those for the counties of Southampton, Sussex, Surry and Prince George, shall meet at Sussex court-house; those for the counties of Brunswick, Mecklenburg and Lunenburg, shall meet at Lunenburg court-house; those for the counties of Dinwiddie, Amelia and Chesterfield, shall meet at Chesterfield court-house; those for the counties of Powhatan, Cumberland, Goochland, Henrico and Hanover, shall meet at Henrico court-house; those for the counties of Prince Edward, Charlotte and Halifax, shall meet at Charlotte court-house; those for the counties of Henry, Pittsylvania and Bedford, shall meet at Pittsylvania court-house; those for the counties of Buckingham, Amherst, Albemarle and Fluvanna, shall meet at Albemarle court-house; those for the counties of Botetourt, Rockbridge, Montgomery, Washington and Kentucky, shall meet at Botetourt court-house; those for the counties of Augusta, Rockingham and Greenbrier, shall meet at Augusta court-house; those for the counties of Accomack and Northampton, shall meet at Accomack court-house; those for the counties of Elizabeth City, Warwick, York, Gloucester, James City, Charles City and New-Kent, shall meet at James City court-house; those for the counties of Middlesex, Essex, King and Queen, King William and Caroline, shall meet at King and Queen court-house; those for the counties of Lancaster, Northumberland, Richmond and Westmoreland, shall meet at Richmond court-house; those for the counties of King George, Stafford, Spotsylvania, Prince William and Fairfax, shall meet at Spotsylvania court-house; those for the counties of Loudoun and Fauquier, shall meet at Loudoun court-house; those for the counties of Culpeper, Orange and Louisa, shall meet at Orange court-house; those for the counties of Shenandoah and Frederick, shall meet at Frederick court-house; those for the counties of Hampshire and Berkeley, shall meet at Berkeley court-house; and those for the counties of Yohogania, Monongalia and Ohio, shall meet at Monongalia court-house; and shall fix on such place in some one of the counties in their district as shall be most proper for situating a grammar school-house, endeavouring that the situation be as central as may be to the inhabitants of the said counties, that it be furnished with good water, convenient to plentiful supplies of provision and fuel, and more than all things that it be healthy. And if a majority of the overseers present should not concur in their choice of any one place proposed, the method of determining shall be as follows: If two places only were proposed, and the votes be divided, they shall decide between them by fair and equal lot; if more than two places were proposed, the question shall be put on those two which on the first division had the greater number of votes; or if no two places had a greater number of votes than the others, as where the votes shall have been equal between one or both of them and some other or others, then it shall be decided by fair and equal lot (unless it can be agreed by a majority of votes) which of the places having equal numbers shall be thrown out of the competition, so that the question shall be put on the remaining two, and if on this ultimate question the votes shall be equally divided, it shall then be decided finally by lot.

The said overseers having determined the place at which the grammar school for their district shall be built, shall forthwith (unless they can otherwise agree with the proprietors of the circumjacent lands as to location and price) make application to the clerk of the county in which the said house is to be situated, who shall thereupon issue a writ, in the nature of a writ of ad quod damnum, directed to the sheriff of the said county commanding him to summon and impannel twelve fit persons to meet at the place, so destined for the grammar school house, on a certain day, to be named in the said writ, not less than five, nor more than ten, days from the date thereof; and also to give notice of the same to the proprietors and tenants of the lands to be viewed, if they be to be found within the county, and if not, then to their agents therein if any they have. Which freeholders shall be charged by the said sheriff impartially, and to the best of their skill and judgment to view the lands round about the said place, and to locate and circumscribe, by certain metes and bounds, one hundred acres thereof, having regard therein principally to the benefit and convenience of the said school, but respecting in some measure also the convenience of the said proprietors, and to value and appraise the same in so many several and distinct parcels as shall be owned or held by several and distinct owners or tenants, and according to their respective interests and estates therein. And after such location and appraisement so made, the said sheriff shall forthwith return the same under the hands and seals of the said jurors, together with the writ, to the clerk's office of the said county and the right and property of the said proprietors and tenants in the said lands so circumscribed shall be immediately devested and be transferred to the commonwealth for the use of the said grammar school, in full and absolute dominion, any want of consent or disability to consent in the said owners or tenants notwithstanding. But it shall not be lawful for the said overseers so to situate the said grammar school-house, nor to the said jurors so to locate the said lands, as to include the mansion-house of the proprietor of the lands, nor the offices, curtilage, or garden, thereunto immediately belonging.

The said overseers shall forthwith proceed to have a house of brick or stone, for the said grammar school, with necessary offices, built on the said lands, which grammar school-house shall contain a room for the school, a hall to dine in, four rooms for a master and usher, and ten or twelve lodging rooms for the scholars.

To each of the said grammar schools shall be allowed out of the public treasury, the sum of   pounds, out of which shall be paid by the Treasurer, on warrant from the Auditors, to the proprietors or tenants of the lands located, the value of their several interests as fixed by the jury, and the balance thereof shall be delivered to the said overseers to defray the expence of the said buildings.

In these grammar schools shall be taught the Latin and Greek languages, English grammar, geography, and the higher part of numerical arithmetick, to wit, vulgar and decimal fractions, and the extraction of the square and cube roots.

A visiter from each county constituting the district shall be appointed, by the overseers, for the county, in the month of October annually, either from their own body or from their county at large, which visiters or the greater part of them, meeting together at the said grammar school on the first Monday in November, if fair, and if not, then on the next fair day, excluding Sunday, shall have power to choose their own Rector, who shall call and preside at future meetings, to employ from time to time a master, and if necessary, an usher, for the said school, to remove them at their will, and to settle the price of tuition to be paid by the scholars. They shall also visit the school twice in every year at the least, either together or separately at their discretion, examine the scholars, and see that any general plan of instruction recommended by the visiters of William and Mary College shall be observed. The said masters and ushers, before they enter on the execution of their office, shall give assurance of fidelity to the commonwealth.

A steward shall be employed, and removed at will by the master, on such wages as the visiters shall direct; which steward shall see to the procuring provisions, fuel, servants for cooking, waiting, house cleaning, washing, mending, and gardening on the most reasonable terms; the expence of which, together with the steward's wages, shall be divided equally among all the scholars boarding either on the public or private expence. And the part of those who are on private expence, and also the price of their tuitions due to the master or usher, shall be paid quarterly by the respective scholars, their parents, or guardians, and shall be recoverable, if withheld, together with costs, on motion in any Court of Record, ten days notice thereof being previously given to the party, and a jury impannelled to try the issue joined, or enquire of the damages. The said steward shall also, under the direction of the visiters, see that the houses be kept in repair, and necessary enclosures be made and repaired, the accounts for which, shall, from time to time, be submitted to the Auditors, and on their warrant paid by the Treasurer.

Every overseer of the hundred schools shall, in the month of September annually, after the most diligent and impartial examination and enquiry, appoint from among the boys who shall have been two years at the least at some one of the schools under his superintendance, and whose parents are too poor to give them farther education, some one of the best and most promising genius and disposition, to proceed to the grammar school of his district; which appointment shall be made in the court-house of the county, on the court day for that month if fair, and if not, then on the next fair day, excluding Sunday, in the presence of the Aldermen, or two of them at the least, assembled on the bench for that purpose, the said overseer being previously sworn by them to make such appointment, without favor or affection, according to the best of his skill and judgment, and being interrogated by the said Aldermen, either on their own motion, or on suggestions from the parents, guardians, friends, or teachers of the children, competitors for such appointment; which teachers shall attend for the information of the Aldermen. On which interregatories the said Aldermen, if they be not satisfied with the appointment proposed, shall have right to negative it; whereupon the said visiter may proceed to make a new appointment, and the said Aldermen again to interrogate and negative, and so toties quoties until an appointment be approved.

Every boy so appointed shall be authorised to proceed to the grammar school of his district, there to be educated and boarded during such time as is hereafter limited; and his quota of the expences of the house together with a compensation to the master or usher for his tuition, at the rate of twenty dollars by the year, shall be paid by the Treasurer quarterly on warrant from the Auditors.

A visitation shall be held, for the purpose of probation, annually at the said grammar school on the last Monday in September, if fair, and if not, then on the next fair day, excluding Sunday, at which one third of the boys sent thither by appointment of the said overseers, and who shall have been there one year only, shall be discontinued as public foundationers, being those who, on the most diligent examination and enquiry, shall be thought to be of the least promising genius and disposition; and of those who shall have been there two years, all shall be discontinued, save one only the best in genius and disposition, who shall be at liberty to continue there four years longer on the public foundation, and shall thence forward be deemed a senior.

The visiters for the districts which, or any part of which, be southward and westward of James river, as known by that name, or by the names of Fluvanna and Jackson's river, in every other year, to wit, at the probation meetings held in the years, distinguished in the Christian computation by odd numbers, and the visiters for all the other districts at their said meetings to be held in those years, distinguished by even numbers, after diligent examination and enquiry as before directed, shall chuse one among the said seniors, of the best learning and most hopeful genius and disposition, who shall be authorised by them to proceed to William and Mary College, there to be educated, boarded, and clothed, three years; the expence of which annually shall be paid by the Treasurer on warrant from the Auditors.

Report, p. 53-5. Surprisingly, no MS copy of this famous Bill has been found and no memoranda or scraps of notes such as TJ left respecting other Bills.

The Acts pertaining to the College of William and Mary fell within Pendleton's share of the revision, but, as TJ explained in his Autobiography, "We thought that . . . a systematical plan of general education should be proposed, and I was requested to undertake it. I accordingly prepared three Bills for the Revisal, proposing three distinct grades of education, reaching all classes. 1. Elementary schools for all children generally, rich and poor. 2. Colleges for a middle degree of instruction, calculated for the common purposes of life, and such as would be desirable for all who were in easy circumstances. And 3d. an ultimate grade for teaching the sciences generally, and in their highest degree" (Ford, I, 66). Within a decade after the work of the Committee of Revisors was begun, TJ regarded the Bill for the More General Diffusion of Knowledge as the most important one in the Report (TJ to George Wythe, 13 Aug. 1786). The exalted declaration of purpose in the preamble remains one of the classic statements of the responsibility of the state in matters of education. But what was new and distinctively Jeffersonian in the Bill was not its advocacy of public education, for in this respect it in fact envisaged a combined system of public and private education; and, indeed, public education was already in practice and had been for some generations in the systems of common schools of New England. But what was new in the Bill and what stamped its author as a constructive statesman of far-seeing vision was the object of seeking out men of genius and virtue and of rendering them "by liberal education worthy to receive, and able to guard the sacred deposit of the rights and liberties of their fellow citizens." This implied the establishment of a ruling *élite* that would promote public happiness by wisely forming and honestly administering the laws; but, though this never became and possibly could not become an explicit object of any democratic society, the important thing about TJ's Bill was that those "whom nature hath endowed with genius and virtue . . . *should be called to that charge without regard to wealth, birth or other accidental condition or circumstance*." The Bill recognized natural gradations and disparities among men; it saw nothing dangerous or inimical to the liberties of the people in accepting and making use of such a natural aristocracy of virtue and talent; and its unique and revolutionary feature, never yet put into practice by any people, was that, in order to permit such a natural aristocracy to flourish freely, it would remove all economic, social, or other barriers that would interfere with nature's distribution of genius or virtue. (See TJ's account of this Bill in *Notes on Virginia*, Ford, III, 251-5; see also R. J. Honeywell, *Educational Work of Thomas Jefferson*, Cambridge, Mass., 1931.) A highly interesting contemporary comment on the Bill is that by William Wirt: "Among other wise and highly patriotic bills which are proposed, there is one for the more general diffusion of knowledge. After a preamble, in which the importance of the subject to the republic is most ably and eloquently announced, the bill proposes a simple and beautiful scheme, whereby science (like justice under the institutions of our Alfred) would have been 'carried to every man's door.' Genius, instead of having to break its way through the thick opposing clouds of native obscurity, indigence and ignorance, was to be sought for through every family in the commonwealth; the sacred spark, wherever it was detected, was to be tenderly cherished, fed and fanned into a flame; its innate properties and tendencies were to be developed and examined, and then cautiously and judiciously invested with all the auxiliary energy and radiance of which its character was susceptible. What a plan was here to give stability and solid glory to the republic! If you ask me why it has never been adopted, I answer, that as a foreigner, I can perceive no possible reason for it, except that the comprehensive views and generous patriotism which produced the bill, have not prevailed throughout the country, nor presided in the body on whose vote the adoption of the bill depended. I have new reason to remark it, almost every day, that there is throughout Virginia, a most deplorable destitution of public spirit, of the noble pride and love of country. Unless the body of the people can be awakened from this fatal apathy; unless their thoughts and their feelings can be urged beyond the narrow confines of their own private affairs; unless they can be strongly inspired with the public zeal, the *amor patriæ* of the ancient republics, the national embellishment, and the national grandeur of this opulent state, must be reserved for very distant ages" (William Wirt, *Letters of a British Spy*, 10th edn., N.Y., 1832, p. 231-2; originally published in 1803).

TJ apparently finished the Bill late in the autumn of 1778, for on 18 Dec. 1778 he wrote to Pendleton about it (his letter is missing, but see Pendleton's reply under date of 11 May 1779). On 15 Dec. 1778 leave was given by the House for the presentation of a Bill "for the more general diffusion of knowledge," and Richard Parker and George Mason were ordered to prepare it; the Bill was presented by Parker on the next day, whereupon the House "*Ordered*, That the public printer do forthwith print and forward four copies of the said act to each county within this Commonwealth" (JHD, Oct. 1778, 1827 edn., p. 117, 120). It is very doubtful whether this order to print the Bill was actually executed; if it was, no copy of it has been found (see Edmund Pendleton to TJ, 11 May 1779 and notes thereon). The Bill was again presented on 12 June 1780, but no further action was taken until, on 31 Oct. 1785, Madison brought it up along with other bills of the Report of the Committee of Revisors. It was considered by the House 6 Dec., was amended 20 Dec., and on 21 Dec. was actually passed by the House under a new title, "An act, directing the mode of appointing aldermen." But, on being referred to the Senate, the Bill died (JHD, May 1780, 1827 edn., p. 14, 44; same, Oct. 1785, 1828 edn., p. 12-15, 74-5, 100, 101). Madison reported a year later, when TJ's Bill was again considered, that the system was carefully considered but not adopted because of the cost involved (Madison to TJ, 4 Dec. 1786; see also Madison to TJ, 22 Jan. 1786).

Madison did not bring in Bill No. 79 with the others reported on 1 Nov. 1786 but it was brought up two weeks later, and, as Madison reported to TJ, it "went through two readings by a small majority and was not pushed to a third one" (Madison to TJ, 15 Feb. 1787; JHD, Oct. 1786, 1828 edn., p. 44). The plan for establishing public schools was not carried to completion until 1796 when the Assembly passed an "Act to Establish Public Schools" (Shepherd, II, 3-5) which retained some of the phraseology of TJ's Bill, especially that providing for the election of aldermen. However, the 1796 Act provided only for primary schools, and the determination of the expediency of establishing such schools was left entirely to the aldermen of each county, borough, or corporation.

80. A Bill for Amending the Constitution of the College of William and Mary, and Substituting More Certain Revenues for Its Support

Whereas a scheme for cultivating and disseminating useful knowledge in this country, which had been proposed by some of its liberal minded inhabitants, before the year 1690 of the Christian epocha, was approved, adopted, and cherished, by the General Assembly, upon whose petition King William and Queen Mary of England, to the crown whereof the people here at that time acknowledged themselves, as a colony, to be subject, by their charter, bearing date the seventh day of February, in the fourth year of their reign, gave license, in due form, to Francis Nicholson, Esquire, Lieutenant Governor of the colony, and seventeen other trustees, particularly named, to found a place of universal study, or perpetual college, in such part of the country as the General Assembly should think fit, consisting of a President, six Professors, and an hundred scholars, more or less; enabled the trustees, and their survivors, to take and hold lands, tenements, and hereditaments, to the yearly value of two thousand pounds, with intention, and in confidence, that, after application of the profits thereof, with such donations as by themselves and others might be made for that purpose, to the erecting, founding, and adorning the college, they should transfer the same to the President and Professors; appointed James Blair, clerk, the first President, and empowered the trustees, and their successors, to elect the succeding President, and the Professors; willed the college, after it should be founded, to be called the College of William and Mary in Virginia; and incorporated the President and masters, enabling them and their successors to take and hold lands, tenements, hereditaments, goods and chattels, to the yearly value of two thousand pounds, of lawful money of England; appointed the trustees and their successors, to be elected in the manner therein prescribed, so as not to be less than eighteen, visiters of the College, with power to nominate one of themselves a rector annually, and to ordain statutes for the government of the College, not contrary to the royal prerogative, the laws of England or Virginia, or the canons of the Church of England; willed that the President and Professors should have a Chancellor, to be nominated, every seventh year, in the manner therein prescribed; granted to the trustees a sum of money, then in the hands of William Byrd, Esquire, the Auditor, received for quitrents, to be applied towards erecting, founding, and adorning the College; and also granted to the trustees, to be transferred to the President and Professors, in like manner as before directed, part of the then royal revenue, arising from the duty upon tobacco exported; and also granted to the said trustees the office of surveyor general of Virginia, with intention, and in confidence, that they and their successors, or the longest livers of them, should receive the profits thereof, until the foundation of the College, and when that should be effected, account for and pay the same or the surplus, above what should have been expended in that work, to the President and Professors; and that thereafter the said office should be held by the said President and Professors. And the said King and Queen, by their said charter, granted to the said trustees ten thousand acres of land on the south side of the Blackwater swamp, and also other ten thousand acres of land in Pamunkey neck, between the forks or branches of York river, with this intention, and in confidence, that the said trustees, or the longest livers of them, should transfer the said twenty thousand acres of land, after the foundation of the College, to the President and Professors; as by the said charter, among other things, relation being thereunto had, may more fully appear. And whereas voluntary contributions towards forwarding this beneficial scheme, the sum whereof exceeded two thousand pounds, sterling, was received by the said trustees, with one thousand pounds, sterling, out of the money arising from the quitrents granted to the use of the said College by Queen Anne, part whereof was applied to the purchase of three hundred and thirty acres of land at the middle plantation, being the same place at which the General Assembly, by their act, passed in the year 1693, had directed the said College to be built, and whereon the same was accordingly built, and the General Assembly, by one other act, passed in the same year 1693, intitled an Act for laying an imposition upon skins and furs, for the better support of the College of William and Mary in Virginia, endowed the said College with certain duties on skins and furs therein specified, which duties were afterwards enlarged and confirmed to the use of the said College, and made payable to the President and Professors by divers other acts of General Assembly. And by one other act passed in the year 1718, the said College was further endowed by the General Assembly with the sum of one thousand pounds, out of the public funds, in the hands of the Treasurer, which was directed to be laid out for the maintaining and educating scholars, and to be accounted for to the General Assembly, from time to time, when required: Which sum was accordingly paid to the said visiters, and by them invested in the purchase of two thousand one hundred and nineteen acres of land, on both sides of Nottoway river, in the counties of Prince George, Surry, and Brunswick, and seventeen negro slaves, to be employed in tilling and manuring the same, and certain scholarships were accordingly established on the said funds; and the General Assembly, by their act, passed in the year 1726, and intitled an Act for laying a duty on liquors, further endowed the said College with an annual revenue of two hundred pounds, for twenty one years, to be paid out of certain duties thereon imposed on liquors, and by one other act, passed in the year 1734, endowed it with the whole of the said duties, during the residue of the said term then unexpired, a part or the whole thereof to be expended in purchasing a library for the said College: And by divers other acts, passed at subsequent times, the Assemblies, for the times being, having continued to the said College the whole of the annual revenues, arising from the said duties, until the first of June, which shall be in the year 1780, to be applied to the funding scholarships, and other good uses, for the support of the said College, and to be accounted for to the General Assembly; and the said General Assembly by of in the year gave a further donation to the said College of to be laid out in purchasing a mathematical apparatus for the said College, which was accordingly purchased. And the said trustees, in pursuance of the trust reposed in them, proceeded to erect the said College, and established one school of sacred theology, with two professorships therein, to wit, one for teaching the Hebrew tongue, and expounding the holy scriptures; and the other for explaining the common places of divinity, and the controversies with heretics; one other school for philosophy, with two professorships therein, to wit, one for the study of rhetoric, logic, and ethics, and the other of physics, metaphysics, and mathematics; one other school for teaching the Latin and Greek tongues; and one other for teaching Indian boys reading, writing, vulgar arithmetic, the catechism and the principles of the Christian religion; which last school was founded on the private donation of the honorable Robert Boyle, of the kingdom of England, and, by authority from his executors, submitted to the direction of the Earl of Burlington, one of the said executors, of the bishop of London, for the time being, and in default thereof, to the said trustees; and over the whole they appointed one president as supervisor.

And whereas the experience of near an hundred years hath proved, that the said College, thus amply endowed by the public, hath not answered their expectations, and there is reason to hope, that it would become more useful, if certain articles in its constitution were altered and amended, which being fixed, as before recited, by the original charters, cannot be reformed by the said trustees, whose powers are created and circumscribed by the said charter, and the said College being erected and constituted on the requisition of the General Assembly, by the Chief Magistrate of the state, their legal fiduciary for such purposes, being founded and endowed with the lands and revenues of the public, and intended for the sole use and improvement, and no wise in nature of a private grant, the same is of right subject to the public direction, and may by them be altered and amended, until such form be devised as will render the institution publicly advantageous, in proportion as it is publicly expensive; and the late change in the form of our government, as well as the contest of arms in which we are at present engaged, calling for extraordinary abilities both in council and field, it becomes the peculiar duty of the Legislature, at this time, to aid and improve that seminary, in which those who are to be the future guardians of the rights and liberties of their country may be endowed with science and virtue, to watch and preserve the sacred deposit: Be it therefore enacted by the General Assembly, that, instead of eighteen visiters or governors of the said College, there shall in future be five only, who shall be appointed by joint ballot of both houses of Assembly, annually, to enter on the duties of their office on the new year's day ensuing their appointment, having previously given assurance of fidelity to the commonwealth, before any Justice of the Peace; and to continue in office until those next appointed shall be qualified, but those who shall be first appointed, after the passing of this act, and all others appointed during the course of any year to fill up vacancies happening by death, resignation, or removal out of the commonwealth, shall enter on duty immediately on such appointment; any four of the said visiters may proceed to business; they shall chuse their own Rector, at their first meeting, in every year, and shall be deemed the lawful successors of the first trustees, and invested with all the rights, powers, and capacities given to them, save only so far as the same shall be abridged by this act, nor shall they be restrained in their legislation, by the royal prerogative, or the laws of the kingdom of England; or the canons or constitution of the English Church, as enjoined in the said charter. There shall be three Chancellors, in like manner appointed by joint ballot of both houses, from among the Judges of the High Court of Chancery, or of the General Court, to enter on their office immediately on such appointment, and to continue therein so long as they remain in either of the said courts; any two of whom may proceed to business; to them shall belong solely the power of removing the Professors, for breach or neglect of duty, immorality, severity, contumacy, or other good cause, and the judiciary powers in all disputes, which shall arise on the statutes of the College, being called on for that purpose by the Rector, or by the corporation of President and Professors, a copy of their sentence of deprivation, being delivered to the sheriff of the county wherein the College is, he shall forthwith cause the Professor deprived to be ousted of his chambers and other freehold appertaining to the said College, and the remaining Professors to be reseized thereof, in like manner and form, and subject, on failure, to the like fines by the said Chancellors, as in cases of writs of habere facias seisinam issued from Courts of Record. But no person shall be capable of being both visiter and Chancellor at the same time; nor shall any Professor be capable of being at the same time either visiter or Chancellor. Instead of the President and six

Professors, licensed by the said charter, and established by the former visiters, there shall be eight Professors, one of whom shall also be appointed President, with an additional salary of one hundred pounds a year, before they enter on the execution of their office, they shall give assurance of fidelity to the commonwealth, before some Justice of the Peace. These shall be deemed the lawful successors of the President and Professors appointed under the said charter, and shall have all their rights, powers and capacities, not otherwise disposed of by this act; to them shall belong the ordinary government of the College, and administration of its revenues, taking the advice of the visiters on all matters of great concern. There shall, in like manner, be eight Professorships, to wit, one of moral philosophy, the laws of nature and of nations, and of the fine arts; one of law and police; one of history, civil and ecclesiastical; one of mathematics; one of anatomy and medicine; one of natural philosophy and natural history; one of the ancient languages, oriental and northern; and one of modern languages. The said Professors shall likewise appoint, from time to time, a missionary, of approved veracity, to the several tribes of Indians, whose business shall be to investigate their laws, customs, religions, traditions, and more particularly their languages, constructing grammars thereof, as well as may be, and copious vocabularies, and, on oath, to communicate, [from time to time to the said president and professors the materials he collects to be by them laid up and preserved in their library, for which trouble the said missionary shall be allowed a salary at the discretion of the visitors out of the revenues of the college.

And forasmuch as the revenue arising from the duties on skins and furrs and those on liquors with which the said college was endowed, by several acts of General assembly is subject to great fluctuations,[1] from circumstances unforeseen, insomuch that no calculation or foresight can enable the said visitors or professors to square thereto the expenditures of the said college, which being regular and permanent should depend on stable funds, be it therefore enacted that the revenue arising from the said duties shall be henceforth transferred to the use of the public to be applied towards supporting the contingent charges of government; and that in lieu thereof the said college shall be endowed with an impost of 9d[2] on every hogshead of tobacco to be exported from this commonwealth by land or water, to be paid to the inspectors, if such tobacco be carried to any public warehouse, by the person receiving the said tobacco from them, and by the said inspectors accounted for on oath to the said President and professors on or before the 10th. day of Octob. in every year with an allowance of 6 per centum for their trouble, and if the said tobacco be not carried to any public warehouse, then the said impost shall be paid collected and accounted for[3] in like manner under the like penalties, and for the same allowance as prescribed by law in the case of skins and furrs exported: which revenue shall be applied in aid of the other funds for the general purposes for which the said college is instituted, and together with them shall be accounted for annually to the General assembly.][4] And that this commonwealth may not be without so great an ornament, nor its youth such an help towards attaining astronomical science, as the mechanical representation, or model of the solar system, conceived and executed by that greatest of astronomers, David Ryttenhouse; Be it further enacted, that the visiters, first appointed under this act, and their successors, shall be authorised to engage the said David Ryttenhouse, on the part of this commonwealth, to make and erect in the said College of William and Mary, and for its use, one of the said models, to be called by the name of the Ryttenhouse, the cost and expence of making, transporting and erecting whereof shall, according to the agreement or allowance of the said visiters, be paid by the Treasurer of this commonwealth, on warrant from the Auditors.

APPENDIX.

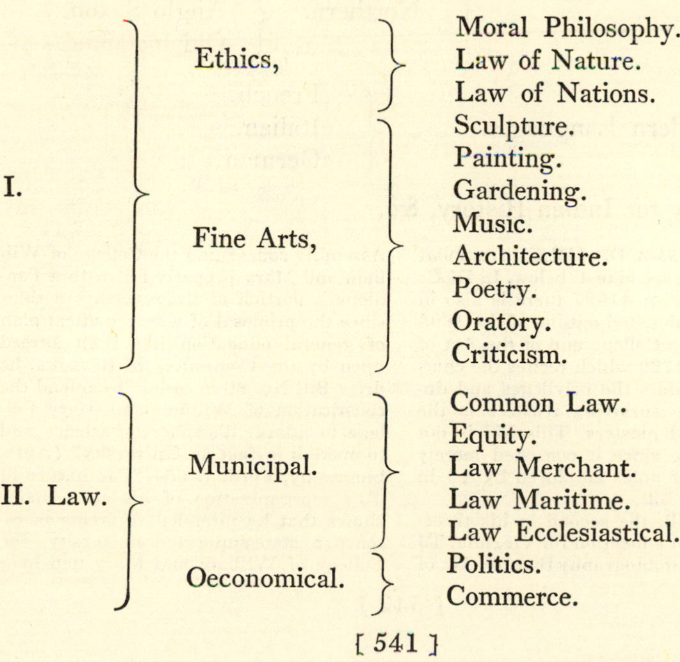

- I.
  - Ethics,
    - Moral Philosophy.
    - Law of Nature.
    - Law of Nations.
  - Fine Arts,
    - Sculpture.
    - Painting.
    - Gardening.
    - Music.
    - Architecture.
    - Poetry.
    - Oratory.
    - Criticism.
- II. Law.
  - Municipal.
    - Common Law.
    - Equity.
    - Law Merchant.
    - Law Maritime.
    - Law Ecclesiastical.
  - Oeconomical.
    - Politics.
    - Commerce.

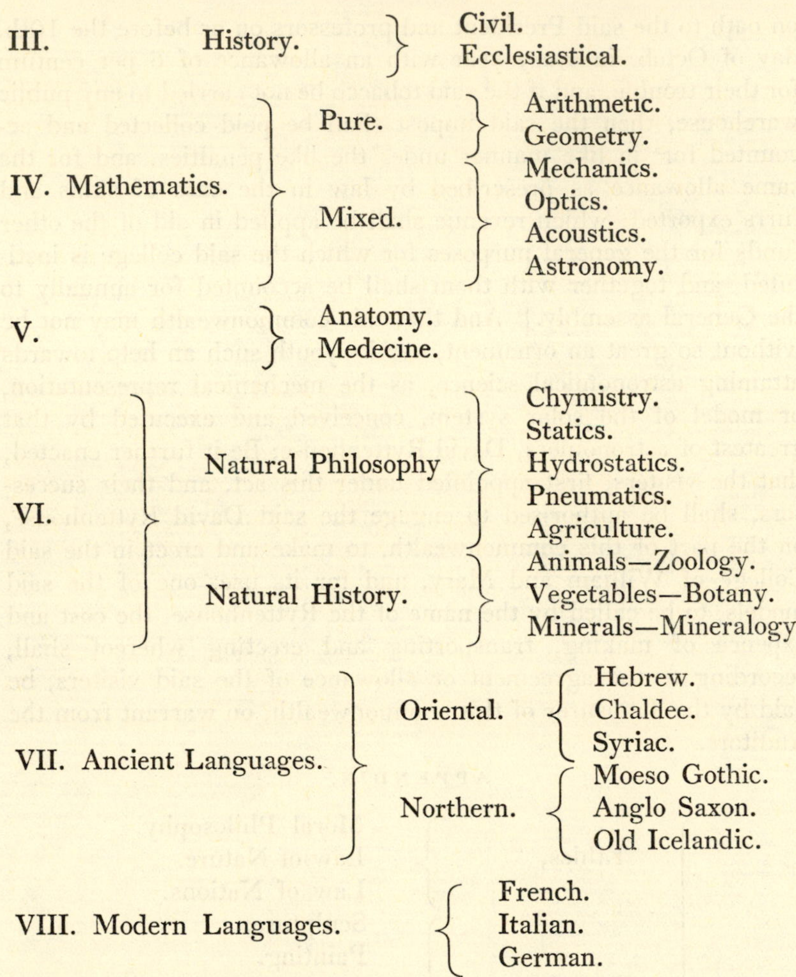

III. History. — Civil. Ecclesiastical.

IV. Mathematics. — Pure. (Arithmetic. Geometry.) Mixed. (Mechanics. Optics. Acoustics. Astronomy.)

V. Anatomy. Medecine.

VI. Natural Philosophy (Chymistry. Statics. Hydrostatics. Pneumatics. Agriculture.) Natural History. (Animals—Zoology. Vegetables—Botany. Minerals—Mineralogy.)

VII. Ancient Languages. — Oriental. (Hebrew. Chaldee. Syriac.) Northern. (Moeso Gothic. Anglo Saxon. Old Icelandic.)

VIII. Modern Languages. — French. Italian. German.

Missionary for Indian History, &c.

Report, p. 55-8. Dft (DLC); fragment in TJ's hand; see note 4, below. In DLC: TJ Papers, 234: 41987 there is also in TJ's hand a detailed outline of the 1693 charter of the College and of the Act of Transfer of 1729 which recites the charter and transfers the privileges and duties from the surviving trustees to the president and masters. This MS is not included here since it consisted merely of a series of notes employed by TJ in drafting the Bill.

Of this Bill, the second in his threefold system of education for Virginia, TJ said in his Autobiography that the Act of Assembly concerning the College of William and Mary properly fell within Pendleton's portion of the revisal, but that, since the proposal of a systematical plan of general education had been agreed upon by the Committee of Revisors, he drew Bill No. 80 in order "to amend the constitution of William and Mary College, to enlarge it's sphere of science, and to make it in fact an University" (Autobiography, Ford, I, 66). The nature of TJ's reorganization of his alma mater shows that he intended to create in essence a state-supported university; the College of William and Mary had long enjoyed some public revenues, yet TJ felt that it was "an establishment purely of the Church of England; the Visitors were required to be all of that Church; the Professors to subscribe it's 39 Articles; it's Students to learn it's Catechism; and one of its fundamental objects was declared to be to raise up Ministers for that church" (same, I, 67). Accordingly, in his provisions both for the government of the College and for the modernization of its curriculum, TJ proposed to secularize the institution, a proposal naturally following upon the relationships between church and state expressed in the famous preamble to the Bill for Establishing Religious Freedom. Even in respect to the professorship endowed by Robert Boyle for the purpose of Christianizing the Indians, TJ proposed to abolish the idea of an Indian school as part of the College and to substitute therefor "a perpetual mission among the Indian tribes." The requirement set up by the founder of this trust would be observed by having the missionary instruct the Indians in the principles of Christianity, but an object that must have been paramount in TJ's mind and certainly one that he returned to many years later was that of having the missionary "collect their traditions, laws, customs, languages, and other circumstances" (*Notes on Virginia*, Ford, III, 256); especial attention was to be paid to languages and, as the Bill stipulated, grammars, vocabularies, and other records accumulated by the missionary were to be deposited in the College library. In spite of these proposed measures for the secularization and modernization of the College, TJ felt that "the religious jealousies . . . of all the dissenters took alarm lest this might give an ascendancy to the Anglican sect and refused acting on that bill" (Autobiography, Ford, I, 67). However, shortly after being elected governor, TJ was also made one of the visitors of William and Mary College and, as such, he was able to bring about some of the changes proposed in his Bill. In his Autobiography he states: "I effected . . . a change in the organization of that institution, by abolishing the Grammar school, and the two professorships of Divinity and Oriental languages, and substituting a professorship of Law and Police, one of Anatomy, Medicine, and Chemistry, and one of Modern languages; and the charter confining us to six professorships, we added the Law of Nature and Nations, and the Fine Arts to the duties of the Moral professor, and Natural history to those of the professor of Mathematics and Natural philosophy" (same, I, 69-70).

This Bill was presented by Madison 31 Oct. 1785, postponed 14 Dec. to next session, and brought up again on 1 Nov. 1786, but apparently no further action was taken on it (JHD, Oct. 1785, 1828 edn., p. 12-15, 92; same, Oct. 1786, p. 16-17).

[1] See note 4 below. In margin of Dft TJ wrote: "see Memor. in Journ. Deleg. May 28. 1777." On 28 May 1777 the rector, visitors, and governors presented a memorial to the House of Delegates, which set forth the financial difficulties under which the College was operating because of the cessation of duties from which it derived its income and praying that the Assembly establish a fund for its support; this memorial was referred to the committee of the whole, but on 12 June the committee was discharged from proceeding thereon (JHD, May 1777, 1827 edn., p. 34-5, 74).

[2] See note 4 below. *Report* reads: "impost of five pounds of tobacco on every hogshead"; opposite this, in the margin, TJ wrote: "£1875," which may have been the total amount he calculated such an impost would produce. At this point also TJ deleted in MS: "shall be paid to the said professors and their successors in all times hereafter."

[3] See note 4 below. Following this point the text of Bill No. 80 as reported by the Committee of Revisors reads: "to the said President and Professors, by the same persons, at the same times, in and under the like manner, penalties and conditions, as prescribed by the laws, which shall be in force at the time, for collecting the duties imposed on exported tobacco, towards raising supplies of money for the public exigencies."

[4] The part enclosed in square brackets (supplied) follows the text of Dft (DLC) noted above, rather than the text of the *Report*. Numerous deletions were made by TJ in Dft, but these were chiefly alterations in phraseology.

81. A Bill for Establishing a Public Library

Be it enacted by the General Assembly, that on the first day of January, in every year there shall be paid out of the treasury the sum of two thousand pounds, to be laid out in such books and maps as may be proper to be preserved in a public library,[1] and in defraying the expences necessary for the care and preservation thereof; which library shall be established at the town of Richmond.

The two houses of Assembly shall appoint three persons of learning and of attention to literary matters, to be visitors of the said library, and shall remove them, or any of them, and fill any vacancies, from time to time, as they shall think fit; which visiters shall have power to receive the annual sums beforementioned, and therewith to procure such books and maps as aforesaid, and shall superintend the preservation thereof. Whensoever a keeper shall be found necessary they shall appoint such keeper, from time to time, at their will, on such annual salary (not exceeding one hundred pounds) as they shall think reasonable.

If during the time of war the importation of books and maps shall be hazardous, or if the rate of exchange between this commonwealth and any state from which such articles are wanted, shall from any cause be such that they cannot be imported to such advantage as may be hoped at a future day, the visiters shall place the annual sums, as they become due, in the public loan office, if any there be, for the benefit of interest, or otherwise shall suffer them to remain in the treasury until fit occasions shall occur of employing them.

It shall not be lawful for the said keeper, or the visiters themselves, or any other person to remove any book or map out of the said library, unless it be for the necessary repair thereof; but the same shall be made useful by indulging the researches of the learned and curious, within the said library, without fee or reward, and under such rules for preserving them safe and in good order and condition as the visiters shall constitute.

The visiters shall annually settle their accounts with the Auditors and leave with them the vouchers for the expenditure of the monies put into their hands.

Report, p. 58.

Bill presented by Madison 31 Oct. 1785, postponed 14 Dec. to next session, and brought up again on 1 Nov. 1786; apparently no further action was taken on it (JHD, Oct. 1785, 1828 edn., p. 12-15, 92; same, Oct. 1786, p. 16-17).

1 The phrase "public library" as here employed is not to be understood as meaning an institution similar to Benjamin Franklin's Library Company of Philadelphia (which TJ must have become acquainted with on his trip north in 1766) or as having the connotation that

public libraries later assumed. This Bill was the third part of his general system of education, and the function of TJ's "public library" is to be explained in that context. In his Autobiography TJ stated that the three grades of education that he proposed were (1) schools for elementary purposes; (2) "Colleges for a middle degree of instruction"; and (3) "an ultimate grade for teaching the sciences generally, and in their highest degree"—this third grade being provided for in a Bill "for the establishment of a library" (Ford, I, 66-7). In a more nearly contemporary account, TJ stated that this Bill "proposed . . . to begin a public library and gallery, by laying out a certain sum annually in books, paintings, and statues (*Notes on Virginia*, Ford, III, 255); however, the Bill provides only for the purchase of books and maps, making no mention of the acquisition of objects suitable to an art museum. The real object of his library was that "of indulging the researches of the learned and curious." It was obviously not intended for the whole reading public or to meet the general reading requirements of the entire community, but to enable those of superior talent to give freer rein to their particular geniuses (see notes to Bill No. 79, above).

82. A Bill for Establishing Religious Freedom

Well aware that the opinions and belief of men depend not on their own will, but follow involuntarily the evidence proposed to their minds; that[1] Almighty God hath created the mind free, *and manifested his supreme will that free it shall remain by making it altogether insusceptible of restraint*;[2] that all attempts to influence it by temporal punishments, or burthens, or by civil incapacitations, tend only to beget habits of hypocrisy and meanness, and are a departure from the plan of the holy author of our religion,[3] who being lord both of body and mind, yet chose not to propagate it by coercions on either, as was in his Almighty power to do, *but to extend it by its influence on reason alone*;[4] that the impious presumption of legislators and rulers, civil as well as ecclesiastical, who, being themselves but fallible and uninspired men, have assumed dominion over the faith of others, setting up their own opinions and modes of thinking as the only true and infallible, and as such endeavoring to impose them on others, hath established and maintained false religions over the greatest part of the world and through all time: That to compel a man to furnish contributions of money for the propagation of opinions which he disbelieves *and abhors*,[4] is sinful and tyrannical; that even the forcing him to support this or that teacher of his own religious persuasion, is depriving him of the comfortable liberty of giving his contributions to the particular pastor whose morals he would make his pattern, and whose powers he feels most persuasive to righteousness; and is withdrawing from the ministry those temporary[5] rewards, which proceeding from an approbation of their personal conduct, are an additional incitement to earnest and unremitting labours for the instruction of mankind; that our civil rights have no dependance on our religious opinions, any more than[6] our opinions in physics or geometry; that therefore the proscribing any citizen as unworthy the public confidence by laying upon him an incapacity of being called to offices of trust and emolument, unless he profess or renounce this or that religious opinion, is depriving him injuriously of those privileges and advantages to which, in common with his fellow citizens, he has a natural right; that it tends also[7] to corrupt the principles of that *very*[8] religion it is meant to encourage, by bribing, with a monopoly of worldly honours and emoluments, those who will externally profess and conform to it; that though indeed these are criminal who do not withstand such temptation, yet neither are those innocent who lay the bait in their way; *that the opinions of men are not the object of civil government, nor under its jurisdiction*;[9] that to suffer the civil magistrate to intrude his powers into the field of opinion and to restrain the profession or propagation of principles on supposition of their ill tendency is a dangerous falacy, which at once destroys all religious liberty, because he being of course judge of that tendency will make his opinions the rule of judgment, and approve or condemn the sentiments of others only as they shall square with or differ from his own; that it is time enough for the rightful purposes of civil government for its officers to interfere when principles break out into overt acts against peace and good order; and finally, that truth is great and will prevail if left to herself; that she is the proper and sufficient antagonist to error, and has nothing to fear from the conflict unless by human interposition disarmed of her natural weapons, free argument and debate; errors ceasing to be dangerous when it is permitted freely to contradict them.

We the General Assembly of Virginia do enact[10] that no man shall be compelled to frequent or support any religious worship, place, or ministry whatsoever, nor shall be enforced, restrained, molested, or burthened in his body or goods, nor shall otherwise suffer, on account of his religious opinions or belief; but that all men shall be free to profess, and by argument to maintain, their opinions in matters of religion, and that the same shall in no wise diminish, enlarge, or affect their civil capacities.

And though we well know that this Assembly, elected by the people for the ordinary purposes of legislation only, have no power to restrain the acts of succeeding Assemblies, constituted with powers equal to our own, and that therefore to declare this act[11] irrevocable would be of no effect in law; yet we are free to declare, and do declare, that the rights hereby asserted are of the natural rights of mankind, and that if any act shall be hereafter passed to repeal the present or to narrow its operation, such act will be an infringement of natural right.

Report, p. 58-9. No MS copy of this famous Bill has been found. Text of Act as adopted in 1785 is in Hening, XII, 84-6. The engrossed MS copy of the Act, on parchment, is in Vi (photostat in TJ Editorial Files); the text in Hening agrees with this authoritative text and also with the text of the official printing in the session laws of Oct. 1785 (*Acts passed at a General Assembly of the Commonwealth of Virginia*, Richmond: Dunlap and Hayes [1786], p. 26-7). For various contemporary printed texts, see note below. Since the printed text of 1779 is reproduced in facsimile in this volume, the text of the *Report* has been followed here so that the slight variations in punctuation and spelling can be noted. The texts of both the 1779 broadside and the 1784 *Report* are obviously different from the MS as TJ would normally have written it, the former employing such spellings as "honours," "labour," &c., and the latter being punctuated in an erratic manner. These variations may be attributed to copyists' or printers' errors. These two texts are the closest we can get to TJ's original, but there is little to choose between them: the most that can be said is that the 1779 broadside is the earliest known text. *Those parts of the Bill that were deleted by amendment are printed in italic type*; it is important to note that this device is employed only as a graphic means of showing at a glance the changes made by the General Assembly and that the text as printed in *Report*, p. 58-9, is entirely in roman type and should, for ordinary purposes, be so quoted.

For a good summary and background of TJ's attitude toward the established Church, dissenting groups, and the relationship of church and state, see Malone, *Jefferson*, I, 274-80. This Bill, which TJ ranked with the Declaration of Independence, might indeed be considered as a necessary consequence of it: as the Declaration of Independence asserted the natural right of a people to choose any form of government conducive to their safety and happiness, so the Bill for Establishing Religious Freedom asserted the natural right of a person to choose his beliefs and opinions free of compulsion. In this sense the famous preamble to TJ's Bill provided philosophical justification, as of natural right, not merely for the ideas of religious toleration and separation of state and church but also for the right of the individual to complete intellectual liberty—"the opinions of men are not the object of civil government, nor under its jurisdiction." TJ later asserted that the effort to disestablish the Church of England in Virginia and to establish religious freedom brought on "the severest contests" in which he had ever been engaged (see Notes and Proceedings on Discontinuing the Establishment of the Church of England, 11 Oct. to 9 Dec. 1776). The effort had resulted in 1776 in a compromise: TJ and his colleagues had failed to obtain repeal of all laws interfering with religious worship and, instead of disestablishing the Church, had only succeeded in exempting dissenters from levies made in behalf of the establishment. From 1776 to 1779 the General Assembly was assailed with petitions for and against further reform. The particular issue was whether the maintenance of churches should be left to voluntary contributions or whether "a general assessment should not be established by law, on every one, to the support of the pastor of his choice" (Autobiography, Ford, I, 54). The Bill for Establishing Religious Freedom, though TJ declared he had drawn it in 1777, was probably not brought forward in these years from 1776 to 1779 because the intense fight over the question of a general assessment made it difficult enough to hold the position that had been gained. However, on 4 June 1779, after TJ had been elected governor, the House ordered Harvie, Mason, and Baker to bring in a bill on this subject. TJ's Bill was presented by Harvie on 12 June, the next day it passed the second reading, and the third reading was postponed to 1 Aug., which killed it for that session (JHD, May 1779, 1827 edn., p. 34, 36, 44, 46).

There is no reference in the Journals of the House of Delegates to the printing of TJ's Bill as introduced at the May 1779 session, but, though attributed to the year 1785 in the bibliographies of Sabin and others, it was printed in the summer of 1779 as a broadside under the title: "*A* BILL *for establishing* RELIGIOUS FREEDOM, *printed for the consideration of the* PEOPLE" (see facsimile reprint in this volume; see also Mazzei to TJ, 19 Mch. 1780). Whether this was done under the authority of the General Assembly or privately by TJ and other supporters of the Bill is not certain, but, though the General Assembly from time to time did print bills that were held over from one session to another so that they could be discussed by the people (e.g., see Bill for Giving the Members of the General Assembly an Adequate Allowance, 12 Dec. 1778), the available evidence seems to support the supposition that it was privately issued. For, if the General Assembly had authorized publication, there would seem to be no reason why such authorization should not have appeared in the Journals, as other similar authorizations did. Also, at the Oct. 1779 session there were several petitions for and against this particular Bill and two of them express doubt as to whether the publication was authorized by the General Assembly or not. A petition from Augusta county expressed approval of "the bill presented to the last Assembly, (and published, as they suppose, for the Consideration of the people) 'for establishing religious freedom' " and prayed that it be enacted into law. Another petition from dissenters in Lunenberg county asserted that they had seen "a bill which they suppose was published by order of the last Assembly, 'for establishing religious freedom' " (this petition, incidentally, supports TJ's assertion that some of the dissenting groups, having gained their point in 1776, went over to the opposition and supported the idea of a general assessment; for the petition of the Lunenberg dissenters approved the Bill and at the same time prayed for the enactment of a general assessment). Other petitions from Essex and Amherst concerned the Bill but did not refer to the fact or the method of its being printed (JHD, Oct. 1779, 1827 edn., p. 20, 27, 32, 37). It seems obvious that, if this Bill had been printed under public authority, that fact would have been known to the petitioners and their memorials to the General Assembly would not, therefore, have expressed doubt on the point. For if the broadside had been printed by public authorization, it would no doubt have been transmitted as such by the clerk of the House or by the executive department. When the printing of *The Report of the Committee of Revisors* was authorized by the General Assembly in 1784, the resolution specifically directed that the pamphlet "be distributed throughout the several counties by the Executive, in such manner as they shall judge most conducive to the end proposed." It is difficult to imagine what motive could have persuaded, or what means could have been employed by, the General Assembly to conceal its authorization of the printing of the broadside if, as on this and other occasions, its object was to have the Bill "printed for the consideration of the people."

The effort to have Bill No. 82 passed separately at the May and Oct. sessions in 1779 was not successful. But in Oct. 1785 this Bill was one of two in the second half of the revisal brought up for consideration and the only one of these adopted (the other was Bill No. 79). Madison reported to Monroe on the day the Bill passed the House: "The Bill proportioning crimes and punishments was the one at which we stuck after wading thro' the most difficult parts of it. A few subsequent bills however were excepted from the postponement. Among these was the Bill for establishing Religious freedom, which has got thro' the H. of Delegates without alteration, though not without warm opposition. Mr. Mercer and Mr. Corbin were the principal Combatants against it" (Madison to Monroe, 17 Dec. 1785, *Writings*, ed. Hunt, II, 205). This was something of an understatement. The Bill was introduced by Madison 31 Oct. 1785, read twice, and referred to the committee of the whole. It was debated and amended by the committee on 15 Dec., and this amendment, which has not been identified, was approved by the House the next day. At the same time another amendment was proposed—that is, that the whole of TJ's preamble be struck out and the following substituted therefor: "Whereas, it is declared by the Bill of Rights, 'that religion, or the duty which we owe to our Creator, and the manner of discharging it, can be directed only by reason and conviction, not by force or violence; and therefore, all men are equally entitled to the free exercise of religion, according to the dictates of conscience, and it is the mutual duty of all to practice christian forbearance, love and charity towards each other' " (JHD, Oct. 1785, 1828 edn., p. 12-15, 93, 94, 95). When Madison reported on this

Bill to TJ, 22 Jan. 1786, q.v., he mentioned the Senate's effort to accomplish the same amendment, but did not refer to that attempted earlier in the House. As an indication of the importance attached to this whole question, it is worth noting that the ayes and noes on this amendment were recorded in the Journals. The amendment failed by a vote of 38 to 66.

On 17 Dec. a motion was made to postpone the third reading of the engrossed Bill until the Oct. session 1786, but this was defeated. The Bill was thereupon read the third time, put to a vote, passed by a majority of 74 to 20, and transmitted to the Senate. The ayes and noes were ordered to be recorded. Those voting in favor of the Bill were: Joshua Fry, Wilson Cary Nicholas, Joseph Eggleston, Samuel Jordan Cabell, Zachariah Johnston, Michael Bowyer, John Trigg, Robert Clark, George Hancock, Archibald Stuart, William Anderson, Hickerson Barksdale, John Clarke (Campbell), Samuel Hawes, Anthony New, John Daniel, Henry Southall, French Strother, Henry Fry, William Gatewood, Meriwether Smith, Charles Simms, David Stuart, William Pickett, Thomas Helm, Christopher Greenup, James Garrard, George Thomson, Alexander White, Charles Thruston, Thomas Smith, George Clendennin, John Lucas, Jeremiah Pate, Ralph Humphreys, Isaac Vanmiter, George Jackson, Nathaniel Wilkinson, John Mayo, Jr., John Rentfro, William Norvell, John Roberts, William Dudley, Thomas Moore, Carter Braxton, Benjamin Temple, Francis Peyton, Christopher Robertson, Samuel Garland, Benjamin Logan, David Scott, William Pettijohn, Robert Sayres, Daniel Trigg, William Hartwell Macon, Griffin Stith, David Bradford, James Madison, Charles Porter, William Harrison, Benjamin Lankford, John Clarke (Prince Edward), Richard Bibb, Cuthbert Bullitt, Daniel Carroll Brent, Williamson Ball, Andrew Moore, John Hopkins, Gawin Hamilton, Isaac Zane, John Tayloe, John Whittaker Willis, Andrew Kincannon, and James Innes.

Those who voted against the Bill were: Thomas Claiborne, Miles King, Worlich Westwood, John Page, Garland Anderson, Elias Wills, William Thornton, Francis Corbin, Willis Riddick, Daniel Sandford, John Gordon, Edward Bland, Anthony Walke, George Lee Turberville, William Garrard, John Francis Mercer, Carter Bassett Harrison, Richard Cary, Jr., Wilson Cary, and Richard Lee.

The Senate amended the Bill and returned it to the House on 29 Dec.; this was precisely the same amendment that had been offered in the House two weeks earlier. This time the amendment failed of adoption by a vote of 35 to 56, a vote that, like the earlier one, reflected opposition to the preamble rather than to the Bill; for the vote in favor of the Bill on 17 Dec. included some (e.g., such a conservative as Carter Braxton) who voted in favor of the amendment on 29 Dec. There was, on the other hand, almost no shifting of position among those whose names are recorded as voting on the amendment on both 16 Dec. and 29 Dec.: Francis Peyton voted in favor of it on the former date and against it on the latter; Anthony New and John Prunty voted against it at first and then for it.

The Senate on 9 Jan. 1786 insisted on its amendment and requested a free conference on the subject of its amendment, to which the House agreed. The managers met on 12 Jan. 1786. The Senate's "objections [to the preamble]," wrote Madison, "were frivolous indeed. In order to remove them as they were understood by the Managers of the H. of D. the preamble was sent up again from the H. of D. [on 13 Jan.] with one or two verbal alterations. As an amendment to these the Senate sent down a few others, which as they did not affect the substance though they somewhat defaced the composition, it was thought better to agree to than to run further risks, especially as it was getting late in the Session and the House growing thin. The enacting clauses past without a single alteration, and I flatter myself have in this country extinguished for ever the ambitious hope of making laws for the human mind" (Madison to TJ, 22 Jan. 1786; JHD, Oct. 1785, 1828 edn., p. 12-15, 93, 94, 95, 96, 115, 117, 134, 135, 138, 139, 143-4, 148). The amendments offered by the Senate, and agreed to by the House on 16 Jan. 1786, are indicated in notes 1, 2, and 4; other amendments made either in the House or Senate are indicated in notes 7, 8, 9, and 11.

Madison and others thought these amendments rendered "the style less elegant, though the sense is not affected" (Hening, XII, 84). But Malone (I, 279) is quite correct in saying that these amendments deleted "some of the more sweeping statements about the supremacy and illimitability of reason; and, as a result, the statute did not rest on quite so broad a base as the one its author had designed."

Ironically, due to TJ himself, it was the text neither of the Bill as originally submitted nor of the Act as finally adopted that was in his day and subsequently most generally accepted as "The Act for Establishing Religious Freedom." In 1776 TJ had revealed his desire to have the world, or at least some of his friends and political associates, know the text of the Declaration of Independence as he had drafted it, and he had sent out several copies that he had laboriously copied by hand. But his pristine text was not printed at all until more than a quarter of a century had elapsed and it never came close to achieving the popularity enjoyed by the text as adopted by Congress. But the Bill for Establishing Religious Freedom fared differently: its full text as drafted by TJ was put into type six years before its altered version was enacted into law. What was more important, TJ, being in France at the time his Bill was adopted, saw to it that the famous declaration was widely distributed. It was not mere pride of authorship but pride of country as well that led him to obtain publication in Europe: "it is honorable for us," he wrote Madison, "to have produced the first legislature who has had the courage to declare that the reason of man may be trusted with the formation of his own opinions" (TJ to Madison, 16 Dec. 1786); in the same letter TJ reported that the Act "has been received with infinite approbation in Europe and propagated with enthusiasm"; that it had been translated into French and Italian, had been sent to most of the courts of Europe, had been inserted in the *Encyclopédie méthodique*, was appearing in most of the publications respecting America, such as those of Brissot, Clavière, and Mazzei; and that it had "been the best evidence of the falshood of those reports which stated us to be in anarchy." Though his motive in promoting publication in Europe was elevated, TJ nevertheless took unwarranted liberties with the authoritative text of this immortal statute, as the following facts clearly prove.

Facsimiles of what TJ in the epitaph that he later drew up referred to as "the Statute of Virginia for religious freedom" are to be found in TJ Editorial Files: (1) *A BILL for establishing* RELIGIOUS FREEDOM, / *printed for the consideration of the* PEOPLE. [Williamsburg, 1779]. Broadside, Boston Public Library, Evans 19350, Swem, "Va. Bibliog.," 7476, and Sabin 100041. (All three bibliographies, apparently assuming that the Bill was published under public authority in the fall of 1785 when the Bill was being debated, assign that date, the place as Richmond, and James Hayes, the public printer, as the printer. Since the Bill was undoubtedly printed in 1779, and was probably issued privately, this assignment should be changed as to place, printer and date, and probably as to publisher); (2) *An* ACT *for establishing* RELIGIOUS FREEDOM, / *passed in the assembly of Virginia in the beginning / of the year* 1786. [Paris, 1786]. Four-page pamphlet. Copy in PHi; another that TJ sent to Van Hogendorp was found by Dr. Howard C. Rice, Jr., in the Van Hogendorp papers, Rijksarchief, The Hague, Sabin 100342. This text, which was sent to various persons by TJ as a separate pamphlet, was also bound in as an appendix to some copies of the first edition of *Notes on Virginia*. It was later included as an appendix to the 1787 Stockdale edition, the 1788 (first American) edition printed in Philadelphia by Prichard and Hall, and in subsequent editions of the *Notes*. The text of (5) below derives from one of these editions. (3) *Acte de la République de VIRGINIE, / qui établit la liberté de Religion.* [Paris, 1786]. Four-page pamphlet, probably printed by Philippe-Denys Pierres (see Ford, II, 237). Copy in NN; another found by Dr. Rice in Van Hogendorp papers, Rijksarchief, The Hague, Sabin 100342; (4) *An* ACT *for establishing* RELIGIOUS / FREEDOM, *passed in the Assembly / of Virginia in the beginning of the year 1786* / [rule] / *Acte de la République de VIRGINIE, / qui établit la liberté de Religion, passé / à l'assemblée de la Virginie au commen- / cement de l'année 1786*. [Paris, 1786]. Eight-page pamphlet found by Dr. Rice, in the Bibliothèque de l'Institut de France, Paris, Sabin 100344; (5) REPUBLICAN NOTES / ON / RELIGION; / AND, / AN ACT ESTABLISHING RELIGIOUS FREE- / DOM, PASSED IN THE ASSEMBLY OF / VIRGINIA, IN THE YEAR 1786. / [rule] / BY THOMAS JEFFERSON, ESQUIRE, / PRESIDENT OF THE UNITED STATES. / [rule] / [ornament] / DANBURY: / PRINTED

BY THOMAS ROWE. / 1803. Twelve-page pamphlet containing extracts from Query XVII, *Notes on Virginia* and (p. 9-11) the text of "*An* ACT *for establishing* RELIGIOUS FREEDOM, / *passed in the Assembly of Virginia, in the beginning / of the Year* 1786," Sabin 35914. This text, as well as the title, obviously derives from that described under (2) above. These various contemporary versions are referred to in the notes below as Text (1), Text (2), &c.

A glance at Texts (2) to (5) above is sufficient to show that they are not derived from the broadside of 1779, or from the *Report* of 1784, or even from the printed session laws of 1785. They are, in the points noted below, at variance with both the Bill and the Act. All of the English texts described above, excluding Text (1) of course, agree. All of the French texts, which vary from the English texts in one important particular but possibly were derived from one of them, agree with each other. Clearly TJ had before him a copy of the Act as adopted when he prepared this English version of 1786; it is equally clear that he also had at hand a copy of the Bill when he produced this curious hybrid text whose stemma embraced those of both Bill and Act. The following variations are to be noted. First, English Texts (2), (4), (5) do not begin, as the Act does, with the phrase "Whereas Almighty God hath created the mind free" but, as the *amended* Bill does, with the words "Well aware that Almighty God hath created the mind free." This incorporates *part* of the amendment indicated in note 1, below, but also restores part of the deleted initial phrase of the Bill. The French texts agree with the English in this variant reading. Second, the deletions made by amendments to the Bill as described in notes 2, 4, and 9 below are all followed in English and French Texts (2) to (5), since none of these texts contains any of the words or clauses deleted in these places or their equivalent. Third, English Texts (2), (4), (5) agree with the Bill rather than the Act as adopted by including the word "very" at the point indicated in note 8, below. Finally and curiously, French Texts (3) and (4) agree with the Bill rather than with the Act in the phraseology of the enacting clause (see note 10, below), reading: "Nous, l'Assemblée générale de Virginie, établissons pour loi. . . ." The English Texts (2), (4), and (5), however, read as follows: "*Be it therefore enacted by the General Assembly* . . . ." which is neither the text of the Bill nor that of the Act as adopted (the latter does not contain the word "therefore"). Ironically, TJ himself, by accepting in part the enacting clause agreed upon by the General Assembly and by retaining the opening words ("Well aware that") of his Bill, did grammatical and structural violence to his great declaration of intellectual and spiritual freedom. It is inexplicable that the English Texts (2), (4), and (5) should have had this fault, and that the French Texts (3) and (4) should not have. The long French preamble beginning "Convaincus que le Dieu tout puissant a créé libre l'esprit de l'homme" is made grammatically and structurally sound when the enacting clause following it reads: "Nous, l'Assemblée générale de Virginie, établissons pour loi. . . ." But the preamble of English Texts (2), (4), and (5) which begins "Well aware that Almighty God hath created the mind free . . . ." is left dangling in mid-air, without a noun or pronoun to depend on, when its enacting clause, instead of following the Bill as TJ drew it with its stately "We the General Assembly do enact," reads "*Be it therefore enacted by the General Assembly.*"

TJ's hybrid English version of 1786, which is neither precisely that of the Bill nor that of the Act, unfortunately triumphed over the more elevated style of the former and over the legally more correct form of the latter. This version, with its unhappily dangling preamble, became established in America by the 1788 edition of the *Notes on Virginia.* The H. A. Washington edition of TJ's *Writings* unfortunately carried the hybrid text, and even the title given it in 1786—"An Act for establishing Religious Freedom, passed in the Assembly of Virginia in the beginning of the year 1786." The Commonwealth of Virginia could go on publishing the authoritative version (e.g., *The Code of Virginia*, Richmond, 1849, p. 358-60); and Ford (II, 237-9) could print the Bill as it was in the 1784 *Report*; but when the most widely used edition of TJ's papers (L & B) repeated the incorrect text used in the Washington edition, that form became so firmly established that the authoritative or the original versions could never hope to displace it. Even scholarly editors of modern texts, such as Adrienne Koch and William Peden (*The Life and Writings of Thomas Jefferson*, New

York, 1944, p. 311-13), continue to repeat the unhappy hybridization of errors that TJ propagated in 1786.

1 The preceding words in italics were deleted by Senate amendment on 16 Jan. 1786. The beginning of the Act as adopted reads: "Whereas, Almighty God hath. . . ."

2 The preceding words in italic were deleted by Senate amendment on 16 Jan. 1786.

3 In his Autobiography TJ wrote: "Where the preamble declares that coercion is a departure from the plan of the holy author of our religion, an amendment was proposed, by inserting the word 'Jesus Christ,' so that it should read, 'a departure from the plan of Jesus Christ, the holy author of our religion' the insertion was rejected by a great majority, in proof that they meant to comprehend, within the mantle of it's protection, the Jew and the Gentile, the Christian and Mahometan, the Hindoo, and infidel of every denomination" (Ford, I, 62). There is no record in the Journals of this particular amendment.

4 The preceding words in italic were deleted by Senate amendment on 16 Jan. 1786.

5 Text (1) reads "temporal," which is clearly what TJ intended. The clerk's or printer's error which caused the *Report* to read "temporary" was repeated in the Act as adopted, thus giving legal sanction to an incorrect usage that TJ could not tolerate. Accordingly in 1786 he restored "temporal" to Text (2), a reading which was followed by the derivatives of that text. The various revisals and codifications of Virginia laws, however, have adhered to the legally correct but otherwise improper "temporary."

6 Text (1) reads: "any more than on our opinions in physicks or geometry." The error of the clerk or printer in omitting "on" in the *Report* was repeated in the Act as adopted. TJ in 1786 restored the preposition to Text (2), but at the same time the word "any" at the beginning of the clause quoted was omitted, a reading followed by the derivatives of that text. It is quite possible that this omission of the word "any" may have been made by the printer of Text (2) for no better reason than that of justifying his lines. While TJ's alterations in the text of the Act were, with this one possible exception, obviously intentional, other contemporaneous texts departed from the wording of the Act with engaging innocence either of a regard for accuracy or of respect for exact legal phraseology. The Act as printed, for example, in the *Virginia Gazette, or American Advertiser* (Richmond: James Hayes) for 22 Feb. 1786 dropped a conjunction, altered spellings, and substituted new words, such as "preacher" for "teacher," "suspicion" for "supposition," "minister" for "ministry," "habit" for "bait," "have" for "hath," and "physic" for "physics." This particular printing is possibly the one that was sent to TJ, though the Act may also have appeared in the *Virginia Gazette and Independent Chronicle* (Richmond: Dixon & Holt) and the *Virginia Gazette & Weekly Advertiser* (Richmond: Thomas Nicholson) and may have been sent to TJ from one of these sources. Certainly the text that was printed by Isaiah Thomas as "from the Virginia Gazette" in Madison's *A Memorial and Remonstrance* (Worcester, 1786) would seem to be derived from another text than that presented in James Hayes' *Virginia Gazette*; for Thomas' text repeats only three of its many vagaries—"preacher," "minister," and "physic." The text that appeared in Hayes' newspaper bore the attestation of John Beckley, clerk of the House, and of H. Brooke, clerk of the Senate. It is quite probable, therefore, that the words "preacher," "minister," and "physic" (as well as the variation indicated in note 10, below) were clerks' errors, just as Beckley's supervision of the printing of the *Report of the Committee of Revisors* had perpetuated such errors as those pointed out in this and the preceding note.

It was Dr. Richard Price, distinguished zealot for the American cause, who surpassed clerks, printers, and even TJ himself in taking liberties with the wording of a Virginia statute. In 1786 Dr. Price distributed copies of the Act in a broadside circular as "an example of legislative wisdom and liberality never before known" (London, 1786; Sabin 100343). This printing was undoubtedly based on Text (2), though the copy of the first edition of *Notes on Virginia* that TJ inscribed and presented to Dr. Price (Paris: privately printed, 1785; this copy now in NjP) does not contain that text. Thus, taking TJ's hybrid version of the Act as his starting point, Dr. Price produced a more extensively altered text that no one, fortunately, seems to have followed. Whatever Dr. Price may have felt about the wisdom and liberality of the legislature that adopted the Act, he indubitably thought that he could improve upon the style of the law. He therefore freely struck out words and phrases, altered others, and provided many variant readings; some of these were indubitable improvements, such as his excision of the word "bait" in an otherwise exalted passage.

[7] The word "also" was deleted by amendment in the House or Senate and "only" substituted for it, which is the reading of the Act as adopted. TJ, however, restored the original reading in Text (2), and this reading was followed by the derivatives of that text.

[8] The word "very" is not in the Act; it may be the amendment made by the House on 16 Dec. or one of those made on 13 Jan.

[9] The preceding words in italic are not in the Act and were probably deleted by the House on 16 Dec. or 13 Jan.

[10] In employing this phraseology, TJ departed from the usual form for the enacting clause. "We the General Assembly of Virginia do enact" is certainly more suited to the elevated style of the Bill than "Be it enacted by the General Assembly"; but, despite Madison's statement that no alterations were made in the enacting clause, the latter is the form that was adopted. Whether this was by amendment in the House or in the Senate is not certain. As noted above, TJ caused Text (2) to read: "Be it therefore enacted . . . ." This does not conform to the text of the Act as adopted, which omits "therefore"; but it does conform to the attested copy of the Act as printed in Hayes' *Virginia Gazette* for 22 Feb. 1786. This seems to confirm the suggestion advanced in note 6, above, that TJ made use of a newspaper text of the Act as he was engaged in preparing Text (2).

[11] The Act reads: "to declare this Act to be irrevocable . . ."; all other texts, except those appearing in revisals and codifications of Virginia law, omit the words "to be." These two words were apparently inserted by amendment, but were deleted by TJ when he prepared Text (2) and are not to be found in any of the derivatives of that text.

83. A Bill for Saving the Property of the Church Heretofore by Law Established

Be it enacted by the General Assembly, that the several tracts of Glebe land, the churches, and chapels, the books, vestments, plate and ornaments, all arrears of money and tobacco, and all property real and personal of private donation, which on the seventh day of October, in the year one thousand seven hundred and seventy six, were vested in any persons whatever for the use of the English church till then established by law, or were due or contracted for, bona fide, on that day, or which since that time have legally become so vested, due, or contracted for, shall be saved in all time to come to the members of the said English church, by whatever denomination they shall henceforth call themselves, who shall be resident within the several parishes as they stood distinguished by metes and bounds on the same day, those of each parish to have the separate and legal property of the said articles belonging to their respective parishes, and to apply them from year to year, by themselves, or by agents to be appointed by themselves as they shall hereafter agree, for and towards the support of their ministry; and that no future change in the form of their church government, ordination of their ministry, or rituals of worship, shall take away or affect the benefit of this saving.

The surviving vestrymen in every parish shall have authority to carry into execution all contracts legally and bona fide made by themselves, or their predecessors, before the first day of January, in the year 1777, and to provide for the payment of all arrears of salaries due to ministers or readers for services performed before that day, by a levy, if they have not already on hand money or tobacco sufficient, and for these purposes may sue or be sued as might have been heretofore where vestries were full.

Where any parish hath been altered in its bounds, the inhabitants thereof shall nevertheless remain liable for their proportionable part of all monies or tobaccoes due, and all contracts legally made, before such division or alteration, to be apportioned on them and levied by the vestry of the respective parish into which they are incorporated by such division or alteration.

And whereas vestries although authorised by law to levy on their parishoners so much only as was sufficient to answer the legal demands on their parish, actually existing, yet frequently levied more, so that there remained on their hands a depositum to be applied to the future uses of their respective parishes, and it may have happened that in some instances such depositums were on hand on the said first day of January, in the year one thousand seven hundred and seventy seven, after all legal demands satisfied, which were then existing, or which by this act are made legal; and also debts may have been owing to some parishes, Be it therefore enacted, that such depositums and debts shall be applied to the maintenance of the poor of such parishes, where it hath not already been done, in case of the poor rates to be levied for that purpose in future; and in the case of any such parish since then divided or altered, or lying in different counties, such easement shall be divided and apportioned in the same way as burthens in a like case are herein before directed to be apportioned. But where any parish has no glebe such depositums and debts, or the proportion thereof, belonging to such parish, shall be applied towards purchasing a glebe, the property and application of which shall be in the same persons and for the same uses, and according to the same rules as would have been by the former part of this act, had the said glebe been purchased before the passing hereof.

Report, p. 59.

This Bill intended to reenact, in more explicit form, the protective clauses inserted in the Resolutions of 19 Nov. 1776 and in the Act of 1776 for exempting the different societies of dissenters, &c. (see Vol. 1, 530-1; Hening, IX, 165). Bill No. 83 was first introduced by John Harvie as a separate Bill on 12 June 1779, but on 14 June its second reading was postponed to 1 Aug. Nothing further was done until, on 31 Oct. 1785, Madison presented it along with others of the revisal; it was postponed 14 Dec. to the next session and brought up again on 1 Nov. 1786, but apparently no further action was taken on it (JHD, May 1779, 1827 edn., p. 34, 44, 46; Oct. 1785, 1828 edn., p. 12-15, 92; Oct. 1786, p. 16-17; see also the Act passed 12 Jan. 1802 "concerning the glebe lands and churches within this commonwealth," Shepherd, II, 314).

84. A Bill for Punishing Disturbers of Religious Worship and Sabbath Breakers

Be it enacted by the General Assembly, that no officer, for any civil cause, shall arrest any minister of the gospel,[1] licensed according to the rules of his sect, and who shall have taken the oath of fidelity to the commonwealth, while such minister shall be publicly preaching or performing religious worship in any church, chapel, or meeting-house,[2] on pain of imprisonment and amercement, at the discretion of a jury, and of making satisfaction to the party so arrested.

And if any person shall of purpose, maliciously, or contemptuously, disquiet or disturb any congregation assembled in any church, chapel, or meeting-house,[2] or misuse any such minister being there, he may be put under restraint during religious worship, by any Justice present, which Justice, if present, or if none be present, then any Justice before whom proof of the offence shall be made, may cause the offender to find two sureties[3] to be bound by recognizance in a sufficient penalty for his good behavior, and in default thereof shall commit him to prison, there to remain till the next court to be held for the same county; and upon conviction of the said offence before the said court, he shall be further punished by imprisonment and amercement at the discretion of a jury.

If any person on Sunday shall himself be found labouring at his own or any other trade or calling, or shall employ his apprentices, servants or slaves in labour, or other business, except it be in the ordinary houshold offices of daily necessity, or other work of necessity or charity, he shall forfeit the sum of ten shillings for every such offence, deeming every apprentice, servant, or slave so employed, and every day he shall be so employed as constituting a distinct offence.

Report, p. 59. Text of Act as adopted is in Hening, XII, 336-7.

Bill was presented by Madison 31 Oct. 1785 and on 14 Dec. postponed to next session; at the Oct. 1786 session it was brought up again, amended by both House and Senate, and passed on 27 Nov. (JHD, Oct. 1785, 1828 edn., p. 12-15, 92; same, Oct. 1786, p. 16-17, 49, 52, 64, 127). The Act as adopted and the Bill as proposed agree except as noted below; Act was suspended until 1 July 1787 (Hening, XII, 410-11).

1 The Act reads: "minister of religion."

2 The Act reads: "or other place of religious worship."

3 The Act reads: "securities."

85. A Bill for Appointing Days of Public Fasting and Thanksgiving

Be it enacted by the General Assembly, that the power of appointing days of public fasting and humiliation, or thanksgiving, throughout this commonwealth, may in the recess of the General Assembly, be exercised by the Governor, or Chief Magistrate, with the advice of the Council;[1] and such appointment shall be notified to the public, by a proclamation,[2] in which the occasion of the fasting or thanksgiving shall be particularly set forth. Every minister of the gospel[3] shall on each day so to be appointed, attend and perform divine service and preach a sermon, or discourse, suited to the occasion, in his church, on pain of forfeiting fifty pounds[4] for every failure, not having a reasonable excuse.[5]

Report, p. 59-60. MS (Vi-U); clerk's copy. MS (DLC) in clerk's hand, endorsed by TJ: "A Bill Concerning Public Fasts." On verso is a series of notes in TJ's hand on the proceedings of the House of Commons on controverted elections. MS (DLC) is referred to below as MS Bill.

Bill was presented by Madison on 31 Oct. 1785 and on 14 Dec. was postponed to the next session; it was brought up at the Oct. 1786 session and was committed to the committee of the whole, but apparently no further action was taken on it (JHD, Oct. 1785, 1828 edn., p. 12-15, 92; same, Oct. 1786, p. 16-17).

1 Instead of the words "throughout this commonwealth . . . of the Council" the MS Bill reads: "throughout this State, shall be in the General Assembly during their Sessions, and in their recess, in the Governor or Chief Magistrate for the time being with the advice of the Council."

2 The MS Bill reads: "Resolution of the Assembly or by a Proclamation of the Governor respectively."

3 The MS Bill reads: "Every Episcopal Minister prefer'd to any Parish in one of his Churches and every other Licenced Minister of the Gospel, at one of the meeting Houses at which he is appointed or accustomed to perform divine Service shall. . . ."

4 The MS Bill has a blank space at this point.

5 The MS Bill adds the following: "one half to the use of the Commonwealth and the other to the Informer, to be recovered with costs by action of debt or information in any Court of Record."

86. A Bill Annulling Marriages Prohibited by the Levitical Law, and Appointing the Mode of Solemnizing Lawful Marriage

Be it enacted by the General Assembly, that marriages prohibited by the Levitical law shall be null; and persons marrying contrary to that prohibition, and cohabiting as man and wife, convicted thereof in the General Court, shall be amerced, from time to time, until they separate. A marriage between a person of free condition and a slave, or between a white person and a negro, or between a white person and a mulatto, shall be null. Where a person, by inquisition taken by virtue of a commission issuing out of the High Court of Chancery, shall be found a lunatic, if, before such person shall be declared of sane mind by the Judges of the said court, or two of them, he or she shall marry, such marriage shall be null. And a marriage between any persons whatsoever, unless it be with such license, and, moreover if both or either of the parties not having been married before, be under the age of twenty one years, with such consent, as herein after directed, shall be null. The marriage license shall be issued by the clerk of the court of that county, in which the woman shall have resided for the last preceeding four weeks, at the least, in this form or to this effect. A B, of the hundred of in the county of and C D, of the hundred of in the county of are hereby licensed to be joined together in matrimony; and shall be signed by the first acting Justice of the Peace, of the same county, who shall then be therein; but the clerk shall not issue the license, until the father or guardian of any party who, not having been lawfully married before, shall be under the age of twenty one years, shall have personally declared, or by writing under his hand and seal, attested by two witnesses, shall have signified, his consent to the marriage to the clerk, which consent the clerk shall certify at the foot or on the back of the license, and shall certify in a separate paper to the Justice of the Peace. Any clerk, required to issue a license without such declaration or signification of a father's or guardian's consent, and doubting whether a party be of full age, or not, may suspend issuing the license until the then next court day of his county, unless he shall be sooner satisfied, when the fact shall be enquired of by a jury, and according to their verdict he shall govern himself in issuing or refusing the license. Any clerk who shall issue a marriage license, when the parties, or either of them, shall be under the age of twenty one years, without such consent, declared or signified as aforesaid, shall be liable to the action of the father or guardian of the infant, or of each infant mentioned in the license, for damages; which damages, in case of a suit brought by the guardian, shall be to the use of the ward; and the clerk shall moreover be deprived of his office. Persons who having obtained such license, as before is directed, shall, in presence of witnesses, declare or yeild their consent to be married together, shall, without further ceremony, be deemed man and wife, as effectually as if the contract had been solemnized, and the espousals celebrated, in the manner prescribed by the ritual of any church, or according to the custom of any religious society, whereof they are members. The clerk issuing licenses shall keep a correct register of them, and the Justices signing them shall report such signature, within six months thereafter, to the court of his county, which report shall be entered by the clerk in such register; and whosoever shall neglect his duty in these particulars, or any of them, shall be amerced.

Report, p. 60. MS (ViU); clerk's copy.

Bill was presented by Madison 31 Oct. 1785 and on 14 Dec. postponed to next session; it was brought up at Oct. 1786 session and passed the second reading, but apparently no further action was taken on it (JHD, Oct. 1785, 1828 edn., p. 12-15, 92; same, Oct. 1786, p. 16-17). This remarkable Bill significantly omits all references to performance of marriage ceremonies under ecclesiastical authority; what was required here was simply the obtaining of a license and the declaration of intent in the presence of witnesses. The 1748 Act concerning marriages (Hening, VI, 81-5), according to whose terms TJ himself was married, required not only a license but also "thrice publication of banns according to the rubric in the book of common prayer"; only ministers could perform the ceremony, though in the event that a parish should not have a minister, the clerk or reader could act in his place.

87. A Bill against Usury

Be it enacted by the General Assembly, that no person shall hereafter, upon any contract take, directly or indirectly, for loan of any money, wares or merchandize, or other commodity, above the value of five pounds, for the forbearance of one hundred pounds, for a year, and, after that rate, for a greater or lesser sum, or for a longer or shorter time; and all bonds, contracts, covenants, conveyances, or assurances, hereafter to be made, for payment or delivery of any money, or goods, so to be lent, on which a higher interest is reserved or taken, than is hereby allowed, shall be utterly void. If any person shall, by any way, or means of any corrupt bargain, loan, exchange, shift, covin, device, or deceit, take, accept, or receive, for the loan of, or giving day of payment for money, wares, merchandize, or other commodity, above the rate of five pounds, for one hundred pounds, for one year, every person so offending, shall forfeit double the value of the money, wares, merchandize, or commodity, so lent, exchanged, or shifted, one moiety to the use of the commonwealth, and the other to the informer, to be recovered, with costs. Any borrower of money or goods may exhibit a bill in Chancery, against the lender, and compel him to discover, upon oath, the money or thing really lent; and all bargains, contracts, or shifts, which shall have passed between them, relative to such loan, or the repayment thereof, and the interest or consideration for the same; and if, thereupon, it shall appear, that more than lawful interest was reserved, the lender shall be obliged to accept his principal money, without any interest, or other consideration, and pay costs, but shall be discharged of all other penalties of this act. Every broker, solicitor, or driver of bargains, who shall hereafter, directly or indirectly, take or receive more than the rate or value of five shillings, for brokerage, or soliciting, the loan or forbearance of one hundred pounds, for a year, or above one shilling for making or renewing[1] the bond or bill, for such loan or forbearance, or for any counter-bond or bill, concerning the same, shall forfeit, for every offence, twenty pounds to the commonwealth and informer, to be recovered, and divided, as herein before is mentioned.

Report, p. 60. MS (ViU); clerk's copy. Text of Act as adopted is in Hening, XII, 337-8.

Bill was presented by Madison 31 Oct. 1785, postponed 14 Dec. to next session, and brought up again at Oct. 1786 session. It was considered by committee of the whole 18 Nov.; the House passed the Bill on 21 Nov. The Senate approved it on 8 Dec. (JHD, Oct. 1785, 1828 edn., p. 12-15, 92; same, Oct. 1786, p. 16-17, 49, 52, 95, 127). The Act as adopted and the Bill as proposed are identical; Act was suspended until 1 July 1787 (Hening, XII, 410-11). See the 1748 "Act to restrain the taking of excessive Usury," whose preamble states that "the high interest of money has been found in all countries where it has prevailed, to impoverish the people, and a great discouragement to trade and industry" (Hening, VI, 101-4); this Act limited the interest rate to 5%; provided double forfeiture for violation; and stipulated the same brokerage fees.

[1] The Act as given in Hening, XII, 337-8, reads, erroneously, "receiving."

88. A Bill to Prevent Gaming

Be it enacted by the General Assembly, that every promise, agreement, note, bill, bond, or other contract, to pay, deliver, or secure money, or other thing, won, or obtained, by playing at cards, dice, tables, tennis bowles, or other game, or by betting or laying on the hands or sides of any person who shall play at such games, or won, or obtained, by betting or laying on any horse race, or cockfighting, or at any other sport or pastime, or on any wager whatsoever, or to repay or secure, money or other thing lent or advanced for that purpose, or lent or advanced at the time of such gaming, sporting, or wager, to a person then actually playing, betting, laying, or adventuring shall be void. Any conveyance or lease of lands, tenements, or hereditaments, sold, demised, or mortgaged[1] to any person for his use, to satisfy or secure money, or other thing by him won of, or lent or advanced to, the seller, leasor, or mortgager, or whereof money or other thing so won, or lent or advanced shall be part or all of the consideration money shall be void.[2]

If any person by playing or betting at any game, or wager whatsoever, in any house public or private,[3] and at any time within the space of twenty four hours, shall loose or win, to or from another a greater sum or any thing of greater value than pounds,[4] the looser or winner, shall be[5] liable to pay ten shillings in the pound, for every pound over and above the said sum of pounds,[4] which he shall so win or lose, and upon information thereof made to any county court, and due proof thereof had, such county court shall levy, upon the goods and chattels of the offenders, the full penalty incurred, to be applied to lessening the levy of the county wherein such offence shall be committed.[6]

Any person who shall bet or play for money, or other goods, or who shall bet on the hands or sides of those who play at any game in a tavern, racefield, or other place of public resort, shall be deemed an infamous gambler, and shall not be eligible to any office of trust or honor within this state.

Any tavern keeper who shall permit cards, dice, or billiards,[7] to be made use of in his house, or shall permit any person to bet or play for money or other goods, in any out-house, or under any booth or arbour[8] upon the messuage, or tenement he possesses, and shall not make information thereof, and give in the names of the offenders to the next court, which may be held for the county, city, or borough, wherein he resides, shall be deprived of his license, and moreover shall pay to the informer one hundred pounds, to be recovered by action of debt in any Court of Record.

Two Justices of the Peace may cause any person not possessing a visible estate, nor exercising some lawful trade or profession, who shall be suspected by them to support himself for the most part by gaming, to come or be brought before them, and if the suspicion, appear upon examination, to be well founded, may require security of him for his good behavior during the term of twelve months, and if before the expiration thereof he shall play for, or bet any money or other thing, at any game whatsoever, he shall be adjudged to have broken the condition of his recognizance.

No person in order to raise money for himself or another, shall publicly or privately put up a lottery of blanks and prizes to be drawn or adventured for, or any prize or thing to be raffled or played for, and whoever shall offend herein shall forfeit the whole sum of money proposed to be raised by such lottery, raffling or playing, to the use of the commonwealth.[9]

This fact shall be in force after due publication thereof, and all other acts respecting gaming stand hereby repealed.

Report, p. 60-1. Text of Act as adopted is in Hening, X, 205-7, with the title "An act to suppress excessive gaming."

See the 1748 Act for preventing excessive and deceitful gaming (Hening, VI, 76-81). The Bill proposed by the Committee of Revisors was brought in as a separate Bill at the Oct. 1779 session and adopted as presented with the exceptions noted below (JHD, Oct. 1779, 1827 edn., p. 13, 25, 28, 46, 49, 51, 66, 67). It was again presented 31 Oct. 1785 by Madison, was postponed on 14 Dec. to the next session, and was brought up again at the Oct. 1786 session; but no further action was taken on it (same, Oct. 1785, 1828 edn., p. 12-15, 92; Oct. 1786, p. 16-17).

1 The Act contains an additional clause extending this proviso to slaves and other personal estate.

2 The Act, instead of voiding these transactions, provides that such conveyances shall "inure, to the use of the heir of such mortgager . . . and shall vest the whole estate and interest of such person in the lands . . . slaves or other personal estate so sold, mortgaged, or otherwise transferred . . . as if such lessor, bargainer, mortgager, or vender had died intestate."

3 Preceding six words are not in Act.

4 The Act reads: "five pounds."

5 In addition to the fine provided for in the remainder of this clause, the Act has this further penalty: "the loser and winner shall be rendered incapable of holding any office, civil or military, within the state, during the space of two years."

6 The Act has the following additional clause: "and upon a conviction before such county court, shall incur the forfeiture hereby inflicted, and be *ipso facto* deprived of his office aforesaid."

7 The Act reads: "or any instrument of gaming."

8 The Act adds: "or other place."

9 The Act has the additional proviso that the presiding justice in the general court and in inferior courts shall give this Act in charge to the grand juries of their courts at the time such juries are sworn. The Act does not specifically repeal previous Acts and provides that it is to go into effect on 1 Mch. 1780.

89. A Bill to Prevent Forestalling, Regrating, and Engrossing, and Sales by Auction

Be it enacted by the General Assembly, that if any person shall buy, or cause to be bought, any goods, wares, merchandize, or victual, which at the time of purchase shall be under carriage or transportation to any market or fair within this commonwealth, to be sold therein, or to any city or town wherein there is no public market established or to any port or harbour of this commonwealth for sale, or shall make any bargain, contract, or promise, for the buying or having such goods, or the pre-emption thereof, before the same shall be in or at the market, fair, city, town, port or harbour, ready to be there sold, or shall persuade any person coming to this commonwealth, or any market therein, to forbear bringing any goods, wares, or merchandize thereto, or use any means or device for the enhancing of the price of any such goods in this commonwealth, or any market therein, every such person offending in either of the said particulars is declared a forestaller. But this act shall not extend to any person living more than two miles[1] from any town within this commonwealth, and purchasing any victuals, goods, or commodities, necessary for the use and consumption of himself and his family, or those in his employ,[2] for one year. If any person shall, by any means, buy, obtain, or get into his possession, in any fair, or market, any victual, that shall have been brought to the said fair or market, to be sold, and shall make sale thereof again, in the same place, or in any other place, within two miles[1] thereof, he is declared a regrater. If any person shall buy within this commonwealth, to sell again, in this or any of the confederating states[3] of America,[4] any goods, wares, merchandize, or victual, which shall have been imported or brought into this commonwealth, from any other place whatsoever, or any commodities, manufactures, or materials for manufacture, raised or wrought within this state, except such purchase be made from the original importer, owner, maker, or manufacturer of such goods, wares, merchandize, victual, commodities, manufactures, or materials for manufacture, respectively, or shall buy to sell again, any victual raised within this commonwealth,[5] every person so offending is declared an engrosser. But this act shall not extend to any person purchasing such articles from one who purchased from the importer, and retailing the same more than twenty five miles from any tide water; nor[6] to any agent of this commonwealth, or of the confederating states of America, or any of them, purchasing necessaries, really and bona fide, for the use of the army or navy, and not dealing in such articles on the account of himself or any other private persons[7] (such agent for the confederating states, or any of them, producing, whensoever called on, sufficient proof of his acting under authority from the confederating states, or some one of them) nor to the managers of any ironworks, purchasing necessaries for the use of those employed about such ironworks, and selling them to such persons;[8] nor to the purchasers of materials for manufacture, which shall be really applied to that use in the family of the purchaser, or some manufactory wherein he is interested; nor to ordinary keepers, purchasing victual to be retailed in their ordinaries, or persons keeping private houses for lodging or entertainment, who may buy any kind of victual, and retail the same in their respective houses after it is prepared and dressed for the table;[9] nor to persons purchasing wheat to grind into flour or malt; nor to bakers purchasing flour, and selling the same in bread; nor to graziers or butchers purchasing live stock, and selling the same after slaughter;[10] nor to the owners of any imported goods sold as being damaged for the benefit of ensurers, or condemned in the Admiralty, and purchased by the said owners. Every person becoming a forestaller, regrater, or engrosser, as before described, shall, on conviction, for the first offence, suffer imprisonment, by the space of one month,[11] without bail or mainprise and forfeit the value of the things so by him bought or sold, and for the second offence shall be imprisoned two months, without bail or mainprise, and shall forfeit double the value of the things so by him bought or sold, and for any such offence afterwards committed shall stand in the pillory for such time as the court shall direct, not exceeding two hours, shall forfeit treble the value of the things by him bought or sold,[12] and be imprisoned at the discretion of the jury convicting him of the said offence; provided such imprisonment doth not exceed three months.[13] No goods, wares, merchandize, victual, commodities, manufactures, or materials for manufacture, imported into this commonwealth, or raised or manufactured within the same (except slaves, stocks, houshold furniture,[14] goods condemned in the Admiralty Court, or goods which being damaged are by the law and custom of merchants to be sold for the benefit of insurers, victual, or goods sold on account and for the benefit of the confederating states of America, or some one of them, goods taken in execution, or upon attachments, or distrained for rent or public taxes, or sold by executors, or administrators) shall be exposed to sale at public vendue, under penalty on each person selling or buying at such vendue, for each article so sold, of double the value thereof. All the penalties hereby inflicted shall be one half to the use of the commonwealth, and the other to the informer; and, where the sum doth not exceed twenty five shillings, shall be recoverable with costs, before any Justice of the Peace, and, where it shall exceed that sum by action of debt or information in any Court of Record, and in such action of debt the clerk shall endorse on the writ, that bail is to be required, whereupon the sheriff shall take sufficient bail for the appearance of the defendant, or be answerable himself, as in other like cases, and the court may either rule the defendant to give special bail, or admit an appearance without as to them shall appear just.[15] This act shall be particularly given in charge to all grand juries, and it shall be made a part of their oath, specially, that they will present all offences against the same coming to their knowledge, which presentments shall be tried in a summary way, by a jury to be impannelled and charged, unless the court, for very good cause to them shewn, shall continue the same.[16]

Report, p. 61-2. Other copies, arranged in the probable order of their dates, are: (1) MS (Vi), being the Bill as introduced 29 Nov. 1777, together with a page of amendments, the more important of which are cited in textual notes; the Bill is in a clerk's hand and the amendments are in the hand of John Tazewell, the former being endorsed: "A Bill to prevent Forestalling, engrossing & Regrating. 1777. Nov: 29. Read the first Time. Read the second Time & commd. to a Com: of the whole on Monday next. To be engrossed." (2) Dft (DLC), in hand of George Wythe, undoubtedly drawn up for the Committee of Revisors, as the following endorsement shows: "Bills to prevent forestalling, regrating and engrossing, and sales by auction. One was copied, with some amendments proposed by T. J. from the act in October session 1777. The other is more approved by G. W. because it is shorter and, as he thinks, contains all that is good in the other" (see Document IV, 2, below). Diagonal line is drawn through text, indicating that it is the one Wythe did not prefer. (3) Dft (DLC), referred to in the endorsement just quoted, is also in the hand of Wythe and was presumably drawn about the time of the foregoing which he rejected; neither was followed by the Committee of Revisors, since the text here given is closer to the Bill introduced 29 Nov. 1777 than to these two. The text which Wythe rejected partly because of its length consists of one page of 26 lines; the text which he approved consists of 25 lines. (4) MS (ViU); clerk's copy as described in Editorial Note, above. (5) Hening, IX, 382-4, which is the Act as adopted Jan. 1778. For convenience, these variant texts are referred to in notes as Text (1), Text (2), &c.

The purpose of this Bill is obvious but was not stated probably because "An act for enabling the publick contractors to procure stores of provisions," which was drawn by a committee consisting of TJ and George Mason and was being considered in the House from Nov. 1777 to Jan. 1778 concurrently with the Bill to prevent forestalling, set forth the same purpose explicitly. The preamble to that Act, whose original Bill, MS (Vi), is in the hand of Mason, stated that "divers persons devoting themselves to Avarice and Extortion, and intending to amass Riches out of the Ruins of their Country, or treacherously to betray it into the Hands of it's Enemies, by forestalling and ingrossing the Provisions necessary for the Sustenance of its Armies in the ensuing Campaign, have industriously bought up, and already got into their Possession, so great a proportion of the Provisions usually brought to Market at this Season, that there is little Hope of our being able to lay up such Stores thereof as will be requisite for the Purposes of the succeeding Year, and some of them refuse to sell the same to the public Agents Contractors and Commissaries or demand such prices as amount to a Refusal, because they wou'd endanger a public Bankruptcy; and others under Pretence of exporting the same for Sale, mean to supply our Enemies therewith" (much of this preamble was struck out by the legislature; see the Act as adopted in Hening, IX, 385-7; see also JHD, Oct. 1777, 1827 edn., p. 93, 96, 101, 102, 103, 106, 107-8, 112-13. On 20 Nov. 1777 TJ was appointed member of a committee to bring in a Bill to prevent forestalling; he presented draft of Bill on 29 Nov. It was later considered by the House and amended; Senate also amended Bill, and House agreed to all save one of Senate amendments; from this one the Senate receded on 8 Jan. 1778 (JHD, Oct. 1777, 1827 edn., p. 35, 49, 93, 94, 101, 103, 107). The exceptions in this Act led to abuses and an amending Act was passed at the Oct. 1778 session (Hening, IX, 580-1); Text (2) and Text (3) were simplified versions of the Bill as first enacted, but the text given here incorporates some of the provisions of the amending Act and was therefore probably selected for inclusion by the Committee of Revisors after Texts (2) and (3) were drawn. Those texts differ greatly in phraseology from all others, but are in substance much the same as the original Act; the chief difference apparently is that Text (3) includes bartering as well as buying and selling in the definitions of forestaller and engrosser. The more important of the variations in the texts considered by the Committee of Revisors are indicated in the textual notes. At the Oct. 1779 session the amending Act of 1778 was revived and continued for another year. At the same time a duty of 2½% was laid upon all goods imported from other states or foreign countries which were intended for sale at vendue within nine months of the date of importation; a prohibition was also laid on owners of such goods and vendue masters to prevent their bidding at sales in order to advance prices, unless bids by vendue masters were bona fide purchases of goods for personal or family use (Hening, X, 157-8). At the session of May 1781 the Act to prevent forestalling was revived and continued for another year; it was not revived again after its expiration (same, p. 425). Bill No. 89 was presented by Madison on 31 Oct. 1785, postponed 14 Dec. to next session, and brought up again on 1 Nov. 1786; apparently no further action was taken on it (JHD, Oct. 1785, 1828 edn., p. 12-15, 92; Oct. 1786, p. 16-17).

[1] Text (1) and Text (5) read: "four miles"; Text (2) originally agreed with these and was altered to "two miles."

[2] Text (1) was amended by the House through the addition of the phrase "or those in his employ."

[3] Text (1) and Text (5) read "United States." Text (2) originally read "United States" and was altered to agree with the text here given. This interesting change was probably made by Wythe, since Text (2) is the text which TJ had approved and since the alteration was probably made as Wythe transcribed it. In all other instances where the text as given here employs the phrase "confederating states" or its equivalent, Text (1) and Text (5) read "United States."

[4] Text (1) reads: "or shall buy within any of the United States to sell again in this Commonwealth," but this was deleted by a House amendment.

[5] The clause "or shall buy to sell again, any victual raised within this Commonwealth" is not in Text (1) or Text (5). The exception allowed in the foregoing, in respect to victuals, led to abuses which were the subject of the amending Act passed in the session of Oct. 1778; under cover of this exception, the Act stated, "a practice hath prevailed of buying up great quantities of victual from those who make and raise the same, and withholding it from the poor and from the publick, until they have agreed to give a very advanced price for the same, which practice is found to be mischievous and oppressive." Accordingly, in respect to victuals, an engrosser was by this Act defined to be merely one who bought within Virginia to sell again in that or in another state any victual raised in the Commonwealth (Hening, IX, 581-3). Hence the clause "or shall buy to sell again, any victual raised within this Commonwealth" was inserted in Bill No. 89 of the *Report* in order to make it conform to this amending Act; both Text (2) and Text (3), though differing in phraseology, embrace the same proviso respecting victuals raised in Virginia. This would seem to indicate that these texts were drawn up after the passage of the amending Act of 1778 and rejected in favor of the present text sometime before 18 June 1779.

[6] The passage "to any person purchasing . . . from any tide water; nor" is not in Text (1), being added through amendment by the House. The Senate offered an amendment at this point to insert, after the word "water," the following: "nor to any person, commissioned by another, to purchase salt for one year's consumption of his family, such purchase not exceeding one peck for each person therein." But the House on 6 Jan. 1778 declined to agree to this amendment, and, two days later, the Senate receded from it (JHD, Oct. 1777, 1827 edn., p. 103, 107).

[7] The passage "and not dealing . . . private persons" is not in Text (1), having been added through amendment by the House.

[8] The passage "nor to the managers . . . to such persons" is not in Text (1), having been added through amendment by the House. The concluding phrase of the amendment as submitted—"at no higher advance than is herein after allowed, to other retailers at the same Distance from Tide Waters"—was struck out along with the matter indicated in note 13, below.

[9] The passage "or persons keeping private houses . . . for the table" is not in Text (1), having been added through amendment by the House.

[10] The passage "nor to persons purchasing wheat . . . the same after slaughter" is not in Text (1) or Text (5). This further exception was added by the amending Act passed at the Oct. 1778 session; however, that Act also contained this further exception: "nor to brewers purchasing barley and converting the same into beer" (Hening, IX, 582). The last exception was not incorporated in Bill No. 89 of the *Report*.

[11] Text (1) has a blank space; the preceding two words are supplied from Text (5). Texts (2) and (3) provide for amercement or imprisonment or both, at the discretion of the jury.

[12] Text (1) reads "shall be set on the Pillory, shall forfeit all his goods and chattels, and be imprisoned at the dis-

cretion of the jury." This severe penalty was struck out by the House; the Act as amended agrees with the present text.

[13] The preceding eight words were added to Text (1) through amendment by the House; at the same time the House deleted the following from Text (1): "Every Person who shall buy in this or any of the United States any goods, wares, merchandize, victual, commodities, manufactures or materials for manufacture from the importer, owner, maker or manufacturer thereof, or who now hath any such goods, wares, merchandize, victual, commodities, manufactures, materials for manufacture or commodities heretofore purchased of any Person whatever, shall be obliged to sell the same again in moderate and reasonable quantities for each Family to those who offer to buy for ready money at not more than the rate of percentum advance on the price paid to the Importer, owner, maker, or manufacturer if the said Articles be either Salt or brown Sugar, and for any other articles at not more than the Rate of percentum advance and the Charges of Carriage or transportation to the place where the purchaser shall store or keep them. And every person refusing so to do shall forfeit for every offence the value of the Articles so refused to the person offering to purchase. But this shall not extend to the publick agents purchasers of materials for manufacture or ordinary keepers so far as they are before excepted, nor to persons reserving so many only of such articles as may be necessary for the use and consumption of themselves and their Families for one Year, nor to the makers or purchasers of Any Tobacco for refusing to sell such Tobacco. Every importer selling in Gross, shall, if he be a resident within this Commonwealth deliver into the Clerks office of his County within days after such Sale a list on Oath of the names of all persons to whom he shall have so sold in gross and the price of each Article respectively; and if he be a foreigner, he shall within the like space of time deliver such list into the naval office of the District in which he shall have entered his vessel on pain of forfeiting in either case value of the goods so sold in gross; such list or a Copy thereof attested by the Clerk or Naval Officer, as the case may be, shall be good evidence in any prosecution at law against any person purchasing such goods and retailing the same again at a higher advance than is hereinbefore allowed."

[14] The words "slaves, stocks, houshold furniture" are not in Text (1); they were added by amendment.

[15] The following clause appears in Text (1) and Text (5) at this point: "All Acts of Parliament and of General Assembly relating to any thing within the purview of this Act are hereby Repealed."

[16] This final sentence is not in Text (1), Text (2), or Text (5); it is in Text (3), though differently phrased.

90. A Bill Constituting the High Court of Chancery

Be it enacted by the General Assembly, that the Court of Equity, called the High Court of Chancery, consisting of the present three Judges thereof, or their successors, to be appointed, when vacancies happen, in manner herein after directed, of whom any two are declared to be a sufficient number to constitute a court, shall be a Court of Record, and have jurisdiction over all persons, and in all causes now depending, and hereafter to be brought, before them, by subpœna in Chancery, and bill in equity, originally commenced in that court, or removed thither by writs of certiorari, where the matter in controversy shall be equal in value to ten pounds, of current money, or two thousand pounds of tobacco, or, of less value, if the Justices of a county, city, or borough or the vestry of a parish be parties, by appeal from the decrees of the court of any county, city, or borough, in Chancery, by habeas corpus, and by any other lawful ways or means. The said court shall also take cognizance of suits for alimony and legacies, and all such other matters as the High Court of Chancery in England, by custom, exerciseth jurisdiction in. Every future Judge of the said court shall be chosen out of the Judges of the General Court, or the Court of Admiralty, or such counsel, if such there be, as shall have attended at the bar of this court, or of the General Court, for seven years, and shall be appointed by commission of the Governor, and, before he enter upon the duties of his office, shall give assurance of fidelity to the commonwealth, and also take the oath of office, following: "You shall swear, that well and truly you will serve this commonwealth, in the office of Judge of the High Court of Chancery; and that you will do equal right to all manner of people, great and small, high and low, rich and poor, according to equity and good conscience, and the laws and usages of Virginia, without respect of persons. You shall not take, by yourself, or by another, any gift, fee, or reward of gold, silver or any other thing, directly or indirectly, of any person or persons, great or small, for any matter done, or to be done, by virtue of your office, except such fees or salary as shall be by law appointed. You shall not maintain, by yourself, or by any other, privily or openly, any plea or quarrel depending in the courts of this commonwealth. You shall not delay any person of right for the letters or request of any person, nor for any other cause, and if any letter or request come to you contrary to law, you shall nothing do for such letter or request; but you shall proceed to do the law, any such letter or request notwithstanding. And finally, in all things belonging to your said office, during your continuance therein, you shall faithfully, justly, and truly, according to the best of your skill and judgment, do equal and impartial justice, without fraud, favour, affection, or partiality. So help you God." Which oath shall be administered in open court, if it be sitting, or, if not, by one of the other Judges who shall give a certificate thereof: And the taking of the said oath, in the former case, or such certificate, in the other, shall be recorded in the said court. And any Judge presuming to execute his office, before he shall have given such assurance of fidelity, and taken the said oath, shall forfeit and pay five hundred pounds, of current money, to the use of the commonwealth. The Judges of the said court shall hold their offices so long as they respectively demean themselves well therein, and shall take precedence in court, according to the order in time of their elections, or nominations in the ballot. This court shall appoint a clerk, when and so often as that office shall become vacant, who shall continue in office so long as he shall demean himself well therein. They shall also appoint a serjeant at arms, who shall continue in office during their pleasure. Any two Judges of the court may appoint a clerk in the room of him who shall die in vacation, to continue in office until the succeeding term. The clerk may appoint an assistant clerk with the approbation of the court, and not otherwise, to continue in office during the pleasure of his principal. The sheriff of that county in which the court shall sit, and his undersheriffs, or such and so many of them as the court shall direct, shall attend, and obey, this court, as the officers thereof. This court shall sit two terms, in every year at the capitol, in Williamsburg, or at or in such other house or place as the General Assembly shall hereafter appoint; or, if the place appointed, or to be appointed, be destroyed, or be in the power of, or in danger of invasion by, a public enemy, or infected with a contagious or pestilential disease, in a recess of the General Assembly, at such place as the Governor, with advice of the Council, by writ of adjournment which he is hereby empowered to issue, shall direct, until further provision be made by law. The terms shall begin on the fifth day of April and September, or, if that be Sunday, then on the next day, and shall be continued eight days, Sunday excluded, each. Before every term, the clerk shall make out a list of all causes depending in court, which are ready for hearing that term, distributing them, in convenient numbers, amongst the days thereof; and shall deliver subpœnas, for summoning witnesses, to any parties who desire them. The said court may be adjourned by one Judge, before the coming of another, for the same number of days, and all matters depending in it, when the court shall not sit in any term, or shall not continue to sit the whole term, shall stand continued to the next term, in the same manner as the General Court may be adjourned by one or two of the Judges thereof, and as matters depending in that court shall stand continued. A Judge of this court, accused of corruption, oppression, or other maladministration, may be impeached thereof by the House of Delegates before the Court of Appeals, and the impeachment shall be prosecuted, and the delinquent punished, in the like manner as in the case of a Judge of the General Court so impeached, if found guilty.

Report, p. 62. MS (ViU); clerk's copy.

See TJ's Bill for Establishing a High Court of Chancery under date of 25 Nov. to 4 Dec. 1776; also the Act as adopted at the Oct. 1777 session, Hening, IX, 389-99. Bill No. 90 only restates that part of the Act of 1777 concerning the organization of the court, its jurisdiction, date of holding sessions; procedural matters which were included in the Act of 1777 were separated by the Committee of Revisors and incorporated in another Bill (see Bill No. 101, below). Bill presented by Madison 31 Oct. 1785, read twice, and on 14 Dec. postponed to Oct. 1786 session; on 1 Nov. 1786 it was brought up again, read twice, and committed to committee of the whole (JHD, Oct. 1785, 1828 edn., p. 12-15, 92; same, Oct. 1786, p. 16-17). Apparently no further action was taken until, at the Oct. 1792 session, an Act was passed "reducing into one, the several acts concerning the High Court of Chancery" (Hening, XIII, 411-22).

91. A Bill Constituting the General Court

Be it enacted by the General Assembly, that the court of common law, called the General Court, consisting of the present Chief Justice, and the four other Judges thereof, or their successors, to be appointed, when vacancies happen, in the manner herein after directed, of whom any three or four are declared to be a sufficient number to constitute the court, shall have jurisdiction over all persons, and of all treasons, felonies, misdemeanors, and other pleas of the commonwealth, except prosecutions for offences against statutes, inflicting less penalties than twenty shillings, or two hundred pounds of tobacco, and in all actions and suits, and other matters, at common law, now depending, and hereafter to be brought before them, by original process, or certiorari, where the things demanded, or damages pretended to have been sustained, in any case, shall be equal in value to ten pounds, of current money, or two thousand pounds of tobacco, or of less value if the Justices of a county, city, or borough, or the vestry of a parish be parties; and by appeals from the judgments, orders, and sentences of the court of a county, city, or borough; and by writs of error, habeas corpus, supersedeas, prohibition, and mandamus; and by any other lawful ways or means. The court, in cases of appeals relating to probates of wills and testaments, establishment or obstruction of ways, and erection of water mills, may examine witnesses, both such as gave testimony in the court below, and others; but in other cases shall proceed in the same manner, as if the cases were removed by writs of error. Every future Judge of the said court shall be chosen out of the Judges of the Court of Admiralty, or such counsel, if such there be, as shall have attended at the bar of this court, or the High Court of Chancery, for seven years, and shall be appointed by commission of the Governor; and, before he enter upon the duties of his office, shall give assurance of fidelity to the commonwealth, and also take the oath of office following: "You shall swear, that well and truly you will serve this commonwealth in the office of a Judge of the General Court; and that you will do equal right to all manner of people, great and small, high and low, rich and poor, according to law, without respect of persons; you shall not take, by yourself, or by any other, privily or openly, any gift, fee, or reward, of gold, silver, or any other thing directly or indirectly, of any person or persons, great or small, for any matter done, or to be done, by virtue of your office, except such fees or salary as shall be by law appointed. You shall not maintain, by yourself, or any other, privily or openly, any plea or quarrel depending in the courts of this commonwealth. You shall not deny or delay any person of common right, for the letters or request of any person, nor for any other cause; and if any letter or request come to you, contrary to the law, you shall nothing do for such letter or request; but you shall proceed to do the law, any such letter or request notwithstanding. And, further, in all things belonging to your said office, during your continuance therein, you shall faithfully, justly, and truly, according to the best of your skill and judgment, do equal and impartial justice, without fraud, favour, affection, or partiality. So help you God." Which oath shall be administered in open court, if it be sitting, or, if not, by one of the other Judges, who shall give a certificate thereof; and the taking of the said oath in the former case, or such certificate in the other, shall be recorded in the said court; and any Judge presuming to execute his office, before he shall have given such assurance of fidelity, and taken the said oath, shall forfeit and pay five hundred pounds, of current money, to the use of the commonwealth. The Judges of this court shall hold their offices so long as they, respectively demean themselves well therein, and shall take precedence in court, according to the order in time of their elections, or nominations in the ballot. The said court shall appoint a clerk, when and so often as that office shall become vacant, who shall continue in office so long as he shall demean himself well therein. They shall also appoint a tipstaff and crier, who shall continue in office during their pleasure. Any three Judges of the court may appoint a clerk, in the room of him who shall die in vacation, to continue in office until the succeeding term. The clerk may appoint an assistant clerk, with the approbation of the court, and not otherwise, to continue in office during the pleasure of his principal. The sheriff of that county in which the court shall sit, and his under sheriffs, or such and so many of them as the court shall direct, shall attend and obey the said court, as the officers thereof. This court shall sit four terms, in every year, at the capitol, in Williamsburg, or at or in such other house or place as the General Assembly shall hereafter appoint, or, if the place appointed, or to be appointed, be destroyed, be in the power of, or in danger of invasion by, a public enemy, or be infected with any contagious or pestilential disease, in a recess of the General Assembly, at such place as the Governor, with advice of the Council, by writ of adjournment, which he is hereby empowered to issue, shall direct, until further provision be made by law. The terms shall begin on the first day of March, June, August, and December, or if that be Sunday, then the next day, and shall continue, the first and third, twenty four natural days, Sundays excluded, each, and the two others, in which treasons, felonies, misdemeanors, and other pleas of the commonwealth only shall be heard and determined, until all the business of those kinds, except such as must be necessarily adjourned, shall be finished. Before every March and October term, the clerk shall enter, in a particular book, all causes and other matters which shall be ready for trial and argument in that term, and wherein there shall have been interlocutory judgments, with the names of the parties, placing those first which were first brought to that stage of their progress, and distributing them in convenient numbers amongst the days of the term, except pleas of the commonwealth, in cases of treason and felony, which shall stand to the first day. One or two of the Judges, if no more attend the first day of any term, shall adjourn the matters depending before the court from day to day, until a sufficient number shall come, if that happen before the hour of four of the clock, in the afternoon, of the sixth day. If the court shall not sit in any term, or shall not continue to sit the whole term, or, before the end of a term, shall not have heard and determined all matters ready for their decision, such matters and all others depending in court shall stand continued, pleas of the commonwealth to any term which shall be next following, and the rest to the March or October term which shall be next following.

Report, p. 63. MS (ViU); clerk's copy.

See TJ's Bill for Establishing a General Court, under date of 25 Nov. to 4 Dec. 1776; also the Act as adopted at the Oct. 1777 session, Hening, IX, 401-19. Bill No. 91 only restates that part of the Act of 1777 which constitutes the general court, defines its jurisdiction, &c. Procedural matters of this court were placed in a separate Bill by the Committee of Revisors (see Bill No. 102, below). Bill presented by Madison 31 Oct. 1785, read twice, and on 14 Dec. postponed to Oct. 1786 session; on 1 Nov. 1786 it was brought up again, read twice, and committed to a committee of the whole (JHD, Oct. 1785, 1828 edn., p. 12-15, 92; same, Oct. 1786, p. 16-17). Apparently no further action was taken until, at the Oct. 1792 session, an Act was passed "reducing into one, the several acts and parts of acts concerning the General Court" (Hening, XIII, 422-7).

92. A Bill Constituting the Court of Admiralty

Be it enacted by the General Assembly, that the Court of Admiralty, to consist of three Judges, any two of whom are declared to be a sufficient number to constitute a court, shall have jurisdiction in all maritime causes, except those wherein any parties may be accused of capital offences, now depending and hereafter to be brought before them, shall take precedence in court according to the order in time of their appointments, and shall be governed in their proceedings and decisions by the regulations of the Congress of the United States of America, by the acts of General Assembly, by the laws of Oleron, and the Rhodian and Imperial laws, so far as they have been heretofore observed in the English Courts of Admiralty, and by the laws of nature and nations. If the regulations of Congress happen to differ from those of General Assembly, the latter are declared to be supreme in cases wherein citizens only are litigants, and the former in all other cases. Every future Judge of this court shall be chosen out of such counsel, if such there be, as shall have attended at the bar of the High Court of Chancery, or General Court, for seven years, and shall be appointed by commission of the Governor, and, at the time he shall give assurance of fidelity to the commonwealth, shall take the oath of office, following: "You shall swear, that well and truly you will serve this commonwealth, in the office of a Judge of the Court of Admiralty; that you will do equal right to all manner of people, great and small, high and low, rich and poor, of what country or nation soever they be, without respect of persons. You shall not take, by yourself, or by any other, any gift, fee, or reward of gold, silver or any other thing, directly or indirectly, of any person or persons, great or small, for any matter done, or to be done, by virtue of your office, except such fees or salary as shall be by law appointed. You shall not maintain, by yourself, or by any other, privily or openly, any plea or quarrel depending in the said court. You shall not delay any person of right for the letters or request of any one, nor for any other cause, and if any letter or request come to you contrary to the law, you shall nothing do for such letter or request, but you shall proceed to do the law, any such letter or request notwithstanding. And finally, in all things belonging to your said office, during your continuance therein, you shall faithfully, justly, and truly, according to the best of your skill and judgment, do equal and impartial justice, without fraud, favour, affection, or partiality." The taking of which oath, or the certificate thereof, shall be registered in the said court. Any judge executing his office, before he shall have taken the said oath, or given assurance of fidelity to the commonwealth, shall forfeit five hundred pounds, of current money, to the use of the commonwealth. This court, or any two Judges thereof, when it is not sitting, shall appoint a Register, an Advocate and a Marshall, when those offices shall become vacant, who shall take the oath of office, and of whom the Register and Marshall shall moreover give bonds, the former in one thousand pounds, and the other in ten thousand pounds, payable to the Governor, or his successors, with sureties to be approved by the court, or two Judges, with conditions that they will faithfully and impartially perform their respective offices, and account for and pay all money which may come to their hands by virtue thereof: Upon which bonds suits may be severally brought for the benefit, and at the costs, of any persons grieved by breach of the conditions, until the damages to be recovered shall be equal to the penalties. The Judge, Register, Advocate and Marshall, shall continue in office so long as they respectively demean themselves well therein. The court shall sit, so often as there shall be occasion, at the capitol, in Williamsburg, until the General Assembly shall appoint another place, or at or in such house or place as the Governor, with advice of the Council, shall, by writ of adjournment direct, in case an accident by fire or tempest, or a pestilential disease, or an enemy shall make it necessary. This court shall have power to order sale of perishable goods to be made at any time, taking sufficient caution for securing the proceeds of the sale to him who shall be intitled to them by the final sentence. Every commander of a ship of war, or other vessel, belonging to the commonwealth, or to any citizen thereof, when he shall be required, shall assist the Marshall of the said court, acting by virtue of the process thereof, to seize and secure any vessel or goods, subject to such process, so as not to violate the right of any other of the United States, or of any state or prince in amity with them. When a citation shall have been served upon the owner or master of a vessel therein mentioned, if no person appear at the return-day, or at such further time as the court, for peculiar reasons, shall appoint, and enter into the litigation, the libel shall be taken for confessed. And if return be made that the master or owner was not found, and no person appear and claim, the court shall make an order, to be published three times in the Virginia Gazette, that the libel be taken for confessed, unless the party interested shall appear and shew cause to the contrary, at a certain day, to be limited in the order, not being less than three, nor more than six, weeks, after the making thereof; and, the said order being so published, if there be no such appearance, before expiration of the time limited, the libel shall be taken for confessed accordingly, caution being given to secure the effects, so that they may be subject to the future order of the court, and the sentence given thereupon shall be published in manner aforesaid: And if the master, owner, or other person interested, at any time, within one year after such last mentioned publication, or, that being omitted, within seven years after sentence, by petition desire that the cause be reheard, and give security for payment of such costs as may be awarded against him, the court shall admit such party to make his defence or claim in the same manner as if he had appeared at the return of the citation, and may give such sentence as they shall think just, and agreeable with the laws prescribed for the rules of their decisions. Commissions for taking the examinations of witnesses may be awarded, and such examinations may be read in the like cases as they may be in an action of common law. In a case where both parties are citizens of the commonwealth, every matter of fact affirmed by the one and denied by the other shall be stated as a formal issue, and tried before the same court by a jury, in like manner as such issue ought to be tried in an action at common law. The court may at any time after, but not before an interlocutory sentence, if they see good cause, require a person pretending a claim to any vessel or goods mentioned in the libel, to give security for the costs which may be occasioned by discussion of the claim, and may refuse to admit him until such security be given, and may award any party to pay costs when they judge it reasonable, unless he be the master, or owner, appearing and making a defence or a claim at the return of a citation; and the like execution for such costs may issue, and there shall be like proceedings thereupon as for costs recovered by judgments in an action at common law, otherwise than that the execution shall bear teste the day of examination, and may be made returnable to any day not less than one month thereafter. In case of a capture from an enemy, if there be a condemnation, and neither of the United States in general, nor the commonwealth in particular, be interested therein, the court shall order the sales to be made, and accounts thereof to be returned, by the libellant, or his agent, if it be his desire. A party thinking himself aggreived may appeal from the final sentence of the court, in case of a capture from an enemy with whom the United States of America are at war, to such court, and in such manner, as is or shall be appointed by Congress, and in any other case to the Court of Appeals, giving bond, with surety, in the latter, to prosecute the appeal, and perform the sentence, if it be affirmed.

Report, p. 63-4. This Bill was prepared by Wythe; see Document IV, Part 5 in the present series.

See TJ's Bill for Establishing a Court of Admiralty, under date of 25 Nov. to 4 Dec. 1776; also the Act as adopted at Oct. 1776 session, Hening, IX, 202-6. Bill No. 92 is a restatement of the Act of 1776, though that clause of the Act which required that the proceedings and decisions of the Court of Admiralty be governed by "English statutes prior to the fourth year of the reign of king James the first" is not included in Bill No. 92; and, under the same general clause, Bill No. 92 includes the following not in the Act of 1776: "and by the laws of nature and nations." This Bill was brought in separately 10 June 1779 and, on 11 June, was read the second time and referred to the committee of the whole. It was again presented by Madison 31 Oct. 1785, read twice, and on 14 Dec. postponed to Oct. 1786 session; on 1 Nov. 1786 it was brought up again, read twice, and committed to committee of whole (JHD, May 1779, 1827 edn., p. 41, 42; same, Oct. 1785, 1828 edn., p. 12-15, 92; same, Oct. 1786, p. 16-17). Apparently no further action was taken until, at the Oct. 1792 session, an Act was passed "reducing into one, the several acts concerning . . . District Courts." This Act included the following: "Those cases in which the court of admiralty heretofore had jurisdiction by law, and which are not taken away by the constitution of the United States, are hereby transferred to the district courts to be proceeded on as the law requires in the said court of admiralty" (Hening, XIII, 432).

93. A Bill Constituting the Court of Appeals

Be it enacted by the General Assembly, that a Court of Appeals, for hearing and determining suits which ought to be instituted there, and for finally deciding those which are herein after referred to that tribunal, shall be holden twice in every year, namely, on the twenty ninth, or, when that shall happen to be Sunday, on the thirtieth, day of March and August, and shall sit, in the whole, six juridical days, successively, each time, unless the business depending before them be sooner dispatched, at the capitol, in Williamsburg,[1] or at such other place as shall be appointed by the General Assembly, or, in their recess, by the Governor, with advice of the Privy Council, in any such emergency as will make the adjournment of any other court, by his writ lawful. The Judges of the High Court of Chancery, General Court, and Court of Admiralty, shall be Judges of the Court of Appeals, of whom the first shall take precedence, and the second be next, in rank and of them[2] shall be a sufficient number to constitute the court. Every Judge, before he exercise this office, shall, in that court, openly give assurance of fidelity to the commonwealth, and take this oath: "You shall swear, that you will well and truly serve this commonwealth in the office of a Judge of the Court of Appeals; and that you will do equal right to all manner of people, great and small, high and low, rich and poor, without respect of persons. You shall not take, by yourself, or by any other, any gift, fee, or reward, of gold, silver, or any other thing, directly or indirectly, of any person or persons, great or small, for any matter done or to be done, by virtue of your office, except such fees or salary, as shall be by law appointed. You shall not maintain, by yourself, or any other, privily or openly, any plea or quarrel, depending in the courts of this commonwealth. You shall not delay any person of right for the letters or request of any person, nor for any other cause; and if any letter or request come to you, contrary to the law, you shall nothing do for such letter or request; but you shall proceed to do the law, any such letter or request notwithstanding. And, finally, in all things belonging to your said office, during your continuance therein, you shall faithfully, justly, and truly, according to the best of your skill and judgment, do equal and impartial justice, without fraud, favour, or affection." This court shall have jurisdiction, not only in suits originating there, and adjourned thither for trials by virtue of any statute, which trials shall be by juries, according to the course of law; but also in such as shall be brought before them by appeals and writs of error, to reverse decrees of the High Court of Chancery, judgments of the General Court, and sentences of the Court of Admiralty, after those decisions shall be final there, if the matter in controversy be equal in value, exclusive of costs, to fifty pounds, or be a freehold, or franchise; and also in such cases as shall be removed before them by adjournment from the other courts before mentioned, when questions in their opinion, new and difficult occur; and moreover in such, wherein appeals to reverse decrees and judgments of the former General Court, and sentences of the Court of Vice-Admiralty, as had not been determined, the one by the King of Great-Britain, in his Privy-Council, the other by the High Court of Admiralty of Great-Britain, before the fifteenth day of April, one thousand seven hundred and seventy six. The court shall appoint a clerk, tipstaff, and crier, the first removable for misbehaviour, the two others at pleasure, and shall be attended by the sheriff of the county in which they sit, as their officer. The party desiring to prosecute such appeal, or writ of error, shall proceed in like manner, and shall be liable to like damages, if the decree, judgment, or sentence, be affirmed, and the said clerk shall issue the like process, for summoning the adverse party, removing the records, suspending execution, and for every other requisite purpose, making those alterations in the form which are necessary to adapt it to the case, as are prescribed and ascertained in case of an appeal or writ of error to reverse the decree, sentence, or judgment, of a county, city, or borough court, and such prosecution shall be commenced within the time limited in the case last mentioned, unless it be such appeal to the said King, or High Court of Admiralty, in which instance the prosecution shall be commenced within twelve months after the first session of the said Court of Appeals shall be ended. The said clerk shall carefully preserve the transcripts of records certified to his court, with the bonds for prosecution and all papers relative to them, and other suits depending therein, docketing them in the order he shall receive them, that they may be heard in the same course, unless the court, for good cause to them shewn, direct any to be heard out of its turn; and shall faithfully record their proceedings and decisions, and certify such as shall be given upon appeals, writs of error, and matters removed by adjournment to the proper courts. A clear and concise state of the case of each party in such appeal, writ of error, or controversy adjourned by reason of novelty and difficulty, with the points intended to be insisted upon, signed by his counsel, and printed, the expence whereof shall be taxed in the bill of costs, shall be delivered to every Judge time enough before the hearing, for his consideration; but the court, if this be neglected, may, nevertheless, hear and determine the matter, and may take into their consideration any thing apparent in the manuscript record, although it be omitted in such printed case; and may give such decree, judgment, or sentence, if it be not affirmed or reversed in the whole, as the court, whose error is sought to be corrected, ought to have given, affirming in those cases where the voices on both sides shall be equal, with an allowance of the costs of appeal to the party prevailing, to be certified, as well as their opinion upon any adjourned question to the court, from which the matter was removed, who shall enter it as their own, and award execution thereupon accordingly.[3]

Report, p. 64-5. Text of Act as adopted in 1779 is in Hening, X, 89-92. This Bill was prepared by Wythe; see Document IV, Part 5 in the present series.

See TJ's Bill for Establishing a Court of Appeals, under date of 25 Nov. to 4 Dec. 1776; also, the Act as adopted at the Oct. 1778 session, Hening, IX, 522-5. Bill No. 93 was brought in separately on 10 June 1779, amended and passed by the House 25 June, and approved by the Senate the next day (JHD, May 1779, 1827 edn., p. 41, 42, 66, 68; Hening, X, 89-92). Despite its adoption in 1779, the Bill was again presented by Madison 31 Oct. 1785, was postponed to Oct. 1786, and no further action was taken (same, Oct. 1785, 1828 edn., p. 12-15, 92; same, Oct. 1786, p. 16-17). At the Oct. 1792 session an Act was passed "for reducing into one act, the several acts concerning the Court of Appeals" (Hening, XIII, 405-11).

1 At this same session, May 1779, the General Assembly authorized removal of the capitol from Williamsburg to Richmond.

2 Act reads: "five of them."

3 Act has an additional clause at this point repealing so much of the Act of 1778 as fell within the purview of this Act.

94. A Bill for Constituting Courts Martial

Be it enacted by the General Assembly, that it shall be lawful for the Governor, with advice of the Council of State, by commission, to be directed to three or more able and sufficient persons to constitute, from time to time, so often as occasion may require, a Court Martial, to which it shall pertain to have cognizance of things touching war out of the commonwealth, and also of things that touch war within the commonwealth, which cannot be determined nor discussed by the common law. Which court shall be holden at such time and place as the said commission shall direct, and shall be governed, in their proceedings and sentences, according to the laws and usages of war, of nature, and nations; and shall have power to adjourn, from time to time, till they shall have heard and determined the offence specified in their commission.

A Marshall also to execute the orders and sentences of the said court, and a clerk to make a minute of their proceedings, shall be appointed by the Governor, to whom the said proceedings shall be returned to be safely kept in the office of the Council of State.

Nevertheless the Governor, with advice of the Council, shall have power to suspend, from time to time, the execution of the sentence of the said court, or finally to annul the same in their discretion.

Report, p. 65.

Bill presented by Madison 31 Oct. 1785, postponed on 14 Dec. to next session, and again brought up at the Oct. 1786 session, but apparently no further action was taken on it (JHD, Oct. 1785, 1828 edn., p. 12-15, 92; same, Oct. 1786, p. 16-17).

95. A Bill Constituting Justices of the Peace and County Courts

Be it enacted by the General Assembly, that the Aldermen to be elected for every county, who by that election shall stand nominated to be Justices for the said county, if they were not such before, shall on the first Monday in   after their election, if fair, if not, on the next fair day, Sunday excluded, laying aside all excuses, other than grievous sickness, convene at the court-house of the county, and there with open doors, between the hours of twelve and three of the clock in the day, nominate to be Justices for the said county, so many of the most honest, knowing, and discreet men dwelling therein, and neither of them being sheriff, clerk of the peace, owner of a tavern in the same county, or keeper of a tavern, as, together with themselves, and those already invested with, and continuing in the said office, will make up the number seven, and so many more as will raise that number, if it be not equal to one for every fifty militia in their county, and shall deliver the said nomination, certified under their hands and seals, to the sheriff of their county, who shall attend for that purpose; and, within fifteen days thereafter, the said sheriff shall carry it to the Governor, under the penalty of one hundred pounds. The Governor, with advice of the Council, shall, immediately thereupon, make out and deliver, to the sheriff, a commission, to be directed to such of the said Aldermen as were not before Justices, and to the persons designed by the said nomination, constituting the said commissioners Justices of the Peace for the same county, in addition to those before officiating; and the said sheriff shall, under the like penalty, deliver the said commission to the clerk of the peace, on or before the court-day next after his return to the said county, a reasonable time being allowed for such return. If any person named in the said commission shall fail before the next nomination of Justices, to qualify himself for executing his office, by giving the assurance and taking the oaths, herein after prescribed, unless he be employed in the service of the public, out of the county, his appointment shall thereupon become absolutely void. And if any person invested with the said office, shall remove out of the county to dwell, or shall forbear to sit in court, during the space of six months, unless such non-performance of that duty be justifiable by reason of the like avocation as aforesaid, or shall personally declare, or by writing under his hand, proved by a credible witness, signify, to the said Aldermen, at their anniversary meeting, that he will not act any longer in the said office, he shall thereupon stand divested thereof. The said Justices shall have the powers of conservators of the peace and authority, moreover, jointly or severally, to take of all those who be not of good fame, sufficient surety for their good behaviour, to the intent that the peace be not broken; and shall certify and return all recognizances by them taken to their next county court, to be continued or discharged as the court shall see cause: but no such recognizance shall be binding longer than twelve months after the taking thereof. Any one Justice shall have power to take cognizance, either on his own view, or on information of the breach of a penal law, if the penalty exceed not twenty five shillings, or two hundred pounds of tobacco, and also to hear and determine any plaint in debt or detinue, or upon trover and conversion if the value of the thing alledged to be detained, or the damage alledged to have been sustained be not more than twenty five shillings, or two hundred pounds of tobacco, proceeding in a summary way, without a jury, after the defendant, by warrant of such Justice, or some other, directed to the constable, shall have been summoned to appear, and answer the information or plaint, and the said Justice, if he shall give judgment against the defendant, shall award a writ of fieri facias to make the penalty, debt, or damages, or of distringas, to compel delivery of the thing recovered, with costs, to be directed to the constable, who shall proceed in the same manner as a sheriff ought to proceed in, when the like writ is directed to him. A court in every county, to be constituted of the Justices for such county, or any four or more of them, and to be called the county court, shall hold their sessions, monthly, at the time and place when and where the court of such county, before the commencement of this act, might lawfully sit. Such county court shall be a court of record, and a court both of common law and of chancery, and shall hold plea of actions, real, personal, and mixt, if the causes of such actions arise within their county, or if the actions be such as are called transitory, and where the value of the thing, claimed in any personal action, shall exceed twenty-five shillings, or two hundred pounds of tobacco, and shall hear and determine pleas of the commonwealth arising, or prosecutions, for crimes and misdemeanors, committed within their county, other than treasons and felonies; and shall hear and determine cases of equity in chancery, when the officer of their own county shall have served the defendants with the subpœnas to answer, unless the original cause of action be of such a local nature that, if it were the subject of a common law suit, it must have been tried in the court of such other county, or in the General Court. Where a bay, river, or other water course divideth two counties, the court and every Justice of the Peace, and officers, of either shall have the same jurisdiction and power upon the water, from the shore of their own county to the opposite shore, as if the whole water were within the body of a county. Every person appointed a Justice of the Peace, before he shall execute the office, shall give assurance of his fidelity to the commonwealth, and, in the court of his county, take this oath: "You shall swear that, in the office of Justice of the Peace, in and for the county of   you shall do equal right to the poor, and to the rich, after your cunning, wit, and power, and after the laws and [st]atutes of the commonwealth. You shall not be of counsel in any quarrel hanging before you. You shall hold your sessions after the form of the statute thereof made. Fines and amercements, that shall happen to be made, and forfeitures which shall fall before you, you shall cause to be entered, without any concealment, and thereof true accounts to be sent to the public Treasurer. You shall not set, for gift, or other cause, but well and truly you shall do your office of Justice of the Peace, in that behalf. You shall take nothing for your office of Justice of the Peace to be done, but of the commonwealth. You shall not direct, nor cause to be directed, any precepts by you to be made, to the parties; but you shall direct them to the sheriff of the said county, or other the officers or ministers of the commonwealth, or other indifferent persons, to do execution thereof. So help you God." And also this other oath. "You shall swear, that well and truly you will serve the commonwealth, and the citizens thereof, in the office of a Justice of the county court of   in Chancery, and that you will do right to all manner of people, great and small, high and low, rich and poor, according to equity and good conscience, and the laws and usages of the commonwealth, without favour, affection, or partiality. So help you God." And whosoever shall execute the office of a Justice of the Peace, before he shall have given such assurance of his fidelity, and taken such oaths as aforesaid, shall forfeit and pay three hundred pounds; one half thereof to the use of the commonwealth, and the other half to him who will sue for the same. Any Justice of the Peace, accused of corruption, oppression, or other mal-administration, may be thereof impeached before the Court of Appeals, by order of the House of Delegates, or upon a presentment of the grand jury of his county; and if he be found guilty, may, by sentence of the said court, be removed from his office a certain time, or be perpetually disabled to hold that, or any other office, in the commonwealth. All matters depending before a county court, if the Justices thereof fail to meet on the day to which they shall adjourn, either in the same session, which they may adjourn from day to day, or in the next month, shall stand continued to the succeeding session, and that although between the two sessions more months than one intervene, and returns of process shall be made to, and parties and others, bound and summoned, shall appear at, such succeeding session, in like manner, and under like penalties for any defaults, as if the month in which it shall be held had been next, in order of time. Process shall not be discontinued, if by any accident there shall not at any time be a sufficient number of Justices to constitute a court. The clerk of every county court shall reside in such county during his continuance in office, or, if he do not the office shall become vacant.

Report, p. 65-6. MS (ViU); clerk's copy.

See TJ's earlier effort to reform the county courts—the Bill for Better Regulating the Proceedings in the County Courts, under date of 25 Nov. to 4 Dec. 1776. That Bill failed of passage because of conservative disinclination to alter established institutions. Any attempt to reform this most important of all local units of government was bound to meet with intense opposition. Under the Constitution of 1776 the county courts were virtually a closed corporation, since the appointive power lay with the governor but was limited to nominations made by the courts themselves. As pointed out above (Vol. 1, 606), these courts were thus almost exempt from local control. They embraced legislative, judicial, and executive functions (thus wholly violating the principle of separation of powers), and, since they held the key office of sheriff under their domination, these courts were the chief bulwark of the established order. Despite the failure of TJ's 1776 Bill and despite Section XV of the Constitution of 1776, the Committee of Revisors apparently decided to assault the main stronghold of the county court system by taking the power of nomination out of the hands of non-elective justices and placing it in the hands of elective aldermen. Madison brought up the Bill on 31 Oct. 1785. Legislation on this subject in 1785 hinged also on the question of courts of assize that TJ had proposed in 1776. The same question came up in 1785, when courts of assize were again defeated. "A reform of the County Courts is the substitute proposed by the adversaries of the Assize," wrote Madison to James Monroe 17 Dec. 1785 (*Writings*, ed. Hunt, II, 205). But Bill No. 95 was not the reform these adversaries had in mind: that Bill had already been postponed to the Oct. 1786 session. The substitute "Act for reforming the county courts, and for other purposes," adopted at the Oct. 1785 session (Hening, XII, 32-6), as Madison wrote to TJ on 22 Jan. 1786, "Requires them to clear their dockets quarterly. It amounts to nothing, and is chiefly the result of efforts to render Courts of Assize unnecessary." This reform Act was amended at the Oct. 1787 session, and in the Oct. 1792 session an Act was passed "to reduce into one the several acts concerning the county and other inferior courts" (same, XII, 467-74; XIII, 449-67). But all of these Acts were primarily concerned with questions of jurisdiction and procedure, not with fundamental reforms of this all-powerful unit of government. Actually the county courts as organized under the Act of 1748 continued virtually unchanged through the Revolution and, in most respects, down to the adoption of the Constitution of 1867 (see A. O. Porter, *County Government in Virginia*, New York, 1947, p. 100-54). Madison brought Bill No. 95 up again in 1786 but no action was taken on it (JHD, Oct. 1785, 1828 edn., p. 12-15, 92; same, Oct. 1786, p. 16-17).

96. A Bill concerning Sheriffs

Be it enacted by the General Assembly, that each county court shall, annually, in the months of July, or August, recommend three persons, named in the commission of the peace, one of whom shall be commissioned by the Governor, or Commander in Chief, with advice of the Council, on the twenty fourth, or twenty fifth, day of October following, to execute the office of Sheriff of such county, for the ensuing year: And if any sheriff so appointed, shall die within the year, the Governor shall and may appoint one of the others recommended, to act as sheriff, in his room: And if any county court shall neglect to recommend persons for the office of sheriff, or if all the persons recommended die within the year, the Governor, or Commander in Chief, with advice of the Council, shall appoint and constitute any one of the Justices, named in the commission of the peace, to be sheriff, and fill up the vacancy, in like manner, in case of his death, within the year. Every person, so appointed sheriff, and refusing to accept and execute the office, shall forfeit twenty pounds, to the use of the county towards lessening the levy; for which penalty judgment may be entered by the court, on the refusal of the person to accept being made in court, otherwise the same may be recovered by information exhibited against the person refusing, and on his conviction, as in other cases: But if the person refusing shall make oath in court, "That he hath used his best endeavours, truly and bona fide, without covin or collusion, to get security for performing of the said office, and cannot obtain such security," he shall thereupon be exempted from the penalty, and a new commission shall be issued, as in case of a vacancy by death. No person, who hath once served as sheriff, or paid his fine, for refusal, shall be liable to the forfeiture aforesaid, until every Justice in the commission of the peace, shall have actually served as sheriff, paid his fine, or discharged himself by oath, as aforesaid; and no member of the General Assembly, during the time of his being such, shall be finable for not accepting the office of sheriff. Every person accepting a sheriff's commission shall, in his county court, enter into two bonds, with good and sufficient sureties, one in the penalty of one thousand pounds, with the following condition: to wit: "The condition of the above obligation is such, that, if the above bound A. B. as sheriff of the county of   shall, by himself, or his deputies, well and truly collect all officers fees and dues, put into his or their hands to collect, and account for, and pay the same, at such time, and in such manner, as is directed by law; shall also well and truly execute, and due return make of, all process and precepts, to him directed, and to him or them delivered, and pay and satisfy all sums of money or tobacco, by him or them received, or which or ought to have been received, upon any such process or precept, to the person or persons intitled thereto; and in all other things shall truly and faithfully execute and perform the said office of sheriff, according to law, during the time of his continuance therein; then the above obligation to be void, otherwise to remain in full force." Which bond shall be payable to the Governor, for the time being, and his successors, and, in his name, or that of his successor, any person injured by a breach of the condition, may, at his costs, prosecute a suit thereon, and recover damages, and be liable to pay costs to the defendant, if a verdict or judgment pass in his favour, or the suit be discontinued: And such bond shall not become void upon the first recovery, or dismission of a first or other suit, but may be put in suit, from time to time, by, and at the costs of any other person injured, until the whole penalty be recovered in such damages. The other bond shall also be payable to the Governor, and his successors, in such penalty as the court shall direct, at least double the amount of the taxes, to be levied in such county, for that year, and with the following condition, to wit: "The condition of the above obligation is such, that, if the above bound sheriff of the county of shall, by himself, or deputies, well and truly collect all taxes and duties directed by law to be collected in the said county, during the time of his continuance in office, also all fines, amercements, and penalties, which he shall be authorised to collect and account for, and pay the same to the public Treasurer, and other persons intitled thereto, at such time, and in such manner, as is directed by law; then the above obligation to be void, otherwise to remain in full force." For breach of the condition of which bond, at the instance, and costs, and for the benefit of any person injured thereby, a suit may be commenced and prosecuted, in the same manner, and subject to the same regulations, as the action upon the first mentioned bond; or the public Treasurer, or any other public or county creditor, upon the second bond, or any officer, upon the other bond, may, by motion to the General Court, or county court, against the obligors, giving them ten days notice of such motion, recover judgment for all money and tobacco collected by such sheriff, or his deputies, and not accounted for to the person or persons respectively intitled to receive them. Every person, before he enters upon his office of sheriff, or under sheriff, shall in open court, give assurance of fidelity to the commonwealth, in the form prescribed by law, and also take the following oath of office, to wit: "I A. B. do swear, that I will do right, as well to poor as rich, in all things belonging to my office of sheriff; that I will do no wrong to any man, for any gift, reward, or promise, nor for favour, or hatred; that I will make due panels of persons able and sufficient, and not suspected, or procured; and that in all other things, I will faithfully and impartially execute the duties of my said office, according to the best of my skill and power. So help me God." A court shall have power, from time to time, to ordain rules for the government, sustentation, and cure of prisoners, and at any time, to remove the jailor, for negligence, or malice, towards them; and the public jailor, whenever that office shall become vacant, shall be appointed by the General Court; but the person, so to be appointed, as well as he who is now in office, shall, nevertheless, have the custody of prisoners committed to the public jail, by any process, order, or decree of the High Court of Chancery, and shall be subject to the directions of that court, with regard to those prisoners. No sheriff shall return, upon any writ to him directed, that the defendant is not found in his bailiwick, unless such sheriff, or his deputy, shall have actually been at the place of residence of such defendant, and, not finding him, shall have left a true copy of the process; or unless such defendant's place of residence is unknown to such sheriff or officer. If the defendant cannot be arrested by the sheriff, and shall be a known inhabitant of another county, the sheriff shall return the truth of the case; and thereupon the process, as to such defendant, shall abate. When any under sheriff shall have served any writ of execution, or other process, he shall endorse thereon the time of service, and subscribe, as well his own name, as that of his principal, to his return thereof, under pain of forfeiting three thousand pounds of tobacco, one half to the commonwealth, and the other to the informer, to be recovered, with costs, by action of debt or information, in any Court of Record. It shall not be lawful for the sheriff, or any other officer, to execute any writ, or other process, upon Sunday, unless it be for treason, felony, or breach of the peace, or to retake a prisoner escaped. Every contract made between a sheriff and any person in his custody, except such as the law prescribes, and except bonds made for repayment of money or tobacco, actually advanced by the former, to discharge the other from imprisonment, shall be void. Every sheriff, for collecting the public and county levies, and paying the same, shall be allowed six per centum. If any person, indebted for taxes, or levies, shall fail to pay the same, by the time limited by law, the sheriff, or collector, may distrain any goods, which shall be found upon the lands whereon the debtor lives, and in his possession, notwithstanding such goods may be comprised in any deed of mortgage; and, if the taxes or levies be not paid, may proceed to the sale thereof, as in other cases of distress; but such sheriff or collector shall not seize slaves on that or any other occasion where other goods sufficient may be had, nor make any unreasonable distresses, on pain of answering damages to the party grieved and full costs. The sheriff shall have power to collect or distrain for any arrears of taxes, levies, or officers fees, which may remain uncollected by his predecessor, at the time of his death, or removal from office; and shall account for the same, in like manner, as for other collections, and be subject to the like remedy, on his failing to account for and pay the same. Every collector shall deliver to the person, from whom taxes, levies, or fees are demanded, or his agent, if present, an account, stating distinctly every article of the demand, and offer to give a receipt for the same, and shall have no power to make distress, before such account and receipt shall have been tendered, where the debtor or his agent shall reside in the county, unless he abscond. If any person committed to jail shall thence escape, on affidavit or proof thereof by the sheriff, or jailer, any Justice of the Peace, if the escape were from a county jail, or, if from the public jail, any judge of the court, by whose authority he was committed, shall and may issue as many warrants as are thought necessary, under his hand and seal, directed to all sheriffs and constables in the commonwealth, reciting the cause of imprisonment, and the time of escape, and commanding every of them, in their respective counties and precincts, to retake such prisoner, and convey and commit him to the jail of the county, wherein such retaking shall be, there to remain until discharged by due course of law; which warrant every sheriff or constable, into whose hands the same shall come, is hereby required to obey; and, on the committment of every such prisoner, so retaken, the sheriff, or jailer, to whom he is committed, shall give a receipt for the body, and shall make return thereof upon the warrant to the court, by whose authority the prisoner was committed. And in case the prisoner was charged in execution, the said sheriff or jailer shall keep him in custody, without bail or mainprize, until he shall have satisfied the debt, or be otherwise discharged by due course of law. If the prisoner shall have been committed for breach of the peace, or behaviour; or shall have escaped before it was determined whether he ought to be tried in the General Court, for some crime he had been charged with, or after it was determined, that he might be tried for such crime in the county court, the sheriff, to whom he shall be committed, after he was retaken, shall cause him to be removed to the jail from whence he escaped; if he escaped after it was determined that he ought to be tried in the General Court, or, being charged with, or convicted of, any crime, escaped from the public jail, then such sheriff shall cause him to be removed to the public jail. No judgment shall be entered against a sheriff, or other officer, in any suit, to be brought for, or by reason of, the escape of a debtor, in his custody, unless the jury, who tries the issue, shall expressly find, that the prisoner escaped with the consent or through the negligence, of such sheriff, his deputy, or other officer; or that he might have been retaken, but that the sheriff, or officer, neglected to make immediate pursuit. In case of any such escape, neither with the consent, nor through the negligence, of the sheriff, the party at whose suit the prisoner was committed, may, by an action on the case, recover damages against any person or persons, by whose aid in any manner he escaped. Any person furnishing a prisoner with instruments, or arms, to facilitate his escape, shall be deemed guilty of a misdemeanour, although no escape shall actually have happened. Where the sheriff of any county shall have cause to suspect, that any person, committed to his jail, for treason, felony, or other capital crime, will attempt to escape, or that others will endeavour to rescue him, such sheriff is impowered and required to impress a sufficient guard, for securing such prisoner, so long as he shall continue in prison, and the expence of such guard shall be levied by the court on the county, and repaid by the public. When any sheriff shall be removed from office, an indenture between him and the new sheriff, for delivering over of prisoners, or an entry upon the records of the county court, of the names of the several prisoners, and causes of their committment, shall be sufficient to discharge the old, and charge the new sheriff, as to such prisoners. Where any under sheriff hath heretofore so proceeded, or shall hereafter so proceed, upon any writ of execution, or other process, in the course of the collection of levies, fees, or penalties, or in making other distresses, as that judgment may by law be thereupon entered against his principal sheriff, upon motion, in every such case, either the creditor, or the sheriff, may, on motion, obtain judgment against the under sheriff, and his securities, his or their executors, or administrators, for such his default, in like manner, upon such notice, and subject to the like execution, as such laws direct against the sheriff.

Report, p. 66-8. MS (ViU); clerk's copy.

Bill presented by Madison 31 Oct. 1785, postponed 14 Dec. to next session, and brought up again 1 Nov. 1786. Apparently no further action was taken on it. However, on 25 Oct. 1785 a bill was ordered to be brought in to amend laws respecting the appointment of sheriffs and Madison presented this bill 9 Nov.; it was enacted into law on 8 Dec. (JHD, Oct. 1785, 1828 edn., p. 12-15, 28, 30, 70, 76, 92, 133; same, Oct. 1786, p. 16-17; Hening, XII, 98). This Act was limited merely to the appointment of sheriffs and was not a comprehensive law such as was contemplated in Bill No. 96. See also the Act of Oct. 1784 (Hening, XI, 463).

97. A Bill for Licensing Counsel, Attorneys at Law, and Proctors

Be it enacted by the General Assembly, that no person, except the Attorney General, shall be permitted by any court to practice therein as a Counsel, Attorney at law, or Proctor, unless he shall heretofore have obtained a license, in the manner prescribed by the law then in force, or until he shall obtain a license, in writing, from three of those, who shall be at that time, Judges of the High Court of Chancery, or General Court: which license, if he produce to them a certificate, from the court of that county, wherein his usual abode shall have been during twelve months next preceeding, that he is a person of honest demeanour, such three Judges are empowered and required to grant, under their hands and seals, if, after examination, it be their opinion, that he is duly qualified. Every Counsel, Attorney, and Proctor, before he shall practice, shall, in some Court of Record, give assurance of fidelity to the commonwealth, and, moreover, in such court, if he shall thereafter obtain a license, shall take the oath following, "I do swear, that I will honestly demean myself in the practice of a Counsel, Attorney, or Proctor, and will execute my office according to the best of my knowledge and ability." A person, who shall have been convicted of treason, felony, forgery, or wilful and corrupt perjury, shall not be suffered to practice, in any court, as a Counsel, Attorney, or Proctor. If the General Court from their own observation, detect any mal-practice in a Counsel, or Attorney, of that court, or if a complaint, in writing, be made to them of such mal-practice in the said Court, or in the court of a county, city, or borough, the party accused shall be summoned to shew cause why an information should not be filed against him; and if such information be ordered, and he be found guilty of the matter therein charged, the said General Court may either suspend his license, during a certain time, or vacate it altogether, as they shall think him to have deserved. And the High Court of Chancery and Court of Admiralty, upon the like detection or complaint of mal-practice in those courts, respectively, shall proceed in the same manner against a Counsel, Attorney, or Proctor, and may inflict the same punishment upon the offender. After the commencement of the year one thousand seven hundred and eighty two,[1] no Counsel, or Attorney at law, practising in the court of a county, city, or borough, shall be permitted by the Judges to practice the same profession in the High Court of Chancery, or General Court.[2]

Report, p. 68. MS (ViU); clerk's copy. Text of Act as adopted is in Hening, XII, 339-40.

Bill was presented by Madison 31 Oct. 1785, postponed 14 Dec. to next session, brought up again 1 Nov. 1786, and passed on 27 Nov. with the single change noted below (JHD, Oct. 1785, 1828 edn., p. 12-15, 92; same, Oct. 1786, p. 16-17, 49, 52, 62, 126). The Act was suspended until 1 July 1787 (Hening, XII, 410-11). See the 1761

Act for regulating the practice of attorneys (same, VII, 397-401).

[1] The words "After the commencement . . . and eighty two" are omitted from the Act of 1786.

[2] TJ may have been the author of this drastic proviso excluding county attorneys from practice in the general court; see TJ to George Wythe, 1 Mch. 1779.

98. A Bill Prescribing the Oath of Fidelity, and the Oaths of Certain Public Officers

Be it enacted by the General Assembly, that every person, by law required to give assurance of fidelity, shall, for that purpose, take an oath in this form,[1] "I   do declare myself a citizen of the commonwealth of Virginia. I relinquish and renounce the character of subject or citizen of any Prince, or other state, whatsoever, and abjure all allegiance, which may be claimed by such Prince, or other state; and I do swear to be faithful and true to the said commonwealth of Virginia, so long as I continue a citizen thereof. So help me God."[2] And no person shall have power to act, in any office, legislative, executive, or judiciary, before he shall have given such assurance, and shall moreover have taken such of the following oaths, if another be not specially prescribed, as adapted to his case. The oath of a Governor. "I   elected Governor of Virginia, by the representatives thereof, do solemly promise and swear, that I will, to the best of my skill and judgment, execute the said office diligently and faithfully, according to law, without favour, affection, or partiality; that I will to the utmost of my power, protect the citizens of the commonwealth in the secure enjoyment of their rights, franchises, and privileges, and will constantly endeavour that the laws and ordinances of the commonwealth be duly observed, and that law and justice, in mercy, be executed in all judgments; and, lastly, that I will peaceably and quietly resign the government, to which I have been elected, at the several periods to which my continuance in the said office is or shall be limited by law, and the constitution. So help me God." The oath of a Privy Counsellor. "I   elected one of the Privy Council of Virginia, by the representatives thereof do solemnly promise and swear, that I will, to the best of my skill and judgment, execute the said office diligently and faithfully, according to law, without favour, affection, or partiality; and that I will keep secret such proceedings and orders of the Privy Council as the Board shall direct to be concealed, unless the same be called for by either House of the General Assembly. So help me God." The oath of one not specially directed to take any other. "I   do solemnly promise and swear, that I will faithfully, impartially, and justly, perform the duty of my office of   according to the best of my skill and judgment. So help me God." The said oaths, to be taken by a member or officer of either House of General Assembly, shall be administered by any member of the Privy Council, and the taking thereof shall be certified to the clerk of such House; and the said oaths to be taken by any other person, if it be not otherwise directed, shall be administered in some Court of Record, or by any Judge or Justice thereof, and the taking thereof shall be recorded in the said court.

Report, p. 68-9. Dft (DLC); in TJ's hand, written on verso of address leaf of letter containing (on recto) draft of Bill for Allowing Salaries to Certain Officers of Government (q.v., May 1779). Endorsed by TJ at top of page: "A Bill prescribing an oath of fidelity ⟨*to the Commonwealth*⟩." Draft is undated, but was drawn by TJ and introduced by him on 29 May 1779. Text in Hening, X, 22-3 agrees precisely with text of *Report*. Differences between Act as adopted in 1779 and draft by TJ are indicated below.

TJ asked for, and obtained, leave on 29 May 1779 to introduce two bills concerning oaths: the present Bill and the Bill permitting those who would not take oaths to be otherwise qualified (Bill No. 119, below). Both were introduced by him the same day and both were adopted at this session. The present Bill passed its second reading on 31 May and was passed by the House on 1 June, TJ carrying it to the Senate, and approved by the Senate the same day (JHD, May 1779, 1827 edn., p. 27, 28, 29). Despite the adoption of Bill No. 98 in 1779, Madison introduced it again 31 Oct. 1785. It was postponed to the Oct. 1786 session, however, and no further action was taken on it (JHD, Oct. 1785, 1828 edn., p. 12-15, 92; same, Oct. 1786, p. 16-17). Bills No. 98 and 119 as enacted in 1779 were incorporated in the Act of 1792 "for reducing into one the several acts prescribing the oath of fidelity" (Shepherd, I, 3-4).

[1] The enacting clause of TJ's draft reads: "Be it enacted by the General assembly that every person appointed to act in any office within this commonwealth legislative, executive, or judiciary by authority from the laws thereof and all persons migrating hither to become citizens of the commonwealth shall take the following oath of fidelity before some court of record, or before some one of the judges of the high court of Chancery or General court to be by such judge certified into his court, to wit:"; the oath, which agrees precisely with the text of the Act as adopted, follows this passage.

[2] Following the oath, TJ's draft has only the following: "Which oath shall be entered of record by the clerk of the said court. No such officer shall be capable of acting in the office to which he shall be appointed until he shall have taken the said oath." Although, on obtaining leave to introduce his Bill on 29 May 1779, TJ was ordered to draft one that would not only prescribe the oath of office but also set forth oaths of office "for certain publick officers," his draft did not cover the latter purpose. Half of the page on which it was written is blank and there is no indication but that the draft is that of a complete Bill. Since there were apparently no amendments offered to his Bill, and since the text of the *Report* agrees precisely with the Act of 1779, it is possible that TJ's fair copy of his draft covered both purposes and therefore prescribed oaths of office for the governor and others. This assumption is supported by the fact that the oaths of office for the governor and for privy councillors were identical with those prescribed by an ordinance of Convention in 1776 and, therefore, there was no need for TJ to make a transcription of these oaths in his draft (Hening, IX, 120).

99. A Bill to Prevent the Sale of Public Offices

Be it enacted by the General Assembly, that if any person shall, for valuable consideration, dispose of any office which concerns the receipt, or the controlment or auditing accounts, of the public revenue, taxes, or duties; the office of Attorney for the commonwealth, clerk of the Council, or of any other public board, clerk of a Court of Record, sheriff, Naval-Officer, Advocate, Register, or Marshal of the Court of Admiralty, or any other public office, which concerns the administration of justice, and for the execution whereof he is intitled to fees or salary; or the deputation of any such office; or any military office; or shall make any bargain for that purpose, the seller, if he be the officer, shall forfeit the office, or, if he have the power of nomination to it, shall be deprived of the office in virtue of which he exerciseth that power; and in either case he in whose behalf the bargain was made shall be forever disabled to hold the office so bargained for; and every bond or contract made upon, or in consequence of, such bargain shall be void; and, moreover, the parties to the bargain shall be punished, by imprisonment and amercement at the discretion of a jury.

Report, p. 69. MS (ViU); clerk's copy.

Bill was presented 31 Oct. 1785 by Madison, postponed 14 Dec. to next session, brought up again on 1 Nov. 1786, considered and amended by committee of the whole 21 Nov., read the third time and rejected on 22 Nov. 1786. Apparently no further action was taken on this Bill (JHD, Oct. 1785, 1828 edn., p. 12-15, 92; same, Oct. 1786, p. 16-17, 53, 54). But see the "Act against buying and selling of offices" passed at the Oct. 1792 session (Shepherd, I, 6-7).

100. A Bill Directing the Method of Proceeding upon Impeachments

Be it enacted by the General Assembly, that the process against any person impeached by resolution of the House of Delegates shall be summons, attachments and distress, bearing teste, the first of them the day of emanation, and the others the return-day of the process preceeding, and shall be issued and signed by the clerk of the said court. A copy of the articles of impeachment shall be delivered to the party accused, whensoever he shall require it, and the court shall from time to time make such rules for compelling him to answer and bringing the matter to issue speedily as to them shall seem reasonable; and every fact so put in issue shall be tried by a jury.

Report, p. 69. MS (ViU); clerk's copy. Bill presented by Madison 31 Oct. 1785, postponed 14 Dec. to next session, brought up again at Oct. 1786 session, and on 1 Nov. read twice and committed to the committee of the whole (JHD, Oct. 1785, 1828 edn., p. 12-15, 92; same, Oct. 1786, p. 16-17). Apparently no further action was taken on it until the session of Oct. 1789, when Bill No. 100 was again brought forward and adopted without alteration (Hening, XIII, 56; see also the Act of 1792, Shepherd, I, 16-17).

101. A Bill for Regulating Proceedings in Courts of Equity

Be it enacted by the General Assembly, that original and subsequent process to bring any person to answer a bill, petition, or information, exhibited in the High Court of Chancery, shall run in the name of the commonwealth, bear teste, in the name of the first Judge of the court, the last preceeding return-day, be issued and signed by the clerk, and be returnable to the first or seventeenth day of the next succeeding, or of the current term, unless another return-day be, in extraordinary cases, specially directed or authorised by some statute; but the day it shall be issued shall be endorsed thereon, and noted in the book wherein the names of the parties shall be first entered. The day of appearance to the process shall be the second day after the end of the term. All process from the court of a county, city, or borough, in Chancery shall run in the name of the commonwealth, bear teste, in the name of the clerk of the peace, the day it shall be taken out, be issued and signed by him, and be returnable to the next succeeding session. If the complainant shall not appear at the day of appearance, in the High Court of Chancery, or at the session, when the cause shall be first called, in any other court, the suit shall be dismissed. The defendant, when he shall first enter his appearance, may give a rule to the complainant to put in his bill, if it shall not have been filed before. When a suit shall be dismissed for want either of appearance or prosecution, the defendant shall recover costs of the complainant. A complainant may have leave, without application to the court, to amend his bill at any time before he shall have replied to the answer, paying to the defendant all his costs occasioned thereby; and if he shall not file the amended bill, within the same time as is allowed for filing the original bill, the suit may be dismissed. Rules to file bills and replications and for other proceedings in the High Court of Chancery, shall be given with the clerk in vacation, and in every other court shall be given with the clerk in sessions, and shall be entered, the former in a book to be kept for that purpose, and the latter with the other proceedings of the court, and every such rule shall be out in one month, so that, if the party make default, the suit may be dismissed, or such order be made as is proper in the case. All proceedings in the clerks office of the High Court of Chancery may, from time to time, be controuled by the court in the succeeding term, who may also set aside dismissions and reinstate causes upon such terms as to them shall seem equitable. If the defendant shall not appear, at the day of appearance, in the High Court of Chancery, or at the session when the cause shall be first called, in any other court, the subpœna having been served upon him, and such service being proved, either by the return of a sworn officer, or by the affidavit of some other person, or if the defendant, having appeared, shall not put in his answer to the bill, before the expiration of three months, in either case an attachment shall be awarded against him; and such attachment, issuing from the court of a county, city, or borough, may be directed to, and shall be obeyed by, the sheriff of any other county. A defendant may swear to his answer before a Judge of the court, in which the suit shall be depending, or before a Justice of the Peace of any county, city, or borough. The defendant, to a cross bill, shall not be compelled to put in his answer thereto, before the complainant, in the cross bill, shall have put in his answer to the other bill; nor shall an attachment be awarded against the defendant to the cross bill for not answering, until the expiration of three months after such answer to the first bill shall have been put in. If the complainant shall not except or reply to the answer, before the end of two months after it shall have been put in, a rule may be given him to reply. Exceptions to an answer, if, before the end of two months after they shall have been filed, another answer be not put in, shall be set down to be argued. The complainant shall pay costs to the defendant, if the answer be adjudged sufficient, and recover them of him, if otherwise; the costs shall be doubled, if a second answer be adjudged insufficient; and if a third be so adjudged, the defendant, besides paying costs, shall be examined upon interrogatories, and be committed until he answer them. When the answer of a defendant, put in after process of contempt served upon him, shall have been excepted to, and adjudged insufficient, if he put not another answer in, at or before the next term, or session, the bill may be taken for confessed, unless it seem reasonable to the court to allow the defendant further time to put in such other answer. If the matter of a plea by verdict be found false, the complainant shall have the same advantage thereof as in case of a verdict in a court of common law. After any issue, made upon a plea, shall have been tried, or any demurrer shall have been over-ruled, no other plea or demurrer to the same bill shall be admitted; but the defendant shall answer the allegations of the bill. If the complainant shall not reply to a plea, or set down a demurrer to be argued, at the end of two months after they shall have been filed, his bill may be dismissed. If the matter of a plea be found true, or a demurrer adjudged good, the defendant shall recover costs; but, otherwise, the complainant shall recover costs to that time; and, unless the defendant put in an answer, before, or at, the end of two months thereafter, the bill shall be taken for confessed, and the matter thereof decreed. Any party may have commissions to take the examinations of his witnesses, and, reasonable notice being given to his adversary of the time and place of executing the commissions, such examination of any witness, who may lawfully be examined viva voce, may be read as evidence at the trial, if the party, at whose instance the witness was examined, shall prove, that he was not in the commonwealth, or was dead, or so infirm that he could not attend personally, and not otherwise. Every matter of fact, affirmed by one party, and denied by the other, in a bill, and answer, or plea, shall be stated as a formal issue, and tried before the same court, by a jury, in like manner as such issue ought to be tried in a court of common law, and upon like evidence as is there admissible, and not otherwise;[1] for trial of which issue the sheriff attending the court shall summon the jury, and the clerk shall issue subpœneas for summoning the witnesses, in the same manner as they do in the courts of common law; and the persons so summoned shall be subject to the power of the court, in the same manner, intitled to the same allowances, and liable to the same penalties, as they are in those courts. Auditors appointed by the court may examine the parties, upon oath, touching any matters in question, and shall have such allowance for their trouble in taking the account as the court shall adjudge reasonable, to be paid by such party as the court shall think justly chargeable therewith. The proceedings of the High Court of Chancery shall be entered and daily drawn up by the clerk, and, the necessary corrections being made, shall be signed the next day, by the presiding Judge, except on the last day of a term, when they shall be signed the same day; and the minutes of the proceedings of every other Court of Chancery shall be entered by the clerk, and signed by the presiding Justice, before the adjournment, and the said proceedings shall afterwards be drawn up at large. The bills, answers, replications, and depositions, in every cause, with the orders, decrees, and other proceedings, of the court, shall be recorded in well bound books, to be carefully preserved. Any two Judges of the High Court of Chancery, when it is not sitting, may grant writs of certiorari, ne exeat, and injunction, in the same manner as the court may grant them. But, before any writ of certiorari, to remove a cause, shall be issued, the party desiring it shall produce an affidavit, that ten or more days notice in writing of the time when, and place where, a motion would be made to the court, or a petition be presented to the two Judges for that purpose, had been given to the adverse party; the truth of the allegations of which petition shall be sworn to, or be otherwise proved; and he shall give bond, with sufficient surety, in such penalty, payable to the other party, as the court, or Judges shall direct, with condition for performing the decree of the court. No writ of ne exeat shall be issued, if the demand be triable in a court of common law; nor before a bill shall have been filed, with affidavits, or other evidence, to prove the allegations thereof to be true; nor before the complainant shall have given a bond, with sufficient surety, in a penalty directed by the court, or Judges, payable to the defendant, with condition for payment of all such damages and costs as shall be recovered by him against the complainant, by occasion of suing out the said writ; which bond shall be delivered to the defendant. On the writ shall be endorsed the penalty in which bond shall be taken in execution thereof. If the defendant satisfy the court or Judges by answer, affidavit, or otherwise, that he hath no design to leave the country, or that he is not indebted to the complainant, the writ shall be discharged. No writ of injunction to the judgment, or proceedings, in any action at common law, shall be issued, unless affidavit, or other proof, be made, that the allegations of the bill are true; nor before bond, with sufficient surety, and in an adequate penalty, payable to the plaintiff in the action, be given, with condition for payment, as well of the debt or damages recovered, or to be recovered, in the action, as of all such costs and damages as shall be awarded to the same plaintiff, in case the injunction be dissolved; which bond shall be delivered to him. Any party may appeal to the High Court of Chancery from a decree of the court of any county, city, or borough, giving bond, within ten days thereafter, with sufficient surety, in an adequate penalty, payable to the adverse party, with condition for performance of the decree, if it be affirmed, or so much of it as shall be affirmed, and for payment of the damages and costs which shall be awarded to the appellee. If the appeal be not entered at the session when the decree shall have been pronounced, the party thinking himself aggrieved may, within three months afterwards, appeal therefrom, lodging for that purpose, with the clerk of the High Court of Chancery, a copy of the proceedings in the cause, and a petition suggesting error in the decree, signed by some counsel attending that court, and also lodging with the petition, a bond, with sufficient surety, in like penalty, and with like condition, as in the other case; and the clerk shall thereupon issue a summons against the appellee, requiring him to appear, and answer the said petition and appeal; and shall also issue a supersedas, when it shall be necessary, to surcease further proceeding, in execution of the decree; and the court shall and may hear and determine the appeal, in the same manner, as if it had been entered at the time the decree shall have been pronounced; and in both cases the bonds shall be delivered to the appellees. In any suit in the High Court of Chancery, against a defendant, residing out of the country, the court may order any other party in the suit to retain the estate or effects of the absent defendant, which he may have in his hands or possession, or so much thereof as shall be sufficient to answer the demand of the complainant, or make such other order, for securing the estate and effects, for that purpose, as shall be thought effectual, unless security, to be approved by the court, be given to perform the decree; the complainant first making affidavit, that the demand is just. If a defendant or other person, against whom a subpœna or other process shall be issued from the High Court of Chancery, shall not cause his appearance to be entered, within such time, and in such manner, as it ought to have been entered, in case the process had been served, affidavit being made, that the defendant is not in the country, or that there is good reason to believe he absconds, to avoid being served with process, the court may make an order, that the defendant appear at a certain day, to be appointed, and a copy of the order shall, within fourteen days, be printed in the Virginia Gazette, and, if he reside in the country, published at the court-house of the county, wherein was his usual abode, within six weeks after making the order, and shall also be posted up at the front door of the house, in which the court shall sit. And if the defendant shall not appear at or before the day appointed, or at or before such further day as the court, if they see cause, shall allow, the court may order the bill to be taken for confessed, and make such decree as shall seem just, and award process to compel the performance thereof, either by immediate sequestration of the real and personal estate and effects of the defendant, or so much thereof as shall be sufficient to satisfy the demand of the complainant, or by causing the estate or effects claimed by the complainant to be delivered to him, or by granting such other relief as may seem proper, according to the nature of the case, and agreeable with the principles of equity; the complainant first giving sufficient security to perform such order, touching the restitution and disposition of the estate and effects, as the court shall make upon the appearance of the defendant, and paying reasonable costs; or if the complainant fail, or be unable to give security, the court may order the estate and effects, sequestered, or whereof possession shall have been ordered to be delivered, to remain under the direction of the court, appointing a receiver thereof, or otherwise, until such further order shall be made as the court shall think just. The court of any county, city, or borough, in Chancery, may proceed in the same manner, against any citizen out of the country, or absconding, to avoid being served with the process of such court, and shall have the same power over his estate and effects as the High court of Chancery, if it appear, to the satisfaction of such inferior court, by affidavit, or of their own knowledge of the fact, and be so entered in their proceedings, that the Defendant had formerly resided within their jurisdiction, and had not removed out of it so long as one year before the subpœna issued. If a defendant, brought before any court of Chancery, by virtue of the process thereof, shall refuse or neglect to enter his appearance, or to appoint an Attorney to act on his behalf, the court may appoint an Attorney to enter an appearance for him; and thereupon such proceedings may be in the cause, as if the defendant had appeared: but no process shall be issued, to compel the performance of a decree, made upon a refusal, or neglect, to enter an appearance, or to appoint an Attorney, before the defendant, if he be in custody, or forthcoming, shall have been served with a copy of the decree. The copy of a decree against a defendant, out of the country, or absconding, made for not appearing, shall be served upon him, if, within seven years after it shall have been made, he return, or become publickly visible, or, in case of his death, upon the heir, devisee, executor, or administrator, representing him, as to the matter in controversy. If the defendant, or his representative, having been served with a copy of such decree, shall, within seven months after the service, or, not having been served with the copy, if he, or his representative, or any person claiming under him, by virtue of any act prior to the commencement of the suit, shall, within seven years after making the decree, appear in court, and petition to be heard, with respect to the matter of the decree, and shall pay down, or give security for payment of, such costs as the court shall think reasonable, the petitioner may be admitted to answer the bill, and issue may be joined, and witnesses on both sides examined, and such other proceedings, decree, and execution, may be thereupon, as there might have been, if the party had originally appeared, and the suit had then been newly begun, or as if the former decree had not been made. But if the defendant, or his representative, having been served with a copy of such decree, shall not, within seven months after the service, or, not having been served with the copy, shall not, within seven years after making the decree appear, and petition, that the cause may be reheard, and pay down, or give security for payment of such costs as the court shall think reasonable, the decree shall stand confirmed against the defendant, and all persons claiming under him, by virtue of any act, subsequent to the commencement of the suit: and the court, at the end of the seven years, may make such further order as shall seem just and reasonable, according to the circumstances of the case. An attachment against a defendant, for a contempt, in not appearing to answer a bill, or in not answering a bill, shall be executed in the same manner as a writ of capias in an action at common law, whereon no direction to take bail is endorsed; and where any such attachment shall appear, by the return thereof, to have been executed, if the defendant shall not appear, or answer, the bill be taken for confessed, and the matter thereof decreed; and if the demand be not ascertained by the bill, and exhibits, or one of them, a jury shall be impaneled to enquire of and assess, the damages, at the following term, or session, in the same manner as in the case of an interlocutory judgment at common-law. In taxing costs, a lawyer's fee shall be allowed to the party who shall recover costs.

Report, p. 69-71. MS (ViU); clerk's copy.

See TJ's Bill for Establishing a High Court of Chancery, under date of 25 Nov. to 4 Dec. 1776; also the Act as adopted at Oct. 1777 session, Hening, IX, 389-99, and notes to Bill No. 90, above. Bill presented by Madison 31 Oct. 1785, read twice, and on 14 Dec. postponed to Oct. 1786 session; on 1 Nov. 1786 it was brought up again, read twice, and committed to committee of the whole (JHD, Oct. 1785, 1828 edn., p. 12-15, 92; same, Oct. 1786, p. 16-17). Apparently no further action was taken, though at the Oct. 1787 session the Act for Establishing a High Court of Chancery was amended in respect to rules of practice and procedure "because justice is greatly delayed by the tedious forms of proceedings, suitors are therefore obliged to waste much time and expence, to the impoverishment of themselves and the state, and decrees when obtained are with difficulty carried into execution" (Hening, XII, 464-7).

1 This important proviso restates in more precise terms the corresponding section of the Act of Oct. 1777. Concerning that Act TJ wrote in his Autobiography: "In that one of the bills for organizing our judiciary system, which proposed a court of Chancery, I had provided for a trial by jury of all matters of fact, in that as well as in the courts of law. He [Edmund Pendleton] defeated it by the introduction of four words only, '*if either party choose*.' The consequence has been, that as no suitor will say to his judge, 'Sir, I distrust you, give me a jury,' juries are rarely, I might

say, perhaps, never, seen in that court, but when called for by the Chancellor of his own accord" (Ford, I, 51). Actually an amendment to this effect was inserted in the 1776 Bill for Establishing a High Court of Chancery, introducing the qualifying words "if either party shall desire it, or the Court shall think proper to direct the same." This amendment was adopted in 1776 and continued in the Bill when it was brought up again in 1777; but it was deleted and is not in the Act as adopted (Hening, IX, 394). TJ remembered the amendment, but forgot that it failed to become law.

102. A Bill for Regulating Proceedings in Courts of Common Law

Be it enacted by the General Assembly, that all writs, given by the twenty-fourth chapter of the statutes, made in the thirteenth year of the reign of King Edward, the first, of England, and heretofore in use, shall continue to be used, in the same manner as if that statute were hereby re-enacted.[1] Actions of account may be maintained against the representatives of deceased guardians, bailiffs, and receivers, and also by one joint tenant, or tenant in common, or his executor, or administrator, against the other, as bailiff for more than his share; and the auditors appointed by the court, in any action of account, may examine the parties, upon oath, touching the matters in question; and shall have such allowance, for their trouble in taking and auditing the accounts, as the court shall adjudge to be reasonable, to be paid by the party against whom the balance of the account shall appear to be. The representatives of a deceased executor, whether rightful or wrongful, who shall have converted to his own use, or wasted the estate of his testator or intestate, shall be chargeable for such conversion or waste of the assets in their hands, in the same manner as their testator or intestate might have been charged. Process, from the General Court, shall run in the name of the commonwealth, be issued and signed by the clerk, and bear teste in the name of the Chief Justice, the preceeding return-day; but the day it issued shall be endorsed thereon, and noted in the book where the names of the parties to the suit are first entered. The return-day of process, issuing from the General Court, to arrest or summon persons to answer in actions real, personal, and mixt, where other days be not in extraordinary cases especially directed or authorised by some statute, shall be the eighth and twenty third days of the March and October terms, and of process, in pleas of the commonwealth, the first day of the term after the emanation; and no process shall be returnable later than to some day of the next term but one after emanation. Process, from the court of a county, city, or borough, shall run in the name of the commonwealth, be issued by the clerk of the peace, bear teste in his name, be signed by him, and, if not an exigent, shall be returnable to the session next after the teste, unless where, if the process be to arrest one in a civil action or suit, such next session will happen within three days after the teste, in which case the process shall be returnable to the session in the month following; and every such process, to arrest one, shall be executed at least three days before the return-day thereof. Process in an action at common law, against the Governor, a member of the Privy Council, a Judge, or a clerk of the High Court of Chancery, General Court, or Court of Admiralty, or a sheriff, shall be summons and distress, and against such Governor, Judge, or clerk, shall issue from the General Court, if the value of the matter in controversy exceed ten pounds; and process in any such action, to arrest a person so privileged, or issuing against such Governor, Judge, or clerk, from any other court, than the General Court, shall be void. Such action against a Governor, Judge, or clerk, shall be tried, if the plaintiff require it, on some day in the term next, or next but one, after the issue shall be joined, unless good cause for deferring the trial be shewn; but if more than two Judges of the General Court be parties or interested, the case shall be adjourned to the Court of Appeals, and be tried before them at their first or second session after the adjournment, if no good cause for deferring the trial be shewn. The second days next after the March and October terms shall be the days of appearance upon process from the General Court, returnable to the eighth and twenty-third days of those terms respectively. Every party to any civil action, not allowed to sue in forma pauperis, unless he be under the age of twenty-one years, or of unsound mind, and in that case his guardian, to be specially assigned by the court, may, by warrant, under his hand or by appointment personally declared in court, empower an attorney to appear for him, and without such authority, entered of record, no attorney shall be permitted to appear, neither shall any act done by him bind the party. Warrants of attorney to confess judgments, or suffer them to pass by default, and releases of error, made before the actions brought, shall be void; and an attorney appearing by such warrant, knowing it to have been made before the action brought, shall forfeit and pay to the defendant the amount of the debt or damages, for which the judgment shall be given to be recovered by action of debt; and shall moreover be liable to his action for damages. In any action, if affidavit be made before some Justice of the Peace, or the clerk who shall issue the writ, that the debt demanded, or the value of the goods detained, or alledged to have been converted to the use of the defendant, or the damage sustained by non-performance of the condition, covenants, promise, or agreement, for which the action is brought, amounts to a certain sum, exceeding ten pounds, if the action be in the General Court, or five pounds, if in the court of a county, city, or borough, or, if a Judge of the court, from which the writ shall issue, certify in writing, under his hand, that the defendant appeared, by affidavit, to have been guilty of a mayhem, or of a violent battery, and ought to give bail in a certain sum, or, if the action be founded upon some act of the General Assembly, requiring the defendant to give bail, the clerk, at the request of the plaintiff, shall endorse on the writ a direction, with his name thereunto subscribed, that the sheriff or officer take bail, in the sum mentioned in the affidavit, or certificate, which shall be lodged with the clerk, or in a sum equal to the forfeiture inflicted by the act, if it be ascertained, or, if not, in the amount of such damage as the plaintiff shall make affidavit, in manner aforesaid, to have been sustained. And the sheriff, or other officer, shall discharge out of his custody, every person arrested by force of such writ, or by a capias, upon an indictment of trespass, or misdemeanor, upon sufficient surety given to appear at such day and place as the writ shall require. And the bonds, executed by the defendant and surety, shall be returned with the writ. And if no direction, to take bail, be endorsed on the writ, in any action personal, the sheriff, or other officer, shall not arrest the body of the defendant, but shall serve him personally with a copy of the process against him; and, if he shall not appear, at the time and place he ought to do so, the plaintiff may proceed against him, in the same manner as if the defendant had entered his appearance. No person shall be out-lawed in any action quare vi et armis. Whensoever a writ of exigent shall be sued out in any civil case, it shall be directed to the sheriff of that county wherein the last place of abode of the defendant was, and, issuing from the court of a county, city, or borough, shall be returnable to the sixth session next after the teste, and shall be audibly read by the said sheriff, who shall also set up copies thereof at the door of the court-house of his county five sessions, successively; and if the defendant be returned five times required, and shall not appear at or before the return of the writ of exigent, the plaintiff may proceed, in the same manner, as he might have proceeded against the defendant, if he had appeared. If a defendant, arrested by force of any process, and enlarged upon giving a bail-bond, with surety, for his appearance, to the sheriff, or other officer, shall not appear accordingly, or offering to appear, and being ruled by the court to put in special bail, shall neither put in such bail, nor surrender himself to prison, the plaintiff may proceed against him, in the same manner, as if the defendant had appeared, and put in special bail; and the sheriff or other officer, shall assign the bail-bond to the plaintiff, at his request, and thereupon the surety shall be subject to the same judgment, and may make the same defence, as the party, for whose appearance he was bound, is subject to, and might have made; but if the surety shall not appear, judgment shall not be entered against him, until ten days at least after a rule, to shew cause to the contrary, shall have been served upon him, or, if he be not found, left at the place of his usual abode, whereof affidavit shall be made and filed; and the surety may, at any time before such judgment, put in a plea in bar thereto, or discharge himself of the action, by bringing the defendant into court, or delivering him into the custody of the sheriff, which he shall have the same power to do, as if he were special bail; or the surety may, at any time after such judgment, by order of the court, obtain an attachment against the estate of the defendant, directed to the sheriff of any county: which estate may be sold, towards satisfaction of the judgment, or may be replaced, in the same manner, as if it had been taken in execution, by writ of fieri facias. The sheriff, or officer, who shall execute process, where special bail is required, neglecting to take and return the bail-bond, or taking such surety for appearance as the court shall judge to be insufficient, shall be liable for the demand, may make defence, and may be relievable against the defendant, or out of his estate, in the same manner as the surety; but every surety shall be deemed sufficient, unless exception be made to him, and a note of such exception be filed, during that term, or session, of the court, to which the process shall have been returned, or at the day of appearance, next after the term, and reasonable notice, in writing, of the exception to be given to the sheriff, or officer, suggested to be liable to justify the surety in some day of the term, or at the session next after the notice, and an affidavit of the notice be made and filed. The recognizances of special bail may be taken by any Justice of the court, in which the action dependeth; and such recognizances, in actions depending in the General Court, may also be taken by any persons, being Justices of the Peace, whom that court shall appoint; and the recognizances shall be transmitted, by those who take them, to such court respectively, where any special bail may be excepted to; and if he be not justified, at the term, or session, next after the recognizance shall have been transmitted, and after reasonable notice, in writing, of such exception, proved, by affidavit filed, to have been given to the party liable, in case the bail be adjudged insufficient, the recognizance shall be discharged, and the plaintiff may proceed in the same manner, as he might have done, if no recognizance had been taken; but if no exception be made, or the bail be not adjudged insufficient, the recognizance shall be as effectual, as if it had been taken in court. Whosoever shall personate another, before any authorised to take bail, shall not only be liable to the action of the party injured, but also be amerced, and imprisoned. Special bail may discharge himself of his recognizance as well before as after judgment against the defendant, either by bringing him in court, and there delivering him up, or by delivering him to the officer who arrested him, or his successor, so as such render, after judgment, be in due time, and so as notice, of a render to the officer, be given to the clerk of the court, where the action was commenced, within such time as a render in court ought to be made; and thereupon such proceedings shall be, as might have been if the defendant had not been bailed. If return of any process, whereon a direction to take bail shall have been endorsed, be made, that the defendant is not found in the bailiwick of the officer, the plaintiff may sue out an attachment against the estate of the defendant, directed to the same officer; and if any of the defendant's estate be attached, and he shall not replevy the same, by giving bond with surety to the officer, with condition for his appearance, at the return of the attachment, or shall not at that time appear and put in special bail, being ruled to do so by the court, the plaintiff may proceed as if the defendant had not appeared, and, judgment being given for him, the estate attached shall be disposed of as if it had been taken by writ of fieri facias. A defendant, arrested by process from the General Court, in any action, not having given a bail-bond, but remaining in custody, and not having put in an attorney to appear for him, shall, by writ of habeas corpus, to be granted to the plaintiff, at his desire, after the day of appearance, and after the declaration filed, be brought before the court, at some certain day, in any term, when, if the defendant, being present at the bar, shall not enter his appearance in person, or put in an attorney to appear for him, and plead, upon a rule given him, to be out before the last day of the term, judgment may be entered against him, as appearing in person. And where a person shall sue forth a writ from the General Court against a prisoner, in the public jail, the defendant, by order of the said court, may be brought before them, by the jailer, at any day of the term; and the same proceedings shall be thereupon, as if the prisoner had been arrested by force of such process; and, in either case, such charge, in court, by declaration, signified by rule to the jailer, shall be a good cause of detention of the prisoner, in his custody, and subject such jailer, suffering an escape, to an action; and a defendant, in prison, by force of process from the court of a county, city, or borough, and brought before such court, by their order, may be charged, in like manner; and the officer, in whose custody he remains, shall have the same power to detain him, and shall be subject to the like action for an escape, as in the case of a prisoner in the public jail. In an action at common law, commenced in the General Court, the defendant, or tenant, at the day of appearance, or whenever he shall afterwards enter his appearance, may give the plaintiff, or demandant, a rule to put his declaration, if it shall not have been put in before; and, after the declaration shall be put in, if the defendant, or tenant, do not plead thereto, before the end of one month, the plaintiff, or demandant, may then give the defendant, or tenant, a rule to plead; and either party, at the end of one month after he shall have put in any pleading, may give the other party a rule to plead further, in answer thereto, until issue be joined; and every such rule shall be entered by the clerk of the court in a book, and shall be out in one month; and, after the expiration of the rule, a nonsuit or judgment, against the party making default, shall be entered by the clerk, in the same book, as an act of the court, in the preceeding term, and shall stand confirmed, unless good cause to the contrary be shewn to the court, on the eighth day of the succeeding term, at which time any judgment entered during that interval, against a defendant, or against a defendant and his surety, or against a defendant and the sheriff, shall be set aside, upon the appearance of the defendant, and by his putting in special bail, if he be ruled to do so, and pleading, and any other proceeding, in the clerk's office may then also be examined, and, being judged erroneous, may be corrected by the court. A dilatory plea, or a plea of non est factum, shall not be received, unless the party offering it make affidavit of the truth thereof, or shew some probable matter to the court to induce them to believe the fact of the plea to be true. The defendant or tenant, in any action, or the plaintiff, in replevin, may, with leave of the court, plead as many several matters thereto, as he shall think necessary for his defence. In an action of trespass quare clausum fregit, the defendant may plead a disclaimer, and that the trespass was involuntary, and that he tendered sufficient amends for such trespass before the action brought; upon which points, or some of them, the plaintiff shall join issue; and if the issue be found for the defendant, or the plaintiff be nonsuited, the plaintiff shall be barred. In an indictment, or information, for a libel, the defendant may plead a justification, and if the jury find the facts contained in the writing, supposed to be a libel, to be true, he shall be acquitted; and where the defendant shall plead not guilty to such indictment, or information, or to any declaration for a libel, or for slanderous words, if, at the time of putting in the plea, he shall file a writing, therein, stating specially, the matters of fact he will endeavour to prove, in his defence, he shall be admitted, on the trial, to give evidence of such of the said matters of fact, as are pertinent to the cause, in mitigation of the fine or damages. In every action of ejectment, commenced merely to try the title of the lessor of the plaintiff to lands or tenements, such lessor, and all persons claiming under him, shall be bound, and finally barred, by a judgment given against the plaintiff, of all right and title to the same lands and tenements, prior to the commencement of the action. An action shall not abate by death of one or more of the plaintiffs, or demandants, or of the defendants, or tenants, if it might afterwards originally be maintained by or against the survivor or survivors, such death being suggested on the record. If either or both the parties die, after verdict, judgment shall be entered, in the same manner, as if they were living. An action shall not abate by death of either party, or of both parties, after an interlocutory, and before a final judgment, if it might, after such death, originally be maintained by or against his or their representatives; but a scire facias shall be sued forth by the living plaintiff, or demandant, or the executor, administrator, heir, or devisee, against the defendant, or tenant, or the executor, administrator, heir, or devisee, representing him or them, respectively, to shew cause why the debt, or other thing demanded, or the damages alledged to have been sustained, should not be recovered; and if the person, against whom the scire facias shall be sued, appearing at the return of the writ, shall not alledge matter sufficient to arrest the judgment, or being returned warned, or, if return being made on two writs of scire facias, that he could not be found in the county, he shall make default, an enquiry of damages shall be made by a jury, which being done, judgment final shall be given, in the same manner, as it might have been, if the parties to the scire facias had been parties to the original action. An action brought in the name of the Governor, in behalf of the commonwealth, shall not abate by his death. All causes, civil and criminal, commenced, and all appeals entered, before the twelfth day of April, one thousand seven hundred and seventy four, wherein George the third, King of Great Britain, or his Attorney General, was a party, or wherein other persons, suing as well on behalf of themselves as of the said King, were parties, and which remain undetermined, and wherein the King's right hath devolved upon the commonwealth, shall stand revived, and be in the same condition as they then were, or, by virtue of any act of General Assembly since made, now are, and may be prosecuted, and in like cases actions upon bonds and recognizances made payable to the said King may be commenced and prosecuted, and execution of judgments recovered by the said King, or his Attorney, or by others who sued on behalf as well of themselves as of the said King, yet remaining unsatisfied, may be done; the name of the commonwealth, or of the Attorney General thereof being inserted in all future forms, where the name of the said King, or of his said Attorney, respectively, ought to have been inserted, if the government of this country, as formerly exercised under the crown of Great Britain had not been dissolved. The court shall give leave to either party to an action, at any time before the trial, to amend his declaration, or other pleading, so that the amendment do not alter the nature of the action, or delay the trial, and the party who desires it pay the costs occasioned thereby. Mistakes and irregular entries by the clerk of a court may, at any time before execution, be corrected and reformed by the same court. In an action upon a bond, or upon a contract, subjecting the party to the payment of a penal sum, for non-performance of a condition, covenant, or agreement, the plaintiff may assign as many breaches as he will, and the jury, upon trial, shall assess damages for such of these as shall be proved to have happened, or judgment upon demurrer, or by confession, or by nil dicit, having been given for the plaintiff, he may suggest the like breaches upon the record, and a jury shall be summoned and charged to enquire of the truth of them, and to assess the damages sustained thereby; and in either case judgment shall be for the penalty, to be discharged by payment of such damages, with the costs, as well as of the damages, which may be thereafter assessed, for other breaches, if any, to be suggested as often as they shall happen, in a writ of scire facias. Judgment, in an action upon a bond, for a debt, shall be for the penalty, to be discharged by payment of the principal debt, with the interest due, and to become due, and costs, or for the costs only, if the defendant shall, before judgment, pay into court, to the use of the plaintiff, the principal debt, with the interest then due. Private statutes may be given in evidence in any case, without pleading them specially. A defendant may plead payment of the principal debt and interest, in bar of an action, upon a judgment, or upon a bond, although the payment shall have been after the time mentioned in the condition thereof, or upon a single bill; and may also plead a tender and refusal, between the time of payment, and the commencement of the action. Where a demurrer shall be joined, in any action, the court shall not regard any other defect or imperfection in the writ, return, declaration, or pleading, than what shall be specially alledged, in the demurrer, as causes thereof, unless something so essential to the action or defence, as that judgment according to law, and the very right of the cause, cannot be given, shall be omitted. Upon an interlocutory judgment, the damages sustained by the plaintiff, shall be inquired of in court; but such inquiry shall not be made, in the General Court, at the term next after the judgment, unless twenty days previous notice thereof be given to the defendant, and affidavit of such notice be made and filed. A question of law, arising upon a special verdict, or upon a special case, stated by counsel on both sides, shall not be argued the same term or session, without consent of parties. The clerk of every court shall issue and deliver subpœnas to all persons requiring them, for summoning witnesses to appear before such court, at such days of any term, or session, as he shall be directed by such persons. No negro, mulatto, or Indian, shall be a witness, in any cause, if either of the parties be a white person. Any party, in an action, may have commissions, to take the examinations of his witnesses; and, reasonable notice being given, to his adversary, of the time and place of executing the commissions, such examination of any witness, who may be lawfully examined, viva voce, may be read, as evidence at the trial, if the party, at whose instance the witness was examined, shall prove, that he was not in the commonwealth, or was dead, or so infirm that he could not attend personally. Any person who having been summoned to appear before the court, or commissioners, to testify, and attending accordingly, shall refuse to give evidence, may be committed to jail, and closely confined, until he shall submit to be examined. Any person summoned to appear before the court, or the commissioners, as witnesses, and failing to attend accordingly shall not only be liable to the party grieved, for damages, to be recovered, by an action on the case, but shall, moreover, forfeit and pay, to the same party, one thousand pounds of tobacco, by rule of court, to be made absolute, unless such rule being served upon him, good cause be shewn to the contrary, at the next term or session. The privilege, from arrest, of any person going to, attending on, or returning from a court of justice, shall continue, from the time of leaving his habitation, until his return thither, provided it exceed not one day for every twenty miles of the distance he must necessarily travel, over and above the time of attendance. Every witness shall be allowed one pound and a half of tobacco for every mile he shall necessarily travel, from the place of his abode, to that he shall have been summoned to appear at, and the same for returning, and his ferriage, and sixty pounds of tobacco for every day he shall attend, in obedience to such summons, to be paid by the party, on whose behalf he shall have been summoned. The forfeiture inflicted by any act of General Assembly, and not thereby otherwise appropriated, if no prosecution be commenced on behalf of the commonwealth alone for the whole, shall be, one half to use of the informer; and in either case, if the defendant be convicted, costs shall be recovered against him. In every action, the party for whom judgment final shall be given, shall recover his costs of suit against the other party, and in case of a non-suit, the defendant or tenant shall, moreover, recover, if the action be in the General Court, five pounds of tobacco, for every mile the place of his usual abode is distant from the place, at which the process, served upon him, shall have been returnable; or, if the action be in any other court, five shillings, to be taxed in the bill of costs. One, of several defendants, joined in the same action of trespass, assault, false imprisonment, or ejectment, who shall, upon trial of the issue, be, by verdict acquitted, shall recover his costs, in like manner as if all had been acquitted. In any personal action, the plaintiff, for whom a verdict shall be found, shall recover no more costs, than the damages assessed by the jury, if these be under forty shillings, unless the title or boundaries of land, or a franchise, shall appear to the court to have been in question, or unless the defendant be convicted of wrongful or unreasonable distress. The clerk, in taxing costs upon a judgment, shall allow, to the party who recovers costs, five pounds, in the General Court, and thirty shillings in any other court, in an action, where the title or boundaries of land shall appear by the proceedings, or shall be declared by the court, and entered on the record, to have been in controversy, on the trial, or fifty shillings in the General Court, and fifteen shillings in any other court, in a different action, not being a petition to recover a small debt, and seven shillings and sixpence, in such petition, for a lawyer's fee, if a lawyer was employed by him. When a dilatory plea, or plea in abatement, shall be overruled, the plaintiff shall recover his costs of suit to that time, a lawyer's fee excepted. In taxing costs against the party from whom they shall be recovered, no office copy, taken out by, or for, the other party, of a writing, filed on behalf of himself, shall be allowed; nor shall the charge of more than three witnesses to the proof of any one matter of fact, be allowed, unless, from the contrariety of evidence, or the great number of witnesses, on the opposite side, or other circumstances the court shall think it reasonable to allow more. In an information, or indictment, for any trespass, or misdemeanor, or in an action against any person concerned in the administration of justice, for what he shall do in execution of his office, or by authority of a statute of the commonwealth, or against one for a penalty incurred by breach of a statute, the defendant, having pleaded the general issue, may, upon trial thereof, give evidence of any special matter, which if it had been pleaded, would have acquitted or justified him. Where there are mutual debts between the plaintiff and defendant, or where either party being an executor or administrator, there are mutual debts between the testator or intestate, and the plaintiff, or defendant, one debt may be set against the other, and such matter may be pleaded in bar, or may be given in evidence upon the general issue, so as, at the time of pleading the general issue, notice, in writing, be given of the particular sum or debt intended to be insisted on, and upon what account it became due; but if either of the debts shall have accrued by a penalty, contained in a bond or specialty, the debt, intended to be set off, shall be pleaded specially, and the amount of the sum due shall be shewn in the plea, and the plaintiff, in case judgment be given for him, shall recover no more than shall appear justly due, after one debt shall be set against the other. No writ of certiorari shall be granted, for removing an action into the General Court, if such action might not have been originally commenced there, nor after an issue shall have been joined; nor before the party praying the writ shall have given the adverse party ten days notice of the time when, and place where application will be made for it, and shall produce an affidavit of such notice; nor unless the reasons for desiring the writ be stated in a petition, to be verified by affidavit, and filed; nor where the action, before removed by certiorari shall have been remanded by writ of procedendo; neither shall such writ issue, before bond be given, with such surety as shall be approved of, and in such penalty, payable to the adverse party, as shall be directed by those who order the writ, with condition, that the party praying it, shall perform the judgment of the court. Such writ may be granted by two Judges of the court, in vacation; but, whensoever granted, shall not be obeyed, if it be not produced to the Judges, to whom it is directed, before issue joined, in the action. Any person apprehending himself to be aggrieved by a judgment of the court of a county, city, or borough, if the debt, or damages, or the value of the goods specifically recovered exclusive of costs, exceed ten pounds of current money, or two thousand pounds of tobacco, or if the title or boundaries of land, or a franchise, shall have been in question may enter and prosecute an appeal, from such judgment, to the General Court. Before the appeal shall be allowed, and before any writ of error, to reverse any such judgment shall issue, bond shall be given, with sufficient surety, and in an adequate penalty, payable to the appellee, or defendant in error, with condition, that the appellant, or plaintiff in error, shall prosecute the appeal, or writ of error, with effect, and perform the judgment of the General Court; which bond, in the former instance, shall be lodged with the clerk of the court below, and, in the other instance, with the clerk of the court above, to be delivered to the obligee. Such bond being given, in the case of an appeal, the clerk of the court below shall forthwith send a transcript of the record to the clerk of the court above, and the same proceedings shall be thereupon, as if the transcript had been removed by writ of error. No appeal or writ of error shall be granted before a final judgment. A writ of error, wherein there shall be a variance from the original record, or other defect, shall be amended, and made agreeable to such record, by the court, to which it shall be returnable. Upon an appeal or writ of error, the court above shall give such judgment as, in their opinion, the court below ought to have given. If the judgment against a defendant, whereby debt, or damages, or goods specifically demanded, shall have been recovered, be affirmed, in every part, the appellee or defendant in error shall recover, of the adverse party, five pounds by the year, from the time of rendering the judgment, for every hundred pounds of such debt, or damages, or of the value of such goods, including the costs, and after that rate for a less sum, or value, or a shorter time, besides the costs of the appeal, or writ of error; if the judgment against a defendant or tenant, whereby any title to lands, or a franchise, shall have been recovered, be so affirmed, the appellee or defendant in error shall recover two thousand pounds of tobacco, besides the costs of the appeal, or writ of error; and if the judgment, against a plaintiff or demandant be so affirmed, the appellee or defendant in error shall recover fifty shillings, besides the costs of the appeal, or writ of error. No writ of error shall be granted in any personal action, if the thing recovered, exclusive of costs, be of less value than ten pounds, of current money, unless it be by special order of the General Court, after ten days notice of a motion, for that purpose, shall have been given to the plaintiff.

Upon quashing any writ of error, for variance from the original record, or other defect, the defendant in error shall recover against the plaintiff issuing the writ the same costs, and in the same manner, as if the judgment had been affirmed. No judgment, after a verdict of twelve men, shall be stayed or reversed, for any defect, or fault, in any writ, original or judicial; or for a variance in the writ, from the declaration, or other proceedings; or for any mispleading, insufficient pleading, discontinuance, misjoining of the issue, or lack of warrant of attorney; or for the appearance of either party, being under the age of twenty one years, by attorney, if the verdict be for him, and not to his prejudice; or for not alledging any deed, letters testamentary, or commission of administration, to be brought into court; or for omission of the words, with force and arms, or against the peace, or for mistake of the christian name, or sur-name, of either party, sum of money, or quantity of merchandize, day, month, or year, in the declaration, or pleading, the name, sum, quantity, or time, being right in any part of the record preceeding; or for omission of the averment this he is ready to verify, or this he is ready to verify by the record; or for not alledging as appeareth by the record; or for omitting the averment of any matter, without proving which, the jury ought not to have given such a verdict, or for any informality in entering up the judgment by the clerk; neither shall any judgment entered upon confession, or by nil dicit, or non sum informatus, be reversed, or a judgment, after enquiry of damages, be stayed, or reversed, for any omission, or fault, which would not have been a good cause to stay or reverse the judgment, if there had been a verdict. The proceedings of the General Court shall daily be drawn up, and entered, by the clerk, in a well bound book, and, having been audibly read by him, in open court, and corrected by the court, shall be signed by the presiding Justice, on the following day, unless it be on the last day of a term, when they shall be signed the same day; which book shall be carefully preserved, with the other records. The minutes of the proceedings of the court of a county, city, or borough, before their adjournment, shall be audibly read by the clerk, in open court, and corrected by the court, and signed by the presiding Justice, and afterwards the proceedings shall be entered at large by the clerk, in a well bound book, to be carefully preserved with the other records. Complete records of the process, proceedings, and judgments of the General Court, in all actions, and of the court of every county, city, and borough, in those actions, wherein there shall be writs of error, or appeals, or wherein the titles or boundaries of lands, or franchises shall be in question, shall be made up by the respective clerks, in books well bound, and carefully preserved with the other records; the records in those actions, wherein the titles or boundaries of lands shall be determined, being entered in distinct books. The clerk of every court shall, on or before the first day of January, annually, transmit a list of the fines imposed on jurors, and others the preceeding year, to the sheriffs of the counties, wherein the delinquent shall dwell, to be collected, received, and accounted for by such sheriffs in the same manner, as taxes; and shall also, before the first day of September, transmit the like lists to the public Treasurer.

Report, p. 71-5. MS (ViU); clerk's copy.

See TJ's Bill for Establishing a General Court, under date of 25 Nov. to 4 Dec. 1776; also the Act as adopted at the Oct. 1777 session (Hening, IX, 401-19) and notes to Bill No. 91, above. Bill was presented by Madison 31 Oct. 1785, read twice, and on 14 Dec. postponed to Oct. 1786 session; on 1 Nov. 1786 it was brought up again, read twice, and committed to a committee of the whole (JHD, Oct. 1785, 1828 edn., p. 12-15, 92; same, Oct. 1786, p. 16-17). Apparently no further action was taken. But see the Act passed at the Oct. 1792 session "reducing into one the several acts concerning the establishment, jurisdiction, and powers of District Courts" (Hening, XIII, 427-49).

[1] In DLC: TJ Papers, 232: 42063 is a MS bill endorsed "A Bill for continuing the use of certain writs" and also "13.E.1.c.24." This entire bill was copied verbatim as the first sentence of Bill No. 102. It was written by the same clerk who transcribed the fragment of Bill No. 64 (q.v.); on its verso TJ jotted down the memoranda that form Part 5 of Document IV in this series.

103. A Bill Directing the Method of Proceeding against, and Trying Free Persons Charged with Certain Crimes

Be it enacted by the General Assembly, that any free person, brought before a Justice of the Peace of a county, and, by the testimony of another free person, charged with treason, or felony, done in such county,[1] shall be committed to jail, by warrant of such Justice, who shall by his precept, order the sheriff to summon the other Justices to meet, in the court-house, at an appointed time, not more than ten, nor less than five days after the commitment; and shall take the recognizance of witnesses, to appear before the said Justices, at that time and place. If the offence shall have been done in another county, the Justice shall, by his warrant, cause the prisoner to be put into the custody of a constable,[2] to be by him conveyed to the next constable, and so from constable to constable,[3] every one of which constables, whilst he shall officiate in execution of this act, may impress so many men, horses, and boats, as shall be necessary for the safe-guard and conveyance of the prisoner, into such other county, and there brought before some Justice thereof, who shall proceed in like manner as if the offender had been brought before him in the first instance.[4] The Justices, so convened, shall be attended by the clerk of the peace, and any four, or more of them, who will act, having examined the witnesses, as well for, as against the prisoner, in his presence, for summoning which witnesses, on behalf of the prisoner, subpœnas shall be delivered to him, or any other for him, desiring them, by the clerk of the peace, and heard his defence, if, in their opinion, the evidence be not sufficient to convict him, shall enlarge him. If it seem to them, that the evidence is sufficient to convict the prisoner, but that the offence is cognizable by the court of the county, they shall take the recognizance of the prisoner, with surety, in such sum as they think proper, to appear before such court, at the next session, in which there will be a grand jury for the same county, or, if he do not give such surety, shall remand him to jail, there to remain until such session, or until he shall enter into the recognizance, with surety before any one of the said Justices, who shall return it to the clerk of the peace. If they shall think the offence cognizable by the General Court only, remanding the prisoner to jail, from whence he shall, by mittimus of two of them, be removed by the sheriff to the public jail, and delivered to the keeper thereof, or, if they think him bailable, admitting him to bail, the Justices shall take the recognizance of the witnesses to appear before the General Court, on the first day of the next term, and, causing the examinations of the witnesses to be taken in writing, shall order them, together with the recognizances, both of the prisoner, if there be any, and of the witnesses, to be transmitted by the clerk of the peace to the clerk of the General Court; and the two Justices, who give the mittimus, when there shall be one, may, by their warrant, empower the sheriff to impress so many men, horses, and boats, in all places he shall pass through, as shall be necessary for the safeguard and conveyance of the prisoner; to which warrant all persons shall yield obedience, and in execution whereof the officer shall proceed as the law directs, in other cases, wherein impressments are authorised. If the Justices shall be of opinion, that the prisoner may be bailed, and shall enter that opinion in their proceedings, and also the sums of money in which he and his bail ought to be bound, he may be bailed, either by them, or by any Justice of the same county, or by any Judge of the General Court, who shall transmit the recognizance to the clerk of the General Court, and grant a warrant for the deliverance of the prisoner; and that warrant being put into the hands of the officer in whose custody the prisoner shall be, he shall thereupon be delivered, if he be detained for no other cause. Any two Judges of the General Court, when it is not sitting, may admit to bail a prisoner, whom they shall think intitled thereto, and grant a warrant for his deliverance, notwithstanding the Justices before whom the examination was, shall have been of a different opinion. When the Justices shall have determined, that a prisoner ought to be tried for an offence, in the General Court, the clerk of the peace shall issue a writ of venire facias, to be directed to the sheriff, commanding him to cause twelve good and lawful men, freeholders of his county, of the neighbourhood of the place where the fact shall have been committed, to come before the Justices of the General Court, at the time the witnesses shall be bound to appear there; which writ shall be executed by the said sheriff; and the freeholders, summoned by virtue thereof, or such of them as appear, and be not challenged, together with so many other good and lawful men of the by-standers[5] as will make the number twelve, or, if the whole array be challenged, twelve of such by-standers, shall be a lawful jury for the trial of the prisoner. After any man shall be indicted of treason, or felony, if he be not already in custody, the sheriff shall be commanded to attach his body, by writ, or by precept, which is called a capias, and if he return, that the body is not found, another writ or precept of capias shall be immediately made, returnable forthwith, in which the sheriff shall be also commanded to seize his chattels, and safely to keep them; and if he return, that the body is not found, and the indictee cometh not, an exigent shall be awarded, and the chattels shall be forfeited; but if he come, and yield himself, or he be taken, before the return of the second capias, the goods and chattels shall be saved. And in all trials for such offences, the prisoner shall have a copy of the indictment, and of the panel of the jurors, who are to try him, whensoever he shall require it before trial or sentence. And when any of the panel shall be challenged by the Attorney for the commonwealth, he shall assign the cause of his challenge, which shall be enquired of according to law. When the grand jury shall have presented, to the General Court, any bill of indictment against one charged with treason, or felony, the court shall cause the offender, if he be[6] forth-coming, immediately, or so soon as conveniently[7] may be, to be arraigned and tried the same term, unless they see good cause to adjourn the trial to the next, and shall allow him counsel to assist him at his trial, if he desire it. Written examinations of witnesses, taken by virtue of commissions, which may be issued by the clerk of the peace, or the clerk of the General Court, on behalf of the commonwealth, or the person charged with treason, or felony, may be read in evidence upon his trial, in the like cases as the examinations, taken by such commissions, may be read on trial of an issue between party and party in the General Court.[8] When any prisoner, committed for treason or felony, and applying to the General Court, by petition, or motion, the first day of the term, shall desire to be brought to his trial before the end thereof, and shall not be indicted in that term, unless it appear, by affidavit, that the witnesses against him cannot be produced in time, the court shall set him at liberty, upon his given bail, in such penalty as they shall think reasonable, to appear before them at a day, to be appointed, of the succeeding term; and he, and every other person, charged with such crime, who shall not be indicted before, or at the second term after he shall have been committed, unless the attendance of the witnesses against him appears to have been prevented by himself, shall be discharged from his imprisonment, if he be detained for that cause only; and if he be not tried at or before the third term, after his examination before the Justices, shall be forever discharged of the crime. The clerk of the peace, when the Justices of his county shall have determined that a prisoner ought to be tried in the General Court, shall deliver subpœnas for summoning his witnesses, to him, or any person on his behalf, requiring them, returnable at the same time as the witnesses for the commonwealth shall be bound to appear; which subpœnas the officers to whom they shall be directed shall obey; and the clerk of the General Court shall cause subpœnas, for the same purpose, and at the like request, to be delivered to the prisoner, or his agent; and the witnesses for the prisoner shall be examined, upon oath, in the same manner as other witnesses. The keeper of the public jail, by warrant of any two Justices of his county, may impress so many men to attend him for the safe-guard of prisoners in his custody, and during such time as shall be mentioned in the warrant, so as no one of them be compelled to attend more than one day in a week; the charge whereof shall be defrayed by the public. In a presentment to the county court, if the penalty of the offence exceed not thirty shillings, or three hundred pounds of tobacco, or, to the General Court, if the penalty exceed not five pounds of current money, or one thousand pounds of tobacco, no information thereupon shall be filed, but a summons shall be issued against the defendant to answer the presentment, and, such summons having been served upon him, or a copy thereof having been left at the place of his usual abode, where the prosecution shall be in the county court, at least ten days before the return day, if he do not appear, judgment shall be entered against him for the penalty; and if he do appear, the court shall, in a summary way, without a jury, hear and determine the matter of the presentment, in the form in which it shall have been made, and give judgment thereupon, according to law, and the very right of the cause, disregarding any exception that may or might be taken to the form of the presentment. Execution of a sentence of death shall not be done in less time than thirty days after judgment shall have been given against the prisoner. All such expences as shall be incurred by the apprehension, committment, examination, and removal of offenders, triable in the General Court only, shall be defrayed by the county wherein the matter shall have been transacted, and reimbursed by the public. The clerk of the General Court shall enter in books, to be kept for that particular purpose, the names of jurors, attending for the trials of prisoners, and the names of witnesses, appearing on behalf of the commonwealth, against them, with accounts of the days they shall have attended, and certify such entries to the Board of Auditors.

Report, p. 75-7. MS (ViU); clerk's copy. Text of Act as adopted in 1786 is in Hening, XII, 340-4.

Bill presented by Madison 31 Oct. 1785, read twice, and on 14 Dec. postponed to next session; it was brought up again on 1 Nov., passed by the House on 27 Nov., amended by the Senate, and on 19 Dec. the Senate amendments were agreed to by the House (JHD, Oct. 1785, 1828 edn., p. 12-15, 92; same, Oct. 1786, p. 62, 102, 107, 150). Except as noted below, the text of the Act as adopted agrees with that of the Bill as proposed by the Committee of Revisors. Enforcement of Act was suspended until 1 July 1787 (Hening, XII, 410-11).

[1] The Act adds here and at other corresponding points in the text: "or corporation."

[2] The Act reads "sheriff" for "constable" at this and corresponding points in the text.

[3] Instead of the words "to be by him . . . to constable" the Act has the following: "to be by him conveyed to the county or corporation where the offence was committed."

[4] The Act includes at this point a clause allowing the sheriff "the same fee per mile for such service as is allowed to sheriffs for removing criminals from a county to the public jail, to be levied and paid by the county wherein the service was performed, and repaid by the public."

[5] The Act adds the following at this point: "being freeholders within this commonwealth."

[6] The Act reads: "not forthcoming"; MS (ViU) agrees with *Report* in giving the correct reading.

[7] The word "conveniently" is not in the Act.

[8] This sentence is not in the Act.

104. A Bill Directing the Method of Trying Slaves Charged with Treason or Felony

Be it enacted by the General Assembly, that the Justices of every county shall be Justices of Oyer and Terminer, for trying slaves charged with treason or felony: Which trials shall be by five at the least, without juries, upon legal evidence, at such times as the sheriffs shall appoint, not being less than five, nor more than ten, days after the offenders shall have been committed to jail. No slave shall be condemned in any such case, unless three-fourths, or more, of the Justices[1] sitting upon his or her trial, shall agree in opinion, that the prisoner is guilty.[2] The value of a slave condemned to die, who shall suffer accordingly; or before execution of the sentence perish, to be estimated by the Justices triers, shall be paid by the public to the owner. One being detained in slavery, and having commenced an action to assert his freedom, shall be prosecuted and tried for any such crime, in the same manner as a freeman ought to be prosecuted and tried.[3]

Report, p. 77. MS (ViU); clerk's copy. Text of Act as adopted in 1786 is in Hening, XII, 345.

Bill presented by Madison 31 Oct. 1785, read twice, and postponed to Oct. 1786 session; brought up again 1 Nov. 1786, amended and passed by the House 30 Nov., and approved by the Senate 2 Dec. (JHD, Oct. 1785, 1828 edn., p. 12-15, 92; same, Oct. 1786, p. 16-17, 55, 67, 82, 127). The Act as adopted agrees with the Bill as proposed except for the important differences indicated below. Enforcement of Act was suspended until 1 July 1787 (Hening, XII, 410-11).

1 Instead of the words "unless three-fourths, or more" the Act reads "unless all."

2 The Act has the following additional clause at this point: "*Provided always*, That when judgment of death shall be passed upon any such offender there shall be thirty days at least between the time of passing judgment and the day of execution, except in cases of conspiracy, insurrection, or rebellion." This, of course, merely extended to slaves the same provision accorded free persons convicted of treason or felony, though, of course, the corresponding section of Bill No. 103 had no such exception for cases of conspiracy, &c.

3 The Act has the following additional clause at this point: "No person having interest in a slave shall sit upon the trial of such slave."

105. A Bill for Reforming the Method of Proceeding in Writs of Right

Be it enacted by the General Assembly, that, for trial of disputed titles to lands in a more simple mode than that which hath most commonly been used of late, the claimant or demandant of an estate in fee simple may sue forth, against the possessor or tenant, a writ of praecipe quod reddat; which issuing from the General Court, shall be in this form, or to this effect: "The commonwealth of Virginia to the sheriff of E, greeting. Command C D, that he, justly, and without delay, render unto A B, tenement containing of land, with the appurtenances in the hundred of [1] in the county of E, which he claimeth to be his right, and whereof he complaineth, that the aforesaid C D doth withhold the possession. And unless he shall do so, then summon the said C D, that he appear before the Justices of our General Court, at on the day of the next court, to shew wherefore he hath not done it. And have you there then this writ. Witness Chief Justice of our said court, at the day of in the year ." And issuing from the court of a county, city, or borough, in the like form with necessary alterations; and shall be directed to the sheriff of that county, or to the proper officer of that city, or borough, wherein the tenant resideth, or that wherein was his last place of abode. Upon which writ the count[2] shall be in this form, or to this effect: "E to wit: A B, by F G, his Attorney, demands against C D tenement, containing of land, with the appurtenances, in the hundred of [1] in the county of E, and bounded by . And whereupon the said A B saith that he hath right to have the tenement aforesaid, with the appurtenances, and offereth proof, that such is his right."

If several tenements be demanded in the same count, the contents, situations, and boundaries, of each shall be inserted therein. To which count the tenant may plead in this form, or to this effect: "And the aforesaid C D, by H I, his Attorney, cometh, and defendeth the right of the said A B, when and where it behoveth him, and all that concerneth it, and whatsoever he ought to defend, and chiefly the tenement aforesaid, with the appurtenances, as of right namely tenement containing of land in the hundred of [1] in the county of E, and bounded by and putteth himself upon the assize, and prayeth recognition to be made, whether he hath greater right to hold the tenement aforesaid, with the appurtenances, as he now holdeth it [or them][3] or the said A B to have it as he now demandeth it [or them]." And to such plea the replication shall be in this form, or to this effect: "And the aforesaid A B, in like manner, putteth himself upon the assise, and prayeth recognition to be made, whether he hath greater right to hold the tenement aforesaid, as he demandeth, or the said C D as he holdeth it [or them]." Whereupon twelve good and lawful men, qualified as jurors are required to be, shall be elected, tried, and charged, as the manner is, to make recognition of the assize; which charge shall be in this form, or to this effect: "You shall say the truth, whether C D hath more right to hold the tenement, which A B demandeth against him, by his writ of right, or A B to have it [or them] as he demandeth." And at the trial, any matter may be given in evidence, which might have been specially pleaded. And upon the verdict, or in the case of a demurrer, the like judgment shall be given, and upon such judgment the like execution awarded, as in case of a writ of right; and the party, for whom judgment shall be given, shall recover his costs of suit; and the demandant, if he recover his seisin, may also recover damages to be assessed by the recognitors of assize, for the tenant's withholding possession of the tenement demanded. Where the praecipe quod reddat shall issue from the General Court, if return thereof be made, that the tenant is not found in the bailiwick of the officer, to whom it was directed, the demandant may sue forth a writ of exigi facias in this form, or to this effect: "The commonwealth of Virginia to the sheriff of E, greeting. We command you, that you cause C D to be required, from county court to county court, until five courts be passed, if he doth not appear; and if he doth appear, then summon him, that he be before the Justices of our General Court, at on the day of the next court, to shew wherefore he hath not rendered unto A B tenement, containing of land, with the appurtenances, in the hundred of [1] in the county of E. And have you there then this writ. Witness Chief Justice of our said court, at the day of in the year ." And when the residence, or last place of abode of the tenant, shall be out of the county, in which the land demanded lieth, a like writ of exigi facias shall also be directed to the sheriff of the latter county, and, in either case, a copy of such writ shall, within four weeks after the teste thereof, be printed in the Virginia Gazette; and the said writ or writs of exigi facias being returned in due form, and being printed as aforesaid, if the tenant shall not appear at the court to which the same is or are returnable, judgment shall be entered, that the demandant recover his seisin against the tenant. Where the praecipe quod reddat shall issue from the court of a county, city, or borough, if return thereof be made, that the tenant is not found in the bailiwick of the officer to whom it was directed, the demandant may sue forth a new praecipe every court, for five courts following, successively, if the tenant be not by one or other of them before summoned; and when the residence or last place of abode of the tenant shall be out of the county, city, or borough, in which the land demanded lieth, a testatum praecipe shall also be directed to the sheriff, or proper officer, of the latter county, city, or borough; and in either case a copy of the first of the said five praecipes shall, within four weeks after the teste thereof, be printed in the Virginia Gazette, and a copy of that, and of every other of them, shall, within fourteen days after the teste of each, be set up at the door of his court-house by the officer to whom it shall be directed, and who, by an endorsement on such writ, shall be required by the clerk to do so, and return of the said five writs being made, that the tenant is not found in the bailiwick or bailiwicks of the officer or officers, to whom they were directed, and that they had been set up as is before directed, and the first of them being printed as aforesaid, if the tenant shall not appear at the court, to which some one of the said writs was returnable, judgment shall be entered, that the demandant recover his seisin against the tenant; but if the tenant against whom, without having appeared, or without having been summoned, any such judgment shall be rendered, shall be out of Virginia, at the time of the suit brought, the judgment shall be no bar to an action commenced by him, or any claiming under him, to be restored to the land recovered, within a year and a day after he or they shall come into the country, or, remaining out of it, within seven years after the judgment; in which action, or in a separate one, damages may also be recovered. If the tenant, whether summoned or not, shall appear, and afterwards make default, judgment shall be entered against him; and if, having been summoned, he shall not appear, the court shall make an order, that, unless he appear at the then next court, or see judgment shall be entered against him, which shall be entered accordingly, if a copy of that order, being delivered to him, or left at the place of his usual abode, fifteen days, or more, before such next court, and affidavit thereof being made, he shall not then appear. If the demandant or tenant, against whom any such judgment shall be rendered, at the time of the suit brought, shall be an infant, a married woman, or a person of unsound mind, the judgment shall be no bar to another action, commenced within five years after attainment of full age, discoverture, or recovery of understanding, or within the same time after the death of such privileged person.

Report, p. 77-8. MS (ViU); clerk's copy. Text of Act as adopted in 1786 is in Hening, XII, 345-9.

Bill presented by Madison 31 Oct. 1785, read twice, and, after being several times put on the calendar for debate, it was killed by being postponed to 31 Mch. 1786. Nevertheless, Madison brought it up again at the Oct. 1786 session. It was amended and passed by the House on 24 Nov. and approved by the Senate 2 Dec. (JHD, Oct. 1785, 1828 edn., p. 12-15, 93, 94, 101; same, Oct. 1786, p. 16-17, 55, 57, 82, 127). The Act as adopted agrees with the Bill as submitted by the Committee of Revisors except as indicated below. Enforcement of Act was suspended until 1 July 1787 (Hening, XII, 410-11).

1 The words "in the hundred of," followed by a blank space, are not in the Act.

2 The Act, incorrectly, reads: "court" for "count."

3 Square brackets are in Bill here and elsewhere.

106. A Bill concerning Partitions and Joint Rights and Obligations

Be it enacted by the General Assembly, that all joint tenants or tenants in common who now are, or hereafter shall be of any estates of inheritance in their own rights, or in the right of their wives, and all joint tenants or tenants in common who now hold, or hereafter shall hold, jointly, or in common, for term of life or years, [and joint tenants, or tenants in common, where one or some of them have, or shall have estates for term of life or years,][1] with others who have, or shall have estates of inheritance, or freehold in any lands, tenements or hereditaments, may be compelled to make partition between them, of such lands, tenements, and hereditaments, as they now hold, or hereafter shall hold, as joint tenants, or tenants in common, by writs de partitione facienda, the forms whereof shall be devised in the General Court and adapted to the cases aforesaid. But no such partitions between joint tenants, or tenants in common, who hold, or shall hold, estates for term of life or years, with others holding equal or greater estates, shall be prejudicial to any intitled to the reversions or remainders after the death of the tenants for life, or after the expiration of the years. If partition be not made between joint tenants, whether they be such as might have been compelled to make partition, or not, or of whatever kind the estates or thing holden or possessed, be the parts of those who die first, shall not accrue to the survivors, but shall descend or pass by devise and shall be subject to debts, charges, curtesy, or dower, or transmissible to executors or administrators, and be considered to every other intent and purpose, in the same manner, as if such deceased joint tenants had been tenants in common. The representatives of one jointly bound with another for payment of a debt, or for performance, or forbearance of any act, or for any other thing, and dying in the lifetime of the latter, may be charged, by virtue of such obligation, in the same manner as such representatives might have been charged if the obligors had been bound severally as well as jointly. Partition may be demanded by one and the same writ, of all the several parcels of land, or other real estate to which the parties have title, and execution thereupon done by the sheriff and jury, as heretofore, or by special commissioners to be appointed by the court, with assent of the parties by allotment to each party of part in each parcel, or of parts in one or more parcels, or of one or more individual parcels, with or without the addition of a part or parts of other parcels as shall be most for the interest of the parties in general. No plea in abatement shall be received in any suit for partition, nor shall it abate by the death of any tenant. After a writ of partition returned, affidavit being made by some credible person, that due notice of the writ had been given to the tenant or tenants to the action, and that a copy thereof had been left with him, her, or them, if he, she, or they could be found, or if not, that such notice had been given to, and copy left with the wife, son or daughter being of the age of twenty one years, or upwards, and at the usual place of abode of such as could not be found, or the person in actual possession not being the demandant of the lands whereof partition is demanded, twenty days or more before the day of return, if the tenant or tenants shall not cause an appearance to be entered, at the time by law appointed, or within one month thereafter, the demandant having filed his, or her declaration, the court may proceed to examine his or her title, and the quantity demanded, and shall give judgment, by default, for so much as he or she shall appear to them to have a right to, and award a writ to make partition, which being executed after eight days notice given to the persons mentioned before, judgment final shall thereupon be given, which shall be as binding as if it had been given after an appearance; and upon a trial, unless any tenant within one year after the first judgment, or being an infant, a married woman, of unsound mind, or out of Virginia, within one year after attainment of full age, death of the husband, recovery of understanding, or return to the country, respectively, by motion to the court, either admitting the demandant's right and purpart, shall shew inequality in the partition, in which case the court may award a new partition to be made, and that in presence of all the parties if they choose to attend it; and the second partition shall be as binding as if the tenant had appeared and pleaded in the first instance, or else shall shew sufficient matter in bar of the partition, or that the demandant hath not title to so much as he or she hath recovered, in which case the court may suspend, or set aside the judgment, and admit the tenant to appear and plead, and the cause shall proceed as if no judgment had been given; and if upon the trial thereof the court shall give the same judgment as the first, it shall stand confirmed, and the person or persons in whose behalf the motion was made, shall be awarded to pay costs. The under sheriff, when the high sheriff cannot conveniently attend, may, in presence of two Justices of the Peace, proceed to the execution of a judgment in partition, by inquisition in due form of law, and the high sheriff shall make the same return as if he had acted in person. They who were tenants of the messuages, lands, tenements, and hereditaments, or any part thereof, before they were divided, shall hold the same of the landlords, to whom they shall be allotted by the partition in severalty, under the same conditions, rents, covenants and reservations, and the landlords shall warrant the several parts unto the tenants as they were bound to do by leases or grants, respectively: And any demandant who was tenant, in actual possession, to the tenant to the action for his purpart of the messuages, lands, tenements and hereditaments, divided by virtue of a writ of partition or any part thereof, shall hold it for the same term, and under the same conditions and covenants when it shall be allotted in severalty.

Report, p. 78-9. MS (ViU); clerk's copy. Text of Act as adopted is in Hening, XII, 349-52.

Bill was presented by Madison on 31 Oct. 1785, postponed 14 Dec. to next session, brought up again at Oct. 1786 session, amended, and passed on 28 Nov. (JHD, Oct. 1785, 1828 edn., p. 12-15, 92; same, Oct. 1786, p. 16-17, 55, 60, 65, 127). Act as adopted and Bill as proposed by Committee of Revisors agree except as noted below; Act was suspended until 1 July 1787 (Hening, XII, 410-11).

[1] The words in square brackets (supplied) are not in the Act as adopted.

107. A Bill for the Speedy Determination of Suits Wherein Foreigners Are Parties

Be it enacted by the General Assembly, that a suit, commenced in the High Court of Chancery, or General Court, by or against a party, who is no citizen of the commonwealth, shall be heard or tried in the term to which the process shall be returned, regularly executed, or so soon afterwards as may be; and, to this end, subsequent process to compel appearance may be returnable to any day of a term, and rules to bring the matter in dispute to speedy issue may be given to expire at any shorter time than what is prescribed in ordinary cases. If such suit be commenced in the court of a county, city, or borough, it may without any other reason, on the motion or petition of either party, be removed by writ of certiorari; and the hearing or trial thereof shall be accelerated by like means as if it had originated in the court to which it shall be removed. And the Court of Appeals, High Court of Chancery, or General Court, shall determine every such suit brought before them by writ of error or appeal, with all the expedition which the necessary forms of their proceedings will allow.

Report, p. 79. MS (ViU); clerk's copy. Bill presented by Madison 31 Oct. 1785, postponed 14 Dec. to next session, brought up again at the Oct. 1786 session, and referred to committee of the whole; apparently no further action was taken on it (JHD, Oct. 1785, 1828 edn., p. 12-15, 92; same, Oct. 1786, p. 16-17).

108. A Bill for Speedy Recovery of Money Due from Certain Persons to the Public

Be it enacted by the General Assembly, that when any person, who hath received or shall receive public money from the Treasurer, for recruiting or paying the army, building, rigging, or furnishing ships or vessels of war, erecting fortifications, buying clothes, provision, arms, or ammunition, erecting or prosecuting public manufactories, or for other public use, hath not applied, or shall not apply the said money accordingly, or hath neglected, or shall neglect to account for and repay so much thereof as shall remain unapplied, upon a motion on behalf of the commonwealth, made to any Court of Record, notice thereof in writing having been given days,[1] or more, to the delinquent, with a state of the matter alledged against him, either by delivering copies of such notice and allegation to him, or leaving them at the place of his usual abode, the said court may give judgment, and award execution against him and his sureties, for so much, as a jury, to be empannelled instantly, unless good cause be shewn for deferring it, for trial of an issue, if he appear, and make it up, or for enquiry of damages, if he appear not, or appearing refuse to make up such issue, shall find to be due from him, on any such account as aforesaid, with damages to be assessed by the jury, and costs. When the Attorney, prosecuting on behalf of the commonwealth, shall commence an action for breach of a contract, which hath been or shall be entered into with government, or with an agent thereof, to supply the army or navy with provision or other articles, at the emanation of the writ, he shall file a declaration, with an assignment of the breaches, which, with the writ, shall be delivered to the officer, to whom that is directed, and served upon the defendant days,[2] or more, before the return day; and on such return day, or on the return day of the subsequent process, in case the preceeding be not legally served, if the defendant appear, and make up an issue, or if he appear not, or appearing refuse to make up such issue, a jury shall be empannelled instantly, unless good cause be shewn for deferring it, to try the issue, or enquire of the damages. And, in like cases, the agents or contractors of the confederating states of America may, by the like remedy, on behalf and in the name of the said states, recover money due to them.

Report, p. 79. MS (ViU); clerk's copy. Text of Act as adopted is in Hening, XII, 352-3.

Bill was presented by Madison 31 Oct. 1785, postponed 14 Dec. to next session, brought up again 1 Nov. 1786, amended by the House, and passed on 28 Nov. (JHD, Oct. 1785, 1828 edn., p. 12-15, 92; same, Oct. 1786, p. 16-17, 55, 60, 65, 127). Act as adopted and Bill as proposed by Committee of Revisors agree except as noted below; Act was suspended until 1 July 1787 (Hening, XII, 410-11).

1 The Act reads: "ten days."

2 The Act reads: "fifteen days."

109. A Bill for Recovering Demands of Small Value in a Summary Way

Be it enacted by the General Assembly, that any debt, or penalty, amounting to more than twenty five shillings, or two hundred pounds of tobacco, and not exceeding one hundred shillings, or eight hundred pounds of tobacco, may be demanded, by petition, to the court of a county, city, or borough. The clerk of the peace shall draw the petition, stating therein how the debt became due, or by breach of what act of General Assembly the penalty was incurred, and shall issue a summons, directed to the sheriff, or other proper officer, commanding him to summon the defendant to appear and answer the petition; and the defendant, being summoned, ten days at least before the return day, and being at the same time served with a copy of the petition, together with a copy of the account, which shall be filed, when the debt shall have arisen by account, the court, if both parties waive the trial by jury,[1] shall and may hear and determine the matter in dispute, in a summary way, and give such judgment as shall appear to be just. And any person may, by petition to be served and tried, in like manner, demand and recover goods detained, or the value of them, and damages for the detention, or damages for goods found by the defendant, and converted to his use, where the goods, with the damages, are not of greater value than one hundred shillings, or eight hundred pounds of tobacco. And whosoever shall bring any other action than a petition, if it appear, either of his own shewing in the declaration, or by the verdict of the jury, that he might have brought a petition, by this act, shall be non-suit.

Report, p. 79. MS (ViU); clerk's copy. Text of the Act as adopted is in Hening, XII, 353-4.

Bill was presented by Madison 31 Oct. 1785, postponed 14 Dec. to next session, brought up again 1 Nov. 1786, amended by the House, and passed 28 Nov. (JHD, Oct. 1785, 1828 edn., p. 12-15, 92; same,

Oct. 1786, p. 16-17, 55, 59, 65, 127). Act as adopted and Bill as proposed by Committee of Revisors agree except as noted below; Act was suspended until 1 July 1787 (Hening, XII, 410-11).

[1] The preceding eight words are not in the Act.

110. A Bill Providing That Actions Popular, Prosecuted by Collusion, Shall Be No Bar to Those Which Be Pursued with Good Faith

Be it enacted by the General Assembly, that if any person hereafter sue with good faith, any action popular, and any defendant, in the same action, plead any manner of recovery by action popular, in bar of the said action, or that he before that time barred any plaintiff in any such action popular, then the plaintiff in the action taken with good faith may aver, that the said recovery in the said action popular was had by covin, or else may aver that the said plaintiff was barred in the said action popular by covin: Then if after the said collusion or covin, so averred, be lawfully found, the plaintiff in that action sued with good faith, shall have recovery according to the nature of the action and execution upon the same, in like wise and effect as though no such afore had been had. Provided alway, that no plaintiff be in any wise received to aver any covin, in any action popular, where the point of the same action, or else the covin or collusion shall have been once tried, or lawfully found with the plaintiff or against him by trial of twelve men and not otherwise.

If the prosecutor of an action, or information, for the recovery of any penalty, not wholly appropriated to the use of such proprietor, shall compound with the offender, or direct such suit or information to be discontinued, unless it be by leave of the court wherein the said suit or information shall be depending, such prosecutor shall be liable for so much of the penalty, to the commonwealth or any other, as they would have been intitled to if the defendant had been convicted.

Report, p. 80. Text of Act as adopted is in Hening, XII, 354-5.

Bill presented by Madison 31 Oct. 1785, postponed 14 Dec. to next session, brought up again 1 Nov. 1786, and passed 28 Nov. (JHD, Oct. 1785, 1828 edn., p. 12-15, 92; same, Oct. 1786, p. 16-17, 55, 57, 65, 127). Text of the Act as adopted and Bill as proposed by Committee of Revisors are the same; Act was suspended until 1 July 1787 (Hening, XII, 410-11).

111. A Bill for Preventing Vexatious and Malicious Prosecutions and Moderating Amercements

Be it enacted by the General Assembly, that every action at common law, or suit in equity, commenced in the name of a person not residing in Virginia, unless he be employed abroad in the service of the commonwealth, or of the United States of America, shall be dismissed, if security be not given with the clerk of the court from whence the process shall issue, or wherein it shall be depending, within sixty days after notice, shall, at any time during such non residence have been given to the demandant, or plaintiff, or his attorney, by some person interested, that such security is required, for payment of the costs and damages which may be awarded to the tenant or defendant, and also of the fees which will become due to the officers of the court. No information for a trespass, or misdemeanor, shall be filed in any court but by express order of the court, entered on record, nor unless the party supposed to be culpable shall have failed to appear, and shew good cause to the contrary, having been required so to do by a summons appointing a convenient time for that purpose, served upon him, or left at his usual place of abode; and the name and sur-name of the prosecutor, and the town or county, in which he shall reside, with his title or profession shall be written at the foot of the information, before it be filed, and of every bill of indictment for any trespass, or misdemeanor, before it be presented to the grand jury; and if the defendant shall appear to shew cause against filing the information, or to answer the information or indictment, and the prosecutor shall not proceed further, or if the defendant shall be found not guilty by the petit jury, or a judgment shall be given for him he shall recover his costs against the prosecutor with an attorney's fee, if one was employed, and the allowances to witnesses to be taxed in the bill of costs, and may have execution for them, as the manner is in civil cases. And in every such information or indictment, the amercement which ought to be according to the degree of the fault and saving to the offender his contenement shall be assessed by twelve honest and lawful men either those by whom the offender shall have been convicted in case of a verdict, or those who shall be empannelled for that special purpose, where judgment shall be given against him upon the argument of a demurrer or by his confession or default. No escheator, sheriff, coroner or other inquisitor, shall hereafter have power of amercement, for default of common summons, save only the Judges of the General Court.[1]

Report, p. 80. MS (ViU); clerk's copy. Text of Act as adopted is in Hening, XII, 355-6.

Bill presented by Madison 31 Oct. 1785, postponed 14 Dec. to next session, brought up again 1 Nov. 1786, amended by both houses, and passed on 29 Nov. (JHD, Oct. 1785, 1828 edn., p. 12-15, 92; same, Oct. 1786, p. 16-17, 55, 60, 65, 66, 127). Text of Act as adopted and Bill as proposed by Committee of Revisors agree except as noted below; Act was suspended until 1 July 1787 (Hening, XII, 410-11).

[1] The Act adds the following: "or the respective county or corporation courts."

112. A Bill Providing a Means to Help and Speed Poor Persons in Their Suits

Where it is intended that indifferent justice shall be had and administered to all the citizens of this commonwealth, as well to the poor as rich, which poor citizens be not of ability, nor power, to sue according to the laws of this land for redress of injuries and wrongs to them daily done, as well concerning their persons and their inheritance, as other causes; For remedy whereof, in behalf of the poor persons of this land not able to sue for their remedy after the course of the law, Be it enacted by the General Assembly, that every poor person which shall have cause of action against any person within this commonwealth, shall have, by the discretion of the court before whom he would sue, writ or writs original, and writs of subpœna, according to the nature of his cause, nothing paying for the same: And that the said court shall direct their clerk to issue the necessary process, shall assign to him counsel learned in the laws, and appoint all other officers requisite and necessary to be had for the speed of the said suit to be had and made, who shall do their duties without any reward for their counsels, help and business in the same.

Report, p. 80. Text of Act as adopted is in Hening, XII, 356-7.

Bill presented by Madison 31 Oct. 1785, postponed 14 Dec. to next session, brought up again 1 Nov. 1786, and passed 7 Dec. (JHD, Oct. 1785, 1828 edn., p. 12-15, 92; same, Oct. 1786, p. 16-17, 55, 57, 92, 127). Text of Act as adopted and Bill as proposed by Committee of Revisors are identical; Act was suspended until 1 July 1787 (Hening, XII, 410-11).

113. A Bill Providing that an Infant May Sue by His Next Friend

In every case where such as be within age may sue, it is enacted by the General Assembly, that their next friends shall be admitted to sue for them.

Report, p. 80. Text as adopted is in Hening, XII, 357.

Bill presented by Madison 31 Oct. 1785, postponed to next session, brought up again 1 Nov. 1786, and passed 28 Nov. (JHD, Oct. 1785, 1828 edn., p. 12-15, 92; same, Oct. 1786, p. 16-17, 55, 57, 65, 127). Act as adopted and Bill as proposed are identical; Act was suspended until 1 July 1787 (Hening, XII, 410-11).

114. A Bill Declaring When the Death of Persons Absenting Themselves Shall be Presumed

Be it enacted by the General Assembly, that any person absenting himself beyond sea, or elsewhere, for seven years successively, shall be presumed to be dead, in any case wherein his death shall come in question, unless proof be made that he was alive within that time. But an estate recovered in any such case, if in a subsequent action or suit the person presumed to be dead shall be proved to be living, shall be restored to him who shall have been evicted; and he may moreover demand and recover the rents and profits of the estate, during such time as he shall have been deprived thereof, with lawful interest.

Report, p. 81. MS (ViU); clerk's copy. Text of Act as adopted is in Hening, XII, 357-8.

Bill presented by Madison 31 Oct. 1785, postponed 14 Dec. to next session, brought up again 1 Nov. 1786, and passed without alteration 1 Dec. (JHD, Oct. 1785, 1828 edn., p. 12-15, 92; same, Oct. 1786, p. 16-17, 61, 65, 71, 127). The Act was suspended until 1 July 1787 (Hening, XII, 410-11).

115. A Bill Prescribing a Method of Protesting Inland Bills of Exchange and Allowing Assignees of Obligations to Bring Actions Thereupon in Their Own Names

Be it enacted by the General Assembly, that if a bill of exchange, for the sum of five pounds, or upwards, dated at any place in Virginia, drawn upon a person at any other place therein expressed, to be for value received, and payable at a certain number of days, weeks, or months after date, being presented to the person upon whom it shall be drawn, shall not be accepted by subscribing his name, with his proper hand to the acceptance, written at the foot, or on the back of the bill, or being accepted in that manner, and not otherwise, shall not be paid before the expiration of three days after it shall become due to the person to whom it shall be payable or his agent, or assigns may cause the bill to be protested by a Notary Public, or if there be no such, by any other person in presence of two or more credible witnesses, for non-acceptance, in the form or to the effect following, written under a fair copy of the bill: "Know all men that I on the day of at the usual place of abode of the above named presented to him the bill of which the above is a copy, and which the said did not accept, wherefore I the said do hereby protest the said bill. Dated at this day of ," or for non-payment after acceptance, in the same form or to the same effect, except that the words "presented to him the bill of which the above is a copy, and which the said did not accept," shall be left out, and instead of them the words, "demanded payment of the bill of which the above is a copy, and which the said did not pay," be inserted: And the drawer, such protest being sent to him, or notice thereof in writing being given to him, or left at the place of his usual abode, within fourteen days thereafter, shall pay the money mentioned in the bill to the person intitled to it, with interest, at the rate of five in the hundred,[1] by the year, from the day of the protest; and he to whom the bill shall be payable, neglecting to procure the protest to be made, or due notice thereof to be given, shall be liable for all costs and damages accruing thereby.

If the bill shall be lost, or shall miscarry, the drawer shall sign and deliver another of the same tenor, sufficient security being given to indemnify him against all persons who may claim under the former. An action of debt may be maintained upon a note or writing, by which the person signing the same shall promise or oblige himself to pay a sum of money or quantity of tobacco to another. Assignments of bonds, bills, and promissary notes, and other writings obligatory, for payment of money or tobacco shall be valid; and an assignee of any such may thereupon maintain an action of debt, in his own name, but shall allow all just discounts, not only against himself, but against the assignor before notice of the assignment was given to the defendant.

Report, p. 81. MS (ViU); clerk's copy. Text of Act as adopted is in Hening, XII, 358-9.

Bill presented 31 Oct. 1785, postponed 14 Dec. to next session, brought up again 1 Nov. 1786, amended by Senate but amendments rejected by House, and passed on 6 Dec. (JHD, Oct. 1785, 1828 edn., p. 12-15, 92; same, Oct. 1786, p. 16-17, 61, 65, 71, 85, 88, 127). Act as adopted agrees with Bill as proposed, except as noted below; Act was suspended until 1 July 1787 (Hening, XII, 410-11).

[1] The Act reads: "five per centum."

116. A Bill for Limitation of Actions

Be it enacted by the General Assembly, that no person shall maintain any action or suit for the recovery of lands or tenements, if such action or suit be not commenced within twenty years next after the cause thereof shall have arisen, unless the plaintiff or demandant, or the person from whom the right is derived were, at the time such cause of action or suit arose, under the age of twenty one years, or a married woman, or of unsound mind, or out of Virginia; in either of which cases the right shall not be barred during the infancy, coverture, insanity, or absence, but shall be barred, if the action or suit be not commenced within five years after the determination of that privilege. No person shall make an entry into lands or tenements, but within twenty years next after the right or title of such entry first descended or accrued, or within five years next after any infant, married woman, or person of unsound mind, or out of Virginia, to whom it so descended or accrued, shall attain full age, be discovert, recover understanding, come into the commonwealth, or die during such privilege; nor shall the operation of this act be hindered by any claim or entry, made within the said twenty or five years, unless an action upon such claim or entry shall be commenced within one year after making thereof; and prosecuted with effect. Actions of debt, grounded upon any lending or contract without specialty, and for arrearages of rent, and actions of trespass quare clausum fregit, of detinue, upon trover, of replevin for taking away goods, for account, and upon the case, other than such accounts as concern the trade of merchandize between merchant and merchant, or their factors, or servants, and suits in the Court of Admiralty for seamens wages, shall not be commenced but within five years, nor shall actions of trespass, or of assault, battery, wounding, or imprisonment, be commenced but within three years next after the causes of such actions or suits respectively shall have arisen; nor shall actions upon the case for words spoken be commenced, but within one year after the words shall have been spoken, or within the like time after the party injured, being under the age twenty one years, a married woman, or a person of unsound mind, or out of Virginia, shall attain full age, be discovert, recover understanding, or come into the country, or after the death of the party so privileged, in cases where the actions or suits may be maintained by executors or administrators. Where any action or suit, commenced within the time before limited for it, shall abate for any cause whatsoever, the plaintiff or demandant, or any person claiming under him, may, by writ of journeys accounts, sued within a year and a day after the abatement, continue the same action. In any of the forementioned actions, if a verdict be found for the plaintiff or demandant, and judgment thereupon be arrested, or if judgment be given for him and afterwards reversed, the plaintiff or demandant may commence a new action for the same cause, within one year and a day after the judgment shall have been arrested or reversed. No judgment at common law, sentence of the Court of Admiralty, or decree in equity, shall be reversed, unless the writ of error, appeal, or suit by bill of review for reversal, be commenced, and with effect prosecuted within five years after the judgment or decree entered of record, or sentence registered, or, if the party intitled to such writ of error, appeal, or bill of review, be under the age of twenty one years, or be a married woman, or of unsound mind, or out of Virginia, at the time of entering the judgment or decree, or registering the sentence, within the same time after he or she shall attain full age, be discovert, recover understanding, or come into the country. Where any person shall be bound by record or specialty, as surety for another, unless it be for the discharge of his duty as executor, administrator, or guardian, or public officer, if no suit be commenced within seven years from the time of his becoming bound, such surety shall be discharged; and every surety, already so bound, shall be discharged, if suit be not commenced within seven years after passing this act. Every prosecution, under a penal act of General Assembly, shall be commenced within two years, if the penalty be wholly appropriated to the use of the commonwealth, and if appropriated to the informer alone, or to the commonwealth and informer, within one year after the penalty incurred. If any person, against whom another shall have cause of action, shall be out of Virginia, or shall abscond, so that he cannot be served with process, the time he shall be so absent, or abscond, shall not be accounted any part of the time of limitation within this act. The four years next after the twelfth day of April, in the year one thousand seven hundred and seventy four, shall not be accounted any part of the time of limitation within this act.

Report, p. 81-2. MS (ViU); clerk's copy.

Bill presented by Madison 31 Oct. 1785, postponed 14 Dec. to next session, and brought up again 1 Nov. 1786; apparently no further action was taken on it (JHD, Oct. 1785, 1828 edn., p. 12-15, 92; same, Oct. 1786, p. 16-17). See the 1776 Act to restrain the operations of the acts for limitation of actions and recording deeds in certain cases, and also its reviving Act of 1777 (Hening, IX, 214-15, 430). With the closing of many of the courts and the expiration of the Act regulating fees on 12 Apr. 1774, deeds for lands, slaves, and other property, which were required to be recorded within a limited period of time, could not be recorded in accordance with this requirement; hence the need for these Acts of 1776 and 1777 to protect those who, "through ignorance or mistake," failed to take out new deeds or were prevented from doing so by the death, refusal, or removal from Virginia of those making the deeds. The period of time excepted by the Act of 1777 in the computation of time for the limitation of actions was not thought to be "sufficiently extended to relieve all those who may justly claim relief" and an Act for this purpose was passed in May 1783 (Hening, XI, 590-1); this Act, which under sufficient proof validated any deed executed after 10 Apr. 1771, was found to occasion "too great and injurious a change in the rules of evidence and the computation of time for the probation of deeds" and was accordingly repealed (same, p. 430).

117. A Bill for Granting Attachments against the Estates of Debtors Removing Privately or Absconding

Be it enacted by the General Assembly, that when any person shall privately remove out of the county he had resided in, or shall abscond so that he cannot be served with process, a Justice of the Peace of the same county, at the request of any to whom he who shall so remove or abscond is indebted, shall and may, by his precept, returnable to his next county court, command the sheriff to attach the goods of the debtor, or so much thereof as shall be sufficient to satisfy the debt demanded and costs, and also to summon any persons, named by the creditor, to appear at the said next court, before the Justices thereof, and render accounts of money, or other things, they owe or have in their hands or power, belonging to the debtor; the said Justice first taking bond of the creditor, with sufficient surety, in a penalty, double the value the debt demanded, payable to the debtor, with condition for the payment of all such costs and damages as shall be awarded to the debtor; which bond shall be at the next court filed with the clerk thereof, to be delivered to the debtor when he shall require it. Goods so attached, shall be replevied, if the debtor, or another for him, shall give bond with sufficient surety, to the sheriff, for appearance of the debtor at the said next court; which bond shall be returned, with the attachment, or, if the debtor shall appear at such next court, and give special bail, the court ruling him so to do. The creditor, at the return of the attachment, shall file his declaration, and thereupon like proceedings shall be in the cause, and, if bond be given for appearance of the defendant, the sheriff or surety shall be subject to like judgment, and be intitled to like relief, as if the defendant had been arrested in an ordinary action. Every garnishee may be compelled to render to the court an account, upon oath, which account shall be entered of record, of all money or goods from him due, or in his hands or power, belonging to the defendant, at the time such garnishee was summoned, and to deliver such goods to the sheriff. If the goods attached be not replevied, and judgment be given for the plaintiff, the said goods, as well as those delivered by the garnishees, shall be sold by the sheriff, in the same manner as goods taken by virtue of a writ of fieri facias, and the proceeds of the sale shall be applied towards satisfying the judgment; and if they be not sufficient, the court shall order the money or goods due from the garnishees, or so much thereof as shall be sufficient, to be applied to the same purpose, which shall acquit the garnishees against the defendant of what they shall pay, by virtue of such order.

Report, p. 82. MS (ViU); clerk's copy. Bill presented by Madison 31 Oct. 1785, postponed 14 Dec. to next session, and brought up again 1 Nov. 1786; apparently no further action was taken on it (JHD, Oct. 1785, 1828 edn., p. 12-15, 92; same, Oct. 1786, p. 16-17).

118. A Bill concerning Inquests

Be it enacted by the General Assembly, that the sheriff of that county in which the General Court shall sit, shall, before every term, summon twenty four good and lawful men, being freeholders in the commonwealth, which he shall have power to do, not only in his own county, but in all places out of it, within the distance of thirty miles from that in which the court shall be held, to appear before the Judges of the said court, on the first day of the said term; and the men so summoned, or any sixteen of them who appear, shall be a grand jury for the body of the commonwealth, and shall have power to enquire of and present all treasons, felonies, and misdemeanors, and other offences whereof that court hath jurisdiction, so that a presentment or indictment by them of an offence committed, in any county, shall be as legal as a presentment or indictment by a grand jury of that particular county could have been. Before each session to be held for every county in the months of February, May, August and November, the sheriff shall summon twenty four good and lawful men of his county, being freeholders therein, and not being owners of, or interested in water-mills, surveyors of highways, ordinary keepers, or constables, to appear before the Justices of the said county at such sessions, and the men so summoned, or those who appear, if more than eight make default, together with so many others of the by-standers qualified in like manner, as will make the number sixteen, shall be a grand jury for the body of that county, and shall have power to enquire of and present all offences therein committed, and cognizable by the said county court. A grand jury shall make no presentment of their own knowledge, unless information of the fact be given by two or more of themselves; and when they make a presentment upon the information of others, they shall write the names of the informants under the presentment. If at any time between the swearing and discharging a grand jury any of them fail to attend the court when required, the others shall proceed to do the business if the number be sufficient, or if not, the court shall command the sheriff to name so many of the persons then present, and qualified to officiate, as with those attending shall make up sixteen, which persons so to be named, having heard the oath of the foreman read, and being sworn as the manner is, shall, to all intents and purposes, afterwards be deemed grand jury men, instead of the defaulters; and every one of such defaulters shall be fined so much money as the court shall judge he ought to forfeit, not exceeding one hundred pounds, unless good cause be shewn to the contrary. For trial of issues in fact, before the Court of Appeals, High Court of Chancery, General Court, Court of Admiralty, and court of every county, city, or borough, the sheriff or other proper officers attending such court, shall, when such Court of Appeals shall so direct, and every day during the term or session of such other court, summon a sufficient number of good and lawful men, qualified, and not privileged in manner herein after mentioned, as well of the bystanders, as of those he can meet with not more than the distance of half a mile from the court-house, to appear before the said court that day and serve as jurors, and juries shall be formed, as they shall be required, of the men so summoned and appearing to be called in the order their names shall stand on the panel, except in an extraordinary case directed by the court to be tried by a special jury, and such juries shall be deemed lawful juries, although they come not from the counties in which the venires shall be laid in the indictments, informations and declarations. Men aged above threescore years, or such as be continually languishing or sick shall not be put in juries, nor shall any without his consent be put in juries in the court of a county, city, or borough, who be not dwelling in such county, city, or borough, nor shall any be a juror on trial of an indictment of treason, felony, or misdemeanor, or in an action wherein the title or boundaries of land, or any franchise shall be in question, who is not a freeholder, nor in any other cause in the Court of Appeals, High Court of Chancery, General Court, or Court of Admiralty, unless he be possessed of a visible estate of the value of one hundred pounds, or in the court of a county, city, or borough, unless he be possessed of a visible estate of the value of fifty pounds. But in case that any indictment be made of felony or of trespass, and thereupon to try the truth thereof, an inquest or proof is to be taken, if one party or the other be strangers it shall be tried by strangers;

and if the one party be a citizen of the commonwealth and the other a stranger, one half of the inquest, or the proof, shall be of citizens and the other half of strangers; and in all manner of inquests and proofs which be to be taken, or made amongst strangers and citizens, the one half of the inquest or proof shall be citizens, and the other half strangers, if so many strangers and foreigners be in the town or place where such inquest or proof is to be taken that be not parties, nor with the parties in the contracts, pleas or other quarrels, whereof such inquest or proof ought to be taken; and if there be not so many strangers, then shall there be put in such inquests or proofs as many strangers as shall be found in the same towns or places, which be not thereto parties, nor with the parties as aforesaid, and the remnant of citizens which be good men, and not suspicious to the one party or the other, notwithstanding that the strangers be not freeholders, nor possessed of visible estates of the value of one hundred pounds or fifty pounds each; but if there be no strangers in the town or place where such inquest or proof is to be taken, then shall there be put in such inquest or proof all citizens. But no exception shall be made to a juror after the jury shall have been sworn. On inquests in the country, sheriffs and bailiffs shall put such as be freeholders of the county, next neighbours, most sufficient, and least suspicious, without denomination before made by any person of the names which by them should be empannelled on pain of being grievously amerced to the commonwealth, and jurors put on any of such inquests shall take nothing (on pain of being discharged from the inquest, and immediately imprisoned by the sheriff) either of meat or drink, from any party, after they shall be summoned, and before the inquest sealed, nor from any other person whatever after the time of coming to the place appointed for their meeting and before the inquest sealed, or before they shall be adjourned, if the business cannot be completed in one day, in which case they may be adjourned by the sheriff, from day to day until such completion. Every freeholder, summoned to serve on any jury, failing to appear, shall be fined four hundred pounds of tobacco to the use of the commonwealth, unless he shall shew good cause to the contrary, being served with a rule so to do. And every sheriff failing to do his duty in summoning a grand jury, shall be fined such sum of money as the court shall judge proper, not exceeding fifty pounds of current money, to the same use. To every juror summoned by virtue of a writ of venire facias, for trial of a prisoner, attending accordingly, the same shall be paid by the public as is paid to witnesses for travelling to and from the General Court, and attending there, with their ferriages. No writ of attaint shall be prosecuted against a jury by pretence of a false verdict: for misbehavior of a jury, as well as for other good cause the Judges who sit at the trial, upon a motion made the same term or session, may, at their discretion, upon such terms as to them shall seem equitable, set the verdict aside, and order a new trial in any case, except an indictment or information wherein the prisoner or defendant shall be acquitted of treason, felony or misdemeanor. If any jurors or juries, or other inquests, take any thing by themselves, or others, to give their verdict and thereof be convicted, such jurors shall not hereafter be put in assizes, juries or inquests, and shall pay each ten times so much as he shall have taken, whereof he that will sue shall have the one half, and the commonwealth the other half. And all the embracers that bring or procure such inquests in the country, to take gain or profit, shall be punished in the same manner and form as the jurors, and if the juror or embracer so convicted, hath not whereof to make satisfaction, in the manner aforesaid, he shall have imprisonment of one year. Also if any juror, after he shall have been sworn in any cause and before he be discharged shall suffer himself to be treated with meat or drink, by either party, or laboured with to give a verdict in favour of either party, otherwise than by the pleading and discussing of the cause in open court, he shall be punished by amercement and imprisonment at the discretion of a jury. Grand juries may be adjourned from day to day during the term or session, until they shall have finished their business. A petit jury in any case, unless it be an indictment of treason or felony, if they be not agreed on their verdict, at the time the court shall adjourn, on the last day of a term or session, shall be discharged of course, and a new trial shall be thereupon. In every case where by law the court is or shall be impowered to give judgment, on a motion against any sheriff, collector, or receiver of public or private money or tobacco, purchasers upon execution, or distress for rent, on bonds for prison rules, or to replevy estates taken in execution, or any other occasion, if the party against whom the motion is made, shall contest the demand, a jury, if he desire one for trial of the matter in controversy upon a short issue made up for that purpose, shall be empannelled and sworn immediately, or if good cause be shewn by the plaintiff to postpone the trial at the next term or session.

Report, p. 82-3. MS (ViU); clerk's copy.

Bill presented by Madison 31 Oct. 1785, postponed 14 Dec. to next session, and brought up again 1 Nov. 1786; apparently no further action was taken on it (JHD, Oct. 1785, 1828 edn., p. 12-15, 92; same, Oct. 1786, p. 16-17).

119. A Bill Permitting Those Who Will Not Take Oaths to Be Otherwise Qualified

Be it enacted by the General Assembly, that any person refusing to take an oath, and declaring religious scruples to be the true and only reason of such refusal, if he will use the solemnity and ceremony, and repeat the formulary, observed on similar occasions, by those of the church, or religious society he professeth himself to be a member of, or to join in communion with, shall thereupon be deemed as competent a witness, or to be as duly qualified to execute an office, or perform any other act, to the sanction whereof an oath is or shall be required by law, and shall be subject to the same rules, derive the same advantages, or incur the same penalties or forfeitures, as if he had been sworn. In presentments, indictments, inquisitions, verdicts, examinations, or other forms, the words, "upon their oath," or "sworn," may be left out, and instead of them, "in solemn form," or "charged," whichever may be adapted to the case, may be inserted; but if the ancient form be adhered to, it shall not be adjudged error.

Report, p. 83. Text agrees precisely with that of Act as adopted at May 1779 session (Hening, X, 28). No MS has been found.

On 29 May 1779 TJ obtained leave to introduce this Bill, which he did the same day (see notes to Bill No. 98, above, introduced at the same time, for which a draft in TJ's hand exists). It was passed by the House on 1 June 1779 and TJ was directed to take it to the Senate along with his Bill Prescribing the Oath of Fidelity. This was TJ's last legislative activity, for immediately thereafter he was elected governor (JHD, May 1779, 1827 edn., p. 27, 29). Bill No. 119 was introduced by Madison on 31 Oct. 1785, read twice, and on 14 Dec. postponed to next session; on 1 Nov. 1786 it was brought up again, but no further action on it was taken until it was incorporated in the Act of 1792 "for reducing into one the several acts prescribing the oath of fidelity" (Shepherd, I, 3-4).

120. A Bill for Regulating the Commencement of the Year, and the Computation of Time

Whereas although the supputation of the year of our Lord, according to which the year beginneth on the twenty-fifth day of March, hath, since the year one thousand seven hundred and fifty-one, been discontinued by the people of this commonwealth, yet the supputation used instead of it, conformable with the usage of all nations with whom they have commerce, hath not been adopted by a proper Legislative sanction; and whereas the calender, used in this commonwealth before the year one thousand seven hundred and fifty-two, hath been discovered to be erroneous, insomuch that the vernal or spring equinox, which, at the time of the general council of Nice, in the year of our Lord three hundred and twenty-five, happened on or about the twenty-first day of March, would happen, in this eighteenth century, on the ninth or tenth day of the same month, and this error, if not remedied, would encrease so as, in process of time, to occasion the several equinoxes and solstices to fall at very different times in the civil year from what they formerly did; which might tend to mislead people, ignorant of the alteration; and whereas a method of correcting the calender, in such a manner, as that the equinoxes and solstices fall nearly on the same nominal days, on which the same happened at the time of the said general council, hath been approved and used in this commonwealth, since the year one thousand seven hundred and fifty-one, but hath not been established by constitutional authority; Be it therefore enacted by the General Assembly, that the first day of January, in every year, which hath happened since the year one thousand seven hundred and fifty-one, as well as in every year which shall happen in time to come, shall be reckoned, taken, deemed, and accounted, to be the first day of the year; and that each new year shall, accordingly, commence and begin to be reckoned, from the first day of every such month of January, next preceeding the twenty-fifth day of March, on which such year would according to the former supputation, have begun or commenced; and that the natural day, which next immediately followed the second day of September, in the year one thousand seven hundred and fifty-two, shall be, as it hitherto hath been called, reckoned, and accounted, to be the fourteenth day of September, the eleven intermediate days of the calender, then in use, being omitted for that time only; and that the several natural days, which followed, and succeeded next after the said fourteenth day of September, shall be, as they hitherto have been, respectively called, reckoned, and numbered, forwards, in numerical order, from the said fourteenth day of September, according to the order and succession of days used in the said calender. And for the continuing and preserving the calender, or method of reckoning and computing the days of the year, in the same regular course, as near as may be, in all times coming; Be it further enacted, that the several years of our Lord one thousand eight hundred, one thousand nine hundred, two thousand one hundred, two thousand two hundred, two thousand three hundred, and any other hundredth years of our Lord, which shall happen in time to come, except only every fourth hundred year of our Lord, whereof the year of our Lord two thousand shall be the first, shall not be esteemed or taken to be bissextile or leap years, but shall be taken to be common years, consisting of three hundred and sixty-five days, and no more; and that the years of our Lord two thousand, two thousand four hundred, two thousand eight hundred, and every fourth hundred year of our Lord, from the said year of our Lord two thousand, inclusive, and also all other years of our Lord, which, by the former supputation, were esteemed to be bissextile or leap years, shall, for the future, and in all times to come, be esteemed and taken to be bissextile or leap years, consisting of three hundred and sixty-six days, in the same sort and manner as is now used, with respect to every fourth year of our Lord. The day increasing in the leap year shall be taken and reckoned of the same month wherein it groweth; and that day and the next going before shall be accounted for one day. In all computations of time, by the month, calender months shall be the measure of computation, unless in cases where the agreement of the parties, or some particular act of Assembly, shall have specially determined otherwise.

Report, p. 84. MS (ViU); clerk's copy. Bill presented by Madison 31 Oct. 1785, postponed 14 Dec. to next session, and brought up again on 1 Nov. 1786; apparently no further action was taken on it (JHD, Oct. 1785, 1828 edn., p. 12-15, 92; same, Oct. 1786, p. 16-17).

121. A Bill Allowing a Bill of Exceptions to Be Sealed

When[1] one impleaded before any court, and in any cause, where appeal[2] lies to a higher court, doth alledge an exception praying that the Justices will allow it, if they will not allow it and he that alledged the exception do write the same exception, and require that the Justices will put their seals in testimony thereof, the Justices or the greater part of them present shall so do; and if such higher court upon complaint made of the said Justices, cause the record to come before them, and the same exception be not found in the roll, and the plaintiff shew the exception written, with the seals of the Justices put to it, the Justices shall be commanded that they appear at a certain day, either to confess or deny their seals. And if the Justices cannot deny their seals they shall proceed to judgment according to the same exception, as it ought to be allowed or disallowed.

Report, p. 84. Text of Act as adopted is in Hening, XIII, 10-11.

Bill presented by Madison 31 Oct. 1785, postponed 14 Dec. to next session, and brought up again 1 Nov. 1786. Apparently no further action was taken on it at this time (JHD, Oct. 1785, 1828 edn., p. 12-15, 92; same, Oct. 1786, p. 16-17). It was passed at the Oct. 1789 session; text of Act as adopted agrees with Bill as submitted by Committee of Revisors except as indicated below.

1 The Act begins with the usual enacting clause.

2 The Act adds at this point: "writ of error or supersedeas."

122. A Bill for Enforcing Performance of Awards Made by Rule of Court

Be it enacted by the General Assembly, that by consent of parties, either personally declared by them, or signified in writing sworn to be their act, by two subscribing witnesses, before a Court of Record, any suit between those parties, in their own rights, may, after issue joined, by rule of such court, be submitted to arbitrators, who shall return their award to the same court, to be there entered of record. And, such award being returned, unless oath be made of some misbehaviour in the arbitrators, or that the award was procured by undue means; or unless the award, upon the face of it, appear contrary to law, the court, proof being made that either of the parties had refused or neglected to perform the award, may order process to issue against him for contemning the rule.

Report, p. 84. MS (ViU); clerk's copy. Bill presented by Madison 31 Oct. 1785, postponed 14 Dec. to next session, and brought up again 1 Nov. 1786. Apparently no further action was taken on it (JHD, Oct. 1785, 1828 edn., p. 12-15, 92; same, Oct. 1786, p. 16-17).

123. A Bill concerning Executions

Be it enacted by the General Assembly, that every action of account render, debt, detinue, deceit, conspiracy, trespass with force and arms, or trespass upon the case, shall be commenced by suing forth the writ called capias ad respondendum, without an original writ or other precept before. Lands, tenements, and hereditaments shall and may by virtue of writs of fieri facias, be taken and sold in satisfaction of judgments. The same actions which will lie against executors or administrators, may be brought jointly against them and the heirs or devisees of the dead person or both, and shall not be delayed for the nonage of any of the parties. The clerk from whose office a writ of fieri facias shall issue upon a judgment against the party convict, or against his executors or administrators, and his heirs or devisees, shall, after the words, "we command you that of the," leave out the words, "goods and chattels," immediately following them, and instead of the latter insert the word "estate," and by virtue of such writ the officer to whom it shall be directed shall, and may proceed in the manner herein after prescribed, to make the debt or damages and costs recovered, first of the goods and chattels, exclusive of slaves, and if there be no such goods and chattels, or not sufficient found in his bailiwick, then of the slaves, and if there be none or not sufficient found in his bailiwick, lastly of the lands, tenements and hereditaments in possession, reversion or remainder, or so much thereof, in one entire parcel, as shall be sufficient, and such part as the owner shall direct if he think proper. Land descended or devised, if before suit brought or process sued out against the heir or devisee it shall have been by him aliened and conveyed to a purchaser with good faith for valuable consideration actually paid, shall not be taken in execution by a writ of fieri facias, but the heir or devisee shall be accountable for the true value thereof, as if it were his proper debt to the creditors of the ancestor or testator; and if the heir or devisee in an action against him, shall plead nothing by descent or by devise at the time of the writ brought, and the plaintiff in his replication shall alledge the contrary, and the issue thereupon joined be found for the plaintiff, and the land appears to have been aliened as aforesaid, the jury shall enquire of the value thereof, and thereupon judgment shall be given and execution shall be awarded for such value: but if judgment be given against the heir or devisee by confession of the action, without confessing the land descended, or upon demurrer, or nihil dicit, it shall be for the debt or damages without enquiry of the land descended or devised. If a writ of capias ad satisfaciendum be not returned and executed, or if a writ of fieri facias appear by the return, either not to have been executed, or to have been partially executed, the clerk at the request of the party suing it out, and if through his means it shall not have been executed, at his costs may issue another writ of the same or a different kind of execution, endorsing thereon the amount of any payment which shall have been made, that the officer may levy or receive no more than what shall then remain due, and the clerk of a county court may, in any case, issue judicial process to the sheriff or other officer of any other county.

Every writ of execution shall bear date at least fifteen days before the return day thereof, and if it issue from the court of a county, city, or borough, shall be returnable to some one of the three sessions of court next after the date. If a defendant shall die charged in execution, the plaintiff or his executors or administrators may proceed to subject the estate of such defendant to execution.

If a sheriff or other officer to whom any writ of fieri facias shall be directed and delivered, take and sell a slave, where sufficient other chattels shall be shewn to him, to satisfy the debt, damages, or costs, or shall take and sell lands, where slaves or other chattels shall be so shewn, or shall make any unreasonable seizures, the officer so offending shall be liable to the action of the party grieved for all damages occasioned thereby, and costs.

Every writ of fieri facias shall bind the property of the lands, tenements, goods and chattels from the time it shall be delivered to the officer, who shall, without fee, endorse on every such writ the day, and time of day when he received the same.

If the owner of goods and chattels, taken in execution by virtue of a writ of fieri facias, shall not pay the debt or damages, and costs, within five days from the seizure, the sheriff or officer on the Sunday next after the expiration of that time, shall give public notice, that at the place appointed in such notice, the said goods and chattels will be exposed to sale by auction on the Wednesday following, causing advertisements for that purpose to be set up at all the churches in his county, not more than ten miles distant from such place.

If the owner of the goods so taken, shall give sufficient surety, or sureties, to the sheriff or officer, to have them forthcoming at the day of sale, the sheriff or officer shall suffer the goods to remain with the owner, at his or her risk, until the day of sale.

If the owner shall, at or before the time of sale, give or tender, to the sheriff or officer, bond with sufficient surety or sureties, for payment of the debt, damages, or costs, with interest for the same, to the creditor, at the end of three months, the sheriff or officer shall restore the estate seized.

If no such bond be offered before or at the time of sale, the sheriff or officer shall proceed to sell so much as will satisfy the demand of the creditor, for ready money or tobacco, as the demand shall be and his fees, and restore the surplus, if any, to the owner; but if the estate cannot be sold for three-fourths of its value, in the judgment of the officer, he may sell the same upon three months credit, taking bond with sufficient surety or sureties, for payment of money or tobacco, with interest to the creditor at the end of three months.

When the goods and chattels, taken in execution by virtue of a fieri facias, shall not be sufficient to satisfy the debt, damages, and costs, and the owner shall not have given such bond with security as aforesaid, for payment thereof, the sheriff or other officer shall, after the expiration of five days from the seizure, give public notice, in the manner before directed, both at the churches, and also at the court-house of his county, on the next court-day, and shall moreover give notice to the owner, if he be in the county, or otherwise to his agent, if any such be known, that at some time appointed in the notice, not less than ninety nor more than ninety-six days from the end of the said five days, the said lands, tenements, and heredita-ments, will be exposed to sale by auction, on the premises, or at such other place, in the same county, as the owner shall, by writing under his hand delivered to the officer, direct.

If the party against whom a judgment shall be entered, have several parcels of land which lie in one and the same county, he or his agent, may, by writing, under his hand, at any time before the day of sale, require the sheriff or officer, to whom a writ of fieri facias upon the judgment shall be directed, to make the debt or damages, and costs, of such of the said parcels as the owner or his agent shall think proper, and if the parcels lie in different counties, the clerk shall and may, at the like request in writing, direct the fieri facias to the sheriff or officer of any county, which the party or his agent (making oath or solemn affirmation that he hath land there) shall particularly mention at any time before the writ shall be delivered to the officer. And if the debt or damages, and costs, be made of any other parcel of land, or of land lying in any other county than that mentioned in such written requisition, the sale of such other parcel, or of the land in such other county shall be void.

If the owner before or at the day of sale, shall not give or tender bond, with sufficient surety or sureties, to the sheriff or other officer, for payment of the money and tobacco, due at the end of three months thence next following, the sheriff or officer shall proceed to sell the said lands, tenements, and hereditaments, for such estate and interest as the party convict shall have therein, or so much thereof as will be sufficient, laid off in one entire parcel, if it may be done, in such place and manner, as he or his agent, if he think proper, shall direct, for ready money or tobacco, as the demand shall be, and the fees; but if the estate cannot be sold for three fourth parts of the value thereof, in the opinion of the officer, he shall sell the same upon three months credit, taking bond of the purchasers, with sufficient surety or sureties, for payment to the creditor.

No sheriff, under sheriff, or other officer, shall buy or bid for any goods, or chattels, lands, tenements, or hereditaments, which he or his principal, or deputy, shall expose to sale by virtue of any fieri facias; and the property of any such thing so bought by him, or by any other to his use, shall not be thereby changed, but the same may be recovered by the former owner, or be made subject to the demands of any of his creditors, unless it shall, before suit brought for that purpose, have been sold with good faith and for valuable consideration to one who had notice that it had been bought in manner aforesaid.

In all sales of land by virtue of an execution, the sheriff or officer shall convey the same to the purchaser, at his costs, by deed in writing, indented, sealed and recorded as the laws direct for other conveyances of lands, which deeds shall recite the execution, purchase and consideration, and shall be effectual for passing to the purchaser all the estate and interest which the debtor had and might lawfully part with in the lands. And in all sales of slaves, upon any execution, the sheriff or officer shall certify on the writ the names of the slaves and of the purchasers.

In every bond to be taken pursuant to this act, for payment of the debt, damages or costs, by the debtor, or by the purchasers on the sale upon credit, it shall be mentioned on what occasion the same were taken, and such bond shall be by the sheriff or officer immediately returned, with the execution, to the clerk's office from whence it issued, there to be safely kept. And if the money or tobacco be not paid, at the time mentioned in the condition, the court, on motion of the creditor, his executors or administrators, shall and may give judgment against the obligors, or the executors or administrators, and heirs or devisees of the principal obligor, for the penalty of their bond, to be discharged by the payment of principal, interest and costs, and thereon award execution; provided ten days previous notice of such motion be given to those against whom judgment is entered. And on such new execution the clerk shall endorse that no security is to be taken, and the sheriff or officer shall proceed to levy the same immediately, first selling the estate of the principal obligor if any can be found, but not taking security for payment at a future day, or selling upon credit as aforesaid.

Also when judgment shall be entered against a sheriff, or other collector for taxes, public, county or parish levies, or officers fees put into his hands to collect, the clerk shall endorse on the execution issued thereupon that no security is to be taken, and the sheriff or officer shall proceed to levy the same immediately, not taking security for payment at a future day, or selling upon credit as aforesaid.

If bond and security be given for the forthcoming of goods taken in execution as before directed, and the debtor, at the time of the sale, shall neither deliver up the same to the sheriff or officer, nor pay or give security for the debt, damages and costs as aforesaid, the sheriff or officer shall endorse the truth of the case upon the execution, and return the bond therewith to the clerk's office; and thereupon it shall be lawful for the court, on the motion of the creditor, his executors or administrators, to give judgment for the penalty of the bond, to be discharged by the payment of the principal, mentioned in the former execution, with interest thereon from the date of the bond, and costs, against the obligors, and thereon to award execution, provided that ten days previous notice of such motion be given to those against whom judgment shall be entered. And on such new execution the clerk shall endorse that no security of any kind is to be taken; and the sheriff or officer shall proceed to levy the same, and keep the estate in his hands until the day of sale, and then shall sell sufficient thereof to satisfy the contents of the execution, not taking any security for the forthcoming of the estate, or for payment at a future day, or selling upon credit as before-mentioned.

If the sheriff or other officer shall levy an execution, writ of attachment, or other distress upon horses or other live stock, and the same shall not be immediately replevied, or security given for the forthcoming thereof, the officer shall provide sustenance for the support of such stock, if he shall remove them, until sold or restored to the owner, the expence whereof, to be settled by the court on the return of the process, shall be allowed to such officer out of the sales, or otherwise by the debtor, or in cases of attachment, if the plaintiff be cast therein, then by such plaintiff.

When any final decree shall be entered for the payment of money or tobacco, or a final order in any court for such payment, the clerk may issue a fieri facias thereupon, against the estate of the debtor, which shall be executed and returned in like manner, and under the same rules and regulations, as are herein before directed in the case of executions upon judgments for debt obtained in the court of law. If any person in custody of a sheriff or other officer, for not performing a decree of any Court of Chancery, whereby money or tobacco is ordered or decreed to be paid, by the person so in custody, to another, shall escape from such sheriff or other officer, he to whom the money or tobacco was ordered or decreed to be paid, or his executors or administrators, may recover the said money or tobacco, by an action of debt against such sheriff or other officer, with costs, in the same manner as if the person so escaped had been in custody upon an execution at common law.

If the sheriff or other officer shall return upon any writ of fieri facias, or venditioni exponas, enquiry, fieri facias in detinue, or withernam in replevin, that he hath levied the debt, damages or costs therein mentioned, or any part thereof, and shall not immediately pay the same to the party intitled thereto or his agent, it shall be lawful for the court from whence such writ issued, upon the motion of such party, his executors or administrators, to give judgment against such sheriff or officer, and his securities, his or their executors or administrators, for the amount of the money and tobacco mentioned in such writ, with interest thereon from the return-day of the writ, and costs, and thereon to award execution, provided that ten days previous notice of such motion be given to those against whom judgment is so entered. And upon such new execution the clerk shall endorse that no security of any kind is to be taken, and the sheriff or officer to whom the same is directed, shall proceed thereupon as is herein before mentioned in other cases of the like endorsement.

Where a writ of execution shall be delivered to the sheriff or officer of another county than that in which the creditor resides, the creditor shall name some person resident in the county wherein the execution is to be levied, to be his agent, for receiving the money or tobacco due thereon, and for giving to or receiving from the sheriff or officer any notices which may be necessary relative to the execution; and the creditor shall avail himself of, and be bound by what the agent shall do therein, in the same manner as if it had been done by himself in person. And if the creditor shall fail to appoint such agent, no judgment shall be entered against the sheriff or officer for the money or tobacco mentioned in the execution, unless it be proved that a demand thereof was made of such sheriff or officer in his county, by the creditor or some other person having a written order from him.

If a sheriff or officer shall fail to return any writ of execution to him delivered, to the office from whence it issued, on or before the return day thereof, the court from whence the execution issued shall and may, on the motion of the creditor, give judgment against such sheriff or officer for any sum not exceeding ten pounds, and costs, to the use of the creditor, and thereon award execution, provided ten days previous notice be given of such motion, and may continue to fine such sheriff or officer, in like manner, from time to time, so often as new notice shall be given, until the execution is returned, or the creditor satisfied his debt, damages, and all costs. And such sheriff or officer shall moreover be liable to the action of the creditor for all damages sustained by his not returning such execution in due time.

At the time of delivering a capias ad satisfaciendum to the sheriff or officer, the creditor if required shall give security to pay the prison fees, which if there be more creditors than one who sue out such executions shall be paid by them in proportion to their debts.

If any person committed in execution shall enter into bond, with sufficient sureties, in the penalty of double the sum due, with condition that he will not depart out of the prison rules or bounds, the sheriff or officer shall allow the prisoner to go at large any where within such bounds. And if after such bond given, the debtor shall escape out of the bounds, it shall be lawful for the court of the county, on the motion of any creditor, or his executors or administrators, to give judgment against the obligors, their several executors or administrators, for the penalty of the bond, to be discharged by the payment of the principal sums mentioned in the execution, with interest from the date of the bond, and costs, and thereupon to award execution, provided ten days previous notice be given of such motion, to those against whom judgment is entered. And every execution upon such judgment shall be issued against the estate of the defendant and levied as herein before is directed; but the clerk shall endorse thereon that no security of any kind is to be taken, and such endorsement shall be observed by the sheriff or officer to whom the same is directed in manner herein before mentioned.

Any person who now is or hereafter shall be committed to jail in execution upon a judgment, shall, on his request, be carried by the sheriff or jailer, either before a Judge of the General Court or any two Justices of the Peace of the county wherein he shall be imprisoned, if it be a judgment of the General Court, or before such two Justices if it be a judgment of the court of a county, city, or borough; and the prisoner may deliver to such Judge or Justices, a schedule of his estate and take the following oath, or being one of the people called quakers or menonists affirm, to the like effect, to wit: "I A. B. do in the presence of Almighty God, solemnly swear, profess and declare, that the schedule now delivered, and by me subscribed, doth contain to the best of my knowledge and remembrance a full, true, and just account and discovery of all the estate, goods and effects to me any way belonging, and such debts as are to me owing, or to any person in trust for me, and of all securities and contracts whereby any money may hereafter become payable, or any benefit or advantage acrue to me or to my use, or to any other person in trust for me; and that I or any other person in trust for me, have not any other lands, money, stock, or other estate real or personal, in possession, reversion, or remainder, wherewith I could satisfy the debt, damages or costs, for which I am charged in execution, or any part thereof. And that I have not directly or indirectly sold, lessened, or otherwise disposed of in trust, or concealed all, or any part of my lands, slaves, money, goods, debts, or effects, whereby to secure the same, to receive or expect any profit or advantage thereof, or to defraud or deceive any creditor or creditors to whom I am indebted. So help me God." And thereupon such Judge or Justices shall order the prisoner to be discharged from his imprisonment, but the creditor or creditors may, at any time afterwards, sue out a scire facias to have execution of any estate the debtor shall thereafter acquire or be possessed of.

The said schedule shall be delivered to, and remain with the clerk of the court from which the execution issued.

All the estate contained in such schedule, for such use and interest as the debtor hath therein, and which he may lawfully part with, saving his or her necessary apparel and utensils of trade, shall be vested in the sheriffs of the counties wherein the estate shall lie or be found, to whom the clerk of the court where the schedule is directed to remain, shall transmit copies thereof, and such sheriffs, respectively, shall sell and convey the estate in their counties to the person or persons who shall purchase, at public sale, upon due notice given, return accounts of sales to the clerk's office, and pay the money, deducting five per centum for their commissions, by order of the court, to the creditors in proportion to their debts.

If the schedule shall contain debts due in money or tobacco to the prisoner, or articles of estate to him belonging, and which are in the possession of any other person or persons, in such case the clerk of the court where the schedule is delivered in, shall immediately issue a summons against each debtor and person having such effects, named in the schedule, reciting the amount of the debt, or the species of goods, and requiring him to appear at the next court to declare on oath, whether the debt, or any, and what part thereof be really due to the prisoner, or what goods and effects of the prisoner he hath. And if any person so summoned as a garnishee, shall fail to appear, the court shall enter judgment against him for the debt, goods or effects mentioned in the schedule, and costs, a lawyer's fee excepted.

But this judgment shall be set aside at the next court, if he shall then appear and contest the demand in which case an issue shall be made up between the parties, to be tried by the jury.

And if any such garnishee shall appear and be sworn, or affirm, being a quaker or menonist, judgment shall be entered for what money or tobacco is acknowledged to be due, or for what goods or effects is acknowledged to be in his or her possession, belonging to the prisoner, and costs as aforesaid, which judgments shall be entered in the name of the sheriff, who shall thereupon proceed to collect or levy the money, and to sell the tobacco and goods for money, returning an account thereof and paying the money as before mentioned, on the sales of the prisoner's estate; for which he shall be allowed over and above his fees, such expences as the court shall judge reasonable, including such fee to a lawyer on the proceeding against the garnishees, as the nature of the case will make just, and if the effects in his hands are not sufficient to reimburse such expences, he shall be paid the balance by the creditor or creditors in proportion to their debts.

Where a garnishee does not acknowledge the whole debt or goods mentioned in the schedule, the sheriff or prisoner shall be at liberty, at any time after, within the times prescribed by the act for limitation of actions and suits, to claim the residue by legal process, and the former judgment shall only be a bar for so much as the garnishee was ordered to pay or deliver.

Where any debtor committed in execution, shall discharge himself by taking the oath or affirmation herein before directed to be taken by insolvent debtors, the sheriff shall not be allowed any other fees for serving the execution, than are or shall be allowed by law for committment and releasement, the maintenance of the debtor, and for selling the effects, and collecting the debts contained in the schedule delivered in by such prisoner of his estate.

In all executions upon judgments for penalties of bonds, or other writings, the commissions of the sheriff or officer for serving the same shall be charged only upon the principal sum, by the payment of which the execution is to be discharged.

In writs of execution in detinue, the commissions shall be allowed upon the value of the goods recovered, and on the damages and costs, and in the writ to have a return of the goods in replevin, the commissions shall be on the amount of the rent avowed for, damages and costs.

Report, p. 84-8. MS (ViU); clerk's copy.

Bill presented by Madison 31 Oct. 1785, postponed various times, and, on 21 Dec., put off until 31 Mch. 1786. It was brought up again on 1 Nov. 1786, but apparently no further action was taken on it at this time (JHD, Oct. 1785, 1828 edn., p. 12-15, 93, 94, 101; same, Oct. 1786, p. 16-17).

124. A Bill concerning Rents and Distresses

Be it enacted by the General Assembly, that any person to whom rent is or shall be due upon a lease for life, may bring an action of debt for such rent in like manner as he might have done if the rent had been reserved or become due upon a lease for years. A landlord, by action on the case, may recover a reasonable satisfaction for the use and occupation of tenements held and enjoyed by another, although there be no agreement by deed between the parties; and if, on the trial of such action, any parol demise, or any agreement, not being by deed, whereby a certain rent was reserved, shall appear, the plaintiff shall not be therefore nonsuited, but may make use thereof, as evidence of the quantity of damage to be recovered. Where a landlord, having only an estate for life in tenements demised to another, shall die before or on the day whereon the rent is reserved payable, the executors, administrators or assigns of such landlord may, by an action on the case, recover from the undertenant the whole of the rent, if the death happened on the day it was payable, or, if the death happen before that day, such a part of the rent as is proportionable to the time the landlord lived of the next preceeding year, or other period in which the rent was growing due. Goods, which lying or being upon tenements demised shall have been taken in execution, unless it be for a debt due to the commonwealth, shall not be removed from thence, before the party, at whose suit the execution was sued out, shall pay or tender to the landlord, or to his agent, such sum of money, or quantity of tobacco, or other thing reserved, as at the time of the taking is or shall be due for the rent of the demised premises, so that it exceed not the rent of one year; and if the landlord or agent accept such year's rent, or so much thereof as is due, the officer to whom the execution was directed shall proceed to levy and pay to the person who sued it out, not only the money or other thing thereby due, but also the rent so advanced. If a lessee for life, term of years, at will, or otherwise, fraudulently convey away his goods from the tenements to him demised, in order to prevent a distress for arrears of rent, the landlord to whom such rent is due, or any person by him for that purpose, lawfully empowered, may, within the space of thirty days after the conveying away, seize such goods, wheresoever they may be found, unless they shall before have been sold, with good faith, and for valuable consideration, to one who was not privy to the fraud, as a distress for the said arrears of rent, in the same manner as he might have done, if they had remained upon the demised premises, and upon the testimony of the landlord, or his agent, before a Justice of the Peace, that there is good cause to suspect the goods so fraudulently conveyed away to be deposited in any house, yard, or other inclosure, such Justice, at the request of the landlord, or his agent, shall and may, by his warrant, authorise such landlord or agent, in company with the sheriff, or under sheriff, or a constable, who shall attend and assist to break and enter such house, yard, or enclosure, in the day time, if the owner or person dwelling there will not permit them to enter without force in order to search for and seize the goods. Those things which by the common-law were not distrainable, either because they could not be rendered again in like plight, or because they were the tools or instruments of the owner's trade or occupation, may hereafter be distrained for rent arrere, and sold in the same manner, as other goods, but shall be kept, as impounded in the place where they shall be found, if they cannot be removed without damage to the owner, until they shall be replevied or sold; and all sorts of emblements and annual fruits growing upon land demised, may be seized as distress for arrears of rent, and when ripe, be cut, gathered, cured, and laid up in barns or proper depositaries on the same land, or, if none be there, in such others as can be procured nearest thereto by the landlord, or his agent, who shall give notice thereof, within the space of one week after the seizure, to the tenant, or leave such notice, in writing, at the last place of his abode, and in convenient time the things so seized shall be sold and disposed of in the same manner as other goods distrained for rent arrere, unless the tenant, or his executors, administrators or assigns, before pay to the lessor or landlord, or his agent, the whole rent arrere, together with the charges occasioned by the seizure. Any person may impound, or otherwise secure a distress, lawfully taken for rent arrere, of whatsoever nature or kind it be, in such place, on the premises, chargeable with the rent, as shall be most fit and convenient for the purpose, and may come and go to and from the place, in order to view the distress, and to sell it and remove it after it shall be sold. A landlord, to whom rent is or shall be due upon a lease determined, may distrain for such rent, in the same manner after as he might have done before, so that such distress be made within the space of six months after the determination of the term, and during the continuance of such landlord's title or interest, and the possession of the tenant from whom the arrears became due. None shall take unreasonable distress, or distrain slaves where other sufficient distress can be had; and if any offend herein, the party grieved may, in an action on the case, recover damages against the wrong doer, with cost of suit. A distress shall not be driven or carried out of the county where it shall have been taken. Upon any pound, breach or rescous of goods distrained or seized as a distress for rent arrere, the person grieved thereby may, in a special action on the case for the wrong sustained, recover treble damages and costs of suit against the offender, or against the owner of the goods, if they be found to have come to his possession or use. The owner of goods distrained and sold, by virtue or colour of this act, or his executors or administrators, if in truth no rent is in arrere or due, may, by an action of trespass, or on the case, to be brought against the person distraining, whether in the right or name of himself, or of another, or his executors, or administrators, recover double of the value of such goods, together with full costs of suit. Where goods shall be distrained for arrears of rent reserved and due, if the tenant or owner of the goods shall, within ten days after the distress taken, and notice thereof, with the cause of such taking, left at the chief mansion house, or other most notorious place on the premises chargeable with the rent distrained for, replevy the same, by giving bond, with sufficient surety, to the sheriff, in the penalty of double the value of the rent demanded, conditioned for prosecuting the suit, with effect, and without delay, and for duly returning the goods distrained, in case a return shall be awarded, the sheriff shall cause the distress to be delivered to the tenant or owner, and shall assign the bond to the lessor or landlord, who may commence an action thereupon in his own name, if the condition be broken, and the person distraining, if he will not suffer the distress to be delivered by the sheriff to the tenant or owner, shall be amerced; and the tenant or owner, in an action of trespass, against the person distraining, may also recover damages; but if the tenant or owner shall not replevy the goods so distrained, within the time and in the manner before mentioned, the landlord shall deliver them to the sheriff, after expiration of the said ten days, who shall take the said goods, and suffer them to be replevied, or sell them in the same manner as if they had been taken by virtue of a writ of fieri facias, applying the produce, in case of a sale, towards satisfaction of the rent demanded, and the expences of the distress and sale, and returning the overplus, if any, to the tenant or owner; and the landlord shall have like remedy against the sheriff for non-payment of the money or tobacco levied, or against the tenant and sureties, who shall have given bond, for producing the goods at the time appointed for sale thereof, or for payment of the rent, interest, and costs, or of the price the goods sold for, as in case of goods taken by virtue of such writ of fieri facias. If any tenant, who shall be in arrere one year's rent, shall desert the demised premises, and leave the same uncultivated or unoccupied, so as no sufficient distress, can be had to countervail the arrears of rent, two or more Justices of the Peace, at the request of the landlord, or of his bailiff, or receiver, may go upon and view the demised premises, and affix, in the most notorious part thereof, notice in writing on what day they will return to take a second view, which shall be at the distance of not less than fourteen days, and if upon such second view, the tenant, or some person on his behalf, shall not appear and pay the rent in arrere, or there shall not be sufficient distress on the premises, then the said Justices may put the landlord into possession of the demised premises; and the lease thereof, as to any demise therein contained only, shall from thenceforth become void; but those proceedings of the Justices shall be examinable in a summary way by the next county court, who are empowered to order restitution to be made to the tenant, together with his expences and costs, to be paid by the landlord if they shall see cause for the same; or, in case they shall affirm the act of the Justices, to award costs, not exceeding five pounds, for the frivolous appeal. The defendant in replevin may avow, or make conusance generally, that the plaintiff in replevin or other tenant of the tenements whereon the distress was made enjoyed the same under a demise or grant, at such a certain rent, during the time wherein the rent distrained for incurred, which rent then was and still remains due, without further setting forth the grant, demise, or title of the landlord. Any tenant, whose estate is determinable upon a life, tenant for years, or at will, guardian or trustee for an infant, or husband seized in right of his wife, or other person claiming under them, who shall hold possession after the determination of his interest, without express consent of the person then immediately[1] intitled, shall be deemed a trespasser. No person shall distrain beasts doing damage upon his land, unless the land be enclosed with a rail fence, five feet high, or with a bank and rail fence, or hedge, the top whereof is eight feet from the bottom of the ditch, the fence or hedge being so close that the beasts could not pass through or under it. When beasts doing damage shall be distrained, and put into a pound overt, the distrainer shall give reasonable notice thereof to the owner, or his agent, or overseer, or leave such notice in writing at the place of his usual abode, if that be distant not more than twelve miles from the pound, but if the distance be greater, or if the owner be not known to the distrainer, the beasts shall be deemed estrays.

Report, p. 88-9. MS (ViU); clerk's copy.

Bill presented by Madison 31 Oct. 1785, postponed 14 Dec. to next session, and brought up again 1 Nov. 1786; apparently no further action was taken on it (JHD, Oct. 1785, 1828 edn., p. 12-15, 92; same, Oct. 1786, p. 16-17). See the 1748 Act for the better securing the payment of rents and preventing the fraudulent practices of tenants and also the 1769 Act amending it (Hening, VI, 9-13; VIII, 332-4).

[1] The MS copy ends at this point.

125. A Bill Providing Remedy and Punishment in Cases of Forcible Entries and Detainers

Be it enacted by the General Assembly, that none make any entry into any lands and tenements, or other possessions, whatsoever but in case where entry is given by the law; and in such case not with strong hand, nor with multitude of people, but only in peaceable and easy manner; and that none who shall have entered into the same in peaceable manner hold the same after with force. And if any do to the contrary, on complaint thereof to any Justices or Justice of Peace, such Justices or Justice, shall take sufficient power of the county, and go to the place where such force is made; and if they find any that hold such place forcibly they shall be taken and put in the jail of the same county, there to abide convict by the record of the same Justices or Justice, until they have paid such amercement as shall be assessed by a jury to be sworn by the Justices or Justice for that purpose. And all the people of the county, as well the sheriff as others, shall be attendant upon the same Justices, to go and assist them to arrest such offenders, upon pain of imprisonment and amercement at the discretion of a jury.

And moreover though that such persons making such entries be present, or else departed before the coming of the said Justices or Justice, notwithstanding the said Justices or Justice in some convenient place, according to their discretion, shall have authority and power to enquire by the people, of the same county, as well of them that make such forcible entries in lands and tenements, as of them which the same hold with force; and if it be found before any of them that any doth contrary to this act, then the said Justices or Justice shall cause to reseize, or to repossess, the lands and tenements so entered or holden as afore, and shall put the party so put out in full possession thereof.

And also when the said Justice or Justices make such enquiries as before, he or they shall make their warrants and precepts, to be directed to the sheriff of the same county, commanding him on behalf of the commonwealth, to cause to come before him or them fit persons to enquire of such entries. And if any sheriff be slack, and make not execution duly of the said precepts to him directed, to make such enquiries, he shall forfeit twenty five pounds, recoverable before any Court of Record, as well by indictment or information, to be taken only for the commonwealth, as by bill at the suit of the party grieved, as well for himself as for the commonwealth, in which case one moiety of the said twenty-five pounds, shall be to the commonwealth, and the other moiety, together with his costs and expences shall be to the party suing.

And moreover, Mayors and bailiffs of cities and boroughs, shall have in the said cities and boroughs like power to remove such entries, and in other articles aforesaid rising within the same, as the Justices of Peace and sheriffs in counties have.

But no restitution upon any indictment of forcible entry, or holding with force, shall be made to any, if the party indicted hath had the occupation, or hath been in quiet possession by the space of three whole years together, next before the day of such indictment so found, and his estate therein not ended or determined; which the party indicted may alledge for stay of restitution, and restitution to stay until that be tried, if the other will deny or traverse the same; and if the same allegation be tried against the party so indicted, then the same party so indicted to pay such costs and damages, to the other party, as shall be assessed by the Judges or Justices before whom the same shall be tried.

Report, p. 89.

Bill presented by Madison 31 Oct. 1785, postponed 14 Dec. to next session, and brought up again 1 Nov. 1786; apparently no further action was taken on it (JHD, Oct. 1785, 1828 edn., p. 12-15, 92; same, Oct. 1786, p. 16-17).

126. A Bill for Repealing Certain Acts of Parliament and of General Assembly

Be it enacted by the General Assembly, that all acts of the Parliament of England, made before the fourth year of the reign of King James the first of England, except such of them as shall be by this General Assembly enacted, in express words, to be in force, shall be, and are repealed, so far as they concern any persons or things in, or belonging to this commonwealth. And it is declared, that every act, either of the said Parliament of England, made in or after the said fourth year of the reign of the said King James, or of the Parliament of Great-Britain, made since the union of the two kingdoms of England and Scotland, so far as any such act concerned or was intended to concern any persons or things in or belonging to this commonwealth, was and is void, and never had any force, further than such act shall have been particularly enacted or allowed by some act of General Assembly to be in force. But no judgment of any court of law, decree of any Court of Equity, or sentence of any Court of Admiralty, founded upon any such act of Parliament, whereof execution hath actually been done, shall be reversed, or deemed null, unless it be for some other cause than the nullity of the said act. And it is further enacted, that all acts of General Assembly, and ordinances of Convention, made before the day of   in this present year of our Lord one thousand seven hundred and   shall be and are repealed, except every such act whereby troops have been raised, and provision made for clothing arming, and subsisting them, and relieving their families; or whereby manufactories on account of the commonwealth have been established or encouraged; or whereby taxes or duties now subsisting have been imposed, or whereby the public Treasurer was empowered to borrow money or issue treasury notes, or any person was empowered to superintend the loan-office of the United American States, or whereby the defective titles of particular persons had been established, and except every such act as confirms and secures the titles to lands in the Northern Neck, held under the proprietor; or as concerns or relates to the lands of, or claimed from Indians; or as concerns or relates to a particular county, parish, town, or corporation, or private persons, only, or so much of such act as is not repealed by some other act; and except also the two ordinances passed at a General Convention of Delegates and representatives from the several counties and corporations of Virginia, held at the capitol, in the city of Williamsburg, on Monday, the sixth day of May, in the year of our Lord one thousand seven hundred and seventy-six, whereof one is intitled "A declaration of rights made by the representatives of the good people of Virginia, assembled in full and free convention, which rights do pertain to them, and their posterity, as the basis and foundation of government," and the other is intitled "The constitution or form of government agreed to and resolved upon by the Delegates and representatives of the several counties and corporations of Virginia."

Report, p. 90.

Bill presented by Madison 31 Oct. 1785, postponed 14 Dec. to next session, and brought up again 1 Nov. 1786; apparently no further action was taken on it (JHD, Oct. 1785, 1828 edn., p. 12-15, 92; same, Oct. 1786, p. 16-17). With the appointment of a new committee to complete the revisal, this general repealing Bill was naturally postponed until that committee's report had been acted upon. But the new committee never reported, the revisal was not completed, and this Bill, of course, was never passed.

Since the Committee of Revisors must have expected their revisal, after approval, to be published as a general code, it is surprising that the two ordinances embracing the Declaration of Rights and the Constitution of 1776 should not have been included in the *Report of the Committee of Revisors*, as they were in The Chancellors' Revisal and in subsequent codes (e.g., those of 1819 and 1849). Perhaps this was because TJ hoped, after completing the revisal of statutory law, to tackle the Constitution, remodel it as he had wanted to do since 1776, and give it the force of substantive law rather than that of a mere legislative enactment by having it adopted by a convention elected by the people.

IV. Appendix

1. Bill Declaring When Laws Shall Be in Force

To prevent all Doubt concerning the Time at which the Laws of this Commonwealth shall take place, and be in Force Be it enacted by the General Assembly, that all Laws, or Acts of Assembly, which shall be made or passed during this, or any future Session, shall take place, and be in Force, from and after the last Day of that Session of Assembly in which they shall have been respectively made or passed, and not sooner: Provided nevertheless, that where any Law, or Act of Assembly, shall particularly declare or specify the certain Date, or Time, at which it is to take Place, or be in Force, that such Law, or Act of Assembly, shall accordingly take Place, and be in Force, from and after the Date, or Time, so declared, or specified, and not otherwise.

And for the more effectual publication of the Laws, and the Information of the People; Be it enacted that the Clerk of every County, after every Session of General Assembly, so soon as he shall have received the Laws made, and passed, in such Session, shall deliver them to the Sherif of his County, taking his Receipt for the same, and such Sherif shall, and he is hereby required, at the next Court after such Laws shall have come to his Hands, and having first made due Proclamation at the Court-House Door, to cause all the said Laws to be publickly and distinctly read, and thereafter return them to the Clerk's office of his County.

MS (DLC); two pages, entirely in George Mason's hand. Endorsed: "A Bill declaring from what time the Laws passed in each Session of Assembly shall take Place, and be in Force; and for the more effectual Publication of the same."

It is probable that this Bill was drawn by Mason for the Report of the Committee of Revisors, but there is no positive evidence to this effect. Its presence among TJ's papers and its object of providing for "the more effectual publication of the Laws, and the Information of the People" seem to be plausible reasons for placing this draft in the revision of 1779. The Committee of Revisors, however, made no use of the Bill and it was never acted upon. Bill No. 2, above, provided that Acts of Assembly should commence and be in force from the date of passage, unless an Act specifically named another date (see Hening, XII, 128-9). This continued to be law in Virginia (*The Code of Virginia*, Richmond, 1849, p. 98).

2. Jefferson's Notes of English Statutes

Statutes doubtful whether to be retained or not.

No. 1.

a 11. or 13.E.1. stat. of Acton Burnel. allowing recognisances before a mayor to have effect of jdmts. & goods for defect of buyers to be delivd. to creditor at appraised value.

b 13.E.1.c.1. the stat. of merchants. supplementory of the last.

c 14.E.3.c.11. supplementory

No. 2. 27.E.3.st.2.c.7. prohibition to export wool, leather, lead.

14.R.2.c.5. do.

No. 1.
d. 27.E.3.st.2.c.5. excluding the justices of Com. law. from things belonging to the staple
e. c.8. merchts. coming to the staple shall be ruled by the law mercht., & not the Com. law. medietas linguae.
f. c.9. supplementory to (a)
g. c.19. justice to be done to merchants from day to day & hour to hour without delay, at the staple.
h. c.20. similar to (g)
i. c.21. constituting officers of the court of the mayor of the staple.
k. c.22. that there shall be correctors in staple towns before whom bargains shall be recorded.
l. c.23. additional to (i).
m. c.24. do.
n. 28.E.3.c.13. additional to (e)
o. 36.E.3.c.7. do.
p. 15.R.2.c.9. confirmn. of (f)
q. 9.H.6.c.24. confirmn. of (n)

1. Jac.c.13. for allowing new execution agt. a memb of parl. discharged from execn. by privilege

Attainder.[1]

Attaint.

Exigent & Utlaria. Idemptilate nominis.

Laws omitted, by me, but necessary to be taken up.

13.E.1.c.7. the latter part of it directing what process in Admeasuremt. of dower. law of Judicial proceedings.

3.E.1.c.47.
6.E.1.c.2
13.E.1.c.40
for parol demurrer. belongs to the law of judicial proceedings.

11.H.4.c.3.
9.H.5.c.4.
14.E.3.c.6.st.1.
8.R.2.c.4.
4.H.6.c.3.
8.H.6.c.12.15.
Jeofails & Amendmts. so much more fully provided for in 32.H.8.c.30. 18.El.14. 27.El.5. 21.Jac.1.13. 16&17.Car.2.8. 4.Ann16. 5.G. 1.13. that properly belongs to another period.

Assises. would belong to L. of judicial proceedings. but may be abolished.

21.H.8.c.19. Avowrie. parvum in multo. a few words in land law, or law of Judicial proceedgs. will do.

the age of consent to marriage 14. in a male, 12 in a female should be extended. perhaps to 18. & 15.

Statutes	Subject
52.H.3.c.11. 3.E.1.c.8. 1.E.3.st.2.c.8.	Beaupleder. belongs to law of Jeofails.
6.E.1.c.4. 13.E.1.c.21.	Cessavit. belongs to land law or law of Pleadings.
33.E.1.st.4. 7.H.7.c.5.	Challenge belongs either to law of Pleadings or Appendix to Criminal law.

Statute	Subject	Remark
3.E.1.c.10.	what sort of men shall be coroners.	these stat. are unnecessary. the 3.E.1.c.10. which is the principal, is only declaratory of the com. l. as may be seen Brit.c.1. written temp. E.1.
4.E.1.st.2.	the duty of a coroner.	
3.H.7.c.1.	do.	
14.E.3.c.8.	Coroners. appendix to criminal law.	
28.E.3.c.6.	how coroners shall be appointed	
1.H.8.c.7.		

Statutes	Subject
13.E.1.c.3.	Cui in vita. law of pleadings.
13.E.1.c.4.	latter part as to ten. by courtesy & for life. l. of pleadings
6.E.1.c.1.14. 6.E.1.st.2. 3.H.7.c.10. 19.H.7.c.20. 23.H.8.c.15. 24.H.8.c.18.	Damages & costs. law of pleadings.
36.E.3.c.1.	Declaration. law of pleadings.
52.H.3.c.29.	Entry. law of pleadings
6.E.1.c.13.	Estrepement. law of Pleadings
13.E.1.c.18.45. 50.E.3.c.6.	Execution. law of Executions.
1.R.2.c.9.	Feoffments l. of Pleadings.
24.H.8.c.5.	Forfeiture. 9. App. to Crim. l.
13.E.1.c.13.	unnecessary. the sher's power being taken away.
1.E.3.st.2.c.17.	do.
	What process.
25.E.3.c.14.st.5.	Indictmts. App. to Crim. l.
11.H.4.c.9.	provided for.
3.H.7.c.1.	foreign to the matter.
12.H.7.c.6.	Merchants.
2.R.2.c.4.	Mariners.
	Money. a necessary subject: but no Eng. stat. worth looking at.
25.E.3.st.5.c.16.	Non tenure. l. of pleadings.
	Parliament. several stat. l. of Elections &c.
	Patents. several stat. some good in them.
	Processe. many stat. l. of Pleadings.

Recognisance & Statute merchant. several stat. a difficult subject.

21.H.8.c.15. Recoveries. insert 3 words into 14.El.c.8.

Redisseisin. several stat. l. of Pleadings.

Receit. l. of Pleadings.

23.H.6.c.10. Sheriff. against farming. l. concerning Sheriffs.

Tenure. several stat. Quia emptores &c. land law.

13.E.1.c.48. View. land law or law of pleadings.

Voucher. several stat. l. of pleadings.

Wager of law. l. of pleadings.

Wards. several stat. a great subject.

Acts of ass. operating from 1st. day of session }
repealing acts never to affect cases happening before repeal[2] }
making absent members pay expences. }

act against impressing but in certain cases

law for cross posts.[3]

bill for establishing English & Grammar schools.[4]

Appendix to Crim. law.[5]

MS (DLC); three pages, entirely in TJ's hand.

These pages represent almost the sole remnant of TJ's memoranda and work-notes for the preparation of his part of the Report of the Committee of Revisors. They are revealing and important and it is to be regretted that what must have been a much larger mass of such memoranda has apparently disappeared; for many of the pungent comments here set forth—"wards . . . a great subject"; "money. A necessary subject: but no Eng. stat. worth looking at"; and "Avowrie. parvum in multo. a few words in land law, or law of Judicial proceedgs. will do."—reveal something of TJ's perceptive mind at work.

[1] It is significant that TJ listed acts of attainder under "Statutes doubtful whether to be retained or not," in view of his Bill to Attaint Josiah Philips and Others, &c., and his later attempt to justify a "proper" use of such acts (q.v., under date of 28 May 1778).

[2] See Document IV, 1, above. Neither the effective dates of Acts of Assembly there proposed by George Mason nor the one here contemplated by TJ was actually written into Virginia law by the Committee of Revisors (see Bill No. 2, above).

[3] This indicates that Bill No. 19 was drawn by TJ.

[4] See Bill No. 79.

[5] See Bill No. 64.

3. Jefferson's Notes of Acts of Assembly Adopted October 1777 and May 1778

Oct. 20. 1777.

* c. 1. to be excluded from the operation of the repealing bill, as are all others marked thus *.[1]

\+ * c. 2. see bill for amending this.

c. 3. unnecessary because fee bill prepared.

\+ c. 5. omit preamble and 2. last clause and copy it verbatim. qu. if not a bill already?

* c. 6.

* c. 7. has been in[. . .]

c. 8. has had effect.

\+ c. 9. copy verbatim.
c. 10. has had effect.
c. 11. see amendments proposed. G. W. has also drawn a bill.[2]
c. 12. expired.
c. 13. other provision made.
\+ c. 14. see bill.
c. 15. bill prepared.
* c. 16.
c. 17. bill prepared.
* c. 18.
* c. 19.
* c. 20.
* c. 21.
\+ c. 22. copy verbatim. See 1778. c. 10.[3]
c. 23. bill prepared.
c. 24. G. W. has drawn a bill.[4]
* c. 25.
c. 26. had effect.
c. 27. provision made.
\+ c. 28. see bill.
* c. 29.
* c. 30.
* c. 31.
* c. 32.
* c. 33.
* c. 34.
* c. 35.

May 4. 1778.
* c. 1.
* c. 2.
* c. 3.
\+ c. 4. see bill.
* c. 5.
c. 6. in G. W's part.[5]
c. 7. provided for.
* c. 8.
c. 9. provided for.
c. 10. same as 1777. c. 22.
c. 11. the principal bill in G. W's part.[6]
c. 12. had effect.
* c. 13.
* c. 14.
c. 15. provided for.
\+ c. 16. ⟨*see bill. should be a general bill establishing other clerkships*⟩ see bill[7]
* c. 17.
c. 18. provided for.
\+ c. 19. draw bill. ⟨*to invest that power in Gov. & council, to enable them to employ superintendants . . . genl. of the navy*

& put down naval commrs & to convert the navy board into a board of trade.⟩[8]

⟨*no slave to be witness*⟩
⟨*not to go from tenements or dwelling of master overseer or employer without pass or token*⟩
⟨*not to keep arms*⟩
⟨*not to pass with arms.*⟩
⟨*riots, routs, unlawful assemblies, trespasses & seditious speeches.*⟩

MS (DLC); two pages, entirely in TJ's hand. The Acts passed Oct. 1777 and May 1778 (here designated as c.1, 2, 3, &c.) are to be found in Hening, IX, 337-443; 445-70.

From this MS it is evident that TJ and Wythe concerned themselves with Acts of the General Assembly, which, according to TJ's Autobiography, fell within Pendleton's division.

1 The repealing Bill is Bill No. 126; the Act excluded is the Act for speedily recruiting the Virginia Regiments, &c.; see Hening, IX, 337-49.

2 This Act corresponds to Bill No. 89; see Hening, IX, 377-80.

3 This Act corresponds to Bill No. 7; see Hening, IX, 428-9 and 462.

4 This Act corresponds to Bill No. 35; see Hening, IX, 431-2.

5 This is the amending Act concerning invasions and insurrections and corresponds to Bill No. 6; see Hening, IX, 458.

6 This is the Act giving speedy remedy to the United States against defaulters; it provided that the United States should have the same remedy against public defaulters as was given to the state. There is, of course, no such Bill in the Revisal, and TJ's remark must have reference to the subject, not to the specific terms of the Act. See Bill No. 108.

7 TJ probably drew this general Bill; see Bill No. 14, above; also, Hening, IX, 467.

8 This Act (same, IX, 470) vested in the commissioners of the navy the power to vary the rates of pilotage according to the exigencies of the times; Bill No. 9.

4. Outline of Bill for Proportioning Crimes and Punishments, &c.

I. Crimes whose punishmt. extends to *Life*.
1. High-treason. Death ⟨*by burying alive. qu.*⟩ by hanging
Forfeiture of lands & goods to Commwth.
2. Petty Treason. Death by hanging.
Dissection.
Forfeitr of half lands & goods to representatives of person killed.
3. Murder. 1. by poyson. Death by poyson.
Forfeitre. of one half as before.
2. in Duel. Death by hanging
gibbeting, if the challenger.
Forfeitre. of one half as before unless the Challengr fell, then to Commw.
3. any other way. Death by hanging
Forfeitre of half as before.
4. Manslaur. 2d offence is murder.
⟨*1st. Labor 7 years.*⟩
⟨*Forfeitre one half as before.*⟩

II. Crimes whose punishment goes to *Limb*.

1. Rape. ⟨2. *Polygamy*⟩ 2. Sodomy.	Castration.
3. Maiming 4. Disfiguring	Retaliation. Forfeiture of half to sufferer.

III. Crimes punisheable by *Labor* &c.

1. Manslaur. 1st. offence.	Labor VII. years. Forfeitre. of half as before.
2. Counterfeiting.	Labor VI. years. Forfeit whole to Commw.
3. Arson. 4. Asportn. of vessels	Labor V. years. Reparation threefold
5. Robbery 6. Burglary	Labor IV. years Reparation. double.
7. Housebreaking. 8. Horse-stealing	Labor III. years Reparation.
9. Grand Larceny.	Labor II. years Reparation ⟨*30. stripes.*⟩ pillory ½ an hour.
10. Petty Larceny.	Labor I. year. Reparation ⟨*15. stripes.*⟩ pillory ¼ of an hour
11. Witchcraft &c.	Ducking 15. stripes.
12. Excusable homicide.	⟨*head & half the beard shaved a year.*⟩ nothing.
13. Suicide.	nothing.
14. Apostacy. Heresy.	nothing.

N (DLC); entirely in TJ's hand, written in a long, narrow column. This document is presented as literally as possible. The italicized words (except those in angle brackets) represent words written by TJ in a hand resembling print, a device he frequently used for emphasis.

TJ later employed this list in preparing Query XIV of the *Notes on Virginia*, copying it almost verbatim in his discussion of the revised code (Ford, III, 250-1). Compare this outline also with the section on crimes and punishments in the Plan Agreed upon by the Revisors at Fredericksburg (Document I in this series) and Bill No. 64. It is important to note that polygamy, though it fell under the drastic penalty set forth in Bill No. 64, was struck from the above list of crimes before that list was revised and employed in *Notes on Virginia*.

5. Memorandum by Jefferson on Bills to be Drafted

⟨*confining prisoner in county jail, to be considd. as obeyg. writ.*⟩
⟨*Presenting? def. & confessing jdmt.*⟩
⟨*deposns. in criminal cases, when to be admitted*⟩
⟨*in bill for specific performnce (as in purchase of lands) have damages for . . .*⟩

T. J. oath of fidelity to be taken by all officers

⟨*fee bill. restrain Sheriff's commn. as the Marshall's in admiralty*⟩

⟨*Jailor's & Sheriff's fees for custody of criminal to be put into fee bill. Attorney's fees.*⟩

⟨*Courts of Chy. to be of record*⟩

⟨*persons disqualified to be justices*⟩

⟨*Sheriff. attorney with same court.*⟩

⟨*clk. of peace. bar innkeepers*⟩

G. W. bill prescribing mode of trial by impeachmt.

T. J. Aldermen to levy county expences & audit accts land law. save right of voting to inhab. of Washingt. Kentucky. Gr. Brier. Ohio Yoh. Monong. for one year aft passing law

G. W. Appeal bill

G. W. Admiralty court

T. J. govmt. of slaves.

T. J. latter half of Ordinances & acts to be divided by session.

T. J. law about public roads.

N (DLC); written by TJ in a narrow column on the verso of "A Bill for continuing the use of certain writs" (see Bill No. 102, note 1). This document has been presented literally. However certain portions of the deleted matter have been so heavily scored out that they are illegible.

Preliminary indexes will be issued periodically for groups of volumes. A comprehensive index of persons, places, subjects, etc., arranged in a single consolidated sequence, will be issued at the conclusion of the series.

THE PAPERS OF THOMAS JEFFERSON is composed in Monticello, a type specially designed by the Mergenthaler Linotype Company for this series. Monticello is based on a type design originally developed by Binny & Ronaldson, the first successful typefounding company in America. It is considered historically appropriate here because it was used extensively in American printing during the last thirty years of Jefferson's life, 1796 to 1826; and because Jefferson himself expressed cordial approval of Binny & Ronaldson types.

✧

Composed and printed by Princeton University Press. Illustrations are reproduced in collotype by Meriden Gravure Company, Meriden, Connecticut. Paper for the series is made by W. C. Hamilton & Sons, at Miquon, Pennsylvania; cloth for the series is made by Holliston Mills, Inc., Norwood, Massachusetts. Bound by the J. C. Valentine Company, New York.

DESIGNED BY P. J. CONKWRIGHT